MEDIUM ÆVUM MONOGRAPHS

EDITORIAL COMMITTEE

K. P. Clarke, A. J. Lappin,
N. F. Palmer, P. Russell, C. Saunders

MEDIUM ÆVUM MONOGRAPHS
NEW SERIES XXIII

A SPORTING LEXICON OF THE FIFTEENTH CENTURY
THE J.B. TREATISE

edited by
DAVID SCOTT-MACNAB

Second, Revised Edition

The Society for the Study of Medieval Languages and Literature

OXFORD · MMXIX

THE SOCIETY FOR THE STUDY OF MEDIEVAL
LANGUAGES AND LITERATURE

OXFORD 2019

http://aevum.space/monographs

© David Scott-Macnab, 2003, 2019

British Library Cataloguing in Publication Data
A catalogue record for this book is available from the
British Library

ISBN-13:
978-0-907570-75-2 (pb)
978-0-907570-96-7 (ebk)

This volume was prepared for publication
by David Scott-Macnab

CONTENTS

PREFACE	vii
SIGLA AND ABBREVIATIONS	xi
INTRODUCTION	1
The *J.B. Treatise*	5
The Witnesses and their Contents	7
The J.B. Elements: Hunting, Hawking and Miscellaneous	8
Principal witnesses of the *J.B. Treatise* and major collections of J.B. material	11
Minor witnesses, containing one or two elements of J.B. material	58
Affinities among the J.B. Elements	74
Tables of Witnesses and their Contents	88
Textual Relationships	90
Development of the *J.B. Treatise*	96
The Context and Purpose of the *J.B. Treatise*	100
Editorial Principles	105
SELECT BIBLIOGRAPHY	106
THE *J.B. TREATISE*	117
PART I BROGYNTYN MS ii.1 (Prk)	119
PART II HARLEY MS 2340 (H)	131
PART III MS HALE 148 (Ha)	143
PART IV MISCELLANEOUS J.B. TEXTS AND ELEMENTS	149
a. Hunting terms – MS Adv	150
b. 'If a hart stands' – MS Am	150

CONTENTS

  c. Names of hawks – MS Harl   150
  d. Beasts of venery and the chase – MS Eg   151
  e. Breeds of dogs – MS Eg   152
  f. Properties of a greyhound – MS Eg   153
  g. Soiling terms – MS T   153
  h. Hierarchy of hawks;
    Hawks' diseases and remedies – MS G   154
  i. Names of wines – MS Dg   158

EXPLANATORY NOTES   161
  Part I MS Prk   161
  Part II MS H   184
  Part III MS Ha   199
  Part IV Miscellaneous J.B. Texts and Elements   206

GLOSSARY   226

APPENDIX I Collective Nouns
    with Index and Explanatory Notes   251

APPENDIX II Carving Terms
    with Index and Explanatory Notes   336

APPENDIX III Resting Terms
    with Index and Explanatory Notes   367

PREFACE

There can be no denying that the work identified as the principal subject of this volume – the *J.B. Treatise* – is burdened with a name that is both cryptic and ungainly: one that is self-evidently a construct of modern scholarship. For reasons that will become apparent, it is a name that has had to be devised because the work it refers to is so fluid and diverse in content that no conventional descriptive title could ever be fitting for all its manifestations. Another reason for the name's invention is that the work was never given an authentic contemporary title when it evolved in the second half of the 15th century. As it happens, however, the more one learns about the work under discussion, the more suitable its synthetic modern title is revealed to be.

To begin by deciphering the initials J.B., these allude to the very mysterious, putative originator of the treatise, or part of it, at least: a person of indeterminate sex, who is referred to in three separate colophons in three independent witnesses as *Dam Iulyans Barnes*, *Iulyan Barne*, and *I.B.* More on this figure later in the Introduction.

Turning to the 'treatise' itself, it will be seen that this is even more elusive than its supposed composer, in that there is no single, authoritative version that can be pointed to as its pre-eminent, let alone its archetypal, representative. It is also impracticable to attempt to construct a definitive version from the surviving witnesses, or to reconstuct a hypothetical urtext. For what has come down to us is an assortment of texts that all draw on essentially the same body of material, but in a variety of different ways, so that several versions of the *J.B. Treatise* are to be found among them.

To complicate matters further, the material that makes up the *J.B. Treatise* itself evolved and developed as it was copied by different scribes, while also maintaining its essential character fundamentally unchanged. In consequence it is possible to say that, amid much variation, at the core of the treatise are expositions of various sorts on the sports of hawking and hunting, with particular emphasis on the terminology appropriate to each. Among the treatise's most recurrent components are lists of 'terms of association' or 'collective nouns' (which grew increasingly imaginative as new phrases were added), 'carving terms' and the well-known 'hierarchy' of hawks and their owners. There is also an accretion of associated information, much of it gnomic – such as the account of the 'properties of a greyhound' – along with a range of more miscellaneous material, such as 'names of wines', and items of a moralising character, such as the mnemonic 'precepts in -*ly*', which enjoin one to 'Arise early, serve God devoutly', and so on. Despite the many different configurations into which this material was assembled, there is little difficulty – as Rachel Hands first suggested in 1967 – in perceiving that common to them all is a recognisable and immensely popular little manual of instruction concerning the language of fieldsports and other matters that *longythe to a yonge gentylle man to haue knowynge of*, as one version claims (Egerton MS 1995).

This eclectic, multifarious manual is frequently found in commonplace books and miscellanies, several containing a high proportion of practical texts, produced in the latter half of the 15th century. Some of its components also occur in a range of other compilations, sometimes as filler, but often because of a perceived affinity with other texts included there. The widespread popularity of the *J.B. Treatise* can be gauged by the relatively large number of manuscripts and early printed books in which it survives, either whole or in part: twenty-six in all. These reveal a work that was constantly being added to, cut back and generally modified to suit the purposes of its different copyists. The result is a potentially baffling array of redactions, which have never before been closely examined in their entirety. Some are patently closely related, but others are so distant from one another that they could arguably be regarded as entirely discrete compositions. For the purposes of this study, I have elected to downplay such differences and to concentrate instead on the congruities – admittedly slight at times – that unite all the different versions as members of a large, heterogeneous family.

There is, however, no simple way of presenting all the notable members of such a family, with all their distinctive features, without some repetition, since even distant cousins may manifest traits that unite and divide them in equal measure. It has also proved impossible to select any particular manuscript as a base text for the entire family group, since there are too many rival witnesses that differ in so many ways that none can justly be elevated above all others as the foremost representative of the treatise. Neither recensionist nor best-text editing methods are of any use in dealing with the entire J.B. corpus, which is why I have opted – in Parts I, II and III of this study – to present three independent versions founded on three base manuscripts, which can be collated with several others that are either directly or distantly related. Not only do these three selected versions – edited from Brogyntyn MS ii.1, Harley MS 2340, and MS Hale 148 – between them encompass almost all the individual J.B. components (or 'elements'), they also exemplify some (though not all) of the major arrangements in which the *J.B. Treatise* is found. It could, with justification, be argued that at least one other version – represented by Trinity College Dublin MS 516, or Beinecke MS 163 – deserves also to be set out in full, but to do so would entail the repetition of very similar material for the sake of showing it in a distinctive arrangement; so too with Egerton MS 1995 and MS Pepys 1047.

I have elected instead to concentrate on documenting the full range and diversity of the J.B. elements, and have accordingly – in Part IV– assembled an assortment of elements that are either unique in themselves, or notably at variance with their equivalents in Parts I–III. These include one element from Trinity College Dublin MS 516, two elements that receive unusual treatment in Egerton MS 1995, and the pair of hawking elements that comprise the entire J.B. contents of the 'Duke of Gloucester' MS.

Finally, Appendices I, II and III contain three of the most recurrent and varied lists of terms – those of 'collective nouns', 'carving terms' and 'resting terms' – collated, and annotated, from all J.B. witnesses.

The resulting arrangement of this volume is somewhat unorthodox, but only through seeking to deal justly with its unconventional subject matter. This has entailed setting out as many formulations of the *J.B. Treatise* as possible, and compiling a complete survey of its variegated contents, both actual and potential, while avoiding excessive duplication. Every extant component and every formulation of the treatise is therefore represented in some form or other – either whole or in part; as a base text or a collated congener; as part of the compilations of the Appendices; or else in extended quotations in the Explanatory Notes. It may be presumed that any section of any witness not set out in one of these ways must be so similar to material already selected for this edition that its inclusion would be repetitious and supererogatory.

In the years that have elapsed since the publication of the first edition of this book in 2003, a number of important reference works and studies have been published, some manuscripts have been recatalogued or have had a change of owner, and I myself learned of a significant additional witness of the *J.B. Treatise* that was unknown to me previously. The present edition takes account of such developments by including relevant new information wherever possible. It also seeks to clarify certain issues that I felt could be better expressed, and takes account of ongoing revisions to the *OED*.

It remains for me to acknowledge and thank the following institutions and bodies for permission to publish the transcriptions contained in this volume:

> The National Library of Wales, for MS Brogyntyn ii.1, fols 184r–192r
>
> The British Library, for Harley MS 2340, fols 47r–51v, Egerton MS 1995, fols 55v, 63r
>
> The Treasurer and Masters of the Bench of Lincoln's Inn, for MS Hale 148, fols 6v–8r

I owe a special debt of thanks to HRH, Prince Richard, The Duke of Gloucester for graciously welcoming me to Kensington Palace and placing several manuscripts at my disposal, including MS G (the 'Duke of Gloucester' manuscript). My transcription of pages 158–161 of that manuscript was originally published by kind permission of His Royal Highness.

I should also like to thank the staff of many libraries who assisted me with my enquiries, among them, Kenneth Dunn Esq., National Library of Scotland; Guy Holborn Esq., Lincoln's Inn Library; Daniel Huws Esq., National Library of Wales; Dr Consuelo Dutschke, Columbia University Library; Dr John Hall, Cambridge University Library; Dr Kristian Jensen, formerly of the Bodleian Library; the staff of Lambeth Palace Library; Alfred Mueller Esq., Beinecke Library; Robert York Esq., The College of Arms, London.

Thanks are also due to Prof. Anthony Edwards, Dr Lotte Hellinga, Prof. Constance Hieatt, Prof. Julia Boffey, Dr James McNelis, Prof. Nigel Palmer, Prof. Ralph Hanna, Prof. Tim Unwin and Dr Allen J. Grieco for answering my queries and offering advice; Julia Bruce for tracking down and forwarding materials that were otherwise inaccessible to me; and Craig MacKenzie and Gabrielle Singleton for proofreading.

Finally, I should like to acknowledge my considerable debt to Prof. John Scattergood, who first alerted me to the J.B. contents of MS T and then encouraged me to work on the *J.B. Treatise*; and to Mrs Rachel Hands, who generously shared her knowledge and personal research materials with me.

David Scott-Macnab

School of Languages
North-West University, Potchefstroom
November 2019

SIGLA AND ABBREVIATIONS

Manuscripts and Early Printed Books containing versions of the *J.B. Treatise* or J.B. material

Addl	London, British Library, Additional MS 33994 ('Ware Manuscript'), fol. 26v
Adv	Edinburgh, National Library of Scotland, MS Advocates 19.3.1, fols 62r, 63r–64v
Am	Oxford, Bodleian Library, MS Ashmole 189 (SC 6777), fol. 211r
BK	Wynkyn de Worde, *The Boke of Keruynge*, 2nd edn (1508, 1513), *STC* 3289, 3290, sig. A1v
BS	Helmingham Hall, Suffolk, 'Tollemache *Book of Secrets*', fols 42r–43r, 44r
C	Cambridge, University Library, MS Ll.1.18, fols 44v–45r
Dg, Dg*	Oxford, Bodleian Library, MS Digby 196, fols 160r–161v, 157v
Eg	London, British Library, Egerton MS 1995, fols 55v–58r, 63r–64v
Ex	Exeter, Exeter Cathedral Library, MS 3533, fols 101v–103v
G	Location unknown, private collection, (*olim* London, Kensington Palace, 'Duke of Gloucester Manuscript'), pp. 158–161
H	London, British Library, Harley MS 2340, fols 47r–51v
Ha	London, Lincoln's Inn Library, MS Hale 148, fols 6v–8r
Harl	London, British Library, Harley MS 541, fol. 225r
HSG	William Caxton, Westminster: two printings of Lydgate's, *The Hors, the Shepe and the Ghoos* (1476–7), *STC* 17019, 17018 [fols 16v–18r]
L	London, Lambeth Palace Library, MS 306, fols 174v–176v
LJ	William Caxton's *Book of Courtesy* (also called *Little John*), 2nd edn, printed by Wynkyn de Worde, Westminster (*c.* 1491–3), *STC* 3304: Bodleian Library, Douce Framents e.4, [sig. b6v]
Pl	New York, Columbia University, Rare Book & Manuscript Library, Plimpton Add. MS 2, fols 3r–5v

Pp	Cambridge, Magdalene College, The Pepys Library, MS Pepys 1047, fols 2r–5v, 20v–23r
Prk	Aberystwyth, National Library of Wales, Brogyntyn MS ii.1 (*olim* MS Porkington 10), fols 184r–192r
Rc	Oxford, Bodleian Library, MS Rawlinson C 158 (SC 12022), endleaf [fol. xi^v]
Rd	Oxford, Bodleian Library, MS Rawlinson D 328 ('Walter Pollard's notebook', SC 15444), fols 171r–173r
Rg	London, College of Arms, MS Arundel 58 ('Robert of Gloucester Manuscript'), endleaves [i^{r-v}, iii^v]
Ry	London, British Library, Royal MS 17 D IV, fols 87r–89r
StA	*The Boke of St. Albans* ('Schoolmaster Printer': St Albans, 1486), *STC* 3308, sigs d3r–d4r, f4v–f8r
StA(2)	*The Boke of St. Albans* (Wynkyn de Worde: Westminster, 1496), *STC* 3309, sigs c5r–v, e2v–e5r
T	Dublin, Trinity College Library, MS 516, fols 35r–36r
W	New Haven, Yale University, Beinecke Rare Book and Manuscript Library, Beinecke MS 163 ('Wagstaff Miscellany'), fols 185r–186r

Manuscripts and Early Printed Books
containing related or analogous material

C*	Cambridge, University Library, MS Ll.1.18, fol. 45r: a list of wines
L2	London, British Library, Lansdowne MS 762, fol. 16r–v: eight Lansdowne group items
(Lansdowne group	See discussion of *StA* in the Introduction, pp. 49–50)
MC	Seven Lansdowne group items handwritten on the blank pages (fols 34v–35r) forming the juncture between two Caxton incunables that have been bound together to form a composite volume: London, British Library, IB.49408 and IB.49437; see Introduction, p. 50
T2	Cambridge, Trinity College, MS O.9.38, fol. 49r: Properties of a good horse
W2	Oxford, Bodleian Library, MS Wood empt. 18 (SC 8606), fol. 60r: Properties of a good horse

Manuscripts containing the *Boke of Huntyng* (*BH*)

K   London, British Library, Additional MS 82948 (*olim* Kensington Palace, 'Kerdeston Hunting Book'), fols 3r–v; ed. Danielsson (1971)

Lm   London, Lambeth Palace Library, MS 491, fols 287r–290v; ed. Zettersten (1969)

Rawl   Oxford, Bodleian Library, MS Rawlinson Poet. 143 (SC 14637), fols 1r–11a^v; ed. Hands, *EHH*, pp. 168–86

(See further Introduction, pp. 3–4)

Works and Websites frequently cited

A-ND   *Anglo-Norman Dictionary*, ed. William Rothwell *et al.* (1992)

Babees Book   *The Babees Book*, ed. F.J. Furnivall (1868, repr. 1997)

BF   Turbervile, George, *The Booke of Faulconrie or Hauking* (London, 1575), *STC* 24324; facs. edn 1969

BH   *Boke of Huntyng*: hunting treatise in *The Boke of St Albans* (1486), sigs e1r–f4r, with manuscript versions Lm and Rawl; facs. edn by Rachel Hands, *EHH* (1975); see Introduction, pp. 3–4, 47–9

Bibbesworth   de Bibbesworth, Walter, *Le tretiz*, ed. William Rothwell (1990); ed. Thomas Wright (1857)

Boke of Nurture   Russell, John, *The Boke of Nurture*, in *The Babees Book*, ed. Furnivall

Book of Secrets   Tollemache *Book of Secrets*, ed. Jeremy Griffiths (2001)

CT   Chaucer, Geoffrey, *The Canterbury Tales*, in *The Riverside Chaucer*, gen. ed. Larry D. Benson (1990)

CV   *The Craft of Venery*, ed. David Scott-Macnab (2009)

DAV   Frederick II, *De arte venandi cum avibus*, ed. Casey A. Wood and F. Marjorie Fyfe (1943)

DHLF   *Le Robert: Dictionnaire historique de la langue française*, ed. Alain Rey (1992)

DMF   *Dictionnaire du Moyen Français (1330–1500)*, online at <www.atilf.fr.dmf>

DNB   *The Dictionary of National Biography*, ed. Sir Leslie Stephen and Sir Sidney Lee (1917)

ABBREVIATIONS

Douay-Rheims *The Vulgate Bible: Douay-Rheims Translation* (2010–13)
EHH *English Hawking and Hunting in 'The Boke of St. Albans'*, ed. Rachel Hands (1975)
eLALME An Electronic Version of *A Linguistic Atlas of Late Mediaeval English* <www.lel.ed.ac.uk/ihd/elalme/elalme.html>
FEW von Wartburg, Walter, *Französisches etymologisches Wörterbuch* (1948–)
Florio Florio, John, *A Worlde of Wordes, or Most Copious, and Exact Dictionarie in Italian and English* (London, 1598)
Godefroy Godefroy, F., *Dictionnaire de l'ancienne langue française du IXe au XVe siècle* (1881–1902)
Graesse Graesse, Johann Georg Theodor, *Orbis Latinus: Lexicon lateinischer geographischer Namen*, rev. edn (1972)
Harley Cook Books *Two Fifteenth-Century Cookery Books*, ed. Thomas Austin (1888, repr. 1964)
IMEV Brown, Carleton and Rossell Hope Robbins, *The Index of Middle English Verse* (1943); Robbins, Rossell Hope and J. Cutler, *Supplement to the Index of Middle English Verse* (1965)
IPMEP Lewis, R.E. et al., *Index of Printed Middle English Prose* (1985)
ISTC Incunabula Short Title Catalogue: <https://data.cerl.org/istc>
LALME McIntosh, Angus, et al., *A Linguistic Atlas of Late Mediaeval English* (1986); see also eLALME
Latham Latham, R.E., *Revised Medieval Latin Word-List from British and Irish Sources* (1980)
LC Phébus, Gaston, *Livre de chasse*, ed. Gunnar Tilander (1971)
Letter-Book G *Calendar of Letter-Books preserved among the Archives of the Corporation of the City of London ... Letter-Book G*, ed. Reginald R. Sharpe (1905)
Manual X Keiser, George R., *Works of Science and Information*, Volume 10 of *A Manual of the Writings in Middle English* (1998)
MED *Middle English Dictionary*, ed. Hans Kurath, Sherman M. Kuhn et al. (1952–2001); also online at <https:quod.lib.umich.edu/m/middle-english-dictionary>
MG *The Master of Game by Edward, Second Duke of York*, ed. Wm. A. and F. Baillie-Grohman (1904)

Modus et Ratio	*Les livres du roy Modus et de la royne Ratio*, ed. A.G. Tilander (1932)
NIMEV	Boffey, Julia and A.S.G. Edwards, *A New Index of Middle English Verse* (2005)
Noble Arte	Gascoigne, George, *The Noble Arte of Venerie or Hunting* (London, 1575), *STC* 24328; facs. edn printed as *Turbervile's Booke of Hunting* (1908)
Noble Cookry	Napier, Mrs Alexander, *A Noble Boke off Cookry* (1882)
Nominale	*Nominale sive verbale*, ed. W.W. Skeat (1906)
ODNB	*Oxford Dictionary of National Biography* (2004); also online at <www.oxforddnb.com>
OED	*Oxford English Dictionary*, online 3rd edn <www.oed.com>
PEB	*Prince Edward's Book of Hawking* (*IPMEP* 194, 741); see further *PEB 1*, *PEB 2* below
PEB 1	*Prince Edward's Book of Hawking* in BL, Harley MS 2340, fols 1r–22v; ed. A.E.H. Swaen (1943–44)
PEB 2	*Prince Edward's Book of Hawking* conflated with medical recipes for hawks in Lambeth Palace MS 306, fols 166r–174v (unpublished); see Introduction, pp. 32–33
PH	*The Proceis of Hawkyng*: hawking treatise in *The Boke of St Albans* (1486), sigs. a2r–d3r; facsimile edn by Rachel Hands, *EHH* (1975); see Introduction, p. 47
Pottage	*An Ordinance of Pottage*, ed. Constance B. Hieatt (1988)
PPF	*The Percy Poem on Falconry* (*NIMEV* 3693; Beinecke MS 163, fols 125r–134r), ed. Bror Danielsson (1970)
Promptorium	*Promptorium parvulorum*, ed. A.L. Matthew (1908, repr. 2002); ed. Albertus Way (1843–65)
SC	*Summary Catalogue of Western Manuscripts in the Bodleian Library at Oxford*, ed. R.W. Hunt et al. (1895–1953)
Secular Lyrics	*Secular Lyrics of the XIVth and XVth Centuries*, ed. Rossell Hope Robbins, 2nd edn (1955)
SGGK	*Sir Gawain and the Green Knight*, ed. J.R.R. Tolkien and E.V. Gordon, 2nd edn (1967)
STC	Pollard, A.W., G.R. Redgrave et al., *A Short-Title Catalogue of Books Printed in England, Scotland and Ireland 1475–1640*, 2nd rev. edn (1976–91)

THawk 1 The *Tretyse off Hawkyng* in the Durham County Record Office (D/X 76/7); ed. Bror Daniellson (1972); see Introduction p. 64

THawk 2 The *Tretyse off Hawkyng* in BL Sloane MS 3488, fols 1r–3r; ed. N.J. Shirley Leggatt (1950); see Introduction p. 64

THawk 3 The *Tretyse off Hawkyng* in CUL MS L1.1.18, fols 55v–58v (unpublished); see Introduction p. 64

THunt The *Tretyse off Huntyng*, ed. Anne Rooney (1987)

Tobler–Lommatz. Tobler, Alfred, and E. Lommatzsch, *Altfranzösisches Wörterbuch* (1925–)

Twiti-A Twiti, William, *The Art of Hunting* in the 'Ashton' MS; ed. David Scott-Macnab (2009), pp. 3–11

Twiti-C Twiti, William, *The Art of Hunting* in BL MS Cotton Vespasian B XII; ed. David Scott-Macnab (2009), pp. 14–19

Twiti-F Twiti, William (Guillaume), *L'art de venerie* (Anglo-Norman text) ed. Gunnar Tilander (1956)

Vulgate *The Vulgate Bible: Douay-Rheims Translation* (2010–13)

Whiting Whiting, B.J., *Proverbs, Sentences and Proverbial Phrases from English Writings Mainly Before 1500* (1968)

Journals, Libraries, Series

Anglia *Anglia, Zeitschrift für englische Philologie*

A-NTS Anglo-Norman Text Society

Archiv *Archiv für das Studium der neueren Sprachen und Literaturen*

BL British Library, London

Bodl. Bodleian Library, Oxford

CUL Cambridge University Library

E&S *Essays & Studies*

EETS, ES, OS, SS Early English Text Society, Extra Series, Original Series, Supplementary Series

ELN *English Language Notes*

MÆ *Medium Ævum*

MLN *Modern Language Notes*

N&Q *Notes and Queries / Notes & Queries*

NLS National Library of Scotland

NM	*Neuphilologische Mitteilungen*
NS	New Series
OS	Original Series
PMLA	*Publications of the Modern Language Association of America*
RES	*Review of English Studies*
SATF	Société des anciens textes français
SN	*Studia Neophilologica*
TCBS	*Transactions of the Cambridge Bibliographical Society*
TCC	Trinity College, Cambridge
TPS	*Transactions of the Philological Society*

Languages

AN	Anglo-Norman
EMnE	Early Modern English
L	Latin
MDu	Middle Dutch
MF	Middle French
MHG	Middle High German
MLG	Middle Low German
MnE	Modern English
OE	Old English
OF	Old French
OI	Old Icelandic
ON	Old Norse

INTRODUCTION

In the earliest decades of printing in England, one of the most popular books to reach the public was *The Book of Hawking, Hunting, and Blasing of Arms*, first printed in St Albans (Herts.) in 1486 (*STC* 3308).[1] That volume, now widely known as *The Boke of St Albans* (hereafter *StA*),[2] consists of four main treatises – on hawking, hunting, coat armour and the blazoning of arms – all texts of a fundamentally practical nature. *StA* may be described as England's first off-the-shelf miscellany: a printed version of a type of book that had previously been assembled by commissioned scribes, or by literate individuals compiling their own 'commonplace books'.[3] The popularity of the book can be judged from the fact that it was reprinted by Wynkyn de Worde in 1496 (*STC* 3309) with the addition of another sporting treatise, on 'fysshing with an angle',[4] and was thereafter reissued whole or in part a further ten times by 1565.[5]

The wide dissemination of *StA*, especially in its later editions, prompted a rapid rise in the reputation of a certain Dame Juliana Berners (Barnes or Bernes), who came to be accepted as the book's author, although her

---

[1] *STC* = A.W. Pollard, G.R. Redgrave et al., *A Short-Title Catalogue of Books Printed in England, Scotland and Ireland 1475–1640*, 2nd rev. edn (London, 1976–91).

[2] The title given to *StA* by the British Library's online Incunabula Short Title Catalogue (ISTC), and by institutions following its nomenclature, is *Book of Hawking, Hunting, and Heraldry*: ISTC No. iB01030000. Regarding date, the printer's penultimate colophon on sig. f²9v claims that this work was compiled ('compy[l]yt') in 1486, and it is conventionally assumed to have been printed in the same year. For a full description, see *English Hawking and Hunting in 'The Boke of St. Albans'*, ed. Rachel Hands (London, 1975; hereafter *EHH*), pp. xiii–xxii; and see further pp. 47–52 below.

[3] I discuss the notion of a commonplace book later in this Introduction.

[4] Sigs g3v–i4v.

[5] *STC* 3309.5–3312.7 and 3313.3, 3313.5. For a useful survey of similar practical books and the milieu in which they were produced, see George R. Keiser, 'Practical books for the gentleman', in *The Cambridge History of the Book in Britain: Volume III, 1400–1557*, ed. Lotte Hellinga and J.B. Trapp (Cambridge, 1999), pp. 470–94. See also E.F. Jacob's remarks on the sections relating to heraldry and fishing: 'The Book of St Albans', in *Essays in Later Medieval History* (Manchester, 1968), pp. 195–213.

name, in fact, belongs only with the hunting treatise, which ends with the colophon, *Explicit Dam Iulyans Barnes in her boke of huntyng* (sig. f4r). For enthusiastic antiquarians, however, this colophon provided evidence of a more extensive authorial presence, and the sporting dame was soon credited with authorship of the whole volume, including even the treatise on fishing added by Wynkyn.[1] According to the historian William Burton (1575–1645), *Dam Iulyans Barnes* was to be identified with 'lady Juliana Berners', daughter of Sir James Berners of Essex, and prioress of Sopwell Nunnery at St Albans, Hertfordshire – a notion accepted as fact by numerous later commentators.[2] In spite of a conspicuous dearth of supporting evidence, Burton's claims were greatly amplified in the 19th century by Joseph Haslewood, who even constructed a speculative pedigree for Dame Juliana and supplied many conjectural details about her life.[3]

All such biographical theorising has long been comprehensively refuted, together with any notion that 'Dame Juliana' could have been the overall author of *StA*,[4] and yet many libraries still catalogue that incunable under her name, and she continues to be cited as author in modern editions of all or part of it.[5] In fact, in recent years, Dame Juliana can be said to have been

---

[1] See Bishop John Bale's catalogue of famous British authors – *Scriptorum illustrium maioris Brytanniae ... catalogus*, 2 vols (Basle, 1557, 1559; facsimile reprint, Farnborough, 1971), I, 611 (Centuria octava, s.v. 'Ivliana Barnes') – in which Bale claims that Dame Juliana, 'illustris fœmina ... heroica mulier', was alive in 1460 and that she was responsible for all five treatises found in Wynkyn's edition of 1496, *StA*(2).

[2] Burton's attribution occurs in a handwritten note on a front endpaper in the copy of *StA* (1486 edn) held by Cambridge University Library, classmark Inc.3.J.4.1 [3636].

[3] *The Book Containing the Treatises of Hawking; Hunting; Coat-Armour; Fishing; and Blasing of Arms. As printed at Westminster by Wynkyn de Worde*, Introduction by Joseph Haslewood (London, 1810), pp. 5–17.

[4] See, for example, William Blades, *The Boke of Saint Albans by Dame Juliana Berners* (London, 1881), pp. 7–15. Blades summarises the development of Dame Juliana's putative biography, and concludes: 'What we really know of the Dame is almost nothing, and may be summed up in the following few words. She probably lived at the beginning of the fifteenth century, and she possibly compiled from existing MSS. some rhymes on Hunting' (p. 13). See also the detailed discussion by Rachel Hands, 'Juliana Berners and *The Boke of St. Albans*', *RES*, NS 18 (1967), 373–86, and Julia Boffey's entry on 'Berners [Bernes, Barnes], Juliana' in the *Oxford Dictionary of National Biography* (*ODNB*), which remedies the many inaccuracies upheld about the dame in past editions of *The Dictionary of National Biography*.

[5] For example, Dame Juliana Berners, *The Boke of Saint Albans, 1486*, facsimile edn, The English Experience, No. 151 (Amsterdam & New York, 1969); *Julians Barnes: Boke of Huntyng*, ed. Gunnar Tilander, Cynegetica 11 (Karlshamn, 1964). The online

purposely resurrected so as to be held up for admiration as an important female author of the late Middle Ages,[1] in spite of there being no new evidence to sustain this proposition.[2] As George Keiser succinctly observes, 'The authorship of Dame Juliana Berners is an enduring myth ...; her identity as a daughter of Sir James Berners of Essex ... was perpetuated by early antiquarians and resists efforts of sound scholarship to cast doubt upon it.'[3]

Just as the whole of *StA* cannot realistically be attributed to Dame Juliana, neither can the verse hunting treatise – the *Boke of Huntyng* – alone, in spite of the colophon attributing it to her.[4] As Rachel Hands has shown, the name Juliana Barnes occurs nowhere else in connection with the *Boke of Huntyng*, which is more usually associated with the legendary figure of Sir Tristram, mentioned near the start of the treatise: 'Wheresoeuere ye fare by fryth or by fell / My dere chylde take hede how Tristram dooth you tell' (*StA*, 1214–15).[5] On the other hand, the dame's name and initials are

---

catalogue of the Bodleian Library cites 'Berners, Juliana, 1388?' as the author of several of its holdings.

[1] See, for example, Marilyn Bailey Ogilvie, *Women in Science: Antiquity through the Nineteenth Century* (Cambridge, MA, 1986, 1993), p. 36, s.v. 'Barnes (Berners), Juliana'; Barry Collett, *Late Medieval Englishwomen: Julian of Norwich, Marjorie Kempe and Juliana Berners*, The Early Modern Englishwoman, Series I, Part 4, Vol. 3 (Aldershot, 2006); 'Juliana Berners' in *Women's Writing in Middle English*, ed. Alexandra Barratt, 2nd edn (Abingdon, 2010), pp. 249–54. Barratt makes no mention of the arguments of William Blades or Rachel Hands, yet finds (p. 249) 'independent corroboration of Dame Juliana's existence' in Sir Henry Chauncy's *Historical Antiquities of Hertfordshire* (1700). The impulse to extol Juliana Berners in this way is not new, as may be judged by her inclusion in Mrs [Mary] Pilkington's *Memoirs of Celebrated Female Characters* (London, 1804), p. 50.

[2] Apart from other considerations, as Julia Boffey notes (*ODNB*, *art. cit.*), the name 'Dam Julyans' could be construed as a corruption of 'Daun Julyan', which would alter the sex of the author.

[3] George Keiser, *Works of Science and Information*, Volume 10 of *A Manual of the Writings in Middle English 1050–1500*, gen. ed. Albert E. Hartung (New Haven, CT, 1998) (hereafter *Manual X*), 3699 [460].

[4] I shall refer to the hunting treatise by its own colophon title – *Boke of Huntyng* – rather than that adopted by Rachel Hands ('the "Tristram" treatise'). Keiser uses versions of both titles: *Manual X*, 3699 [460].

[5] All references are to Hands's lineated facsimile edition, *EHH*. Tristram is also mentioned in all three manuscript versions of the treatise: London, Lambeth Palace Library, MS 491, fols 287r–290v (Lm); Oxford, Bodleian Library, MS Rawlinson Poet. 143, fols 1r–11(a)v (Rawl); London, British Library, Additional MS 82948 (*olim* Kensington Palace, Duke of Gloucester, 'Kerdeston Hunting Book'), fol. 3r–v (K).

elsewhere manifestly associated with other material, which the compiler of *StA* used as filler for the final leaves of his book's hawking and hunting sections: sigs d3r–4r and f4v–8r. The nature of this 'additional material' in *StA* is very diverse, but at its heart is a collection of instruction, lore and terminology relating to hawking and hunting. The most common item in this compilation is a list of collective nouns, or 'terms of association', which occupies sigs f6r–7r in *StA*. A similar list in MS Pepys 1047 (Pp) ends with the colophon, 'Explicit Iulyan Barne' (fol. 5v); and, in Harley MS 2340 (H), another such list closes with the colophon, 'Explicit I.B.' (fol. 51v).[1] It would seem highly likely, under the circumstances, that the initials *I.B.* and the name *Iulyan Barne* are connected; furthermore, that they belong with the list of collective nouns and, through it, with the little collection of hawking and hunting information in which such lists normally occur.

Given the combined testimony of all these sources, we may plausibly deduce that the name *Dam Iulyans Barnes* is misplaced in *StA*: that it originally belonged with the 'additional material' that follows the *Boke of Huntyng*, and was transferred by the book's compiler to the end of the hunting treatise for reasons that we can only guess at. One credible suggestion is that the compiler was influenced by the long passages in the *Boke of Huntyng* in which a mother – a 'dame' – instructs her child, and that he associated this figure with the *Dam Iulyans* mentioned in what we may presume to have been the colophon to his 'additional material'.[2]

Having dispensed with Dame Juliana's adventitious connection with *StA*'s hunting treatise, we are faced with an entirely new issue: why, or how,

---

Modern editions of these texts have been published by: Arne Zettersten, 'The Lambeth manuscript of the Boke of Huntyng', *NM*, 70 (1969), 106–21; Hands, *EHH*, pp. 168–186; Bror Danielsson, 'The Kerdeston "library of hunting and hawking literature" (early 15th c. fragments)', in *Et Multa et Multum: Beiträge zur Literatur, Geschichte und Kultur der Jagd*, ed. Sigrid Schwenk *et al.* (Berlin, 1971), pp. 47–59 (54–6). Other works, of a later date, also attribute the *Boke of Huntyng* to Tristram, rather than to Dame Juliana, as Hands shows: *EHH*, pp. lvi–lvii.

[1] In yet another manuscript – Lambeth Palace MS 306 (L), which is closely related to MS H – the initials 'jb', written large, have been added in a later hand, probably of the 16th century, above the start of a composite hawking treatise, followed by a number of items of JB material. MS L is discussed in more detail below.

[2] The presence of a female instructor is apparent in lines 1214–1528, 1731–1846 of the *Boke of Huntyng*. For further analysis, see Hands, 'Juliana Berners', pp. 381–4, and *EHH*, pp. lvii–lx, as well as my discussion of *StA* below. M.Y. Offord observes that the name 'Iulyans' (in *StA*) is a strange form that probably represents a compositor's error for 'Iulyane' or 'Iulyana': review of *Julians Barnes: Boke of Huntyng*, ed. Tilander, in *MÆ*, 35 (1966), 150–3. Indeed, 'Iulyane' would nicely match the 'Iulyan' of Pp.

her name became linked with lists of collective nouns and the other material that usually accompanies them. Unfortunately, there is no evidence to sustain anything beyond speculation in this regard, so I shall not attempt to answer that tantalising riddle. My aim, instead, is to examine the range of material associated with 'Juliana Berners' or 'J.B.' in sources other than *StA*. For convenience, I shall follow the convention adopted by Rachel Hands and refer to this as the 'J.B. material'. And, where there seems justification in doing so, I shall refer also to the *J.B. Treatise*, reserving this title for those cases where a substantial body of J.B. material takes on a coherent, unified form, as it does in several of the manuscripts that form the basis of this study.

THE *J.B. TREATISE*

As matters stand, the J.B. material has the curious distinction of being both familiar and obscure: some of it is well known to scholars, and even to the wider public, while a great deal remains generally unexplored. The reasons for this are probably twofold: in the first place, the material has usually been examined in a piecemeal fashion, with only one or two of its constituent items receiving attention at any one time; secondly, it has often been approached by way of *StA*, whose version is the best known. As a result, a very imperfect conception of the J.B. material has developed, not least because the form in which it occurs in *StA* is corrupt or problematic in several ways. For one thing, the J.B. elements in *StA* are interspersed with items from another source belonging to the so-called 'Lansdowne group' of texts (discussed further below in relation to *StA*),[1] which has created uncertainty over what should count as J.B. material and what not. It is therefore unfortunate that scholars have long used *StA* as their primary point of reference when identifying or alluding to the J.B. material,[2] even though versions of it occur in at least twenty-four other 15th-century sources (twenty-two of them manuscripts) that are all independent of *StA*.

---

[1] The 'Lansdowne group', so-named after BL, Lansdowne MS 762, is described more fully later in this Introduction. See also Hands, *EHH*, pp. liv–lv; Keiser, *Manual X*, 3703–4 [473–80].

[2] See, for example, Daniel Huws, 'MS Porkington 10 and its scribes', in *Romance Reading and the Book: Essays on Medieval Narrative presented to Maldwyn Mills*, ed. Jennifer Fellows, Rosalind Field *et al*. (Cardiff, 1996), pp. 188–207 (esp. p. 191), where Huws refers to the J.B. material as 'texts occuring in Dame Juliana Berners's *Boke of St Albans*'.

Perhaps the best-known feature of the J.B. material overall is its lists of collective nouns, which were the subject of a major study by John Hodgkin in the early 20th century. Hodgkin collated and examined the collective nouns that occur in *StA* and twenty-two other witnesses dating from the 15th to the 19th centuries.[1] However, only seven of his witnesses are medieval manuscripts, while many of the books he cites derive from *StA*, and so have little independent value.

A few years later, Hodgkin published another study of J.B. material – the carving terms – which he traced in *StA* and thirteen other witnesses up to 1691.[2] That study includes only three manuscripts, as well as several printed books that are either later editions, or derivatives, of *StA*.

For decades, Hodgkin's studies defined the field, with scholars publishing more lists of these two sets of terms as further manuscripts came to light.[3] In the process they invariably overlooked other, adjacent J.B. material in those manuscripts, together with the evidence it provided for the existence of a small, popular treatise.

This pattern was broken only in 1967, when Rachel Hands first mapped out the contents of eleven manuscripts containing what she called 'the "J B" treatise',[4] and again in 1975 when she published her annotated facsimile edition of *StA*, together with an analysis of 22 witnesses of the 'J.B. group' of texts.[5] Understandably, however, *StA* provided the main focus for Hands's analysis: she was interested in the J.B. material for the light it could cast on *StA*, and so had no need to collate or compare the J.B. texts in a systematic way for their own sake. That will be the task of the present study, which includes three witnesses that were not known to Hands, and another that she excluded from her survey because of its late date.[6]

---

[1] John Hodgkin, 'Proper terms: An attempt at a rational explanation of the meanings of the collection of phrases in *The Book of St. Albans*, 1486', *TPS*, 26:3 (1909), 1–187 (hereafter 'Terms I').

[2] John Hodgkin, 'Proper terms. II. "Tearmes of a keruer"', *TPS*, 27:1 (1914), 52–94, and 27:2 (1916), 123–37 [95*–109*] (hereafter 'Terms II').

[3] See, for example, Hope E. Allen, 'The fifteenth-century "associations of beasts, of birds, and of men": the earliest text with "language for carvers"', *PMLA*, 51 (1936), 602–6. Other studies are noted in the appropriate sections below.

[4] Hands, 'Juliana Berners', pp. 384–6 (p. 384).

[5] Hands, *EHH*, pp. xlv–liv, *passim*. Keiser describes the J.B. group as 'the invention of Rachel Hands', but nevertheless accepts her name for it, along with her account of its salient features: *Manual X*, 3701 [465].

[6] Unknown to Hands in 1975 were MSS BS, Ex and T; and she paid little attention to Wynkyn de Worde's Bole of Keruyng (*BK*).

THE WITNESSES AND THEIR CONTENTS

There are currently twenty-six known witnesses containing J.B. material, of which twenty-two are 15th-century manuscripts, three are incunables of the 15th century, and one is an early printed book of the early 16th century. For most purposes, the 1486 printing of *StA* may be considered the latest text of any value to the present study. So influential was this volume that all rival versions of the J.B. material were overshadowed and soon disappeared from view. Hence my exclusion of the many printed books containing J.B. material derived from *StA* that are listed by Hodgkin.[1] However, a few later printed books – such as *The Boke of Keruyng* – contain one or more items of J.B. material for which no manuscript tradition survives, and these have been included even though they postdate *StA*.

Principal witnesses and major collections of J.B. material

1. Adv – NLS, MS Advocates 19.3.1, fols 62r, 63r–64v
2. Dg / Dg* – Bodl., MS Digby 196, fols 160r–161v; fol. 157v (Dg*)
3. Eg – BL, Egerton MS 1995, fols 55v–58r, 63r–64v
3a. Ex – Exeter Cathedral, MS 3533, fols 101v–103v
4. H – BL, Harley MS 2340, fols 47r–51v
5. Ha – Lincoln's Inn, MS Hale 148, fols 6v–8r
6. HSG – Caxton's two printings of Lydgate's *The Hors, the Shepe and the Ghoos* (1476–77), [fols 16v–18r]
7. L – Lambeth Palace, MS 306, fols 174v–176v
8. Pl – Columbia University, Plimpton Add. MS 2, fols 3r–5v
9. Pp – Magdalene College, Cambridge, MS Pepys 1047, fols 2r–5v, 20v–23r
10. Prk – National Library of Wales, Brogyntyn MS ii.1, fols 184r–192r
11. Rd – Bodl., MS Rawlinson D 328, fols 171r–173r
12. Rg – College of Arms, MS Arundel 58, endleaves [i^{r-v}, iii^{v}]
13. *StA* – *The Boke of St Albans* (1486), sigs d3r–d4r, f4v–f8r
14. T – Trinity College, Dublin, MS 516, fols 35r–36r
15. W – Yale University, Beinecke MS 163, fols 185r–186r

---

[1] I have also excluded witnesses that contain *only* one or more of the 'miscellaneous' elements (defined below), and that otherwise have nothing to connect them with the *J.B. Treatise*; for example, Trinity College, Cambridge, MS O.9.38 (cited by Hands), which contains only the 'Properties of a good horse', among a range of disparate contents.

Witnesses with one or two J.B. elements

16. Addl – BL, Additional MS 33994, fol. 26v
17. Am – Bodl., MS Ashmole 189, fol. 211r
18. BK – Wynkyn de Worde's two printings of *The Boke of Keruyng* (1508, 1513), sig. A1v
19. BS – Helmingham Hall, 'Tollemache *Book of Secrets*', fols 42r–43r, 44r
20. C – Cambridge University Library, MS Ll.1.18, fols 44v–45r
21. G – [Location unknown], 'Duke of Gloucester MS', pp. 158–161
22. Harl – BL, Harley MS 541, fol. 225r
23. LJ – Caxton's *Book of Courtesy* (or *Little John*), 2nd edn, printed by Wynkyn de Worde (*c.* 1491–93), [sig. b6v]
24. Rc – Bodl., MS Rawlinson C 158 (SC 12022), endleaf [fol. xi^v]
25. Ry – BL, Royal MS 17 D IV, fols 87r–89r

Each of these witnesses will be described in detail, and in the above order, in the pages following.

The J.B. Elements: Hunting, Hawking and Miscellaneous

Between them, the witnesses listed above contain twenty items (or 'elements') of J.B. material, sixteen of which are concerned with the subjects of hunting and hawking.[1] There are also four elements of a more miscellaneous nature, two of them patently moralistic in tone. As I shall argue, the hunting and hawking elements comprise the real core of the *J.B. Treatise*, whereas the other, 'miscellaneous', elements are essentially extraneous to it. It would seem that these extraneous items accrued to the treatise as it was copied and assembled by different scribes, and that they eventually became inseparable from it – which means that they have to be included in my analysis. Nevertheless, they remain of an essentially different order when compared with the hawking and hunting elements, and need to be recognised as such.

---

[1] In identifying these twenty elements I have adopted many of the names used by Rachel Hands in *EHH*, pp. xlvi–xlviii. However, I have compressed some of her categories, where there are two closely related elements that always occur together (e.g. Hands's 'names of dogs' and 'work of different hounds' become my 'Breeds of dogs'), and I omit others that I consider even more tenuously associated with the J.B. material proper (e.g. the 'bishoprics of England': Keiser, *Manual X*, 3702 [471]).

The J.B. elements listed below are described in more detail later in this Introduction (see 'Affinities among the J.B. Elements' below). As will be seen, many of them have more than one form, and nowhere do they all occur together in a single witness. They are found instead in a variety of combinations, or even just singly.

Hunting

1. **Collective nouns** (or 'collectives') – for many categories of animals, birds and humans:
   A herde of hartys, A herde of bukkys, A herde of cranys ... (MS H).
2. **Soiling terms** – for describing a hart's attempts to escape its pursuers by plunging into a pond or stream (<OF *soil, souil*, 'a wallow'):
   The hunt hath cast of a braas of alauntes to a herd of hertes ... (MS Ha)
   A herte, yf he be chased, he wil desire to a reuer ... (MS T).
3. **Resting terms** – describe how different animals and humans retire to rest or sleep (in some cases, to mate):
   An harte is herborowyde, A knyth is herborowyde ... (MS H).
4. **Carving terms** – describe the dismemberment of a range of different animals, birds and fish, as well as their preparation and cooking:
   A dere brovkyne, A gose reyryde, A cappone sawsyd ... (MS Prk)
5. **Beasts of venery and the chase** – a catalogue of different game animals and vermin:
   There ben .iiij. bestys of venery: the hare, the harte ... (MS Ha).
6. **Breeds of dogs** – mainly hunting dogs and how the different breeds are used:
   There bythe grayhoundys, basterdys, mongrellys ... (MS Prk)
   The hunte schall haue help. There byn grehundis ... (MS Ha).
7. **The hunter** – an account of a hunter's accoutrements and horn calls:
   I wold se a hunt with a horn hongyng abowte his nek ... (MS Ha).
8. **Properties of a greyhound** – a gnomic list of the essential features of a greyhound:
   A greunde schuld haue a congres hede, a ladys nek ... (MS Ha)
   Thy grehounde moste be heddyd lyke a snake ... (MS Eg).
9. **Hunting terms** – for describing how different animals are hunted:
   An herte is chased, An hynde is chased, A bock is ronnon ... (MS Adv).
10. **If a hart stands** – describes the demeanour of three types of deer:
    Yf an herte stande, he stallethe; Yf a bucke stande ... (*HSG*).

Hawking

11. ***Hierarchy of hawks*** – a hierarchical list of hawks and their 'owners' according to social status:
    There is an egle, a vaweture and a melowne ... (MS G)
    Thre hawkys longyn for a emperour ... (MS H).

12. ***Hawks' diseases and remedies*** – an inventory of the principal maladies suffered by hawks, and their cures:
    These bene þe infirmyteis of euery hawke ... (MS G)
    An havke hathe in þe hede þe ree, þe frounce ... (MS Prk).

13. ***Choosing a hawk*** – important features to look for when choosing a hawk:
    Take a lyttyll goshauke, a schorte schene, an opyn fote ... (MS H)
    To chese an hauke: take a lytyll goshauke ... (MS Ex).

14. ***Ages of a hawk*** – lists the different names used of a hawk as it matures:
    An hawke is callyd an nyes, a bowere, a brawncher ... (MS H).

15. ***A hawk's foot and feathers*** – sets out the technical names used of a hawk's foot and feathers:
    The talons of the fote: the fyrst ys the pouns afore ... (MS Ex)
    The tokynnys of þe fote ... (MS H).

16. ***Flying terms*** – the correct terminology for describing the different ways in which a hawk may fly at game:
    The hawke fleyth to þe vve, þat is whan þe hawke hath fowndyn hyr game ... (MS H)
    Now ye must lerne youre termys of haukyng. Youre hauke fleyth to the fowle ... (MS Ex).

Miscellaneous

17. ***Precepts in '-ly'*** – a set of moral apothegms:
    Aryse erlly, And serve god dewoutly ... (MS Prk).

18. ***Four things to dread*** – a set of moral apothegms:
    There ys iiij þingys þat euery wyis man owȝte to drede ... (MS Prk).

19. ***Properties of a good horse*** – a gnomic list of the essential features of a horse:
    There longithe to a good hors xv mannere of condycyons ... (MS Prk).

20. ***Names of wines*** – a list of different types of wines:
    londwyne, Reynesshe wyne, wyne of Cavelence ... (MS Dg).

Principal witnesses of the *J.B. Treatise* and major collections of J.B. material

1. Adv – Edinburgh, National Library of Scotland, Advocates Library, MS 19.3.1 ('the Heege Manuscript'): late 15th century (*c.* 1480), paper, 216 folios (viii+216+xvi), *c.* 210 × 140 mm.[1] There are four items of J.B. material, constituting a slightly fragmented version of the *J.B. Treatise*, on fols 62r and 63r–64v:

A tryppe off deere[2]
i. Carving terms
[fol. 62v: largely blank with some unrelated scribbles][3]
ii. Hunting terms
iii. Resting terms
iv. Collective nouns (136 phrases)

Adv is a miscellany of very diverse material, including three romances, a prose *Life of St Catherine*, part of Lydgate's *Lyfe of Oure Lady*, a collection of religious lyrics and an anthology of humorous material, such as the burlesque romance *The Huntyng of the Hare* (*NIMEV* 64). The manuscript, which originated in the north-east Midlands,[4] consists of thirteen (possibly fourteen) quires,[5] comprising nine booklets, mostly in the hand of Richard

---

[1] Adv and its contents are described in full by Gisela Guddat-Figge, *Catalogue of Manuscripts Containing Middle English Romances* (Munich, 1976), pp. 127–30; Philippa Hardman, 'A mediaeval "library in parvo"', *MÆ*, 47 (1978), 262–73; Philippa Hardman, *The Heege Manuscript: A Facsimile of National Library of Scotland MS Advocates 19.3.1*, Leeds Texts and Monographs (Leeds, 2000), pp. 1–57. The online catalogue of the NLS <manuscripts.nls.uk> dates the manuscript *c.* 1480.

[2] All major headings, subheadings and colophons relating to J.B. material are indicated by means of italic type. Guddat-Figge transcribes this particular heading as 'A tryppe off þe eore' (*Catalogue*, p. 128), which makes no sense (see my further discussion below).

[3] Discontinuities in a witness – such as blank pages or extraneous items – are described within square brackets.

[4] Restrictions of space have made it impracticable to include a comprehensive analysis of the usual issues regarding language and dialect in the present survey of J.B. witnesses. In many cases, the relevant information could not be satisfactorily presented without considerable explication, and it has therefore been omitted altogether rather than being offered selectively or in a condensed form that might appear deficient.

[5] Hitherto, all descriptions of Adv have treated folios 48–67 as comprising a single quire, the fourth in the codex (4^{20}). However, careful examination of the manuscript by Kenneth Dunn Esq. of the NLS has convinced him that these folios may actually

Heege (Heeg, Hyheg), with some contributions by John Hawghton and several other unnamed contemporary copyists.[1]

As Philippa Hardman has shown, each booklet consists of a major work, such as a romance or a saint's life, followed by an assortment of shorter pieces that fill up the remaining leaves – a clear indication that, singly and together, these booklets were all conceived and executed according to a deliberate editorial plan.[2] They are plain and workmanlike in appearance, and the wear and soiling of their outer leaves show that they were well used before being bound together as a single volume. Interpretations of the original function of these booklets vary: Julia Boffey and John Thomson suggest that they may have circulated among local readers or book compilers looking for material to incorporate in their own collections;[3] whereas Thorlac Turville-Petre proposes that the entire collection may have been produced on commission, perhaps for the Sherbrooke family of Oxton, Nottinghamshire, as a complete, small library – in the words of H.S. Bennett, a 'library *in parvo*' – since its 'contents seem to cater for the complete needs of a family: spiritual, practical and recreational'.[4] Once the nine booklets were bound up together, the resulting volume appears to have been used as a commonplace book by later owners, whose scribbles and additions can be found on various leaves that were originally left blank.[5]

---

comprise two quires, 4^{16} (fols 48–63) and 5^4 (fols 64–67), with the break falling in the middle of the *J.B. Treatise*. I am very grateful to him for pointing this out to me.

[1] For the notion of a booklet, which may consist of one or more quires, see P.R. Robinson, 'The "Booklet": A self-contained unit in composite manuscripts', *Codicologica 3: Essais Typologiques* (Leiden, 1980), pp. 46–69; Ralph Hanna III, 'Booklets in medieval manuscripts: further considerations', *Studies in Bibliography*, 39 (1986), 100–111.

[2] Hardman, 'Library in parvo', pp. 262–73.

[3] Julia Boffey and John J. Thompson, 'Anthologies and miscellanies: production and choice of texts', in *Book Production and Publishing in Britain 1375–1475*, ed. Jeremy Griffiths and Derek Pearsall (Cambridge, 1989), pp. 279–315 (esp. pp. 295–7).

[4] Thorlac Turville-Petre, 'Some medieval English manuscripts in the north-east Midlands', in *Manuscripts and Readers in Fifteenth-Century England*, ed. Derek Pearsall (Cambridge, 1983), pp. 125–41 (esp. pp. 133–9). H.S. Bennett, *Chaucer and the Fifteenth Century* (Oxford, 1947), p. 165.

[5] I use the term 'commonplace book' to designate a miscellany compiled over time by a single scribe for his/her own edification. For discussion of what constitutes a commonplace book, see *Secular Lyrics of the XIVth and XVth Centuries*, ed. Rossell Hope Robbins, 2nd edn (Oxford 1955), pp. xxviii–xxx; A.G. Rigg, *A Glastonbury Miscellany of the Fifteenth Century: A Descriptive Index of Trinity College, Cambridge, MS. O.9.38* (Oxford, 1968), pp. 24–6, along with Rossell Hope Robbins's review of

Heege himself contributed the J.B. material towards the end of the manuscript's fourth booklet (fols 48–67), most of which is taken up by *Sir Isumbras*, *The Lay Folk's Mass Book* and a number of poems and proverbs. Heege signs his name at three points in this booklet, on fols 56v, 60v and 67v. The J.B. material begins at the top of fol. 62r with a two-line, boxed, pen-flourished red lombard initial (of mediocre calligraphic quality) introducing the phrase *A tryppe off deere*, written at least twice as large as what follows.[1] This phrase is incongruous for several reasons. In the first place, it makes a poor heading for the Carving terms that follow immediately after; if anything, its formulation suggests that it belongs with the Collective nouns that commence on fol. 63r. Yet, neither in Adv nor anywhere else, are deer ever classified as a 'trip': they are invariably a 'herd'.[2]

The Carving terms on fol. 62r are set out like the rest of the J.B. material, in long lines across the entire width of the page, with virgules separating the phrases. Two lines are, however, only half filled, perhaps indicating that Heege found parts of his exemplar unreadable and intended to tease out the missing phrases later, but failed to do so.[3] The Carving terms come to an end three-quarters of the way down fol. 62r and are followed by an inexplicable interruption: the verso of this leaf is largely blank, except for a few scribbles and pen-trials in several hands, mostly towards the top of the page.

The remaining three items of J.B. material (nos ii–iv) start again at the top of fol. 63r with a short passage found nowhere else: a set of eleven phrases describing how different animals are hunted or caught (the Hunting terms). Then come the Resting terms and, finally, the Collective nouns, which conclude half-way down fol. 64v, where a medicinal recipe *For a malaundre* in a different hand fills most of the remaining space on that page. On fol. 63r, lines drawn across the page separate the different J.B. elements from one another; at the foot of fol. 64r, two phrases of the Collective nouns have been corrected by another hand.

Rigg's book in *Anglia*, 89 (1971), 140–3, especially p. 141; Boffey and Thomson, 'Anthologies', pp. 292–3; Guddatt-Figge, *Catalogue*, pp. 25–8.

[1] Palaeographical and codicological terms used in the present edition can be consulted in Denis Muzerelle's illustrated, multi-lingual website, *Vocabulaire Codicologique* at <http://vocabulaire.irht.cnrs.fr/>.

[2] See Appendix I, no. 59, and the associated note.

[3] Gaps are also to be found elsewhere, as at the foot of fol. 64r, where Heege has written only *A mysbelefe of*, the end-noun *peynters* being supplied by a different hand.

It is difficult to assess whether all the J.B. elements in Adv were copied from a single exemplar, and so represent a unified version of the *J.B. Treatise*. The question arises on several counts: first, because of the unusual ordering of the elements, with the Carving terms preceding all others; elsewhere the Carving terms always occur later in the sequence, usually after the Collective nouns (see, for example, Eg, *HSG*, Pl, Prk, Rd, *StA*, T, W). Secondly, there is the unusual phraseology of the Carving terms, which employ an imperative construction (for example, 'Breke the dere'), as against the semi-passive participial form (for example, 'a deer broken') found in most other versions. This imperative construction appears elsewhere only in Wynkyn de Worde's *Boke of Keruynge* (*BK*) and the Tollemache *Book of Secrets* (BS) – nos 18 and 19 below. Finally, there is the mystery of the blank page separating the Carving terms from the rest of the J.B. material.

Perhaps Heege had two sources at his disposal: one containing the list of Carving terms (i), and the other the remaining three items (ii–iv), and he wanted to signal this by leaving fol. 62v blank.[1] Or perhaps he thought he could find further carving terms to add to his list, and so left space to fill at a later stage.[2] Yet again, maybe he simply made a blunder in copying, perhaps through working on loose bifolia while the remainder were being proofread. The issue cannot be satisfactorily resolved and, in any case, Heege has kept the four items of J.B. material close together to produce an acceptable, if unconventional, version of the *J.B. Treatise*.[3]

Adv's lists of Collective nouns, Carving terms, and Resting terms are all contained in Appendices I–III respectively. Its unique list of Hunting terms (item ii) is transcribed in Part IVa below.[4]

---

[1] Cf. the Brome manuscript (Yale University Library, MS 365), in which leaves between items are left blank: Boffey and Thomson, 'Anthologies', p. 311/86n.

[2] Cf. the actions of Robert Thornton in leaving space in one of his collections (BL Add. MS 31042) for the completion of the *Northern Passion* from a better exemplar: Boffey and Thomson, 'Anthologies', pp. 300, 315/114n.

[3] Hardman observes that the items following *Sir Isumbras* (including the J.B. material) 'appear to have been written over a period of time, for the ink and size of the hand vary considerably from item to item': 'Library in parvo', p. 266. While this is true, the four elements of J.B. material clearly belong to the same period of copying.

[4] It will be seen that I employ initial capitals to designate the different J.B. elements (as in 'Carving terms'), but lower-case throughout when considering the material contained by an element genrically: 'more carving terms'.

2. Dg / Dg* – Oxford, Bodleian Library, MS Digby 196: second half of the 15th century, with a table of contents from the 16th century (fol. 1), paper and vellum, 197 folios (197+iv), c. 295 × 220 mm. It contains a unified *J.B. Treatise* on fols 160r–161v,[1] consisting of:

  i. Collective nouns (50 phrases)
  ii. Beasts of venery and the chase
  iii. Breeds of dogs
  iv. Soiling terms
  v. Resting terms
  vi. Hierarchy of hawks
  vii. Names of wines
  viii. Ages of a hawk
  ix. Hawks' diseases and remedies

There is also an additional short list of collective nouns (20 phrases) on fol. 157v, which I refer to as **Dg***. This list is accompanied by an asterisk (a *signe-de-renvoi*), which matches another, larger asterisk together with the phrase *ex parte precedenti* ('from the preceding part'),[2] at the end of the main list of collectives on fol. 160r.

Dg appears to be a commonplace book with very varied contents, including a lapidary, verses, historical and religious texts, the prophesies of Merlin, a genealogical table of English kings, and a *Mappa mundi*, among other items.[3] Many leaves have been cut out, others survive as mere fragments, and there are also some insertions, such as the two small bifolia (fols 20–23) containing prophecies and poems, including 'The taxe hath tened vs alle' on Jack Straw's rebellion (*NIMEV* 3260).

Most of the manuscript appears to be the work of a single scribe, who added to his book in a variety of scripts and inks, probably over a long period of time. The entire manuscript has been foliated at least twice, first in pencil and later in ink (with occasional ink and pencil additions).

---

[1] Through some accident of miscopying, the scribe left fol. 160v blank. I have disregarded this gap in my analysis of Dg because it falls in the middle of the Soiling terms. In other words, it does not suggest that the J.B. material in Dg might derive from more than one source – as is the case with Adv, Eg and Pp.

[2] MS: 'ex parte precedonti'.

[3] For a full list of contents, see William D. Macray, *Catalogi Codicum Manuscriptorum Bibliothecæ Bodleianæ*, Part 9: Digby (Oxford, 1883), cols. 212–18. One notable item is a continuation of Ranulf Higden's *Polychronicon*; see John Taylor, *The Universal Chronicle of Ranulf Higden* (Oxford, 1966), pp. 116, 159, 178.

According to a pencil note by William Macray on the inside of the front cover board, the manuscript was originally bound in a confused manner, and was re-ordered and renumbered by him in 1880.

Macray's rearrangement does not affect the two adjoining quires that contain the two sections of J.B. material – the short list of collectives on fol. 157v (Dg*), and the remainder of the treatise on fols 160r–161v. These two quires maintain their original sequence and position relative to one another, albeit with new folio numbers. Even so, it is not immediately clear which of the two sections of J.B. material was written first. The short list of collectives on fol. 157v appears at the bottom of the leaf, under four lines of Latin verse, and in the middle of a chronology of English kings, beginning with the accession of Richard II and ending with the death of Henry V (hence, 1377–1422). It would appear that the scribe came to the end of the fourth year of Henry V on fol. 157v, drew a line under his text, and wrote the four lines of Latin verse. At a later stage he added the list of collectives, which are in a different ink (now badly faded). He also continued his chronology of kings on fol. 158r, ending half-way down that page with the year 9 (*recte* 10) Henry V (1422): 'And so he ended at Boys vyncent and as a Cristen Prynce to God passed owte of this wrecched world on whose sowle God have mercy Amen'. The verso of fol. 158 is blank, as is the recto of fol. 159 (the last leaf of the quire); however, on the verso of fol. 159 is a set of Latin verses on the deaths of the twelve apostles.[1]

The following quire opens with the main *J.B. Treatise*, which has been carefully executed and neatly laid out. The text commences at the top of the page with a list of Collective nouns (item i) written, like the rest of the treatise, in long lines across the width of the page. It is introduced by a raised lombardic initial followed by flourished ascenders in the first line. The items that follow are mostly separated from one another by a line of space, and generally begin with one-line initials. The overall effect is a formality that is absent from many other parts of the manuscript. At first sight, this section appears to be written in a different hand from the shorter list of collectives on fol. 157v (Dg*). It is manifestly in a different ink (the ink of the short list is extremely faded), and has been written with a differently cut quill. And yet, even though the faintness of the ink of the Dg* list makes comparison of the two hands extremely difficult, they appear to have many similarities, especially in the execution of the letters *R* and *S*, and in the semi-circular titulus that indicates an omitted *n*.

---

[1] My account of the quiring at this point is open to correction; the manuscript has been stab-bound, making it difficult to see exactly where quires begin and end.

Features such as these incline me to believe that the Dg* collectives are by the same scribe who penned the full *J.B. Treatise*, and that some time elapsed between the execution of these two items. As I have already observed, the main list of collectives (on fol. 160r) ends with a cross-reference in the same ink and script as the Dg* list on fol. 157v. This suggests that the scribe added the Dg* list to the manuscript *after* having copied the full *J.B. Treatise*, and that he positioned it so as to be conveniently near to the full treatise. This hypothesis may also explain why there is no repetition between the two lists of collectives, and why the Dg* list is notably different from any other: it may have been selectively copied by the scribe who saw it as supplementing his main list.[1] The Dg* list is also noteworthy for containing items that are found elsewhere only in C (no. 20 below), and in three Anglo-Norman glossarial texts.[2] As with C, this list appears to draw on a different tradition from that which supplied the main J.B. lists of Collective nouns.

Dg's *J.B. Treatise* is closely related to the version preserved by Rg: the first seven elements of Dg match those in Rg, although neither manuscript has been copied from the other: see Rg (no. 12 below) for more details. There is also a close relationship between the Dg–Rg pair and Prk (no. 10 below): six elements of Dg (ii, iii, iv, vi, viii and ix) and four of Rg (ii, iii, iv and vi) match the sequence and contents of their equivalents in Prk almost exactly – albeit that all three versions are dialectically perceptibly dissimilar.[3] Within this sequence, the close correspondence of Dg's hawking elements (vi, viii, ix) to those of Prk (x, xi, xii) highlights the anomalous presence of element vii (the Names of wines) in the middle of Dg's hawking material. (Rg matches Dg in having the Names of wines follow the Hierarchy of hawks, but ends at that point.)

The arrangement of the J.B. material in these manuscripts suggests that Dg (along with Rg) probably derives from a lost witness (hypothetically MS θ), whose scribe somehow skipped from the Hierarchy of hawks (Dg–Rg: vi) to the Names of wines (Dg–Rg: vii) – perhaps by turning two

---

[1] Five end-nouns are common to both lists, but the collective nouns with which they are paired are different in each case. The list of collectives on fol. 157 was first described and published by Rachel Corner [= Hands], 'More fifteenth-century "terms of association"', *RES*, NS 13 (1962), 229–44.

[2] See MS C below for more information.

[3] It will be seen that Prk lacks item v (the Resting terms) in the Dg–Rg sequence, but that is because that element occurs earlier in Prk, having derived from another version of the treatise (Pl).

leaves of his exemplar (hypothetically MS δ) at the same time – before realising his mistake and returning to the hawking material (Dg: viii, ix).[1]

As a corollary, we may suppose that Prk derived its last six elements – and especially its three hawking elements – directly or indirectly from MS δ, thereby preserving them in the correct, unbroken sequence. Strictly, the Names of wines in its entirety should be omitted from any discussion of the *J.B. Treatise*. However, because it occurs in two manuscripts (Dg, Rg), and falls in the middle of the J.B. material in one of them (Dg) – and may furthermore yet be found to occur in the same place in other witnesses, still undiscovered – I have included it for the sake of completeness.

Finally, it should be observed that Dg's Resting terms (v) are closely related to the version in Ha, though there is nothing else to connect these two witnesses.

The six elements in Dg that overlap with Prk are collated in the textual notes accompanying the transcription of Prk in Part I below. Of the remaining three elements, the Collective nouns and Resting terms are incorporated in Appendices I and III respectively, while the Names of wines is set out in a separate transcription (collated with Rg) in Part IVi.

3. **Eg** – London, British Library, Egerton MS 1995: late 15th century, paper, 223 folios, *c.* 275 × 205 mm. It contains two separate collections of J.B. material on fols 55v–58r, and 63r–64v, consisting of:

> *Note ye the properteys that longythe to a yonge gentylle man to haue knowynge of suche thyngys that longythe vnto hym that he fayle not in hys propyr termys that longythe vnt[o] hym as hyt shalle folowe hereynne wrytynge &c*
> i. Properties of a greyhound
> ii. Collective nouns (106 phrases)
> iii. Carving terms
>
> [fols 58v–62v: various items, including *The Lytylle Childrenes Lytil Boke* (*NIMEV* 1920); prognostications in Latin; list of the bishoprics of England][2]

---

[1] See 'Textual Relationships', Group 2, later in this Introduction.

[2] Rachel Hands includes the list of English bishoprics (see Keiser, *Manual X*, 3702 [471]) on fol. 62v in her list of Eg's J.B. contents. I have excluded this item as extraneous to the *J.B. Treatise* proper, and because of the arrangement of the manuscript itself: this list precedes the heading on fol. 63r that introduces the second set of J.B. elements.

*For a yong gentylle man to know the termys of venery
and the crafte whythe the .iiij. bestys of venery*
iv. Beasts of venery and the chase
v. Breeds of dogs
vi. Soiling terms
vii. Hierarchy of hawks

*Gret huntyng by ryuers and wode
makythe a manys here to growe thorowe hys hoode.*[1]

Eg is a miscellaneous collection of some fourteen items in verse and prose that are variously edifying and instructive. Its contents include an assortment of poems on diverse topics – including several by Lydgate, such as his *Dietary* (*NIMEV* 824), and his account of the *sotelties* presented at the coronation banquet of Henry VI in 1432 (*NIMEV* 1929) – together with proverbs, recipes, statistics and lists of various sorts. There is also historical matter, such as the verse *Siege of Rouen* (*NIMEV* 979) and a prose chronicle of London that is conventionally known as *Gregory's Chronicle* after its putative (but now disputed) author, William Gregory (sometimes called Gregory Skinner) of the Skinner's Company, who was mayor of London in 1451–2.[2]

Because of its purported association with William Gregory, Eg has also been called 'William Gregory's Commonplace Book', and has been described as a work assembled over many years.[3] However, its professional appearance suggests otherwise. Specifically, the entire volume is carefully written in a clear, mixed Anglicana – with distinctive abbreviations, flourishes and letter-forms – that is almost certainly the hand of a single (probably professional) scribe. Decoration is also stylistically remarkably consistent, with capitals tipped in red, along with red paraphs and large red

---

[1] *NIMEV* 1014.5; Whiting H22.

[2] For a comprehensive description of the manuscript, see David R. Parker, *The Commonplace Book of Tudor London: An Examination of BL MSS Egerton 1995, Harley 2252, Lansdowne 762, and Oxford Balliol College MS 354* (Oxford, 1998), pp. 17 ff. An important earlier account is in *The Historical Collections of a Citizen of London in the Fifteenth Century*, ed. James Gairdner, Camden Society, NS 17 (London, 1876), pp. i–v. The issue of Gregory's authorship is discussed by, among others, Mary-Rose McLaren, *The London Chronicles of the Fifteenth Century: A Revolution in English Writing* (Cambridge, 2002), pp. 29–33.

[3] *The Middle English Poem 'Erthe upon Erthe'*, ed. Hilda M.R. Murray, EETS OS 141 (London, 1911), pp. xii, 29; *Secular Lyrics*, ed. Robbins, p. xxix; *Historical Collections of a Citizen*, ed. Gairdner, p. iii.

lombard initials throughout, the latter having been supplied by a rubricator following guide letters left by the scribe.[1] In certain places, the scribe has even returned to write words within an initial – such as the phrase *mons dei* written in black ink over the large red initial *A* on fol. 57v (see also fol. 58r). The manuscript also lacks any features that might be considered typical of a collection compiled accretively (as would a commonplace book), such as blank pages, pen-trials, jottings or interleavings. In short, all evidence indicates that Eg was very likely written down over a relatively brief period of time, probably as a commission, by a professional scribe, who could also have been the rubricator.[2]

The J.B. material in Eg is noteworthy for several reasons. In the first place, although it shows broad family resemblances with versions in other witnesses, it is independent of all of them. The organisation of the material is also unique, with almost every element set out as a list (in other witnesses, items i, v and vi are usually written in long lines). Then there is the division of the material into two discrete parts (fols 55v–58r, 63r–64v), suggesting that it derived from two sources, both now unknown. Finally, the scribe's headings are novel, with their emphasis on providing instruction for young men in the use of terminology that they ought to have at their command. No other J.B. text is so explicit in setting out its didactic intentions, or in stating that its contents form a necessary part of the knowledge and vocabulary of a 'gentylle man'. Although there are some amusing items among the Collective nouns, the overall serious instructive purpose of this little collection cannot be doubted.

In contrast with their novel style of presentation, the J.B. elements in Eg are generally fairly orthodox in content. Three, however, I consider sufficiently distinctive to warrant their own transcriptions: accordingly, Eg's Beasts of venery and the chase, Breeds of dogs, and Properties of a greyhound are set out in Parts IVd, IVe and IVf below. The Collective nouns and Carving terms are incorporated in Appendices I and II, and the remaining elements are sufficiently similar to those of other transcribed texts to merit no further special attention.

---

[1] In the text of the *J.B. Treatise*, the lombard initials are three, six, nine and even thirteen lines high.

[2] Because of these features, Julia Boffey and Carol M. Meale refer to Eg as a 'commercially produced *commonplace-type* book' (emphasis mine): 'Selecting the text: Rawlinson C. 86 and some other books for London readers', in *Regionalism in Late Medieval Manuscripts and Texts*, ed. Felicity Riddy (Cambridge, 1991), pp. 143–69 (p. 149).

3a. Ex – Exeter, Exeter Cathedral MS 3533: mid- to late 15th century; parchment and paper in a 19th-century binding; 106 folios, with two pairs of modern endleaves at front and rear (ii+106+ii), foliated continuously 1–108 (including the two endleaves at the rear); *c.* 210 × 135 mm, with large variations in the written area. The codex is chiefly a legal miscellany with some extraneous treatises appended, one of them being a unified *J.B. Treatise* of six distinct elements devoted entirely to hawking information (fols 101v–103v):[1]

> For to kepe haukys
> i. Hawks' diseases and remedies
> ii. Choosing a hawk
> iii. Ages of a hawk
> iv. A hawk's foot and feathers
> v. Flying terms
> vi. Hierarchy of hawks

Ex has been described in detail in two major catalogues, as well as in an article I published in 2007, and that information need not be repeated here.[2] Briefly, the manuscript consists mainly of legal texts written by a number of scribes from the middle of the 15th century to about 1485, this date being recorded on fol. 70r. Then come two works on heraldry (fols 79v–101r) and, finally, the *J.B. Treatise*, which appears to have been added to fill up space in the final quire, and so can be dated to the last quarter of the 15th century. The treatise itself has been neatly and professionally written in 25 to 30 long lines per page, with wide spaces between paragraphs. It begins with a two-line red lombard initial, and most paragraphs commence with capitals (including *ff* for capital *F*) slashed with red.

In terms of its contents, the *J.B. Treatise* in Ex is of considerable interest for several reasons. In the first place, it shows strong affinities with the hawking material in MSS H and L and, to a lesser extent, with that in Pp.

---

[1] The unusual number (3a) assigned to this manuscript in my list of J.B. witnesses is a consequence of my discovering it after the first edition of this volume had gone to press. The information given here is a shortened version of my full description in 'An autonomous and unpublished version of the *J.B. Treatise* in Exeter Cathedral MS 3533', *MÆ*, 76 (2007), 70–84. I am grateful to the editors of *Medium Ævum* for permission to reproduce information from that article here.

[2] Historical Manuscripts Commission, *Report on Manuscripts in Various Collections*, 4 vols (London, 1901–1907), IV, 33 ff.; N.R. Ker *et al.*, *Medieval Manuscripts in British Libraries*, 5 vols (Oxford, 1969–2002), II, 837–39; Scott-Macnab, 'An autonomous and unpublished version of the *J.B. Treatise*' (2007).

This is most apparent in the arrangement of Ex's six items, for they occur in a sequence that is found elsewhere only in the cognate pair H–L. There is also close agreement with H and L, and to a lesser extent with Pp, in the the ordering of the diseases and remedies for hawks; on the other hand, Ex shows a strong correspondence with Pp in the opening formula for that item: *To helpe an hauke of dyuerse sykenesse* (Ex), *To helpe an hawke of dyvers sekenes* (Pp).

With regard to the Hierarchy of hawks, Ex matches H and L with its short account of an emperor's hawks, but varies from them in later details, sometimes considerably. (For more details, see 'Affinities among the J.B. Elements' later in this Introduction.)

It is therefore clear that Ex (the later witness) cannot have descended from the H–L pair, or, for that matter, from any other known recension. Ex exhibits too many significant variations – including words, phrases and statements found nowhere else, as well as errors and omissions – for this to be possible. Ex also contains several distinctive terms that suggest that it is a collateral descendant of H and L – for example, *aglye* against *akyllys* in H, *pelaundyr* (*polyon* H), *stoke-coluer* (*stokedowfe* H). These factors suggest a shared distant ancestor of the hawking items common to Ex, H–L and Pp – an archetype (or hypearchetype) that I have designated α in the relevant stemma (see Textual Relationships, Group 1, later in this Introduction).

The fact that Ex contains six hawking items and none relating to hunting (not even the Collective nouns) lends further weight to my hypothesis that the hawking and hunting sections of the *J.B. Treatise* originally existed separately, until they were brought together to form a new composite treatise – as I propose we find in H, for example. This would mean that Ex, in spite of its late date, preserves an early form of the J.B. hawking elements: in other words, a short treatise on the subjects of hawks and hawking that existed before their eventual association with 'Iulyans Barne' or 'I. B.'.

Since I have already published a fully annotated edition of Ex's *J.B. Treatise* in *Medium Ævum*,[1] no part of it is represented here, though I do refer extensively to it in the Explanatory Notes on H.

---

[1] Scott-Macnab, 'An autonomous and unpublished version of the *J.B. Treatise*' (2007).

4. H – London, British Library, Harley MS 2340: mid-15th century, vellum, 60 leaves (foliated i+59),[1] *c*. 130 × 100 mm.[2] H contains an early version of the *J.B. Treatise* on fols 47r–51v, and closes with an important J.B. colophon on fol. 51v:

i. Hawks' diseases and remedies
ii. Choosing a hawk
iii. Ages of a hawk
iv. A hawk's foot and feathers
v. Flying terms
vi. Hierarchy of hawks

Now of venery lerne wele ȝour termys

vii. Beasts of venery and the chase
viii. Soiling terms
ix. Resting terms
x. Collective nouns (45 phrases)

Explicit I.B.

H is a pocket-sized codex consisting almost entirely of sporting texts. Except for a few later scribbles and additions on blank leaves, the entire volume appears to be the work of a single scribe, who also provided red-ink headings and red-ink punctuation throughout. The manuscript opens with a six-line blue lombard initial with red pen flourishing, and has several more smaller blue initials with red flourishing throughout. Quires 1–3 contain a copy of *Prince Edward's Book of Hawking* (*PEB*: fols 1–22v),[3] and quires 4–6 present a collection of remedies for hawks (fols 23r–45r) that are unrelated to the J.B. or *PEB* remedies.[4] As W.L. Braekman observes, the latter independent compendium of hawking remedies consists of the same basic text copied twice (fols 23r–34r, 34v–45r), with some minor variations

---

[1] The blank, unnumbered front 'endleaf' is actually the first leaf of the first quire, an n⁶ gathering.

[2] For a full description, see *A Catalogue of the Harleian Manuscripts in the British Musuem*, 4 vols (London, 1808–1812), II, 346.

[3] The Harleian text of *PEB* – hereafter *PEB 1* – has been published by A.E.H. Swaen, 'The booke of hawkyng after Prince Edwarde Kyng of Englande and its relation to the Book of St. Albans', *SN*, 16 (1943–4), 1–32. For a survey of other witnesses of *PEB*, see Hands, *EHH*, pp. xxiii–xxx; Keiser, *Manual X*, 3697 [452].

[4] See *Of Hawks and Horses: Four Late Middle English Prose Treatises*, ed. W.L. Braekman, Scripta 16 (Brussels, 1986), pp. 17–37.

and additions in both sections.[1] These remedies end on fol. 45r, and so do not fill the sixth quire, which ends with fol. 46. Fol. 45v is blank; fol. 46r contains a remedy for toothache in a later hand, and its verso is blank.

The J.B. material falls in the seventh quire, originally a gathering of eight leaves, one of which is missing: fols 47–53. Since the J.B. text fails to fill this quire, it is followed by miscellaneous later additions: an inscription in the sixteenth-century hand of Richard Raulle, who also attempts to imitate the J.B. colophon (fol. 52r); and a variety of recipes (some of which have been struck out), including 'to make a pultus', 'to temper bird-lime', 'for the pine in a haukes fote' (fols 52v–53v). Finally, the eighth quire, of six leaves (fols 54–59), is mostly blank, except for scribbles, pen-trials and a fragment of verse (fol. 55r).

H's binding makes it difficult to verify which leaf of the seventh quire is missing, but it seems likely to be the first. That would account for the abrupt start of the J.B. material, without a suitable heading introduced by a coloured initial (such as the scribe provides for other works in the manuscript), or even any introductory remarks. The text simply commences with the title, in red ink, for the malady with which the Hawks' diseases and remedies usually begins: *For þe ree of an hawke*. Any attempt to suggest what might have preceded this remedy can be no more than speculative, but the affinities that H shows with Ex and Pp make it possible that a heading and opening formula, such as we find in Ex/Pp, could be (part of) what is missing.[2]

It is noteworthy that the six hawking elements with which H's *J.B. Treatise* begins are found in exactly the same order in two other manuscripts, L and Ex, of which Ex is the later and more distant relation (see no. 3a above). L (no. 7 below), on the other hand, also contains the same four hunting elements as are found in H, and close comparison of the two indicates that L must be descended from H, possibly via an intermediary.

One other witness needs to be mentioned at this stage: Pp (no. 9 below), some sections of which show broad correspondences with H. Other passages, however, are markedly different, indicating that the kinship between the J.B. materials in H and Pp is fairly distant, and that the two belong to collateral branches of the same family.

---

[1] *Of Hawks and Horses*, ed. Braekman, p. 15. *PEB 1* and the independent hawking remedies are conflated by *MED* under the stencil '**Bk Hawking* (Harl)'.

[2] 'For to kepe haukys / To helpe an hauke of dyuerse sykenesse' (Ex, title and line 1); see my article in *MÆ* (2007), p. 77, and see further the Explanatory Notes to H below.

As it stands, the J.B. material in H, though acephalous, can be deemed to constitute an established, unified version of the *J.B. Treatise* – sufficiently so for it to stand as one of the base manuscripts for this study (see Part II). And yet there are also clues that might suggest that the hawking and hunting sections had separate origins, making it possible that H may itself be a composite assemblage – perhaps even the first in which these sections were brought together. It is especially noteworthy that the hunting elements (vii–x) are introduced by their own heading (at the foot of fol. 50r), and that they close with the colophon attribution to 'I.B' (fol. 51v). This raises the question as to whether the statement *Explicit I.B.* refers to *all* the preceding material, including the hawking elements that start on fol. 47r, or perhaps only to the hunting elements themselves. It is also worth noting that this colophon occurs after the Collective nouns, for that is precisely where a similar colophon (*Explicit Iulyan Barne*) occurs in Pp – where, moreover, it is completely divorced from that manuscript's hawking material.

As I argue elsewhere in this Introduction, the surviving evidence seems to indicate that the name and initials of Iulyan Barne/I.B. originally belonged with the Collective nouns, which may have formed the nucleus of a little compendium of hunting elements that once existed separately from the hawking elements, but was conjoined to them at an early stage to form one of many versions of the *J.B. Treatise*. This is not to suggest that H has a privileged position in the hierarchy of J.B. texts; merely to recognise that it is one of the earliest in which this conjoining occurs. (See further my discussion of Pp, and 'Development of the *J.B. Treatise*' below.)

5. Ha – London, Lincoln's Inn Library, MS Hale 148: late 15th century, parchment, 67 leaves, *c.* 190 × 125 mm. Ha contains a coherent, unified *J.B. Treatise* on fols 6v–8r, comprising:

   i. Collective nouns (50 phrases)
   ii. Beasts of venery and the chase
   iii. The hunter
   iv. Breeds of dogs
   v. Soiling terms
   vi. Resting terms
   vii. Properties of a greyhound
   viii. Hierarchy of hawks
   ix. Hawks' diseases (but no remedies)

Ha is taken up almost entirely by William Lyndwood's compendium of canon law, the *Provinciale, seu constitutiones Anglie* of 1433/4 (fols 9–67), and by a table of contents for this work (fols 1r–6r).[1] The *J.B. Treatise* was added to the empty leaves at the end of the first quire (1^8), which the table of contents failed to fill. It begins at the top of fol. 6v and ends half-way down fol. 8r; then come three lines of text in a later hand that appear to have been deliberately expunged, and are consequently unreadable.[2] The verso of fol. 8 (the last of the gathering) is blank.

All the material in the first quire is written without embellishment in black ink only – in marked contrast to the text of the *Provinciale* itself, which commences on the first leaf of the second quire and has decorated initials of blue ink, with elaborate marginal ornamentation in red. Both Joseph Hunter and N.R. Ker ascribe the *Provinciale* to a (Secretary) hand of the 15th century, and the *J.B. Treatise* to a later, mixed Anglicana (English hybrida) hand from the close of that century.[3] Should this judgement be accurate, it is worth noting that the two hands are remarkably similar: they are identical in size and general appearance, and employ the same marks of abbreviation, many of which are distinctive, such as a reversed α-shaped titulus to indicate an omitted *m* or *n*. Also distinctive and identical in both texts are the tailed superscript *u*, the form of hyphen used when words break across two lines, the curled final *t* and *n*, and an elongated *s*-shaped diacritic over the letter *i*. In short, it seems possible that the *J.B. Treatise* may not be from a significantly later date than the *Provinciale* and may even have the same provenance.

Be that as it may, the *J.B. Treatise*'s *raison d'être* in this codex is to provide filler for a number of blank leaves, and it is unrelated to the rest of the manuscript's contents. Although it has no heading or colophon, the treatise has been carefully executed in a neat, professional hand. The Collective nouns are written as a list in two columns, but everything else is written in paragraphs of long lines that are separated from one another by approximately two lines of space. One- or two-line black-ink initials are used at the start of each paragraph.

---

[1] See further the descriptions by Joseph Hunter, *A Catalogue of the Manuscripts of the Honourable Society of Lincoln's Inn* (London, 1838), p. 142 (MS XXVII); Ker, *Medieval Manuscripts*, I, 135.

[2] The only distinct letter is the initial *S* of the first word, which has the appearance of a 16th-century hand. Ultraviolet light may reveal more.

[3] Hunter, *Catalogue*, p. 142; Ker, *Medieval Manuscripts*, I, 135.

No other manuscript contains a collection of J.B. material exactly matching Ha. There is a general similarity with the ordering of elements in the Dg–Rg pair, but the wording of the elements themselves is often noticeably different. Ha has a somewhat stronger affinity with Rd, which has four of Ha's elements (ii–v) in precisely the same order, and internal similarities suggest that both recensions belong in the same sub-family, though there are also disagreements indicating that neither manuscript derives from the other.

It is unfortunate that Ha's *J.B. Treatise* ends somewhat abruptly with only the first part of what is normally a two-part element: the Diseases and remedies of hawks (ix); the concluding words *et cetera*, which appear to have been added later, suggest that someone noticed the absence of the remedies at an early stage. Ha here sets out what appears to be a truncated version of the diseases and remedies found in G and Ry, although it descends from neither of those manuscripts.

It is possible that Ha's version of the *J.B. Treatise* may itself be a conflation from more than one source: for example, there is no other manuscript in which the Properties of a greyhound (vii) occurs in the same position. Nevertheless, there is also a purity and simplicity about Ha, in that it contains nothing that is not clearly connected with hunting and hawking – unlike the Dg–Rg pair, for example, which intrudes the Names of wines amongst its sporting elements, or other texts that include a number of the 'miscellaneous' elements. It is for reasons such as these that I have selected Ha to provide one of the principal texts set out in full in this study (see Part III below).

6. *HSG* – John Lydgate, *The Hors, the Shepe and the Ghoos*, twice printed by William Caxton in 1476–77 (*STC* 17019, 17018). A small quarto booklet, without title page, signatures or catchwords, printed throughout in Caxton's type no. 2. It contains a short *J.B. Treatise* of five elements on the final two leaves of its second gathering (fols 16v–18r, or b8v–b10r of b^{10}):

    i. Collective nouns (106 phrases)
    ii. Resting terms
    iii. 'If a hart stands'
    iv. Carving terms
    v. Soiling terms

Only two substantial copies of this incunable survive: a near-perfect specimen in Cambridge University Library (*STC* 17018), lacking fols 1 and 6; and a perfect copy in the Pierpont Morgan Library, New York, (*STC* 17019).[1] For many years, *STC* 17018 was considered to be the first edition, while *STC* 17019 was believed to have been printed later, and they were dated 1477 and 1477–78 respectively.[2] However, it is now accepted that *STC* 17019 is the earlier of the two impressions, and that both belong to the period 1476–77 rather than 1477–78.[3] Although later, *STC* 17018 is preferable for my purposes in that it avoids (or corrects) a significant error in the Soiling terms of *STC* 17019,[4] and for that reason I have adopted the Cambridge text (*STC* 17018) for all citations in this study.

HSG originally consisted of 18 leaves in two quires: a^8 b^{10}. Like other Caxton pamphlets of this date, it would not have had a title page, which means that the missing first leaf can be presumed to have been blank.[5] It contains the text of Lydgate's poem *The Hors, the Shepe and the Ghoos* (*NIMEV* 658) on fols 2r–14v, followed by the moralising poem *Hit is ful hard to knowe ony estate* (*NIMEV* 1629: fols 15r–16r), combined with two Lydgate stanzas, previously known as the 'Halsham Ballad' (*NIMEV* 3504, 3436).[6] The remaining leaves of the second quire are then taken up by the

---

[1] There is also a fragment of six leaves (fols 2–7) of *STC* 17019 in Cambridge University Library, catalogue no. 4069, and a fragment of four leaves (fols 4–5, 9, 18) of *STC* 17018 in the British Library, shelf-mark IB. 55016. The latter was discovered by William Blades in 1859, in the binding of Caxton's 1478 edition of *Boece*, in the library of the King Edward VI Grammar School in St Albans. The discovery is described in full in Blades's *The Biography and Typography of William Caxton* (London, 1877), p. 213n.

[2] Thus in *STC*, vol. 1. See also Gordon Duff, *Fifteenth Century English Books* (Oxford, 1917), nos 261, 262.

[3] See *STC*, III, 38–9, 289, 331. The case for revising the chronology of these two editions was put by Lotte Hellinga, *Caxton in Focus* (London, 1982), pp. 63–8, 80–3, and by Paul Needham, *The Printer & the Pardoner: An Unrecorded Indulgence Printed by William Caxton for the Hospital of St. Mary Rounceval, Charing Cross* (Washington DC, 1986), pp. 83–91. On a possible lost ancestor to both surviving versions of this incunable, see my article, 'Caxton's printings of *The Horse, the Sheep and the Goose*: Some observations regarding textual relationships', *TCBS*, 13 (2004), 1–13.

[4] See the explanatory note to Part IVg, line 6, below.

[5] Authorities differ in their foliation of this short pamphlet, depending on whether they count the missing first folio or not. I have followed the formula set out by Duff (*Fifteenth Century Books*, no. 261), which takes account of the phantom first folio; this also accords with the pencil foliation in the Cambridge copy.

[6] This composite poem appears also in Huntington MS 144, into which it was apparently copied from *STC* 17018. See Curt F. Buhler, 'Lydgate's *Horse, Sheep and*

J.B. Treatise (fols 16v–18r), with the verso of the final leaf remaining blank. It is important to recognise that the type-facsimile printed by M.M. Sykes for the Roxburghe Club was not derived from this edition, but from the Pierpont Morgan impression when it was held by the library of Yorkminster.[1]

HSG is doubly noteworthy for being among the very earliest books printed by Caxton in England, and also for containing the first printed text of the *J.B. Treatise* – earlier even than that found in *StA*. The fact that the treatise is here used as filler should not, however, be over-emphasised; of much greater significance is Caxton's decision to use it in the first place. We may speculate that the J.B. elements he chose are admirably suited to the rustic setting established by Lydgate's poem of a debate between a horse, a sheep and a goose. But no less important would be his assessment of the desirability of the J.B. material to potential buyers – a judgement seemingly confirmed by his need to reprint the pamphlet within a year,[2] and for Wynkyn to follow suit with three further known editions by 1500 (*STC* 17020–17022), all containing the same basic version of the *J.B. Treatise* as that originally printed by Caxton.[3]

Caxton's version of the *J.B. Treatise* is itself unusual for including the three-line passage 'If a hart stands', which I have catalogued as a separate J.B. element although, as I point out later, it could easily be regarded as an extension of the preceding Resting terms. The only other J.B. collection in which this item occurs is the fragmentary Am (no. 17 below), which appears in any case to have been copied from *HSG*. The origins of this item remain undiscovered, as does Caxton's copy-text for the four other J.B. elements assembled in *HSG*.

And yet there are some manifest similarities between Caxton's printed text and two manuscript versions, T and W. In particular, all three preserve a unique version of the Soiling terms, with no variations between them.

Goose and Huntington MS. HM 144', *MLN*, 55 (1940), 563–70.

[1] *The Hors, the Shepe & the Ghoos*, reprinted by M.M. Sykes for The Roxburghe Club (London, 1822); this is not a true facsimile, as a photographic facsimile would be, though it is sometimes referred to as such. With the exception of the four leaves discovered by Blades in a Caxton binding, all other copies of these incunables survived in *Sammelbände* that were disbound in the 19th century – as described with much other interesting information by Alexandra Gillespie, 'Caxton's Chaucer and Lydgate quartos: miscellanies from manuscript to print', *TCBS*, 12 (2000), 1–25 (at pp. 5–7).

[2] For more on Caxton's commercial sagacity and strategies, as well as the similarity of his quartos to manuscript booklets, see Gillespie, 'Caxton's quartos', pp. 12–17.

[3] The J.B. material as printed in Wynkyn's editions is little different from Caxton's, except for minor variations of orthography.

More generally, *HSG*, T and W also contain the same four major elements – the Collective nouns, Resting terms, Carving terms and Soiling terms – which together seem to have constituted a small, compact rendition of the *J.B. Treatise*. Regrettably, the similarities between *HSG*, T and W go no further, making it impossible to establish any direct connections between them.[1]

One final affiliation to be observed is that *HSG*'s Collective nouns were reproduced in the second edition of Caxton's *Book of Courtesy*, or *Little John* (*LJ*), as printed by Wynkyn de Worde in 1491–93 (see no. 23 below). All that remains of that work, however, is a fragment of a printer's proof, bearing only the last fifteen collectives.

The only part of *HSG* to be independently represented in this edition is the gnomic set of lines 'If a hart stands', which is collated with Am in Part IVb. In addition, *HSG*'s Soiling terms are collated with T and W in Part IVg. Its remaining elements – the Collective nouns, Carving terms, and Resting terms – are all fully incorporated and annotated in Appendices I–III.

7. **L** – London, Lambeth Palace Library, MS 306: mid-15th to 16th century, paper, 202 folios (i+202+ii), *c*. 295 × 215 mm. There is a collection of J.B. material on fols 174v–176v, consisting of:

　　i. Hawks' diseases and remedies
　　ii. Choosing a hawk
　　iii. Ages of a hawk
　　iv. A hawk's foot and feathers
　　v. Flying terms
　　vi. Hierarchy of hawks
　　vii. Beasts of venery and the chase
　　viii. Resting terms
　　ix. Collective nouns (54 phrases)
　　　　Explicit
　　x. Carving terms (in a different hand)

Viewed in its entirety, L is a very miscellaneous compilation made up of three distinct parts. The earliest is a collection of eight booklets (consisting of 20 quires) composed around 1460, largely by a single scribe (fols 1–48,

---

[1] There is also considerable similarity between the Carving terms of W and *HSG*, but the other elements in both W and T – aside from the Soiling terms – are more distant from their congeners in *HSG*.

114–187).[1] These eight booklets contain a variety of works, such as a chronicle of England, the romance *Lybeaus Desconus*, *St Gregory's Trental*, *The Wright's Chaste Wife*, love lyrics, and historical and religious poems. There is also a version of *Prince Edward's Book of Hawking* uniquely combined with a set of additional hawking remedies, that blend directly into the J.B. material (described in more detail overleaf). Most of these booklets originally ended in blank leaves, which were subsequently filled with writings (many of them on medical and botanical subjects) in several 16th-century hands. The presence of independent sets of leaf signatures in most of these booklets suggests that they were originally compiled as discrete items.[2]

Interposed between fols 48 and 73 of the 15th-century compilation described above is the second distinct part of the manuscript – namely, three quires of historical material (fols 49–72), mostly in the hand of the antiquary John Stow (*c.* 1525–1605), who also added occasional notes elsewhere. Finally, the third part of the codex consists of a printed text: Caxton's *Life of St Winifred* of 1484/5 (*STC* 25853), in two gatherings that have been bound in at the rear (fols 188–202).

It is now difficult to assess whether the eight earliest booklets were initially brought together in the 1460s, as Maldwyn Mills suggests, or whether they remained as loose quires until they were bound up with Stow's writings and the Caxton gatherings in the 16th century, as Guddat-Figge claims.[3] Since these early quires have no worn or grubby outer leaves to suggest that they circulated independently, Mills's conclusion seems the more plausible. At any rate, it is clear that the entire codex was not

---

[1] For the notion of a manuscript booklet, which may consist of one or more quires, see my discussion of Adv above. According to Guddat-Figge, *Catalogue*, pp. 218–226, the 15th-century booklets comprise: (I) fols 1–48; (III) 73–113; (IV) 114–126; (V) 127–131; (VI) 132–141; (VII) 142–165; (VIII) 166–177; (IX) 178–187.

[2] L has been described in detail by James Gairdner, *Three Fifteenth Century Chronicles*, Camden Society, NS 28 (London, 1880), pp. i–xv; Montague Rhodes James and Claude Jenkins, *A Descriptive Catalogue of the Manuscripts in the Library of Lambeth Palace* (Cambridge, 1930–2), pp. 421–26; *Lybeaus Desconus*, ed. M. Mills, EETS os 261 (London, 1969), pp. 2–3. The two latter studies conflict in their collation of the manuscript's first sixteen quires, with Mills counting fol. 113 as a singleton. A third collation can be found in the hand-written annotations to the James and Jenkins catalogue kept in Lambeth Palace Library. Of these three collations, I find that of Mills to be the most authoritative. See also Guddat-Figge, *Catalogue*, p. 225 for details on the manuscript's leaf signatures.

[3] *Lybeaus Desconus*, ed. Mills, p. 3; Guddat-Figge, *Catalogue*, pp. 225–26.

originally a commonplace book, as has been been claimed for it; it became a commonplace book only after assuming its present, composite form when bound in its entirety in the 16th century.[1]

As indicated briefly above, the J.B. material is to be found in one of the original 15th-century quires, a gathering of 12 leaves foliated 166–177.[2] It forms part of a unique conflated text, consisting of three separate items: (a) *Prince Edward's Book of Hawking*, (b) some additional remedies for hawks, and (c) the J.B. material – all of which appear to derive from MS H, although probably not directly. Whoever assembled this composite work clearly saw it as a comprehensive treatise on falconry (*PEB* + the extra hawking remedies + the J.B. hawking material) with some useful hunting information attached (J.B. items vii–ix). There is a long introductory paragraph, not found in H, which begins, *This is the maner to kepe haukes and to rewle them in all poyntis*, together with a comprehensive table of contents (fol. 166r–v), which contains a total of 174 headings, up to and including the J.B. Hierarchy of hawks (item vi). In other words, the table of contents does not include the J.B. hunting elements, which were perhaps considered interesting but extraneous. The entire text is carefully written in a cursive Secretary hand, with red-ink headings that flow directly into the paragraphs they introduce.

No other version of this combined material is known, but there is an intriguing possibility that a manuscript that once belonged in the collection of the bibliophile Richard (C.F.G.R) Schwerdt (*ob*. 1939) may contain something similar – a surmise based entirely on the description of that manuscript in Schwerdt's 4-volume catalogue:

> Berners (Juliana) Dame. Manuscript on Falconry circa 1450. English (21.6 × 13.5 cm). 7 ll. This manuscript closely resembles 2340 of the Harleian collection in the British Museum, except that on the first page ... 24 lines occur before the passage "This is þe manr to kepe hauks [...]" which marks the beginning of the Harleian version. The resemblance between the two manuscripts ceases at the end of page 12 of the present one, and the text on pp. 13–14 is entirely different and ends abruptly.[3]

---

[1] See Hands, *EHH*, p. xxiv; R.H. Robbins, review of Rigg's *Glastonbury Miscellany*, p. 141.

[2] Booklet VIII in Guddat-Figge's system.

[3] C.F.G.R. Schwerdt, *Hunting, Hawking, Shooting, Illustrated in a Catalogue of Books, Manuscripts, Prints and Drawings*, 4 vols (London, 1928–37), II, 317.

That manuscript was sold by Sotheby's in 1946 and its present whereabouts are unknown.[1]

The person who assembled the composite treatise described above has skilfully blended its different components to avoid repetition. In the first place, he has combined *Prince Edward's Book of Hawking* and the additional hawking remedies to form an entirely new text (referred to hereafter as *PEB 2*),[2] which runs from fol. 167r to fol. 174v, and ends with a paragraph describing how to treat a hawk with a flesh wound: *For an hauke wounded* (cap. 162).[3] There then occurs the rubric, *For an sperhauke*, which is not one of the numbered headings and is not in the table of contents. There is nothing distinctive about this heading to indicate a transition to new material, but that is exactly what happens here, for the remedy that it introduces marks the start of the J.B. material.

The transition is relatively seamless, since the J.B. material commences with its own account of Hawks' diseases and remedies (item i), and this follows on naturally from the remedies of *PEB 2*. Even in attaching the J.B. material, the compiler continues to exercise his editorial skills, for he omits J.B. remedies that repeat information already provided by *PEB 2*. It is clear that the compiler saw the J.B. hawking material as integral to his composite hawking treatise, for he continues to supply numbered red-ink headings, all of which are reflected in the initial table of contents. The last of these headings, cap. 174, introduces the final J.B. hawking element, the Hierarchy of hawks, with the words, *Ther beth dyuers haukes for euery astate and for other men of degre*. The hierarchy runs to the foot of fol. 175, where, it would seem, the entire hawking treatise comes to an end, although there is no *explicit* or closing remark that terminates it unequivocally.

The J.B. hunting material – which, as I have mentioned already, is not included in the table of contents, but is written by the same scribe – begins at the top of fol. 176r with a red lombard initial *T* introducing the Beasts of venery and the chase. That item is written in long lines, but the next two items (the Resting terms and Collective nouns) are written in two columns, below which a boxed *Explicit* marks the end of the text. Later, however, a

---

[1] The sale of the manuscript is recorded in the Sotheby Sale Catalogue for 11–12 March 1946, lot 2183. I discuss the matter further in 'Hawking information in the Tollemache "Book of Secrets"', *N&Q*, 51 (2004), 348–50. See also Hands, *EHH*, p. xxvi.

[2] I regard this as a composite text, distinct from the unamplified version found in MS H (= *PEB 1*). See further, Keiser, *Manual X*, 3697 [452].

[3] The equivalent passage occurs in H, fol. 18r–v, almost nine pages before the end of the text; see *PEB 1* (ed. Swaen), p. 18.

different scribe expanded the list of collectives with eight additional phrases, and went on to add the final element – the Carving terms – on the verso of fol. 176.[1] Thereafter, a third scribe, writing in a small, spiky hand, corrected several items in the Carving terms, and added one further phrase to the list of Collective nouns.[2]

It is not immediately clear how the compiler of this entire section of the manuscript viewed the J.B. hunting material that follows his composite hawking treatise. The fact that he failed to include it in his table of contents suggests that he may have seen it as extraneous; on the other hand, the fact that he placed his only *explicit* after the hunting section could suggest an implied acceptance that the hunting material is connected with what precedes it. There is no corresponding ambiguity in the actions of the scribe who contributed the Carving terms: he must have recognised the J.B. material for what it was and realised that a list of carving terms could justly be appended to it: indeed, that such a list belonged with it.

Given the composite nature of the entire text to which the J.B. elements have been conjoined, it seems best to categorise L as containing a collection of J.B. material – uniquely assimilated into a new, larger work – rather than a version of the *J.B. Treatise*. The J.B. elements in L may ultimately derive from the *J.B. Treatise* in H, but they have here been made part of something entirely novel, which needs to be recognised for what it is.

A final noteworthy feature of L's composite hawking treatise is that the letters 'jb' (written as large minuscules) have been added in a 16th-century hand above the start of the table of contents on fol. 166r, together with folio numbers at top right on the recto of each leaf, up to fol. 176.[3] Whoever was responsible for these additions appears to have recognised the text for its associations with J.B./Juliana Barnes and decided to flag it as such.

---

[1] The J.B. hunting items and the carving terms are transcribed in part or in full by O.S. Pickering and V.M. O'Mara, *The Index of Middle English Prose, Handlist XIII: Manuscripts in Lambeth Palace Library* (Cambridge, 1999), p. 23.

[2] This is also pointed out by Corner, 'More terms', p. 16. The second scribe fills much of the available space at the end of the gathering with two items on the diet of nightingales, and a third on discerning the sex of a lark (fols 176v–177v). The gathering closes with a hymn to the Virgin on fol. 177v (*NIMEV* 2397), perhaps in the hand of the third scribe. The hands of the second and third scribes appear to be of the early 16th century.

[3] This 16th-century foliation runs 1–11 on fols 166–176. There is also a separate 15th-century signature sequence at bottom right of the first six leaves only, running A1–6.

8. Pl – New York, Columbia University, Rare Book and Manuscript Library, Plimpton Add. MS 2: *c.* 1450 (or perhaps a little later), parchment, 6 leaves, 160 × 60 mm (holster format). Pl contains six items of J.B. material on fols 3r–5v,[1] consisting of:

   i. Collective nouns (105 phrases)[2]
   ii. Precepts in *-ly*
   iii. Resting terms
   iv. Carving terms
   v. Four things to dread
   vi. Properties of a good horse

Pl is an unusual compilation. It begins with three liturgical items in Latin and English (fols 1v–2v), proceeds to the J.B. material (fols 3r–5v), and ends with two devotional poems in English (fol. 5v).[3] The J.B. material and the final two devotional poems are all in the same, fairly formal, mixed Anglicana hand, and have been rubricated with one- and two-line lombard initials and the red-tipping of capitals. The manuscript as a whole has been pricked and ruled, and the scribe of the rubricated section (fols 3r–5v) has left one-line spaces between paragraphs and groups of items.

The J.B. material itself is presented in an unusual way, in that the Collective nouns, Resting terms and Carving terms are set out in groups of five or six phrases, with each group introduced by its own red lombard initial. The nine Precepts in *-ly* are also grouped together and are introduced by a single red lombard initial. Nowhere else are these J.B. elements

---

[1] Fols 1r and 6r–v are blank, and until relatively recently only the surfaces containing writing (fols 1v–5v) were numbered with the page sequence 1–9. The manuscript has, however, now been assigned folio numbers for all six leaves.

[2] Only 100 phrases of collectives are actually legible on fols 3r–4r; five have been lost through damage to the upper edge of several leaves, but have been included in my tally of 105. There are also two additional phrases containing collectives among the Resting terms on fol. 4v.

[3] Pl is described briefly by S.A. Ives, who dates the manuscript *c.* 1450: 'Corrigenda and addenda to the description of the Plimpton manuscripts as recorded in the De Ricci Census', *Speculum*, 17 (1942), 33–49 (p. 46). See also W.H. Bond and C.U. Faye, *Supplement to the Census of Medieval and Renaissance Manuscripts in the United States and Canada* (New York, 1962), pp. 324–25. I am very grateful to Mrs Rachel Hands and Dr Consuelo Dutschke of Columbia University Library for assisting me in my early work on this manuscript. It can now be viewed in its entirety on the Digital Scriptorium website, where it is dated to the second half of the 15th century: <http://www.digital-scriptorium.org>.

presented in such a manner, except in MS Prk, which also has its collectives arranged in groups of five. Other similarities indicate a strong relationship between Pl and Prk, for Prk contains exactly the same set of six elements in precisely the same order, although it then goes on to provide another six elements not found in Pl (see Prk, no. 10 below).

The relationship between the two manuscripts is not immediately obvious. At first sight, Pl appears to be an abridged version of Prk, as Rachel Hands suggests.[1] However, internal evidence indicates that Pl is unlikely to have derived from Prk. For instance, Pl contains several phrases that are wanting in Prk, as well as forms of words that are unlikely to have derived from their very distinctive counterparts in Prk.[2] Pl also preserves the correct wording of at least one statement that is corrupt in Prk: cf. *þat ys on þe curs off owre holy fader* (Pl), against *þat is vone of oure holly fadyre* (Prk).

On the other hand, there is nothing in the items that Prk shares with Pl that could not have originated in Pl. It therefore seems more likely that Prk derived some of its material, by at least one intermediary, from Pl, and conflated this with a further set of J.B. elements from another source (which would mean that Pl must be earlier than the date of 1470 assigned to Prk). For all the above reasons, no part of Pl is independently presented in this study. Nevertheless, all its J.B. material is fully collated with Prk in Part I below, and is discussed where appropriate in the Explanatory Notes.

9. Pp – Cambridge, Magdalene College, The Pepys Library, MS Pepys 1047: late 15th century (after 1471), paper, 23 folios (i+23+i), *c.* 180 × 125 mm. Pp contains two sections of J.B. material on fols 2r–5v and 20v–23r, together with an important J.B. colophon on fol. 5v:[3]

    i. Collective nouns (146 phrases)

    Explicit Iulyan Barne

    [fols 6r–20v: charms, recipes, remedies etc.]

    To helpe an hawke of dyvers sekenes
    ii. Hawks' diseases and remedies
    iii. Choosing a hawk
    iv. Flying terms

---

[1] Hands, *EHH*, p. 13.

[2] Cf. *boyys, vn ioyneteyd, spolyyde* (Pl), against *baeyis, vn gynttyte, spyllyde* (Prk).

[3] Pp also contains a version of the Precepts in *-ly* on fol. 1r, which I have disregarded because it is clearly unconnected with either of Pp's two sets of J.B. items.

v. Hierarchy of hawks
vi. Beasts of venery and the chase
*Here endys hawkyng with medsyns and castyng
and all that longys to goode hauke kepyng*[1]

Pp is a single-quire booklet, originally of 24 leaves, one of which (no. 14) has been excised.[2] Its contents are of a generally miscellaneous nature, but there is a strong preponderance of recipes, remedies and associated material, such as charms against ailments. There are also a few moralising items, and other writings offering information of a different kind, such as a set of prognostications for the coming year depending on the day of the week on which Christmas falls (fol. 23r–v).[3]

The entire manuscript is the work of a single scribe, writing in a fairly cursive, but open, mixed Anglicana hand. Although there are no signs of ruling, and although some items are written in a more cramped manner than others,[4] the overall style of execution is fairly formal, with wide spaces separating paragraphs, and red-ink headings throughout. In short, Pp shows all the signs of having been carefully assembled and copied over a relatively short period, probably as a commission, rather than evolving over time as an accretive collection, as would be the case if it were a commonplace book or a household miscellany.[5] There is a tantalising clue that the manuscript may have been owned by a woman because of the deliberate obliteration

---

[1] *NIMEV* 1197.2.

[2] The manuscript is described in detail by Rosamond McKitterick and Richard Beadle, *Catalogue of the Pepys Library at Magdalene College Cambridge*, Volume V: Manuscripts, Part i: Medieval (Cambridge, 1992), pp. 8–9. The entire manuscript has also been reproduced in facsimile, with a modern English translation (not always reliable), by Gerald A.J. Hodgett: *Stere Htt Well: A book of medieval refinements, recipes and remedies from a manuscript in Samuel Pepys's library* (London, 1972).

[3] The genre is discussed briefly by Rossell Hope Robbins, 'Medical manuscripts in Middle English', *Speculum*, 45 (1970), 393–415 (at p. 397); for verse accounts of the same idea, see *NIMEV* 1905.

[4] See, for example, fols 22r and 23r.

[5] McKitterick and Beadle describe Pp as 'a household book', which I take to mean a household miscellany: *Catalogue of the Pepys Library* (V. i), p. 8. For the notion of a household miscellany as a collection of texts assembled over a period of time by several members of a household, see Boffey and Thompson, 'Anthologies', p. 294. Although Pp's contents may be broadly typical of such collections, its mode of production must have been quite different.

of an antifeminist phrase in the list of collective nouns;[1] however, Pp bears no evidence of patronage or ownership before being acquired by Samuel Pepys, probably shortly before 1700.

Although Pp contains that vitally important colophon *Explicit Iulyan Barne*, I have categorised it as containing J.B. material rather than a *J.B. Treatise* because of the division of its material into two distinct sections that are separated by 29 pages of unrelated matter (fols 6r–20v). It seems likely that the scribe had two different J.B. sources at his disposal (or perhaps an exemplar that was itself compiled from separate sources), since these two J.B. sections belong to entirely different traditions that are found together nowhere else.

Turning first to the five items comprising the second section (ii–vi), these are tantalisingly similar to their equivalents in H and L, and, to a lesser extent, Ex. Specifically, the Hawks' diseases and remedies (ii) and the Hierarchy of hawks (v) show stronger affinities with H and L than with any other version. What is more, the accounts of Choosing a hawk (iii) and Flying terms (iv) occur elsewhere only in H, L and Ex. In general, this entire cluster of items in Pp looks remarkably like a truncated, and slightly corrupted, version of H. And yet the disagreements between Pp and H are so numerous, and of such a character, that it has proved impossible to collate Pp with the transcription of H in Part II below, except in relation to the Beasts of venery and the chase (vi). The evidence yielded by a close comparison of texts indicates that this second cluster of elements (ii–vi) cannot have descended from H, and so must belong to a collateral branch of the same family.

There is a further striking correspondence between Pp and H in the form of their J.B. colophons and where these are located. It would seem more likely than not that there is some connection between Pp's *Explicit Iulyan Barne* and H's *Explicit I.B.*, especially since both colophons fall at the end of the Collective nouns in their respective manuscripts. In this regard, Pp is superior to H for preserving intact a vital attribution that has – in all likelihood and for reasons unknown – been abbreviated in H. But there are other issues to consider as well.

Matters are complicated by Pp's first J.B. section – the list of Collective nouns and its colophon – which cannot have descended from H or any of its congeners. As I explain below ('Affinities among the J.B. Elements'), the lists of collectives fall into one of two categories: long lists and short lists,

---

[1] We can infer from the sequence in other lists that the deleted phrase is most likely to have been 'An impatience of wives'. See further Appendix I, no. 219 and note.

which differ, not only in the number of phrases they contain (45 in H, 146 in Pp), but also in terms of their preferred expressions. For example, where H, along with other short lists, has 'a chattering of starlings', 'a team of swans', 'a flight of larks', and 'a truelove of turtles', Pp agrees with most other long lists in offering 'a murmuration of starlings', a herd of swans', 'an exalting of larks', and 'a dole of turtles'. An important implication is that the origin of Pp's J.B. colophon becomes rather more mysterious. In the absence of additional evidence, we must suppose that at some point during the evolution of the lists of collectives (both long and short varieties), the name *Iulyan Barne* (abbreviated as *I.B.*) became attached to them as a putative originator, and that Pp and H independently preserve this attribution. It is regrettable that nothing more precise can be said about the origins of Pp's list of collectives, as it shows no close affinity with any other known version.

Although Pp could arguably have been included as a separate text in this edition, its contents have been dealt with as follows: the Collective nouns are collated with all other J.B. versions in Appendix I, and the remaining material is discussed and quoted extensively in the notes on H (Part II). The entire text – indeed, the entire manuscript – can also be read in Gerald Hodgett's facsimile edition, *Stere Htt Well* (1972).

10. Prk – Aberystwyth, National Library of Wales, Brogyntyn MS ii.1 (*olim* MS Porkington 10): *c.* 1470, paper and parchment, 211 folios in 26 quires, quarto, *c.* 140 × 105 mm.[1] Prk contains a conflated version of the *J.B. Treatise* on fols 184r–192r, consisting of:

  i. Collective nouns (107 phrases)[2]
  ii. Precepts in *-ly*
  iii. Resting terms
  iv. Carving terms
  v. Four things to dread

---

[1] For a full description of this manuscript and its contents, see Daniel Huws, 'MS Porkington 10 and its scribes', pp. 188–207, esp. pp. 190–1. Although Huws's article in many ways supersedes the two earlier standard accounts of this manuscript, they remain important: Auvo Kurvinen, 'MS. Porkington 10: description with extracts', *NM*, 54 (1953), 33–67; Guddat-Figge, *Catalogue*, pp. 73–8. High-quality images of the entire codex, named 'A Middle English Miscellany', can be viewed on the Digital Gallery of the National Library of Wales website: <https://www.llgc.org.uk>.

[2] This tally excludes the two additional phrases that form part of the Resting terms; see the text of Prk at I/126–7.

vi. Properties of a good horse
vii. Beasts of venery and the chase
viii. Breeds of dogs
ix. Soiling terms
x. Hierarchy of hawks
xi. Ages of a hawk
xii. Hawks' diseases and remedies

Prk is a miscellaneous collection, mostly in English, of a diverse range of material, including numerous poems and songs, a table of eclipses, a treatise on limning, medical recipes, a life of Saint Catherine, and one of only two known versions of *Sir Gawain and the Carl of Carlisle* (*NIMEV* 1888). Although the first quire (fols 1–10) seems originally to have been compiled independently of the rest, it was completed by one of the scribes involved in assembling the entire codex, and became an integral part of the whole at an early stage.

Overall, Prk shows all the signs of having been written and assembled deliberately, and with great care, rather than growing haphazardly over time. Disregarding the first quire, the manuscript is the work of eight scribes, of whom two contributed the great majority of items as well as rubricating the text and tidying up the work of others by filling blank leaves at the ends of quires.[1]

Although Prk has sometimes been categorised as a commonplace book,[2] it does not conform to the standard definition of such a work – that is, an anthology assembled over time by one person. Nor is it a 'household miscellany' – a collection put together by several members of a household – as proposed by Boffey and Thomson.[3] Internal evidence suggests instead that Prk was perhaps commissioned as a library piece: a one-volume 'library *in parvo*', as Adv has been called. There are, however, no clear indications as to who its patron might have been; the manuscript's language is

---

[1] See Huws, 'MS Porkington 10 and its scribes', pp. 190–3, 198. In addition to the eight scribes already mentioned, the hands of a further eight scribes are apparent in the (possibly extraneous) first quire alone. Huws argues convincingly that one of the two principal scribes ('scribe O' in his nomenclature) is probably the shaper of the entire collection: *ibid.*, pp. 198–9.

[2] For example, Rigg, *Glastonbury Miscellany*, p. 26.

[3] Boffey and Thompson, 'Anthologies', p. 294. See also Jeremy Griffiths' definition of a household miscellany as a volume 'in which the tastes of an individual compiler may be less evident than the activity of a number of individuals over a period of time, presumably in a provincial household': *Tollemache 'Book of Secrets'*, p. 4.

distinctively of the West Midlands, but Welsh names appearing in marginal scribbles show that it had reached Wales by the early 16th century.[1]

The *J.B. Treatise* falls on the last three leaves of quire 23 (fols 184–6) and the first six leaves of quire 24 (fols 187–92). It is preceded by a prose account of *The Siege of Jerusalem* (fols 157v–184r) in the same hand – that of 'scribe O', the putative organiser of the whole codex. The remainder of quire 24 consists of three shorter pieces – the political poem *The Cock in the North* (*NIMEV* 4029), a satirical letter, and a list of gifts to the pope from the lords of Venice – all in the hand of 'scribe J', the second of the manuscript's two main scriveners. There is every indication that the *J.B. Treatise* was regarded as an important text in Prk, and was not simply added as a filler item, as occasionally happens elsewhere (for example, MS Ha). Not only has it been copied by the manuscript's principal scribe, but its style of execution is formal throughout: the scribal hand (a hybrid Secretary) is neat and precise, the text begins with a two-line red lombard initial, line capitals are touched in red,[2] and the transition from quire 23 to 24 is carefully marked by means of catchwords placed prominently in a cartouche.

This is the longest known version of the *J.B. Treatise* and, in many ways, the most fully developed. Although it has fewer hawking elements than H and L, it contains more elements overall than any other witness. Close analysis of these elements reveals that they have been assembled from two distinct traditions: the first six elements are almost identical to the complete text of Pl (even down to the arrangement of the collective nouns in groups of five); conversely, the next six elements are closely related to most of what is found in the cognate pair Dg–Rg.[3]

Prk and Pl are indubitably closely related, with Prk probably deriving by way of at least one intermediary from the earlier Pl (see my discussion of Pl above); by contrast, there is no direct link between Prk and Dg–Rg, apart from the close similarity of their shared material. It is not possible to say

---

[1] The name 'H. Hatton', which is written conspicuously in a scroll on fol. 52v, may be associated with the Hatton family of Hatton, near Runcorn (Cheshire). The earliest Welsh name is that of 'John ap D[afyd]d', written in what appears to be an early 16th-century hand on fol. 26r; see Huws, 'MS Porkington 10 and its scribes', pp. 204–5; Kurvinen, 'MS. Porkington 10', p. 37.

[2] Huws maintains that this scribe was responsible for most of the rubrication and decoration in the manuscript: 'MS Porkington 10 and its scribes', p. 198.

[3] The similarity with Dg is greatest, with Prk's final six elements (vii–xii) matching the sequence in Dg almost exactly. Prk omits only the Collective nouns and Resting terms of the Dg sequence, and for good reason: they are included among Prk's first six elements, derived from Pl.

when the two parts of Prk's *J.B. Treatise* were first brought together: perhaps Prk was copied from an exemplar in which all the items had already been assembled as they appear here; or perhaps the scribe's exemplar contained only the first six elements (from Pl), to which he added the final group of six elements from another source (now lost) related to Dg–Rg.[1]

An immediate consequence of this conflation of materials is that it alters the status of two elements – (v) Four things to dread and (vi) Properties of a good horse – that might otherwise be dismissed as being extrinsic to the *J.B. Treatise* proper. In Pl, for example, these two 'miscellaneous' elements are written after the Carving terms, and could therefore be regarded as having been adventitiously appended to the J.B. material. In Prk, the addition of a further six elements from the Dg–Rg group effectively locks the two doubtful elements within an entirely new hybrid version of the *J.B. Treatise*, with the result that they must henceforth be treated as having become integral to it.

Owing to the manifest significance of Prk's *J.B. Treatise* in the corpus of surviving witnesses, it was a natural choice as one of the three main versions presented by this study. See Part I for the complete text, collated as appropriate with Pl, Dg and Rg.

11. Rd – Oxford, Bodleian Library, MS Rawlinson D 328 ('Walter Pollard's notebook': SC 15444): 14th–15th centuries, parchment and paper, 207 leaves (ii+207+ii, foliated 1–194), mostly measuring *c.* 220 × 150 mm.[2] Rd contains a collection of J.B. material on fols 171r–173r, composed of:

A litel boke of doctrine for ionge gentil men
  i. Collective nouns (153 phrases)
  Longing for keruers
  ii. Carving terms
  [added later]
  iii. Beasts of venery and the chase
  iv. The hunter
  v. Breeds of dogs
  vi. Soiling terms

---

[1] Perhaps my hypothetical MS δ: see the description of Dg above, and my discussion of 'Textual Relationships' (Group 2) later in this Introduction.

[2] For a comprehensive description and collation of Rd, see David Thomson, *A Descriptive Catalogue of Middle English Grammatical Texts* (New York and London, 1979), pp. 290–315.

Rd is a composite codex of two distinct parts. The first consists of six leaves of parchment (fols 1–6) from the turn of the 14th/15th centuries, containing Cato's *Distychs*; the second part, which is entirely of paper, is a commonplace book from the second half of the 15th century, compiled by Walter Pollard of Plymouth, a teacher at Exeter Grammar School, who notes his ownership of the manuscript in 23 Hen VI (1444/5) on fol. 179r. Only the second part will concern us further here.

The contents of Pollard's book are extremely diverse, since he added to it over a period of some forty years – the last date in his hand being 1483 (fol. 189v). The material that Pollard collected includes verses, moralising items, domestic notes, and a good many grammatical and didactic items, among them notes on individual words, a treatise on spelling, and a text of the *Informacio* by the grammarian John Leylond (Leyland, Leland: fols 8r–15v).[1] It is not difficult to see why the J.B. material should have appealed to Pollard, with his professional interest in language and terminology. Indeed, only a few leaves separate the J.B. material from an obviously scholarly item: a treatise on figures of speech (fols 176r–179r).

The J.B. material falls in the manuscript's fourteenth quire (the thirteenth of Pollard's book), consisting of fols 169–179(a).[2] I have not categorised this material as a distinct version of the *J.B. Treatise* because it is clearly an amalgam from two separate sources that Pollard drew on at widely different times. First to be set down were the Collective nouns and Carving terms (i–ii), which were carefully written as a single continuous list in two columns on fols 171r–172r. A line drawn beneath the last carving term indicates the conclusion of this material. Beneath this line appears the second group of four J.B. elements (iii–vi) in a different ink and in a hand of markedly different appearance; the overall execution is also noticeably more casual. This group of items runs to fol. 173r, where the Soiling terms end abruptly; the verso of this leaf is blank, as is fol. 174r. In spite of the pronounced difference in appearance of the first and second groups of elements, they are very likely both the work of Pollard, who is known to have written in

---

[1] See *ODNB*, s.v. John Leylond [Leyland, Leland] (*ob.* 1428). For more about both Leylond and Pollard, see further *An Edition of the Middle English Grammatical Texts*, ed. David Thomson (New York and London, 1984), pp. xii, 61–2, 76–80, 164–76.

[2] Fol. 179(a) is a blank leaf that follows fol. 179 and has not been included in the manuscript's modern pencil foliation. There are many such unnumbered leaves, some of them still uncut bifolia, which need to be taken into account when calculating a collation for this manuscript.

a variety of styles, and whose script changed considerably as he got older.[1] It therefore seems likely that Pollard added the second group of elements at a much later stage in his life, after recognising their connection with the Collective nouns and Carving terms that were already present in his book.

Internal evidence confirms that Rd's two groups of J.B. elements have different origins. The first group (items i–ii) belongs broadly with the likes of *StA* and T, while the second (iii–vi) shows notable affinities with Ha, both in its ordering and in the wording of the elements themselves. These affinities are sufficiently strong for items iii–vi to be collated with Ha in Part III below. Incompatabilities of date and minor textual disagreements show that neither Rd nor Ha could have derived the other. There must therefore have been a common original, as yet undiscovered: the hypothetical MS λ described below under 'Textual Relationships', Group 3.

No part of Rd is represented independently in this edition. However, in addition to the collation of four of its elements with Ha in Part III, the Collective nouns, Carving terms and Resting terms are collated with all other versions in Appendices I–III.

12. Rg – London, College of Arms, MS Arundel 58 (also known as the 'Robert of Gloucester MS'): first half of the 15th century, with J.B additions from the second half of the same. This is a folio manuscript of about 342 parchment leaves (*c.* 345 × 240 mm), preceded by three unfoliated parchment endleaves that measure *c.* 345 × 130–190 mm; I shall refer to these endleaves as fols i–iii. The binding also includes three paper flyleaves at the front and five at the rear, all of a later date and all blank, which I have ignored for the purposes of this discussion. The parchment endleaves at the front of the codex contain a compact version of the *J.B. Treatise* on fols i^{r-v} and iii^v, consisting of:

    i. Collective nouns (49 phrases)
    ii. Beasts of venery and the chase
    iii. Breeds of dogs
    iv. Soiling terms
    v. Resting terms
    vi. Hierarchy of hawks
    vii. Names of wines

---

[1] See Thomson, *Descriptive Catalogue*, pp. 290–1 for a brief account of Pollard's varied writing styles.

Since the *J.B. Treatise* occurs only in Rg's endleaves, I shall not attempt to describe the remainder of this manuscript beyond observing that it consists of three texts, of which the first is by far the longest.[1] They are: (1) A version of Robert of Gloucester's metrical *Chronicle of the History of England* (*NIMEV* 727), including its own table of contents and several interpolations in prose and verse (fols 1–251), followed by (2) the romance *Richard Coeur de Lion* (*NIMEV* 1979: fols 252–334) – both elaborately decorated with illuminated initials and other embellishments; (3) verses on the kings of England, accompanied by painted medallions of English monarchs from William I to Henry IV (*NIMEV* 444: fols 335–42). Overall, these texts distinguish the manuscript as one devoted to 'historical' matter.[2]

It needs to be observed at once that the parchment endleaves i–iii have been sewn into the manuscript in a confused order so that the J.B. material appears to start – on fol. i^r – in the middle of the list of Breeds of dogs (item iii). As a result, W.H. Black, who catalogued the manuscripts of the College of Arms library in the early nineteenth century, asserts that Rg's endleaves are missing a leaf, on the assumption that the beginning of the text had been lost.[3] In fact, the 'lost' text begins on fol. iii^v, from where it runs unbroken onto fol. i^r. Once this is recognised, the elements comprising the *J.B. Treatise* readily fall into place (as indicated in my list of its contents above), and the original arrangement of the endleaves can be easily deduced. Taking their current sequence as i, ii, iii, they would originally have been arranged in the order iii, i, ii.

It would appear that the three endleaves originally belonged in a quire of at least six leaves (three bifolia), of which the first leaf survives as fol. iii. This leaf is significantly darker and more worn than the others, indicating that it was once the outer leaf of a well-used booklet. Its recto is mostly blank, except for some scribbled words, practice flourishes, a few short lines of Latin, and the heading *Epithitis* ('Epithets') written prominently at the top in a 16th- or 17th-century hand. The *J.B. Treatise* itself starts on the verso of this leaf (fol. iii^v), filling it and breaking off at the bottom in mid-

---

[1] The manuscript needs to be refoliated; it has an archaic ink foliation that runs to 342, but some leaves have been lost from this sequence, while others have been added within it (e.g. fol. 15c).

[2] The final section, containing the verses on the kings of England, appears to have been compiled separately from the rest of the manuscript, but was bound up with it at an early stage. For a fuller description of Rg, see Guddat-Figge, *Catalogue*, pp. 215–17.

[3] William Henry Black, *Catalogue of the Arundel Manuscripts in the Library of the College of Arms* (London, 1829), p. 104.

sentence. The J.B. text resumes, as I have observed, without interruption at the top of what is now fol. i^r and continues overleaf on fol. i^v, where it breaks off about half-way down, after completing the Names of wines. Fol. ii has been severely trimmed lengthwise so that it is even narrower than fols i and iii; its recto bears a few lines of writing in a 16th-century hand (including the name S*ir* Frances Dalp‹..›rey), and its verso is completely blank. The conjugate leaves of fols i and ii have been trimmed down to mere stubs, which have been folded back on themselves so that they precede the endleaves; the conjugate of fol. iii must have been even more severely trimmed, for its stub is difficult to find in the binding.

In spite of being relegated to the recycled endmatter of a large, prestigious volume, these few leaves show all the signs of having originally been conceived as a well-made booklet. Margins are frame-ruled in red – except on fol. ii^v – and the *J.B. Treatise* itself is carefully written in a professional Secretary book hand of the late 15th century. At some point the text was even corrected, albeit minimally, by another contemporary hand.[1]

It is clear, however, that neither the treatise nor the booklet containing it was completed, for what we have in Rg is a fragmentary version of the longer text found in Dg. Its contents match those of Dg almost exactly, to the end of the Names of wines, at which point Rg lacks Dg's last two elements: the Ages of a hawk, and the Hawks' diseases and remedies.[2] Minor textual details show, however, that Rg could not have derived from Dg, either directly or indirectly; this is especially evident in the several places where Rg preserves a coherent account of a passage that is confused in Dg. Close comparison of the textual evidence indicates that both probably derive from a common antecedent, now lost: the hypothetical MS θ, which I discuss in greater detail in relation to Dg (see no. 2 above).

In conclusion, Rg is of relatively minor significance as an independent witness of the *J.B. Treatise*, but nevertheless offers some useful insights into its overall development and diffusion. No part of Rg is independently represented in this edition; however, items ii–iv and vi are collated with the main text of Part I, item v with the main text of Part III, and item vii with the main text of Part IVi. In addition, its Collective nouns and Resting terms are collated with all other versions in Appendices I and III.

---

[1] For example, on fol. iii^v, the word *Otere* ('Otter') is added in the margin, with a caret beside the original *Othe*.

[2] Dg's last two elements occur also in Prk, together with the version of the Hierarchy of hawks common to both Rg and Dg. It would seem that these three elements together formed a distinct little cluster of J.B. hawking material that is partially preserved in Rg.

13. StA – *The Boke of St Albans*, first compiled and printed in 1486 by the so-called 'Schoolmaster Printer' of St Albans, Herts.: *STC* 3308. This famous incunable is a four-part manual of 90 folio leaves, offering instruction in hawking, hunting, coat-armour, and the blazoning of arms; it contains two sets of signatures, which run a–c^8, d^4, e–f^8; ^{2}a–b^6, ^{2}c–e^8, ^{2}f^{10}. For the purposes of this study, only the first two parts of *StA* will be considered – namely, the treatises on hawking and hunting, which occupy the leaves bearing the first signature sequence, a2–f8.[1] It is here that *StA*'s J.B. material is found, divided into two distinct sections: the first occurs at the end of the hawking treatise, on sigs d3r–4r; and the second (interspersed with a variety of other items) at the close of the hunting treatise on sigs f4v–8r. In other words, the main disposition of texts in *StA* is as follows:

sigs a2r–d3r	Hawking treatise – *The Proceis of Hawkyng* (*PH*)[2]
sigs d3r–4r	J.B. Hierarchy of hawks
sigs e1r–f4r	Hunting treatise – *The Boke of Huntyng* (*BH*)[3]
sigs f4v–f8r	J.B. hunting material, combined with other items that are extrinsic to the J.B. collections

The J.B. material itself consists of the following ten elements, beginning with a colophon that ends the hawking treatise (*PH*), and introduces the J.B. Hierarchy of hawks:

[sig. d3r] *Here endyth the proceis of hawking. And now foloys the naamys of all maner of hawkys & to whom they belong*

i. Hierarchy of hawks

[sigs d4v–f4r: *The Boke of Huntyng*, which ends with the colophon *Explicit Dam Iulyans Barnes in her boke of huntyng*]

---

[1] For a full description of *StA*, see Hands, *EHH*, pp. xiii ff.

[2] I have adopted this name from the colophon on sig. d3r: *Here endyth the proceis* ['treatise'] *of hawkyng*. The text is based largely on *PEB* and a Latin hawking treatise known as *Dancus Rex*, ed. Gunnar Tilander, Cynegetica IX (Lund, 1963). See further, Hands, *EHH*, pp. xxiii–xxxii. The distinctiveness of the *StA* hawking treatise is not sufficiently highlighted by Keiser, *Manual X*, 3913 [452].

[3] Keiser, *Manual X*, 3699, 3915–6 [460] calls this work by two names: (i) *Dame Julyans Barnes Boke of Huntyng*, and (ii) *Sir Tristram's Boke of Huntyng*.

[sig. f4v]
Bestis of the chace of the swete fewte & stinking
ii. Beasts of venery and the chase

The namys of diuerse maner houndis
iii. Breeds of dogs

The propreteis of a good grehound
iv. Properties of a greyhound

The propretees of a goode hors
v. Properties of a horse

[sig. f5r: Moralising apothegm: 'Well trauelid women ner well trauelid hors wer neu*er* goode']][1]

vi. Precepts in *-ly*

Merke wele theys .iiii. thynges
vii. Four things to dread

[sig. f5v: Six sets of moralising verses:
(1) 'Who that makith in Cristynmas a doog to his larder' (*NIMEV* 4106); (2) 'Fer from thy kynnysmen keste the' (*NIMEV* 761); (3) 'Who that byldys his hous all of salowes' (*NIMEV* 4101); (4) 'Ther be .iiii. thynges full harde for to knaw' (*NIMEV* 3521.5; cf. Whiting, *Proverbs*, T185); (5) 'Too wyues in oon hous' (*NIMEV* 3818); (6) 'Who that mannyth hym with his kynne' (*NIMEV* 4106.5)][2]

The compaynys of beestys and fowlys
viii. Collective nouns (164 phrases)

Here folow the dew termys to speke of breekyng or dressyng of dyuerse beestis and fowlis &c And thessame is shewed of certayn fysshes
ix. Carving terms (including a sub-heading: *Now of fysshes*)

---

[1] Whiting, W501; Keiser, *Manual X*, 3703 [472].

[2] Keiser, *Manual X*, 3703–4 [475–480]; see also George R. Keiser, 'A new text of, and new light on, the *Supplement to the Index of Middle English Verse*, 4106.5', *N&Q*, 43 (1996), 15–18.

ye shall say thus
x. Resting terms

[Shires and bishoprics; provinces of England: sig. f8r][1]

While it is possible that the *StA* compiler employed a single manuscript source in which the hawking treatise (*PH*), the hunting treatise (*BH*), and all the 'additional' material (the J.B. items, the moralising apothegm, the moralising verses, and the list of shires and bishoprics) were all present, and perhaps even disposed as they are in his printed book, no such copy-text has yet been found. Indeed, surviving manuscripts of all the relevant texts indicate that the *StA* compiler probably had at least three different sources at his disposal containing, respectively, *PH*, *BH*, and some or all of the J.B. and other additional materials. It is even very likely that this additional matter came from more than one source, as is discussed in more detail below.

So much for the general picture. A more specific conundrum for the present study is how the J.B. material and the other items that I have labelled as extraneous to it were disposed in the compiler's source(s), together with the associated question of when, and by whom, they were first brought together. These issues are central to defining what is, and what is not, 'J.B. material' in *StA*.

The ten items of the Lansdowne group

Beginning with the Properties of a good horse (item v) on sig. f5r, and ending with the six sets of moralising verses overleaf (sig. f5v), *StA* contains ten items that have, variously, either a tenuous connection with the *J.B. Treatise,* or none at all. As Rachel Hands has proposed, it seems likely that all ten items belong together as a self-contained group, and may have existed in an entirely separate source from the one that supplied the *StA* compiler with his J.B. material.[2] Evidence for this is to be found in BL, Lansdowne MS 762, fol. 16r–v (MS L), which contains eight of these ten items in precisely the same sequence as they occur in *StA*.[3] This manuscript

---

[1] Rachel Hands (*EHH*, p. 167/2044n) includes these two lists in her tally of J.B. elements, but I have excluded them for reasons adduced below. See also Keiser, *Manual X*, 3702 [471].

[2] Hands, *EHH*, pp. xlv–xlvi, liv–lv.

[3] The Lansdowne text, which omits the 'Four things to dread' and 'Who that mannyth hym' of the *StA* sequence, has been published in *Reliquiæ Antiquiæ*, ed. T. Wright and J.O. Halliwell, 2 vols (London, 1841–3), I, 232–3.

supplies a name for the collection of items under discussion: 'the Lansdowne group'.[1]

Further support for Hands's hypothesis comes from a composite codex of two Caxton incunables that have been bound together, and into the middle of which have been written seven of the Lansdowne group items found in *StA*, in essentially the same order.[2] The codex in question (indicated hereafter by the siglum MC) consists of Caxton's printings of a French translation of the *Meditationes circa septem psalmos pœnitentiales* by Cardinal Petrus de Alliaco (Pierre d'Ailly), and a French translation of the *Cordiale quattuor novissimorum*, ascribed to Gerard van Vliederhoven.[3] The seven Lansdowne group items occur on a blank opening formed by fol. 34v of the *Meditationes* and fol. 1r of the *Cordiale* (or fols 34v–35r in the pencil foliation of the entire volume), and have been dated on palaeographic grounds to the turn of the 15th/16th centuries.

Assorted verbal variations indicate that the versions of the Lansdowne-group items in *StA*, MS L and MC are all independent of one another, which lends further credence to the notion that we are dealing with material that circulated as an autonomous little collection.[4] It would therefore make sense to exclude all ten items under discussion from any catalogue of *StA*'s J.B. contents – and yet there is also good cause *not* to do so. Three of these items occur also in Pl and Prk, where they are integral components of the *J.B. Treatise*, and for that reason I have accepted them as occasional members of the J.B. set – though only, as in *StA*, when they are interwoven with items that are unequivocally of the J.B. group, or so closely contiguous with them as to be inseparable. The three items in question are: the Properties of a good horse (v), the Precepts in *-ly* (vi), and the account of Four things

---

[1] Hands, *EHH*, pp. liv–lv; Keiser, *Manual X*, 3703–4 [472–480].

[2] Omitted are the Properties of a good horse, the apothegm about 'Well trauelid women' and the set of verses on 'Four things hard to know'. The text is reproduced by Curt F. Bühler, 'Middle English apothegms in a Caxton volume', *ELN*, 1 (1963), 81–4.

[3] British Library, shelf-marks IB. 49408 and IB. 49437. Though undated, both incunables have been assigned to Caxton's later years at Bruges (up to 1475/6). The *Meditationes* was formerly thought to have been printed by Colard Mansion, but this attribution has been rejected; see L.A. Sheppard, 'A new light on Caxton and Colard Mansion', *Signature*, NS 15 (1952), 28–39; *Catalogue of Books Printed in the XVth Century now in the British Museum*, ed. George D. Painter, Part IX.ii (Belgium) (London, 1967), p. 131. See also Hands, *EHH*, pp. liv–lv.

[4] Rachel Hands remarks of the Lansdowne group that, 'In content it is very different from most of the J.B. material, offering social comment and proverbial counsel rather than instruction and information ...': *EHH*, p. lv.

to dread (vii).[1] The remaining seven items – the moral apothegm on sig. f5r and the six sets of moralising verses on sig. f5v – I have excluded as interlopers.

The knotty question of J.B. status applies also to the two final items in *StA*: the list of shires and bishoprics, and the list of provinces of England, both to be found on sig. f8r. Rachel Hands counts the shires and bishoprics as a J.B. element because analagous lists occur also in Eg (fol. 62v) and Harl (fol. 227v). But it seems to me that both items are alien to the essential interests of the J.B. treatise, namely, hawking and hunting. I would argue, furthermore, that the lists of bishoprics in both Eg and Harl have no more than a fortuitous proximity to the J.B. material, and that the same is true of *StA*. I have therefore excluded both items from my list of *StA*'s J.B. contents, and from my overall catalogue of J.B. elements in this study.

The J.B. material in StA

It will be clear from the above discussion that *StA* does not contain a coherent, integrated *J.B. Treatise*, but a melange of J.B. elements that are independent of all known manuscripts. Occasional general similarities can be observed with other versions – such as Rd's Collective nouns – but no extant manuscript stands out as a close family member, or even a partial source for *StA*, let alone a possible copy-text.

To complicate the issue even further, the way the J.B. material has been broken up and arranged in *StA* makes it is difficult to determine whether the compiler used one or more J.B. sources, and whether these contained diffuse collections of J.B. items or distinct versions of the *J.B. Treatise*. Another enigma is to be found in the fact that *StA* includes the Hierarchy of hawks, but no other J.B. hawking elements. Perhaps, as Rachel Hands argues, the compiler omitted all other J.B. hawking material because it would have repeated information already present in the main hawking treatise, *PH*; but it is also possible that his exemplar simply did not contain any.[2] Issues such as these are impossible to resolve, since no known manuscript can be adduced as evidence.

In many ways, *StA* contains the most confused assembly of J.B. material, for not only are the J.B. elements disordered and interspersed with extraneous items, but the collective nouns themselves are listed in an

---

[1] In cataloguing the J.B. contents of other witnesses, I have excluded some of these elements where they are clearly unconnected with the J.B. material: for example, the Precepts in -*ly* in Pp (fol. 1r) and in T (fol. 27r).

[2] Hands, *EHH*, p. liv.

idiosyncratic sequence that often disjoins the little groups into which they are normally arranged.[1] It is therefore unfortunate that the J.B. material became best known through this, its first printed version, and the numerous later editions and derivative printed works inspired by it. Despite its widespread influence, the best that can be said for *StA* is that it is an important witness to one or more lost J.B. manuscripts, and perhaps even a lost *J.B. Treatise*. On its own, it is a poor and potentially misleading representative of the treatise, which is why it could not serve as a base text within the present study. Nevertheless, its importance cannot be doubted, as my frequent references to it will confirm.

All references to *StA* are to the first edition of 1486, as lineated in Hands's facsimile edition (*EHH*). Where it is necessary to cite Wynkyn's second edition of 1496 (*STC* 3309), the abbreviation *StA*(2) will be used.

14. T – Dublin, Trinity College Library, MS 516: *c*. 1450–71, parchment and paper, 223 leaves, *c*. 210 × 140 mm. It contains a compact version of the *J.B. Treatise* on fols 35r–36r:[2]

De venatoribus in Anglicis
i. Collective nouns (146 phrases)
ii. Soiling terms
iii. Resting terms
This longeth to a keruer
iv. Carving terms

T is a commonplace book compiled by John Benet, a cleric who was vicar of Harlington (Beds.) from 1443 to 1471, and who died some time before November 1474.[3] It has a wide variety of contents, including political and religious poems, prophesies in prose and verse, *mirabilia* and *memorabilia*,

---

[1] The ordering of *StA*'s collectives most likely indicates the manner in which the compositor read two columns of entries in his exemplar (i.e. across, rather than down, the page), as Rachel Hands explains: *EHH*, p. lii.

[2] I have excluded the Precepts in *-ly* on fol. 27r as belonging to a collection of moralising items in the manuscript that has nothing to do with the *J.B. Treatise*.

[3] From October 1471 until his death, Benet was rector of Broughton (Bucks.). See G.L. Harriss, 'A fifteenth-century chronicle at Trinity College Dublin', *Bulletin of the Institute of Historical Research*, 38 (1965), 212–18; and G.L. and M.A. Harriss, 'John Benet's chronicle for the years 1400 to 1462', in *Camden Miscellany*, Vol. XXIV, Camden Fourth Series, 9 (1972), 151–233, especially pp. 153–8.

and is perhaps best known for the chronicle composed by Benet for the years 1400–1462.¹

Since Benet was in the habit of signing his name and writing dated notes throughout the manuscript, it is fairly clear when and where its different sections were compiled. In general, the greater part of the manuscript can be assigned to Harlington in the 1460s, and most of it is in Benet's own clear, cursive Anglicana hand. Some sections were not written out by Benet himself, but were almost certainly collected and incorporated by him.² The whole manuscript was then bound as a book, very likely by 1468, after which Benet set about rubricating his work. He also added various items that can be dated from 1468 to 1471, but did not rubricate these additions.³

The *J.B. Treatise* occurs towards the end of the fourth quire (fols 31–39), and falls among other items that were completed by 1461.⁴ However, the two leaves containing the treatise (and the account of Exodus on fol. 36v) stand out from the folios around them by having no rubrication, so they could be a later addition. Perhaps their contents were written down after Benet rubricated his book, or perhaps these leaves represent a bifolium inserted into the fourth quire after the book was first bound – the tightness of the binding makes it difficult to tell. At any rate, the *J.B. Treatise* is in

---

¹ For descriptions of T (*olim* MS E.5.10), see T.K. Abbott, *Catalogue of the Manuscripts in the Library of Trinity College Dublin* (Dublin, 1900), pp. 78–79; Marvin L. Colker, *Trinity College Library Dublin: Descriptive Catalogue of the Mediaeval and Renaissance Latin Manuscripts*, 2 vols (Aldershot, 1991), II, 976–1002, esp. p. 980; John Scattergood, 'Trinity College MS 516: A clerical historian's personal miscellany', in *Makers and Users of Medieval Books: Essays in Honour of A.S.G. Edwards*, ed. Carol M. Meale and Derek Pearsall (Cambridge, 2014), pp. 121–31. I am very grateful to John Scattergood for drawing my attention to this manuscript and generously allowing me to use his own research notes in the preparation of this study.

² For example, the long extract from John of Legnano's *De Bello* (fols 76r–107v), items on the Old Testament and ancient history (fols 123r–126v), and notes about the Archbishops of York and the domestic affairs of Jervaulx Abbey (fols 208r–219v).

³ For example, the section updating his chronicle on fol. 189r. See Harriss and Harriss, 'John Benet's chronicle', p. 157: 'The underlining of passages in the book and the marking of annals in the chronicle were both done in red in Benet's hand after the book had been assembled. Passages of an analogous character which have not been rubricated are all of a date subsequent to 1468.'

⁴ The *Mirabilia Angliae* on fol. 34r–v is dated 1459, and on fol. 75v there is a signature alongside the date 1461.

Benet's own hand, and was part of the manuscript when it was foliated and had its contents listed in the late 15th century.[1]

The *J.B. Treatise* is a rather curious item in this book, being unlike anything else in it. One must assume that Benet copied the treatise, either because it interested him, or because he felt that its information was useful; perhaps he felt that it would be advantageous to him, as a country vicar, to have a greater command of the language of both the hunt and the high table. The text itself was probably copied from a single source (now lost), since it is written continuously without the interposition of extraneous items, as happens in Eg and Pp. In places, it shows similarities with Adv, though the connection goes no further than that. Of greater significance are T's correspondences with *HSG* and W, since it shares with them a version of the Soiling terms found nowhere else. In terms of its overall contents, T contains the same four elements as W, and four of the five elements found in *HSG* – albeit in a different order, and not always with the same level of agreement as pertains to the Soiling terms. As I have already argued in relation to *HSG*, this set of four elements probably constituted a distinctive, short rendition of the *J.B. Treatise* focusing solely on hunting, as the heading *De venatoribus in Anglicis* in T affirms.

T contains an outstanding example of this little version of the treatise, and it is with regret that I have decided not to include an annotated transcript of the entire text in the present study. The task would, however, have been supererogatory given that T's Collective nouns, Resting terms and Carving terms are all included in the full collations of Appendices I–III. I have, however, provided a separate transcription of T's Soiling terms, collated with *HSG* and W in Part IVg.

15. W – New Haven, Yale University, Beinecke Rare Book and Manuscript Library, Beinecke MS 163 ('Wagstaff Miscellany'): 14th to mid-15th century, parchment, 193 leaves, *c.* 290 × 200 mm.[2] There is a compact version of the *J.B. Treatise* on fols 185r–186r:

---

[1] The undated 15th-century contents list, which is not in Benet's hand, appears on fols 191r–192v.

[2] W is described in detail by Barbara A. Shailor, *Catalogue of Medieval and Renaissance Manuscripts in the Beinecke Rare Book and Manuscript Library, Yale University*, 3 vols (Binghamton, NY, 1984–1992), I, 216–23. The entire manuscript can be viewed online in the Digital Collections of the Beinecke Library website, under the title 'Wagstaff miscellany': <http://beinecke.library.yale.edu>.

i. Collective nouns (132 phrases)
ii. Carving terms
iii. Resting terms
iv. Soiling terms[3]

W is a composite manuscript of two discrete parts. The first (fols 1–186) is a miscellaneous collection of diverse material from the mid-15th century; the second (fols 187–193) consists mainly of a list of emperors, kings and archbishops in a hand of the 14th century. In the discussion that follows, only the first part of the manuscript will be referred to.

W contains a diverse range of texts in English and Latin, including three works concerning parliament,[4] a Latin version of the story-cycle *The Seven Sages of Rome*, medical, veterinary and cooking recipes,[5] instructions on how to improve wine,[6] a treatise on astronomy, two major spiritual works, hymns, a smattering of verses, and manuals of instruction on hawking, hunting and the care of horses. As Barbara Shailor observes:

> The contents of the volume are fascinating: it has everything a fifteenth-century member of the English gentry might want or need to know of a scientific, legal or medical nature, with much more inserted wherever space would permit.[7]

The appearance of the manuscript is very varied. Decoration is sporadic and often workmanlike, with touches of red ink at the ends of sentences, headings underlined in red or blue, and two- or three-line coloured lombard initials, some ornamented with red or blue flourishes, a few of which are much more professionally executed than others.

---

[3] Shailor associates the first three J.B. elements with the contents of a 1561 edition of *StA* (presumably William Copland's: *STC* 3312.5), and therefore mistakenly sets them apart from the Soiling terms: *Catalogue*, p. 221, nos 34, 35.

[4] Discussed in some detail by Margaret Laing, 'John Whittokesmede as parliamentarian and horse owner in Yale University Library Beinecke MS 163', *SELIM: Journal of the Spanish Society for Mediaeval Language and Literature*, 17 (2010), 7–78 (pp. 13–22).

[5] The cooking recipes have been examined by Constance B. Hieatt, 'Recipes from Beinecke MS 163', *Yale University Library Gazette*, 61 (1986), 15–21, and published by her in *An Ordinance of Pottage: An Edition of the Fifteenth Century Culinary Recipes in Yale University's MS Beinecke 163* (London, 1988).

[6] Published by Mary-Jo Arn, 'The emendation of wine: wine recipes from Beinecke MS 163', *Yale University Library Gazette*, 64 (1990), 109–23.

[7] Barbara A. Shailor, 'A Cataloguer's view', in *The Whole Book: Cultural Perspectives on the Medieval Miscellany*, ed. Stephen G. Nichols and Siegfried Wenzel (Ann Arbor, 1996), pp. 153–67 (p. 164).

It is now generally accepted that W was probably compiled and owned by its principal scribe, who wrote his name in red as 'Whittokesmede' in three places.[1] This is thought to be John Whittokesmede III (*c.* 1405–1482/3),[2] a prominent gentleman-landowner in Wiltshire, who was also a lawyer and an active member of parliament, which could account for the presence of the three works on parliamentary matters.[3] Other hands are interspersed with that of Whittokesmede, indicating that he used one or more professional scriveners to add material, and sometimes to complete an item that he had begun.[4] Several other hands, probably of a later date, are responsible for adding yet more material in blank spaces. According to Margaret Laing and the online eLALME,[5] a total of twelve hands can be distinguished in the manuscript, some of them contributing only an item or two.[6]

As a whole, W is noteworthy for containing a high proportion of practical manuals, such as the treatise *Medicines for Horses* (fols 50r–55v),[7] which commences with a two-line red lombard initial, and has its headings underlined in red. Even more interesting for our purposes is the presence of two important sporting texts, both of which have been afforded coloured decorations by a professional rubricator. The first of these is a verse treatise on hawking, which has come to be known as *The Percy Poem on Falconry* (*PPF*) (fols 125r–134r), and of which this is the only known copy.[8] The

---

[1] Thus on fol. 59r. The form 'Whittokysmede' appears on fol. 14v, where it has been partially effaced, and on fol. 101v. Margaret Laing argues that there is only one principal scribe, not two as claimed by Shailor. She describes his hand and lists the sections that can be attributed to him: Laing, 'John Whittokesmede', pp. 9–10.

[2] The name is often modernised as 'Whittocksmead', but I have followed Margaret Laing and others in using one of the forms found in W.

[3] Whittokesmede's energetic career is described in detail by J.T. Driver, 'The Career of John Whittokesmede, a Fifteenth-Century Wiltshire Lawyer and Parliamentary "Carpet-Bagger"', *The Wiltshire Archaeological and Natural History Magazine*, 92 (1999), 92–99. See also the timeline provided by Laing, 'John Whittokesmede', pp. 74–78.

[4] For example, Whittokesmede begins the verse treatise on hawking on fols 125r–126v, but it is completed (fols 126v–134r) by another scribe.

[5] 'An Electronic Version of *A Linguistic Atlas of Late Mediæval English*': <www.lel.ed.ac.uk/ihd/elalme/elalme.html>; see LP (Linguistic Profile) 5291.

[6] Laing, 'John Whittokesmede', pp. 9–10.

[7] Not identified by Shailor as such: *Catalogue*, p. 218, no. 14. For a description of this treatise, see Keiser, *Manual X*, 3692 [441]; Laing, 'John Whittokesmede', pp. 22–5. Another recension of this text occurs in MS G (q.v.), and a fragmentary copy in MS C.

[8] The poem begins with the line, 'Thu that art a gentilman' (*NIMEV* 3693). See Bror Danielsson, 'The Percy Poem on Falconry', *Studier i Modern Språkvetenskap*, NS 3

start of the poem is marked with a three-line blue lombard initial with red pen flourishing, and has two more such initials marking important divisions in the text (fols 131v, 133v). Immediately following is a copy of the prose hunting treatise *The Master of Game* by Edward, Second Duke of York (fols 134v–178v),[1] a work that is also decorated with two- and three-line red-flourished blue initials, and that terminates towards the end of the manuscript's penultimate quire (no. XXVII in Shailor's catalogue).

A number of items, all far more informally executed, follow *The Master of Game*, the longest of these being a *Confessio* of the Seven Deadly Sins (fols 179r–183v), which required the addition of another quire (XXVIII^6: fols 181–86). Then, very close to the end of that final quire, we find the *J.B. Treatise* (fols 185r–186r) in Whittokesmede's own hand (Hand A in the eLALME analysis), written in light-brown ink and without decoration of any kind.[2] It may be considered no more than wishful thinking to suppose that the *J.B. Treatise* was added to the manuscript owing to a perceived correspondence with the major sporting texts that precede it, were it not associated with hunting and hawking in several other sources as well.

The J.B. items are written without interruption in two columns, starting at the top of fol. 185r and ending about a quarter of the way down the second column on fol. 186r, with gaps of varying widths separating the different elements. The remaining space on fol. 186r is taken up by two unrelated items, each in a different hand: *A meddyson for þe stoune y-prouyd* and some Latin verses on the judgement of Paris.

I have categorised W as containing a version of the *J.B. Treatise* because of its many similarities with *HSG* and T. The Carving terms, in particular, are closely related to those in *HSG*, and W's version of the Soiling terms is matched only by *HSG* and T. As a group, *HSG*, T and W bear witness to the existence of a popular, compact formulation of the *J.B. Treatise*, albeit one that lacks any hawking elements. (See further my discussion of this point in relation to *HSG* and T above.)

No part of W is independently represented in this edition; however, its Soiling terms are collated with those of *HSG* and T in Part IVg; and its Collective nouns, Carving terms and Resting terms are collated with all other versions in Appendices I–III.

(1970), 5–60; Keiser, *Manual X*, 3697 [451].

[1] Keiser, *Manual X*, 3700 [462].

[2] See eLALME, LP 5291, for a summary of Hand A's copying stints.

Minor witnesses, containing one or two elements of J.B. material

16. Addl – London, British Library, Additional MS 33994 ('Ware MS'): 15th–17th centuries, paper, 26 leaves, *c.* 175 × 130 mm.[1] There is only one, short element of J.B. material, with its own heading, on fol. 26v:

Distretacio rerum[2]

i. Collective nouns (10 phrases)

Addl is a miscellaneous collection that was originally bound up with three other manuscripts, now separated from it and classified as Additional MSS 33991, 33992 and 33993. It contains four main items from widely different periods: a Latin treatise on the history of the Irish language in a 17th-century hand, together with notes in Spanish on the early history of the church in Ireland; a printed treatise, *De officio admirallitatis Anglie*; and a fragmentary copy of *The Parlement of the Thre Ages* (fols 19r–26v) in a hand of the late 15th century. *The Parlement of the Thre Ages* concludes three-quarters of the way down fol. 26v and is immediately followed by a short list of collective nouns, written in two columns and in the same hand. The two words of the heading – *Distretacio rerum* – are positioned so that each is above a column of collectives.

The leaves of this manuscript survive as singletons pasted onto stubs in a modern binding, so it is impossible to estimate the original quiring and so to judge whether the collectives might have continued on another leaf. It is very possible that they did, since the few terms that survive on fol. 26v belong with the long versions of these lists (as in T) rather than the short ones (as in Ha). Perhaps these terms were appended to *The Parlement of the Thre Ages* because of their perceived association with hunting, the scribe having been inspired by the long hunting episode in that poem. But they may, equally, be no more than serendipitous filler material.

17. Am – Oxford, Bodleian Library, MS Ashmole 189 (SC 6777): late 15th century, paper, 219 folios, *c.* 215 × 145 mm. Am contains three J.B. elements on fol. 211r:

---

[1] The manuscript and its contents are described by M.Y. Offord in her edition of *The Parlement of the Thre Ages*, EETS os 246 (London, 1959), pp. xiv–xv. Offord refers to Addl as the 'Ware MS', after Sir James Ware (*ob.* 1666), the Irish antiquary in whose collection it once belonged.

[2] Read *Distractio rerum*, 'the division of things'.

i. Resting terms
ii. 'If a hart stands'
iii. Carving terms

This quarto volume is a composite assemblage of four disparate parts that are completely unrelated, except for their preponderant interest in astrology, astronomy, calendars and related topics.[1] The first three parts (fols 1–200) have no bearing on this study, and will therefore be discussed no further. The fourth part, consisting of fols 201–19, is a collectanea of manuscript fragments on astrology and the astrolabe, as well as sundry prognostications, one of them a fragment of verse prophecies for the coming year depending on the day of the week on which Christmas falls (*NIMEV* 1995/8–10: fol. 210r–v).

This is immediately followed by the J.B. material – written in the same hand as the verse prophecies – on fol. 211r, a leaf that has been neatly ruled by drypoint into two columns. The text breaks off prematurely, however, at the bottom of the first column, leaving the second column empty; the verso of the leaf is blank.[2]

By any measure, the J.B. material is strikingly out of place in Am. It was probably included because it was written on one leaf of a bifolium, whose conjugate (fol. 210) contains the prognostications that were the real interest of the person who assembled this little collection of manuscript leaves.[3] The J.B. items are noteworthy for being essentially identical with their congeners in *HSG* (all of which occur on fol. 18r of that incunable), though Am breaks off after only thirteen carving terms – of the nineteen in *HSG* – and omits entirely the Soiling terms that come after the Carving terms in the printed work. Also lacking in Am are *HSG*'s Collective nouns, although these may have existed on another bifolium that is now lost.

In contrast with what it lacks, Am is the only J.B. witness other than *HSG* to preserve the curious little element 'If a hart stands', although the version in Am shows signs of scribal confusion. Am's version of this element is collated with the better text of *HSG* in Part IVb below.

---

[1] For full descriptions of Am, see William Henry Black, *A Descriptive, Analytical and Critical Catalogue of the Manuscripts Bequeathed unto the University of Oxford by Elias Ashmole* (Oxford, 1845), cols 150–3; L.M. Eldredge, *The Index of Middle English Prose: Handlist IX* (Cambridge, 1992), pp. 4–6 (with the manuscript erroneously cited as SC 6666).

[2] The three J.B. items are transcribed in full by Eldredge, *Handlist IX*, p. 6.

[3] Fols 210 and 211 are now physically disjoined, but show all the relevant signs of belonging together.

Given the broadly similar dates of Am and *HSG*, and the intriguing duplication of contents on both manuscript leaf and printed page, it is conceivable that the J.B. material in Am derives from *HSG*, though descent from a common original is also possible. Whatever its exact lineage, Am is undoubtedly cognate with *HSG* and is treated accordingly in the remainder of this study.

18. *BK* – Wynkyn de Worde, *The Boke of Keruynge*, 1508, 1513: *STC* 3289, 3290.[1] Although this printed book dates from the (early) 16th century, I have included it because it opens (sig. A1v) with an unusually worded item of J.B. material that probably derives from a lost manuscript:

Termes of a Keruer
i. Carving terms

The feature that makes *BK*'s Carving terms distinctive (though not unique) is that they employ an imperative construction that occurs elsewhere only in Adv and BS; for example, *Alaye that fesande (BK)*. (As can be seen in Appendix II, formulations that use past participles – such as *A fesawnte alet (StA)*, *A fesaunt y-aled* (T) – are far more common.) Since neither Adv nor BS could have been the source of the *BK* list, some other copy-text, now lost, must have been used.

The main work in Wynkyn's book is an adaptation of the *Boke of Nurture* by John Russell, usher and marshal to Humphrey, Duke of Gloucester (*ob.* 1447), and has nothing to do with the *J.B. Treatise*.[2] It would seem, however, that whoever compiled *BK* (Wynkyn himself, perhaps) saw a connection between the J.B. Carving terms and the sections of the *Boke of Nurture* relating to 'þe connynge of kervynge' of fish and flesh,[3] and accordingly appended a list of the J.B. terms as a sort of preface or phraseological primer.

---

[1] Except where otherwise indicated, all references are to the second edition of 1513, as printed in *The Babees Book*, ed. Frederick J. Furnivall, EETS os 32 (London, 1868, repr. 1997), pp. 261–86.

[2] Russell's *Boke of Nurture* is printed in *The Babees Book*, pp. 115–99. Neither the J.B. Carving terms nor Wynkyn's main text bear any relation to BL MS Additional 37969, fols 2–8, contrary to the impression given by Laurel Braswell in her survey of 'Utilitarian and scientific prose', in *Middle English Prose: A Critical Guide to Major Authors and Genres*, ed. A.S.G. Edwards (New Brunswick, NJ, 1984), 337–87 (p. 365). The Additional MS text that Braswell alludes to is a courtesy book, printed by R.W. Chambers (ed.), *A Fifteenth-Century Courtesy Book*, EETS os 148 (London, 1914).

[3] *Babees Book*, pp. 137–46.

The *BK* compiler also drew on the J.B. phrases to construct sixteen headings for instructions on the preparation of different types of birds, as in the following: 'Alaye that fesande. Take a fesande, and reyse his legges & his wynges as it were an henne, & no sauce but onely salte.'[1] These headings do not belong to Russell's original *Boke of Nurture*, although it should be noted that a number of J.B. carving verbs are to be found in instructions in Russell's work – which suggests that they were in general use, and not simply imaginative inventions of the compilers of the J.B. lists, as they are sometimes suspected of being. I discuss such issues further below, in the Explanatory Notes to Appendix II.

BK's Carving terms are not set out separately in this edition, but are included in the full catalogue of Carving terms in Appendix II.

19. BS – Helmingham Hall, 'Tollemache *Book of Secrets*': late 15th or early 16th century, paper, 65 leaves (foliated 1–64, with fol. 41 included twice), *c.* 155 × 115 mm.[2]

BS contains one item of J.B. material on fols 42r–43r and 44r, with a blank leaf (fol. 43v) inexplicably interrupting its unity:

    i. Carving terms

BS is a type of commonplace book with a diverse range of contents, most of which are of a conspicuously practical nature. They include, among other things, instructions on gluing pages that are torn, a recipe for book glue, a treatise on lace-making, planting-patterns for herbs, a list of medicines, instructions on how to restore a dovecote, and the dimensions of a man's shirt.[3] There is also a smattering of texts on sporting subjects, including a few sentences from the hawking treatise *PEB* (fol. 14v), a treatise on fishing with an angle (fols 20r–25r), four remedies for the ailments of hawks (fol. 41*r),[4] and the list of J.B. Carving terms.

The main texts appear to be the work of a single scribe (or perhaps two scribes at most) writing a very varied Anglicana hand. The book's

---

[1] *Babees Book*, p. 275 (see pp. 275–7). These headings occur on sigs B1r–B2r of Wynkyn's book.

[2] The manuscript is described and reproduced in facsimile in *The Tollemache 'Book of Secrets': A Descriptive Index and Complete Facsimile*, ed. Jeremy Griffiths, completed by A.S.G. Edwards (London, 2001). See especially pp. 1–7, 281–3. I am very grateful to Prof. A.S.G. Edwards for alerting me to this manuscript as Griffiths' edition was going to press.

[3] For a full list of contents, see *Tollemache 'Book of Secrets'*, pp. 9–11.

[4] I follow Griffiths in referring to the second fol. 41 as fol. 41*.

earliest known owner was Catherine Tollemache (*ob.* 1620), who notes her ownership on the inside of its front wrapper.[1] This manuscript is notable for containing no purely literary texts, leading Jeremy Griffiths to categorise it as 'an ancestor of the type of exclusively practical household book or manual that culminates in Mrs Beeton's *Book of Household Management*'.[2]

The remedies for hawks on fol. 41*r are unrelated to any comparable remedies found in the J.B. group of texts, *PEB* or *StA*.[3] At the time of writing, I have been unable to identify the tradition to which they belong, but am confident that they are unconnected with the J.B. Carving terms that they precede. One reason for this conclusion is that the leaf bearing the hawking remedies is a singleton among seven stubs (four before and three after), and its verso is blank.[4] There is therefore no continuity between the hawking remedies and the carving terms in the manuscript; and, since these items are found nowhere else together, it is plausible to deduce that they probably derived from different sources. I have accordingly decided to regard the close proximity of these two items as entirely coincidental and have therefore omitted the BS hawking remedies from my catalogue of the manuscript's J.B. contents, and shall refer to them no further.

The carving terms themselves are strangely disposed, with a blank leaf (fol. 43v) separating the terms for animals and birds from those for fish. In spite of this hiatus, the carving terms belong together and appear to have come from a single source, for they all maintain a distinctive imperative construction, which occurs elsewhere only in Adv and *BK*. The similarity with *BK* is particularly strong, but BS differs in one vital respect: it contains the names of nineteen sauces interspersed among the carving terms. These names of sauces occur nowhere else in the J.B. set, and may represent a personal contribution by the BS scribe.

---

[1] She has been identified with the Catherine who married Lionel Tollemache, 1st Baronet, in 1581: Tollemache '*Book of Secrets*', pp. 2–3.

[2] Tollemache '*Book of Secrets*', pp. 4–5. See also the comments of Julia Boffey on this manuscript and the concept of the 'household book' generally: 'Bodleian Library MS Arch. Selden. B.24 and definitions of the "household book" ', in *The English Medieval Book*, ed. A.S.G. Edwards, Vincent Gillespie and Ralph Hanna (London, 2000), pp. 125–34.

[3] Griffiths remarks that there are 'generally similar' remedies in *PEB* with 'further general parallels' in *StA*, and goes on to list several J.B. texts containing accounts of hawks' diseases and remedies (*Tollemache 'Book of Secrets'*, pp. 27–28). This is potentially misleading, since the BS and J.B. remedies are not congeners and have nothing in common beyond their shared subject-matter.

[4] For a collation of the manuscript, see *Tollemache 'Book of Secrets'*, pp. 281–82.

The BS Carving terms are included in Appendix II, with the names of sauces noted in the textual apparatus.

20. C – Cambridge, Cambridge University Library, MS Ll.1.18: second half (perhaps third quarter) of the 15th century, paper, 129 leaves (some very fragmentary), *c.* 225 × 145 mm.[1] C contains only one element of J.B. material on fols 44v–45r:

i. Collective nouns (73 phrases)[2]

C is a type of household miscellany with a diverse range of contents, including a legal formulary, medical recipes, an assortment of moral and religious sentences, and texts on heraldry, history, geography and household management. It consists of sixteen quires disposed among five separate booklets, which appear to have been compiled by one principal scribe over a period of many years, with two other hands contributing a few major items. George Keiser speculates that the codex may have been 'compiled under the direction of a household officer, probably with clerical training, who had responsibility for producing such documents for an ecclesiastical or lay lord', and suggests a provenance of Southwell (Notts.), with a possible association with the influential Lancashire families of Booth and Worsley.[3] Another, very similar suggestion is that the principal scribe 'was a member or servant of the religious community at the collegiate church of Southwell, near Newark in Nottinghamshire.'[4]

The second booklet, consisting of fols 19–73, contains a number of works of a strongly practical nature, among them *The Ordinance of Pottage* and

---

[1] C is described in detail in the online resource 'Scriptorium: Medieval and Early Modern Manuscripts Online' <scriptorium.english.cam.ac.uk>, and in the earlier *A Catalogue of the Manuscripts Preserved in the Library of the University of Cambridge*, 6 vols (Cambridge, 1856–1867), IV, 17–19. The most recent modern pencil foliation takes account of numerous missing leaves, and so runs from fol. 3 to fol.150, even though only 129 leaves (some severely mutilated) remain extant.

[2] Rachel Hands includes a further element, 'The shappe of a greyhounde', which occurs on fol. 55r: see *EHH*, p. xlix. However, this bears little relation to J.B. accounts of the Properties of a greyhound. Moreover, it is clearly part of the *Tretyse off Hunting* (fols 48r–55v), since it is positioned before the closing colophon of that work. See *The Tretyse off Huntyng*, ed. Anne Rooney, Scripta 19 (Brussels, 1987), p. 56. C's list of collectives has been published by Corner, 'More terms', pp. 231–2.

[3] Keiser, 'Practical books for the gentleman', pp. 478–80.

[4] Scriptorium, <scriptorium.english.cam.ac.uk>, 'Manuscript Full Description'.

other recipes (fols 19r–42r, 42v–44v),[1] the only known copy of *The Tretyse off Huntyng* (*TH*: fols 48r–55r), *The Tretyse off Hawkyng* (fols 55v–58v),[2] a fragmentary collection of hawking remedies of unknown provenance (fols 59r–61v),[3] and a fragment of *Medicines for Horses* (fols 63r–72v, of which fols 63–65 are so badly damaged that little can be gleaned from them). This booklet originally consisted of three quires (3^{16}, 4^{16} and 7^{12}) but at an early stage quire 4^{16} was augmented by the insertion of the hunting and hawking treatises – each occupying its own quire (5^6 and 6^{4+1}) – after fol. 47 (originally 4_{13}), producing a composite gathering of 27 leaves.[4] It is in this fourth quire that the J.B. collectives are to be found, written in three narrow columns between a set of cooking recipes (fol. 44v) and a list of wines (fol. 45r). Like much else in the manuscript, the collectives are executed in a very informal style, though the hand is undoubtedly that of a practised scrivener.

C's list of Collective nouns is something of an anomaly in that it bears a general resemblance to several versions in the J.B. group (specifically, the short lists of collectives), but also contains many phrases that do not belong within the wider J.B. tradition. Some of these phrases occur also in Dg* (the short supplementary list found in Dg) and in a group of three Anglo-Norman texts, whose roots are in an older, entirely separate tradition: *Nominale sive verbale* (CUL MS Ee.4.20), *Femina* (TCC MS B.14.40), and the *Tretiz* of Walter de Bibbesworth (BL MS Arundel 220 and CUL MS

---

[1] C's text of *The Ordinance of Pottage* differs markedly from that in MS W, as is noted by Hieatt (ed.), *Pottage*, p. 13.

[2] The title appears on fol. 55v, while a colophon on fol. 58v reads *Explicit tractatus de hawkyng*. This treatise – hereafter *THawk 3* – is derived partly from *PEB*. Analogous texts occur also on a fragment of parchment roll preserved in the Durham County Record Office (*THawk 1*), and in BL, MS Sloane 3488, fols 2v–3r (*THawk 2*). The Cambridge text remains unpublished, but the Durham and Sloane texts have been published, respectively, by Bror Danielsson, 'The Durham treatise of falconry', *Studier i Modern Språkvetenskap*, 4 (1972), 21–37, and N.J. Shirley Legatt, 'The Book of St. Albans and the origins of its treatise on hawking', *SN*, 22 (1950), 135–45. See also Hands, *EHH*, pp. xxv–xxviii. The treatment of *PEB* and its derivatives and analogues by Keiser in *Manual X* needs to be thoroughly updated; see 3697 [450] ('The Durham Treatise of Falconry'); 3697–8 [452] ('Prince Edward's Book of Hawking').

[3] Transcribed by Braekman (ed.), *Of Hawks and Horses*, pp. 39–48, and discussed by Hands, *EHH*, p. xxv. These remedies bear the heading *Here begynneth the tretyse off the sekenes off haukes & off þe salues & remedyes for þe sayd sekenessez*, and end imperfectly on fol. 61v. They probably continued on to fol. 62, which is missing.

[4] For a schematic representation, see Rooney, *The Tretyse off Huntyng*, p. 12; also Scriptorium, <scriptorium.english.cam.ac.uk>, 'Collation Diagram'.

Gg.1.1).[1] In its entirety, however, the list in C has no known analogue, and it could arguably be considered too divergent to merit being included in the J.B. group. I have, nevertheless, decided to incorporate it because, whatever other influences it shows, C's list of collectives is plainly dominated by the J.B. tradition.

Conversely, I have excluded the list of wines that follows immediately after the collectives on fol. 45r since it is unrelated to the J.B. 'Names of wines' found in the cognate pair Dg–Rg, and is in any case alien to the *J.B. Treatise* proper. Nevertheless, the presence of this list in C is interesting, for a similar contiguity of material in a hypothetical precursor of Dg–Rg could account for way that the Names of wines became attached to the J.B. material in those manuscripts. I refer to C's list of wines frequently in the explanatory notes on the Names of wines in Part IV.i, using the siglum C*.

21. G – [Location unknown: private collection.] Formerly in the possession of Prince Richard, Duke of Gloucester, hence 'Duke of Gloucester MS' (*olim* York House MS 45): late 15th century, parchment, 142 leaves (i+142+i), *c.* 240 × 175 mm. The entire codex, including two endleaves, has been paginated in pencil to p. 288; the manuscript itself, excluding endleaves, therefore consists of pp. 3–286. It contains two items of J.B. material on pp. 158–161:

　　i. Hierarchy of hawks
　　ii. Hawks' diseases and remedies

Until 2006, this manuscript was located in the library of the Duke of Gloucester at Kensington Palace, London. It was sold by Christie's of London on 26 January 2006, and is now in an anonymous private collection.[2] Previously, it was in the collection of Richard Schwerdt, whose catalogue describes it in some detail.[3]

---

[1] Modern editions are cited in the Explanatory Notes for Appendix I. The *Nominale* is a glossary in Anglo-Norman and English; *Femina* is a general Anglo-Norman primer for English children; and Bibbesworth's *Tretiz* is an Anglo-Norman primer concentrating on terminology appropriate to husbandry and manorial record-keeping. See Corner, 'More terms', pp. 16–17, for further comments on the similarities that C and Dg* show with the Anglo-Norman texts.

[2] Christie's Sale 7300, lot 501.

[3] Schwerdt, *Hunting, Hawking*, II, 357–59. See also the *Sotheby Sale Catalogue*, 11–12 March 1946, lot 2254. It was at this auction that the former Duke of Gloucester (Prince Henry) acquired the manuscript. For a more thorough, modern description, see

G is of considerable interest to this study because it is an anthology of texts pertaining to what might be termed 'country matters'. Its contents include manuals on forest laws in Latin and English (pp. 165–81), a long list of names that might be given to hunting hounds (pp. 185–96),[1] three separate texts on on horses, including *Medicines for Horses* (pp. 197–221),[2] a treatise on agriculture (*Godfridus super palladium*: pp. 225–250), Þe *Tretice of Nicholas Bollard* on grafting and planting trees (pp. 250–258),[3] and a copy of the *PEB* hawking treatise (pp. 259–286).[4] The first eight gatherings of the codex also contain a copy of Edward of York's hunting treatise *The Master of Game* (hereafter *MG*, pp. 1–157). This ends on the recto of a leaf (p. 157) with an account of a boar's tusks, and how they might be interpreted as *a tokyn of a grete boore*.[5] The J.B. material begins – in a different, smaller hand – on the verso of the same leaf (p. 158), and was plainly used to fill up some of the empty pages of the last gathering of *MG* (8^{10} of the codex). The last J.B. remedy for hawks ends near the top of p. 161, and is followed by several additional remedies in another, much less formal hand (perhaps of the early 16th century), which fill the page. Pages 162–3 are blank, as is the last page of the gathering (p. 164), except for the inscription 'This book has been long in the possession of the Dansey Family of Brinsop Court, Herefordshire, April 15th 1770'.

The J.B. items in G are virtually identical to their congeners in Ry. Both manuscripts contain the same two elements, and even the same versions of them; they alternate between masculine and feminine pronouns in the same places, and even share a few unusual terms – for example, *hew(e)* instead

---

my article, '*The Names of all Manner of Hounds*: A Unique Inventory in a Fifteenth-Century Manuscript', *Viator*, 44 (2013), 339–68 (pp. 347–51).

[1] Scott-Macnab, '*The Names of all Manner of Hounds*', 357–68.

[2] See Kelly-Anne Gilbertson, *An Edition of the Fifteenth-Century Treatise 'Medicines for Horses'* (unpubl. PhD Diss., University of Bristol, 2017). This treatise occurs also in MS W (q.v. above), and as a fragment in MS C.

[3] *Geoffrey of Franconia's Book of Trees and Wines*, ed. W.L. Braekman, Scripta 24 (Brussels, 1989); W.L. Braekman, 'Bollard's Middle English book of planting and grafting and its background', *SN*, 57 (1985), 19–39.

[4] *PEB* occupies the manuscript's final two gatherings, which show many signs of having been produced separately from the rest of the codex; the text is discussed briefly by Hands, *EHH*, pp. xxiv–xxv.

[5] Chapter 35 in the manuscript; see *The Master of Game by Edward, Second Duke of York: The Oldest English Book on Hunting*, ed. Wm. A. and F. Baillie-Grohman, (London, 1904), pp. 80–82.

of the more common *view*.¹ What is more, both manuscripts employ the J.B. material as filler at the end of *MG* – which ends at precisely the same point in both. Internal evidence suggests strongly that the J.B. material in Ry was copied from G,² which makes it very possible that Ry's text of *MG* also derives from G, though this cannot be verified without a thorough comparison of the two *MG* texts – a task beyond the scope of the present enquiry.³

A further notable feature of both G and Ry is that their shared version of the Hawks' diseases and remedies is found nowhere else among the J.B. texts and could therefore, arguably, be rejected as alien to the 'true' J.B. tradition. On the other hand, the prefatory account of a hawk's diseases matches the version that appears in Ha, where it breaks off without progressing to the remedies themselves. Since the descriptions of diseases and remedies normally go together, it seems likely that the text in Ha is truncated, and that the missing remedies could have been the same as those in G–Ry. It therefore makes sense for these remedies to be admitted as yet another variant in the whole range of J.B. materials.

Turning to the Hierarchy of hawks (element i), this is broadly related to the version that appears in Ha, but not sufficiently so to establish a firm connection between the two manuscripts. Instead, G's Hierarchy of hawks shows strong correspondences with Rc, where it is inexplicably combined with the Breeds of dogs. It seems likely that G and Rc derive this element from a common original, the hypothetical MS μ in my discussion of 'Textual Relationships', Group 5, below.

Owing to the novelty of the J.B. contents of the cognate pair G–Ry, I have included an annotated transcription in Part IVh below, with G as the base manuscript.

---

¹ Part IVh, line 24, below.

² Ry omits some significant words and short passages found in G (e.g. part of the list of animals hunted by an emperor's 'hawks': IVh, lines 1–4). Where Ry has words and phrases that are lacking in G, these can all be explained as minor scribal interpolations.

³ I am grateful to Dr James McNellis of Wilmington College, Ohio, for many helpful comments on this topic. In his view, G and Ry contain sibling versions of *MG*, perhaps descended (or copied) from Huntingdon Library MS EL65 B63 (*olim* EL 1123): James I. McNellis III, *The Uncollated Manuscripts of 'The Master of Game': Towards a New Edition* (unpubl. PhD Diss., University of Washington, 1996), pp. 107–9. See my further comments in relation to Ry (no. 25) below.

22. Harl – London, British Library, MS Harley 541: 15th–17th centuries, paper, 232 leaves (foliated to 229), *c.* 215 × 150 mm. The manuscript contains one item of J.B. material on fol. 225r:

i. Collective nouns (48 phrases)[1]

Harl is a composite codex containing an immensely varied collection of material from the 15th to the 17th centuries.[2] I shall not here attempt to describe the entire volume, but shall concentrate on a section at the rear consisting of 23 leaves from the 15th century. These leaves fall into two distinct groups: fols 207–214, which contain verses; and fols 215–229, which are dominated by lists, including the names of mayors and sheriffs of London (fols 215r–219v), parish churches of London (fols 220v–224v), *gates of þe cytee of London* (fol. 224v), the J.B. Collective nouns (fol. 225r), and *þe hallis þat longe to þe cytee of London* (fols 225v–226v), among other items. Although it seems likely that all 23 leaves belong together as a set, they cannot now be examined for quiring as each leaf has been separated from its conjugate and glued to a stub sewn into the modern binding.

The group of leaves containing lists (fols 215–229) was compiled by two principal scribes, with the J.B. collectives contributed by the more prolific of the two.[3] The J.B. list bears a general resemblance to other short lists of collectives (as, for example, in Ha), but derives from none of them, making it impossible to speculate whether the scribe might have had a fuller exemplar of the *J.B. Treatise* to hand. What seems most likely is that he was not interested in these terms for their bearing on fieldsports, but for their capacity to contribute an additional list to the anthology that he was assembling. Curiously, his collaborator then thought it relevant to append, below the collectives, a list of five names for hawks, which is found nowhere else among the J.B. group: these names are set out for the sake of completeness in Part IVc below. Finally, yet another contemporary scribe added two extra phrases to the initial list of forty-six Collective nouns.[4]

---

[1] For reasons that I have already adduced, I dismiss the list of English bishoprics on fol. 227v as extraneous to the *J.B. Treatise* proper.

[2] A full description is provided by the *Catalogue of the Harleian Manuscripts in the British Museum*, I, 346.

[3] This scribe wrote out most of the longer items, including 'the mayors and sheriffs of London' and 'the parish churches of London'. The second scribe contributed 'the halls of London', but usually filled up blank spaces left by the first scribe. A third scribe added an *ABC* on fol. 228r, but nothing else.

[4] These two phrases are squeezed into tight spaces, making the hand difficult to identify, but its majuscule *A* is distinct from that of both other scribes.

23. *LJ* – Caxton's *Book of Courtesy* (also called *Little John*), 2nd edn, printed by Wynkyn de Worde in *c*. 1491–93: *STC* 3304. Oxford, Bodleian Library, Douce Fragments e.4.

All that remains of this incunable is a set of two quarto leaves printed on one side only, and therefore in all probability representing the half-sheet of a printer's proof. Although now separated, the two leaves can be presumed to have been joined, and to have been intended to be folded into a bifolium. One leaf bears the signature bb (representing b1r), together with some text of the *Book of Courtesy*, while the other leaf (presumably b6v of a six-leaf gathering)[1] has one item of J.B. material:

i. Collective nouns (15 phrases)

The list of collectives is immediately followed by the words, *Here endeth a lytyll treatyse called the booke of curtesye or lytyll John. Enprynted atte westmoster*. Below is a small version of Caxton's device, but printed upside-down, presumably the reason for the printer's rejection of this sheet. This metal-cut device, which shows Caxton's cypher surrounded by a border of flowers, was never used by Caxton, but is known to have been used by Wynkyn for several early works. The typeface is Caxton's no. 6, which was also used by Wynkyn until 1493.[2]

LJ's fifteen J.B. Collective nouns match the final fifteen collectives in Caxton's *HSG* (no. 6 above). It seems very likely that Wynkyn copied these phrases from the earlier Caxton volume, for they are laid out exactly as in *HSG*. Although it is impossible to tell how many more of the collectives might have been included in the complete *LJ*, we may reasonably presume that Wynkyn used all the preceding phrases, which take up a complete opening in *HSG* (fols 16v–17r). In short, *LJ* may be regarded as a fragmentary derivative of *HSG*; it is also another example of how the J.B. collectives were used as filler when the main text itself failed to take up all the available space in a final gathering.

---

[1] Blades, *Life and Typography of Caxton*, II, 235–6, concludes that the completed book 'probably consisted, like Caxton's early editions, of a 4^n and a 3^n, making 14 leaves'. See also Duff, *Fifteenth Century Books*, no. 54.

[2] See E. Gordon Duff, *Early English Printing: A Series of Facsimiles of all the Types used in England during the XVth Century, with Some of those used in the Printing of English Books Abroad* (London, 1896; repr. New York, 1970), pp. 6–9, and plate 39b. Also, Ronald B. McKerrow, *Printers' and Publishers' Devices in England & Scotland 1485–1640* (London, 1913), No. 2. I am very grateful to Dr Kristian Jensen, formerly of the Bodleian Library, for assisting me in my enquiries about the dating of these leaves.

24. Rc – Oxford, Bodleian Library, MS Rawlinson C 158 (SC 12022): predominantly early 14th century, with one extraneous leaf from the 13th century, and the J.B. material inscribed on an endleaf in a hand of the second half of the 15th century; vellum, 122 folios (xii+122+vii), *c.* 345 × 240 mm.[1]

The front endleaves consist of ten paper folios that belong to the book's early-modern binding and are numbered in pencil from i–ix (*sic*).[2] They are followed by two vellum leaves (numbered x–xi), which measure *c.* 335 × 230 mm. Two items of J.B. material, preceded by their own heading, occur on the verso of the second vellum endleaf (fol. xi in the current pencil foliation):

> *These ben the namys of alle maner hawkis*
> i. Hierarchy of hawks
> ii. Breeds of dogs

Since the J.B. material occurs on a single endleaf, I shall not describe the remainder of this manuscript, beyond observing that it contains only one principal text: the legal treatise *De legibus et consuetudinibus Angliæ* of Henry de Bracton (*ob.* 1268), which occupies fols 1–121.[3] This is immediately followed by a single vellum leaf (fol. 122) purporting to record a perambulation of the forests of Essex in 9 Hen. III (1224/5).[4]

The two vellum endleaves that are of interest to the present study constitute a bifolium added to the book as part of an early binding, possibly its first. The vellum is very thick and stiff, and bears no signs of having been

---

[1] The manuscript is described briefly by William D. Macray, *Catalogi Codicum Manuscriptorum Bibliothecæ Bodleianæ*, Part 5: Rawlinson, 5 vols (Oxford, 1862–1900), II, p. 71.

[2] The present binding antedates the manuscript's arrival at the Bodleian in the 1750s. The binding and paper endleaves appear to be of the late 17th century: the watermark of a crowned shield is almost identical to no. 1786 (Holland, *c.* 1690) recorded by Edward Heawood, *Watermarks, Mainly of the 17th and 18th Centuries*, Monumenta Chartæ Papyraceæ I (Hilversum, 1950). The seven unnumbered endleaves at the rear of the codex are of the same paper as those at the front.

[3] Published as *Henrici de Bracton: De legibus et consuetudinibus Angliæ, libri quinque*, ed. Sir Travers Twiss, Rolls Series 70, 6 vols (London, 1878–83).

[4] Published in *The Early Charters of the Augustinian Canons of Waltham Abbey, Essex, 1062–1230*, ed. Rosalind Ransford, (Woodbridge, 1989), pp. 129–131, no. 203. Ransford suggests a tentative date for the perambulation of March 1227, since the text appears to postdate Henry's declaration of his coming-of-age in February 1227.

ruled or otherwise prepared for writing. The recto of fol. x, the outermost leaf, was clearly affixed to the original front board as a pastedown, but there is no record of when it was unglued. The verso of fol. xi is its hair-side, and it is here that the J.B. text has been written, presumably after these leaves were made part of the binding.

The choice of J.B. elements assembled here is curious, for these two items are not normally associated with one another, and are nowhere else combined as they are here. Furthermore, the Hierarchy of hawks has such strong similarities with the corresponding passages in Ry and G that one would expect it to be followed by the Hawks' diseases and remedies, as in those manuscripts. Perhaps the scribe deliberately excluded other material for the sake of marrying a pair of lists – one of hawks and one of dogs – though it is not clear where he might have found the latter.

The second J.B. element, the Breeds of dogs, bears some similarity to the versions in Ha and Rd, but its closest analogue is undoubtedly to be found in *StA*. Unfortunately the text in Rc is framentary, breaking off halfway down the page with the word *prykered*. *StA* provides the remainer of this phrase – *prikkerid curris* 'prick-eared curs' (that is, dogs with pointed ears)[1] – together with a long statement about the small pups favoured by ladies (*StA*, lines 1859–61).

Little more can be deduced about Rc's selection of J.B. material, where it came from, and why it should have been written down on the flyleaf of de Bracton's legal treatise. Nevertheless, this small, fragmentary text is an important witness to the sheer range of formulations of J.B. material that must have been circulating in the later 15th century.

25. Ry – London, British Library, MS Royal 17 D IV: second half (perhaps third quarter) of the 15th century, parchment, 91 leaves, *c.* 260 × 175 mm.[2] There are two items of J.B. material, each supplied with its own heading, on fols 87r–89r:

> *Here ben the names of all maner of hawkes and to whom and to what maner of men they longe to.*
>
> i. Hierarchy of hawks

---

[1] See *MED*, s.v. *prik-ered* (adj.): 'having erect or pointed ears'.

[2] The manuscript is described by Sir George Warner and Julius P. Gilson, *British Museum: Catalogue of Western Manuscripts in the Old Royal and King's Collections*, 4 vols (London, 1921), II, 251.

Thise ben the remedies ayenst all maner infirmiteis of all maner of hawkes.

ii. Hawks' diseases and remedies

[Followed by two sets of additional remedies for hawks, of unknown provenance, written in spaces left by items written earlier: fols 88v–91r, 89r–90r]

Ry consists principally of an elegant copy of Edward of York's hunting treatise *The Master of Game* (*MG*, fols 1r–85v), written by a single scribe, and decorated throughout with coloured initials that are flourished in red and blue. Apparently finding that he was left with two blank leaves at the end of his final quire, the scribe went on to add a short prose account of horn-blowing (fol. 86r–v), entitled *How the hunter shal blow after the cawse requireth*, the origins of which are obscure.[1] Thereafter, he added the J.B. material, which was presumably intended to complete the quire (up to fol. 87) but overshot the mark, necessitating the addition of a final gathering of four leaves (fols 88–91).

Having completed the Hawks' diseases and remedies three lines from the top of fol. 89r, the same scribe went on to add a further set of hawking remedies, of an unknown provenance, beginning in the space left below the J.B. text on fol. 88v, and continuing to fol. 91r. These remedies are longer and more complex than the J.B. remedies, which makes them easy to distinguish. They also include more general information about hawking, as is indicated by the heading *To lerne to drawe to kepe & knowe gosehaukes & ... oper braunchers & nyas* (fol. 90v). The scribe appears to have been concerned about running out of space, for his hand is far more cramped when writing this second set of remedies. Even so, he left some space at the bottom of each page, and this was subsequently filled on fols 89r 90r by a third set of remedies, added in a 16th-century hand. Neither of these additional sets of remedies has been transcribed for this study, and neither will be analysed further.

It remains only to observe that the additional hawking remedies complete the codex. The final page of the last gathering (fol. 91v) contains some scribbled proverbs, a Latin riddle, pen-trials and two 16th-century inscriptions: *anno 1557. H.B.*; and *Richarde brennynge is the possessor of thys booke*, the latter repeated several times.

---

[1] The text is not mentioned by the Baillie-Grohmans in their brief account of this manuscript (*Master of Game*, p. 240), nor is there any separate category for treatises on horn-blowing in Keiser's *Manual X*.

As I have already observed in relation to G (no. 21 above), there are considerable similarities between Ry and G. Although G, in its entirety, has a much greater range of contents than Ry, both manuscripts contain textually cognate versions of *The Master of Game*, which concludes at precisely the same point in both: the account of how to judge a 'grete boor' by the size and appearance of its tusks.[1] This is followed by the J.B. material, either immediately afterwards (G) or very soon after (Ry), and here too there is close agreement between the two.

Briefly, Ry's Hierarchy of hawks is identical to the corresponding item in G and closely related to that in Rc. More significantly, Ry's account of Hawks' diseases and remedies is found nowhere else apart from G. Close comparison of the J.B. contents of the two manuscripts suggests strongly that Ry descends from G, but it is not impossible that the two are siblings derived from a common original – the conclusion reached by James McNellis in relation to their two versions of *The Master of Game*.[2] Since I have been unable to undertake more than a cursory examination of *MG* in these two manuscripts, I shall continue to treat G as the parent of Ry on the basis of my comparison of their J.B. material.

Paradoxically, the J.B. material is much better set out in Ry than it is in G. The scribe has taken the trouble to provide headings for both J.B. items (where G has none), and has also added marginal legends indicating the disease for which each remedy is intended. Even though the decoration lavished on *The Master of Game* has not been extended to this part of the codex, the same careful style of execution is apparent.

In spite of Ry's superior appearance, however, its J.B. text is less authoritative than that of G, which is why I have selected G as the base manuscript for the presentation of this material in Part IVh below.

---

[1] The end of chapter 36 in Ry, chapter 35 in G; *Master of Game*, p. 82.

[2] McNellis, *The Uncollated Manuscripts of 'The Master of Game'*, pp. 107–8; see my discussion of G above.

AFFINITIES AMONG THE
J.B. ELEMENTS

The twenty J.B. elements (the items that make up the *J.B. Treatise* in its many different forms) are discussed below in the following order:

I. Hunting elements
(1) Collective nouns; (2) Soiling terms; (3) Resting terms; (4) Carving terms; (5) Beasts of venery and the chase; (6) Breeds of dogs; (7) The hunter; (8) Properties of a greyhound; (9) Hunting terms; (10) 'If a hart stands'.

II. Hawking elements
(11) Hierarchy of hawks; (12) Hawks' diseases and remedies; (13) Choosing a hawk; (14) Ages of a hawk; (15) A hawk's foot and feathers; (16) Flying terms.

III. Miscellaneous elements
(17) Precepts in *-ly*; (18) Four things to dread; (19) Properties of a good horse; (20) Names of wines.

In representing relationships between the different versions of each element, the following conventions are observed. Sigla enclosed within square brackets comprise a group of texts with strong, but varied, affinities. Within that group, witnesses linked by a dash are closely related (such as ancestors and their direct descendants, as well as siblings), whereas those separated by commas are recognisably, but more distantly, related in ways that cannot be readily established. For example, [H–L, Ex, Pp], [Ha, Rd].

Sigla that are not enclosed by square brackets represent unrelated members of a broad group possessing no special affinities with one another.

In all cases, sigla are listed in alphabetical order, with bracketed sets receiving precedence, thus: [Adv, *BK*], [Pl–Prk], Eg, L.

Some of the J.B. elements catalogued here are not included in Keiser's inventory of the contents of 'The J.B. and Lansdowne Groups' in *Manual X*, 3701–3704 [465–480]; some are recorded elsewhere in that volume, and some are not identified at all. In the descriptions that follow, cross-references to *Manual X* are provided wherever possible.

INTRODUCTION 75

I. Hunting elements

1. Collective nouns – A list of phrases containing collective nouns (terms of association) for animals, birds and many orders of human society.[1] There are two main types: (a) long lists ranging from 105 to 164 phrases;[2] (b) short lists, usually of about 45 to 50 phrases, but also including two lists – those of C and Dg*, with 73 and 20 phrases respectively – whose contents and structure set them somewhat apart from others of this type.

(a) Long lists: [*HSG–LJ*], [Pl–Prk], Addl, Adv, Eg, Pp, Rd, S*t*A, T, W

(b) Short lists: [C, Dg*], [Dg–Rg], [H–L], Ha, Harl

Not only are most of the long lists (type a) independent of one another, they also show considerable individuality, presumably because they were constantly being developed and enlarged by enthusiastic copyists. Although Addl and *LJ* contain only a few phrases (ten and fifteen respectively), internal evidence indicates that both are probably fragmentary versions of long lists; Addl cannot be linked with any other version, but *LJ* is undoubtedly cognate with *HSG*. The only other cognate pair among the long lists is that of Pl–Prk, in which phrases are arranged in groups of five – a practice found nowhere else. Among the remainder, there are only broad similarities between certain lists (such as Adv and T; Rd and S*t*A), but no correspondences strong enough to indicate any further close family groups among them.

Disregarding C and Dg*, the short lists (type b) are generally more consistent than the long ones; all have considerably fewer comical entries and all include the distinctive phrase 'a herd of bucks', which occurs in none of the long lists. Several other phrases can be considered characteristic of the short lists, though some occur occasionally in the long lists (for example, 'a diving of atteals', 'a mute of hounds', 'a *sord* of mallards', 'a team of oxen').

Other differences over terminology set the short lists apart from the long ones, as can be seen in the following formulas (terms in square brackets belong to the long lists): 'a clowder [cluster] of carls [churls]', 'a team [herd] of swans', 'a team [paddeling] of ducks, 'a chirming [chirm] of

---

[1] See Keiser, *Manual X*, 3702 [470]; Hodgkin, 'Proper Terms' (I).

[2] Pl probably had 105 phrases, but only 100 survive intact owing to damage to the manuscript. I have nevertheless included it in these statistics.

goldfinches', 'a flight [exalting/exaltation] of larks', 'a chattering [murmuration] of starlings'.

There are more identifiable affinities among the short lists, including two independent cognate pairs, [Dg–Rg] and [H–L]; only Ha and Harl stand on their own with no definite affiliations.

Although neither C nor Dg* can be the precursor of the other, they are noteworthy for containing phrases found nowhere else in the J.B. group, but reminiscent of the collectives in three Anglo-French glossarial texts – *Nominale*, *Femina* and Bibbesworth's *Tretiz* (referred to in my discussion of C earlier in this Introduction).

Three versions of the J.B. Collective nouns are set out in Parts I/1–107, II/197–241 and III/1–50. In addition, all phrases from all J.B. sources are collated and annotated in Appendix I.

2. Soiling terms – A short account of a particular juncture in a hart hunt when the quarry plunges into a body of water, such as a pond or stream, to escape its pursuers. In doing so, the hart is said, in the technical vocabulary of the hunt, to 'soil (itself)', that is, 'to go to water'– the verb is usually intransitive, sometimes reflexive.[1] This little passage also sets out many other terms associated with the act of 'soiling'. Two main types can be discerned: (a) long versions, which commence with the formula, *A hont hath cast a covpull of aloundys to a herd of harttes* (Prk); (b) short versions that begin, *A hert yf he be chased he wil desire to a reuer* (T).

(a) Long versions: [Dg–Rg, Prk, Rd], Eg, H, Ha

(b) Short versions: [*HSG*, T, W]

Turning first to the short versions (type b), these all consist of seven statements that are remarkably similar, in spite of there being no evidence that any of them could have descended from another. They are also noteworthy for introducing five statements with a conditional *if* (+ subjunctive): for example, *yf he take ouer þe reuer he crossyth* (T).

The long versions (type a) are generally less consistent, and use a *when* + indicative introductory construction: for example, *when he swymmythe ouer he crossythe* (Prk). The cognate pair Dg–Rg show signs of corruption in their opening lines (which are preserved intact by Prk). The fragmentary

---

[1] See note I/189–200 below for further discussion of the verb *soilen*. Hands (*EHH*, pp. xlvi ff.) uses the expression 'hunting terms' for this element.

Rd shows considerable similarity with Rg, but since it ends abruptly after only three statements, its affiliations are difficult to establish with certainty.[1]

Both Eg and Ha belong broadly with the Dg–Rg grouping, but contain minor omissions and variations that set them apart: for example, *braas of alauntes* (Ha) against *covpel of alovndes* (Dg); *vp on the water* (Eg) against *vp aȝeynst the water* (Dg). Finally, H differs from all others in this group by changing the perspective of the 'observer', locating him on the river bank towards which, rather than away from which, the hart is fleeing: *whan he cummyth ouer* (H) against *whan he swymmethe over* (Dg).

Note that four of the long versions (Dg, H, Ha, Rg) proceed to the Resting terms using a distinctive linking couplet, *a hert flype, a fawcon flype* (Dg), indicating a tradition in which these two elements were conjoined. Prk preserves only the line about the falcon flying and uses it to introduce the Hierarchy of hawks, since the Resting terms appear earlier in Prk's sequence of J.B. elements.

Four versions of the Soiling terms are set out in Parts I/189–200, II/174–82, III/70–8 and IVg.

3. Resting terms – A list of up to eighteen statements containing terms, each appropriate to a specific animal, for referring to the action of retiring to sleep, rest or (occasionally) mate; many of these terms are also applied to different orders of human society.[2] Several lists go on to include a number of terms that might best be described as indicating characteristic actions of certain people or animals – for example, *a heyron stalkyth* (H). There are five main types, disposed among fourteen witnesses:

(a) W

(b) [Pl–Prk], *StA*, T

(c) [Dg–Rg, Ha], [H–L], Eg

(d) [Am–*HSG*]

(e) Adv

W, the sole representative of type a, has only six statements, all of them active in construction: *An herte herboryth*. W's list is the shortest and may

---

[1] Another pattern of correspondences indicates that Rd should broadly be grouped with Ha (see elements 5, 6 and 7). With the Soiling terms, however, Rd's truncated text shows the greatest correspondence with Rg.

[2] The J.B. Resting terms are not recognised as an independent category in Keiser's *Manual X*, but are included as a sub-category (IV) of 'Proper Terms': 3702 [470].

represent the earliest form of this item, as it does not intersperse animals and humans as all the others do.

The texts of type b come together by beginning with a set of five or six statements containing active verbs, and then changing to present participles:

A herte harboreth ...
A hare in a forme schulderynge or ellis lenynge (T).

Of these, the cognate pair Pl–Prk show strong agreement, while *StA* and T each have their own distinctive phrases that set them apart from the others.

Type c texts are united by beginning with statements employing a quasi-passive construction, which is later abandoned in favour of an active verb:

A hert ys herborowred ...
A cony syttethe (Dg)

Although Dg (twelve statements) and Rg (ten statements) form a cognate pair in terms of their overall J.B. contents, they exhibit some disagreements over this particular element; indeed, Dg is here closer to Ha (also with twelve statements). The versions of the other cognate pair, H–L, are virtually identical, with fourteen statements each. Finally, Eg stands on its own as the shortest of this type with only nine statements.

Type-d texts, represented only by the cognate pair Am–*HSG*, are unique in beginning with a pair of statements about the hare and the dove – the first employing a present participle, and the second an active verb – before going on to the hart, the animal with which these lists normally begin:

An hare in his forme is sholdring or lening
A douue sitteth
an Herte is herbored (*HSG*, fol. 18r)

Type-d texts have eight statements in all, and they are followed by three statements (found only here) commencing *Yf an herte stande he stalleth* (*HSG*), which could be considered an extension of the Resting terms, but which I have elected to treat as a separate element, named after its opening formula: 'If a hart stands' (no. 10 below).

Adv, the sole representative of type e, has the longest list, consisting of eighteen statements, several of which occur nowhere else. Its first four statements – relating to hart, knight, hind, and lady (in that order) – use a quasi-passive construction (as in *An hert harburght*), but all the rest employ active verbs, beginning with the statement *A buck lodgeth*.

Three versions of the Resting terms are set out in Parts I/118–27, II/183–96 and III/79–90. In addition, all statements containing resting terms, from all J.B. sources, are collated and annotated in Appendix III.

4. Carving terms – A list of up to 41 statements containing terms for the dismemberment of specific animals, birds and fish, either at table or in the kitchen, or even in the field.[1] There are two main types: (a) long lists that include carving terms for fish; (b) short lists that refer only to animals and birds.

(a) Long lists: [Adv, *BK*, BS], [Pl–Prk], Eg, L, Rd, *StA*, T

(b) Short lists: [Am–*HSG*, W]

Among the long lists (type a), only Pl and Prk form a cognate pair; Adv, *BK* and BS are all independent of one another, but are united in presenting their information by way of a distinctive imperative construction, as in *vndo the dere* (Adv). Elsewhere, the carving verb is invariably expressed as a past participle in a quasi-passive construction: for example, *A crane dysplayd* (Am), *A crane ys dysplayde* (Eg). The five remaining versions of the type-a lists form a loose group with no firm relationships between any of them.

Of the short lists (type b), the cognate pair Am–*HSG* show strong similarities with W, though the latter is undoubtedly independent of them.

One version of the J.B. Carving terms is set out in Part I/128–56. In addition, all statements containing carving terms, from all J.B. sources, are collated and annotated in Appendix II.

5. Beasts of venery and the chase – A catalogue of game animals that divides them into three main orders: 'beasts of venery', 'beasts of the chase of the sweet foot', and 'beasts of the chase of the stinking foot'.[2] Variations between the different versions of this element are relatively minor, but are sufficient to indicate two main types: (a) longer versions that explain several of their terms; (b) shorter versions that generally avoid explication.

(a) Long versions: [Dg–Rg, Prk], Eg

(b) Short versions: [H–L, Pp], [Ha, Rd], *StA*

The main distinguishing characteristic of the long versions (type a) is that they gloss three key words: *elk*, *spyccard* and *baud*. As elsewhere, Prk shows strong affinities with Dg–Rg, though it disagrees on a key issue:

---

[1] The J.B. Carving terms are not recognised as an independent category in Keiser's *Manual X*, but are included as sub-categories (II, III) of 'Proper Terms', 3702 [470]. See also *Manual X*, 3682 [406] for Wynkyn de Worde's *Boke of Kervyng*.

[2] Keiser, *Manual X*, 3702 [467]. These categories of animals are examined in detail below; see, especially, the notes to Prk I/171 ff.

whether the ages of the elk and spyccard are measured in years or hundreds of years. In this regard, Eg agrees with Dg–Rg, but is otherwise very different, especially because of its unique additional remarks and the way it is set out on the page (see Part IVd).

Among the short versions (type b), only H–L and Pp gloss the term *spyckard* (Pp), *spytard* (H) as a hart of 100 years; what is more, they agree in their definition against all the long versions. Although there are notable differences between Ha and Rd, they clearly preserve the same basic text, and so form a subgroup of their own. St*A* stands on its own, but agrees with all the other short versions by including the 'white rat' (ME *whitret, whitrat* = a stoat or ermine; but *waturrate*, 'water rat' in Pp), which is wanting in all the long versions.

Four versions of the Beasts of venery and the chase are set out in Parts I/171–81, II/165–73, III/51–8 and IVd.

6. Breeds of dogs[1] – There are two main types: (a) long versions that typically list thirteen different 'breeds' of dogs, and then proceed to describe the characteristic activities of five categories of hunting hounds;[2] (b) short versions that simply list the dogs (up to fourteen of them).

(a) Long versions: [Dg–Rg, Prk], Eg

(b) Short versions: [Ha, Rd], [Rc, St*A*]

Among the long versions (type a), Dg–Rg and Prk come together as a distinct subgroup, although Prk stands somewhat apart from the Dg–Rg pair. Eg, though containing much the same information as the other long versions, is distinctive in being arranged as a list rather than in long lines, and because of its unique additional remarks (see Part IVe).

The short versions (type b) fall into two subgroups, among which no witness is directly descended from another. Rc breaks off abruptly but is clearly a truncated version of St*A*, with correspondences found nowhere else. Ha and Rd have their own strong parallels, though they differ over certain terms: for example, *myddynges kurris* (Ha) against *dunghylle curres* (Rd).

---

[1] Keiser, *Manual X*, 3702 [468].

[2] Rachel Hands sometimes categorises the account of canine hunting activities as a separate element, calling it 'the work of different hounds': *EHH*, p. xlvii, nos 5 and 8 (but cf. p. xlvi, no. 3). However, since this supplementary passage always occurs with the Breeds of dogs, I have elected to treat it as an extension of that element.

Ha and Rd also come together in linking this element to the one preceding it in their sequence of J.B. items: 'The hunter' (see no. 7 below). However, Rd stands alone in furnishing a unique link with its next element, the Soiling terms, by means of a single line that recreates some of the sound-effects of a hunt: 'With *Tro to tro, Ware, ryot, Ware*!'

Three versions of the Breeds of dogs can be found in Parts I/182–8, III/66–9 and IVe.

7. The hunter – A short paragraph that begins with a description of a huntsman and his accoutrements, before listing the horn signals that he should be able to sound under various circumstances. There is only one type of this element, preserved in two manuscripts.[1]

(a) [Ha, Rd]

Ha and Rd are broadly similar in their rendering of this item, but there are occasional omissions in Rd and some minor variations of terminology: for example, *belte* (Ha) against *gurdylle* (Rd). They also agree in employing the same formula – *The hunte schall haue help* ... (Ha) – as a link with the following element, the Breeds of dogs (no. 6 above).

The text of 'The hunter' as preserved in Ha is set out in Part III/59–65.

8. Properties of a greyhound – A gnomic account of a greyhound, in which the animal's features are defined by means of comparisons with other creatures.[2] Medieval French and English hunting manuals contain several independent renditions of the same idea,[3] but they are all unrelated to the J.B. versions, which fall into two main types: (a) a collection of rhyming couplets found in two independent witnesses; (b) a prose description that survives in only a single witness.

(a) Rhyming couplets: Eg, *StA*

(b) Prose description: Ha

Eg and *StA* exhibit considerable disagreement and are clearly unrelated, except that they preserve different versions of the same basic text, which

---

[1] Rachel Hands refers to this element as 'names of various horn calls': *EHH*, pp. xlvi–vii, nos 2, 7. In my view, the horn calls are listed as part of a hunter's accomplishments, hence my preferred name for the element.

[2] See Keiser, *Manual X*, 3702 [469].

[3] See the notes to Ha: III/91ff. below.

begins, *A grehounde shulde be heded like a snake and necked like a drake* (*StA*, 1863: *NIMEV* 42.5). *StA* also contains a supplementary set of doggerel verses tracing the development of a greyhound (*The first yere he most lerne to fede. / The secund yere to felde hym lede* ...),[1] which is not in Eg.

The prose account found in Ha commences, *A greunde schuld haue a congres hede, a ladys nek* ..., as well as five lines of doggerel verses similar to, though shorter than, the version in *StA*.

Two versions of the J.B. Properties of a greyhound are set out in Parts III/91–100 and IVf.

9. Hunting terms – A short list of only eleven lines containing terms describing the ways in which different game animals are typically hunted: 'A hart is chased ... a wolf is trapped', and so on.[2] This J.B. element occurs in one form only, in a single manuscript:

(a) Adv

The J.B. Hunting terms in Adv are set out in Part IVa.

10. 'If a hart stands' – The shortest of all the J.B. elements, this consists of only three brief statements that describe the typical demeanour of three types of deer – hart, buck and roe – in terms of how each 'stands'. It occurs in two closely related sources immediately after their Resting terms.

These three statements could arguably be regarded as an extension of the Resting terms, but I have elected to treat them as constituting an autonomous J.B. element.

(a) [Am–*HSG*]

The version preserved in *HSG* (collated with Am) is set out in Part IVb.

---

[1] *StA*, ll. 1866–73 (*EHH*, pp. 80–81).
[2] Rachel Hands refers to this element as 'terms for hunting different beasts': *EHH*, p. xlix, no. 18.

II. Hawking elements

11. Hierarchy of hawks – A list in which various falcons, hawks and other large raptors are allocated to different orders of human society, as in the well-known statement, *Ther is a goshawke, and that is for a yeman* (*StA*).[1] There are two main types: (a) long versions, which begin with an introductory paragraph about an emperor's three 'hawks' and what they kill,[2] before launching into the main hierarchy itself; (b) short versions, which reduce the account of an emperor's raptors to a mere line or two.

(a) Long versions: [Dg–Rg, Prk], [G–Ry, Rc], Eg, Ha, *StA*

(b) Short versions: [H–L, Ex], Pp

With the exception of Ha, the long versions (type a) are all very similar, but nevertheless fall into certain distinct subgroups. Dg–Rg and Prk are virtually identical except for a few minor variations; so too are G–Ry and Rc. Although *StA* and Eg contain essentially the same information as the Dg–Rg subgroup, each is sufficiently different in its own way to exclude it from that set. By comparison, Ha stands noticeably apart: it begins with a fairly standard account of an emperor's birds, but follows this with a simple list of hawks and makes no attempt to assign these birds to different members of human society – normally the very *raison d'être* for this element.

Of the short versions (type b), the cognate pair H–L exhibit two slightly different approaches to the same basic material, the main distinction being the way that each entry is introduced, with the syntax of H being inverted in L, thus: *A tersell for a ȝeman* (H), against *For a yoman a tarssell* (L). Ex is essentially the same as H, though the phrasing of some statements is different, and one attribution (of the goshawke) is both surprising and unique. Pp also contains much the same information (with variations), but is the shortest of the b-group.

Four versions of the Hierarchy of hawks are set out in I/201–24, II/142–63, III/101–14, and IVh/1–25.

12. Hawks' diseases and remedies – An account of the different diseases that can afflict a captive hawk, together with remedies for each condition. Three main types are apparent: (a) a short list of a hawk's principal ailments and the parts of the body they affect, followed by suitable remedies; (b)

---

[1] Keiser, *Manual X*, 3701 [466].

[2] An emperor's three 'hawks' are the eagle, the vulture, and the milan: see I/201–4 and the associated notes.

a set of remedies not preceded by the introductory list of illnesses, and often somewhat different (in wording at least) from those of type a; and (c) a prefatory list of illnesses, worded slightly differently from the version found in the a-group, followed by a collection of remedies that are markedly different from those of either types a or b.

(a) [Dg, Prk]

(b) [H–L, Ex], Pp

(c) [G–Ry], Ha

The two versions that constitute type a are virtually identical in wording, although they occur in formulations of the *J.B. Treatise* that are only distantly related. (See below under 'Textual Relations', Group 2.)

Of type-b texts, the cognate pair H–L contain some discrepancies because L omits several remedies that appear in H; however, those that occur in both manuscripts match closely. Ex contains essentially the same remedies, with a few omissions and some rephrasing. And although Pp clearly belongs with others of this group, it is much shorter and presents its remedies in a different order.

The texts of type c bear witness to an entirely different tradition, with a distinctive preliminary list of diseases, and many remedies that are found nowhere else. The cognate pair G–Ry agree closely,[1] and Ha stands apart since it contains only the list of diseases and none of the remedies.

Four different versions of the Hawks' diseases and remedies are set out in Parts I/229–70, II/1–100, III/115–23 and IVh/26–84.

13. Choosing a hawk – A short account of the bodily features, such as length of tail and wings, that indicate a worthwhile hawk or falcon. There is only one main type, which occurs in three manuscripts.

(a) [H–L] Ex, Pp

The two texts forming the cognate pair H–L show strong agreement. Ex and Pp contain essentially the same information as H–L, but differ in a few details, such as *louryng browys* (Ex), *lowryng browes* (Pp), against *lowryng hyen* (H), *lowryng ien* (L). Ex also omits any reference to *the sere*

---

[1] Rachel Hands makes no comment about the remedies in G, but refers to those in Ry as being 'similar in content to those of the J.B. treatise, but not in actual wording': *EHH*, pp. xlviii–l (nos 11, 22). Rather than excluding these remedies, I have elected to include them as constituting a major variant within the J.B. group.

and replaces þe beke, þe ye, þe fote (H) with the fote, þe yee, the fethyr. Pp lacks the description of a falcon, and ends with a statement found in none of the other witnesses: *thes ben the tokyns and synes*.

The version found in H (collated with L) is set out in Part II/101–6.

14. Ages of a hawk – A list of terms for the different life stages of a maturing hawk (for instance, *nyes* = eyas, an unfledged chick), together with names that a fully grown bird might be given through association with certain quarries (for example, 'pheasanter'). Although all versions contain much the same information, they fall into two main types:

(a) [H–L], Ex

(b) [Dg, Prk]

The three representatives of type a are slightly longer than those of type b, principally because they separate the names given to a hawk in its first year from those applied later. The cognate pair H–L show strong agreement, but both are marred by confusions that are clarified by Ex, in many ways the best exemplar of this item.

The two representatives of type b, Dg and Prk, are essentially the same, albeit with some lexical variations, such as *byttonnere* (Prk), *butorer* (Dg).

Two versions of the Ages of a hawk, those of Prk (collated with Dg) and H (collated with L), are set out in Parts I/225–8 and II/107–11 respectively.

15. A hawk's foot and feathers – A list of technical terms for referring to a hawk's foot and feathers. There is only one version of this element, occurring in three witnesses:

(a) [H–L], Ex

The two representatives of the cognate pair H–L contain essentially the same text, with minor omissions and variations apparent in L. Ex expresses this information slightly differently, and in a few places shows corruption, which is easily corrected from H.

The version in H (collated with L) is set out in Part II/112–24.

16. Flying terms – An expository, but not particularly lucid, account of the terms used for the different ways in which a hawk may pursue and capture its quarry. There is one main type, which occurs with considerable lexical variation in four witnesses, all of which exhibit confusion or corruption:

(a) [H–L] Ex, Pp

The cognate pair H–L show strong agreement, setting them apart from both Ex and Pp. As elsewhere, Ex is more cogently expressed, but shows confusion over important terms. Pp contains a condensed version of this item, which nevertheless occasionally clarifies issues in other witnesses.

The version preserved in H (collated with L) is set out in Part II/125–40.

III. Miscellaneous elements

17. Precepts in '-ly' – A set of moral apothegms based on adverbs ending in *-ly*, beginning 'Arise early / And serve God devoutly'.[1] There are many variants of this item, which was evidently very popular with medieval compilers. It occurs in several manuscripts of the J.B. group, but often at some remove from their J.B. material (for example, Pp, fol. 1r).[2] Where the Precepts in *-ly* occur in close association with other J.B. elements, two main types are apparent, both corresponding to *NIMEV* 324: (a) a long version of some sixteen precepts; (b) a short version of only ten maxims.[3]

(a) Long: *StA*

(b) Short: [Pl–Prk]

As I argue elsewhere, this item does not belong in the *J.B. Treatise* proper, but has to be acknowledged because of the way in which it has become incorporated in the formulations of the treatise found in Pl and Prk. There is close agreement between Pl and Prk, except that Pl transposes a pair of lines and lacks another line through physical damage to the manuscript.

The long version of *StA* is less secure in its right of inclusion in this catalogue of J.B. elements since it very likely derives from a non-J.B. source. However, I have elected to include it because of the difficulty of disentangling it from adjacent J.B. items.

The version in Prk (collated with Pl) is set out in Part I/108–17.

18. Four things to dread – Another collection of moral aphorisms (without rhyme) that has become attached to the J.B. material.[4] It occurs with little variation in three J.B. witnesses:

---

[1] Keiser, *Manual X*, 3703 [473].

[2] See the notes to Prk: I/108–17.

[3] Similar verses are listed as *NIMEV* 317, 3087, 3102.

[4] See Whiting, T124, 'Four Things to be dread of every wise man'; Keiser, *Manual X*, 3703 [474].

(a) [Pl–Prk], *StA*

The two texts forming the cognate pair Pl–Prk are almost identical, and are also essentially similar in content to *StA*. However, *StA* includes a long Latin maxim that is lacking in the two manuscripts (*Quia indignacio regis vel principis mors est*), and is also worded a little differently.

The version in Prk (collated with Pl) is set out in Part I/157–61.

19. Properties of a good horse – A set of fifteen comic gnomic maxims, ostensibly for assessing the qualities of a horse.[1] The topos is a popular one with many variants, including collections of eighteen, twenty-five and fifty-four properties, as well as analogues in French, German and Dutch.[2] It appears with little variation in three J.B. witnesses:

(a) [Pl–Prk], *StA*

Once again, the two texts forming the cognate pair Pl–Prk are almost identical, and also match *StA* in terms of content. However, there are occasional differences of terminology, as in *faire of here* (*StA*), against *a fayre tras* (Prk).

The version in Prk (collated with Pl) is set out in Part I/162–70.

20. Names of wines – A list of fifty-six wines which, though essentially alien to the *J.B. Treatise*, has nevertheless become attached to it in two witnesses that form a cognate pair:

(a) [Dg–Rg]

Unsurprisingly, the two versions of this item are identical in content, although they show interesting variations in their spelling of proper nouns, especially place names.

The version preserved in Dg (collated with Rg) is set out in Part IVi.

The two 'Tables of Witnesses and their Contents' overleaf provide a comparative overview of the issues examined in the foregoing sections, and a foundation for the discussion of textual relationships that follows.

---

[1] Keiser, *Manual X*, 3692 [440].

[2] See the notes to Prk (I/162 ff.) and Rachel Hands, 'Horse-dealing lore, or a fifteenth-century "Help to discourse"?', *MÆ*, 41 (1972), 230–39, esp. pp. 233–4; also *EHH*, p. 151/1874n.

TABLES OF WITNESSES AND THEIR CONTENTS

Contents of witnesses with strong affinities or direct kinship

Am	HSG	LJ	Dg	Rg	G	Ry	H	L	Ex	Pl	Prk
	1a	1a	1b	1b	11a	11a	12b	12b	12b	1a	1a
3d	3d		5a	5a	12c	12c	13a	13a	13a	17b	17b
10a	10a		6a	6a			14a	14a	14a	3b	3b
4b	4b		2a	2a			15a	15a	15a	4a	4a
	2b		3c	3c			16a	16a	16a	18a	18a
			11a	11a			11b	11b	11b	19a	19a
			20a	20a			5b	5b			5a
			14b				2a	3a			6a
			12a				3c	1b			2a
							1b	4a			11a
											14b
											12a

Key to J.B. elements

1. Collective nouns
2. Soiling terms
3. Resting terms
4. Carving terms
5. Beasts of venery and the chase
6. Breeds of dogs
7. The hunter
8. Properties of a greyhound
9. Hunting terms
10. 'If a hart stands'
11. Hierarchy of hawks
12. Hawks' diseases and remedies
13. Choosing a hawk
14. Ages of a hawk
15. A hawk's foot and feathers
16. Flying terms
17. Precepts in *-ly*
18. Four things to dread
19. Properties of a good horse
20. Names of wines

The sub-groups of each element (represented as a, b, c, etc.) are described in the preceding pages.

Contents of witnesses with more distant affinities, or none

Addl	Adv	BK	BS	C	Dg*	Eg	Ha	Harl	Pp	Rc	Rd	StA	T	W
1a	4a	4a	4a	1b	1b	8a	1b	1b	1a	11a	1a	11a	1a	1a
	9a					1a	5b		+	6b	4a	+	2b	4b
	3e					4a	7a		12b		5b	5b	3b	3a
	1a					+	6b		13a		7a	6b	4a	2b
						5a	2a		16a		6b	8a		
						6a	3c		11b		2a	19		
						2a	8b		5b			+		
						3c	11a					17a		
						11a	12c					18a		
												+		
												1a		
												4a		
												3b		

In the above table, the symbol + is used to indicate the presence of unrelated material that breaks the continuity of the J.B. items.

TEXTUAL RELATIONSHIPS

Drawing together the main threads of the foregoing discussion, we find that the surviving J.B. witnesses are so diverse in content that it is impossible to map their relationships to one another on a single stemma. Only eight witnesses, in four separate pairs, can with certainty be counted as directly related, namely H–L, Pl–Prk, *HSG–LJ* and G–Ry. But not one of these pairs is even distantly related to any of the others, though all of them show affinities, to a greater or lesser extent, with one or more other witnesses. Close analysis of those other witnesses reveals a complex web of correspondences and divergences, for some that agree in terms of two or more elements often disagree over others; and several witnesses that show no similarities in most respects may preserve the same basic formulation of an element found nowhere else. For example, the hawking material in Pp shows affinities with H and L that are suggestive of a shared distant ancestor; yet working against this agreement is Pp's long list of collectives, which is entirely different from the short variety found in H and L. Similarly, while Ha and Rd show considerable agreement in respect of four elements, it is with Dg and Rg that a fifth element in Ha shows greatest similarity.

What this means is that there is no straightforward way of characterising – let along representing schematically – the textual relationships of all the witnesses that have come down to us: there are simply too many unaccountable variations among them, indicating that we are missing many more pieces of the puzzle than we currently have to show of it. What we can attempt to do, however, is to establish which witnesses belong together in broad family groups, some as collateral descendants, others as siblings, usually of one or more hypothesised ancestors.

To that end, the following descriptions summarise relationships that can be deduced on the basis of similarities between some or all of the witnesses' contents: relationships that the accompanying, very provisional and simplified, stemmata attempt to represent schematically. It must be stressed that these stemmata make no attempt to follow the traditional rules for stemmatics; the different lengths of stems, for example, are not indicative of the distances of witnesses from archetypes or ancestors. In all respects, these stemmata are intended to do no more than provide graphic representation of complex relationships that can be difficult to summarise in words.

Categorising the J.B. witnesses in terms of correspondences in their contents yields eight groups.

Group 1: H–L, Ex, Pp

This is one of the most important groups by virtue of two witnesses, H and Pp, that preserve J.B. colophons. Its other main features are as follows:

Ex and H contain slightly different renditions of the same six hawking elements.

Pp contains five of these same hawking elements worded rather differently, but still sufficiently alike to suggest that Ex, H and Pp all derive their hawking material from a common source – represented as α.

H also contains five hunting elements, the last of which is a short list of collectives that ends with the colophon *Explicit I.B.*

Pp contains a long list of collectives that is separated from the hawking elements, and so appears to derive from a different source; this ends with the colophon *Explicit Iulyan Barne.*

It seems likely that the short list of collectives in H represents an early formulation of this element, and that the longer list in Pp is a later, amplified form of it. That both lists end with what appear to be related versions of the same colophon suggests that some comparable attribution must have existed in a common, distant source (the original short list of J.B. collectives) – represented as β. From this grew the amplified longer list (β‡) that was incorporated into Pp.

H is a direct ancestor of L.

In L, the J.B. material derived from H has been incorporated into a new, larger work based on *Prince Edward's Book of Hawking*; furthermore, some J.B. elements are reordered and reworked, which very likely indicates a lost intermediary – indicated as γ.

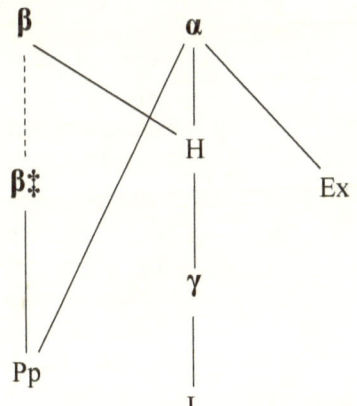

α – Archetype of J.B. hawking treatise

β – Short list of collectives

β‡ – Longer, amplified list of collectives

γ – Possible intermediary in which some J.B. items were rearranged and altered

Group 2: Pl–Prk, Dg–Rg

Pl is the proximate source of a significant portion of Prk's J.B. contents.

At first sight, Pl, with seven elements, appears to be an abbreviated version of Prk, which has thirteen. But internal evidence, and the later date of Prk, show that the relationship is in fact the reverse: that Prk draws on the seven items in the earlier Pl, and combines them with a further six items of hunting and hawking information from one or more other sources – indicated as δ – to produce a new, conflated collection of J.B. material.

Dg appears to be the antecedent of Rg, which ends imperfectly with only seven of Dg's nine elements, but internal evidence suggests rather that Dg and Rg are siblings, deriving from a lost source – indicated as θ.

There are strong correspondences between Prk and Dg in that they share the same six elements of hunting and hawking information (interspersed with two other items in Dg) that Prk derives from δ. These six items are, moreover, sufficiently similar for them to collatable. This agreement suggests that Dg and Rg's common ancestor, θ, can be connected to δ, whose hypothetical existence as a distinct little collection of J.B. items becomes a little more certain.

The two items that Dg does not share with Prk – the Names of wines and a set of Resting terms – can be accounted for as follows. It is possible that δ contained the Resting terms found in Dg, and that these were omitted from Prk because an equivalent item had already come down to it from Pl. As for the Names of wines, these may have existed in δ, and been ignored by the Prk compiler, or they could have been introduced by θ, which would explain why they are found only in Dg and Rg.

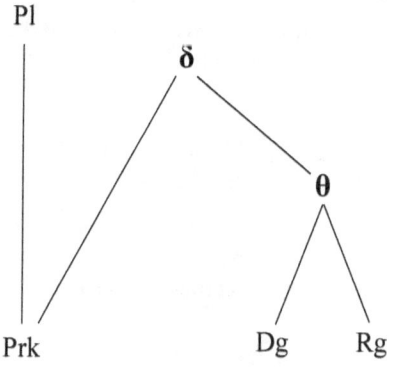

δ – Archetype containing six hunting and hawking items

θ Lost common ancestor containing the Names of wines and a set of Resting terms

Group 3: Ha, Rd, (*StA*)

Ha and Rd share comparable versions of four hunting elements (of the six elements in Rd and the nine in Ha), in precisely the same sequence. They differ in other respects, such as the fact that Rd has a long list of Collective nouns, whereas Ha has a short one.

It is possible that these four shared elements circulated as a distinct little cluster of J.B. material, which is represented as λ.

A further correspondence that I have not attempted to plot graphically is to be found between the lists of collectives in Rd and *StA*. Not only do Rd and *StA* have the longest lists of this element (164 phrases in *StA*, 153 in Rd), their lists contain phrases found nowhere else: see Appendix I, nos 12, 18, 71, 129, 177, 202.

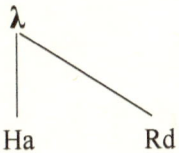

λ – Ancestor containing a cluster of four hunting items shared by Ha and Rd

Group 4: *HSG–LJ*, Am, T, W

The fragmentary nature of *LJ* makes it impossible to tell if it was typeset from *HSG* or from another exemplar in the Caxton/Wynkyn printshop, but that the two witnesses are closely related is unquestionable.

Am, which also appears to be fragmentary, shares three elements with *HSG*, and here too a close relationship is apparent, since one of those elements ('If a hart stands') is found nowhere else. It is impossible to tell whether Am is copied from *HSG* (the better text), or whether both descend from a lost, common source. For the sake of simplicity, I have represented *HSG* as the forebear of both *LJ* and Am.

Standing somewhat apart are T and W, which show notable similarities with one another: they have four elements in common, three of which are of the same type. They also share four elements with *HSG*, of which two are of the same type, including one (the Soiling terms) in a formulation that is found nowhere else. Somewhere in the distant past must lie a common original that has undergone various mutations in its transmission over time. This is indicated as π.

Group 4

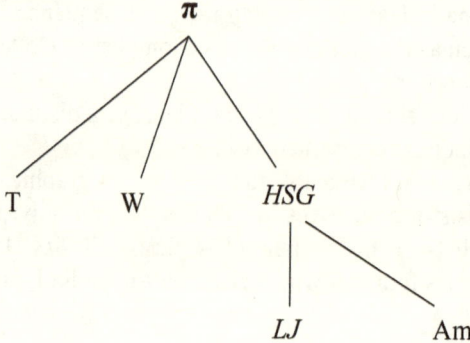

π – Archetype containing four hunting items shared by T, W, and *HSG*

Group 5: G–Ry, Rc, *StA*

G and Ry, which consist of only two hawking elements each, appear to be related by linear descent, with G being the parent.

More distantly related is Rc, which contains the same version of the Hierarchy of hawks as G–Ry (derived from µ), but also a version of the Breeds of dogs that aligns it with *StA* (derived from ω).

StA is, of course, a witness of such complexity that it would need a stemma all of its own, which I shall not attempt to provide here.

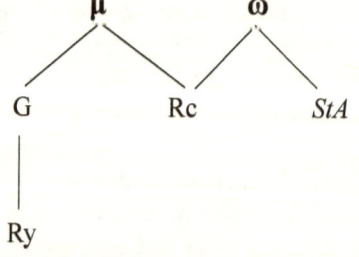

µ – Close ancestor containing the Hierarchy of hawks that Rc shares with G

ω – Remote ancestor containing distinctive version of the Breeds of dogs that Rc shares with *StA*

Group 6: Adv, *BK*, BS

Adv, *BK* and BS come together in sharing the same distinctive formulation of Carving terms expressed as imperative verbs, although Adv contains many more J.B. elements than the other two.

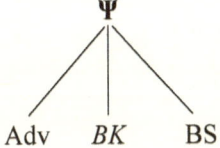

ψ – Remote ancestor containing Carving terms using an imperative construction

Group 7: C, Dg*

C and Dg* show an unusual commonality in their Collective nouns. Although the list in C is somewhat longer than the one in Dg*, both contain phrases found nowhere else; see Appendix I, nos 35, 39, 45, 68, 81, 170, 183, 207.

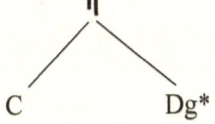

η – Remote ancestor containing a distinctive set of Collective nouns

Group 8: Addl, Eg, Harl

Addl, Eg, Harl form a group only insofar as they show no affinities with any other witness, and so stand apart.

Addl   Eg   Harl

DEVELOPMENT OF THE
J.B. TREATISE

The twenty-six surviving witnesses of J.B. material constitute a surprisingly wide range of manuscripts and early printed books, including heterogeneous miscellanies (such as Adv and Prk), personal commonplace books (such as Rd and T), collections of sporting manuals (such as G and H), and a variety of other compendia. The sheer number of these witnesses attests to the widespread popularity of the J.B. material in the second half of the 15th century, yet the scarcity of clear lines of kinship among them indicates also that there must have been many more versions in circulation than have come down to us. It is to be hoped that more witnesses will come to light in the future, thereby allowing us to plot more connections, and so achieve a greater comprehension of the complex relationships that pertain between witnesses than is currently possible. For the time being, those relationships can be best understood through close scrutiny of the various affinities that exist between individual J.B. elements, as described earlier in this Introduction, for those elements were often transplanted from one kindred group of texts to another as scribes and compilers assembled their own preferred anthologies of J.B. material.

Seen together, the surviving witnesses demonstrate just how varied the J.B. material could be, both in the form of the individual elements and the combinations into which they might be arranged. This has profound implications for any attempt to define the *J.B. Treatise*, which has to be conceived as having rather fluid boundaries; and that, in turn, can easily give rise to disagreements about what to categorise as a mere collection of J.B. material, and what to recognise as a version of the treatise itself. It needs to be recognised that the J.B. material is protean by nature, and that any attempt to analyse it will inevitably be fraught with the difficulties of trying to pin down such an entity.

The character and diversity of the witnesses nevertheless allow us to surmise that there was a range of J.B. materials in circulation in the later 15th century, consisting of single elements and groups of elements, which scribes and compilers drew on as they pleased for their own purposes. In the process, these elements were constantly being modified, developed and amplified, as well as being rearranged with other elements, and even combined with extraneous items that probably merely abutted them in an earlier copy-text.

Circumstantial evidence suggests that the first element to emerge as a distinct unit was the Collective nouns, for analogous lists of such phrases were assembled as early as the 13th century for inclusion in didactic Anglo-Norman glossarial texts, such as *Femina* and Bibbesworth's *Tretiz*.[1] Brief, elementary lists of collectives for the principal animals of the chase also appear in medieval hunting manuals, such as William Twiti's *The Art of Hunting*, originally written in Anglo-Norman in the first quarter of the fourteenth century, and later translated into Middle English. Twiti presents a simple list of collectives in the following exchange between an experienced huntsman and his apprentice:

How many herdes be there of bestes of venery?

Sire, of hertis, of bisses ['hinds'], of bukkes & of doos.
A soundre of wylde swyn; a bevy of roos.[2]

Similarly, *Prince Edward's Book of Hawking* (*PEB*) sets out the collectives for the foremost quarries of an austringer as part of an excursus on the terminology of the sport: 'And ye schull say "I have founde a couey of pertriche, a beuey of quayles, and eye of fesauntes".'[3]

The *PEB* list is later amplified by the derivative *Tretyse off Hawkyng*, which assembles an altogether more varied list of collectives:

Thow sal say 'hole-fotyd fawlis ['fowls'] lyeng' and noȝt 'sittyng'. And we will go on feld and fynd a covy of partrikkes, or a nee of fesaundes, a covpell of fowle, lyenge and not sittyng. For all hole-foted fewles lyggys in [this] kynd of speche.[4] So dos partrik, fesaund and whayle ['quail']. And þu sal say 'a bevy of whayles' and of heronnis [and] of rocum ['roes']. And a herd of cranes and of dere. A company of gese and of ladyes. And a flok of larkis and of schepe.

How many is a covi of partrykkes?

Als many as hawntis in a place and kepis hem togedir passyng II, and so of fesaundes and of whayles and of all odir as said before.

---

[1] See above under MS C (no. 20).

[2] Twiti, *The Art of Hunting*, Cotton MS, ll. 170–72, in *The Middle English Text of 'The Art of Hunting' by William Twiti*, ed. David Scott-Macnab (Heidelberg, 2009), p. 19. A similar but slightly longer list occurs also in *BH*, ll. 1257 ff.

[3] *PEB 1* (ed. Swaen), p. 9 (fol. 7r; punctuation mine).

[4] 'Whole-footed fowl' are waterfowl with webbed feet.

How few may be a covy?

þu may say III resonabely and no fewer. For II is a copil euermore and III is a herd of dere and no fewer. For if þu se II dere and no mo þu may say 'þer pasturs II dere, II hertis, II bukkis, II roesse'. And so of all kynd of hem etc. Vt in Tristram.[1]

One can see in these different texts that inventories of collective nouns became an increasingly prominent feature of medieval sporting manuals, of both hunting and hawking. There is, moreover, a clear pattern of development from the short, simple tally set out by Twiti to the far more extended list of *The Tretyse off Hawkyng*, which goes beyond its immediate needs in relation to the sport of hawking to include deer, geese and ladies. A distant but noticeably similar pattern can be observed in the J.B. lists of collectives, which focus initially on game animals before broadening out to embrace a range of other categories – including birds, domestic animals and classes of human society – many of which are allotted collective nouns that are patently contrived, and often ingenious and humorous. The parallels are strong enough to suggest that the J.B. collectives may have developed from a sporting manual similar to *The Tretyse off Hawkyng* through a process whereby they were first separated as a discrete item, then augmented to produce both the serious short lists and the more imaginative long lists.

We may also deduce that the J.B. collectives did not develop on their own, but as the core element of a little treatise on hunting terminology. As I have observed already, the Collective nouns are the most common of the J.B. elements, occurring in nineteen of the twenty-six known witnesses. In fourteen of these, we find the collectives combined with elements relating to the hunt;[2] and in three witnesses (Eg, H and T), they are preceded by headings that explicitly mention hunting, such as *De venatoribus in Anglicis* (T). Unfortunately, there is insufficient consistency in the pattern of elements among surviving witnesses to indicate reliably how the *J.B. Treatise* first came into being, and equally no possibility of reconstructing an archetype from them. In general, however, it can be said that the J.B. Collective nouns correlate very strongly with a cluster of up to four other

---

[1] *THawk 1* (ed. Danielsson), p. 36, lines 234–47 (punctuation mine); cf. the slightly different wording of *THawk 2* (ed. Leggatt), pp. 143–4. These quotations from Twiti and the *Tretyse off Hawkyng* may be considered typical of the treatment of collective nouns in hawking and hunting manuals of the period. It will be apparent that they bear little relation to the J.B. lists of such terms, either in their arrangement or their extent.

[2] Adv, Dg, Eg, H, Ha, *HSG*, L, Pl, Prk, Rd, Rg, *StA*, T, W.

hunting elements – the Beasts of venery and the chase, Carving terms, Resting terms and Soiling terms – as can be seen most clearly in Dg, H, *HSG*, Rg, T and W.

Among these witnesses, *HSG*, T and W are noteworthy for coming together with essentially the same four major hunting elements: Collective nouns, Carving terms, Resting terms and Soiling terms. Such congruity is found nowhere else in the *J.B.* group, and clearly represents one of the major configurations that the *J.B. Treatise* could assume. It is tempting to suppose that this group of witnesses preserves something of the *J.B. Treatise* in its original form, before it began accumulating hawking elements. But such a hypothesis would be difficult to sustain on the basis of surviving evidence alone. All that can be said with certainty is that other witnesses – such as Dg and H – show clearly that the hunting elements were conjoined at an early stage to one or more hawking elements, to form a composite little treatise on the fieldsports of hunting and hawking.

Other items, with no obvious connection to those sports, must have come later, through a mixture of eccentric scribal choices and errors in copying (such as turning two pages in an exemplar – which, as I have suggested, may account for the inclusion of the Names of wines in Dg). Yet it would be a mistake to be entirely dismissive of extraneous elements such as the Precepts in *-ly* and the Names of wines. Many things that strike the modern reader as blatant incongruities could be perfectly acceptable to medieval sensibilities – as can be seen, for example, in the long moralising exhortations that take up most of the later pages of John Fitzherbert's *Book of Husbandry* (1523).[1] For all practical purposes, then, anthologies of J.B. material and the *J.B. Treatise*, in its various forms, are best characterised in terms of their combined hawking and hunting contents, although several are either predominantly, or even exclusively, concerned with the sport of hunting, and one (Ex) wholly focused on hawking.

One final, tantalising, piece of evidence to consider is the positioning of the two 'J.B.' colophons in H and Pp. The former has the formula *Explicit I.B.* at the end of its Collective nouns, which is also the final element of its J.B. contents. Likewise with Pp, the list of Collective nouns closes with the colophon *Explicit Iulyan Barne*, even though this item is located at some remove from the rest of the J.B. material. The evidence is inconclusive, but

---

[1] Fitzherbert proceeds from advising the reader on how 'To nourishe all maner of stone fruite, and nuttes', to 'A shorte information for a yonge gentyl-man that entendeth to thryue', with much more along similar lines in what follows; *The Book of Husbandry by Master Fitzherbert*, ed. Walter W. Skeat (London, 1882), p. 90.

it could suggest that the name Juliana Barnes, in its various formulations, may have been attached specifically to the Collective nouns. And if the Collective nouns initially formed the nucleus of a little cluster of hunting elements, then that may account for the association between Dame Juliana and the subject of hunting as we find asserted by *StA*'s colophon, *Explicit Dam Iulyans Barnes in her boke of huntyng* (sig. f4r) Such a connection, if well known at the time, could have played some part in motivating the *StA* compiler to transplant the name 'Iulyans Barnes' from his exemplar's J.B. material to the *Boke of Huntyng* itself.

THE CONTEXT AND PURPOSE OF THE *J.B. TREATISE*

In his survey of 'Practical books for the gentleman' in the late Middle Ages, George Keiser suggests very plausibly that Wynkyn de Worde's 1496 reprinting of *StA*, with the addition of a treatise on 'fishing with an angle', only a decade after the original had been compiled at St Albans, 'attests to an audience eager for access to works of practical writings'.[1] This audience, he concludes, consisted principally of 'the English landholding classes and those responsible to them', especially clerics, 'often children of the gentry themselves, who shared the interests and aspirations of the laity they served'.[2] Keiser's essay is of special interest to the present study because he discusses six codices containing J.B. material (including *StA*), though without examining their J.B. contents in particular.[3] Those J.B. contents, as I have argued, comprise one of the most desirable little handbooks of the late 15th century; one so popular, in fact, that it was included in *HSG*, one of the very first books to be printed by Caxton at Westminster, and in *StA*, the first off-the-shelf miscellany of practical texts to be printed in England.

That little handbook – the *J.B. Treatise* – is an unusual compendium in that it contains practical information of a singular kind, utterly different in nature from what we find in more familiar practical works, such as *The Proprytees and Medycynes for Hors*,[4] *The Master of Game*, and *Prince*

---

[1] Keiser, 'Practical books', p. 470.

[2] *Ibid.*, pp. 472, 482–3. Note that Keiser refers to *StA* in its entirety as *The book of hawking, hunting, and blasing of arms*, and also by the potentially confusing abbreviated title *The book of hawking*.

[3] Keiser (*ibid.*) discusses C, Eg, G, W, *BK* and *StA* in varying degrees of detail.

[4] *STC*, 3290, 3291.

Edward's Book of Hawking. It is worth examining the character of this information and exploring some of its implications for our understanding of the purpose, context and reception of the *J.B. Treatise.*

Perhaps the most noteworthy feature of the various J.B. elements is that the majority present their information in the form of lists of terms. Very few depart from this rule, especially among those concerned with hunting; here, only the Soiling terms and 'The hunter' are noticeably different in that they set out their terminology by means of short discursive passages that evoke a sense of context. The same is generally true of the hawking elements: all are lists, with the notable exception of the Hawks' diseases and remedies – the only item in the entire collection that contains genuinely practical information.

In short, although I have characterised the *J.B. Treatise* as a practical work, it is not really a text that one would want to turn to for instruction about medieval hawking and hunting techniques – and this would have been as true in the Middle Ages as it is today. The *J.B. Treatise* differs from most other practical books, and from all the other English treatises on hawking and hunting, in that it provides information about the terminology of these sports, but offers little to no instruction concerning their actual practices. It is therefore more like a compendium of terms – a lexicon for hawkers and hunters – than anything else. I would hazard further that the treatise may have been especially popular among persons who had no real interest in the practicalities of fieldsports, but wished to be conversant with the specialised argots of such aristocratic pursuits.

The reason why such a text should have been so popular at this time may be found in the enormous changes taking place in rural England, and in the composition of rural English society, from the middle of the 14th century. These included the gradual abandonment of direct demesne farming and the emergence of a class of rich peasant farmer leasing demesne lands from large landowners; the widespread conversion of arable land into pasture as the demand for English wool grew ever greater through the 15th century; and the associated rapid growth of several new classes of landholder consisting, on the one hand, of enterprising men of the countryside (including petty dignitaries and manorial officers such as bailiffs and reeves), and, on the other hand, of wealthy urbanites, such as merchants and lawyers, who took up rural leases for the first time, built imposing residences and established powerful dynasties, both locally and nationally.[1]

---

[1] For more information about these developments, see Leonard Cantor, 'Introduction', *The English Medieval Landscape*, ed. Leonard Cantor (London, 1982), 17–24 (especially

These new landholders were often self-made men, hungry for social advancement and passionate about the means for maintaining it. We can imagine such men being thirsty for knowledge, especially of the sort contained in the books of practical instruction that burgeoned in the 15th century, and of which the *J.B. Treatise* is a notable, though idiosyncratic, representative. Of course, the new landed classes need not have been the only group with an interest in such texts, but their need for knowledge about the countryside and country pursuits might have been the most acutely felt.

Regrettably, only three J.B. manuscripts have yielded the names of their original owners, through which definite information can be gained about their exact origins; and only four others contain useful clues about the families or persons for whom they may have been composed. (Others, of course, contain names of scribes and indications of general provenance through linguistic forms, but this is of limited use in determining the precise social milieu in which they were composed.) Yet even in this small sample we can see that interest in the *J.B. Treatise* stretched far beyond the traditional hawking-and-hunting landed classes. It is noteworthy that the following list of the individuals and families who either compiled, or are believed to have commissioned, J.B. manuscripts yields the name of only one member of the landed gentry, alongside those of a schoolmaster and a clergyman. Another contains clues that it was commissioned for a late 14th-century mayor of London:

Walter Pollard, schoolmaster, Exeter (Rd)
John Benet, clergyman, Bedfordshire (T)
John Whittocksmead, MP, Wiltshire gentry (W)

? An unknown mayor of London (Eg)[1]
? Sherbrooke family, Nottinghamshire gentry (Adv)
? Tollemache family, Suffolk gentry (BS)
? Booth or Worsley family, Lancashire gentry (C)

How such people used the information in the *J.B. Treatise* is impossible to tell, though we can be sure that they would not have learned enough to

---

pp. 20–23); Alan R.H. Baker, 'Changes in the later Middle Ages', in *A New Historical Geography of England*, ed. H.C. Darby (Cambridge, 1973), 186–247 (especially pp. 187–218).

[1] Previously thought to be William Gregory (*ob. c.* 1467); see McLaren, *London Chronicles*, pp. 29–33, for an analysis of the evidence. She concludes (pp. 32–3) that the author of the chronicle and its putative 'extension' 'seems to have been a mayor'.

make them competent falconers or hunters. A studious reader of the treatise would, however, have become familiar with a useful range of hunting and hawking terms, as well as a sense of when and how to use them. He would also have discovered an amusing little *aide mémoire* on the salient features of a good horse, and another concerning the vital attributes of a greyhound. And not only would he have learned the names of the most significant diseases that could afflict a hawk, he would have had a handy list of remedies with which to direct the servants attending his mews.

We may plausibly infer that information of this sort would have been invaluable to prosperous urbanites new to the countryside, aspiring landholders of any background, and upwardly mobile clergymen eager to be acquainted with the 'gentle' but arcane phraseology of the traditional aristocracy. The milieu in which the *J.B. Treatise* circulated was full of such people, and I would argue that it was among them that the treatise achieved its greatest popularity. The urgency of their need may be glimpsed in the following exchange between Kno'well, an old gentleman, and his nephew, Stephen, in Ben Jonson's play *Every Man in His Humour*, first performed in about 1598:

Stephen Uncle, afore I go in, can you tell me an' he have e'er a book of the sciences of hawking and hunting? I would fain borrow it.

Kno'well Why, I hope you will not a-hawking now, will you?

Stephen No wusse; but I'll practice against next year, uncle. I have bought me a hawk, and a hood and bells and all; I lack nothing but a book to keep it by.

Kno'well Oh, most ridiculous.

Stephen Nay, look you now, you are angry, uncle. Why, you know, an' a man have not skill in the hawking and hunting languages nowadays, I'll not give a rush for him. They are more studied than the Greek or the Latin. He is for no gallant's company without 'em.[1]

---

[1] Ben Jonson, *Every Man in His Humour: A Parallel Text Edition of the 1601 Quarto and the 1616 Folio*, ed. J.W. Lever (London, 1971). The text quoted is that of the 1616 edition, I.i.32–44.

Of particular interest here is Stephen's emphasis on the need for skill in 'hawking and hunting *languages*' (my emphasis)[1] – precisely the sort of information contained in concentrated form in the *J.B. Treatise*, and clearly still highly sought after in Jonson's day, little more than a century after the period in which that small, compact and adaptable manual was being enthusiastically copied throughout England.

For the ambitious Stephen, mastery of the terminology of hawking and hunting is a guarantee of social acceptance, especially among the gallants of his day – an aspiration that Johnson uses for comic effect. By contrast, in real life, and at much the same time, the ability to sound knowledgeable about horses, hounds, hawks, and hunting was a matter of life and death for the Jesuits Robert Southwell and John Gerard, who employed such linguistic skills to pass themselves off as country gentlemen as they moved about the land in search of souls needing their ministry. A typical example from Gerard's autobiography relates how he pretended to be looking for a lost hawk to account for his presence in a particular area:

> As soon as my companion had left, I came out of the wood by a different path. I had gone only a short distance when I saw some country folk coming toward me. Walking up to them I asked whether they knew anything about a stray hawk; perhaps they had heard its bell tinkling as it was flying around. I wanted them to believe that I had lost my bird and was wandering about the countryside in search of it. This is what falconers do. And they would not be surprised because I was a stranger here and unfamiliar with the lanes and countryside; they would merely think that I had wandered here in my search.[2]

As this example demonstrates, confidence was key to safeguarding the masquerade. For Gerard and Southwell, as much as for Stephen, a handy little terminological primer such as the *J.B. Treatise* would have been invaluable in ensuring their credibility.

---

[1] The earlier 1601 Quarto lacks this emphasis, reading simply, '... an' a man have not skill in hawking and hunting nowadays ...': *ibid.*, p. 14 (I.i.39).

[2] John Gerard, S.J., *The Autobiography of a Hunted Priest* (San Francisco, 2012), pp. 13–14. See also Anne R. Sweeney, *Robert Southwell: Snow in Arcadia: Redrawing the English Lyric Landscape 1586–1595* (Manchester, 2006), pp. 109–10.

EDITORIAL PRINCIPLES

All transcriptions in this volume, whether from manuscripts or early printed books, observe the following editorial principles.

Capitalisation and punctuation are modern. Manuscript punctuation is not reproduced, with the exception of paragraph marks, for which I have used the paraph, or pilcrow (¶), throughout.

The Tironian nota for *et* is represented by the ampersand, but all other contractions, suspensions and abbreviations have been expanded and indicated by italics. These include the upward curl on final *m*, *n* and *r*, which has been transcribed as *e* where there is strong evidence to read it thus, or as *-er* or *-yr* according to a scribe's ususal orthographic practice; likewise, the looped downward stroke at the end of a word, which has been transcribed as *-es* or *-ys* based on spellings elsewhere in the text. Other marks that appear to be otiose are generally ignored (such as the horizontal stroke through *l*, *ll* and *h*), unless there is corroboration that the scribe's preferred spelling requires such marks to be taken into account.

The contracted forms *wt*, *wtt* and *w^t* are all expanded as w*ith* (without a *t* in roman type) for reasons of legibility; and the tailed *z* is transcribed as *z*, not *3*. Superscript letters that are not part of a contraction, as in þ^e, þ^i, þ^{is}, are silently normalised. Except in later printed works, if *y* (or a character of similar appearance) is used in place of þ, the distinction is ignored and þ is used instead.

Words elided with a preceding indefinite article have been silently emended (for example, *afayre* = *a fayre*). Other word-divisions have in most cases been standardised according to modern practice, with the manuscript reading supplied in the apparatus. Left unaltered are words whose meaning would change to a greater or lesser extent if they were modernised (for example, *gentylle man*), as well as those where the *n* of the indefinite article *an* has been transferred to the beginning of the following noun (for example, *a neygule* = 'an eagle').

In general, minimal alterations have been made to the text, though obvious scribal errors and omissions are corrected [in square brackets] and noted in the apparatus. Letters in ⟨angled brackets⟩ are conjectural or doubtful, either because the original letters have been lost through physical damage, are obscured by ink blots, or were poorly formed by the scribe.

In recording variations between a base manuscript and other witnesses collated with it, the textual apparatus ignores minor variations such as *a*/*an*; *and*/*&*; *it*/*yt*/*hit*; *on-*/*un-*/*vn-*; *woll*/*will*; þ/*th*; *-3-*/*-gh-*; *3-*/*y-*.

SELECT BIBLIOGRAPHY

J.B. Texts and Texts of Associated Material

Allen, Hope E., 'Fifteenth-century associations' = 'The fifteenth-century "associations of beasts, of birds, and of men": the earliest text with "language for carvers"', *PMLA*, 51 (1936), 602–6.

Berners, Dame Juliana, *The Boke of Saint Albans, 1486*, The English Experience, No. 151 (Amsterdam and New York, 1969).

The Book Containing the Treatises of Hawking; Hunting; Coat-Armour; Fishing; and Blasing of Arms. As printed at Westminster by Wynkyn de Worde, Introduction by Joseph Haslewood (London, 1810).

Bühler, Curt F., 'Middle English apothegms in a Caxton volume', *ELN*, 1 (1963), 81–4.

Burton, T.L., 'Terms' = 'Late fifteenth-century "terms of association" in MS. Pepys 1047', *N&Q*, 25 (1978), 7–12.

Corner, Rachel, 'More terms' = 'More fifteenth-century "terms of association"', *RES*, NS 13 (1962), 229–44.

de Worde, Wynkyn, *The Boke of Keruynge*, 2nd edn (1513), in *The Babees Book*, ed. F.J. Furnivall, EETS os 32 (London 1868), pp. 261–86.

English Hawking and Hunting in 'The Boke of St. Albans': A facsimile edition of sigs a2-f8 of 'The Boke of St. Albans' (1486), ed. Rachel Hands, Oxford English Monographs (London, 1975).

Hodgkin, John, 'Terms I' = 'Proper terms: An attempt at a rational explanation of the meanings of the collection of phrases in *The Book of St. Albans*, 1486', *TPS*, 26:3 (1909), 1–187.

———, 'Terms II' = 'Proper terms. II. "Tearmes of a keruer"', *TPS*, 27:1 (1914), 52–94; 27:2 (1916), 123–37 [95*–109*].

Kurvinen, Auvo, 'MS. Porkington 10: description with extracts', *NM*, 54 (1953), 33–67.

[Lydgate, John], *The Hors, the Shepe & the Ghoos*, reprinted by M.M. Sykes for The Roxburghe Club (London, 1822).

Scott-Macnab, David, 'An autonomous and unpublished version of the *J.B. Treatise* in Exeter Cathedral MS 3533', *MÆ*, 76 (2007), 70–84.

Stere Htt Wel: A Book of Medieval Refinements, Recipes from a Manuscript in Samuel Pepys's Library, trans. Gerald A.J. Hodgett, (London, 1972).

The Tollemache 'Book of Secrets': A Descriptive Index and Complete Facsimile, ed. Jeremy Griffiths, completed by A.S.G. Edwards, The Roxburghe Club (London, 2001).

Hawking and Hunting Texts

Albertus Magnus, *De animalibus libri XXVI: Nach der Cölner Urschrift*, ed. Hermann Stadler, 2 vols (Münster, 1920).
Baillie-Grohman, see *The Master of Game by Edward, Second Duke of York*.
Bert, Edmund, *Bert's Treatise of Hawks and Hawking for the First Time Reprinted from the Original of 1619*, Introduction by J.E. Harting (London, 1891).
Cox, Nicholas, *The Gentleman's Recreation: In Four Parts, Viz. Hunting, Hawking, Fowling, Fishing* (London, 1677); facsimile edn (East Ardsley, 1973).
The Craft of Venery, in *The Middle English Text of 'The Art of Hunting' by William Twiti*, ed. David Scott-Macnab, pp. 20–27.
Danielsson, Bror, 'The Percy Poem on Falconry', *Studier i Modern Språkvetenskap*, NS 3 (1970), 5–60.
——, 'The Kerdeston "library of hunting and hawking literature" (early 15th c. fragments)', in *Et Multa et Multum: Beiträge zur Literatur, Geschichte und Kultur der Jagd. Festgabe für Kurt Lindner*, ed. Sigrid Schwenk, Gunnar Tilander and Carl Arnold Willemsen (Berlin, 1971), pp. 47–59.
——, 'The Durham treatise of falconry', *Studier i Modern Språkvetenskap*, NS 4 (1972), 21–37.
de la Buigne, Gace, *Le Roman des deduis*, ed. Åke Blomqvist, Studia Romanica Holmiensia 3 (Karlshamn, 1951).
Edward [Plantagenet], 2nd Duke of York [aka Edward of Norwich], *The Master of Game*, see *The Master of Game by Edward, Second Duke of York*.
Frederick II, Holy Roman Emperor, *The Art of Falconry: Being the 'De arte venandi cum avibus' of Frederick II of Hohenstaufen*, trans. and ed. Casey A. Wood and F. Marjorie Fyfe (Stanford, CA, 1943; repr. 1981).
Gascoigne, George, *The Noble Arte of Venerie or Hunting* (1575); facsimile edn printed as *Turbervile's Booke of Hunting 1576* [*sic*], Tudor & Stuart Library (Oxford, 1908).
A Jewell for Gentrie, see T.S.
Julians Barnes: Boke of Huntyng, ed. Gunnar Tilander, Cynegetica 11 (Karlshamn, 1964).
Leggatt, N.J. Shirley, '*The Book of St. Albans* and the origins of its treatise on hawking', *SN*, 22 (1950), 135–45.
Les livres du roy Modus et de la royne Ratio, ed. A.G. Tilander, 2 vols, SATF (Paris, 1932).

The Master of Game by Edward, Second Duke of York: The Oldest English Book on Hunting, ed. Wm. A. and F. Baillie-Grohman (London, 1904).

McNellis, James I. (III), *The Uncollated Manuscripts of The Master of Game: Towards a New Edition* (unpubl. PhD diss., University of Washington, 1996).

Le menagier de Paris, ed. Georgine E. Brereton and Janet M. Ferrier (Oxford, 1981).

The Middle English Text of 'The Art of Hunting' by William Twiti, ed. David Scott-Macnab, Middle English Texts 40 (Heidelberg, 2009).

Of Hawks and Horses: Four Late Middle English Prose Treatises, ed. W.L. Braekman, Scripta 16 (Brussels, 1986).

The Percy Poem on Falconry, see Danielsson, Bror (1970).

Phébus, Gaston, *Livre de chasse*, ed. Gunnar Tilander, Cynegetica 18 (Karlshamn, 1971).

Swaen, A.E.H., 'The booke of hawkyng after Prince Edwarde Kyng of Englande and its relation to the *Book of St. Albans*', *SN*, 16 (1943–44), 1–32.

Tardif, Guillaume, *Le livre de l'art de faulconnerie e des chiens de chasse* (1492), ed. Ernest Jullien, 2 vols (Paris, 1882).

Three Anglo-Norman Treatises on Falconry, ed. Tony Hunt, Medium Ævum Monographs, NS 26 (Oxford, 2009).

The Tretyse off Huntyng (Cambridge University Library MS L1.1.18, fols. 48r–55v), ed. Anne Rooney, Scripta 19 (Brussels, 1987).

T.S., *A Jewell for Gentrie* (London, 1614); facsimile edn, The English Experience, No. 890 (Amsterdam and Norwood, NJ, 1977).

Turbervile, George, *BH = The Booke of Faulconrie or Hauking* (London, 1575), facsimile edn, The English Experience, No. 93 (Amsterdam and New York, 1969).

Twiti, Guillaume, *L'art de venerie: La vénerie de Twiti: le plus ancien traité de chasse écrit en Angleterre*, ed. Gunnar Tilander, Cynegetica 2 (Uppsala, 1956).

Twiti, William, *The Art of Hunting*: in *The Middle English Text of 'The Art of Hunting' by William Twiti*, ed. David Scott-Macnab, pp. 3–19.

Zettersten, Arne, 'The Lambeth manuscript of the *Boke of Huntyng*', *NM*, 70 (1969), 106–21.

Other Texts and Collections of Texts

Antiquitates Culinariæ, see Warner, Richard (1791).

The Babees Book, ed. Frederick J. Furnivall, EETS OS 32 (London, 1868, repr. 1997).

Bestiary: Being an English Version of the Bodleian Library, Oxford, M.S. Bodley 764, trans. Richard Barber, (Woodbridge, 1993).

Bibbesworth, Walter de, *Le tretiz*, ed. William Rothwell, A-NTS, Plain Texts Series, 6 (London, 1990).

——, 'The Treatise of Walter de Biblesworth', in *A Volume of Vocabularies Illustrating the Condition and Manners of our Forefathers ... From the Tenth Century to the Fifteenth*, ed. Thomas Wright (London, 1857), pp. 142–74.

The Boke of Curtasye (BL, Sloane MS 1986), in *The Babees Book*, ed. F.J. Furnivall, pp. 297–327.

Borde (Boorde), Andrew, *The Breuyary of Helthe* and *A Dyetary of Helth*, in *The First Book of the Introduction of Knowledge made by Andrew Borde*, ed. F.J. Furnivall, EETS, ES 10 (London, 1870).

Calendar of Letter-Books preserved among the Archives of the Corporation of the City of London at the Guildhall: Letter-Book G, circa A.D. 1352–1374, ed. Reginald R. Sharpe (London, 1905).

Caxton, William, *Lyf of Charles the Grete*, ed. Sidney J.H. Herrtage, EETS ES 36, 37 (London, 1880–81).

Chaucer, Geoffrey, *The Riverside Chaucer*, 3rd edn, gen. ed. Larry D. Benson (Oxford, 1990).

The Commodyties of England, see Fortescue, Sir John.

Cotgrave, Randle, *A Dictionarie of the French and English Tongues* (London, 1611; facsimile repr., Menston, 1968).

Curye on Inglysch: English Culinary Manuscripts of the Fourteenth Century, ed. Constance B. Hieatt and Sharon Butler, EETS ss 8 (Oxford, 1985).

An Edition of the Middle English Grammatical Texts, ed. David Thomson (New York and London, 1984).

Femina: Now First Printed from a Unique MS. in the Library of Trinity College, Cambridge, [ed.] William Aldis Wright, The Roxburghe Club (Cambridge, 1909).

Femina (Trinity College, Cambridge MS B.14.40), ed. William Rothwell (Aberystwyth and Swansea, 2005), available online from The Anglo-Norman On-Line Hub <www.anglo-norman.net/texts/femina.pdf>.

Fitzherbert, John, *Booke of Husbandrie* (London, 1598); facsimile edn, The English Experience, No. 926 (Amsterdam and Norwood, NJ, 1979).

[Fitzherbert, John], *Master Fitzherbert's Book of Husbandry, Reprinted from the Edition of 1534*, ed. Walter W. Skeat (London, 1882).

Florio, John, *A Worlde of Wordes, or Most Copious, and Exact Dictionarie in Italian and English* (London, 1598; facsimile edn, Hildesheim, 1972).

[Fortescue, Sir John], *The Commodyties of England*, in *The Works of Sir John Fortescue, Knight*, ed. Thomas (Fortescue) Lord Clermont, 2 vols (London, 1869).

For to Serve a Lord, in *The Babees Book*, ed. F.J. Furnivall, pp. 366–77.

Gerard, John, *The Herball or Generall Historie of Plants* (London, 1597); facsimile edn, The English Experience, No. 660B, 2 vols, (Amsterdam and Norwood, NJ, 1974).

The Hunted Hare, in *Secular Lyrics*, ed. Rossell Hope Robbins, pp. 107–110.

The Hunttyng of the Hare, ed. David Scott-Macnab (q.v.), *Anglia* (2010).

Langland, William, *The Vision of William Concerning Piers the Plowman*, ed. Walter W. Skeat (Oxford, 1886; repr. 1961).

The Laud Troy Book, ed. J. Ernst Wülfing, EETS os 121, 122 (London, 1902–03).

The Libel of English Policy, in *Political Poems and Songs relating to English History, Composed during the Period From the Accession of Edw. III. to that of Ric. III.*, ed. Thomas Wright, 2 vols, Rolls Series (London, 1859–61), II, 157–205.

Malory, Thomas, *Works*, ed. Eugène Vinaver, 2nd edn (Oxford, 1977).

Middle English Metrical Romances, ed. Walter Hoyt French and Charles Brockway Hale, 2 vols (New York, 1964).

Middle English Verse Romances, ed. Donald B. Sands, (Exeter, 1986; repr. 1996).

Napier, Mrs Alexander (Robina), *A Noble Boke off Cookry* (London, 1882).

Nominale sive verbale, ed. Walter W. Skeat, *TPS*, 25:3 (1906), pp. 1*–50*.

An Ordinance of Pottage: An Edition of the Fifteenth Century Culinary Recipes in Yale University's MS Beinecke 163, ed. Constance B. Hieatt, (London, 1988).

Palsgrave, John, *Lesclarcissement de la langue francoyse* (London, 1530): ed. F. Génin, *L'éclaircissement de la langue française par Jean Palsgrave* (Paris, 1852).

The Parlement of the Thre Ages, ed. M.Y. Offord, EETS os 246 (London, 1959; repr. 1967).

Paston Letters and Papers of the Fifteenth Century, ed. Norman Davis, 2 vols (Oxford, 1971–76); Part 3, ed. Richard Beadle and Colin Richmond, EETS ss 22 (Oxford, 2005).

The Political Songs of England, from the Reign of John to that of Edward II, ed. and trans. Thomas Wright, Camden Society, os 6 (London, 1839).

The Promptorium Parvulorum: The First English–Latin Dictionary, ed. A.L. Mayhew, EETS es 102 (London, 1908; repr. 2002).

Promptorium parvulorum sive clericorum: dictionarius anglo-latinus princeps, ed. Albert Way, 3 vols, Camden Society, os 25, 54, 89 (London, 1843, 1853, 1865).

Reliquiæ Antiquæ: Scraps from Ancient Manuscripts, ed. Thomas Wright and James Orchard Halliwell, 2 vols (London, 1841–43).

Russell, John, *The Boke of Nurture*, in *The Babees Book*, ed. F.J. Furnivall, pp. 115–99.

Scott-Macnab, David, '*The Hunttyng of the Hare* in the Heege Manuscript', *Anglia*, 128 (2010), 102–23.

Secular Lyrics = *Secular Lyrics of the XIVth and XVth Centuries*, ed. Rossell Hope Robbins, 2nd edn (Oxford, 1955).

Shakespeare, William, *The Oxford Shakespeare: The Complete Works*, 2nd edn, gen. eds Stanley Wells and Gary Taylor (Oxford, 2005).

Sir Gawain and the Green Knight, ed. J.R.R. Tolkien and E.V. Gordon, 2nd edn, rev. Norman Davis (Oxford, 1967; repr. 1979).

Sir Orfeo, in *Middle English Verse Romances*, ed. Donald B. Sands, pp. 185–200.

The Squire of Low Degree, in *Middle English Metrical Romances*, ed. W.H. French and C.B. Hale, II, 721–55.

Trevisa, John, *On the Properties of Things: John Trevisa's Translation of 'Bartholomæus Anglicus: De Proprietatibus Rerum'*, 3 vols, ed. M.C. Seymour *et al.* (Oxford, 1975–88).

Two Fifteenth-Century Cookery Books: Harleian MS. 279 (ab. 1430), & Harl. MS. 4016 (ab. 1450), with Extracts from Ashmole MS. 1429, Laud MS. 553, & Douce MS. 55, ed. Thomas Austin, EETS os 91 (London, 1888; repr. 1964).

The Vulgate Bible: Douay-Rheims Translation, ed. Swift Edgar and Angela M. Kinney, 6 vols, Dumbarton Oaks Medieval Library (Cambridge, MA, 2010–13).

Warner, Richard, *Antiquitates Culinariæ, or Curious Tracts relating to Culinary Affairs of the Old English* (London, 1791; repr. London, 1981).

White, T.H., *The Book of Beasts* (London, 1954).

Wright, Thomas, *Anglo-Saxon and Old English Vocabularies*, 2nd edn, rev. Richard Paul Wülcker, 2 vols (London, 1884).

Studies

Ap Evans, Humphrey, *Falconry for You* (London, 1960).

Bator, Magdalena, *Culinary Verbs in Middle English*, Studies in English Medieval Language and Literature, 46 (Frankfurt-am-Main, 2014).

Bennett, H.S., *Life on the English Manor: A Study of Peasant Conditions 1150–1400* (Cambridge, 1960).

Blades, William, *The Life and Typography of William Caxton, England's First Printer*, 2 vols (London, 1861–63); rev. and reissued as one volume: *The Biography and Typography of William Caxton* (London, 1877; repr. Totowa, NJ, 1971).

Boffey, Julia and John J. Thompson, 'Anthologies and miscellanies: production and choice of texts', in *Book Production and Publishing in Britain 1375–1475*, ed. Jeremy Griffiths and Derek Pearsall (Cambridge, 1989), pp. 279–315.

Childs, Wendy R., *Anglo-Castilian Trade in the Later Middle Ages* (Manchester, 1978).

Fifteenth-Century Attitudes: Perceptions of Society in Late Medieval England, ed. Rosemary Horrox, (Cambridge, 1994).

Francis, A.D., *The Wine Trade* (London, 1972).

Gillespie, Alexandra, 'Caxton's Chaucer and Lydgate quartos: miscellanies from manuscript to print', *TCBS*, 12 (2000), 1–25.

Guddat-Figge, Gisela, *Catalogue of Manuscripts Containing Middle English Romances* (Munich, 1976).

Hands, Rachel, 'Juliana Berners and *The Boke of St. Albans*', *RES*, NS 18 (1967), 373–86.

Hands, Rachel, 'The names of all manner of hawks, and to whom they belong', *N&Q*, NS 18 (1971), 85–8.

Hardman, Philippa, 'A mediaeval "library in parvo"', *MÆ*, 47 (1978), 262–73.

Harting, James Edmund, *Bibliotheca Accipitraria* (London, 1891, repr. 1964).

Heidenreich, Manfred, *Birds of Prey: Medicine and Management*, trans. Dr Yvonne Oppenheim (Oxford, 1997).

Hohnerlein-Buchinger, Thomas, *Per un sublessico vitivinicolo: La storia materiale e linguistica di alcuni nomi di viti e vini italiani* (Tübingen, 1996).

Huws, Daniel, 'MS Porkington 10 and its scribes', in *Romance Reading and the Book: Essays on Medieval Narrative Presented to Maldwyn Mills*, ed. Jennifer Fellows, Rosalind Field et al. (Cardiff, 1996), pp. 188–207.

James, Margery Kirkbride, *Studies in the Medieval Wine Trade*, ed. Elspeth M. Veale (Oxford, 1971).

Keiser, George R., 'Practical books for the gentleman', in *The Cambridge History of the Book in Britain: Volume III, 1400–1557*, ed. Lotte Hellinga and J.B. Trapp (Cambridge, 1999), pp. 470–94.

Lachiver, Marcel, *Vins, vignes et vignerons: histoire du vignoble français* (Paris, 1988).

Lockwood, W.B., *The Oxford Book of British Bird Names* (Oxford, 1984).

McLaren, Mary-Rose, *The London Chronicles of the Fifteenth Century: A Revolution in English Writing* (Cambridge, 2002).

Rigg, A.G., *A Glastonbury Miscellany of the Fifteenth Century: A Descriptive Index of Trinity College, Cambridge, MS. O.9.38* (Oxford, 1968); reviewed by Rossell Hope Robbins, *Anglia*, 89 (1971), 140–3.

Scott-Macnab, David, 'A re-examination of Octovyen's hunt in *The Book of the Duchess*', *MÆ*, 56 (1987), 183–99.

———, 'Burlesque romance and the bourgeoisie', in *Noble and Joyous Histories: English Romances, 1375–1650*, ed. Eileán Ní Cuilleanáin and J.D. Pheifer (Dublin, 1993), pp. 113–35.

———, 'Hawking information in the Tollemache *Book of Secrets*, *N&Q*, 51 (2004), 348–50.

———, 'Caxton's Printings of *The Hors, the Shepe and the Ghoos*: Some Further Considerations', *TCBS*, 13 (2004), 1–13.

———, '*The Names of all Manner of Hounds*: A Unique Inventory in a Fifteenth-Century Manuscript', *Viator*, 44 (2013), 339–68.

———, 'Middle English *counter-riuere*', *Anglia*, 134 (2016), 604–16.

———, '*A Hors shulde haue ... a dry hede*', *N&Q*, 64 (2017), 22–24.

Simon, André L., *The History of the Wine Trade in England*, 3 vols (London, 1964).

Thomson, David, *A Descriptive Catalogue of Middle English Grammatical Texts* (New York and London, 1979).

Tilander, A.G., *Glanures lexicographiques*, Skrifter utgivna av Kungl. Humanistika Vetenskapssamfundet i Lund (Acta Regiae Societas Humaniorum Litterarum Ludensis), 16 (Lund, 1932).

Unwin, Tim, *Wine and the Vine: An Historical Geography of Viticulture and the Wine Trade* (London and New York, 1991).

Woodford, M.H., *A Manual of Falconry*, 4th edn, updated by Roger Upton (London, 1987).

Yalden, Derek, *The History of British Mammals* (London, 1999).

Modern Reference Works

Anglo-Norman Dictionary, ed. William Rothwell, Louise W. Stone, T.B.W. Reid et al. (London, 1992); rev. 3rd edn online at <www.anglo-norman.net/>.

Boffey, Julia and A.S.G. Edwards, *A New Index of Middle English Verse* (London, 2005).

Catalogue of the Harleian Manuscripts in the British Museum, 4 vols (London, 1808–1812).

The Dictionary of National Biography: From the Earliest Times to 1900, ed. Sir Leslie Stephen and Sir Sidney Lee, 22 vols (London, 1917).

Dictionnaire du Moyen Français (1330–1500); consulted online at <http://www.atilf.fr/dmf>.

Duff, E. Gordon, *Fifteenth Century English Books: A Bibliography of Books and Documents Printed in England and of Books for the English Market Printed Abroad* (Oxford, 1917).

Französisches etymologisches Wörterbuch, see von Wartburg, Walter.

Godefroy, F., *Dictionnaire de l'ancienne langue française du IXe au XVe siècle*, 10 vols (Paris, 1881–1902).

Graesse (Grässe), Johann Georg Theodor, *Orbis Latinus: Lexicon lateinischer geographischer Namen des Mittelalters und der Neuzeit*, rev. by Friedrich Benedict, Helmut Plechl and Sophie Charlotte Plechl, 3 vols (Braunschweig, 1972).

A Manual of the Writings in Middle English 1050–1500, gen. ed. Albert E. Hartung (New Haven, CT, 1967–).

Incunabula Short Title Catalogue (ISTC): available online at <http://istc.bl.uk>.

Index of Middle English Verse = (1) Carleton Brown and Rossell Hope Robbins, *The Index of Middle English Verse* (New York, 1943); (2) Rossell Hope Robbins and J. Cutler, *Supplement to the Index of Middle English Verse* (Lexington, 1965).

Jamieson, John, *Dictionary of the Scottish Tongue* (1808), abridged by John Johnston, rev. by John Longmuir (Edinburgh, 1867).

Keiser, George R., *Manual X = Works of Science and Information*, Volume 10 of *A Manual of the Writings in Middle English 1050–1500*, gen. ed. Albert E. Hartung (New Haven, CT, 1998).

Ker, N.R. *et al.*, *Medieval Manuscripts in British Libraries*, 5 vols (Oxford, 1969–2002).

Latham, R.E., *Revised Medieval Latin Word-List from British and Irish Sources, with Supplement* (London, 1980; repr. 2008).

Lewis, R.E, N.F. Blake and A.S.G. Edwards, *Index of Printed Middle English Prose* (New York and London, 1985).

McIntosh, Angus, M.L. Samuels and Michael Benskin, *A Linguistic Atlas of Late Mediæval English*, 4 vols (Aberdeen, 1986); also available online as eLALME: <http://lel.ed.ac.uk/ihd/elalme/elalme.html>.

Middle English Dictionary, ed. Hans Kurath, Sherman M. Kuhn *et al.*, (Ann Arbor, 1952–2001); also online via the Middle English Compendium portal: <https://quod.lib.umich.edu/m/middle-english-dictionary/>.

Oxford English Dictionary, 3rd edn, online at <www.oed.com>.

Oxford Dictionary of National Biography: From the Earliest Times to the Year 2000, ed. H.C.G. Matthew and Brian Harrison, 60 vols (Oxford, 2004); available online at <www.oxforddnb.com>.

The Oxford Dictionary of English Etymology, ed. C.T. Onions, G.W.S. Friedrichsen and R.W. Burchfield (Oxford, 1969).

Pollard, A.W. and G.R. Redgrave, *A Short-Title Catalogue of Books Printed in England, Scotland and Ireland 1475–1640*, 2nd edn, rev. by W.A. Jackson, F.S. Ferguson and Katharine F. Pantzer, 3 vols (London, 1976–91).

Le Robert: Dictionnaire historique de la langue française, ed. Alain Rey, 2 vols (Paris, 1992).

Schwerdt, C.F.G.R., *Hunting, Hawking, Shooting, Illustrated in a Catalogue of Books, Manuscripts, Prints and Drawings*, 4 vols (London, 1928–37).

Summary Catalogue of Western Manuscripts in the Bodleian Library at Oxford, ed. R.W. Hunt *et al.*, 7 vols (Oxford, 1895–1953).

Tobler, Adolf and Erhard Lommatzsch, *Altfranzösisches Wörterbuch*: *Adolf Toblers nachgelassene Materialien*, ed. Erhard Lommatzsch, continued by Hans Helmut Christmann (Berlin, 1925–).

Upton, Clive, David Parry and J.D.A. Widdowson, *Survey of English Dialects: The Dictionary and Grammar* (London and New York, 1994).

von Wartburg, Walter, *Französisches etymologisches Wörterbuch: eine Darstellung des galloromanischen Sprachschatzes* (Tübingen, 1948–); also online via the atilf portal: <apps.atilf.fr/lecteurFEW/>.

Whiting, Bartlett Jere, with Helen Wescott Whiting, *Proverbs, Sentences and Proverbial Phrases from English Writings Mainly before 1500* (Cambridge, MA, 1968).

The *J.B. Treatise*

PART I
BROGYNTYN MS ii.1 (Prk)

Contents	Collated with
Collective nouns	Pl
Precepts in -*ly*	Pl
Resting terms	Pl
Carving terms	Pl
Four things to dread	Pl
Properties of a good horse	Pl
Beasts of venery and the chase	Dg, Rg
Breeds of dogs	Dg, Rg
Soiling terms	Dg, Rg
Hierarchy of hawks	Dg, Rg
Ages of a hawk	Dg
Hawks' diseases and remedies	Dg

[COLLECTIVE NOUNS]

A herd of harttus   f. 184r
A herd of all ma*nn*ere dere
A herd of wrennys
A herd of swannys
A herd of cra*n*nys   5

¶ A ny of feysandys | f. 184v
¶ A covey of parttrygys
A bevy of rossys
A bevy of ladys
A bevy of quayllys   10

¶ A cegee of betterys
A cege of herronns
A spryng of teyllys
A sort of mallarttus
A dyssayt of lappwyn*n*gys   15

¶ A mosture of peycokys
A faulle of wodcokys
A walke of snyttys
A co*n*ngregacone of plouerys
A cowert of cottys   20

¶ A nost of mene
A hoste of sparrovs | f. 185r
A feyllyschype of yovmeyne

A swarme of byne
A chyrme of goldfynchys   25

¶ A wnkyndnys of rawynnys
A byldynge of rookys
A morthere of crowys
A clatteryng of chov3this
A mormeracyone of staris   30

¶ A exsalttynge of larkys
A pyttyvsnys of turtyllys
A wache of ny3ttyn*n*galys
A mutacyone of þrestyllys
A typingys of pyis   35

¶ A cete of grayis
An erthe of foxis
A byrre of connys | f. 185v
A nest of rabettys
A lyttere of whelpus   40

A route of kny3ttys
A rovte of woluys
A pryd of lyonnys
A lcpc of leberttys
A slothe of bayris   45

[*1–45 collated with Pl*]
1 A ... harttus] *phrase lost, leaf damaged* Pl   2 ma*nn*ere] *om* Pl   8–9] *transposed* Pl
11 betterys] byttorys Pl   14 mallarttus] mawlardeys Pl   16 mosture] mowster Pl
17 wodcokys] wodcokekys Pl   22 sparrovs] sparowys Pl   23 yovmeyne] yemen Pl
24 of] *add* go canc MS; byne] been Pl   26 wnkyndnys] vnkyndenys Pl   29 chov3this]
chow3eys Pl   35 typingys] tydyngys Pl   37 An ... foxis] *phrase lost, leaf damaged* Pl
38 byrre] bere Pl   40 lyttere] letur Pl   41 kny3ttys] knghtty‹s› (*hole in leaf*) Pl
42 woluys] wolleuys Pl   45 bayris] berys Pl

A harres of horssys
A stode of marys
A rage of colttys
A pase of assys
A barrene of mullys 50

A syngelare of borys
A sondyre of wyld swyne
A dryfte of tame swyne
A clovdyre of tame cattys | f. 186r
A dovt of wyld cattys 55

A leys of grayhoundys
A brace of hovndys
A kennel of racchys
A covpul of spannelis
A sawt of a lyone 60

A pontyfycalle of prelettus
A stat of prynsys
A dyngnete of chennans
A trothe of barrovns
A charge of curattys 65

A bomynabul sy3te of movnkys
A supereflovite of nonnys
A preys of preysttys
A skoue of fyche
A skole of clarkys 70

| A cast of bred   f. 186v
A cast of havkys of þe toure
A fly3t of goshavkys
A fly3t of cormmeravnttys
A fly3t of dowys 75

A centtans of iugys
A ellequens of laweris
A damnynge of iurrears
A good-awyse of borges
A fayth of marchandys 80

A drovfe of neyte
A trype of gayte
A floke of schepe
A gagulle of gyse
A gagulle of wemene 85

A clvsture of grappus
| A clostyr of nottys   f. 187r
A clostyr of chourllys
A triete of covrtears
A bost of sovdears 90

A skolke of freris
A skolke of thewys
A skolke of foxys
A rafulle of cnavys
A rafulle of baeyis 95

[continued overleaf]

[46–95 collated with Pl]
46 horssys] hors Pl 54 clovdyre] clowder Pl 55 dovt] dowte Pl 60 sawt] sowte Pl; lyone] lyonen Pl 63 dyngnete] dyngyyte Pl 66 movnkys] monnkys (kys *super*) Pl 67 supereflovite] superfluete Pl 68 preys] pres Pl; preysttys] pres⟨t⟩ys Pl 71–5 A cast ... dowys] *transposed with next five phrases* Pl 74 cormmeravnttys] cavmerawntys Pl 78–80 A ... marchandys] *lost, leaf damaged* Pl 79 good-awyse] goodawyse MS 81 drovfe] drove Pl; neyte] nete Pl 82 gayte] gete Pl 84 gyse] gesse Pl 85 wemene] wmen Pl 86 clvsture] clowster Pl; grappus] *add catchwords* A Clustyr of nottys MS 89 triete] i *super* MS, thret Pl 90 sovdears] sawdyarys Pl 92 thewys] thevys Pl 95 baeyis] e *super* MS, boyys Pl

A tharfe of þreysschars
           A lache of carttars
           A squat of davberis
           A neuertreyuyng of iovghelars
100   A powertte of harppers
           A mallapertnys of pedlers
           A lying of pardnars

           A lavȝttyre of hostelers
           A prommes of tappestrs
105   A skoldynge of kemmyssteris
           A fyȝttynge of beggars
f. 187v | A dysworschype of stottys

                    [PRECEPTS IN -LY]

           ¶ Aryse erlly,
           And serve god dewoutly;
110   Go by þe way sadly,
           Answsere þe peppull demurely,
           Go to þy mete appetently,
           And to þi soppere soborly,
           And arys temparatly,
115   And to þi bede meryly,
           And be þerin iocondlye,
           And slepe sovrly.

[*96–117 collated with Pl*]
96 tharfe] thrave Pl;   þreysschars] thrachearys Pl   101–2 A mallapertnys ... pardnars] *om* Pl   103 lavȝttyre] lawȝeterys Pl   105 kemmyssteris] kemstarys Pl   108 Aryse] A Ryse MS   109 And] *om* Pl;   dewoutly] de woutly MS   111 Answsere ... demurely] *lost, leaf damaged* Pl;   demurely] de murely MS   112 þy] þe Pl;   appetently] apyte⟨...⟩ (*leaf damaged*) Pl   113–4] *transposed* Pl   113 And] *om* Pl   114 And] *om* Pl;   temparatly] temperally Pl   115 And] *om* Pl   116 And] *om* Pl;   þerin] þer in MS   117 sovrly] sewrely Pl

[RESTING TERMS]

      A hart harborowth,
      A kny3t herborovthe;
120 A boke logythe,
      A squyer*e* logythe;
      A roo beddyte,
      A yoman beyddyte;
      A har*e* in her*e* forme schold*er*ynge or*e* leynnyng;
125 A connye syttynge;
      A trype of harrys;
      A trase of harrys.

[CARVING TERMS]

f. 188r | A der*e* brovkyne
      A gose reyryde
130 A cappon*e* sawsyd
      A swane i-lyfte
      A herne dysme*m*myrde
      A peycoke dyswygurte
      A corllowe vngynttyte
135 A bytter*e* vntachyd
      A fayssant i-illyde
      A mallard vnbrassyde
      A conny vnlassyde
      A pygyne i-thyide
140 A quaylle i-thyide
      And alle smalle brydys

                                             [*continued overleaf*]

[*118–141 collated with Pl*]
122 beddyte] bedythe Pl   123 beyddyte] bedythe Pl   124 here] hys Pl; scholderynge] schol|deryng, deryng *repeated super* Pl   ore] *om* Pl   127 A trase of harrys] A trasse of a hare Pl   128 brovkyne] y broken Pl   129 reyryde] y reryde Pl   130–1] *transposed* Pl   132 herne] heron Pl   133 dyswygurte] dysvygoryd Pl   134 vngynttyte] vn gynttyte MS, vn ioyneteyd Pl   135 vntachyd] vn tachyd MS   136 i-illyde] y ellyde Pl   137 vnbrassyde] vn brassyde MS   138 vnlassyde] vn lassyde MS

A pyge heddyte and sydyte
A lame scholdyrt
A hene i-spyllyde
145   A chekyne i-frosschyde

A lamppray cordyt in gallantye
A gret heyle callyd a rostere or ellys a spychecoke
And all ellys small in sorraye
f. 188v   A samon i-chynyd |
150   A pyke i-splate
A carpe i-tronchnide
A trout i-gobenyd
A cheyuen fynnyde
A perche and a roche i-schallyd
155   A tenche in iolly
A plays i-savssyd

[FOUR THINGS TO DREAD]

There ys iiij þingys þat euery wyis man [ow3te] to drede:
þat is vonne [þe curs] of oure holly fadyre þe poppe; þe
sekonde ys þe indyngnacyone of a prynce; þe þred is þe
160   euyle wylle odyre þe fawyr of a iuge; þe fowrthe ys þe
mutacyone or a schlandure of a commente.

[*142–161 collated with Pl*]
144 i-spyllyde] spoylyde Pl   145 frosschyde] frocheyd Pl   146 A lamppray ... gallantye] *lost, leaf damaged* Pl   147 A gret heyle] *lost, leaf damaged* Pl;   or] other Pl;   spychecoke] spyche coke MS   148 And all ellys small in sorraye] A alle oþer ellys y calyde e‹lly›s *(hole in leaf)* yn sorrey Pl   149 i-chynyd] chynyde Pl   150 i-splate] y splyte Pl   151 i-tronchnide] trownsonnyd Pl   152 i-gobenyd] gobbonde Pl   153 fynnyde] y vynyde Pl   154 i-schallyd] scalyd Pl   155 iolly] iele Pl   157 iiij þingys] iiij maner of thynge Pl;   wyis] i *super* MS;   ow3te] *om* MS, *sic* Pl   158 þe curs] *om* MS, *sic* Pl   159 a prynce] aprise Pl   161 or] & Pl;   schlandure] schalndure MS; sclawnder Pl

[PROPERTIES OF A GOOD HORSE]

There longithe to a good hors xv ma*nn*ere of condycyons; þ*at* is, iij of a man*e*, iij of a woma*n*, iij of [a] har*e*, iij of a foxe, iij of a na⟨s⟩. Þe iij of a man*e* ys to be provd & hardy
165   and bold; þe iij of a woma*n* ys to have a fayr*e* brest, a fayr*e*
f. 189r tra⟨s⟩ and essye to leppe on*e*; þe iij of a | har*e* ys to have a leyne hede and gret ʒeyin and þ*er*[with] wel rennyng away; þe iij of a fox ys to have a fayr*e* tayle, schort heyris and þ*erw*ith a good trote; þe iij of a nas ys to have a byege
170   chyne, a flat lege and þ*erw*ith a good hoffe.

[BEASTS OF VENERY AND THE CHASE]

¶ Ther*e* byne iiij beystys of ve*n*nery: þe hert, þe har*e*, þe wolfe and þe wyld bor*e*. Of venery þ*er* byne no moo. Ther*e* byne beyst*ys* of chace of þe swete foote and allsoo of þe stynkynge fut. Þis byne of þe swete fut: the boke,
175   þe doo, þe roo-boke and þe roo-doo, the ber*e*, þe rayndeer*e*, þe elke (þ*at* is t⟨o⟩ s⟨a⟩y, a hart of ij wyntur*e* age), þe sp⟨y⟩carde (þat is to say, a hart of iij wynture aage). And þis byne þe best*ys* of þe stynkynge fute: the folmard, þe

---

[*162–170 collated with Pl*]
162 longithe] langhe Pl   163 a woman] awman Pl   163–4 a foxe] afoxys Pl; 164 na⟨s⟩] *binding* MS   164–5 provd ... bold] prewde bold & hardy Pl   165 woman] wman Pl;   a fayre] affayres Pl;   166 tra⟨s⟩] *binding* MS;   one] apen Pl   167 and gret ʒeyin] a gret yyn Pl;   þerwith] *om* Pl   away] a way MS   168–170 tayle ... chyne a] *lost, leaf damaged* Pl   169 þerwith] þer with MS;   byege] e *super* MS   170 þerwith] þer with MS, *om* Pl

[*171–178 and 179–181 (overleaf) collated with Dg, Rg*]
171 byne iiij] beth fowre Rg;   vennery] fenery Rg   172 bore] baore (o *super*) Dg   venery] fenery Rg;   byne] be Dg, beth Rg   173 byne] be Dg, beth Rg   173–4 of þe swete ... swete fut] *om* Rg   174 boke] bukke Dg, bugke Rg, *add* & Rg   175 roo-boke] robugke Rg;   bere] *add* & Dg,Rg;   rayndeere] rayn deere MS   176 elke] heelke Dg, helke Rg;   t⟨o⟩ s⟨a⟩y] *large stain* MS;   ij wynture age] ij*e* (*add* C *del* Dg) wynter of age Dg,Rg;   age] *add* And Dg   177 sp⟨y⟩carde] *large stain* MS;   iij wynture] iij*e* wynter Dg,Rg   177–8 And ... fute] *om* Rg   178 þis] ther Dg;   þe bestes] *om* Dg

fechowe, þe bade (þat is to say a ca⟨t⟩e of þe movnttayne)
180   þe gray, þe foxe, þe wessole, þe mertrone, þe squerelle, þe
      otture, þe stote and þe polcate.

[BREEDS OF DOGS]

f. 189v   ¶ There bythe grayhoundys, basterdys, | mongrellys and
           mastyffys; and [a]lanndys, lymmorous, spannellys and
           rachys; kennettys, terryars, bochere hovndis & dovnghyll
185   currys; and smalle poppys for ladys chambureys.

Allondys bythe cast of, lemors drawith, kennettys
rennyt[h]e, spannyellys reytornnyth, teeryovrs vndure
þe grond fechyng þe fox or þe graye.

[SOILING TERMS]

      ¶ A hont hathe i-cast a covppull of alonndys to a herd
190   of harttys;
      he blowith comfortynge his hovnndys;
      þe alonndys chassythe þe herte oute of þe herde;
      þe hert takythe þe watter, þane he swllyt⟨h⟩;
      when he swymmythe dovne, he flettythe;
195   when he swymmythe vpe aȝey⟨nst⟩ þe watter, he
          breykythe or beyttyþ;

---

179 ca⟨t⟩e] *smudge* MS   181 otture] othe, *add* otere *in margin in diff. hand* Rg;   þe stote] *om* Rg
[*182–196 and 197–200 (opposite) collated with* Dg, Rg]
182 bythe] ben Dg   grayhoundys] *add* & Dg, and Rg   mongrellys and] mangreynnes & Dg, mene Rg   183 and¹] *om* Dg,Rg   alanndys] lanndys MS; *add* & Dg,Rg
184 kennettys] *add* & Dg, and Rg   bochere] bocheres Dg   185 ladys] lady Rg
186 bythe] ben Dg   lemors] *add* lymov *canc* Dg   187 rennythe] rennyte MS, rennethe Dg, rennyth Rg   188 grond] growne Rg;   fechyng] sessyn Dg, sesyn Rg   or] & Dg, and Rg   189 i-cast] cast of Dg,Rg   a herd] and herde Rg   191–2] *transposed* Dg
191] *add ante* ?þe *canc* Dg   192] *om* Rg   chassythe] chese Dg   193] *add* ?& þan (*obscured by overwriting*) Dg   swllyt⟨h⟩] *binding* MS, swyles Dg, sweylys Rg
194 swymmythe] *olim* svymmythe MS   dovne] *add* þan Dg   flettythe] fleyth Rg
195 aȝey⟨nst⟩] *large stain on MS*, ayens Rg   196 breykythe] brekyt Rg

when he swymmythe ouer, he crossythe;
when he [reytornnythe, he] reycrossythe;
when he [takythe] þe maynelond, he flyth;
200   a favcone flyith.

[HIERARCHY OF HAWKS]

¶ There longythe iij havkys to a emparovre: a neygule, a
watter and a mellannd. Þe sympul|lyst of thes wyll sleye
a hynd calfe or a dooys favne, a roo-doo or an elke, a crane,
a bustterd, a storke, a foxe in a playne grovnd. And þis
205   bene note enlurryd nodyre reycleymyd; the cavs why,
þey be soo pondors but to þe perche portatyfe: there-to
þey byne gouernyd.

These havkys byyne of þe tovre:
A garfavkone and a tarsselet garfavkone for a kynge,
210   A favkone ientyl & a tarselet ientylle for a pryns,
A favkone of þe roche for a duke,
A favkone perygryne for a norle,
A basterd for euyrey lord,
A sakore & a sakorret for a kny3te,
215   A lannyr and a lanneret for a squyer,

197 ouer] add ?þanrth MS; om Dg,Rg   198 reytornnythe he] returnethe/returnyth he Dg,Rg   reytornnythe canc MS, he om MS   199 takythe] taketh/takyth Dg,Rg, canc MS;   maynelond] meenlond Rg;   flyth] fly3þe Dg, fleyth Rg; add A hert [fr canc] fly3þe Dg, A hert fleyth Rg   200 flyith] fly3þe Dg, fleyth Rg

[201–215 collated with Dg, Rg]
201 a neygule] a egel Dg, & egle Rg   202 watter] vature Dg, nature Rg   203 hynd] hyndes Dg, hyndys Rg   or¹] om Dg,Rg   dooys] doo ys MS,Rg, doys Dg   or²] om Dg,Rg   elke] necke Rg   204 bustterd] add s canc Dg   in a playne grovnd] om Rg, om a Dg   205 bene] be Dg, byth Rg   note] nowth Rg   the cavs] be cavse Dg   206 be] byth Rg   soo] add provd canc MS   pondors] pondorose Dg, ponderos Rg   perche] om Rg   portatyfe] pertetyue Rg   207 byne] be Dg, beth Rg   208 These] There MS   These havkys byyne] Ther be hawkes Dg, There buth haukes Rg   þe] om Dg   209 and] om Rg   tarsselet] add a MS   211 roche] rocke Dg   212 a norle] a erle Dg, an erle Rg   213 euyrey] eny Dg   214 & a] add sacr canc Dg   kny3te] kyny3the (n super) Dg   215 a³] om Rg

A marlyone for a lady,
An hobby for a yovnge squyere;
This byn⟨e⟩ havkys of þe toure þat fleythe [fro] þe lure.

There [is] a goshavke for a povre genttylmane,
220　A tersell for a good yomane,
A sparhavke for a pryste,
f. 190v　A musket for a hallywatter | clarke.
Þey byne of anodyr kynde: thay flye to wyue, to þe quarraye and to þe fare iuttye.

[AGES OF A HAWK]

225　Furst an havke ys callyd a nyes, a bowere, a branchere,
a rammage havke, a ventteremuere, a mard-haye, an hagarde.
Allso a havke his cleypyd a partrygere, a faysanddare,
a gellonder, a nanauer, a byttonnere, an herrovnneer.

[HAWKS' DISEASES AND REMEDIES]

¶ An havke hathe in þe hede þe ree, þe frounse; þe pokys
230　& þe mytys abovt þe ȝeye lyddys; & in þe cheste, þe
fyllavndyrs and þe aglys; in þe brayle, þe pere and þe

[*216–224 collated with Dg, Rg*]
217 hobby] hobe Rg　a] *om* Rg　218 byne] e *smudged* MS, be Dg, beth Rg　fro] ?frove MS, for Dg, fro Rg　219 is] *om* MS, ys Dg,Rg　a¹] *om* Rg　for] for for Rg　genttylmane] man Rg　220 tersell] thercel Dg　good] *om* Rg　223 byne] be Dg, buth Rg　thay ... wyue] thay wyue to flye MS, þey fle to (vywe *canc*) vewe (*super*) Dg, thes fleyth to vywe Rg　224 fare iuttye] furre getey Dg, fur ioty Rg
[*225–231 collated with Dg*]
225 a nyes] a yesse Dg　226 mard haye] merdehay Dg　227 faysanddare] fesaunter Dg　228 gellonder] genoner Dg　nanauer] naneuer Dg　byttonnere] butorer Dg, *add* & Dg　herrovnneer] hayrenner Dg　229] *add ante* Also Dg　hede] *add* these sekenes Dg　frounse] frovse Dg　230 abovt] a bovt MS　lyddys] *add* & þe fyllavndyrs *canc* MS　&²] *om* Dg

craye; in þe wyngys and þe legys and þe fete: þe pyne,
þe polione, þe crampe and þe pyes.

235   For þe ree. Take daysys and rawe honne and stampe heme
togaydure, and pute hit in þe havkys palleys.

f. 191r   Anodyre for þe same. Take staffwysavkyre & make a
povdyre þerof & temppure | hit with wyne and swet
mylke and put hit in þe forsayd matter.

240   ¶ For þe frovns. Cast þe havke and pyke ovte þe frovns
with ane hassylle wand; and weche þe forsayd place with
wynegure. & povdore þe same place with leyne marttylmas
byfe mad in povdyr, oþer with povdore of sandragone.

For þe poxe and þe myttys & alle odyre wermyn. Take þe
povdyre [of] orpamente.

245   ¶ For þe fyllavndyrs. Take þe iuse of sovthornwood &
weche þerwith here mete, or ellys in marys mylke; &
ȝeyte vus yovre havke to doubbe his mete in safrovne.

For þe aglys. Take þe gale of a rede coke, reyservynge a
part of þe leuyre, and ȝeyfe hit þe havke to ete.

250   ¶ For þe pere. Take oke pollypodyi and saxfrage &
parslye rottys, and sethe heme in fayre reynnynge watter,
f. 191v   and weche | his mete þerin.

[232–252 collated with Dg]
232 and¹] om Dg   þe²] add legys canc MS   234 stampe] scrape Dg   235 togaydure] to gaydure MS, to gedir Dg   236 Anodyre] A nodyre MS   staffwysavkyre] stavesacre Dg   a] om Dg   237 þerof] þer of MS,Dg   238 forsayd] for sayd MS   240 wand] styke Dg   forsayd] for sayd MS   with] add w canc Dg   241 wynegure] vynecreke Dg   241-2 leyne ... povdyr] powder made of leene of martylmasse beeffe Dg   242 oþer] or Dg   sandragone] sawnddragone Dg   243 poxe] pockes Dg   and] om Dg   244 of] om MS, sic Dg   246 þerwith] þer with MS, þer wythe Dg   in] with Dg   247 vus] vse Dg   248 þe¹] super MS;   of] of of MS   250 saxfrage] saxifrage Dg   251 parslye] percoly Dg   252 his] her Dg   þerin] þer in MS, þerwith Dg

For þe craye. Take þe glayre of a nnegge and weche þerin here mete.

255 ¶ For þe pellyone. Tak a pote lyde vssyde, and heyte hite, and þerwith an[o]ynt here fete.

¶ For þe pyne. Take a lyttyll bagge of salte & bynd hit one þe perche where schoe schalle iouke.

For þe crampe. Take a hanffulle of chyuerys and stampe
260 heme; & with þe iuse thereof weche here hoot þerin tryse.

For þe pyis þat sodenlye wylle froo yow dye. Take maydynewort and isope [and] lawandere, and ordenne iij or iiij stonnys and putt heme in þe fyere tyle þay be rede hoot. And þene put þe erbbys and þe stonnys in a pane,
265 and sete þe havke one a lowe perche þat þe flawyre and þe wappure maye smyte into here hede.

¶ A genneralle medsone. Take butter of a covee of voone blee & take safforoune and sugure and medylle heme
f. 192r togedure. | And put hit in a boxe, and ȝeyfe youre havke
270 a bechynge [þerof] in þe mornnynge and in þe euenynge.

Et Cetera

[253–271 collated with Dg]
253 a nnegge] annegge MS   þerin] þer in MS   255 pellyone] polyon Dg   256 þerwith] þer with MS   anoynt] anynt MS, anoynte Dg   257 bagge] bagege MS, bagge Dg   259 hanffulle] handful Dg   chyuerys] clyveres Dg   260 heme] yt Dg;   thereof] there of MS;   weche] whaysche Dg;   þerin] þer in MS;   tryse] thryes Dg   262 maydynewort] maydyne wort MS;   and¹] om Dg;   and²] om MS,Dg   263 þe] add fvyre canc Dg;   be] ben Dg   264 And¹] om Dg;   þan put þe herbes] twice, first canc Dg   þe²] om Dg   265 flawyre] flauour Dg   265–6 and þe wappure maye] om Dg   266 smyte] add vppe Dg   into] in to MS   267–8 of a covee of voone blee] of oo ble cowe Dg   268 and¹] om Dg   269 togedure] to gedure MS   hit] hem Dg   270 þerof] om MS, sic Dg   in þe²] at Dg   271] om Dg

PART II
HARLEY MS 2340 (H)

Contents	**Collated with**
Hawks' diseases and remedies	L
Choosing a hawk	L
Ages of a hawk	L
A hawk's foot and feathers	L
Flying terms	L
Hierarchy of hawks	L
Beasts of venery and the chase	L, Pp
Soiling terms	—
Resting terms	L
Collective nouns	L

[HAWKS' DISEASES AND REMEDIES]

For þe ree of an hawke.

f. 47r

Take þe iusse of daysys and hony & put it in þe palat of þe hawkis mowthe & stope þe hole of þe rofe of þe mowþe. Or ellys take þe powdir of staffisakyr w*ith* .iij. dropys of
5 whyth Rocell wyne or ellys fayr*e* watyr.

For þe frownce in þe mowþe & in þe throte of an hawke lyke to a scall.

Take a lytyll clowte of lynen cloþe & bynd it to a hesyll styke & wete it in vynegir & wach it well þ*er*with. Or
10 powdyr it w*ith* þe powdir of sandragon, or w*ith* þe powdir made of martymes befe brent apon a tyle-ston to powdyr, & do it to þ*a*t place.

For all man*er* of vermen.

Powdir þi hawke w*ith* orpyment.

15 ### For þe filawndyrs.

3e schall ken it be þe gapyng. Wach þan þi hawkys mete w*ith* maris mylke or w*ith* þe iusse of sothyrnewode & gyfe hyr mych saforne i*n* hir mete.

For þe akyllys i*n* þe hawkis bake þat ben wormys.

20 3e schall knowe whan sche scremyth sodenly heryng no chyrmyng of no byrde. Take þe leuyr of a rede koke & þe gall hangyng þ*er*apon & late hyr hete it at onys fyrst i*n* þe mornyng for a bechyng, sche fastyng aftyr þ*a*t an owr*e*.

[1–23 collated with L]
1] For ... hawke] *om* L, *add* For a sperhauke L   2 palat] pallet L   3 rofe of þe] *om* L   4 Or] Other L;   staffisakyr] stafficare L   5 Rocell] Rochell L;   ellys] *om* L   6–18 For ... mete] *om* L   9 þerwith] þer with MS   11 apon] a pon MS   19 wormys] *add* C .lxiij L   20 scremyth] scrilleth L;   sodenly] *add* hafeyng *canc* MS   21 no byrde] birdes L   22 hangyng] *om* L;   þerapon] þer apon MS   23 bechyng] baitinge L

For þe pere – þat is whan þe hawke
proferyth for to mute & may not.

Take perspere, saxifrage, | perselly rotis, polepody of an oke, & boyle all þes in fayre rennyng watir and þerin wach þi hawkys mete. Put þis into a nerthyn poot, ellys þe watir wyll stynke of þe brasse, and spend þerof dayly.

For þe craye.

Take þe gleyre of a negge & wasch hir mete þerin, & þat is remowntyng for hyre.

For þe polyon þat is a swellyng abofe þe gesse.

Take þe lyde of a poot, or a trene ladyll, and hold it aȝen þe fyre tyll þat it frye owte þerof grese, and þerwith anoynt it.

For þe pyn þat growyth vndir þe ball of þe fote
lyke a pese or more, or a lyttyll note, and þat
brennyth so sore sche may not stande þeron.

Take a bagge of salte & bynd it to þe perch þat sche may stand þeron, & þat schall drye it vp anon.

For þe crampe þat wyll make hir to streke whan
sche puttyþe owte hyr fote, or hir lege, or hir wyng,
& may not drawe it aȝen withowte grete payne.

Take þe iusse of clyuerse or hayryfe sych as ȝe fede gese with (all is on), & gyfe it hyr.

[24–46 collated with L]
24 þe²] thine L   25 for] om L;   not] add C lxiv L   26 perspere] prosper and L
27 rennyng] ranynge L;   þerin] þer in MS,L   28 þi] thine L;   mete] add & And L;
into] in to MS, in L;   poot] pott L   29 spend] ocupie;   þerof] þer of MS,L   30–2 For
... hyre] om L   31 þerin] þer in MS   33 abofe] a bofe MS;   gesse] add C .lxv. L
34 poot] pott L;   aȝen] a ȝen MS, a gayne L   35 þat ... grese] that the grece frye oute
ther of L;   þerof] þer of MS;   and þerwith] þer with and MS, and ther with L   36 anoynt]
a noynt MS,L   37 pyn] pynne L   38 or a lyttyll note] om L   39 so sore] that L;
þeron] þer on MS,L; add C. lxvj. L   40 perch] perke L   41 þeron] þer on MS;   anon]
a non MS,L   42–6 For ... hyr] om L   44 aȝen] a ȝen MS;   withowte] with owte MS

For þe pyis – þat is whan þi hawke fallyth downe sodenly of on | þi hande or of þe perke.

Take heyhond, horhonde, lauandyr cotyn & rosemary, & take hote flyntys owte of þe fyre & kest hem in a pan with herbys, þat þe smoke may go vp to þe hawke .ij. days or .iij. & sche schall be hole.

For þe ree, þe frownce, þe fylawnder[s], þe aglys, þe pere, þe cray.

Take frech buttyr of a cowe of on ble, & claryfye it, & put þerto sewgir-candey & safyrne & a lytyll gyngyr. & put hem togedyr in a box & gyfe it 3our hawke, and sche wyll cum sonere to 3ow for þat þan for flech.

The sekenes of þe pyis: it is a swyuenyng in þe hede þat makys hyr to fall downe from þe hande & from þe perke also.

For to make þe hawke to breke hyr castyng.

As thus, yf þat sche hase receuyd .ij. or .iij., take þe rote of celedony & dubbe it in hyre mete & sche [schall] cast it. Also powdyr of pepyr, cast it on hyre mete euer as sche fedyth, & þat schall make hyr to cast.

An hawke must hafe castyng whan sche is flyyng, | and wederyng in þe sonne; for & sche be wedir-seke, sche wyll hafe but lytyll lust to hyr game.

The good castyng [that] is for a dull hauke is þe shauyng of an hesyll styke. Federys is more kynd for hyr; fayre lynyn cloþe is good; whyth blankett sekyth hyr nerrer (not to mych þerof for dryyng of þe hawke).

[47–73 collated with L]
47 þi] thine L   48 on ... perke] the fist C lxvij. L   49 heyhond, horhonde] honde L; rosemary] rose mary MS   51–2 .ij. days or .iij.] ij. or thre daies L   53–61 For ... also] *om* L   53 fylawnders] fylawnder MS   57 togedyr] to gedyr MS   62 þe] an L castyng] *add* C .lxviij. L   63 þat] *om* L;   hase receuyd] hathe resceyued L;   .iij.] thre L   64 celedony] colodony L;   it in hyre mete] his mete therin L;   sche schall] schall *om* MS, he shall L;   65 Also] *add* cast L;   cast it] *om* L   66 to] *om* L   70] *add ante* Whate castynge is best for an hauke C .lxix. L;   castyng] cas-|tyng MS;   that] *om* MS, *sic* L   72 whyth] white L   73 nerrer] to nere L;   þerof] þer of MS,L;   dryyng] dryenge L

*To prefe weþer þat ʒour hawke be
clene enseymyd or non.*

Take hir blanket & yf it be ʒelow þe hauke is seymy; þat
is to sey, sche is fatt. And yf it be blake, sche is bruschyd.
And yf it be grene, sche is gleymyd – and þat is lyke to a
tysyke & is schorte wynedyd.

Also whan þi hauke is gorchyd & hir bely crowyth
it engenderyth þe pere; þan hyre mute wyll be blake &
than it woll stynke fowle.

*A medycyn whan þat ʒour hawke castyþe
hir mete & may not endue.*

Take an hege sparow, or anoþer sparow or ellys a lytyll
chekyn, & gyfe it þi hauke in hir fote. And euer as sche
brekyth it, put þeron womannys mylke, & latt hyr neuyr
hafe bot smale gorgys & ofte. & þat mete þat sche cast
onys fede hyr no more þeron, bot gyfe hyr anoþer maner
of flech.

Take a stokedowfe or anodyr dowfe, & holde hyr be
þe leggys & bete hyre with a roode & þat schall make þe
blode þerof to spryng and | to swell. Þan strype of þe
federys of þe brest, & latt þi hauk fede a lytyll þeron. &
put womannys mylke þerapon, for þat is remowntyng.
& porke is a goode mete for an hauke & a remowntyng.

Also for þe ree.

Take peletyr of Spayne, & whan þi hawke fedys, gyfe hyr
a lytyll þerof & sche schall spryng þe watyr owte of hyr
hede in þi face.

[74–100 collated with L]
74] .j. *in margin* MS;   prefe weþer þat ʒour] knowe for an L   75 enseymyd] y¹ *super*
MS;   non] not C .lxx. L   78 bruschyd] brused L   80 þi] thine L;   gorchyd] gorged
L;   crowyth] crewith L   81 &] *om* L   83 A medycyn] *om* L;   þat] *om* L   84 endue]
add C lxxj L;   85 hege] hedged L;   anoþer] a noþer MS,L   86 þi] thine L
87 þeron] þer on MS,L   88 cast] castith L   89 þeron] þer on MS;   anoþer] a noþer
MS,L   91 anodyr] a nodyr MS,L   92 roode] rod L   93 þerof] þer of MS,L;
Þan] and L   94 þi] thine L;   a lytyll þeron] theron alitell L;   þeron] þer on MS
95 þerapon] þer apon MS, theron L   96–100 & porke ... face] *om* L   99 þerof]
þer of MS

[CHOOSING A HAWK]

For to chese an hawke.
Take a lyttyll goshauke, a schorte schene, an opyn fote, a grete beke, a wyde mowþe, lowryng hyen; the sere abofe þe beke, þe ye, þe fote acordyng all of on colowre; a long tayle, schorte wyngys, wele crossyng. A facon: a schorte tayle, long wynkys, a schorte schene & long wyngys.

[AGES OF A HAWK]

An hawke is callyd an nyes, a bowere, a brawncher, a ramage hawke, a mure-de-hay; all þe fyrst ȝere a sore hauke; an entyrmuer, a muer, an hagberte. An hawke is callyd a pertrichere, a fesoner, a moser (þe glede), a ielonere (hennys), an aneuer of dokys, an heyroner.

[A HAWK'S FOOT AND FEATHERS]

The tokynnys of þe fote. Þe fyrst is þe pownce afore, þe talon is behynde, þe mydyll sygnett is þe key of þe foote.
Now þe federys of þe hawke. He hath a cuttelle, a sorselle – at þe poynte of þe wyng þe long fedyr; þe flaggys; þe mantellettys þat coueryth all þe body.
In þe tayle of þe hauke, *in* þe myddys þerof, þer is couerkele federis & all þe toþer | ben syde federys, and

---

[*101–118 collated with L*]
101] .ij. *in margin* MS;   For] Fo L;   hawke] *add* C .lxxij. L   102 schene] shynne L;   opyn] apyn L   103 lowryng] low-|ryng MS;   hyen] ien L   abofe] a bofe MS, a boute L   104 ye] þe L   106 wynkys] wynges L;   schene] shynne L;   & long wyngys] *om* L   108 hawke] *add* and L;   mure-de-hay] muredehay MS, murdeheye L   109 entyrmuer] entirmewer L;   a muer] *om* L;   hagberte] hogberd L   110 a moser] a mosher of hennes L;   þe glede] *super* MS, *om* L   111 ielonere] ioloner L;   hennys] *super* MS, *om* L;   an aneuer] a vento L;   of dokys] *super* MS   112 afore] a fore MS,L   113 talon is] talonis MS, talowne is L;   behynde] be hynde MS;   115 a sorselle] *om* L   116 þe¹] thei L;   þe²] *om* L   117] þerof] þer of MS,L   118 couerkele] couercle L;   ben] bethe L

comynly þer passyth not .xij. fedyrs in þe tayle. Þe whyte
type on þe hende is clepyd þe flowre of þe tayle.
 Vndyrneyth þer ben smale whyte feders þe wych is
clepyd þe brayle. Yf so be þat it be fowle of hyr mute,
3our hawke hath þe pere & is seke. Sche must be holpyn
with medycynnys.

[FLYING TERMS]

 Termys how 3our hawke fleyth.
The hawke fleyth to þe vve, þat is whan þe hawke hath
fowndyn hyr game; to þe quarre, whan þe ostregere hath
fowndyn. He must be ware weþer þe fowle be moryng or
fletyng, ellys he my3th dysseyfe þe hawke whan sche
schall flye.
 The hawke flyyth to ferre iotee, þat is to sey whan
þe hawke hath not fowndyn hyr game, nor þe ostreger
neyder, but it spryngyth or sordyth vp sodenly be hym.
 The iotte ferre is whan þe cownteryuer layth ouyr þe
fowle to yowe; & 3yt lat not þe tapyr [sesse till] þe hauke
sese þe fowle.
 All þe whyle þat þe hauke is vndyr & þe fowle soryth
vp, 3our hauke is at a vantage. Whan þat þe hauke is
aboue, þan þe fowle for ferde anewyth into þe watyr, þan
þe fowle soylyth.
 Now here ben 3our termys, lere or be lewde.

[*119–141 collated with L*]
120 on] of L; clepyd] cle-|pyd MS   121 Vndyrneyth] vndyr neyth MS,L   122 brayle] brailles L   123 sche] he L;   holpyn] holpe L   124 medycynnys] medicyne   125] iij *in margin* MS;   fleyth] *add* C lxxiij L   128 fowndyn] founde L;   weþer] for L   129 fletyng] *add* or L   132 fowndyn] founde L   133 neyder] noþer L;   it] she L;   sordyth] sorgeth L;   sodenly be hym] hir selfe sodeynly L   134 iotteferre] iote fer L;   cownteryuer] counter reuer L;   layth] lithe L   135 tapyr] tabur L;   sesse till] *sic* L, serse to MS   137 þat] *om* L   138 vantage] *add* ¶ and L;   þat] *om* L   139 aboue] a boue MS;   into] in to MS, to L   140 soylyth] solchith L   141 Now ... lewde] *om* L

[HIERARCHY OF HAWKS]

f. 50r | Thre hawkys longyn for a emper*our*: þat is to say, an egkyl, a wautour*e*, a millon*e* – neþer luryd nor reclaymyd for heuy.

145 There ben hawk*ys* of towr*e*, þat is to sey:
A gerefacon*e* and a tarselet of þe same for a kyng.
A facon*e* ientyll, a terselet þer*o*f for a pr*i*nce.
A facon*e* of þe rocke, a terselet þer*o*f for a duke.
A facon*e* per*e*gryne, a terselet þer*o*f for a nerle.
150 A bastarde w*ith* a terselett for a lorde.
A sakyr and a sakyrret for a kny3th.
A layner and a laynerett for a sqwyer.
A lese of marlyons for a lady.
A hoby or a taselett of þe same for a sq*u*ier of þe fyrst
155   hede to make þe larke to tapyse.

A gosehawke for a pore man.
A tersell for a 3eman.
A sp*er*awke for a prest.
A muskett for an halywatyr clarke.
160 A kesterell for a knafe.

An aby hawke is canvas mayle, a lovyng hauke & an harde, þat may indur*e* mych sorowe & comynly þei be þe hardyest.

[*142–163 collated with L*]
142] *add ante* Ther beth dyuers haukes for euery astate and for other men of degre C .lxxiiij. Fyrst L;   Thre] iij. L;   longyn for a] longe to an L   143 egkyl] *fully visible only under ultraviolet light* MS, egill L;   wautoure] vautour L   145–6 for a kynge] L *places these words at the start of the sentence*   146 for a] *add* kny3th *canc* MS   147–160] L *places the phrase* 'for a [...]' *at the start of each statement*   147 ientyll] gentill and L;   þerof] þer of MS, of the same L   148 rocke] *add* and L;   þerof] þer of MS, of the same L   149 peregryne] *add* and L;   þerof] þer of MS, of the same L   150 bastarde] bostarde L   151 and] with L;   sakyrret] sokerett L   152 layner] laynett L;   and a laynerett] *om* L   153 lese] lesshe L;   marlyons] merlyons L   154 hoby] *add* or MS;   or a taselett of þe same] *super* MS;   taselett] terslet L   155 tapyse] tappice L   157 tersell] tarssell L   159 halywatyr] holywater L   160 knafe] knave L   161 aby] abbay L   162 indure] endure with L   163 be] ben L;   hardyest] hardest L

164   *Now of venery lerne wele ȝour termys*

[BEASTS OF VENERY AND THE CHASE]

f. 50v | There ben .iiij. bestys of venery: the hare, the harte, the wolfe and þe wylde bore. Of venery þer ben no moo. There ben bestys of þe chase of þe swete fute, and bestys of þe chase of þe styngande fute. The buke, þe doo, þe bere, þe reynedere, þe elke, þe spytard (þat is an harte of
170 an .C. ȝere holde): all þes ben of þe swete fute. There ben bestys of þe styngand fute: þe fulmard, þe fechewe, þe catt, þe gray, þe fox, þe wesyll, þe marteron, þe sqwirell, þe whyterache, þe otyr, þe stote & þe polcate.

[SOILING TERMS]

A hunte hath i-cast of a copyll of alondys to an herde
175   of hartys;
þe harte takys þe watyr, than he soyelys;
& whan he goþe with þe streme, than he fletys;
whan he cummyth vp aȝen, than he brekyþe or betys;
whan he cummyth ouer, he crossyth;
180   whan he retornyth to þe todyr syde, he recrossyth;
whan he takyth þe maynelonde, he fleyth;
An harte flyth, an fawcone flyth.

[*164–173 collated with L, Pp*]
164 Now ... termys] *red-ink flourishes on either side of this heading indicate a major division* MS, *om* L,Pp   165 the hare, the harte] the herte þe hare Pp   166 and] *om* Pp   bore] *add* and Pp;   þer ben] the byth Pp   167 ben] byth Pp   167–8 bestys² ... chase] *also* Pp   168 styngande] stynkand L, stynkyng Pp;   fute] *add* ¶ Off the swete fute is L   169 bere] doer L;   reynedere] reyne dere MS,Pp;   spytard] spyckard and Pp   170 an .C.] a hounder Pp;   ȝere] winter L;   holde] olde L,Pp;   all ... fute] *om* L, mistakenly written as a heading with* 'all' *omitted* Pp   170–1 There ben] Thes ben the L;   There ... fute] *om* Pp   171 styngand] stynkande L   fulmard] fulmer L;   fechewe] fychew Pp   172 þe catt] *om* Pp;   wesyll] wheysyll Pp   173 whyterache] white racche L, waturrate Pp;   þe stote] *om* L;   &] *om* Pp;   polcate] *add* And all thes byn gamys of the stynkyng foote Pp

[*174–182 collated with no other witness*]
178 aȝen] a ȝen MS   180 retornyth] retor-|nyth MS

[RESTING TERMS]

An harte is herborowyde,
A knyth is herborowyde;
185   A bukke is logged,
A sq*u*ier is logged;
A roo-buke is beddyd,
A ȝeman is beddyd;
f. 51r |A har*e* is formyd schulderyng or leneyng;
190   A boye is beddyd brawlyng;
A cony syttyth;
A p*ar*car*e* walkyth;
A p*er*terych lythe;
A fesawnte stalkyth,
195   A crane stalkyth,
A heyron stalkyth.

[COLLECTIVE NOUNS]

A herde of hartys
A herde of bukkys
A herde of cranys
200   A herde of corlewis
A herde of wrennys
A bevee of roys
A bevee of q*u*aylys
A beve of ladys
205   A nye of fesawnt*ys*

[*183–205 collated with L*]
183–8] *red-ink braces link pairs of statements employing the same verb* MS   183] *add ante and canc* MS;   herborowyde] herbrowed L   184 herborowyde] herbrowed L   185 logged] logid L   186 logged] logid L   188 ȝeman] yoman L   189 formyd] fourmed L;   leneyng] lendyng MS, lenynge L   192 parcare] parker L   194–6] *three statements linked by a red-ink brace* MS   194 fesawnte] feysand L   197–241] *red-ink braces link pairs of phrases employing the same collective noun* MS   198] *add* A herde of harys *in different hand* L   202 roys] rooys L   203 qaylys] Q *retraced by different hand* L   205 fesawntys] feysantes L

A couy of p*a*rt*ri*kkys
A rowte of wolfys
A rowte of knytys
A sovneder of wyld swyn
A chermyng of goldfy*n*chys   210
A chateryng of sterlyngys
A ost of men
A ost of sparowys
A gagyllyng of gese
A gagyllyng of wome*n*   215
A floke of schepe
A trype of gete
A huske or a downe of harys
A haras of horse
A haras of harlott*y*s   220
A teme of oxyn
A teme of swa*n*nys
A teme of dukys

A fly3th of dowfys
A fly3th of larkys   225
A sculke of foxys
A sculke of freyrs
A sculke of theuys
A sege of heyro*n*nys
A sege of botowrys   230
A spryng of telys
A sorde of malardys | f. 51v
A doppyng of scheldrakys
A dyvyng of autelys
A dysseyte of lapwynk*y*s   235
A onkyndenes of ravynnys
A trewloufe of turtyllys
A clustyr of grapys
A clustyr of nottys
A clowdyr of carlys   240
A clowdyr of cattys

Lat catt*es* scrate carlys w*ith* sorow iwys,
Lerne or be lewde – I tell þe thys.

Explicit I. B.

[206–244 collated with L]
206 partrikkys] partriches L   208 knytys] knyghtis L   209 sovneder] gendir L
211 sterlyngys] staris L   217 of] *add* l *canc* MS   218 downe] dove L (*?error for* done *misread as* doue)   224 dowfys] dovis L   227 freyrs] freris L   230 botowrys] bettoris L   232 sorde] sorte L   233 doppyng] drowping L   240 clowdyr] cluster L
241 cattys] *add* Explicit L; *also add eight further phrases* [a charme of bees, a cast of brede, a cast of havkes, a carfe of pantlars, a blast of hvnters, a stalke of fosters, a mvsycion of synger‹s›, a melody of harpers ‹&› luters], *followed by a list of 33 carving terms, all in a different hand* L   242–4 *om* L   242 iwys] I wys MS

PART III
MS HALE 148 (Ha)

Contents	Collated with
Collective nouns	—
Beasts of venery and the chase	Rd
The hunter	Rd
Breeds of dogs	Rd
Soiling terms	Rd
Resting terms	Dg, Rg
Properties of a greyhound	—
Hierarchy of hawks	—
Hawks' diseases	—

[COLLECTIVE NOUNS]

A herd of hertes   f. 6v
A herde of cranes
A herde of bukkys
A herde of kurloews
A herde of wrennes   5
A beuy of ladyes
A beuy of rooes
A beuy of quayles
A nye of faysandis
A couy of partryches   10
A rowt of knyght*es*
A rowt of wolfes
A sundir of wyld swyn
A singler of bores
A chyrmyng of goldfynches   15
A chiteryng of stares
A hoste of sparowes
A hoste of men
A gagelyng of wemen
A gagelyng of gyees   20
A flok of schyp
A trip of geette
A husk of hares
A down of hares
A haras of horses   25
A teme of oxn
A teme of swa*n*nes
A teme of wyld dokes
A flyght of larkes

A flyght of swalows   30
A flyght of doues
A skulk of foxes
A skulk of freres
A abhominable syght of monkes
A sup*er*fluite of nu*n*nes   35
A state of prystes
A dignite of chanones
A sege of herones
A sege of bytorus
A spryng of teles   40
A swerde of malardis
A doppyng of herreles
A dyuyng of awteles
A deceyte of lapewyng*es*
A vnkyndenes of rauenes   45
A trewloue of turteles
A mewte of hundees
A thru*m* of greundes
A clowdir of catt*es*
A clowdr*e* of karles   50

30] *start of column 2* MS   32 skulk] skulf MS

[BEASTS OF VENERY AND THE CHASE]

| There be iiij bestes of the venary: the hert, the hare, the wolf and the wyld bore. Of venary they be no moo. There be bestis of the chase of the swete fewte, and bestis of the chase of the stynkyng fewte. The buk and the doo, the roo and the roo-buk, the bere and the reynedere, the elk and the spytard. The folemard and the fuche, the bad, the grey, the fox, the wesell, the martryn, the squirell, the whitrath, the otter, the stotte and the pollecatte.

[THE HUNTER]

I wold se a hunt with a horn hongyng abowte his nek, his wodeknyff by his side, his hoke on his belte byhynd his baak to receyue his dog for the bowe yn hys lyeme; that kyndely cowde blow the pryce of an herte, the deth of an hare, the deth of an otter, and the deth of a wolf, to the chate and rechate, wyth the motis and strakes that longeth thereto.

[*51–65 collated with Rd*]
51 be] ben Rd;   the venary] wenery Rd;   the hert, the hare] *reversed* Rd   52 bore] bare MS, bore Rd;   they be] ther byth Rd;   moo] more Rd   53 chase] chache Rd;   swete] swe-|te MS, swyte Rd;   fewte] fot Rd   54 chase] chache Rd;   fewte] fote as Rd;   and] *om* Rd   54–5] the roo and the roobuk] the ro bucke and the roo doo Rd   55 roo-buk] roo buk MS;   reynedere] reyne dere MS,Rd;   and^3] *om* Rd   56 spytard] specard Rd, *add* And thus ben off the stynkynge fote Rd;   folemard] fulmarde Rd;   and] *om* Rd   57 whitrath] wyȝthe rache Rd   58 and] *om* Rd;   pollecatte] polle catte MS, *add* And here byn a schrwyd flocke Rd   59] *add ante* Sum of thes bythe chasabylle & sum bithe vne chasabylle Rd;   wold] *om* Rd;   with] v^t Rd;   hongyng] *om* Rd abowte] a bowte MS,Rd   60 his hoke on his belte] a hoke vp one hys gurdylle Rd;   byhynd] by hynd MS,Rd   61 receyue] reseve *super* Rd   62 cowde] cowthe Rd 62–3 the deth of an hare] *om* Rd   63–4 to the chate and rechate] tho the chache and to rechace Rd;   motis] notys Rd;   and strakes] and w^t the scharkes Rd   65 longeth] long Rd;   thereto] there to MS,Rd

[BREEDS OF DOGS]

66   The hunte schall haue help. There byn grehundis and
          bastardis, mongerellis and mastiues, alondis and lymures,
          spaynellis and rechis, kenettis and terowres, bocheres
          hundis, myddynges kurris and smale puppes for ladis.

[SOILING TERMS]

70   The hunt hath cast of a braas of alauntes to a herd of
              hertes;
          he blowyth confortyng his hundis;
          the herte takith the water, the hert sowles;
          whan he swymmes down, he fletis;
f. 7v   when he is vp the ryuer, he brekith or | beteth;
75   when he is ouer the ryuere, he crosseth;
          when he returneth, he recrosseth;
          when he takith the megnelonde, he fleth;
          a hert fleth, a faucon fleth.

[66–78 collated with Rd]
66 The] Thys Rd;   There] *add* to *canc* MS   67 mongerellis] mangrellys Rd;   and[1] *om* Rd;   alondis] and loundes Rd;   lymures] lemores Rd   68 rechis] rachys Rd;   terowres] terours Rd   68–69 bocheres hundis] bochere howndys and Rd   69 myddynges] dunghylle Rd;   puppes for ladis] poppys of lades chambers W[t] Tro to tro Ware ryot Ware Rd   70 of] *om* Rd;   braas] copylle Rd;   herd] hert Rd   71 confortyng] comfortynge Rd;   hundis] howndys Rd   72 the herte takith] the hertys that takyt Rd;   water] reuer Rd   73–78] *om* Rd, *text breaks off suddenly*   73 he[2]] *add* flyth *canc* MS   75 crosseth] ?cresseth MS   76 returneth] retur-|neth MS   77 megnelonde] megne londe MS

[RESTING TERMS]

      A hert is herborowid,
80   A knyght [is] herborowid;
      A buk is logged,
      A squier is loggid;
      A roobuk is beddid,
      A yeman is beddid;
85   A hare is formyd schulderyng or lenyng;
      A knaue lyght in his bedde braulyng;
      A cony sittid;
      A boy walkyth;
      A parterich lithe;
90   A faysand stalkyth.

[PROPERTIES OF A GREYHOUND]

      A greunde schuld haue a congres hede, a ladys nek, a liones brest, a sowes ribbe. Y-bakkid like a plowe beme, y-trussid byhynd like an ox bytwen the hornes, y-hangid like a hare, y-howghid like a sikill; a cat*tes* fote, a rat*tes* tayle: then is
95   the greund good to assayle.

      The first ere, fede fede; the secu*n*d yere, a-fyld lede;
      the iij yere, 'Hay! Go bette!'; the iiij yere, w*ith*oute lette;
      the v yere, gode ynow; the vj yere, hold the plow;
      the vij yere, carte sadill; the viij yere, plowe padill;
100   the ix yere, he may avayle greybichies to assayle.

[*79–90 collated with Dg, Rg*]
79 herborowid] herborowred Dg, herbrowyd Rg   80 is] *om* MS;   herborowid] herbowred Dg, herbrowyd Rg   81 buk] bugke Rg   82 A ... loggid] *om* Rg   83 roobuk] robugke Rg   84 A ... beddid] *om* Rg   85 formyd] furmyd a Rg   86 lyght] lyʒthe Dg, lyth Rg;   in his] on ys Rg   87 cony] conynge Rg;   sittid] syttethe Dg, Rg
88 walkyth] walkyd Rg   89 lithe] lyethe Dg, lyth Rg

[*91–100 collated with no other witness*]
90 faysand] fesavnte Dg, fesante Rg   93 byhynd] by hynd MS;   bytwen] by twen MS
97 iij] *followed by an indecipherable mark, possibly a pen-rest blot* MS;   withoute] with oute MS   98 ynow] y now MS   100 avayle] a vayle MS

[HIERARCHY OF HAWKS]

Thre haukes longeth to an emp*e*ro*u*r: an egle, a vowto*ur* and [a] melonne. The simplest of thus iij haukes will scle an hyndis calf, a dooeys fowne, a rowe, an elk, a crane, a bustard, a stork and a fox in a playn grond. And they be not lurid neydir reclaymid: the cause whi, they be so pondrews, saue to a perch portatiff bytwix ij men.

There be haukis of the tour*e*: a gerfaucon & tassell, and a faucon ge*n*tell, and a faucon of the rock, a faucon p*e*regryne, a saker and a sakeret, a lan*er* and a laneret, a merlyon and | a hoby. They be haukis of the tour*e*, and all they fle fro the lure.

There ys a gossehauke and a tarssell, a sparhauk and a musket. They fle to the vewe, to the qwarre, to the vnguyte and to the gytte ferr*e*.

[HAWKS' DISEASES]

Yet haukes haue infirmites. An hauke hath in the hede the rye and the frounce; the pokkes and the mytis aboue the yee lidis; in the nek and in the mantelett*es*, the lyse; and in the cheste, the felaundres; and in the bak, the egles; in the brayell, the per*e*; and in the tewell, the cray; and in the whyng*es*, legg*es* and fete: the polyon, the pyn, the crampe and the peys.

Ostriger*e*, faukener*e*, speruer*e* and mylonere in Englond so wyse.

Et cetera

[101–124 collated with no other witness]
101 emperour] u *super* MS   104 bustard] bus-|tard MS   106 bytwix] by twix MS
107 haukis] hau-|kis MS   108 gentell] gen-|tell MS;   rock] rook MS   109 saker] sa-|ker MS   116 and the frounce] and in the frounte MS;   aboue] a boue MS
117 mantelettes] mante-|lettes MS   122 mylonere] my-|lonere MS

PART IV
MISCELLANEOUS JB TEXTS AND ELEMENTS

Contents	Collated with
a. Hunting terms – Adv	—
b. 'If a hart stands' – *HSG*	Am
c. Names of hawks – Harl	—
d. Beasts of venery and the chase – Eg	—
e. Breeds of dogs – Eg	—
f. Properties of a greyhound – Eg	—
g. Soiling terms – T	*HSG*, W
h. Hierarchy of hawks – G	Rc, Ry
Hawks' diseases and remedies – G	Ry
i. Names of wines – Dg	Rg

PART IV — MISCELLANEOUS

a. Hunting terms – MS Adv

f. 63r
An hert is chased
An hynde is chased
A bock is ronnon
A dwo is shotte
5 An hare is coursed
A bore is vexed
A wolfe is trapped
A beyre is beyted
A fox is halowed
10 A grey is beseged or assauted
A cony is hayed or feretted

b. 'If a hart stands' – *HSG*

f. 18r
Yf an herte stande, he stallethe;
Yf a bucke stande, he herkenythe;
Yf a roo stande, he fereth.

c. Names of hawks – MS Harl

f. 225r
A gossehauke
A tassell
A sperrehauke
A muskett
5 A hay-de-mew

---

a. Hunting terms – Adv
1–2] *2-line symbol (? a paraph) in right margin* 11] *last entry followed by a line drawn across the page*

b. 'If a hart stands' – *HSG* **(collated with Am)**
1 stallethe] stalkethe Am 3 fereth] ferech Am

c. Names of hawks – Harl
1 gossehauke] gosse hauke 3 sperrehauke] sperre hauke

d. Beasts of venery and the chase – MS Eg

f. 63r *For a yong gentylleman to knowe the termys of venery
and the crafte, whythe the .iiij. bestys of venery.*

    The herte,
    The hare,   Of venery there
    The wolfe,   bynne nomore.
    And the wylde bore.

5   The bestys of the chasse as hyt apperythe:
    The bucke,
    The doo,
    The roobucke,
    The roodoo,
10   The bere,
    And the raynedere;
    The elke – that ys to say, a herte of CC wyntyr age;
    ¶ The spyarde – that ys to say, a herte of CCC wyntyr of age.

    The fulmer,
15   The fechewe,
    The catte of the mountayne,
    The gray,
    The fox,   Alle thes benne of the
    The wesylle,   stynkyng fute or
20   The martorn,   stynkyng chasse, for
    The squyrelle,   the[y] wylle bothe clym
    The ottyre,   and crepe as for the
    The polkatte.   substaunce of hem.

---

d. **Beasts of venery and the chase – Eg**
t For] *1-line red lombard initial F*;   gentylleman] gentylle man;   the .iiij. bestys of] *underlined in red*   1–3 The] *3-line red initial T*   1–4] *four phrases linked by braces*   5–10 The] *6-line red initial T*   11 raynedere] rayne dere   12–20 The] *9-line red initial T*   13 ¶] *red-ink paraph*   17–23] *seven phrases linked by braces*   22–3 The] *2-line red initial T*

e. Breeds of dogs – MS Eg

f. 63r

¶ *There ben grehoundys for game and many othyr dyuers houndys, sum honeste & sum profytabylle,*

f. 63v

as | hit shalle folowe here in wrytynge &c.

    Fyrste a grehounde,
    A bastarde grehounde,   Alle thes ben take
    A mongrelle,   in to the lesse.
    A mas⟨t⟩owe,
5   Aloundys,
    Lymoure.

    ¶ Spaynellys,
    Racchys,   Alle thes wylle range for
    Kenettys,   to raysse vppe the game.
10   Teerors.

    ¶ Bocher houndys,
    Dunghylle currys,
    Ande smalle popys for ladys chambers.

    Aloundys ben caste,
15   Lymors drawyn,
    A blodehounde or a dogge for the bowe drawythe,
    Kenettys rennyn,
    Spaynellys retryuyn,
    The terer gothe vndyr the grounde for to festyn
20   the fox or the graye.

---

e. **Breeds of Dogs – Eg**

t ¶] *red-ink paraph*   1–6] *six entries linked by brace*   1 Fyrste] *1-line red initial F*   7–10] *four entries linked by brace*   7 ¶] *red-ink paraph*   11 ¶] *red-ink paraph*; Bocher houndys] Bocherhoundys   13–18] *6-line red initial A; scribe wrote two guide letters, one at line 13, the other at line 16, but the rubricator supplied only one initial*   16 blodehounde] blode hounde

f. Properties of a greyhound – MS Eg

f. 55v

The condyscyons of a grehounde ande of hys propyrteys.

Thy grehounde moste be heddyd lyke a snake, ⎤
I-neckyd lyke a drake, ⎟
I-brestyde lyke a lyon, ⎟
I-sydyd lyke a noynon, ⎟
5   I-fotyde lyke a catte, ⎟
I-taylyd lyke a ratte; ⎦
Thenne ys the grehounde welle i-schapte.

g. Soiling terms – MS T

f. 35v   A herte, yf he be chased, he wil desire to a reuer;
also sone as he takeþ þe reuer, he soyleth;
yf he take ouer þe reuer, he crossyth;
yf he returne, he recrossyth;
5   yf he take with þe streme, he flittyth;
yf he take agayne þe streme, he beteth or elles brekþ;
yf he take þe lond, he fleeth.

f. Properties of a greyhound – Eg
t hys] *add* propyrmyng *canc*   1–6] *lines linked by red-ink brace*   4 I-sydyd ... noynon] *add ante* I-fotyd lyke a noynon *canc by rubricator*

g. Soiling terms – T (collated with *HSG*, W)
1 A] An W   be] *om* W   to] *add* haue *HSG*   reuer] rewer W   2 also sone] Assone *HSG*   soyleth] suleth *HSG*   3 take] *add* thritte W   he²] *add* co *canc* MS   4 he²] *add* soyleth yf *canc* MS   5] *add ante* And *HSG*   flittyth] fleteth *HSG*, fletyth W   6 agayne] a gayne MS, ayenste W   elles] *om* W   brekþ] breketh *HSG*, brekyth W   7 fleeth] fleyth W, *add* Explicit *HSG*

h. Hierarchy of hawks;
Hawks' diseases and remedies – MS G

[*Here ben the names of all man*er *of hawk*es. *And to whom and to what maner of men they longe to.*]

p. 158 | There is an egle, a vaweture and a melowne. Þe sempliste of þeis iij. woll sle an hynde calfe, a doys fowne, a roo-doo, an elke, a crane, a bustarde, a storke, a swan, a fox *in* playne grounde. And þeis iij. be not enlurid ne reclaymed
5 bicause þei be so ponderous þ*at* to perche portatife þei be goue*r*ned; & þeis iij. longyn to an emp*er*oure onely & to none oþ*er* man.

Ther*e* is a ierfawkyn & a tarsell of a ierfawkyn; þeis bene for a kynge.
10 Ther*e* is a fawkyn gentill & a tarsell gentill; þeis bene for a prynce.
Ther*e* is a fawkyn of þe rokke for a duke.
Ther*e* is a fawkyn p*er*egrine for an erle.
Ther*e* is a bastarde þ*at* is for a lorde.
15 Ther*e* is a sacre & a sacrett for a kny3t.
Ther*e* is a laner & a la[n]rett for a squyer*e*.
Ther*e* is a merlyne for a lady.
Ther*e* is an hobye for an inffaunt.
Theis bene þe hawkis of þe towre & fle for þe lewre.

h. **Hierarchy of hawks; Hawks' diseases and remedies – G (collated with Rc, Ry)**
t Here ... to] *sic* Ry, *om* MS, These ben the Namys of Alle Man*er* Hawkis Rc   1 There is an] A Rc;   vaweture and] vawtier & Rc   2 þeis] thez Rc;   doys fowne] doo is fawne Rc   3 an elke, a crane] and Ry   3–4 a storke ... grounde] *om* Ry   4 þeis iij. be not] thees ben nought Rc   5 bicause] by cause Ry;   þei be] they are Rc, they ben Ry;   þat] *om* Rc;   to] *add* the Ry;   portatife] portatiffes Rc   6 &¹] And Ry;   longyn] longyth Rc, longith Ry;   &²] and Ry   6–7 onely ... man] *om* Rc   8 &] *om* Rc, and Ry;   ierfawkyn²] ierfawlyn Ry   10 &] *om* Rc, and Ry   12 rokke] *add* that is Rc;   duke] duc Ry   13 a] *om* Rc;   peregrine] *add* that is Rc;   an erle] a erle Rc   15 &] *om* Rc;   sacrett] *add* thees ben Rc;   kny3t] kniyght Ry   16 laner] lanare Rc;   &] *om* Rc, and Ry;   lanrett] lawrett MS, lanarett Rc, lanret Ry, *add* þes ben Rc   17 merlyne] merlione Rc   18 is] *om* Rc;   an] a Rc   19 þe hawkis] hawekis Rc;   &] and Ry;   for þe] forþe MS;   lewre] leure Rc

20   There is a goshawke for a ʒeman,
        A tarsell for a pore man,
        A sparowehawke for a preste,
        A muskett for a holy watir clerke.
        Theis bene of oþer kynde, for þei fle to þe hewe, to þe
25   qwerre, to þe forget and to þe grete sore.

        These bene þe infirmyteis of euery hawke. First, in þe hede,
        þe ree and þe frownce; abowte þe ye ledis, þe pokkis &
p. 159 þe mytes; in þe nekke and þe manteletis, | þe lice; in þe
        cheste, the felaundirs; in þe back, þe ageles; in þe braile,
30   þe peere and þe cray; and in þe whyngis, leggis & fete,
        þe pelyownde, þe peyne, þe crampe and þe pyes.

        Theis bith þe remedyes aʒenst all maner
        infirmyteis of all maner of hawkis.

        First for þe ree. Take deise and rewe and honye; medell hem
35   togedirs & put hit in [the] palys [of hir mouthe].

        Anoþer for þe same. Take mustarde & put hit in hire
        nostrellis & in hire eres & þe same ofte in þe roffe of hire
        mowþe; and ʒeve hire nessthe tirynge þerwith, and ʒif hit
        brekith sche schall be hole or ellis neuer. And ʒif þou haue
40   no mustarde, take powdire of gyngere & venegir.

---

20 There is] *om* Rc;   goshawke] goushauke Ry;   ʒeman] ʒoman Rc, yoman Ry
21] *add* Ther is Ry;   pore] pouer Ry   22] *add* Ther is Ry;   sparowehawke] sparowe
hawke MS, sparehauke Rc, sparhawke Ry   23] *add ante* Ther is Ry   24 for] *om* Rc;
to þe hewe] *om* Rc   25 forget] furgett Rc;   grete sore] gettffurre Rc, getsore Ry
26–31] *add in margin with brace* the seekenes of euery hawke Ry   27 abowte] a boute
Ry;   ye ledis] *add* and MS, eye liddes and Ry;   &] and Ry   28 manteletis] *add* and
MS,Ry   29 cheste] chiste Ry   back] *add* and MS,Ry   30 &] and Ry   31 pelyownde]
polyownde Ry   32–3] *add in margin with brace* the Remedies for the seeknes Ry
32 bith] ben Ry   34–40] *add in margin with brace* For the Ree Ry   34 First *om* Ry;
deise and] dayse & Ry;   and²] & Ry   35 togedirs] to gedirs MS, to gider Ry;   &] and
Ry;   the] *super* Ry, *om* MS;   of hir mouthe] *sic* Ry, *om* MS   36 Anoþer] Item Ry
38 þerwith] þer with MS, ther w^t Ry;   ʒif hit] if it Ry   39 schall be] shalbe Ry;
ʒif] if Ry

Anoþer for þe same. Take þe tere of hony & put hit in þe palate of hire mouþe & but hit woll breke soo geve hire mustarde.

For þe fronse. Take a quele & pike oute clene þe pith and wessche h*i*t clene w*ith* venegir*e*, and put vppon powdir of sancdragon, or ellis powdir*e* of martemasse befe.

Anoþ*er* for þe same. Take iiij. penywi3t of penyworte, iiij. penywi3t of þe rotes of sage, and a *d* of brewseworte, & a *d* of smegrene, & put he*m* togedirs. Þen take of May-buttir*e* & melt hit ou*er* þe fir*e* & caste þ*er*-to þe ioiste of þeis erbis; & þen put þ*er*-to ij. *d* of hony & halfe a *d* of sugire & a *d*-worþe of powdir gyngir*e* & a *d*-worþe of canell. And þen 3eve þi hawke þ*er*of as ofte i*n* a day as | thow wilte till sche be hole. For þe frounce growith in þe stomake & not i*n* þe mouþe.

For þe pokkis, mytis & lice. Powdere þe hawke with the powdir*e* of orpemente.

For þe felawndirs. Wessche þe hawke w*ith* maris mylke, or ellis iuse of suthernwode, & gefe h*ur* moche saferon in hir*e* mete.

41–3] *add brace in margin* Ry   41 Anoþer] Item Ry   42 geve] yeve Ry   44–55] *add in margin with brace* For the fronse Ry   44 and] *om* Ry   45 wessche] wasshe Ry; powdire] pouder Ry   46 martemasse] martmas Ry   47 Anoþer] A noþer MS; Anoþer for þe same] Item Ry;   iiij ... penyworte] *om* Ry;   penywi3t] peny wi3t MS   48 penywi3t] peny wi3t MS, peny weight Ry;   sage] sawge Ry;   d] *add* weight Ry   49 d] *add* weight Ry;   togedirs] to gedirs MS, to gider Ry   50 þer-to] þer to MS, ther to Ry; ioiste] iuse Ry   51 þer-to] þer to MS;   d[1]] *add* weight Ry;   halfe a d of] half d weight of Ry;   sugire] *add* and d weight of powd*er* of sugre *canc* Ry   52 worþe[1,2]] weight Ry;   powdir] *add* of Ry   53 þi] the Ry;   þerof] þer of MS;   till] *add* that Ry   54 frounce] fronse Ry   56–7] *add in margin with brace* For þe pokkes Ry   56 lice] *add* Take and Ry   58–60] *add in margin with brace* For the felandres Ry   58 felawndirs] felandres Ry, *add* take and Ry   59 ellis] *add* with the Ry;   gefe] gif;   saferon] sauffron Ry   60 hire] *om* Ry

Anoþer for þe same. Take womanis mylke of a knave childe & þe seconde rynde of ellerun þat is grene, & seþen hem togedirs & wessche hire mete þerynne, & þat schall hele him.

65 Anoþer for þe same. Take semen lumbricorum & sugire roce & put hit in a reppe with hire soper, & hit schall sle hem in one ny3t.

For þe ageles. Take þe gall of a rede cok hengynge on a parte with þe lyuer & 3eve hit him fastynge, abidynge
70 aftirwarde fastynge at þe leste an oure.

For þe pere. Take perspere, polypody (oþerwise callid okefern), percely rotis & saxefrage. Boyle þem togedirs in rennynge watire in a pot of erþe, and with þe iuse wessche þe hawkis mete.

75 For þe cray. Wessche þe mete of þe hawke in þe gleyre of an egge.

For þe polyownde. Take a potte lid & holde hit to þe fire till hit swete, and anoynte therewith your hawkis fete; or ellis
79 take oyle dolive.

61–7] *add in margin with brace* For the felandres Ry   61 Anoþer] Item Ry;   knave] man Ry   62 ellerun] elderne Ry;   seþen] sethe Ry   63 togedirs] to gedirs MS, to giders Ry;   þerynne] þer ynne MS   65 Anoþer ... same] Item Ry;   lumbricorum] limbricorum Ry   66 soper] souper Ry;   hem] *sic* Ry, him MS   68–70] *add in margin with brace* For þe angeles Ry   68 ageles] angeles Ry   69 parte] perche Ry;   abidynge] a biding Ry   70 aftirwarde] aftir-|warde MS;   oure] houre Ry   71–4] *add in margin with brace* For þe pere Ry   71 perspere, polypody] pers perepolypody MS, pers pere polypody Ry;   oþerwise] oþer wise MS   72 togedirs] to ge-|dirs MS, to giders Ry   73 erþe] yerthe Ry   75–6] *add in margin with brace* For the cray Ry   75 cray] *add* Take & Ry;   gleyre] clere Ry   77–9] *add in margin with brace* For þe polyounde Ry   77 polyownde] poliownde Ry;   potte lid] pottelid MS, potlyd Ry   78 therewith] there with MS, þer wt Ry   79 dolive] olyve Ry

p. 161 | For þe peyne. Ordeyne a bagge of salte and bynde h*i*t to þe perche where he schall ioke.

For þe pies. Take iij. peses of solondon and put theyme in þe hawkis mowþe, and put hir*e* in a chambir*e* and take
84   away þe loynes.

i. Names of wines – MS Dg

f. 161r   *These been names of wynes*
    londwyne
    Reynessh*e* wyne
    wyne of Cavelence
    wyne of Bunne
5   wyne of Cherow
    wyne of Rennca
    wyne of Elceter
    wyne of Tromyn
    wyne of þe Neker
10   muscaden
    mownterose
    tribiane
    greke
    coorze
15   romanyske
    wyne de Grecia
    wyne de India

80–1] *add in margin with brace* For þe peyne Ry   80 peyne] *add* take and Ry   82–4] *add in margin with brace* For þe pyes Ry   82 pies] pyes Ry;   solondon] selondon Ry; theyme in] hem in to Ry   83 put] doo Ry

i. Names of wines – Dg (collated with Rg)

t been] beth Rg,   of] *add* dyuerse Rg   1 londwyne] londvyne Rg   2 Reynesshe wyne] Reynesshewyne MS   2–3] reynisvyne of | of cauelense Rg   3 wyne] *om* Rg   5 Cherow] terow Rg   6 Rennca] ronnca Rg   8 Tromyn] tromyy Rg   9 þe] *om* Rg   11 mownterose] Mounte rose Rg   16 de Grecia] of greke Rg

PART IV — MISCELLANOUS

wyne de Tartarea
wyne de Sclauonia
romeney of Modon 20
malmesey of Candyne
wyne of Roodes
wyne de Bare
wyne de Calab*ria*
vermulond 25
vernache
wyne fyane
grekeseke
wyne of Mamorant
wyne of Gemerant 30
wyne of Arphax
wyne of Cosderam
mategors
r*e*spoyse
ruptarge 35
caprike
teynt
tyre
bastart
clarrey 40

osey
ypoc*ra*s
pyament
wyne de Lepe
vinn*e* cottinn 45
wyne de Algarbe
wyne de Tullouse
wyne de Robedore
wyne de Bilbowe
wyne de Cayser 50
wyne de Paytors
wyne cute
wyne de Bayon*e*
Rochel
Burgoyn*e* wyne 55
Gascon*e* wyne

18 de Tartarea] of cartaria Rg   19 de] of Rg   20 romeney of Modon] romayy of modyne Rg   21 Candyne] candyse Rg   22 Roodes] Rodys   23 de Bare] of debayre Rg   24 de Calabria] calabr ya Rg   25 vermulond] vermelone Rg   26 vernache] vernage Rg   27 wyne fyane] vynefyage Rg   28 grekeseke] greke (fyle *canc*) feke Rg   29 Mamorant] mamorante *scraped and corrected* Rg   31 Arphax] ar plax Rg   33 mategors] mategrow Rg   34 respoyse] respyese Rg   39 bastart] bastord Rg   45 vinne cottinn] Wyne Cottene Rg   48 Robedore] Robodore Rg   49 Bilbowe] byllow Rg   51 de Paytors] paytew Rg   55 Burgoyne wyne] bur gayne vyne Rg   56 Gascone wyne] & vyne of gaskyne for þe beste Rg

EXPLANATORY NOTES
PARTS I–IV

The notes that follow refer only occasionally to the Collective nouns, Carving terms and Resting terms found in the texts set out in Parts I–IV, as full notes on those items, collated from all J.B. sources, are included in Appendices I, II and III respectively. In order to avoid repetition, these notes also omit any detailed discussion of the complex relationships that exist between the different versions of each constituent element – a topic analysed in full in the Introduction. Nor do they catalogue every possible variation, addition or omission to be found in the different versions of this material, but comment only on those that are most significant.

PART I – MS Prk

The J.B. text begins two-thirds of the way down fol. 184r, with a 2-line red lombard initial *A*, with no break after the explicit for the previous text, *The Siege of Jerusalem*. There is no heading or introductory statement. For a full description of Prk, its version of the *J.B. Treatise* and its closest analogues, see the survey of all J.B. witnesses in the Introduction.

I/1–107 Collective nouns. Prk and Pl stand alone in presenting their collectives nouns in groups of five (with one group of seven: lines 96–102). With 107 entries, the Prk list of collectives belongs with other long versions of this item, although it falls well short of the longest lists, in *StA* and Rd, which have 164 and 153 entries respectively. For typical short versions of this element, see H (II/197–241) and Ha (III/1–50); and see Appendix I for a complete, alphabetic collation of the J.B. Collective nouns, together with explanatory notes.

I/108–17 Precepts in -*ly*. The ten Precepts in -*ly* are separated from the preceding list of collective nouns by a one-line break (the manuscript is clearly ruled), and there is a large, red paraph in the margin beside the opening line. Each apothegm is written on a separate line, as in this edition, and the text is essentially identical to that of Pl. A longer version, of sixteen statements, occurs also in *StA*, where it is written in long lines across the page. The *StA* version is broadly similar to that in Pp (fol. 1r), which has seventeen statements, but which I have left out of this discussion because of its dissociation from the other J.B. material in that manuscript. For that reason, too, I have disregarded the equivalent version in T (fol. 27r).

Comparable renditions of this item (*NIMEV* 324) can be found in the following manuscripts, none of them a member of the J.B. group: BL Additional MS 37049, fol. 86r; BL MS Lansdowne 762, fol. 16v (L2); BL MS Sloane 747, fol. 65v; BL MS Sloane 775, fol. 56v; BL MS Sloane 1360, fol. 232r; BL MS Stowe 850, fol. 1r; Oxford, Balliol College MS 354, fol. 159v; also the composite Caxton volume MC, fol. 34v. The Lansdowne version has been printed in *Reliquiæ Antiquæ*, I, 233, and in *Babees Book*, p. 359.

Among the J.B. manuscripts, other versions of this item occur at a distance from the J.B. material also in Eg (fol. 78r), Adv (fol. 175r) and Rd (fol. 143r). The Eg text accords with *NIMEV* 317, whereas Adv and Rd both contain *NIMEV* 3087, the latter found also in Bodleian MS Tanner 407; see *The Commonplace Book of Robert Reynes of Acle: An Edition of Tanner MS 407*, ed. Cameron Louis (New York and London, 1980), pp. 179–80, 392–6. For yet other renditions, see *NIMEV* 799, 3102; also Whiting, *Proverbs*, G259: 'Serve God devoutly, *etc.* (*varied*)'.

I/118–27 Resting terms. The ten resting terms (including the final two, which belong properly with the collectives) run straight on from the Precepts in -*ly*, without any line break or mark to distinguish them. Cf. the different versions in H (II/183–96) and Ha (III/79–90), and see Appendix III for a full discussion of these terms.

I/128–56 Carving terms. The twenty-nine phrases of carving terms begin at the top of fol. 188r and continue overleaf to about a third of the way down the leaf. By including terms for fish, Prk's list belongs with other long versions of this item. See Appendix II for a full discussion of its contents.

I/147–8 The naming of large and small eels occurs only in Prk and Pl. See Appendix II, nos 44, 45.

I/157 ff. A line break separates the carving terms from all that follows in Prk. From this point on, everything is written in long lines, with red paraphs introducing some elements but not others.

I/157–61 Four things to dread. This set of apothegms appears also in *StA*, sig. f5r (lines 1891–7) under the heading *Merke wele theys .iiii. thynges*; and, with some variations, in MC, fol. 34v. The *StA* version is listed by Whiting, T124. The text of Prk has two large lacunae, which I have filled from Pl.

The passage has its basis in Ecclesiasticus (Sirach) 26:5–7: 'A tribus timuit cor meum et in quarto facies mea metuit: Delatura civitatis et collectio populi et calumniam mendacem super mortem omnia gravia.' (Douay-Rheims: 'Of three things my heart hath been afraid, and at the fourth my face hath trembled: The accusation of a city, and the gathering together of the people: And a false calumny, all are more grievous than death.') All citations of the Vulgate and the Douay-Rheims English translation come from *The Vulgate Bible: Douay-Rheims Translation*, ed.

Swift Edgar and Angela M. Kinney, 6 vols, Dumbarton Oaks Medieval Library (Cambridge, MA, 2010–13).

I/157 Cf. *StA*: Ther be .iiij. thynges principall to be drad of euery wise man'; MC reads: 'Ther be fower thynges to be marked of euery wyseman'.

I/159 *indyngnacyone of a prynce StA* adds *Quia indignacio regis vel principis mors est*, 'Since the displeasure of a king or a prince is death'. MC has the supplementary Latin dictum but lacks the phrase *vel principis*. Cf. Proverbs 16:14: 'Indignatio regis nuntii mortis et vir sapiens placabit eam.' (Douay-Rheims: 'The wrath of a king is as messengers of death: and the wise man will pacify it.')

I/159–60 *þe euyle wylle odyre þe fawyr* Cf. *StA*: 'the fauor or the will'. MC is even briefer: 'the thyrd ys the fauour of a judge'.

I/161 *þe mutacyone or a schlandure of a commente* This should probably read, 'a schlandure or þe mutacyone of a commente'; i.e. 'a slander or the revolt of a commonalty'. Cf. *StA*: 'The .iiij. is sclaundre & the mutacion of a comynalte'; MC: 'the forthe ys the slander of the mutacion of a cominalite'. *MED* lists the form *commente* as a recognised variant of ME *communite* (s.v.).

I/162–70 Properties of a good horse. Similar versions of this gnomic set of observations on the properties of a good horse occur also in *StA*, sig. f5r, and in the following non-J.B. manuscripts: Trinity College, Cambridge, MS O.9.38 (T2), fol. 49r; BL MS Lansdowne 762, fol. 16r (L2); Bodl. MS Wood empt. 18 (W2), fol. 60r. These are all essentially the same in terms of their content, yet T2 is the most similar to Pl–Prk in minor details of presentation and terminology. The text of T2 is printed by Rigg, *Glastonbury Miscellany*, p. 74; that of L2 in *Reliquiæ Antiquæ*, I, 232–33; and that of W2 by Rachel Hands, 'Horse-dealing lore, or a fifteenth-century "help to discourse"?', *MÆ*, 41 (1972), 230–39 (p. 238). There are also longer and more elaborate English versions of this item, as well as French, German and Dutch analogues – on which, see Hands, *ibid.*, p. 234. As Hands observes (*loc. cit.*), these all belong to the genre of 'numerical apothegms' described by Ernst Robert Curtius, *European Literature and the Latin Middle Ages*, trans. Willard R. Trask (London, 1953), pp. 510–14.

I/165–6 *a fayre tras* 'a good quantity [fig. "head"] of hair'. Cf. 'a fayer creste' (T2); 'fair of hair' (*StA*, L2); 'fair heir' (W2).

I/166–7 *a leyne hede* 'a lean head' – i.e. one that gives the impression of emaciation in that the skin clings tightly to the underlying bone, as Albertus Magnus explains in his *De animalibus*, lib. XXII, tract. 2, cap. 1, § 38. The adjective *lene* appears also in T2, as against 'a dry head' in *StA*, L2 and W2 (although W2 also has *lene* interpolated above *dry*, apparently by the same scribe). The two words convey the same meaning here (see *MED*, *drie* adj.(1) 3b), and we find both applied to the love-lorn Arcite, of whom Chaucer says, 'lene he wex and drye as is a shaft' (*CT*, I.1362).

See further David Scott-Macnab, 'A hors shulde haue ... a dry hede', *N&Q*, 64 (2017), 22–4.

I/169–70 *a byege chyne, a flat lege* Presumably this means that a horse should have a sturdy back and a haunch that is smoothly contoured; see *MED, flat* adj. 1. (a).

I/171–181 Beasts of venery and the chase. A red paraph marks the start of this item in the manuscript. Represented here is a long version, comparable with that of Eg (IVd), but distinct from the short versions of (a) H–L and Pp (II/165–73), and (b) Ha and Rd (III/51–8). Prk shows a strong affinity with Dg–Rg at this point, though with a crucial disagreement about the ages of the *elke* and the *spycarde* (see notes below).

The central distinction made in this little passage between three classes of hunted animals – beasts of venery, beasts of the chase 'of the sweet foot', and beasts of the chase 'of the stinking foot' – has no exact parallel in any hunting treatise. In William Twiti's *The Art of Hunting* and the amplified redaction known as *The Craft of Venery* (*CV*), the four J.B. beasts of venery (hart, hare, wolf and boar) are grouped together as animals hunted in the same way, though they are not given any specific appellation; see Twiti-A, 11–12 and *CV*, 10–11, in *The Middle English Text of 'The Art of Hunting' by William Twiti*, ed. David Scott-Macnab (Heidelberg, 2009). By comparison, *BH*, 1218–20, does categorise these four animals as beasts of venery, and distinguishes them from five 'beasts of the chase': the buck, the doe, the fox, the marten and the roe (1221–5). Of everything else, it continues, 'Rascall ye shall hem call' (1226–7).

In his *Select Pleas of the Forest* (Selden Society, 13 (1901), pp. cxiv–cxv), G.J. Turner observes that the division between beasts of venery and beasts of the chase has nothing to do with the concepts of forest and chase, or the laws relating to them, as John Manwood tried to prove in his *Treatise of the Lawes of the Forest* (London, 1615; facs. edn, Amsterdam, 1976). Instead, the distinction seems to reflect different hunting methods, with beasts of venery being dislodged by means of a limer (a tracking dog), and beasts of the chase pursued by the pack without being first tracked by a limer. (See Glossary s.v. *lymoure*.) The treatises are somewhat obscure on this point, but see *CV*, 10–16 and the original Anglo-Norman version of Twiti's treatise, *L'art de venerie* (Twiti-F, 5–20): Guillaume Twiti, *La vénerie de Twiti*, ed. Gunnar Tilander, Cynegetica 2 (Uppsala, 1956).

Yet even if this were the underlying rationale for these categories, many of the animals mentioned by the *J.B. Treatise* are incongruous. The wolf, for example, was probably extinct in England and Wales by the mid-14th century (see Derek Yalden, *The History of British Mammals* (London, 1999), p. 166), and both reindeer and 'elk' owe their presence in this passage more to literary convention than to English sporting practices (see notes below). In short, the J.B. categories of venery and chase seem to be repetitions of a rather time-worn tradition, which even finds its way into *BH* (1218–27), only to be contradicted there by the more plausible assertion that only three animals are *vpreryde* with a limer: hart, buck and boar,

'And all other beestys that huntid shall be / Shall be sought and founde with ratchis [running hounds] so fre' (*BH*, 1365–7).

I/171–2 *þe wolfe* See my comments above on the incongruity of the wolf in a list of game animals of the 15th century. Not only were wolves by then extinct south of the Scottish border, they had been despatched as vermin since Saxon times. Cf. the statement 'A wolfe is trapped' in the J.B. Hunting terms found in Adv (IVa/6).

I/174 ff. *swete foote ... stynkynge fut* Both terms refer to the track or spoor left by an animal, but have different origins. In the case of *foote* (<OE *fōt*), the sense of 'footprint', 'track' probably developed under influence from ME *fute, fewte*, a 'track' (<OF *fuite*, 'flight'). The confusion of the two words is apparent in the fact that both appear in Prk. Other texts are more consistent: Dg, Ha, and *StA* use the form *fewte*; H, L and Eg use *fute*; Pp and Rd have *fo(o)te*. The distinction between the 'sweet' and 'stinking' groups appears to be between animals that leave a moderate scent, and those whose scent is strong. Eg (IVd) also calls the latter *stynkyng chasse*, and observes that animals of this category 'wylle bothe clym and crepe for the substaunce of hem'. There is broad general agreement among the J.B. texts about which animals belong in each category, though *StA* mistakenly transposes otter and marten with roebuck and roedoe.

The distinction between beasts of the 'sweet foot' and those of the 'stinking foot' is not repeated in any English hunting treatise, although *MG* occasionally alludes to the fox and other vermin as 'stinkyng beestis' (p. 78; *bestes puanz* in Edward of York's source, the *Livre de chasse* (*LC*) of Gaston Phébus, ed. Gunnar Tilander, Cynegetica 18 (Karlshamn, 1971), p. 156, line 35). In the earlier *Livres du roy Modus et de la royne Ratio* (*c*. 1376–7), a work now conventionally attributed to of Henri de Ferrières, animals are divided into five *bestes douches* (= *douces*, 'sweet') and five *bestes puans* ('stinking'), with hart, hind, buck, roe and hare assigned to the first category, and wild boar and sow, wolf, fox and otter to the second. See *Modus et Ratio*, ed. A.G. Tilander, 2 vols (Paris, 1932), I, cap. 74–80. Earlier in the same work, these two groups of animals are called *bestes rouges* and *bestes noires* respectively (cap. 2, lines 3–16). It should be noted, however, that *Modus et Ratio* makes these distinctions primarily for allegorical and moralising reasons, so there is no obvious relevance to the J.B. groupings. (See also IVd/17–23n below.)

I/175 *þe rayndeere* Although English travellers to Scandinavia may have seen reindeer in the wild, it seems unlikely that many English writers or sportsmen would have had a very precise notion of what the animal was, other than some sort of exotic deer. Even Gaston Phébus admits, 'J'en ay veü en Nouroegue et Xuedene ['Norway and Sweden'], et en a oultre mer, mais en romain pais en ay je pou veüz' (*LC*, cap 2, line 14). As Tilander suggests, the reindeer that Gaston claims to have seen in *pays roman* were probably imported animals kept in a park (*ibid.*, Glossaire, s.v. *romain*). Interestingly, Edward of York omits Gaston's entire chapter on reindeer when making his translation (*MG*) of *LC*, and the animal is not mentioned in any other English hunting manual until the 16th century, when George Gascoigne describes 'the Raynedeare', but declares 'I will treate no more of him, bicause I do not remember that I euer heard of any in this our Realme of England: it may be that there be some in Ireland ...': *The Noble Arte of Venerie or Hunting* (hereafter *Noble Arte*), facsimile edn published as *Turbervile's Booke of Hunting 1576* (Oxford, 1908), p. 145.

By contrast, reindeer are frequently referred to in works of imaginative literature, sometimes perhaps simply for the sake of alliteration, as in the line 'The roo and the rayne-dere reklesse thare ronnene' (*Morte Arthure*, ed. Edmund Brock, EETS os 8 (London, 1865; repr. 1904), line 922). In other cases, the animal seems intended to evoke an aura of somewhere remote and exotic, as in the following description of a park offered by a poet-lover to his lady: 'I myght speke of a parke of bestys with horn / Thantelope reynder and vnicorn / Iclosed with marble xxti myle a boute / A thousand panters and bukkys yn a route / With elkys hertys white and blake / Tristeth wel of venyson was no lakke' (Eleanor Prescott Hammond, 'How a lover praises his lady', *Modern Philology*, 21 (1923–4), 379–95, lines 142–7). For a range of other literary references, see *MED*, s.v. *rein-der* n.

I/176–7 *elke* The name of some sort of deer, probably obscure even in the 15th century, and not to be confused with the huge Irish elk (*Megaloceros giganteus*), which disappeared from the British Isles about 2000 BC (Yalden, *History of British Mammals*, p. 165). Like the reindeer, the elk was most likely an animal considered strange and exotic, as in the love poem quoted above in note I/175. Prk's explanation that it is a two-year-old male red deer is the most plausible of the J.B. versions, although most hunting manuals prefer the term *brocket* for that animal: Twiti-A, 35; *CV*, 71; *BH*, 1232. In *MG*, a two-year-old stag is a *bulloke*, with *broket* indicating a three-year-old (p. 17). Eg, Dg and Rg all define the elk as being 200 years old: 'a hert of ij^c wynter of age' (Dg). This probably represents scribal error, influenced by the traditional belief in the stag's longevity, as is described by John Trevisa: 'And the hert lyueþ most longe tyme passynge an hundred ȝere, as it was yknowe by hertes þat were ytake an c. ȝere after Alisaundres deþ þe whiche he hadde ymarked wiþ byes [collars] of golde.' *On the Properties of Things: John Trevisa's Translation of 'Bartholomæus Anglicus: De Proprietatibus Rerum'*, 3 vols, ed. M.C. Seymour et al. (Oxford, 1975–88), II, 1177. There is no evidence outside the J.B. tradition that 'elk' was a name used of a two-year-old stag.

þe *spycarde* Only Prk defines this animal as a three-year-old stag. In Eg, Dg and Rg, it is an animal 300 years old: 'a hert of iij^c wynter age' (Dg). Conversely, in H, L and Pp, the name indicates a 100-year-old stag: 'A herte of a hounder yere olde' (Pp). The name appears variously as *spycard* (Dg), *spykard* (Rg), *spyckard* (Pp), *specard* (Rd), *spyccard* (StA), *spytard* (H, Ha), *spitard* (L), and *spyarde* (Eg). The underlying form is probably ME *spaiard* (<AN *espeyard*), 'a three-year-old male red deer'; see Twiti-F, 42; Twiti-C, 35 (*spayer*); Twiti-A, 35 (*espayard*), *CV*,

78; *BH*, 1233 (*spayad*). The form *spycarde* shows the influence of ME *spike*, 'a spike', 'a pointed metal object', while *spytard* is influenced by ME *spite*, 'a spit', 'a sharp rod' – in both cases alluding to the short, sharp, unbranched antler of a young stag. Neither *spycarde* nor *spytard* is recorded by *MED*, but see *OED* s.vv. *spyccard* n. and *spittard* n., as well as *spitter* n.[1] for a later development which corresponds to modern German *Spiesser* (also *Spiesshirsch, Spitzhirsch*) <MHG *spiss* 'a young stag with short, unbranched antlers'; see David Dalby, *Lexicon of the Mediæval German Hunt* (Berlin, 1965), s.v. *spiz* (sm).

I/178–81 Missing from the beasts of the 'stinking foot' in Prk, Eg, Dg and Rg, is the 'white rat', or stoat (also known in its winter coat as the ermine); see H (II/173, and associated note) and Ha (III/57).

I/178–9 *the folmard, þe fechow* 'the foumart, the fitchew' – both synonyms for the polecat, which is mentioned again in line 181. Prk's *fechow* appears also as *fuche* (Ha, Rd) and *fyches* (*StA*).

I/179 *þe bade* A type of wildcat; *MED*, s.v. *badde* n.(1) (b), reads 'the wild cat'. Cf. *the bad* (Ha, III/56), *the baude* (*StA*, 1853). Dg and Rg explain that this animal is a mountain cat, and Eg substitutes 'The catte of the mountayne' (IVd/16). Hands (*EHH*, p. 149/1853n) suggests that 'the leopard or panther is intended here', but the European wildcat (*Felis silvestris*), an animal common in Britain during the Middle Ages, seems more likely. See *MG*, p. 39, where Edward of York refers specifically to English wildcats, and the editors' observations on pp. 209–10; see also Yalden, *History of British Mammals*, pp. 175–7.

I/182–8 Breeds of dogs. A red paraph marks the start of this item, of which Prk preserves a long version. See also the equivalent texts of Ha (III/66–9) and Eg (IVe), together with associated notes. Many of the dogs listed here are discussed by the Baillie-Grohmans in the Appendix to *MG*: pp. 115–212.

I/182 *grayhoundys* A name that encompassed a number of breeds of swift gaze-hounds, including the shaggy Irish wolfhound and the smooth-coated Italian greyhound; see *MG*, pp. 62–63, 142–5.

basterdes Cf. Eg, which reads 'bastarde grehounde' (IVe 2). It seems that any mixed breed is intended here. The juxtaposition of 'bastards' and 'mongrels' is similar to the use of synonyms for the polecat in lines 178–9.

I/183 *mastyffys ... alanndys* 'mastiffs ... alaunts'. Mastiffs were large, heavy-set canines popular as guard dogs, for bull-baiting and for hunting wild boar. The illustration in *LC* shows these dogs with bared teeth and enormous spiked collars (p. 138). In *MG*, Edward of York devotes a short chapter to mastiffs as if they were a separate breed, but he also uses the term *mestifis* when alluding to a variety of alaunt – *Alauntz of þe bochere* – used by boar hunters; see *MG*, pp. 65, 68 and note I/184 below.

Edward of York speaks principally two main varieties of alaunts: *alauntz gentil* and *alauntz ventreres* (*alanz veautres* in *LC*, p. 125). Both types were large, fierce dogs used for hunting deer and boar: 'for a good alaunt shuld renne also fast as a greihounde, and eny beest þat he myȝt come to he shuld hold wiþ his sesours [teeth] and nouȝt leue it, for an alaunt of his nature holdeth faster his biteng þan should iii greihoundes ... and þerfore it is þe best hounde for to hold and for nyme al maner beestis and hold myȝtely' (*MG*, p. 64). Chaucer mentions these dogs in a brief but evocative image of Lycurgus, king of Thrace, who is surrounded by 'white alauntz, / Twenty and mo, as grete as any steer, / To hunten at the leoun or the deer' (*CT*, I.2148–52), in *The Riverside Chaucer*, gen. ed. Larry D. Benson (Oxford, 1990).

I/184 *rachys, kennettes* Small hunting dogs that hunt by scent, sometimes also called 'running hounds'; see Appendix I, nos 104, 166 and notes.

bochere hovndis Edward of York refers to 'Alauntz of þe bochere':

> ... þat byn called greet bochers houndis þe which bouchers holde for to helpe hem to bryng here beestis, þat þei byn in þe cuntre for ȝif an oxe escapid from þe boochers þat leden hym his houndes wold go take hym, and holde hym to his master were come and shuld helpe hym to benynge [*r*. brynge] hym agayn to þe toun. Þei byn of litel cost for þei etyn þe foule þinges in þe boochiers rowe, and also þei kepen her maisters hous, þei byn good for þe batyng of þe bole and huntyng of þe wild boore. (*MG*, p. 65)

I/184–5 *dovnghyll currys* 'dunghill curs', i.e. dogs that scavenge on rubbish dumps. Cf. 'myddynges kurris' in Ha (III/69).

I/185 *smalle poppys for ladys chambureys* 'small "puppies"' (*sc.* lapdogs). A 'puppy' in this obsolete sense is 'A small dog kept as a lady's pet or plaything', and is not to be confused with 'A young dog', a sense first attested in 1567: *OED*, s.v. *puppy* n. 1.a. and 1.b. Cf. *StA*: 'smale ladies popis that beere a way the flees, and dyueris smale sawtis'.

I/186–8 These three lines describe the actions associated with different types of hunting dogs: *bythe cast of*, 'are cast off', 'slipped (released) from their leashes'; *drawith*, 'search for a quarry by scent'; *rennythe*, 'run' (after the quarry); *reytornnyth*, 'return' (to the hunter); *fechyng*, 'retrieving'. Spaniels were trained to swim out to waterfowl that had fallen into water after being struck by a hawk, and to return with these to the falconer; see *MG*, p. 66. The action ascribed to terriers in Dg and Rg is *ses(s)yn*: 'sieze'.

I/189–200 Soiling terms. A red paraph marks the start of this item, of which Prk preserves a long version, characterised by the opening statements about the hunter casting off a couple of alaunts, and then blowing to encourage his hounds. Cf. the equivalent texts of H (II/174–182), Ha (III/70–78), and T (IVg), together with associated notes. The purpose of this little passage is to set out the correct terminology for describing the actions of a hunted hart when it 'soils', i.e. takes refuge in a body of water – a pond, river or the like. (The verb 'to soil' – ME *soilen* – is a technical hunting term derived from the noun *soile*, 'a wallow', 'a water-refuge', itself a loan-word from OF: see Godefroy, *souil* s.m., Tobler–Lommatz., *soil* s.m.) In doing so, the hart attempts to throw its pursuers off its scent by going some way upstream or downstream before crossing to the opposite bank, or, cunningly, returning to the very bank from which it had fled.

Trevisa refers to this episode in the following words: 'And whanne þe hert is arered [started] he fleeþ to a ryuer oþer to a ponde. And if he may swymme ouer þe water he takeþ comfort and strengþe of coldnesse of þe water and scapeþ þe hunters' (*Properties of Things*, II, 1178). Edward of York provides a much longer description beginning, 'And whan he [the hart] is wery and hoote þan he gooþ to yeeld hym and soilleþ hym to some grete Ryvere' (*MG*, pp. 19–20). Another account occurs in *BH*, lines 1545–68, but this employs a set of terms entirely different from those found in the J.B. texts; in *BH*, for example, the hart is said to 'descende' rather than 'soil'. See also the independent *Tretyse off Huntyng* (*TH*), 90 ff. The hunting treatises, together with Trevisa, indicate that the hart will take to water towards the end of the hunt, when it is hot and tired. By contast, the J.B. texts give the impression that the hart heads straight for water, though this is probably only a consequence of their compressed style of presentation.

Elsewhere, a waterfowl is also said to 'soil' when it plunges into water to escape a pursuing hawk; see H (II/140, 176) and T (IVg/2).

I/189–92 The way in which this hunt begins, with the alaunts launched directly at a herd of harts, differs from the standard procedure described in the treatises, whereby a limerer (a tracker, who uses a limer, or tracking dog) first seeks out a specific animal, and then dislodges it ahead of the running hounds; see, for example, *MG*, p. 83 ff. Perhaps this shows that stags were hunted in more ways than the manuals, with their emphasis on chivalric sportsmanship, reflect. In Dg, the order of the second and third statements (Prk, 191–2) is reversed, and Rg omits Prk's third statement altogether.

I/194 'When he swims downstream, he fleets'. *MED*, s.v. *fleten* v.(1), records the meanings 'to float, drift, swim', but not the specific sense 'to swim, move downstream'. The latter sense is also absent from *OED*, s.v. *fleet* v.[1].

I/196 The terms 'break' and 'beat' appear to be synonymous in indicating the action of swimming upstream. This sense of ME *beten* appears to be a calque from OF *batre*, 'to beat', used in the sense 'to swim', 'to plunge through water'. See, for example, the description of the hart's soiling in *LC*, p. 63: 'Et, si en tout le pais n'a grosse riviere, il [the hart] va as petites et *batra* ou amont ou aval, selon ce que plus li plaira, demie lieue ou plus sanz venir a l'une rive ne a l'autre' (emphasis mine; see also *LC*, p. 76). In French, therefore, the stag could 'beat' up or down a stream.

Comparing this with Edward of York's translation, it is interesting to see that Edward retains *beat* for the hart's passage upstream, but uses another term (*foile*) for its motion downstream (the equivalent of J.B. *fleten*): 'And ȝif in þe cuntre is no grete Ryuere he goþ þan to þe litel, and shal bete vp þe water or foile doun þe water as hym likeþ best ...' (*MG*, p. 19; see *MED*, *foilen* v.(2) 3). Elsewhere, however, Edward uses *beat* to refer to the roe's flight *down*stream as well as upstream: 'Whan he hath bete þer inne long, vpward or downward ...' (*MG*, p. 26).

OED, s.v. *beat* v. 20 (b), glosses the verb as having the intransitive hunting sense, 'to take to the water and go up the stream', which it presents as a variation on the notion 'To run hither and thither in attempting to escape'. It also records the verb used transitively in expressions such 'to beat the stream, a brook etc.' But it does not connect any of these citations with the idea of swimming (through) a watery obstacle. A possible later example of such a signification may be found in *The Tempest* (II.i.119–21), when Francisco tries to assure Alonso that his son may not have drowned: 'Sir, he may live. / I saw him beat the surges under him / And ride upon their backs.' *The Oxford Shakespeare: The Complete Works*, 2nd edn, gen eds Stanley Wells and Gary Taylor (Oxford, 2005).

The verb *break*, which is here said to be synonymous with *beat*, occurs also in *BH* in the description of the hart fighting its way upstream – 'Ayen the water his way eeuen iff he hent / Then brekyth he water [Þen brekes he þe water: MS Rawl] ther to take yow tent' (1565–6) – but otherwise appears to be confined to the J.B. texts.

To complicate matters, *OED* has confused this usage with another, very similar expression, 'to beak water or soil', meaning 'to leave the soil': see *OED*, s.v. *break* v. 20. b. Thus Gascoigne: 'When he [a hart] goeth quite through a ryuer or water, we say he breaketh Soyle'; similarly, '... the huntesmen them selues may seeke to finde where the Harte hath forsaken the soyle (which huntesmen call breaking the water) ...' (*Noble Arte*, pp. 243, 116). It should be noted, however, that the sense 'to leave the water', exemplified in *Noble Arte*, is a later development, closely related to the sense 'to break covert or cover: to start forth from a hiding place' (*OED*, *break* v. 20. a.), and *OED* is mistaken to cite *BH* (named *Bk. St. Albans*) as an instance of its use.

I/197–9 Prk shows confusion in these lines. Some words have been mistakenly cancelled by expunction and others have been inserted in the wrong places. The text is, however, easy to reconstruct from other witnesses, not least Pl. See further H (II/174–182), Ha (III/70–78), and T (IVg) below.

I/199 *flyth* 'flees', 'takes flight', with equivoque on 'flies', duly exploited in the next statement, 'a falcon flies'.

I/200 *a favcone flyith* Prk omits the additional statement 'a hert flyȝþe' (Dg), which precedes this statement in Dg, Rg, H and Ha, to form a couplet that rounds off the soiling terms and, in the case of Prk, introduces the hawking items that follow. See H (II/182) and Ha (III/78) below.

I/201 ff. At this point Prk turns from hunting to falconry, on which topic the following preliminary observations summarise some key concepts.

Birds of prey that are trained for taking wild quarries are commonly divided into two main categories: falcons, otherwise known as 'long-winged hawks', or simply 'long-wings'; and true hawks (accipiters), also known as 'short-winged hawks', or simply 'short-wings'. Some modern authorities also use the term 'broadwings' to refer to birds of prey that have wings that are somewhat wider than those of a hawk, but not as long as a falcon, especially buzzards of the genus *Buteo*. See, for example, Emma Ford, *Falconry* 2nd edn (Botley, 2008), pp. 26–7.

Falcons have relatively short tails and wings that taper to sharp points at their tips; the toes are long and slender. Their characteristic method of hunting is to rise high in the air, circle, and and then 'stoop' (i.e. swoop down) at considerable speed on their prey, which often includes other birds in full flight, the quarries being killed or disabled by a glancing blow of the falcon's hind talons. Those used for sport are, in declining order of size: gyrfalcon (or gerfalcon), peregrine falcon, lanner, saker, hobby, merlin and kestrel. In falconry, such birds are released to soar to a height where they can 'wait on' for prey roused for them by the falconer. They are trained to return to the lure – a leather bag decked with wings and bait, which is swung in circles through the air by the falconer – when they fail to make a kill.

True hawks (short-wings) have broad wings and long tails, adapted for an entirely different style of hunting. They approach their prey by stealth, often in woodlands, or using whatever cover is available, and then accelerate to make a short, fast attack. They invariably 'bind' to their prey, killing it by piercing it with their powerful talons; a sparrowhawk will also sometimes break its quarry's neck with its beak in flight. Those used for sport are the goshawk and the smaller sparrowhawk, both of which are trained to fly directly at game from the hawker's gloved fist. In the Middle Ages, they were also trained to fly from a convenient perch while the hawker crept forward to rouse up a quarry. These birds are trained to return to the hawker's fist (rather than to a swung lure) if they fail to make a kill.

It will be apparent that the term *hawk* can be used in general of both falcons and true hawks, though *falcon* is always restricted to long-wings, and in medieval usage often refers specifically to the peregrine falcon. The terms *falconry* and *hawking* are interchangeable; so too are *falconer* and *hawker*, although modern usage favours the former. In contexts where greater specificity is important, however, *falconer* may be reserved for a person who flies long-wings, and *hawker* for one who flies short-wings. In addition, the now rare name 'austringer' (<OF *austruchier*, OF *ostour*, 'goshawk') indicates someone who flies a goshawk, with the even rarer 'sperviter' (<OF *esperveteur*, OF *espervier*, 'sparrowhawk') referring to the owner of a sparrowhawk.

In discussing these issues, I endeavour to distinguish between falcons and hawks, falconers and hawkers, wherever possible, and to use the name austringer where it appears in the text under discussion. Sometimes, however, it is necessary to use the terms *hawk, hawker* and *hawking* generically in a way that includes falcons and those who fly them.

I/201–24 Hierarchy of hawks. A red paraph marks the start of the Hierarchy of hawks, which is set out in long lines across the writing area. Together with the Collective nouns, this is one of the best known elements of the *J.B. Treatise*, especially for the phrase 'a goshawk for a yeoman', which occurs in some versions (see note I/219 below). In *StA*, the hierarchy has been separated from the J.B. material proper and placed at the end of the hawking treatise (sigs. d3v–d4r), thereby gaining an undeserved air of authority, especially among antiquarians and scholars unaware of its true origins. As Rachel Hands has convincingly shown, this hierarchy is one of the most contrived and 'literary' of the J.B. elements, making it extremely unlikely to have been a guide to actual practice: 'The names of all manner of hawks, and to whom they belong', *N&Q*, NS 18 (1971), 85–8; *EHH*, p. 116/1162n.

In essence, the hierarchy separates raptors into three possible categories: 'hawks of an emperor', 'hawks of the tower' (i.e. falcons), and 'other hawks' (i.e. true hawks). Those of the latter two categories are then ordered according to size, and each is apportioned to a member of human society in descending order of rank. This provides a pleasant conceit, but one that could not have been intended seriously, as will become apparent in the notes that follow.

The J.B. Hierarchy of hawks is quite different from, and must not be confused with, the hierarchy of raptors set out in Richard Holland's comic fable *The Buke of the Howlat* (c. 1450; *NIMEV* 1554), in which a number of birds are assigned ranks from human society. In that poem, the eagle is designated an emperor, gyrfalcons are dukes, falcons are earls acting as marshals to the emperor, and goshawks are 'governouris of þe gret oist' (ll. 313–38): Richard Holland, *The Buke of the Howlat*, ed. Ralph Hanna, Scottish Text Society (Woodbridge, 2014), p. 67. For a thorough examination of this poem's date and literary heritage, see *ibid.*, pp. 23 ff.

I/201–7 The three raptors assigned to an emperor – eagle, vulture and milan (kite), here somewhat misleadingly all called 'hawks' – are not treated as birds that can be used for sport by any medieval European hawking treatise. These birds are described and discussed in varying degrees of detail by Frederick II of Hohenstaufen (d. 1250) and Albertus Magnus (d. 1280), for example, but nowhere are they treated as trainable hunting birds, although eagles have long been used in that way throughout the Eurasian Steppe, from Kazakhstan to Mongolia. See Frederick II's *De arte venandi cum avibus* (henceforth *DAV*): *The Art of Falconry ... of Frederick II of Hohenstaufen*, trans. & ed. Casey A. Wood & F. Marjorie Fyfe (Stanford, 1961), pp. 28, 109 (also pp. 525–6 on hunting with eagles); Albertus Magnus, *De Animalibus Libri XXVI*, ed. Hermann Stadler, 2 vols (Münster, 1920), II, 1433–7, 1501–2, 1513. Matters were no different in Renaissance England, as may be judged by George Turbervile's *Booke of Faulconrie or Hauking* (1575; henceforth *BF*), facs. edn (Amsterdam and New York, 1969), pp. 3–24, 45. We may plausibly conclude that eagle, vulture and milan are most likely grouped together in the J.B. hierarchy as the most suitable birds for the most important ruler because of their greater size, rather than for their usefulness or popularity for medieval hawkers. In spite of this caveat, there are undoubtedly valid snippets of information preserved in these lines. (See also the unexplained reference to an 'egle horne' discussed in the note following.)

I/201 *neygule* Albertus Magnus describes a number of different types of eagle, of which the most easily identifiable is the golden eagle: *De Animalibus*, pp. 1433–7. For a translation, see Albert the Great, *Man and the Beasts: De animalibus (Books 22–26)*, trans. James J. Scanlan (Binghamton, 1987), pp. 194–6. The eagle's identification as 'king of the birds' and its ancient and widespread associations with imperial authority need no amplification.

In spite of the lack of evidence of eagles being used in 'hunting', the romance *The Squire of Low Degree* (in *Middle English Metrical Romances*, ed. W.H. French and C.B. Hale, 2 vols (New York, 1964), II, 721–755) contains a reference to an 'egle horne' as a bird suitable for 'hauykyng by the ryvers syde' (lines 774, 776). The term is a mysterious one that has yet to be satisfactorily explained. Perhaps the location of the poem, in Hungary, accounts for the inclusion of this exotic bird.

I/202 *watter* Most likely, 'vulture', *pace MED*, which glosses this word (s.v. *vature* n.) as 'A species of hawk' – an unsatisfactory proposition given that the relevant passage is concerned wholly with the largest birds of prey. *StA* reads *bawtere*, but all the manuscripts have this word beginning with *v* or *w* (including Rc, *vawtier*, which Hands transcribes as *bawtier*: *EHH*, p. 116/1166n. The sheer number of variant forms for *vulture* cited by *MED* is instructive. It is unlikely that the bestiary notion of the vulture as an ungainly scavenger of carrion could have influenced its inclusion in this list. Even the description of Albertus Magnus is unflattering in claiming that a vulture is barely able to lift itself off the ground even with three or more leaps, which makes it easy to catch: 'et ideo tribus saltibus vel pluribus vix a terra elevatur et ideo antequam elevetur, frequenter capitur' (*De Animalibus*, p. 1513). The species of vulture that would have been most familiar to medieval Europeans would have been the bearded vulture, or lammergeier (*Gypaetus barbatus*), the largest European bird of prey, with a wingspan of up to 10 feet, and its closest relative, the Egyptian vulture (*Neophron percnopterus*), which is still found in parts of southern Europe.

mellannd Probably the milan, or kite (<MF); see *OED*, *milan* n.[2] (first attested 1484). Other forms of this word in the J.B. texts are *melonne*, *melowne*, *millone* (see Glossary s.v. *millone*). Turbervile distinguishes two sorts of kites, while also revealing an important consideration, which is that kites were a favourite quarry of falconers:

They flee with the Sacre at two sortes of Kytes, that is, to the Kite royall, which is called by the Frenche man, the (*Mylan Royall*) and at one other kinde of Kyte, called the Blacke Kyte, (the *Mylan Noyer*) whiche is farre the more nimble byrde of the two ... (*BF*, p. 45)

The 'Kite royall' that Turbervile refers to here is most likely the red kite (*Milvus milvus*, formerly *Milvus regalis*), which was formerly regarded as a pest and exterminated from large parts of the British Isles. Perhaps the relatively large size of the kite (it has a wingspan of some 70 inches) and its elegant soaring flight led to its inclusion in the list of 'hawks' suitable for an emperor.

There remains some uncertainty, however, over the exact identity of the milan, and whether it is the same as the *milion* (*mylyon* – the form used in Ex), an obscure bird of prey adopted from the Middle East: see A.G. Tilander, *Glanures lexicographiques* (Lund, 1932), p. 170; Hands, 'Names of all manner of hawks', p. 86/4n. Neither name (*milan, milion*) is attested by the *MED*.

I/203 *elke* Glossed as a two-year-old stag in line 176, but see my comments on this novel definition in the relevant note above.

I/204 *bustterd* The great bustard (*Otis tarda*), formerly found in Britain, though not any more. Eg reads: 'a bustarde, othyrwyse namyde a derefoule' – the latter word unrecorded by either the *OED* or the *MED*, s.v. *der* n.

playne grovnd 'level, open ground' – precisely the sort of terrain in which an eagle needs to be flown at a quarry. Wild eagles habitually soar and stoop down on their prey, but captive eagles cannot be trained to 'wait on' in flight for quarry to be roused for them. In consequence, they are flown from the fist, usually at terrestrial game, since they have not the opportunity to gain sufficient height and speed to stoop at flying birds.

I/205 *enlurryd ... reycleymyd* Although this statement gives the impression that *enlured* and *reclaimed* are semantically distinct, they are but two terms for the same action, namely, that of recalling (a bird) to the lure. The term *reycleymyd* can also mean 'tamed', which is how Hands reads it (*EHH*, p. 116/1169n), while also observing that this fails to make sense, for these birds would have to be tame in order to be flown at game in the first place. It seems likely that there is confusion here, perpetuated by scribal ignorance. Eg offers a mysterious variation that does nothing to make matters clearer: 'And thes hawkys benne not namyd or callyd vnto the lewre, the cause ys for they ben ouyr heuy & ponderos for any man to bere.'

I/206–7 *þe perche portatyfe* A portable perch, which may have been something like the device now known as a 'cadge', an oblong wooden frame with legs, on which several hawks can perch simultaneously. It could also have been a large wooden beam, supported at either end by trestle legs, of the type illustrated in the Vatican Codex of *DAV*; see plate 36 (facing p. 3). See further Ha (III/106), which describes the 'portable perch' as an item carried between two men. The import of these lines is that the emperor's 'hawks', being too heavy (*pondors*) to be recalled by means of

EXPLANATORY NOTES — PART I 175

a lure, are trained 'to [return to] a portable perch'. Eg states this explicitly: 'But they ben made ['trained'] vnto the perke portatyf and ther by they benne gouernyde'.

I/208-18 Described in these lines are falcons, known as 'hawks of the tower' because they soar to a great height and circle there waiting for their prey; see *The Parlement of the Thre Ages*, l. 213: 'And than the hawteste in haste hyghes to the towre'. In the present context, the word *tower* conveys the conflated senses of 'a lofty structure or point' (<OE *tūr*, OF *tor, tour*) and 'a circling motion' (<OF *tor, tour, tourn*): see *MED, tour* n.(1) and n.(2), and Godefroy, s.v. *tourn*, s.m.

The name for each type of bird refers to the female, with the male indicated either by *tercel / terselet* or a diminutive form of the species name, such as *sakret*. This follows from the fact that female falcons (and hawks) are generally bigger than the males, making them the preferred sex to train for pursuing game. The term *tercel* (<OF *tercel*, L *tertius*, 'third') is variously attributed to the fact that the male is about a third smaller than the female, or to the folk-belief that the third egg in a clutch contains a male chick.

I/209 *garfavkone* The gyrfalcon (gerfalcon), or gyr, the largest of the falcons.

I/210-12 All three birds referred to here are but one species: the peregrine falcon. Medieval and Renaissance authors regularly distinguished between different classes of peregrine, with the 'falcon gentle' being considered the finest. See, for example, Frederick II, *DAV*, pp. 110/6n, 124-5, where 'true gentle falcons' *(falcones gentiles absolute* [*sic*]) are acknowledged to be the same species as other peregrines *(gentiles peregrini)*, but are nevertheless distinguished on several points. So too Turbervile, *BF*, pp. 35-8, where the author takes pains to distinguish the 'haggard falcon' from the 'falcon gentle', though both names refer to the peregrine. According to Tilander, the adjective 'gentle' is 'qualificatif du faucon bien proportionné et bien affaité': *Glanures lexicographiques*, p. 127, s.v. *Gentil*. The peregrine is the falconer's bird *par excellence*, capable of exceeding speeds of 150 mph in its stoop, and so prompting rhapsodic descriptions of its aerobatic displays. See *OED*, s.v. *peregrine* adj. & n., and Hands, *EHH*, p. 117/1181n, for discussions of the origins of its name.

I/213 *basterd* A cross-breed of some kind: the exact nature of this bird is unclear. In *StA*, it is allocated to a baron.

I/217 *StA* assigns the hobby to a 'yong man'; G, Rc and Ry give it to an 'infant'; but Eg, Ex, Dg and Rg agree with Prk that it belongs to a young squire. Cf. H, L and Pp, which have 'a (young) squire of the first head'.

I/218 *þat fleythe fro þe lure* Prk reads *?frove þe lure* (the form of the preposition is obscure and seems likely to represent scribal error). Cf. Eg, Ha and Rg (*fro*), Dg, Rc, Ry (*for*). The import of this statement must be that hawks of the tower are recalled by means of a lure, or, as *StA* has it, 'theys ... ben both ilurid to be calde and reclaymed' (1194-5).

I/219–24 Described in these lines are the two short-winged hawks – goshawk and sparrowhawk – that were the staple of the medieval English hawker. The English treatises on hawking, such as *PEB*, *PH* and PPF, are devoted almost entirely to these two birds, and we know from the correspondence of the Pastons that the men of this family flew goshawks; see *Paston Letters and Papers of the Fifteenth Century*, ed. Norman Davis, 2 vols (Oxford, 1971–76), I, 450–2, 579–84.

I/219 The different J.B. texts are far from unanimous in their allocation of the goshawk, with only Dg agreeing with Prk; others give it to a 'gentleman' (Pp); a 'poor man' (H, L, Rg); a 'yeoman' (Eg, G, Rc, Ry, *StA*) and *a mene man þat hath lyuelode* [rent or income] (Ex). This should be proof enough of the unreliability of the widespread assumption that Chaucer's Sir Thopas is hilarious for going hawking with so 'ignoble' a bird as the goshawk: see J.M. Manly, 'Sir Thopas: a satire', *Essays & Studies*, 13 (1928), 52–73 (p. 67); Laura Hibbard Loomis, 'Sir Thopas', in *Sources and Analogues of Chaucer's Canterbury Tales*, ed. W.F. Bryan and G. Dempster (London, 1958), 486–559 (p. 508/5n). By his admiring comments on the goshawk, no less an authority than the Holy Roman Emperor, Frederick II of Hohenstaufen, a noted authority hawks and hawking, shows that he did not consider the bird as suitable only for persons of low status: *DAV*, p. 110. If further proof were needed that men of rank flew these birds, there are the letters of Edward I concerning goshawks (among others) in the royal mews: Frédéric Joseph Tanquerey, 'Lettres du Roi Edward I à Robert de Bavent, King's Yeoman, sur des questions de vénerie', *Bulletin of the John Rylands Library*, 23 (1939), 487–503, nos 3, 5, 15, 16.

I/220 The tercel referred to here is presumably that of a goshawk. In G, Rc, Ry and *StA*, this bird goes to a 'poor man'; a 'yeoman' in H, L, Ex and Rg; and a 'gentleman' in Pp. Only Dg agrees with Prk. Eg omits the tercel goshawk altogether.

I/222 Most lists end with the musket, or male sparrowhawk, but H and L add the kestrel (see II/160). *StA* and Ex agree that the musket belongs to a holywater clerk, but Eg is less specific, with just 'clerke'.

I/223 4 *wyuc ... quarraye ... fare iuttye* Some or all of these terms appear in a number of different forms, and without explication, also in Dg, Rg, G, Rc, Ry and Ha (see III/113–4 and IVh/24–5, together with the textual variants noted there). They are, however, expounded as part of the J.B. 'flying terms' in H, L and Ex, and are discussed in the notes on H (II/125 ff.) below. *StA* reads: 'And theis be of an oder maner kynde, for thay flie to Ouerre [*read* Querre] and to fer iutty and to iutty fferry' (1201–2).

Eg is notable in closing the list of short-winged hawks, and the Hierarchy of hawks as a whole, with the following observations (fol. 64v):

> Ande thes ben made vnto the fyste ande fle w*ith* hyr fre wylle yf they benne in ther prosp*er*yte for to make game vnto hyr mayster more þen for any gredynys of mete for they ben noo rayuyners.

¶ And sum of the hawkys afore sayde wylle be made vnto the fyste welle inowe but they moste haue grete labyr to bryng them there-to &c.

I/225 ff. Ages of a hawk. There is nothing to distinguish this element, the Ages of a hawk, from the preceding Hierarchy of hawks in the manuscript. See also the equivalent text of H (II/107–111). In *PH*, the naming starts at an even earlier age: 'first thay been egges, and afterwarde they bene disclosed hawkys' (17–18). For hawkers, it has always been vitally important to be able to state at what age a bird was first caught and trained, as this can often have a bearing on its temperament and disposition, as well as the type of training it gets. Clearly, the older the bird the more difficult it can be to subdue. Many of the names listed here continue to be used by modern hawkers. For example, a male goshawk that is introduced to humans as a nestling will be known as an 'eyas tiercel goshawk', and will retain this label throughout its life, though gaining additional descriptions of its age, such as 'of three seasons'.

I/225 *a nyes* 'an eyas', an unfledged hawk (<AN <OF *niais*, a nestling); see *MED*, s.vv. *eies* n., *eie* n.(3). Godefroy records *niais* only as an adjective, but see Walter von Wartburg, *Französisches etymologisches Wörterbuch* (Tübingen 1948–; hereafter *FEW*), VII, 113–15, s.v. **nidax*; also *Anglo-Norman Dictionary*, ed. William Rothwell et al. (London, 1992; hereafter *A-ND*), s.v. *niais* s. The word is unquestionably used as a noun in *Modus et Ratio* (I, cap. 114, ll. 36–7: 'l'autre est apelé niais, ch'est chelui qui a esté priz u ny'. See also *Modus et Ratio*, cap. 90, ll. 25–6; *Le menagier de Paris* (*c.* 1394), ed. Georgine E. Brereton and Janet M. Ferrier (Oxford, 1981), p. 163, §39. The hawking treatise in *StA* (*PH*) offers a curious false etymology for this name: 'An hawke is calde an eyes of hir eyghen, for an hauke that is broght vp vnder a bussard or a puttocke [kite], as mony be, hath wateri eyghen' (lines 377–84).

a bowere, a branchere a 'bougher', a 'brancher' – names for fledglings that have started to move out of the nest. Both terms are explained in *PEB 1*, pp. 5–6, and *PH*, 26–31: 'Anoon be kynde they will draw somwatt out of the nest and draw to bowis, and come agayn to ther nest. And then thay be clepit bowessis [boughers]. And after saynt Margaretis day [20 July] thay wil flie fro tree to tree, and then thay bene calde brawncheris.' The distinction between these two stages in a hawk's development is not made by Turbervile, who writes only of branchers: *BF*, p. 69. Other (modern) authorities use the term *bowiser* (not attested in *OED*); see, for example, James Edmund Harting, *Bibliotheca Accipitraria* (London, 1891, repr. 1964), p. 220, s.v. *bowiser*. (See also next note.)

I/226 *a rammage havke* 'a wild hawk' (<AN <OF *ramage*, 'wild', 'untrained') – another name for a fledgling that has been caught before its first moult. In his *Livre de l'art de faulconnerie* (1492), Guillaume Tardif considers the term to be synonymous with 'brancher', for he claims, 'Nyais oyseau est celui qui est prins

ou nid. Branchier est celui qui suit sa mere de branche en branche, qui est aussi nommé ramage': *Le livre de l'art de faulconnerie e des chiens de chasse*, ed. Ernest Jullien, 2 vols (Paris, 1882), I, 31. The same opinion is expressed in the *Menagier de Paris*, pp. 163–4, §39, and by Turbervile, *BF*, pp. 31, 69. But for *Modus et Ratio* they are not the same. Concerning sparrowhawks (*espreviers*), we are told, 'l'un est apelé ramage, ch'est chelui qui a esté a soi longuement; ... le tiers est apelé branchier, c'est celui qui est nouvelement yssu du ny' (cap. 114, 35–40; see also cap. 90, 23–30).

a ventteremuere 'an intermewer'. This term originally denoted a hawk that was in the process of moulting: a half-mewed hawk, a 'part-mewer' (<OF *entre* + *mué*), as in *Modus et Ratio*, I, cap. 90, lines 23–5: 'Il sont faucons de pluseurs manieres: les uns sont muiers de bois, les autres sont sors, les autres sont entremués et tiennent du sor.' By implication, the word came to mean 'a hawk taking on – or already in – its first adult plumage'; hence, a hawk in its second year. According to Turbervile, '... they are called (Entermewers) or Hawkes of the first cote, that is from the middle of May, till ... December ... for that they cast the old, and haue new feathers' (*BF*, p. 32); see also *OED*, s.vv. *intermewed* adj. *intermewer* n. To complicate matters, modern falconers use the expression 'intermewed hawk' for one that has moulted in captivity – a particularised sense that is not recorded by the *OED*; see M.H. Woodford, *A Manual of Falconry*, 4th edn (London, 1987), p. 146.

a mard-haye A hawk that has moulted in the wild. The term is a corruption of Anglo-Norman *muer de haie* <OF *mué de haye*, literally, 'hedge-mewed' – an expression used adjectivally, as in 'le falcon muer de haie' (*Three Anglo-Norman Treatises on Falconry*, ed. Tony Hunt, Medium Ævum Monographs, 26 (Oxford, 2009), p. 23). The derived English noun must therefore denote 'a hedge-mewer' – a sense more recognisable in the form *mure-de-hay* of H (II/108) than in the inverted formulation *hay-de-mew* of Harl (IVc/5). The expression is rare in ME and is not recorded by *MED*. But see the letter written by John Paston III on 24 November, 1472, explaining to his brother, John II, that he cannot use the hawk sent to him because she is a 'mwer [*sic*] de haye': *Paston Letters*, no. 356, lines 1–7. The French expression *mué de haye* (plural *muez de haye*) appears several times in *Le menagier de Paris* (pp. 164–5, §§40–42), and *Modus et Ratio* has the variant *muyer de bois* (I, cap. 97, line 2) along with the plural *muiers de bois* (I, cap. 90, line 24; cap. 114, line 32). Later French falconers speak also of *mués de champs*; see Woodford, *Manual of Falconry*, pp. 186–7.

an hagard a 'haggard' (<OF *hagard*) – a hawk caught when in its adult plumage; hence, one that has moulted at least once in the wild. Such birds are notoriously difficult to tame, as Edmund Bert affirms: 'the Haggart ... hath liued long at liberty, hauing many things at her command, and she is therefore the harder to be brought to subiection and obedience': *An Approved Treatise of Hawkes and Hawking* (London, 1619), p. 3 [sig. B2r]; see *Bert's Treatise of Hawks and Hawking*, facs. edn with introduction by J.E. Harting (London, 1891). There is considerable uncertainty over

the origins of this word, which is not recorded by the *MED*. The popular derivation from Hebrew *agar*, 'a stranger', is implausible (see Woodford, *Manual of Falconry*, pp. 183-4). The *Oxford Dictionary of English Etymology*, ed. C.T. Onions *et al.* (Oxford, 1969), suggests an association with Germanic *hag* (cognate with OF *haie*), 'hedge', though this is doubted by the editors of the *OED*, s.vv. *haggard* adj. and n.². On the other hand, see *Le menagier de Paris*, which defines an 'Esprevier hagart' as one 'qui est mué de haye' (p. 165 § 42).

I/227-8 Presumably, these six names describe a hawk in terms of the prey it is most accomplished at catching: hence, 'partridger', 'pheasanter', 'geliner' (see below), 'ennewer' (see below), 'bitterner' and 'heroner'. The expressions 'herroner' and 'partridger' appear in Turbervile, *BF*, pp. 28, 188.

gellonder An obscure term, probably formed on AN *geline*, 'a hen' (<OF). In other J.B. versions the word appears also as *genoner* (error for *gelloner* – Dg), ielonere (H), ioloner (L). In H (II/111), the word *hennys* is interpolated above the line in the same hand.

a nanauer an 'enewer': a hawk that forces waterfowl – specifically ducks according to H (II/111) – to dive into a river or other body of water in an attempt to escape. Cf. H (II/138-9): 'Whan þat þe hauke is aboue, þan þe fowle for ferde anewyth into þe watyr' (intransitive use); *PH*, 1101-2: 'ye shall say then yowre hawke hath ennewed the fowle in to the ryuer' (transitive). The form of this word in Prk shows signs of corruption not apparent in Dg's *naneuer*.

I/229 ff. Hawks' diseases and remedies. A red paraph in the middle of the line marks the start of this item in Prk. See also the equivalent texts of Ha (III/115-21) and G-Ry (IVh 26-84); also, the somewhat different material of H-L, Pp (II/1-100), which lacks the initial list of diseases and the anatomical areas they affect.

I/229-33 All versions of this passage show some degree of confusion and corruption, but Prk is better than most. Twelve afflictions are listed here, to which Ha, G and Ry add 'the lice' found in a hawk's neck and mantle (the plumage of its back): III/117; IVh/28. Some of the conditions named in this list, such as pin and cramp, are readily identifiable, and are known by the same names to this day. Others are more difficult to translate into modern veterinary terms, for their names encompass a variety of ills – none more so than the diseases attributed to 'worms', both filanders and 'aiguils', as discussed in detail below. For more information about the principal ailments of hawks from a modern viewpoint, see Woodford's, *Manual of Falconry*, pp. 148-65; Humphrey Ap Evans, *Falconry for You* (London, 1960), pp. 123-34. A comprehensive scientific text is that of Manfred Heidenreich, *Birds of Prey: Medicine and Management*, trans. Dr Yvonne Oppenheim (Oxford, 1997).

þe ree 'rye' (AN *ré*), a malady that causes a hawk to suffer congestion of its nares (nostrils) and a 'swollen' head. According to various treatises, the condition is caused by a deficiency of 'hot' (i.e. fresh) meat (*PH*, 113), or by a lack of 'tiring' (tough meat for tearing at): *PPF*, 109-111. In *Cheape and Good Husbandry* (1614), II.xi,

p. 131, Gervase Markham ascribes the rye to a head cold, or to inadequate cleaning of the hawk's beak and nares after feeding. Now obsolete, the term *rye* clearly covered a multitude of ills, including head colds, rhinitis, and other conditions described at length by Turbervile as 'Apostumes of the head' and 'the distillation and swelling of a hawkes heade' (*BF*, pp. 227–33).

þe *frounse* 'frounce', a canker or sore in the mouth and throat (ME *frounce* <OF *fronce*). *PEB 1* claims that 'The frounce comythe when a man fedith his hauk with porke, cat oþer kydde, iiij melys arewe [= *aroue*, 'in succession']' (p. 8), and describes also how the growth may 'wox as grete as a note', indicating that 'þere is a grub þerin' (p. 7; see also p. 14, and *PH*, 96–112). In modern usage, the term *frounce* indicates a grey, scaly growth on the hawk's tongue and the roof of its mouth, extending into the throat in advanced cases and causing the bird great difficulty in eating – a condition caused by the protozoon *Trichomonas gallinæ*. Some medieval texts appear to describe that condition, while others apply *frounce* rather more loosely to a variety of maladies producing lesions or growths in the mouth and throat, including infections of candida yeast and *Capillaria* worms (see þe *fyllavndyrs* below and IVh/44–6). See further Heidenreich, *Birds of Prey*, pp. 128–32, 141–2).

þe *pokys* & þe *mytys* 'pocks' or eruptions, especially about the eyes, caused directly or indirectly by external parasites such as red mites. These mites attack the cere, nares and eyelids, causing irritation and prompting the hawk to scratch the affected areas, which results in sores, or pocks.

þe *fyllavndyrs* 'filanders', threadlike worms (<OF *filandre*; cf. OF *fil*, 'a thread'), described by Turbervile as being 'smal as threedes, & one quarter of an ynche long' (*BF*, p. 252). One of the independent remedies in H declares that, 'Þe fylawndyrs be ... longe smale wormys w^t rede hedes an ynch long, and þei cum of onkynde mete and of onclene mete': *Of Hawks and Horses*, p. 36 §32. These are very likely the parasitic threadworms known today as *Capillaria*, which are endemic in hawks and can become problematic if the bird's resistance is lowered. They then increase dramatically, infesting the lower intestine and even the upper oesophagus and crop. This would accord with the description given by Tardif in his *Livre de l'art de faulconnerie*, pp. 111–12: 'Filandres sont petis vers. Quatre especes y a de filandres: l'une est en la gorge de l'oyseau, l'autre au ventre, l'autre aux rains, la quatriesme est nommée aguilles, qui sont bien petis vers.'

þe *aglys* Any of a variety of parasitic worms. The different forms of this word, which appears to be always used in the plural, suggest considerable scribal uncertainty: *akyllys* (H), *aglye* (Ex), *egles* (Ha), *ageles* (G). These all represent corruption of OF *aiguille*, signifying (i) a needle, (ii) a variety of intestinal worm that has the appearance of a needle. The distinction between such worms and filanders (described immediately above) is unclear, and we see that Guillaume Tardif (quoted above) regards *aguilles* (*sic*) as a particularly small type of *filandres*. At another point (p. 135), he says that they are 'autrement nommées lumbriques'.

The same parasite is probably what we find referred to in *PPF* as *aggelons* (lines 43, 145, 150) <OF *aiguillon*, 'a small worm'.

In other texts, the word takes on other forms, under the influence of OF *anguille* (L *anguilla*) 'an eel'. Thus, *PH* refers to 'A medecyne for wormys called anguellis' (989) – rendered *anguilles* in *PEB 1* (p. 14), *anguillis* in L (fol. 173r) and *angeles* in Ry (see note IVh/68–70 below). None of these terms survived in English beyond the 15th century, for when Turbervile compiles his *Booke of Faulconrie*, he supplies the following heading: 'For the disease called in french the (Aiguils) an euill worse than the Filanders, for which I know no apt English terme, and therfore must borow the french terme of mine Author'. He continues:

> There are found a kind of Filanders which are called (*Aiguilles*) bycause they be sharpe like a needle, shorter and more perillous than are the great Filanders, for ... they pearce the bowels & creepe vp to the hart, so that your hawke perisheth of them, if she be not regarded in time. (*BF,* pp. 318–9)

It is likely that these names for worms encompassed a range of parasites, including tapeworm, ascarids (a form of roundworm) and gapeworm, the latter appearing in an infected bird's trachea. This may explain why the J.B. texts locate the filanders and 'aiguils' variously in the chest and back.

brayle 'abdomen', 'bowels'; not to be confused with the leather strap (called a 'brail') that is used by modern falconers to immobilise the wing of a restless hawk: see Woodford, *Manual of Falconry*, p. 180. *MED*, s.v. *brail* n. (b) cites a number of ME hawking texts to support its definition 'the belly or rump of an animal', a gloss that fails, however, to distinguish between *belly* in terms of its possible internal and external referents; i.e. 'stomach' as opposed to 'underside'. Such a distinction is important for making sense of texts that describe different forms of constipation and their symptoms (see further below). In a number of works, it is clear that the word, especially when given a plural marker, refers to the soft feathers on a bird's abdomen; e.g. *PEB 1*, p. 14: 'and here foundement woll defile her brael'; *THawk 2*, p. 143: 'this hauke is engowted [speckled] in þe brayles ende'; *THawk 1*, ll. 110–11; *PH*, 308–11; II/122 below and associated note. In the context under discussion, however, it would seem that *brayle* refers to the internal workings of the hawk's abdomen where constipation – *þe pere and þe cray* (see next note) – can occur. See also III/119–20 and note.

þe pere and þe cray Two forms of constipation: *pere* <OF *pierre*, 'stone'; *cray* <OF *craie*, 'chalk'. According to *PEB 1* (p. 7), *PH* (93–4) and *PPF* (21–3), a hawk has 'the cray' when it cannot mute (i.e. pass faeces), though it may be more accurate to say that the mutes or faeces are passed with difficulty. A healthy hawk is able to 'slice' or eject its mutes to a distance of several feet, whereas a bird with bowel problems will strain to pass hard mutes, or else it will pass thick, chalky mutes, which clog the feathers around its 'tewel', or vent (cloaca). Turbervile names the

former condition (characterised by hard mutes) 'the stone', and the latter (chalky mutes) 'the Cray' or 'the stone Craye', explaining:

> You must vnderstand y^t there are .ij. sorts of diseases in hawks, called by the name of the stone: & scarsly dothe the one come without the other. The one keepeth beneath in their tuels, & the other in their bowels & panels ['intestines']: & they may be cured bothe togither. Some cal this disease ye Cray. (*BF*, pp. 311–12)

þe *pyne* 'pin', a hard, painful nodule that grows on the underside of a hawk's foot: a form of corn. Turbervile describes it thus: 'The Pynne is a swelling disease, that doth resemble sharpe nayles, rysing vp in the bottome or palme of the Hawkes foote: and by reason it doeth so muche in shape resemble a nayle, by meane of the sharpnesse thereof, those swellings are called by the Falconers of Italie *Chiodetti*, as a man woulde terme them in English, small nayles ...' (*BF*, p. 260).

þe *polione* A swelling of the lower leg; or, according to H, 'a swellyng abofe þe gesse' (II/33), referring to the jesses or leather anklets tied onto the legs of captive birds. Ex describes the condition as 'a swellyng abowte the knees' (27). This suggests a condition brought on by 'bating' – when a hawk attempts to fly off its perch, but is brought up by the leash secured to its jesses. It may then flap around wildly, straining against the leash and causing bruising or swelling of its legs. The affliction is named only in the J.B. texts, and then with some variation: *pellyone* (I/255); *polyon* (H, L); *pelyownde, polyownde* (G), *pelaundyr* (Ex, 27). The rarity of this word makes its origins difficult to trace, but it may be related to *poleine* (or *polayn*), the name given to a piece of armour protecting the knee (see *MED, poleine* n.(3); *OED, poleyn* n.¹; *SGGK*, 576). This supposition receives some support from *PH*, 267–9, which prefaces its account of a hawk's anatomy as follows: 'to begynne at hir fete and goo vpwarde as knyghttis been harnesside and armeed, & so we shall enarme her'.

þe *crampe* 'cramps' – a mysterious affliction, often suffered by eyasses removed from the nest too early; older birds are also affected if allowed to become too cold. As *PH* observes: 'The croampe [*sic*] commyth to an hawke with takyng of colode [*recte* colde] in hir yowthe. Therfore it is goode for an hawke to kepe hir warme: yonge and hoold' (636–8). Cramps are serious in a hawk, as they can easily lead to paralysis and death.

þe *pyes* A condition that causes a hawk to lose coordination and fall from its perch (see II/47–8, 59–61) – possibly what Turbervile calls 'Apoplexye, or falling euill', brought on by overheating or overexertion (*BF*, pp. 225–7), though see also his discussion of giddiness, 'the falling sicknesse' and 'swymming in the head of a Hawke' (*BF*, pp. 233–6, 309–10). Modern hawkers refer to 'fits', or 'epileptiform fits', which afflict short-wing hawks far more than falcons; the causes are usually dietary, as described in Woodford's *Manual of Falconry*, pp. 161–2. As far as I have been able to ascertain, the word *pyes* occurs only in the J.B. texts. It may seem strange that a condition described as a 'swyuenyng in þe hede' by H (II/59–60) should here be located in the feet; presumably, this reflects the hawk's inability to stand upright on its perch.

I/234 ff. The recipes that follow are all written in continuous long lines of prose in the manuscript; some begin with a red paraph. In Dg, they also form a single block of text and are separated from one another by a double virgule.

I/235 *palleys* 'palace' – the palate or roof of the mouth (<OF *palais*); see *OED*, s.v. *palace* n.²; *MED*, s.v. *palas* n. Tardif, *Livre de l'art de faulconnerie*, p. 107, has a recipe 'Contre chancre ou palais de la bouche de l'oyseau' (this malady presumably being what English texts refer to as 'the frounce').

I/237–8 *swet mylke* 'fresh milk'.

I/239–40 *cast* 'hold, restrain'. Modern falconers use this very word to describe the act of restraining a hawk in order to administer medicine or to carry out some other operation (e.g. Woodford, *Manual of Falconry*, pp. 162, 180), yet the particularised sense is not defined by *OED* (though see under *cast* v. 59). The operation described here appears to entail removing the scab on a 'frounce' to expose the wound beneath to medicaments.

I/241–2 *marttylmas byfe* 'Martinmas beef' – i.e. the flesh of an ox slaughtered on St Martin's feast day (Martinmas, 11 November) and salted for winter provision. Such meat was believed to have curative or restorative properties.

I/244 *orpamente* 'orpiment', or yellow arsenic. *PH* directs the austringer to blow orpiment onto the hawk through a quill, 'a penne' (498–9), in order to kill mites and lice. Most English texts are somewhat blasé in their attitude towards this poisonous substance; but cf. *Le menagier de Paris*, p. 169 §56, which takes a more considered approach and suggests safeguards; also, Turbervile, *BF*, pp. 359–60.

I/245–7 *weche* 'wash'. It was standard practice to soak a hawk's meat in water and then wring it out to remove the blood and, with it, much of the nourishment. The resulting 'washed meat' kept the bird's delicate stomach working, but allowed it to become hungry enough to want to hunt. Here the hawk's meat is washed in juice extracted from the crushed leaves of the herb southernwood, or in mare's milk.

I 247 *vus yovre havke ... safrovne* 'accustom your hawk to having its meat flavoured with saffron'. See also H (II/18), G (IVh/59–60): '& gefe hur moche saferon in hire mete'.

I 250 *oke pollypodyi* 'oak polypody', the name given to the common variety of polypody (*Polypodium vulgare*), and similar ferns, found growing on trees, especially oaks; also known as 'oak-fern' (IVh/72). See *OED*, s.vv. *polypody* n.¹, *oak fern* n.

I/253 *þe glayre of a nnegge* 'the white of an egg'.

I/255-6 See G (IVh/77-9) and H (II/34-6) for more information that can help to make sense of this cryptic instruction. The advice is to anoint the hawk's leg with fat released by heating a well-used pot lid, presumably of cast iron. The procedure is mentioned also in *PPF*, 173-8.

I/258 *iouke* 'jouk' = 'roost', 'sleep': the correct term for these actions when performed by a hawk.

I/259 *chyuerys* Read *clyuerys* – i.e. clivers or cleavers, also known as goosegrass; see note II/42-6 below.

I/261 *For þe pyis ... dye* This sentence must be corrupted; Dg is even more confused: 'ffor þe pyes take sodeynly wol fro ʒou dye take mayden wort ...'. It is possible that *sodenlye* is a misreading of *solondon, selondon*, 'celandine' – the plant recommended as a cure for this ailment by G (IVh/82). See my account of *þe pyis* towards the end of note I/229-33 above, and see H (II/47-8) for a more helpful description of the symptoms of this condition.

I/262 *lawandere* Cf. H (II/49), which recommends lavender cotton, an entirely different plant, but perhaps what was originally intended here.

I/270 *a bechynge* 'a beaching' – a falconer's term indicating 'a beakful', by implication, a mere morsel or a small meal. See Turbervile, *BF*, 84: 'feede hir with Pullets flesh earely in the morning asmuch [*sic*] as shall be sufficient for a beaching'. Harting, *Bibliotheca Accipitraria*, p. 219 gives the modern form of this word as *bechins* (not attested by *OED*). However, see *OED*, s.v. beach v.[2] (first attested 1575): 'to give a beakful to (a young bird)'.

PART II – MS H

The *J.B. Treatise* in MS H is acephalous: it begins abruptly at the top of fol. 47r without any general heading or introductory remarks. As I observe in the Introduction, a leaf is missing from this quire, and it is tempting to speculate that it might have been the preceding one, containing a heading similar to those we find in two closely related versions, Pp and Ex. These read, respectively:

'To helpe an hawke of dyvers sekenes' (Pp, fol. 20v)
'For to kepe haukys / To helpe an hauke of dyuerse sykenesse' (Ex, fol. 101v)

L, which appears to be a lineal descendant of H, is unhelpful at this point because of the way in which the beginning of the J.B. remedies for hawks (the Hawk's diseases and remedies) have been blended with the end of the previous item in that manuscript.

The notes that follow will quote extensively from Ex, which has been published separately (Scott-Macnab: 'An autonomous and unpublished version of the *J.B. Treatise*', *MÆ*, 2007), and from Pp, which clearly belongs to the same broad tradition as H and L, but is too divergent to be collated with them.

II/1 ff. Hawks' diseases and remedies. Like Pp and Ex, H does not preface this item with the short passage containing a general overview of hawks' diseases, as found elsewhere – as in Prk (I/229–33), Ha (III/115–21) and G (IVh/26–31). Unlike the absence of a heading, this does not appear to be the result of the manuscript having lost a leaf, but rather a deliberate shaping of the material.

In order to avoid repetition, the following notes on H's Hawks' diseases and remedies do not repeat information already provided in relation to Prk (I/229–70), but do address any new issues that arise in H. Additional comments on avian diseases and remedies will also be found in the notes on G (IVh/26–84).

II/1–5 Pp reads: 'For the ree: Take the iuse of a dasy and hony and put hit yn the pallet of the mowth that hit may stoppe the holes that ben yn the rofe of þe moth' (fol. 20v). Ex comments that 'the ree ... ys a grete desees yn euery hauke wythowte he be well ykapte' (1–2).

fayre watyr 'clean, fresh water'.

II/6–12 Pp reads: 'For the frons in the throte þat is lyke a skall: Take a hassyll stycke and pyke hit owte and wasch hit with vyneagyr; set a litill clowte on the styk*es* ende and powdyr hit w*ith* sodyn drayon or with pouder of martymase beef; bryn hit on a tyle stone and make powder of, and do hit there as tho has wasched the sore' (fol. 20v).

tyle-ston A masonry tile used in the preparation of food and medicine after being heated in a fire. There are frequent references to this utensil in *The Liber de Diversis Medicinis in the Thornton Manuscript*, ed. Margaret Sinclair Ogden, EETS OS 207 (London, 1938); see, for example, p. 17, lines 12, 15; p. 19, line 16.

II/13–14 Pp reads: 'For all maner vermyn on a hawke, wasche hyr and powder hire with ortment' (fol. 20v). Ex lacks this advice on 'vermin' (i.e. lice and mites). In his *Treatise on Birds*, Adelard of Bath (*c.* 1080–1150) warns his nephew that consorting with prostitutes is a sure way of infesting his hawks with parasites: 'meretricum frequentatio tineosos ex contactu accipitres facit'. *De avibus tractatus*, §2, in *Adelard of Bath. Conversations with his Nephew: On the Same and the Different, Questions on Natural Science, and On Birds*, ed. and trans. Charles Burnett *et al.* (Cambridge, 1998), p. 240.

II/15–18 This recipe is wanting in Pp and L, but not in Ex, which is a little clearer than H: 'For the felaunders, y schall tell yow the knowlech of tham: ye shall know hyt by the gapyng of youre hauke' (14–15). The reference to gaping suggests an infestation of gapeworm, the nematode *Syngamus trachea*. These worms inhabit a bird's trachea and can interfere with breathing if they become sufficiently numerous;

the bird then 'gapes' by opening its mouth and glottis wide to draw breath: see Heidenreich, *Birds of Prey*, p. 145. Again, this shows how some medieval names for hawks' diseases could cover a range of ailments.

II/19–23 This recipe is wanting in Pp. By locating these worms in the hawk's back, H agrees with Ha (III/118), G (IVh/29) and Ex (17). Cf. Prk (I/230–1), which has them occurring in the chest.

II/24–9 Pp reads: 'for the peere whan the hauke pro*fyrs* to mewte and may not: Take prosp*er*, saxifrage, polypody and p*er*celly rotys and a nege, and boyle hym yn fayre rynnyng wat*er*. When they ben sodyn put them yn a potte of vrth, and wasche thy hawkys [mete], and spend hit as þe nedys, a lytyll and a litell at onys; probatu*m* est' (fols 20v–21r). (I have supplied the word *mete* from Ex to make better sense of this passage.) Ex reads much the same, and agrees with Pp, against H, in omitting any reference to the stink of brass.

ellys þe watir ... brasse Presumably this mixture of herbs reacts with metalware, producing an unpleasant odour and taste, which would be offensive to a hawk.

II/30–2 This recipe is essentially the same in Ex and Pp.

II/33–6 Pp reads: 'for the polyner*e* that ys a swellyng above the gesse: Take the cover of a potte and hold hit to þe fyr*e* tyll ther*e* cum grece out of hit & ther*e* with noynte hir fete ofte' (fol. 21v). Cf. Ex, 27–29: 'For the pelaundyr that ys a swelling abowte the knees: ... and wyth the grese ye schull anoynt the haukys leggys oftymys.' Only H and L suggest heating a wooden ladle (*a trene ladyll*) as an alternative to a pot-lid.

II/37–41 This description of, and remedy for, the *pyn* is wanting in Ex and Pp.

II/42–6 This remedy is wanting in L. Pp reads: 'For the crawmpe that wyll make hir to streche and make hyr to put owte hir fote, and may not gette hete agayn but w*ith* moche payne: Take the iuse of clythes that geese be made fatte therwyth, and wasche hir mete with the iuse þerof tyll sche be hole' (fol. 21r). Cf Ex, 30–33: 'For the crampe þat wyll make a hauke to streche here lymmys ...'.

clyuerse or hayryfe 'cleavers or hairif' – both names for goosegrass, a climbing plant that was often fed to geese, and which is also known colloquially as 'Sticky Willie' for its remarkable ability to cling to the clothing, hair or fur of passing people or animals. Pp uses yet another name for it: *clythes*, 'clithers'. Cf. *clythen* (Ex, 32), which is reminiscent of *clitheren*, the form used by John Gerard in his *The Herball or Generall Historie of Plants* (London, 1597; facs. edn Amsterdam and Norwood, NJ, 1974); see further *OED*, s.v. *clithers* n.; *MED*, s.v. *cliver* n.(2).

II/47–52 Pp reads: 'For þe pies: That ys whan the hauke fallyth adown sodynly fro the fyst or fro the perche. Take heyhoue, horehounde, lavender coton and rosemary; put all thes yn a [potte *canc*] pan & lay thereyn hote brynnyng flyntes stones above the herbes, and set hit vnder þe haukes perche that the smoke therof may cum into the hawke & so sche schall be hole yn haste' (fols 21r–v). Ex refers to this malady as *the payse*, and recommends 'kyre ose or fond lauender coten' (34–5); see my discussion of those terms in 'An autonomous and unpublished version of the *J.B. Treatise*", p. 82/35n.

heyhond Read *heyhoue* ('hayhove', or ground ivy); the scribe has mistakenly appended *hond(e)* from the end of the next word, *horhonde* ('horehound', a herb). L is even more confused, reading, 'Take honde, lavender cotton'.

Although H, L, Ex and Pp provide more information about the 'pies' than other J.B. texts, their revelation that the condition causes a hawk to fall off its perch is not especially helpful as this could be symptomatic of any number of ailments. Even so, the J.B. recipes for aromatic inhalations suggest an attempt to treat a head-cold or a form of congestion, such as sinusitis, causing disorientation and giddiness – the 'swyuenyng in þe hede' referred to in lines 59–60; see also Prk (I/261–6), and cf. G (IVh/82–4). The term *pies* does not occur in *PEB*, *PH*, or any other English manual of falconry of which I am aware.

II/53–61 This recipe is preserved by Ex, but is wanting in L and Pp; it may be compared with the 'general medicine' in Prk (I/267–70). The sugar-candy referred to here is crystallised sugar, made by repeated boiling and slow evaporation. The description of the 'pies' in lines 59–61 appears to belong with the previous recipe (lines 47–52), and to have been mistakenly transferred to this location by miscopying.

II/62 ff. Described here is a recipe for a hawk that has failed to 'cast' or regurgitate rough material fed to it to cleanse its 'pannel' or stomach. In the wild state, all raptors regularly regurgitate pellets of indigestible material, such as feathers, fur and pieces of bone, and their stomachs secrete a mucus that aids this process. Captive birds need regularly to be fed roughage, called 'casting(s)', to purge the stomach of excess mucus. Such roughage might consist of whole birds or small animals, or, as described in *PEB 1*, p. 6, and *PH*, lines 69–75, strips of coarse woollen cloth called 'blanket' inserted into pieces of meat. Such material is later regurgitated as an oblong pellet, also called 'a casting'.

Pp reads: 'for to make yo*ur* hawke breke hi*r*e castyng: As thus, yf sche have resavyd .ii. or iij castyng*es*, take the rote seledyn and dyppe hir mete ther yn and sche schall caste. Also, take podur of pepur wyll make hir caste. A hawke moste have castyng and bathyng & wethuryng; and gode castyng for dulle hawke ys the scrapyng of dull hasull stycke' (fol. 21v). See also Ex, 43–47. Like Pp, Ex mentions the benefits of scrapings from a hazel stick and omits the other options: feathers, linen cloth, etc.

II/63 *receuyd* 'eaten, ingested, swallowed', a sense recognised by *MED*, s.v. *receiven*, v. 3b, 4a. Presumably, the hawk has twice or thrice eaten material to make it cast and has failed to do so.

II/64 *dubbe it in hyre mete* 'disguise, hide it in her meat': *MED*, s.v. *dubben* v. 3b.

II/68 *wederyng* 'weathering', exposure to open air and light – a term still in use, together with associated expressions such as 'weathering shed' and 'weathering ground'; see Woodford, *Manual of Falconry*, pp. 9–10.

II/72–3 *sekyth hyr nerrer* L reads 'seketh hir to nere'. The expression is not especially clear, but may mean 'probes her more closely', i.e. 'cleanses her more thoroughly'; hence the advice to limit its use, 'for dryyng of þe hawke'. See *MED*, *sechen* v. 3c: 'examine (a wound), probe'.

II/74 ff. This paragraph describes how to assess whether one's hawk has excess body fat after being kept inactive in the mews during its moult, or whether it has been purged of this fat – 'enseamed' – by diet and casting. Pp, which clarifies an obscurity in H and L but is also at variance with those texts, reads: 'To preve an hauke whethure sche be insamyd or no: Take hyr of a rowgh blanked and gyf hyr yn castyng and yf hit be yelow sche ys yn samyd; and yf hit be blake scho ys brosyd withyn, that ys to say sche ys fatte' (fol. 21v). See also *PEB 1*, p. 21, under the heading 'For to enseyme an hawke'; Turbervile, *BF*, pp. 115–7, 215–7; Ap Evans, *Falconry*, pp. 149–52; *MED*, s.v. *enseimen* v.

Ex shows evidence of confusion or corruption here by stating, 'The sekenes of þe pere ys a swellyng yn the hede' (52–3). Perhaps the scribe confused *þe pere* (constipation) with *the payse* = *pies* (giddiness); see note II/47–52 above.

II/76–8 *Take hir blanket* 'Take (and examine) the threads of blanket regurgitated by the hawk'; the meaning of this cryptic statement is disclosed by Pp (quoted above). However, note how H and Ex disagree with Pp over the different colours manifested by regurgitated castings and what these indicate about the health of a hawk (Ex agrees with H about the significance of yellow and black castings, but omits to mention green). Modern authorities agree that any discolouration indicates the presence of excess 'grease', or else a digestive disorder: Ap Evans, *Falconry*, p. 151; Heidenreich, *Birds of Prey*, pp. 78–9. See also Turbervile, *BF*, pp. 115–7, 213–7, for further information about enseaming a hawk, and diagnosing its condition by the colour of its castings.

seymy 'fat'. This adjective is not in *MED*, but see the noun *seime* (<OE *seim*, OF *saime*), 'grease, lard'.

bruschyd ?'bruised, hurt' (<ME *brisen*); or, ?'purged' (<ME *brushen*, 'to brush clean'). This description of a black casting need not have any logical connection with the question of purging the hawk of its fat. Interpretation is complicated by Pp's statement that a black casting indicates the presence of fat (see note II/74 above).

II/78–9 *gleymyd* 'congested with the oily mucus of the stomach' – a substance that falconers still call 'gleam' or 'gleaming' (see Woodford, *Manual of Falconry*, pp. 149, 183), though this is not attested by the *OED*, which treats the word in its different forms as obsolete. See s.v. *gleim* n., *gleimy* adj.

II/83 ff. This passage describes a condition in which a hawk regurgitates its food, and not just the indigestible portions; the result is that it 'may not endue', i.e. 'cannot digest' (its food). There is some confusion about the term *endue*, which appears in *PEB 1*, p. 9, to be synonymous with the action of 'putting-over', i.e. passing food from the crop to the stomach. In *PH*, however, the two actions, though closely related, are clearly distinguished (lines 224–37), as they are by Turbervile, *BF*, pp. 332–4. *MED* (s.v. *endeuen* v.(1) 2) relies solely on *PEB 1* for its definition of this word, and so fails to recognise its range of possible meanings.

The equivalent passage in Pp is here considerably shorter: 'And yf your hauke cast hye [*r*. hyr] mete & may not indew: Take hote mete and gode whyll hit ys quycke; and yf hit be a chekyn plucke of the skyn of the brest and put womans mylke apon. And when sche cast*es* hir mete gyff hir no more thereof' (fols 21v–22r).

Ex, 54–65, is worded somewhat differently from both H–L and Pp, for example: '& euer as sche plumys þervppon put þeron womanys mylke, & lett here neuer yn þe sekenes haue grete gorgys, butt smalle and oft'. Ex also contains the instructions about beating a dove with a rod, but with this wording: 'Also take a stocke-coluer or a pegyon ...' (59). And Ex has a great deal more to say about the benefits of pork and the relative qualities of different types of fat: 'Porke ys good mete and all maner thyng þat beryth grece ys good mete for a hauke, for hyt ys not hangyng [sticky] but euermore slakyng [easing] & losyng [loosening]; and talow ys fadde [unwholesome] & byndyng [constipating]' (63–5). This passage in Ex is found nowhere else in the J.B. hawking remedies.

II/87 *womannys mylke* This ingredient occurs in other recipes for sick hawks – see G (IVh/61); *PPF*, 217–20; BS, p. 93 – as well as in remedies for humans, but has received little comment until recently; see R.A. Buck, 'Woman's milk in Anglo-Saxon and later medieval medical texts', *Neophilologus*, 96 (2012), 467–85.

II/88 *gorgys* 'meals'; the term derives from the notion of filling the bird's crop, or 'gorge'; see *MED*, *gorge* n. 1c, 2a.

II/97 ff. This recipe for the ree is lacking in L and Pp, but not in Ex, which claims (mistakenly) that it is 'for the necke-ache'. The remedy appears to describe a means for relieving a hawk of congestion of the head. Pellitory of Spain is recommended for the ree also in the *Book of Secrets* (p. 94), though the advice there is to rub the sick hawk's beak with the root of this herb.

Ex goes on to provide instructions, unique among the J.B. remedies, on how 'to mew youre hauke redely'; i.e. how to assist it in its annual moult (69–74). The passage reads a bit like a charm, as it recommends cutting up a snake and cooking it with grains of barley, then feeding the barley to a chicken, and finally feeding the chicken to the hawk, 'and he schall be muyed anon'.

II/101 ff. Choosing a hawk. Described here are the distinguishing features of goshawk and falcon respectively, the most important being a long tail and short wings for the former, and a short tail and long wings for the latter. The opening statement, 'Take a little goshawk', may represent an instruction to capture an eyass, the age at which these birds are normally secured for training.

Pp lacks the last sentence referring to a falcon. Under the heading *To chese an hauke gode*, Pp reads 'Take a lytill gooshauke with a schorte chynne and a napyn fote, a grete beke, a wyde mowth, with lowryng browes, the sere, the ey, the fote acordyng of a colure; a long tayle, schorte wyngys well crossyng; thes ben the tokyns and synes' (fol. 22r).

II/102 *schorte schene* Probably referring to that part of the lower leg that lacks feathers, rather than to the whole of the leg below the knee. Goshawks have long legs overall.

an opyn fote Presumably, 'bare, lacking in feathers', unlike the feathered feet of many owls. See *MED, open* adj. 1d.

II/103 *lowryng hyen* 'louring eyes'. One of the most distinctive features of a goshawk is its gimlet eyes, with irises that change with age from yellow to orange and finally red. The bird also has dark 'eyebrows' – the 'lowryng browes' of Pp and Ex – which emphasise its fearsome appearance. T.H. White describes this aspect of his own goshawk in the following colourful terms: 'But that luminous eye (his main feature; it glared out, a focus to all the rest of him, from under furrowing brows, the optic of an insane assassin) ...'; *The Goshawk* (London, 1951, repr. 1960), p. 75.

II/103–4 *the sere ... colowre* In modern usage, *cere* refers to the wax-like membrane above a hawk's beak, pierced by its nares; in ME, the word referred also to the bare skin surrounding the bird's eyes, and the skin of its lower legs and feet; see *MED, sere* n.(1). In a healthy bird these features are all bright yellow, a colour that gets darker with age.

II/106 *long wynkys ... & long wyngys* The repetition of 'long wings' suggests confusion. Cf. L: 'A faukon a shortt taill longe wynges a shortte shynne'; Ex, 78: 'A faukyn: a schort tayle, a long whyng'.

II/107 ff. Ages of a hawk. There are no marks or spaces in the manuscript to separate this account of the Ages of a hawk from the preceding item. See also the somewhat different version in Prk (I/225–8) and the associated notes, where most of the terms introduced by this passage are discussed.

II/108–9 *sore hauke* a 'sore-hawk': a juvenile, under a year old – literally, a red hawk, so called after the distinctive red-brown plumage of a bird that has never moulted (<OF *sor*, 'sorrel, reddish-brown'). *PH* refers to such birds as being 'in thare sore aage' (line 250; see also lines 360–5). According to Tardif, *Livre de l'art*

de faulconnerie, p. 31, 'Sor est appellé à sa couleur sorete, celui qui a volé et prins devant qu'il ait mué'.

muer a 'mewer' – a hawk that has moulted at least once. This is most likely a general term, rather than one that indicates a specific age greater than that of the intermewer. Cf. *PEB 1*, p. 19: 'If thu lovyste wel thi hauke put here not in mewe to late; for if it be a sore hawke put here in the month of februare and if it be a mewere put her in the month of Januare'. This passage refers to the practice of placing a hawk in a sheltered enclosure – the mews – where it can safely moult (or 'mew') its feathers, an annual event lasting up to six months, from January or February to August or September.

an hagberte a 'haggard', a hawk in its adult plumage (see note I/225 above). Ex adds 'þan no faukener can tell þe age of her' (81).

II/110–11 There is corruption or confusion evident here, as indicated by the presence of three phrases *þe glede, hennys* and *of dokes* interpolated above the line. L adds to this confusion, rather than clarifying it, by reading: 'a mosher of hennes, a ioloner, a vento of dokis'. In H, *a moser* may indicate 'a mouser', a hunter of mice; see *MED, mousere* n.(1), <ME *mous* <OE *mus*. Alternatively, it could be formed from ME *mose* (<OE *mase*), the name given to the titmouse and similar small birds. Mice and small birds are both typical prey of a kite, here referred to as *þe glede*. For *ielonere* and *aneuer*, see note I/227–8. The phrase 'mosher of hennes' in L is obscure. Pp lacks the entire passage.

The equivalent lines in Ex (81–3) are useful for purposes of comparison: 'Than aftyr, a hauke ys callyd a pertryger, a fesonder, a moyser (that ys when sche kyllyth foule as a rauen, a boserd, a glede); releuer ys of hennys and dokys.' See my comments in 'An autononmous version of the *J.B. Treatise*', p. 83.

II/112 ff. A Hawk's foot and feathers. There are no marks or spaces in the manuscript to separate this account of a hawk's foot and feathers from the preceding item. L, likewise, lacks any heading or separator.

II/112–13 A hawk has four toes: three anterior and one posterior. In modern parlance, these are all loosely called 'pounces', 'claws' or 'talons', though sometimes 'talon' refers specifically to the hard nail at the end of each toe. Modern falconers also use these words more precisely, restricting 'claws' to the toes of a short-winged hawk, and 'talons' to those of a falcon. In the *J.B. Treatise, pownce* appears to indicate all three anterior toes, and *talon* the posterior toe – a distinction found also in Turbervile, *BF*, pp. 30, 60, *passim*. By contrast, *PH* is more specific, limiting *pownces* to the innermost anterior toe on each foot. The anterior middle toes it calls the 'loong sengles', and those outermost the 'pety sengles' (cf. *Le menagier de Paris*, p. 152 §15, which refers to 'la grant et petite sangle'). On each foot, the middle toe is also called the 'key or closer', for reasons explained by *PH*: 'For what thyng som euer it be þt yowre hawke strenyth, open that sengle and all the fote is oppen' ['For whatever it is that your hawk grasps, open that toe and the whole foot will open'] (lines 282–3; see lines 270–84). In H, the term 'sygnett' ('sign') perpetuates the metaphor established by the initial reference to the 'tokens' of the foot.

L is identical to H, but Pp lacks this information. Ex (84–5) shows some variation: 'The talons of the fote: the fyrst ys the pouns afore, the talent byhyend; the myddyll sygnet, þe lytyll sygnet ys þe princypall key of the fote.'

II/114–6 These three lines name some of the feathers that are significant on a hawk: *cuttelle*: any of the ten primary flight feathers on each wing (in *PH*, 330, they are called 'beam feathers'); *sorcelle*: the sarcel or pinion feather, the first of the primary flight feathers (cf. *PH*, 330–2); *flagges*: the secondary flight feathers on a hawk's wing, also known as 'cubitals'; *mantellettys*: 'mantles', a rare word, probably indicating a bird's dorsal plumage generally, as distinct from its chest feathers, which are often of a different colour. *OED* records the singular noun *mantle* in this sense, but its first citation dates from 1840 (s.v. *mantle* n. sense 10, *Ornithol.*). The related verb 'to mantle' is more widespread, indicating the way a hawk stretches out each wing in turn, together with the corresponding leg; see *OED*, *mantle* v. 3; *PH*, 207–9. Neither word appears in *MED*, but doubtless both derive from OF *mantel*, *manteau*, 'a tunic, kirtle, covering'. See also *Le Robert: Dictionnaire historique de la langue française*, 2 vols, ed. Alain Rey (Paris, 1992; hereafter *DHLF*), s.v. *manteau* n.m.: 'Dès le moyen âge, *manteau* ... désigne en zoologie (1225) la région dorsale du pelage d'un animal lorsqu'elle est de couleur différente du reste. On l'emploie aussi en parlant d'un plumage (1636) ...'.

L omits the sarcel to give a slightly different version of this passage: 'he hathe a cuttell at the poynte of the wynge the longe feders'. The mixture of singular ('a cuttell') and plural ('feders') is potentially confusing, and probably indicates the rarity of the term *cuttell(e)* (literally, 'a knife', 'a blade') in English. The word is taken directly from OF, where it was often used in the plural, as in Guillame Tardif's *Livre de l'art de faulconnerie*, p. 89: 'les pennes grosses des eles, qu'on nomme couteaulx'; also, *Le menagier de Paris*, p. 152 §15: 'bons cousteaulx, bonnes longues plumes'. According to an Anglo-Norman treatise, there are six of these feathers: 'Li cutels, ces sunt les .vi. plus longes pennes des eles aprés le cessel': *Three Anglo-Norman Treatises*, p. 95. See also Frederick II, *DAV*, I.50 (p. 83): 'The most external of these ten [primaries] is called the swing feather (*saxellus*). This feather and those preceding it are shaped and fashioned like knives. The noticeably wider portion represents the handle ... and the narrower part that is outermost suggests the blade of the knife.' The word *cuttell(e)* appears in no other English hawking treatise and is unrecorded in this sense by both *MED* and *OED*.

The sarcel (Frederick II's *saxellus*) is one of the most important feathers for a hawk, contributing to the power and agility of its flight. It is also significant because it is the last wing feather to moult and, as *PH* states, 'An hawke is neuer full ferme nor redy forto drawe owte of mew vnto tyme his sercell be full groyn [grown]'

(724–5). This feather should not be confused with those called 'serceaux' in OF: i.e. the four innermost, or tertiary, feathers of the wing.

II/118 *couerkele federis* The two central feathers of the tail, which cover and protect all the others when the bird is at rest; in modern parlance, the 'deck feathers'. These grow straight out in a direct line with the bird's spine, whereas the other feathers of a hawk's tail (or 'train' in the language of the sport) can be fanned out sideways. *PH* is mistaken in claiming that there is only one deck feather, which it calls the 'Beme feder' (289–94). For a full description of these feathers, see Frederick II, *DAV*, I.53 (p. 90); also *Three Anglo-Norman Treatises*, p. 95: 'Li cuvercle, ces sunt deus maynes pennes de la cowe dount le un kevre le autre a la feze.'

II/122 *brayle* collectively, the under-tail feathers (<AN *brael* <OF *braiel*, 'a belt, girdle'; perhaps, in a transferred sense, 'belly'). H reads *brayle*, against *brailles* L. In Ex the word is also singular in form: 'All the small whyte feders vndyr the tayle byn callyd þe brayle' (93). Cf. *PH*, 308–11: 'an hawke hath long smale white federis hangyng vnder the tayll, from hir bowell downe warde, and the same federis ye shall call the brayles or the brayle federis'; also, *PEB 1*, p. 14: 'and here foundement woll defile her brael'. An Anglo-Norman treatise explains why these feathers might be called 'a belt': 'Ly brayol, ceo est une cisurette [a stripe] de plume blaunche aval le fundament desouz la cowe': *Three Anglo-Norman Treatises*, pp. 95–96; see also *ibid.*, pp. 93, 103, 115. *MED*, s.v. *brail* n. (b), does not recognise this sense of the word, and is very likely mistaken in its choice of citations to illustrate its gloss, 'the belly or rump of an animal'. See further note I/229–33 above.

II/123 *þe pere* the 'stone', a form of constipation, 'medycynnys' for which are prescribed in I/250–2, II/24–29, IVh/71–4. The reference to befouled feathers suggests that the hawk may be suffering from 'the cray' rather than 'the stone' – or else that both terms were used somewhat loosely; see note I/229–33 above.

II/125–40 Flying terms. These comprise a brief and rather cryptic account of some of the different circumstances under which a hawk (not a falcon) will encounter game (in these cases, waterfowl), and the appropriate terms for referring to them. This item occurs also in L and, with variation, in Ex and Pp. A much longer account that uses many of the same terms, but defines them very differently, is found in the *StA* hawking treatise, *PH*, 1059–1131 (q.v. and see also Rachel Hands's notes: *EHH*, pp. 114–5).

In essence, all the J.B. versions show signs of confusion and corruption, with definitions truncated and apparently often misapplied. The fact that H–L, Ex and Pp are not directly related suggests that this corruption must have existed in a common ancestor. The terms themselves are found also at the end of the long versions of the J.B. Hierarchy of hawks – see Prk (I/223–4), Ha (III/113–4), G (IVh/24–5) and *StA*, 1201–2 – but without explanation beyond a brief statement that they refer to the flight of short-winged hawks rather than falcons.

Ex and Pp have very similar headings, which are not found in H–L: 'Now ye must lerne youre termys of haukyng' (Ex, 96), 'Now ye moste lern the termys of haukyn' (Pp, fol. 22r). In other respects, however, Ex (96–109) and Pp diverge frequently. It will be seen that the flying terms in Pp (quoted here in full) constitute a much shorter passage than in H.

> Youre [hauke] flyght to þ[e] feuue, that ys when the hauke has found hir game hir selfe and ensursyth to fle; when we say sche fleyth to the qwarre when the ostryger hath founde he most be ware whet[h]er the fowle ly styll or ellys [fleyng *canc*] fletyng for ellys he myght lyghtly be begyld and hit spryng owte sodenly by hym; whyle the hauke ys vnder the fo[w]le he has the wantage; and as sche anew hit into þe water then sche soylys. (Pp, fol. 22r)

(For this use of the verb *soylys* ['plunges into the water'], cf. my discussion of the J.B. Soiling terms in note I/189–200 above.)

II/126–30 *fleyth to þe vve ... to þe quarre* 'flies to the view ... [flies] to the quarry'. The two notions expressed here are slightly better explained by Ex: 'Youre hauke fleyth to the fowle, that ys when the hauke hathe founde here game here-sylf and enforsyd here-sylf to flee therto. She fleyth to þe querre when the ostriger hathe founde' (103–5). Matters are complicated by *PH*, which transposes these definitions. In other words, *PH* asserts that a hawk 'flies to the view' when the austringer has found prey and summons his hawk – trained to wait at a distance – towards him. As the hawk approaches, the austringer shouts or beats a small drum to rouse the prey, which is then seized by the hawk: *PH*, 1070–1081. Conversely, a hawk 'flies to the quarry' when it sights prey itself, 'and flie preuy li vnder hedges or law bi the grownde, and nym oon of hem or thay rise' (*PH*, 1111–5). *PH* offers these explanations with more authority than the J.B. texts, which are also rather muddled in describing a hawk's flight 'to the quarry'. In the absence of further evidence on which to base a judgement, it can only be said that *PH* and the J.B. texts contradict each other, and that the former may be the more trustworthy.

II/128–9 *moryng or fletyng* ?'stationary or swimming (away)'. Pp reads 'ly styll or ellys fletyng', and Ex has 'moryng – þat ys to sey dyuuyng [*r*. dyuyng] – or fletyng' (99). The participle *moryng* is obscure, but may be adapted from OF *morer*, 'to tarry, linger'. This would fit the context, in which the austringer is warned to be aware of the behaviour of the intended quarry. If it is stationary, he will be able to rouse it when his hawk approaches; but if it is swimming around (or away), it might have found refuge by the time he needs to rouse it for the approaching hawk. This does not, of course, account for Ex's gloss 'diving'.

II/131–3 *flyyth to ferre iotee* The wording in H suggests that this is when game rises suddenly near the hawk, but omits to say how the hawk or austringer should react. Ex explains the situation more fully, though it uses a different (probably corrupted) term altogether: 'The hauke fleyth to þe forehed [*sic*], þat ys to sey when þe hauke hath not found nothyr the ostrynger, but þe fowle spryngyth vppe sodenly by hym' (101–2). By contrast, L seems to suggest that it is the hawk that rises up suddenly: '... when the hauke hathe not founde hir game nor the ostreger noþer, but she spryngeth or sorgeth vp hir selfe sodeynly'.

In none of these cases is it clear how the expression *ferre iotee* (*Fer lutty PH*, 1060) would have originated, except perhaps from OF *jeter*, 'to throw', 'cast' (a hawk). Cf. Pp, quoted above, where the term *ferre iotee* is omitted and the account of sudden flight is elided with that of flying 'to the quarry'. Once again, the J.B. texts are at odds with *PH*, which defines the expresion *fer iutty* as indicating a kill on the bank of the river or pond opposite to that on which the austringer is located: 'Iff yowre hawke nym the fowle at the fer side of the ryuer or of the pitt from yow, then she sleeth the fowle at the fer iutty' (lines 1082–4). In this case, *jutty* is recognisable as a possible variant of *jetty*, and appears to indicate a waterside embankment or bank, which makes more sense than the J.B. explanation. See *OED*, s.v. *jutty* n.; *MED*, s.v. *gete* n.(3)(a); and note II/134–6 following.

II/134–6 *iotte ferre* Uncertainty over the meaning of *ferre iotee* in line 131 is not much lessened by H's account of its converse, the *iotte ferre* (*iote fer* L, *otyffery* Ex, *lutty ferry PH*, 1097), which appears to be when an assistant (*þe cownterryuer*) drives a bird towards the austringer by beating a drum (*tapyr*). Ex (103–6) provides more detail that does not entirely agree with, or contradict, the very abbreviated presentation of H:

> The otyffery [*r*. ioty fery] ys when þe hauke commyth to becke, as yn thys wyse: ye schall lett a man holde youre hauke whyle ye aspye the foule; and when ye haue spyed the foule, ye schall make a becke to youre hauke. But be well ware þat þe foule se nott the tabour tyll þe tyme þat þe hauke fyend þe foule.

In other words, according to Ex, a hawk may find itself having to fly at a bird that has not first been located, and that flies up suddenly nearby (the *ferre iotee / forehed*); or the hawk may be summoned to fly at a bird that has been stalked by the austringer, and that is made to fly up by the beating of a drum (the *iotte ferre / otyffery*).

A somewhat simpler (and perhaps more logical) explanation is supplied by *PH*, 1084–86, which declares that a hawk kills its prey 'at the iutty ferry' when it brings it to ground on the near side of the river, rather than the far side (the 'fer iutty'). But this does little to account for the origins or etymology of *iotte ferre*. The expression is both rare and extremely obscure, and was perhaps not fully understood even in the 15th century, as is indicated by the evident confusion in G and Ry (see IVh/25).

cownteryuer (*counter reuer* L) An assistant or beater tasked with driving waterfowl towards the austringer – especially from the opposite bank of a river, as is described in *PEB 1*: 'and when he shall fle þer moste be a counterreuere to make the foule spyn [turn] so when þe hauke schall come jn, he shall carie it to londe' (p. 12). The word occurs only in H and L, and in some of the longer versions of *PEB*. The noun is unrecorded in Old French and Anglo-Norman, but Gace de la Buigne employs the verb *contreriv(er)er* twice in the allegorical section of his *Roman des deduis*, ed. Åke Blomqvist, Studia Romanica Holmiensia, 3 (Karlshamn, 1951), ll. 2321–29. The *MED*, s.v. *contrevure* (b), is surely mistaken in glossing *counterreuere* in both H and *PEB* as 'a contrivance of some sort', similar to a 'stratagem' and a 'contriver' (ME *contrevour*). The word is more plausibly descended from Anglo-Latin *contrariveator* (also *contraripator*), the name used for a servant that assisted the English kings when they went hawking for waterfowl; see Robin S. Oggins, *The Kings and Their Hawks* (New Haven and London, 2004), pp. 31, 75; R.E. Latham, *Revised Medieval Latin Word-List from British and Irish Sources* (Oxford, 1980, repr. 2008), s.v. *contrariveator*. For a thorough analysis, see my article 'Middle English *counter-rivere*', *Anglia*, 134 (2016), 604–16.

tapyr 'tabor', a small drum. It is not immediately clear in this passage whether the *cownteryuer* or (more likely) some other assistant is beating the tabor, a common piece of equipment in medieval falconry. *PEB 1* also describes the use of a tabor as a means of training a hawk and drawing it to its prey (p. 12). The practice is described in detail by Turbervile (*BF*, pp. 191–94), and illustrated in a *bas-de-page* tinted drawing on fol. 151r of *Queen Mary's Psalter* (BL Royal MS 2 B VII), which shows a servant beating a tabor to drive ducks into the air; reproduced by Oggins, *The Kings and Their Hawks*, p. 195.

II/137–40 The meaning of these lines is comparatively straightforward: the hawk should approach its quarry from below lest it escape by plunging into some water. Cf. *PH*, 1099–1102: 'And if it happyn ... the fowle for fere of yowre hawke woll spryng and fall ayen in to the ryuer or the hawke sees [?'sees' or 'seizes'] hir, and so lie styll and dare not arise, ye shall say then yowre hawke hath ennewed the fowle in to the ryuer'. See also the phrase 'an aneuer of dokes' in line 111 of the present text, and cf. *The Parlement of the Thre Ages*, 245: 'when digges [ducks] bene enewede'.

II/140 *soylyth* 'takes refuge in the water'; cf. the J.B. Soiling terms, especially II/176 and note I/189–200 above.

II/141 *lere or be lewde* Proverbial; see Whiting, L157, and the final colophon at line 243.

II/142 ff. Hierarchy of hawks. In H, the hierarchy of hawks is written as a list, with line capitals slashed with red. H, L, Ex and Pp preserve short versions of this list, as against the long versions found in Prk (I/201–24), Ha (III/101–14) and G (IVh/1–25). Ex (110–125) comes closest to agreeing with H, but contains a notable formulation that sets it apart (see note II/156–7). Pp is shorter than the others, assigning only the eagle to an emperor, and containing only fourteen entries overall.

In spite of their close relationship, H and L are strikingly different in one respect: whereas H structures its entries along the lines *A saker and a sakret for a knight*, L consistently inverts the syntax to form phrases that read *For a knyght, a sakyr with a sokerett*, and so on. Although H has no heading for this item, L supplies 'Ther beth dyuers haukes for euery astate and for other men of degre'; and Pp has: 'Euery man after his degre'. For the principal notes on this item, see notes I/201–24 above.

II/143–4 *neþer luryd ... heuy* So too L; lacking in Pp; Ex reads 'for hyt nedeth nott' (111). This obscure statement is marginally clearer in certain other versions; see note I/205 above.

II/150 *bastarde* Pp reads *wasterd*.

II/154–5 Pp has 'a yonge squyere of þe fyrst hede'; Ex 'a ʒong squyer'. Only H, L and Ex refer to the hoby making the lark 'tapis' – i.e. 'take cover'.

II/156–7 As I have already mentioned in relation to Prk, there is some disagreement about who should get the goshawk. Owing to the dominant influence of *StA*, the notion that the goshawk is a yeoman's bird has become fixed in the popular imagination and continues to be repeated like a mantra (see, for example, Robert Kenward, *The Goshawk* (London, 2010), p. 255). However, Pp reads 'A goosehauke for a gentylman / A tersell for the same'; and Ex contains a formulation found nowhere else: 'A goshauke for a mene man þat hath lyuelode' (122) – i.e. a poor man who has rent, or income. See further note I/219 above.

II/160 Ex and Pp both lack this statement apportioning a kestrel to a knave (i.e. a young boy). It is another phrase from the J.B. Hierarchy of hawks that has acquired a life of its own in the modern world, thanks in part to Barry Hines's novel *A Kestrel for a Knave* (1968).

II/161–3 Only H, L and Ex contain this short account of an *aby hawke* (*abbay hauke* L), though what precisely is meant by the phrase is unclear; *MED* (s.v. *abi hauk* n.) declares rather vaguely, 'A kind of hawk'. The statement that it is (understand 'has') *canvas mayle* (canvas-coloured breast-feathers) is also problematic in terms of determining what colour is intended. According to *PEB 1*, p. 9, and *PH*, a hawk can have three colours of 'mail': 'Hawkes haue white maill, canuas maill or rede maill. And som call rede maill "iren mayll". White maill is soone knawe. Canuas maill is betwene white maill and iron maill. And iron maill is varri rede' (*PH*, 245–8). *OED* glosses *canvas* n. 7.b. (marked by a dagger as obsolete) as 'light-grey', but this seems doubtful given the statement in *PH* that canvas lies between (or is a combination of) white and red. That suggests a light brown or russet colour, or perhaps the overall effect of speckled brown-and-white breast feathers typical of sparrowhawks.

Ex ends at this point with the word *Explicit*.

II/164 Red flourishes on either side of this heading indicate a major division in the text, probably to indicate a change of focus from hawking to hunting terminology.

II/165 ff. Beasts of venery and the chase. H here preserves a short version of the Beasts of venery and the chase, as opposed to the long versions of Prk, Dg–Rg (I/171–81) and Eg (IVd). These lines should be compared with the slightly different short account found in Ha and Rd (III/51–8), and the entirely dissimilar version in *StA* (1847–54). The text of Pp is here so similar to H and L that I have, for once, elected to include it in the collation in the apparatus. The majority of explanatory notes on this item and its terminology will be found in relation to Prk (notes I/171–81 above).

II/168–9 H, L and Pp stand alone in omitting the roebuck and the roe(doe) from the beasts of the chase of the 'sweet foot'; cf. Prk (I/175), Ha (III/54–5), Eg (IVd/8–9), *StA*, 1852.

II/169–70 H, L and Pp stand alone in explaining that a *spytard* (*spyckard* Pp) is a 100-year-old hart. Other versions declare, variously, that it is a three-year-old, or a 300-year-old, male deer; see note I/176–7 above.

II/172 *þe catt* Wanting in Pp. Elsewhere, this animal is referred to as a *bade* or mountain cat; see note I/179.

II/173 *þe whyterache* (*the white racche* L; *þe waturrate* Pp – both faulty). For the form of the word that appears in H, read *whyterathe* (i.e. ME *whit-rat*), 'white rat' – a name used of the stoat, known in its white winter coat as the ermine (*Mustela erminea*). Cf. *whitrath* (Ha, III/57), *whitrat* (*StA*, 1854) and *wyȝthe rache* (Rd). The *Promptorium* has *Whytte rate* as a headword but provides no Latin gloss. As *OED* observes, s.v. *whitret* | *whitterick* n., the name came to be used also of the weasel, but this was probably a later development (the *OED*'s citations are not clear in this regard). There is no mention of the 'white rat' in any of the long versions of the Beasts of venery and the chase.

Pp ends by stating, 'And all thes byn gamys of the stynkyng ffoote'. On the following leaf (fol. 23r) it has the colophon: 'Here endys hawkyng w*ith* medsyns and castyng / And all that longys to goode hauke kepyng'.

II/174 ff. Soiling terms. There is no break in the manuscript, or any other marker, to indicate the start of a new element here. The entire passage is wanting in both L and Pp.

H here preserves a long version of the J.B. Soiling terms, somewhat different from the other long versions in Prk, Dg–Rg (I/189–200) and Ha (III/70–8), and significantly so from the short version of T, *HSG* and W (IVg). The majority of explanatory notes on this element and its terminology will be found in relation to Prk above.

H's presentation of its Soiling terms from line 178 onwards is unique in using the expression *cummyth up / over*, thereby describing the hart's actions as if one were watching the animal's approach, rather than its flight away. Like the other long versions of this element, H contains the opening statement about the hunter casting off his alaunts (II/174–5), but omits the next two statements – found in Prk and Dg – about the hunter blowing the horn, and the alaunts separating the hart from the rest of the herd (see I/193–2).

II/182 The line-capital *A* of this couplet is touched with red, suggesting the start of a new element. There is also a deleted *and* before the phrase *An harte is herborowyde* of the next line, indicating that the scribe was unsure whether the couplet formed part of the Soiling terms or the Resting terms that follow.

II/183–96 Resting terms. The Resting terms are written as a list, with matching phrases linked by red-ink braces and a red slash on the line-capital *A* of every statement. See the notes in Appendix III for a full discussion of these terms.

II/197–241 Collective nouns. The Collective nouns continue without a break from the preceding Resting terms, with matching phrases linked by red-ink braces and a red slash on the line-capital *A* of every phrase. See the notes in Appendix I for a full discussion of these phrases.

II/242 ff. The first apothegm of the colophon, *Lat cattes scrate carlys with sorow iwis*, is not recorded by Whiting, but the second (*Lerne or be lewde*) is, under L157. (See also line 141 where this sentiment is first stated.) The initials of the explicit are decidedly 'I.B.', not 'g.B.' as printed by Hodgkin, 'Terms I', p. 56.

PART III – MS Ha

The J.B. material starts at the top of fol. 6v without any heading or preliminary remarks. For a full account of this manuscript and its version of the *J.B. Treatise*, see the survey of all J.B. witnesses in the Introduction.

III/1–50 Collective nouns. The list of Collective nouns is written in two columns, which are not equal in length. The second column ends about two-thirds of the way down the page. See Appendix I for detailed notes on these phrases.

III/32–33 The phrase 'a skulk of thieves' normally occurs at this point in the list, to form a trio with foxes and friars; see Prk (I/91–3), H (II/226–8) and Appendix I, no. 207.

III/51 ff. Beasts of venery and the chase. The account of Beasts of venery and the chase in Ha is very similar to the version preserved in Rd, but notably different in presentation. Whereas in Ha this item is written in a single paragraph of long lines, in Rd the animals are set out in a list beneath the opening phrase *Ther ben .iiij bestys off wenery*, which is underlined, as for a heading. Moreover, whereas Ha neglects to identify which animals are of the 'sweet foot' and which of the 'stinking foot', Rd introduces the latter group with *And thus ben off the stynkynge fote*. Together, Ha and Rd preserve a distinctive short version of this element, somewhat different from the other short accounts in H–L, Pp (II/165–173) and *StA* (1847–54), and different also from the long versions in Prk, Dg–Rg (I/171–81) and Eg (IVd). The majority of explanatory notes on this element and its terminology will be found in relation to Prk and H (notes I/171–81 and II/165–73 above).

III/58 Rd closes its list of Beasts of venery and the chase with the statement *And here byn a schrwyd flocke*. There is then an interval, followed by, *Sum of thes bythe chasabylle & sum bithe vnechasabylle*, which both introduces the next element, 'The hunter', and refers back to the preceding Beasts of venery and chase. There is a clear implication, not duplicated in Ha, that the two elements belong together.

III/59 ff. The hunter; Breeds of dogs In Ha, a wide interval separates the paragraph containing the next two items – 'The hunter' and 'Breeds of dogs' – from the preceding material. The only other witness in which The hunter occurs is Rd. This little passage describes a huntsman and his accoutrements, followed by some of the horn calls that he should be able to sound. The figure that emerges is not that of a noble hunter, but rather a hunt servant, and specifically a limerer – one who leads a limer, or bloodhound.

III/60–1 This reference to a hook on the hunter's belt (*gurdylle* Rd) as a means of securing the leash (*lyeme*) of his hound is unique, as far as I know. His 'dog for the bow' is a limer specifically trained to accompany an archer, both to locate a quarry and to track it once shot; this animal is the equivalent of the poacher's *berselett* in *The Parlement of the Thre Ages* (see p. 38/39n). The term 'dog for the bow' appears also in Eg (IVe/16) and in Chaucer's description of the evil summoner in *The Friar's Tale*: 'For in this world nys dogge for the bowe / That kan an hurt deer from an hool yknowe / Bet than this somnour knew a sly lechour' (*CT*, III.1369–71). See also the amusing episode in Malory, when 'a grete hunteresse' shoots a sleeping Lancelot in the buttock after she had 'abated her dogge for the bowghe at a barayne hynde': *Works*, ed. Eugène Vinaver, 2nd edn (Oxford, 1977), XVIII, 21 (p. 643).

III/62 *pryce, deth* These are both horn calls used to signal the success of a hunt. In *MG*, only the most important personages may blow the *prise* (ME *pris* <OF *prise*, 'seizure, capture'), though the *deth* can be sounded by anyone present at the kill: *MG*, pp. 98–9, 111. In *SGGK*, hunters blow the *prise* for both the slain deer (1362) and the boar (1601), and the *Craft of Venery* advises that the signal should also be used of the hare: 'and þu schalt blow þe prise homward', for 'well ʒe wytten þat all feyre wordez of venery risen of þe hare' (*CV*, 73–5; see also 154–6; Twiti-F, 149–50, 162; Twiti-A, 105–6; Twiti-C, 134–5, 146–7, 149–50). The J.B. passage implies that the *prise* is reserved for the hart, with the 'death' being used for lesser beasts.

III/64 *chate* A rare word in English, derived from AN *chater*, 'to sound the horn'; see Twiti-F, 103: 'vous devez chater en la manere'. Confusion of *c* and *t* yields *chace* (both verb and noun) in Middle English: see Twiti-A, 80, Twiti-C, 73, and *MED, chace* n.(e). Twiti uses the word generically for any horn call, so it is interesting to find the J.B. passage implying that the 'chate' may have become a specific signal, complementing the 'rechate' (see the following paragraph).

rechate A horn signal for summoning or encouraging hunters and hounds, and for calling them together at the close of a hunt; also known as the 'recheat' and the 'rechace'. See Twiti-C, 83; *MED, rechate* n. For the verb, see *CV*, 117, 169. I discuss this word further in my article, 'A re-examination of Octovyen's hunt in *The Book of the Duchess*', *MÆ*, 56 (1987), 183–99 (esp. pp. 188–9).

motis and strakes 'individual notes and complex passages' blown on a hunting horn.

III/66–9 In both Ha and Rd, the account of The hunter runs straight into the Breeds of dogs, the two items forming a single paragraph in which they are linked by the statement *The hunte schall haue help* (*Thys hunt schalle haue holp*, underlined, Rd). For the purposes of this edition, I have elected to separate them, since in all other J.B. witnesses the Breeds of dogs stands alone. Ha preserves a short version of this item, slightly different from the other short versions found in *StA* (1855–61) and Rc, and more distinct from the long versions of Prk, Dg–Rg (I/182–8) and Eg (IVe). Further observations on the contents and terminology of this element will be found in the notes relating to Prk (notes I/182–8 above).

III/69 *myddynges kurris* StA and Rc both refer to *myddyng dogges*, followed by two breeds not mentioned in the other texts: *tryndeltayles and prikherid curris* (thus *StA*; the text in Rc is damaged and breaks off at the word *prykered*). These names designate, respectively, 'trundle-tails' (mongrels with curly tails) and 'prick-eared curs' (low-bred dogs with upright ears).

smale puppes for ladis Cf. *smal poppys of lades chambers*, Rd, and see note I/185 above. StA stands alone in referring to *smale ladies popis that beere a way the flees, and dyueris smale sawtis*. In Rd, there follows a short imitation of the sound-effects of the hunt, including both a horn signal and the shouts of a hunter: 'With *Tro to tro, Ware, ryot, Ware*!'; this provides a link to the next item, the Soiling terms, which commences with the hunter casting off his dogs.

It is interesting to find this very call reproduced in *MG*, p. 41, in a passage concerning dogs that are distracted by conies: 'What [racche] þat renne[þ] to a cony in ony tyme, hym ouȝt to be astried [reproved] sayeng to him lowde, *Ware, riot, ware!*', for non oþer wilde best in Engelond is callid ryott sauff þe conynge alonly' (punctuation and emendations mine). See also *MED*, s.v. *riot(e)* n. 5.

III/70 ff. Soiling terms; Resting terms In Ha, a wide interval separates the paragraph containing the next two items (the Soiling terms and the Resting terms) from the preceding material. The Soiling terms in Ha belongs broadly with other long versions, such as those of Prk (I/189–200) and H (II/174–82), against the short version preserved by T (IVg/1–7). However, certain words and phrases set it apart, such as *a braas of alauntes*, i.e. 'a brace', as opposed to 'a couple' in Prk and H; indeed, the precise wording of Ha's version of the Soiling terms aligns it more closely with Rg than with Rd – of which the latter is in any case fragmentary, breaking off at *The hert sowlys*.

III/79–90 There is no interval in the manuscript between the Soiling terms and the Resting terms, which together form a single paragraph, in which the Resting terms are written in long lines across the page. See Appendix III for a full discussion of these phrases.

III/91 ff. Properties of a greyhound A wide interval separates the Properties of a greyhound – written as a single paragraph of long lines – from the preceding material. It will be seen that there are two parts to this passage: an initial prose account of a greyhound's main features, which are established by means of comparisons with other animals (lines 91–95); and a set of doggerel couplets on the development and ageing of a greyhound (lines 96–100). Among the J.B. versions, only Ha contains this prose description of a greyhound's features, as opposed to the rhyming couplets found in *StA* (1862–5) and Eg (IVf). Entirely unrelated versions of the topos appear also in some French and English hunting manuals, notably the *Tretyse off Huntyng*, ll. 247–53, and Gace de la Buigne's, *Roman des deduis*, lines 8829–44. Gace's verses were rendered as prose by Gaston de Foix (*LC*, cap. 18), whence they were adapted and translated into English by Edward of York (*MG*, p. 62):

> ... here eynne shuld be reed or blak as of a sparhauke, þe eerys smal and hie in þe maner of a serpent, þe neke grete and longe bowed as a swannes nek, his paas ['chest'] greet and opyn, þe heere vndir his chyn wel hangyng adoun, in þe maner of a lyoun, hey shuldres as a roo buk, þe forlegges streght and greet inow and nought too hie legges, þe feet straught and rounde as a Catte, and greet clees, a long hede as a Cowe, and wel a[u]aled [?'lowered'], þe boone and þe joyntes of þe Chyne greet and hard as þe chyne of an hert.

Keiser, *Manual X*, 3920 [469] links Ha's short prose recital of the properties of a greyhound with the version titled *The shappe off a greyhounde* found at the end of the *Tretyse off Huntyng* in MS C (fol. 55r). But the two texts contain few similarities, apart from treating the same idea in broadly similar terms, as the first few lines of C's version will show: 'Wytte wele þat a greyhound behoueth to haue þis shappe: þe hede off a conger, þe eyen off a lyone, þe nekke off a swanne, þe brestbone off a stede ...' (*THunt*, p. 56). It will also be seen that C's portrayal of a greyhound makes a number of comparisons (with a *stede*, a *cheuerall*, a *bore*, and an *holyfaunt*) that are not found in Ha.

Turning to the doggerel couplets of lines 96–100 in Ha, these are similar to an equivalent, but longer, set of verses in *StA* (1866–73, quoted where appropriate in the notes following), though there is otherwise no strong relationship between the two texts.

III/92 *a sowes ribbe* Probably implies that the greyhound should have a burly, well-rounded ribcage. The next simile, *y-bakkid like a plowe beme*, alludes to the strong, central wooden beam of a plough, which curves in a manner reminiscent of an animal that stands higher at the shoulder than the rump; see the illustration of a plough-beam in John Fitzherbert's *Booke of Husbandrie* (1598; facs. edn, Amsterdam and Norwood, NJ, 1979), Book I, pp. 5, 7. *StA* reads *chyned like a beme* (line 1865), which is less specific and so rather more cryptic. See further *MED*, s.vv. *bem* n. 3.(b), *plough* n. 1c.

III/92–3 *y-trussid byhynd like an ox bytwen the hornes y-hangid like a hare* Two enigmatic statements in which there may be corruption or something missing. The first comparison is probably intended to evoke the neat, compact form of a greyhound's posterior, including its testicles; cf. *MG*, p. 62: 'a lytel pyntel ['penis'] and litel honging ballokis and well trussed nye þe ars'. The second may suggest a long-haired dog; cf. *MG*, p. 62: 'þe heere vndir his chyn wel hangyng adoun'. As the Baillie-Grohmans point out, greyhounds at this time came in many varieties, including some with long or curly coats; the smooth-haired Italian greyhound was only one of many types: *MG*, pp. 142–5. See also the miniature depicting greyhounds in Bibliothèque Nationale, MS français 616, fol. 46v; reproduced in *The Hunting Book of Gaston Phébus*, Introduction by Marcel Thomas and François Avril (Graz, 1994; repr. London, 1998).

III/94 *y-howghid like a sikill* 'hocked like a sickle'. The simile evokes the rounded curve of the greyhound's hind legs, but directly contradicts *MG*, which declares, 'þe hoghes streight, and not crompyng [curving] as of an oxe' (p. 62).

III/97 *'Hay! Go bette!'* Hunting calls which imply that the greyhound is ready for employment in the chase. See Chaucer's *Legend of Dido*, 1212–13: 'The herde of hertes founden is anon, / With "Hay! Go bet! Pryke thow! Lat gon, lat gon!"'. In *StA*, the greyhound's second and third years are described differently: 'The .iij. yere he is felow⟨.⟩lyke. The .iiij. yere ther is noon sike' (*StA*, 1867–8).

III/98 *hold the plow* Enigmatic. The phrase may indicate that the greyhound is useful as a guard dog ('guards the plough'), or that it follows its master when ploughing. There is clearly some progression from this to *plowe padill* in the dog's eighth year (see below), but the meaning is somewhat unclear.

III/98–100 When it comes to a greyhound's seventh year, *StA* diverges:
The .vii. yere he will avayle greie bikkys for to assayle. The .viij. yere likladill. The .ix. yere cartsadyll. And when he is commyn to

that yere, haue hym to the tanner. For the beest hownde that euer
bikke hade, at .ix. yere he is full badde. (1869–73)

In these lines, *StA* describes a steady deterioration, with the dog falling prey to
'lick-ladle' (a parasite), and then being of no more use than a cart-saddle (the small
saddle that supports the shafts of a cart drawn by a cart horse). According to *StA*,
a greyhound of this age may as well be sent to the tanner as it is well past its best.
In Ha, by comparison, the dog is put to bitches only when he is capable of no
other useful work. The term *plowe padill* (99) must refer to the small spade-like
implement used for clearing clods of earth off a ploughshare, though the relevance
is not immediately obvious; see *MED*, s.v. *padel* n.(1), and *plough-patil*, s.v. *plough*
n. 1c (e).

III/101 ff. Hierarchy of hawks. A wide interval separates the paragraph containing the next two elements – the Hierarchy of hawks and Hawks' diseases,
written as continuous long lines – from the preceding material. Ha preserves a
unique rendition of the Hierarchy of hawks, which belongs broadly with the other
long versions, typified by Prk (I/201–224) and G (IVh/1–25), as against the short
versions represented by H (II/142–63). The initial account of the emperor's 'hawks'
is unremarkable, but the subsequent list of falcons and hawks is unique in omitting
to link these birds to specific classes of human society. For further discussion of
this element and its terminology, see the notes to the equivalent passages in Prk, H
and G cited above.

III/113–4 *vewe ... gytte ferre* See notes I/223–4 and II/126–36 *et seq.* above for
a discussion of the four expressions listed here, which are elswehere set out as
part of the J.B. Flying terms. The term *vnguyte* is an inexplicable corruption of an
obscure term, which appears variously as *far iuttye* (I/224), *ferre iotee* (II/131),
forget (IVh/25), *fer iutty* (*StA*, 1202), *Fer Iutty* (*PH*, 1060).

III/115 ff. Hawks' diseases. There is no interval in the manuscript between the
Hierarchy of hawks and the account of Hawks' diseases: both are contained in the
same continuous block of prose. Ha is noteworthy for preserving the preliminary
list of diseases, but none of the remedies that normally follow. The wording of this
short passage shows that it belongs to the same tradition as G and Ry (IVh/26–31),
against that of Prk and Dg (I/229–33). In many ways, Ha preserves the most
coherent version of this little list of diseases, with statements and phrases found
nowhere else. All the important terms are examined in the notes on Prk (I/229–33).

III/116 *aboue* Probably an error for *aboute* (the eye lids), as in Prk (I/230) and G
(IVh/27). Lice and mites are most likely to be found in the feathers all around the
eye, rather than only above it.

III/117 Prk and Dg lack this allusion to lice infesting a hawk's neck and mantle-feathers; cf. I/230 above.

III/118 *egles* Variant (?corruption) of an obscure term for parasitic worms, appearing elsewhere as *aglys* (Prk), *akyllys* (H), *aglye* (Ex), and *ageles* (G); see note I/229–33. Cf. H (II/19), G (IVh/29) and Ex (17), which also locate these worms in the hawk's back, as against Prk, which, perhaps more plausibly, states that both the filanders and the 'aiguils' are found in a hawk's chest (I/230–1).

III/118–9 *in the brayell, the pere ... cray* 'in the abdomen the stone, and in the tewel [vent, cloaca] the cray': see my discussion of the majority of these terms in note I/229–33 above. Ha stands alone in associating the cray with the hawk's 'tewel'; in doing so, it identifies the main symptom of this condition: the fouling of that area with thick, chalky mutes.

III/122 *speruere and mylonere* 'sperviter and milaner': i.e. persons who fly sparrowhawks and (?) milans ('kites') respectively, and matching the preceding names, 'ostreger' (= austringer) and 'falconer'. The word *speruere* usually refers to a sparrowhawk, but appears also as a proper name, such as 'Adam Sperver', presumably referring to the holder's occupation: see *MED*, *sperver* n. (a) (b). *PH* refers to such hawkers as *speruiteris* or *sparuiters* (514, 518, 1025), and *PPF* has *sparfutere* (225).

The second term, *mylonere*, is problematic in that there is no firm evidence outside the often fanciful J.B. Hierarchy of hawks (see note I/201–7 above) that kites were flown at game (their claws are too weak to grasp prey larger than a small lizard), while, conversely, kites (and other slow-flying birds of prey, such as owls) were themselves a favourite quarries of falconers. Perhaps *mylonere* is an error for ?*myrlonere*, ?*merlyonere*, 'one who flies a merlin' (see *MED*, s.v. *merlioun* n). This small falcon was less commonly used than its larger cousins, the peregrine and the lanner, but was a respectable sporting raptor in a way that the kite has never been.

The J.B. text is immediately followed by three lines of prose in a neat hand that appears to be of the 16th century. However, the writing is too faded to read and appears to have been deliberately expunged. It may yield some interesting information under ultraviolet light, but I have been unable to examine the manuscript using such an aid.

PART IV – MISCELLANEOUS J.B. TEXTS AND ELEMENTS

This section presents a number of J.B. elements that are either not represented in the three main versions of the *J.B. Treatise* set out in Parts I–III, or are significantly at variance with the equivalent passages in those texts. Also included are the entire J.B. contents of MS G (IVh); an unusual, but related, short item that is found only in MS Harl (IVc) – the Names of hawks; and the Names of wines found in MSS Dg and Rg. It is hoped that having these items set out in this way will allow the full diversity of the corpus of J.B. materials to be shown, without undue repetition of passages already adequately represented in Parts I–III.

IVa Hunting terms – MS Adv

This list of eleven short statements is unique to Adv; it falls between the Carving terms and the Resting terms and is written with two statements per line. Like so much else in the *J.B. Treatise*, it presents a hierarchy, running from the most valued beasts of the chase (hart and hind) to the least significant (badger and cony). Most of its terms are precise and informative – sometimes evocative, as with *vexed* – but the distinction between *chased* and *run* (*ronnon*) for hart and buck respectively seems a little contrived.

IVa/4 *A dwo is shotte* Cf. the deer hunt in *SGGK* (lines 1154–66), where harts and bucks are allowed to go free, while hinds and does are driven towards waiting bowmen.

IVa/5 *coursed* A technical hunting term indicating that this animal is hunted with gazehounds, i.e. dogs that hunt by sight. The verb, which is rare at this time, derives from the noun *course*, 'a run', 'a chase' (with dogs), as in Chaucer's *Knight's Tale*, where Theseus sets off to hunt a hart and 'wol han a cours at hym or tweye' (*CT*, I.1694). Even more relevant is the burlesque *Hunting of the Hare* (*NIMEV* 64; a poem, incidentally, unique to Adv), in which a yeoman spies a hare and says to a fellow, 'Yf ye have ony grehowndus, hom with yow to bryng, / A cowrs þer schall ye have': see David Scott-Macnab, '*The Hunttyng of the Hare* in the Heege Manuscript', *Anglia*, 128 (2010), 102–23 (lines 23–4).

For a brief discussion of hare-coursing in the Middle Ages, see my article 'Burlesque romance and the bourgeoisie', in *Noble and Joyous Histories: English Romances, 1375–1650*, ed. Eiléan Ní Cuilleanáin and J.D. Pheifer (Dublin, 1993), 113–35 (pp. 130–1). See also *MED*, *cours* n. 2b. The particularised hunting sense of the verb in Adv is unrecorded by *MED*, and the first citation in *OED* is 1550 (and 1552 for the gerund): s.v. *course* v. 1; *coursing* n.[1] 2.

IVa/10 *beseged ... assauted* Both terms evoke the laborious effort required to dig a badger out of its set. Cf. the phrase 'a *sawte* of greys' (i.e. an ?'assault') in Appendix I, no. 88, and the associated note.

IVa/11 *hayed or feretted* Indicating, respectively, that a cony is either caught with nets ('hays' <AN *haie*) or drawn out of their warrens by means of a ferret on a leash. Both terms show how, during the Middle Ages, conies were 'harvested' for their meat and fur rather than hunted as sport animals. See the comments of Edward of York: 'Of conynges speke I not for no man hunteth for hem but ʒit it be bisshhunters [fur hunters], and þei hunte hem with ferettis and wiþ long smale haies' (*MG*, p. 41). For an example of the large-scale harvesting of conies, see the instructions of Edward the Black Prince for 'Simon Forestier, keeper of the prince's chase of Rysing', to kill 1000 rabbits for a feast to be held in May 1362: *Register of Edward the Black Prince*, 4 vols (London, 1930–33), IV, 433 (18 April 1362).

IVb 'If a hart stands' – *HSG*

Found only in *HSG* and Am, these three short statements present yet another hierarchy, this time among England's three species of deer. The overall effect is gnomic, or perhaps proverbial, and not entirely clear, but the implication seems to be that a hart stands impassively, whereas a buck will be seen to be listening intently (?anxiously), and a roe fears constantly for its life.

As I have already remarked, this item could plausibly be treated as an unorthodox extension of the Resting terms: in both *HSG* and Am, these lines follow on immediately from the Resting terms and are in certain respects similar in content. On the other hand, the independent origin of these three lines is indubitable, which is why I have treated them as constituting a separate J.B. element.

Am contains a number of errors, which is why the better text of *HSG* (collated with Am) is presented here.

IVc Names of hawks – MS Harl

As is explained in the Introduction, this list of five names for different types of hawks is interpolated below the Collective nouns in Harl, probably to fill up space. For that reason, and because it is found nowhere else, I have not catalogued it as a separate J.B. element, and have included it here only for the sake of completeness, since it cannot be presented anywhere else.

There is nothing remarkable about the first four names, which refer, respectively, to female and male goshawk, then female and male sparrowhawk. The fifth name, *hay-de-mew*, is, however, rare in Middle English, and is unattested by the *MED*. The particular form is also unusual, since it is an inversion of the original construction,

AN *muer de haie* 'hedge-mewed', as a designation for a hawk that has been caught after moulting in the wild; cf. *mard-haye* (Prk, I/226), *mure-de-hay* (H, II/108). These terms are all discussed further in note I/226 above.

IVd Beasts of venery and the chase – MS Eg

Eg preserves a singular rendition of this element, which belongs, broadly, with the other long versions found in Prk and Dg–Rg (I/171–81). Although there is little that is different in the information presented here, the entire passage is noteworthy for its heading (which refers to terminology that a young gentleman might need to know), the novel way in which this information is arranged, and the supplemental comment on beasts of the 'stinking foot'. For typical short versions, see H (II/165–73) and Ha (III/51–8). The majority of explanatory notes on this item and its terminology will be found in relation to Prk above (notes I/171–81).

IVd/5 In other versions, these animals are referred to as 'beasts of the sweet foot', an expression wanting in this account.

IVd/12–13 The ages assigned to these two animals vary considerably; see note I/176–7 above.

IVd/17–23 The brace should extend up to line 15 so as to include the fulmard, fitchew and cat of the mountain, but is here represented as drawn in the manuscript. Eg is unique in referring to these animals as being 'of the stinking chase', rather than 'of the stinking foot', and explaining that they are so called because they creep and climb. Implicit in this exposition is a medieval hunter's disdain for animals that cannot give the hounds a good run, and which then attempt to escape by climbing a tree or fleeing underground. By contrast, beasts of venery and those of the 'sweet foot' will run far, and the best of them will turn at bay to confront their pursuers in mortal combat (for example, hart and boar).

Cf. the dismissive comments of Edward of York, who refuses to discuss 'vermin', such as martens and polecats, 'for no good hunter gooþ to woode wiþ his houndes in entente to hunte for hem ne þe wylde Cat neiþer' (*MG*, pp. 40–1).

IVe Breeds of dogs – MS Eg

Eg preserves an unusual rendition of this element, which belongs, broadly, with the other long versions found in Prk and Dg–Rg (I/182–8). For typical short versions, see Ha (III 66–9) and *StA* (1855–61). As with its treatment of the Beasts of venery and the chase (IVd), Eg is notable for the way in which it sets out this material (in the form of a list), as well as for its heading and supplemental comments, which are found nowhere else. The distinction between dogs that are led on a leash (1–6) and those that run free (7–10) is particularly interesting, though a little misleading since many of the first group are at some point let off the leash when required to pursue a quarry. The majority of explanatory notes on this passage and its terminology will be found in relation to Prk above (notes I/182–8).

IVe/2 Eg alone refers to a 'bastard greyhound'; elsewhere, the animal mentioned at this point is simply a 'bastard', as in Prk (I/182).

IVe/16 The 'dog for the bow' is not mentioned in any other J.B. version of this item. Allusions to this type of tracking dog are relatively rare in Middle English, and its identification here as a bloodhound is unique. See further note III/60–1 above.

IVe/19 *festyn* Read *fettyn*, 'retrieve' [<OE *fetian*]. Other texts read *fechyng* (Prk), *ses(s)yn* (Dg, Rg): see I/188.

IVf Properties of a greyhound – MS Eg

This version of the Properties of a greyhound, written in rhyming couplets, bears some resemblance to the equivalent passage in *StA*, which reads:

A Grehounde shulde be heded like a Snake,
and necked like a Drake,
Foted like a Cat,
Tayled like a Rat,
Syded lyke a Teme,
Chyned like a Beme. (1863–5)

In Eg, the material is laid out as verse, whereas *StA* presents it as a continuous paragraph of long lines (not as represented above). The resemblance ends there, for *StA* continues with an account of the development of the greyhound up to its ninth year in doggerel verses – a shorter set of which verses occurs also in Ha (III/96–100).

The rhyming couplets of Eg and *StA* that praise a greyhound through comparisons with other animals are different from the unrhymed comparisons found in Ha (III/91–5), not only because of their rhymes, but also because Ha makes ten comparisons, against the six of Eg and *StA*. See further the notes to lines III/91–100 above.

IVf/4 'Sided like an onion'; the comparison suggests the wide, rounded ribcage of a greyhound. Hands interprets *StA*'s 'syded lyke a teme' as alluding to some wooden implement that forms part of the gear for harnessing animals to a plough, harrow or wain; see *EHH*, p. 150/1865n, and *OED*, s.v. *team* n. 9.

IVg Soiling terms – MS T

T preserves a short version of the J.B. Soiling terms, as against the long versions already furnished by Prk (I/189–200), H (II/174–82) and Ha (III/70–78). Found only in *HSG*, T and W, the short versions are remarkably consistent, far more so than the more numerous long versions. What chiefly distinguishes the short versions is the absence of up to three statements describing the start of a hunt in which a hunter looses a pair of alaunts at a herd of harts. The short versions are also more specific in declaring that the hart plunges into a river, as against the more indefinite 'water' of the long versions. Another distinctive feature of the short versions is their use of an *if* + subjunctive clause, where others use a *when* + indicative construction (see Ha, III/70–78). In other respects, however, the short versions present exactly the same terms for the different actions a hart may take once it has 'soiled', and these are discussed in the notes to Prk (I/189–200).

IVg/6 In the first (*olim* second) edition of *HSG* (*STC* 17019), this line reads 'Yf he take agayn the streme he beteth or els beeketh'. Clearly, *beeketh* is a printer's error for *breketh* – not, as *OED* claims, a nonce example of an obscure, undefined 'term of the chase' (s.v. *beek* v.²). I discuss this issue, and its implications for our understanding of Caxton's early printing of pamphlets at Westminster, in greater detail in my article, 'Caxton's Printings of *The Hors, the Shepe and the Ghoos*: Some further considerations', *Transactions of the Cambridge Bibliographical Society*, 13 (2004), 1–13.

IVh Hierarchy of hawks; Hawks' diseases and remedies – MS G

Edited here in their entirety are the two J.B. items found in G up to the point where a 16th-century hand begins adding supplementary hawking remedies near the top of p. 161. The text has been collated with Ry, again excluding numerous additional remedies, even though these are written in the same hand and style as the J.B. material for a further five pages in that manuscript (Ry, fols 89r–91r). Also included in the collation is Rc's Hierarchy of hawks.

IVh/title The title does not occur in the base manuscript (G), and is here supplied from Ry. A shorter version appears also in Rc: *These ben the namys of alle maner hawkis*.

IVh/1–25 In G, the scribe has written some of this material in long lines (1–11, 18–25) and some as a list (12–17). In Rc, the whole item forms a single block of long lines. Only in Ry has it been arranged with due care, with the introductory paragraph about the emperor's 'hawks' written in long lines, and the subsequent hierarchy set out as a list.

G contains a long version of the hierarchy, different from that in Prk (I/201–224) and Ha (III/101–14), and different also from the short versions typified by H (II/142–63). For the principal notes on this element, see Prk (notes I/201–24) above.

IVh/18 *inffaunt* So too Ry and Rc, but no other version assigns the hoby to an infant. In Prk, Dg, Rg and Eg, the hoby belongs to a young squire (I/217); in H, L and Pp, to a (young) squire of the first head (II/154–5); and in *StA* to a young man.

IVh/20–21 G, Ry, Rc and *StA* all agree at this point in allocating the goshawk to a yeoman, and its tercel to a poor man. But cf. H (II/156–7), which says precisely the reverse.

IVh/24 *fle to þe hewe* A formula wanting in Rc, but not in Ry. The usual form of this locution is 'fly to the view' (*wyue* Prk, I/223; *vve* H, II/126; cf. *PH*, 1070). *Hewe* may be considered a corruption of *vewe*, or perhaps a deliberate alternative, meaning 'hue', as in 'a call, shout'; see *MED*, *heue* n.(2) and *PH*, 1070–81, which describes flying 'to the vewe' as follows: The austringer sets down his hawk and crawls towards a quarry; once he can see the quarry, he summons his hawk by waving a hand or stick, and as it approaches he shouts to drive up the game for his hawk. Perhaps *hewe* alludes to such calling out. However, note also the different definition of 'flying to the view' set out briefly in H (II/126–7) above.

IVh/25 *þe forget, þe grete sore* Both expressions are corrupted in G, as well as in Ry and Rc, most likely as a result of scribal misunderstanding. The first term, *forget* (*furgett* Rc), must derive from 'far jutty' (cf. I/224, II/131–3); and *grete sore* (*getsore* Ry; *gettfurre* Rc) from 'jutty far/ferry' (cf. II/134–6; *StA*, 1202; *PH*, 1085). The original of G's *grete sore* may have read ?*gete fere*. See further the analysis of these expressions in the notes to H (II/131–6) above.

IVh/26 ff. Hawks' diseases and remedies. G and Ry preserve a version of the Hawks' diseases and remedies found nowhere else. The initial list of diseases (lines 26–31) shows strong correspondences with the equivalent list in Ha (III/115–21), but is also significantly different in that it lacks the coherence found in that witness. This has been rectified in the edited text, but will be apparent in the following diplomatic transcription of G, which reveals debasement of the text as well as scribal ignorance of its meaning.

> These bene þ^e Infirmyteis of eue*ry* hawke first in þe | hede þ^e Ree .
> And þ^e frownce abowte þ^e ye ledis . And þe | Pokkis & þ^e mytes in
> þe nekke . And þ^e manteletis and | þe lice i*n* þ^e cheste . The felaundirs
> i*n* þ^e back . And þ^e Ageles | i*n* þ^e braile þ^e peer*e* and þ^e Cray . And
> i*n* þ^e whyngis leggis & | fete þ^e pelyownde þ^e peyne þ^e Crampe and
> þ^e pyes.

IVh/26–31 The diseases listed here are discussed in full in relation to Prk (I/229–33) and Ha (III/115–21). In Ry, the name of each disease is highlighted by decorative underlining.

IVh/31 *pelyownde* Also *polyownde* in line 77 and *poliownde* (Ry), denoting a swelling on the lower leg of a hawk. The more usual forms of this rare word are *polione* (I/233), *polyon* (II/33) and *pellyone* (III/120), while the variant *pelaundyr* occurs in Ex, 27. The form found here and in Ry, with its *-ownde* ending, may represent remodelling of the the word under the influence of *wound* to suggest a condition caused by some injury.

peyne Read *pyene*; i.e. *pyne*, 'pin' – a hard nodule or growth on the underside of a hawk's foot. This mistake is repeated in line 80, as well as in Ry.

IVh/32–3 In the manuscript, these lines belong to the preceding list of hawks' ailments. I have separated them to form a heading.

IVh/34 ff. In Ry, individual remedies and groups of remedies are supplied with a brace and a legend in the margin, such as *For the ree*.

IVh/35 *palys* 'palace' = the palate, roof of the mouth; cf. *palleys*, Prk (I/235).

IVh/38 *tirynge* 'tiring', a piece of tough meat given to a hawk to tear at for exercise. In this case, the remedy calls for the tiring to be 'nesh' (i.e. soft).

IVh/38–9 *ȝif hit brekith* See further H (II/99–100), which describes what might happen when the rye 'breaks': 'sche schall spryng þe watyr owte of hyr hede in þi face'.

IVh/44–6 This treatment for the frounce is very similar to the remedies prescribed by Prk (I/239–42) and H (II/6–12). All are suggestive of a candida yeast infection, or thrichomoniasis or 'canker' (the modern terms for frounce), caused by the protozoon *Trichomonas gallinae*.

The J.B. accounts of the founce should be compared with those in *PEB 1*, pp. 7, 14, and *PH*, lines 96–108, which describe cutting open the frounce lesion to remove 'a grubbe'. The latter clearly describe a different sort of frounce, probably a *Capillaria* (worm) infestation of the mouth, where the worms have burrowed into the mucous membrane and laid their eggs, a condition described and illustrated by Heidenreich, *Birds of Prey*, pp. 141–2. *Capillaria* worms were better known to medieval falconers as 'filanders', when they infested the lower digestive tract; see note I/229–33 above.

IVh/47 *iiij. penywiȝt of penyworte* 'four penny-weight of pennywort', although it is possible that *penyworte* is a mistake occasioned by its similarity to *penywiȝt*. The ingredient specified by Ry at this stage is *iiij peny-weight of the rotes of sawge*. Ry is more consistent in specifying 'a *d*-weight' where G has just 'a *d*' or 'a *d*-worþe'.

The name 'pennywort' denotes several types of creeping plant with round leaves, some growing in crevices of rocks and walls, others in marshy ground; see *OED*, s.v. *pennywort* n.

IVh/49 *May-buttire* Hands (*EHH*, p. 99/158n) quotes an illuminating passage from Gervase Markham's *English Huswife* (1615), p. 113, on the preparation and properties of this form of unsalted butter, manufactured in the month of May.

IVh/50 *ioiste* Read *ioisse*, 'juice'.

IVh/54–5 *For þe frounce growith ... not in þe mouþe* A strange statement, since it contradicts G's earlier, correct observation that the frounce manifests in a hawk's head (lines 26–7; more correctly, the mouth). Perhaps these lines should be understood as expressing a belief about the origins of the disease, rather than its final location.

IVh/58 The instruction to wash a hawk in mare's milk if it is suffering from filander worms is surely a mistake, although it is repeated by Ry. The equivalent recipe in Prk (I/245–7) makes more sense by stating that the hawk's meat (rather than the hawk itself) should be washed in this way.

IVh/62 *þe seconde rynde of ellerun þat is grene* 'the pith of green [young] elder'. Both bark and pith of this common shrub were frequently used for medicinal purposes; the branches of a young plant are abundant in pith.

IVh/65 *semen lumbricorum* Most likely, wormseed, a name given to several plants, but especially hog's fennel (*Peucedanum officinale*), considered effective as a purge for intestinal worms; see *OED*, s.v. *wormseed* n. 1, and Tony Hunt, *Plant Names of Medieval England* (Cambridge, 1989), p. 315, s.v. *Worm-Seed*. In his *Herball or Generall Historie of Plants* (London, 1597), Gerard refers to a variety of 'Towers Mustard' by the names 'English Woormseed' and 'Treacle Wormeseede' (pp. 212–4). Of another plant, which he calls 'Holy Wormwood', Gerard says:

> This Wormwood called Sementina & Semen sanctum ... is that kinde of Wormwood which beareth that seede which we haue in vse, called Wormseede. ... the seede is called euery where Semen sanctum, Holie seede, and Semen contra Lumbricos: in English Wormseed; the herb it selfe is also called Wormseed, or Wormseedwoort. (pp. 941–2).

sugire roce 'rock sugar', i.e. crystallised sugar, which is referred to as 'sugar-candy' in H (II/56). Sugar-candy was often used as a laxative for hawks, and is still sometimes administered to a constipated bird. The more unscrupulous falconer might also dose a bird with sugar to loosen its bowels and so ensure a sufficiently keen appetite for hunting – a practice now strongly discouraged.

IVh/66 *reppe* Read ?*roppe*, 'intestine'; see *MED*, *rop* n.(1). A hawk was sometimes given medication hidden in a short length of fowl intestine, as in the following recipe in L (fol. 172v), also for the filanders: 'Take the iuse of neppe [turnip] and putt it in a smale gutt of a capon or of an henne and knytt bothe the endis with a threde and fastinge latte hir resseyue it all hote'. A similar recipe occurs also in *PEB 1*, p. 10.

IVh/68 ff. The next five recipes show a strong resemblance to comparable remedies in Prk and H, but the similarity ends at line 81.

IVh/68–70 Cf. Prk (I/248–9) and H (II/19–23). Ry stand alone in referring to the worms to be treated by this remedy as *angeles*, rather than *ageles*, *aglys* and the like. See the comments in note I/229–33 above.

IVh/71–4 Cf. Prk (I/250–2) and H (II/24–9).

IVh/75–6 Cf. Prk (I/253–4) and H (II/30–2).

IVh/77–9 Cf. Prk (I/255–6) and H (II/33–6). Only the G–Ry pair suggest olive oil as an alternative to the grease sweated from a pot-lid.

IVh/80–1 Cf. Prk (I/257–8) and H (II/37–41). G and Ry stand alone in referring to the 'pin' as the *peyne*, probably as a consequence of scribal misunderstanding of the term.

IVh/82–84 With this recipe for the 'pies', G (together with Ry) diverges again from Prk and H. The instruction to *take away þe loynes* refers to short leather leashes (called 'lunes') that were attached to the ends of a hawk's jesses (i.e the anklets, usually of soft leather or silk, that were worn permanently by a captive bird). Jesses themselves had a free end several inches long, which a hawker would wind about his fingers when carrying a bird. The lunes were attached to the jesses by means of swivels or special knots for a variety of reasons, usually to do with securing a bird to its perch, to a long training leash (the creance), or simply to give the hawker more to hold on to when moving about with a bird on his fist.

Frederick II describes the use of a single leash that joins both jesses, which is how modern hawkers accomplish the same operation: *DAV*, pp. 139–40 (see also *DAV*, pp. 138–9, for a comprehensive description of jesses). However, medieval and Renaissance English texts refer frequently, if not consistently, to *loines* in the plural, as in *PH*, 522–32: '... because the lewnes shulde be fastened to theym with a payre of tyrettis [swivels]'. See also Malory, *Works*, VI, 16 (p. 169): 'And so sir Launcelot ... was ware of a faucon com over his hede fleyng towarde an hyghe elme, and longe lunes aboute her feete. And ... the lunes overcast aboute a bowghe; and ... she hynge by the leggis faste'; Turbervile, *BH*, p. 129: 'and let hir be loose from all hir furniture, that is without either loynes or cryaunce'.

MED is correct in tracing ME *loine* to OF *longe*, *loigne*, 'a leash', but is mistaken when it confuses the plural form of the word with a hawk's jesses: s.v. *loine* n. (2)

(b). The editors were perhaps influenced by the *OED* (s.vv. *loyn* n., *lune* n.[1]), which also fails to account adequately for the particularised plural sense in which the word was used.

IVi Names of wines – MS Dg

This list of wines occurs only in the cognate pair Dg–Rg and is in certain respects the item most peripheral to the dominant interests of the *J.B. Treatise*. Even so, it can be seen as containing information pertinent to the *properteys that longythe to a yonge gentylle man to haue knowynge of* (Eg), and is a good example of the passion for list-making and cataloguing so typical of the treatise overall.

A similar, but independent and shorter, list of thirty-one wines appears under the heading *Vinne de Burdeux* immediately after the list of Collective nouns in MS C (fol. 45r), and, bracketed beside it, is a separate record of prices for wines and spices. For reasons I have already adduced, I have excluded C's list of wines from my catalogue of J.B. material, but nevertheless refer to it from time to time for purposes of comparison using the siglum C*.

Another list – though only of sweet wines – appears in John Russell's *Boke of Nurture* (117–20):

> The namys of swete wynes y wold þat ye them knewe: / Vernage, / vernagelle, wyne Cute, pyment, Raspise, Muscadelle of grew, / Rompney of modon, Bastard, Tyre, O[z]ey, Torrentyne of Ebrew. / Greke, Malevesyn, Caprik, & Clarey whan it is newe.

And in the romance *The Squire of Low Degree* the King of Hungary attempts to console his grieving daughter with promises of numerous delights, including a wide selection of wines (lines 753–62):

> Ye shall haue rumney and malmesyne, / Both ypocrasse and vernage wyne, / Mountrose and wyne of Greke, / Both algrade and respice eke, / Antioche and bastarde, / Pyment also and garnarde; / Wyne of Greke and muscadell, / Both claré, pyment, and rochell. / The reed your stomake to defye, / And pottes of osey set you by.

Several of these wines are also mentioned in Bodleian MS Rawlinson C 86 (quoted by Furnivall (ed.), *Babees Book*, p. 202), and in the *Dyetary of Helth* (1542) and *Breuyary of Helthe* (1547) by Andrew Borde (Boorde), works that are all quoted in the notes below. (For Andrew Borde's works, see *The First Book of the Introduction of Knowledge made by Andrew Borde*, ed. F.J. Furnivall, EETS ES 10 (London, 1870).)

Informative as these passages may seem, they contain several difficulties that are apparent also in the J.B. list of wines. For although many of the wines named by them are well known, others – such as *mountrose* – remain obscure, and some can have misleading names, such as *wyne of Greke*, which indicates wines (often Iberian) made in the Greek manner. A special difficulty of the J.B. list is the sheer number of wines that are identified by place-names, some of which appear fanciful, such as 'wine of India'. Several place-names have proved to be too obscure to link with modern names, though all have been checked in a range of sources, including J.G.T. Graesse *et al.*, *Orbis Latinus: Lexicon lateinischer geographischer Namen des Mittelalters und der Neuzeit*, 3 vols (Braunschweig, 1972; hereafter referred to as Graesse). In time, these names may prove to be valuable indicators of wine-growing regions or wine-exporting towns supplying the English wine trade. But that is a field of enquiry beyond the scope of the present volume. The history of the medieval English wine trade is a complex subject, regarding which the following brief remarks will need to suffice.

In the 14th and 15th centuries, England imported wines from five main regions: France (especially England's own Aquitanian provinces), Germany, the Iberian peninsula, Italy and the eastern Mediterranean. The wines of northern Europe were generally dry and light, and had a very limited life (less than a year), while those of the eastern Mediterranean were heavier, sweeter and lasted far longer owing to their higher alcohol content. (Cf. Borde's *Dyetary*, p. 255, which distinguishes between the 'meane [i.e. light] wines' of Gascony and France, and 'hote wynes', such as 'wyne greke'.) Most naturally sweet wines (*vina dulcia*) – including rumney, malmsey and 'Greek' – came originally from Cyprus, Greece and the Levant, but were successfully imitated in Italy, Spain and Portugal, from where they were exported in ever-increasing quantities, especially after the Ottoman conquests of Greece, Crete, Cyprus and Rhodes. The hot climates of southern Iberia and Italy, and south-eastern France, also produced some strong dry wines, among them the notorious 'wine of Lepe', the effects of which are described in graphic detail by Chaucer's Pardoner (see note IVi/44 below).

Although medieval records and regulations often distinguish between different types of wines, many wine names appear to have been applied quite loosely, with consequent difficulties for modern interpreters. It will be seen from the notes below that scholars disagree over the origins of osey and vernage, while the terms 'Gascon wine' and 'wine of Bayonne' are probably more or less synonymous. Historical studies have revealed a great deal about the quantities of wine imported into England during the later Middle Ages, and by whom. They have been less successful in determining the character and origin of many wines, except in rather vague outline. This may be inevitable when wines are named according to their port of embarkation, such as 'Rochel', but further research may yet reveal much useful information on this subject. For although some wines are now somewhat obscure, they undoubtedly belonged within a finely judged hierarchy, as is evident in works such as the anonymous *La disputoison du vin et de l'iaue* (1305–77) and Henri d'Andeli's *Bataille des vins* (?c. 1223/1240), in which wines are praised or condemned according to their perceived qualities. Both poems, and the topos to which they belong, are examined by James Holly Hanford, 'The medieval debate between wine and water', *PMLA*, 28 (1913), 315–67 (esp. pp. 329–33).

Further information on medieval wines generally can be found in the following works: Wendy R. Childs, *Anglo-Castilian Trade in the Later Middle Ages* (Manchester, 1978), especially pp. 126–36; A.D. Francis, *The Wine Trade* (London, 1972), pp. 4–24; Margery Kirkbride James, *Studies in the Medieval Wine Trade* (Oxford, 1971); Marcel Lachiver, *Vins, vignes et vignerons: histoire du vignoble français* (Paris, 1988); André L. Simon, *The History of the Wine Trade in England*, 3 vols (London, 1964), especially I, 263–92; Tim Unwin, *Wine and the Vine: An Historical Geography of Viticulture and the Wine Trade* (London and NY, 1991), pp. 166–204; Rolf Sprandel, *Von Malvasia bis Koetzschenbroda: Die Weinsorten auf den spaetmittelalterlichen Maerkten Deutschlands* (Stuttgart, 1998); Thomas Hohnerlein-Buchinger, *Per un sublessico vitivinicolo: La storia materiale e linguistica di alcuni nomi di viti e vini italiani* (Tübingen, 1996); Susan Rose, *The Wine Trade in Medieval Europe: 1000–1500* (London, 2011).

Medieval port and city records are another useful source of names for wines, and there is undoubtedly much that can be learned from them. For my purposes I have confined my attention to the *Calendar of Letter-Books ... of the City of London at the Guildhall*, especially *Letter-Book G* (1352–1374), ed. Reginald R. Sharpe (London, 1905), which yields, for example, the following proclamation for 1373 (fol. 312v) concerning the setting of a reasonable price for sweet wines:

> The price of wine fixed by the Mayor ... Vernage at 2*s* a gallon; Ryvere, Mawvesie, and Romeneye at 16*s*; Candye, Trubidane, Mountrosse, Greek, Creet, Province and Clarre at 12*d*.

Keiser, *Manual X*, 3681 [402–404], deals briefly with texts concerned with wines, but limits his attention to works that can be called 'Treatises on Wine', including those containing recipes for restoring wines or for making wine-based drinks. In consequence, inventories of wine names, such as the J.B. list under discussion here, receive no mention.

It remains to be observed that the J.B. Names of wines is notable for omitting any mention of Bordeaux wine, although this was one of the most important of English wine imports, especially up to 1453, when England lost control of the city of Bordeaux and of Guyenne as a whole. It seems unlikely that this omission reflects the loss of England's Aquitanian provinces, since the J.B. list includes Gascon wine, and the wines of Bayonne and La Rochelle. On the importance of Bordeaux as a centre of the medieval wine trade, see Lachiver, *Vins*, pp. 112–23; Francis, *Wine Trade*, pp. 7–8; Unwin, *Wine and Vine*, pp. 197 ff.

IVi/1 *londwyne* 'land-wine'; presumably, a name for any locally produced wine; see *MED*, *lond* n. 3b.

IVi/2 Rhenish wine was a staple of the English wine trade. The name referred broadly to wines exported from Frankfurt, Mainz and Cologne, and included wines from throughout the Rhine region, as well as Alsace. Although Moselle wine – sometimes referred to as *oblinquo* – was also traded down the River Rhine, it was generally distinguished from Rhenish: Simon, *History of the Wine Trade*, I, 281. Andrew Borde remarks that 'there is lytle read [red] Renyshe wyne, except it growe about Bon, beyonde Colyn': *Breuyary*, p. 75.

IVi/3 *Cavelence* Place-name for a location that remains to be identified. It bears a similarity to Cavallicensis, one of the Latin forms used of Cavaillon in the Vaucluse (see Graesse, s.v. *Cabellio*), but the identification is speculative.

IVi/4 *Bunne* Probably the city of Bonn on the Rhine; see Graesse, s.v. *Bonna* (variously also Bun(n)a), and cf. the quote from Borde's *Breuyary*, referring to this city, in note IVi/2 above.

IVi/5 *Cherow* Place-name for a location that remains to be identified. The variant *terow* in Rg is unhelpful in determining the intended location.

IVi/6 *Rennca* Place-name for a location that remains to be identified. It is reminiscent of Rensis, one of the Latin names for Rhens in the Rhine valley (see Graesse, s.v. *Rensensis*), but the variant *ronnca*, employed by Rg, makes this uncertain.

IVi/7 *Elceter* The name is suggestive of Elisatia, or Alsace, an area renowned for the high quality of its wines; see Graesse, s.v. *Alisatia*; Unwin, *Wine and Vine*, p. 185.

IVi/8 *Tromyn* Place-name for a location that remains to be identified. The variant *tromyy* in Rg is unhelpful in determining the intended location.

IVi/9 *þe Neker* Most likely, the Neckar valley of southern Germany, well known for its vineyards.

IVi/10 *muscaden* 'muscadel', a sweet wine made from muscat grapes.

IVi/11 *mownterose* An unidentified type of wine. The name appears variously as *mayntrose* (C*), *Mountrose* (*Squire of Low Degree*, 755) and *Mountrosse* (*Letter-Book G*, fol. 312v).

IVi/12 *tribiane* Probably trebbiano, a white Italian wine of Tuscany and Marche; see Unwin, *Wine and Vine*, p. 169. This may be the same as the 'Trubidiane' mentioned in *Letter-Book G*, fol. 312v.

IVi/13 *greke* A sweet, heavy wine, originally from Greece and Cyprus, but later made elsewhere in the same style. Wines of this type, exported from southern Italy, were often called 'Greek', doubtless also because of the names used of this area:

'Graecia Magna, Graecia Parva, Grecia Maior'. See Simon, *History of the Wine Trade*, I, 282–83; Graesse, s.v. *Graecia Magna*; and see also the note on *wyne de Grecia* (IVi/16) below. The name 'Greek' appears also in *Letter-Book G*, fol. 312v, beside 'Creet'.

IVi/14 *coorze* It seems very likely that this is the wine referred to by Borde as 'wyne course' (*Dyetary*, p. 255) and 'wyne Qoorse' (*Breuyary*, p. 75). The name is obscure, but may be related to Italian *corso*, defined by John Florio as 'a kind of wine in Corsica': *A Worlde of Wordes, or ... Dictionarie in Italian and English* (London, 1598; facs. edn Hildesheim, 1972), s.v. *Corso*. In both Dg and Rg, the word appears as *coorʒe*, which I have read as containing a tailed *z* rather than a yogh <ʒ>.

IVi/15 *romanyske* The *-isk* suffix indicates 'Romanish' = 'Roman', 'from Rome'. The word is not recorded by the *MED*, but *OED*, citing Borde (1542), suggests that this is another name for *Romanesco* (first attested c. 1566), a wine produced in the area around Rome (see *OED*, s.vv. *Romanesco*, n. 1, *romanisk* n.). Indeed, Borde mentions this wine in both his *Dyetary* (*romanysk*, p. 255) and *Breuyary* (*Romaniske wyne*, p. 75), and in both cases as a separate item from rumney (see note IVi/20 below), with which it should clearly not be confused.

IVi/16 *wyne de Grecia* (*wyne of greke* Rg) This may simply be an expanded form of the name *greke* (see IVi/13), or it may refer specifically to a variety of sweet wine made from over-ripe grapes in northern Portugal, called *vinho de Grecia* – a name that reflects the general origin of sweet wines in the eastern Mediterranean. The name appears twice in the *Squire of Low Degree* (755, 759) and is briefly discussed by Francis, *Wine Trade*, p. 19. See also Borde's allusion to *wyne greke* (*Dyetary*, p. 255).

IVi/17–18 India is an unlikely source of wine; Tartary perhaps a little less improbable. It may be that the compiler was indulging in a bit of whimsy, or showing off his knowledge of geographical names, or perhaps alluding to some exotic wines from the farthest fringes of the Mediterranean basin, or even the Black Sea. Genoa held a number of commercial bases in the southern Crimean peninsula, for example, of which the most important was Caffa (modern Feodosia), a major centre for trade with the Mongol states in eastern Europe and Central Asia. (I am grateful to Allen J. Grieco of Villa I Tatti – The Harvard University Center for Italian Renaissance Studies – for drawing my attention to this possibility.) There is also the chance that an eastern European wine reached England through Hanseatic traders operating on the Vistula River (see Unwin, *Wine and Vine*, fig. 32). But these issues remain speculative, and, more to the point, I have found no mention of wines from India or Tartary in any other miscellany, let alone in records of imports or sales in England. For Tartary, Rg reads *cartaria*, which could suggest scribal distrust or uncertainty on the issue.

IVi/19 Slavonia – the fertile agricultural region of northern Croatia between the Drava and Sava rivers – is not well known as a source of wine in medieval England; see my comments on India and Tartary above.

IVi/20 *romeney of Modon* Rumney (or romney), a sweet wine from Modon (now Methóni) in the far south-west Peloponnese. C* has both 'Romendy' and 'Romendy de moden', and *MED*, s.v. *romenei(e* n. includes a number of interesting quotations. In Italy this wine was known as *romania*, and is described by Florio as 'a kind of excellent wine in Italy like malmesie': *Worlde of Wordes*, s.v. *Romania*. See also Hohnerlein-Buchinger, *Per un sublessico vitivinicolo*, pp. 71–4, where *romania* is examined as a sub-category of *malvasia*. Records show that by the 15th century, after the Ottoman conquest of Greece, rumney was being imported from Spain, which suggests that it was being imitated there, along with other sweet styles of wine, such as malmsey and bastard (see Childs, *Anglo-Castilian Trade*, p. 128, and notes IVi/21 and 39 below).

IVi/21 *malmesey of Candyne* (*malmesey of candyse* Rg; *malvesy* C*). The place-name most likely refers to Crete, known in Latin as 'Candia', and in ME and EMnE as 'Candy'; see Graesse, s.v. *Candia*; *OED*, s.v. *candy* n.². The wine itself is one of the best known sweet varieties. Originally known as *malvasia* (OF *malvesie*), it came initially from Napoli di Malvasia (modern Monemvasia) in the south-eastern Peloponnese, later from Crete, and then Iberia. Cf. *Mawvesie* in *Letter-Book G*, fol. 312v.

IVi/22 *Roodes* As the Ottoman Empire spread into south-eastern Europe in the 15th century, the islands of Rhodes, Crete and Cyprus became increasingly important sources of the strong, sweet malmesy and rumney wines exported to northern Europe – until they too fell in 1522, 1571 and 1622 respectively.

IVi/23 *de Bayre* (*debayre* Rg) The place-name suggests the port-city of Bari, in south-east Italy.

IVi/24 Calabria, the region comprising the 'toe' of Italy, was a source of heavy, sweet wines made in the Greek and Cypriot styles.

IVi/25 *vermulond* (*vermelone* Rg) Obscure; the name is not found in other English lists and is not attested by the *MED* or *OED*. It refers perhaps to an Italian wine, since it occurs here among others from that region. The name may also signify a wine with the bright-red colour of vermilion (<ME *vermiloun, vermulon*).

IVi/26 *vernache* Both Rg and C* give the more usual form of this word: *vernage* (<Italian *vernaccia*), indicating a strong, sweet wine, believed to have originated in the Piedmont and Liguria regions of northern Italy. See also Hohnerlein-Buchinger, *Per un sublessico vitivinicolo*, pp. 156–8. In England, the name *vernage* appears to have been used also of a type of spiced wine, probably made from the Italian wine

of that name. There is an unpublished recipe entitled 'vernage' in MS Harley 2378, for an unsweetened spiced wine (*Curye on Inglysch*, ed. Constance B. Hieatt and Sharon Butler, EETS ss 8 (London, 1985), p. 221, s.v. *vernage*); and in Chaucer's *Merchant's Tale* vernage is listed with two other spiced wines drunk by January as stimulants before joining May in bed: 'He drynketh ypocras, claree, and vernage / Of spices hoote t'encreesen his corage' (*CT*, IV.1807–8).

IVi/27 *wyne fyane* Perhaps 'fine wine' is intended here (as in *Promptorium*, s.v. *ffyne wyne*) – a designation that could mean either 'of superior quality' or 'refined, clarified'; cf. *MED*, *fin* adj.; *finen* v.(3) 1. (a). There were elaborate recipes for refining wines, a set of which occurs coincidentally in MS W, fols 122v–123v; Mary-Jo Arn, 'The emendation of wine: Wine recipes from Beinecke MS 163', *Yale University Library Gazette*, 64 (1990), 109–23. Working against this interpretation, the form *fyane* in Dg is troublesome and the variant *vynefyage* in Rg is unhelpful.

IVi/28 *grekeseke* (*grekefeke* Rg) The name suggests a dry Greek wine, as opposed to the sweet wines that are usually associated with that region.

IVi/29–32 The locations indicated by the place-names Mamorant, Gemerant, Arphax (*arplax* Rg) and Cosderam have proved too elusive to be identified with any degree of certainty.

IVi/33 *mategors* (*mategrow* Rg) Obscure, yet to be identified.

IVi/34 *respoyse* 'raspis', a sweet wine, according to Russell, *Boke of Nurture*, 118, where the name appears as *Raspise*; elsewhere, *respice* (*Squire of Low Degree*, 756), *Raspez* (C*), and see *MED*, *raspise* n. The *Promptorium*, s.v. *Rospeys*, defines this as a rose-coloured wine: *Vinum rosatum*. Borde remarks that 'All maner of wynes be made of grapes, excepte respyse, the which is made of a bery' (*Dyetary*, p. 254) – the implication being that it is made from 'raspis' or raspberry, a notion that can in all likelihood be dismissed as folk etymologising. The *OED*, s.v. *raspis* n.[1], suggests a more probable connection with Latin *raspatum*, OF *rapé*, *vin raspé*, wine made from rape, or marc, the skins and other parts left behind after grapes have been pressed. See further Latham, s.v. *raspatum*; *FEW*, XVI, 671, s.v. *raspôn*.

IVi/35 *ruptarge* An Iberian wine, very likely the 'Ryptage' listed as one of the products of Portugal ('the kynges lond of Portyngale and Algarbe') in *The Commodyties of England* (c. 1451), a work formerly ascribed to Sir John Fortescue; *The Works of Sir John Fortescue, Knight*, ed. Thomas (Fortescue) Lord Clermont, 2 vols (London, 1869), I, 549–54 (p. 554). Childs observes that 'Cornish royal officials sometimes called the white they handled "Rubidage" [not attested in *OED*]; this usually came in on northern ships so is almost certainly from the northern coast, and is possibly a corruption of Ribadeo [a coastal town in north-west Spain], or of Ribadavia [a town in south-west Spain on the Rio Miño], which furnished popular wines in England in the sixteenth century' (*Anglo-Castilian Trade*, p. 127). The available evidence is too slight to come to any firm conclusion, but the congruences between *ruptarge, ryptage* and *rubidage* may be worth worth noting. See also my discussion of *wyne de Robedore* in note IVi/48 below.

IVi/36 *caprike* A sweet wine, probably originally from the eastern Mediterranean but later associated with the Iberian peninsula. *The Commodyties of England* (p. 554) names 'Capike' as a Portuguese wine. The name suggests an early connection with the island of Capri (Caprae, Capria); see *MED, caprik* n.; Graesse, s.v. *Capraria insula*; Russell, *Boke of Nurture*, 120.

IVi/37 *teynt* (*Taynte* C*) 'tent', a dark-red wine from Spain: *MED, teint* n.(2); *OED, tent* n.[4] (first attested 1542).

IVi/38 *tyre* A sweet wine of the Levant, possibly from Syria, exported from Tyre in the Lebanon.

IVi/39 *bastart* 'bastard', a sweet (or sweetened) wine, usually from Spain, but also exported from Portugal according to *The Commodyties of England*, where it is mistakenly referred to as 'Bascarde' (p. 554). See also *The Libel of English Policy* (*c.* 1436), which lists 'wyne bastarde' among the commodities of Spain: in *Political Poems and Songs relating to English History*, ed. Thomas Wright, 2 vols, Rolls Series (London, 1859–61), II, 157–205 (p. 160). The name suggests a blend of some sort, which may be why the *MED* claims (s.v. *bastard* n. 3c) that this was a fortified wine. The *OED* is more circumspect, stating only (s.v. *bastard* n. 4) that the name was used historically to indicate 'A sweet kind of Spanish wine, resembling muscadel in flavour', though it goes on to claim that the term was also 'sometimes applied to any kind of sweetened wine'. *A-ND* includes a quotation showing *bastard* used adjectivally to denote a (French) wine (*vin bastard*) that has been enhanced in some way: 'Vin de La Rochelle bastart est fort et sec, et douç en en savour' (s.v. *bastard* a.). See further Francis, *Wine Trade*, pp. 18–19.

IVi/40 *clarrey* 'clary', a sweet, spiced wine; see *MED*, s.v. *clare* n.(1). Clary was usually sweetened with honey, unlike hippocras, for which sugar was generally used. For recipes, see *Curye on Inglysch*, p. 145, no. 205, and pp. 148–9, nos 4, 6. André Simon remarks that, 'Blends of different wines and mixtures of spices, honey and herbs with wine were frequently resorted to to disguise the natural harshness and acidity of wines drunk quite new, as was the prevalent custom throughout the Middle Ages' (*History of the Wine Trade*, I, 290).

In this case, there can be no doubt about the word's meaning, but matters can become confused when the form *claret* is used. This too can denote clary (see *MED*, s.v. *claret* n.(1) (a); *OED*, s.v. *claret* n.1), but also *vins claret*, which the *OED* explains (s.v. *claret* n.[2]) were 'wines of yellowish or light red colour, as distinguished alike from "red wine" and "white wine"; the contrast with the former ceased about 1600'.

IVi/41 *osey* There has been a great deal of speculation about this name and its possible connections with Alsace (<OF *Aussay, Aussois, Auxois*), Auxerre (<OF *Aucoirre*), or the Auxois region; see, for example, *Babees Book*, p. 206/10n, Francis, *Wine Trade*, p. 18. These notions are all strongly refuted by Simon, *History of the Wine Trade*, I, 287–9, and the issue has been dealt with comprehensively by M.J. Freeman, '"Pots of Osey": Portuguese wine in late medieval England and its place of origin', in *De mot en mot: Aspects of medieval linguistics*, ed. Stewart Gregory and D.A. Trotter (Cardiff, 1997), 17–36. As the *OED* indicates (s.v. *osey* n.), the name denotes 'Any of several, probably often sweet, Portuguese wines from the Lisbon area' (<Azoia, a region near that city).

The *OED*'s definition accords well with the evidence from medieval English sources, for Russell lists osey as a sweet wine (*Book of Nurture*, 119), and most medieval English references to osey occur in association with other Peninsular wines: for example, the anonymous author of *The Libel of English Policy* lists it as one of the products of Portugal: 'Here londe hath oyle, wyne, osey, wex and greyne' (p. 163).

IVi/42 *ypocras* 'hippocras': a sweet, spiced wine, which takes its name from the conical cloth bag, known as "Hippocrates' sleeve", through which it was filtered. For recipes, see *Curye on Inglysch*, p. 143, no. 199; pp. 148–9, no. 5.

IVi/43 *pyament* 'piment': a sweet, spiced wine. For a recipe, see *Curye on Inglysch*, p. 154, no. 17.

IVi/44 *wyne de Lepe* A strong white wine from the wine-producing region around the town of Lepe in south-west Spain, near the border with Portugal. This wine was notorious for being used by unscrupulous taverners to adulterate more expensive wines, a practice alluded to in Chaucer's *Pardoner's Tale* (*CT*, VI.563 ff.): 'This wyn of Spaigne crepeth subtilly / In othere wynes, growynge faste by ...'. The region may have produced other strong wines, since records show the arrival of 'sweet wines of Lepe' in England in 1406: Childs, *Anglo-Castilian Trade*, p. 127.

IVi/45 *vinne cottinn* (*wyne cottene* Rg) I have found this name nowhere else, and it is not recorded by either the *MED* or the *OED*. Perhaps it alludes to wines from the Cotentin peninsula of north-west Normandy, a topic explored by Alfred Butot, *De la consommation et du commerce du vin en Normandie, particulièrement en Basse-Normandie et en Cotentin, pendant la guerre de Cent Ans* (Paris, 1938). (I am very grateful to Allen J. Grieco for this helpful suggestion.)

IVi/46 *wyne de Algarbe* So too Rg. C* reads simply *Algarve*, and the *Squire of Low Degree* (l. 756) refers to *algrade*. Clearly, the Algarve of southern Portugal is intended. As citations in the *OED* (s.v. *Algarbe* n.) show, the place-name itself was usually sufficient to designate the region's wines, making the explanatory *wyne de* component redundant.

IVi/47 Toulouse, located on the upper reaches of the River Garonne, was one of several sources of *Haut Pays* wines, commonly exported from Bordeaux – but only after the Bordelais had first shipped all their own produce. As a result, wines of the *Haut Pays* were usually 'racked', or stored, during winter and shipped the following spring; see Unwin, *Wine and Vine*, pp. 197–9. Francis comments further, '... in later centuries the difficulties to which High Country wines continued to be subject led to experiments in the art of preparing and maturing wine' (*Wine Trade*, p. 9; see pp. 7–9, 12).

IVi/48 *wyne de Robedore* (*wyne de Robodore* Rg; ?*Rybdure* C*) The place-name in this phrase is one that I have found nowhere else. It appears to be an English adaptation of Ribadeo, the name of a wine-exporting town on the north-west coast of Spain, with the element *Rob-* showing remodelling based on the name *Robert*. It is very likely also related to the term *Rubidege* that was sometimes used by Cornish officials for white wines from northern Spain (Childs, *Anglo-Castilian Trade*, p. 127), and perhaps a variant name for *ruptarge*, discussed above in note IVi/35. Comparable remodelling of the name of another Spanish wine to yield native English-sounding forms can be seen in *Rob Dauie*, *Roberdany*, *Ribadavy* and *Rob-o-Dauy* < Ribadavia (derived from the important wine-producing centre of that name); see *OED*, s.v. *Ribadavia* n.

The adaptation of the name Ribadeo suggested here should be compared with Ribadavia, another Spanish wine named after an important wine-producing centre, but remodelled to yield the native English-sounding forms *Rob Dauie*, *Roberdany*, *Ribadavy* and *Rob-o-Dauy*; see *OED*, s.v. *Ribadavia* n.

IVi/49 *Bilbowe* The coastal towns of the Basque region were important Spanish trade centres. Bilbao was well known as a source of wine and other commodities; see Childs, *Anglo-Castilian Trade*, pp. 127, 152–4.

IVi/50 *wyne de Cayser* Enigmatic. As can be seen from Graesse, s.vv. *Caesaria* and *Caesaris*, the place-name in this phrase could signify any of a variety of locations, so its intended referent here is uncertain.

IVi/51 *wyne de Paytors* (*wyne paytew* Rg) Wine of Poitou. The region was well known for its wines, which were mostly exported from the port of La Rochelle. See further note IVi/55 below, and Francis, *Wine Trade*, p. 7. For a range of ME forms of the name *Poitou*, including *Peiters* and *Paiters*, see *MED*, s.v. *Peitou* n.

IVi/52 *wyne cute* (*wyne cutte* Rg) The name given to wine (or, preferably, must) reduced to half or a third of its original volume by being boiled (OF *cuit* <*cuire*, 'to cook, boil'), known in Latin as *sapa*, Italian *vino cotto*. According to Florio's *Worlde of Wordes*, *vin cótto* [*sic*] is 'a kinde of sodden [boiled] wine which we call cute, to put into other wines, to make them keepe the longer'. See also *MED*, s.v.

cute adj., and Furnival's note on 'wyne Cute' in Russell's *Boke of Nurture*, line 118: *Babees Book*, p. 203.

IVi/53 *Bayone* The coastal town of Bayonne, close to the Franco–Spanish border, was a significant port for the export of Gascon produce, including wine, to England and elsewhere. The expression 'wine of Bayonne' is unlikely to refer to a specific variety of wine, but rather Gascon wine in general imported to England from Bayonne. See my comments on Gascon wine in note IVi/56 below.

IVi/54 *Rochel* The city of La Rochelle was the primary port of embarkation for wines of Aunis and Poitou destined for England and elsewhere. Wines coming from La Rochelle were judged to be better than those of Picardy, but slightly inferior to the wines exported from Bordeaux (Francis, *Wine Trade*, p. 7; Childs, *Anglo-Castilian Trade*, p. 128). See also *The Libel of English Policy*, which refers to the fleet of Flanders sailing 'Into the Rochelle, to feche the fumose [vaporous] wine' (p. 162).

IVi/55 *Burgoyne wyne* According to Simon (*History of the Wine Trade*, I, 276), Burgundian wine reached England only occasionally and in no significant quantities; its presence in this list is therefore noteworthy.

IVi/56 *Gascone wyne* Cf. *vyne of gaskyne for the best* Rg; *red wyn de gascone* C*. The wines of Gascony figured prominently in England, where they were deemed to be superior to the wines of La Rochelle. In the second half of the 14th century, the maximum retail price for Gascon wine (as well as Spanish wine and osey) was fixed at 6d a gallon, as against 4d for the best Rochelle (see Childs, *Anglo-Castilian Trade*, p. 126). According to Yves Renouard, Gascon wines were 'a luxury commodity', which '... were expensive and could only be afforded by the rich and well-to-do: *grands seigneurs*, the clergy and the bourgeoisie': 'The Wine Trade of Gascony in the Middle Ages', in *Essays in French Economic History*, ed. Rondo Cameron (Homewood, IL, 1970), 64–90 (p. 88).

The gradual loss of England's Aquitanian territories, culminating in the defeat at Castillon in 1453, greatly diminished wine imports from Bordeaux and Gascony. Although foreign traders continued to supply England with some wine from these regions, the shortfall was rapidly filled by increased imports from Iberia – as described by James, *Medieval Wine Trade*, p. 84.

GLOSSARY

The Glossary is selective and applies only to the texts set out in Parts I–IV. Appendix entries are all examined separately in the detailed notes accompanying each appendix.

Any common word that is recognisably similar to its modern form is not glossed, unless it is used in an archaic or specialised sense that warrants identification. All significant spelling variants are included, but minor discrepancies – as with *i/y*, *u/v* – are ignored if an otherwise identical form has already been cited. Verbs are listed under their infinitive form if one occurs in the text; otherwise, under one of their inflected forms, to which others are cross-referred. Where there are several variant spellings of the same word, the headword used is either that which is most recognisable, or closest to the relevant lemma in the *MED*.

Past participles commencing with *i-* or *y-* are listed as an inflection under the base form of the verb, if one exists; otherwise, the participle is treated as a headword ignoring the prefix, so that, for example, *i-gobenyd* will be found under G. In some cases, where it is arguable whether a past participle is being used adjectivally, the word is labelled according to its grammatical form rather than its possible semantic value.

Brief etymologies, in square brackets, are provided only for certain notable words, viz. those that are particularly obscure, or whose forms are here all significantly different from the lemma employed by the *MED*; so too for words that are used in a sense not recognised by *MED*, or omitted altogether from that work. Further details about such words are to be found in the Explanatory Notes – especially the note occasioned by the first occurrence of a particular word. In all cases where a Middle English form is cited, this indicates the lemma used by the *MED*.

In the alphabetic sequence, ȝ (yogh) comes immediately after G, and þ (thorn) follows T. Vocalic and consonantal *i* are distinguished and listed separately under I/Y and I=J. Vocalic and consonantal *v* in initial position are distinguished under V=U and V=V, but medial *u* always precedes medial *v* regardless of phonetic value. In all cases where *y* is simply a spelling variation for *i*, it is alphabetised accordingly.

A separate list of place-names follows the main glossary.

GLOSSARY

Abbreviations used in this Glossary

AN	Anglo-Norman	OE	Old English
adj.	adjective	OF	Old French
adv.	adverb	pa.p.	past participle
attrib.	attributive use	pa.t.	past tense
aux.	auxiliary	perh.	perhaps
conf.	conflated, conflation	pl.	plural
conj.	conjunction	poss.	possessive
dim.	diminutive	ppl.adj.	participial adjective
fig.	figurative(ly)	pr.	present
ger.	gerund	pr.p.	present participle
imp.	imperative	prep.	preposition
impers.	impersonal	prob.	probably
ind.	indicative	pron.	pronoun
infl.	influenced	refl.	reflexive
interj.	interjection	sg.	singular
lit.	literally	spec.	specifically
L	Latin	subj.	subjunctive
ME	Middle English	v.	verb (infinitive unless otherwise specified)
n.	noun		
n.col.	collective noun	var.	variant
obsc.	obscure	2/3	2nd/3rd person

A

& *conj.* and I/230, passim.
& *prep.* if II/68.
aby hawke *n.* a type of hawk (exact sense obscure) II/161. [ME *abi hauk*.]
agayne, aȝen, aȝenst *prep.* against II/34; IVg/6; IVh/32.
ageles, aglys, akyllys, egles *n. pl.* parasitic intestinal worms I/231, 248; II/19, 54; III/118; IVh/29, 68. [<OF *aiguille* 'a needle'.] See also ANGELES.
aȝen *adv.* again II/44, 178.
akyllys *n. pl.* See AGELES.
alauntes, alanndys, allondys, alonndys, alondys, aloundys *n. pl.* alaunts, alans: large, fierce dogs used for hunting deer and boar I/183, 186, 189; II/174; III/67, 70; IVe/5, 14. [ME *alaunt*.]
also *adv.* ~ *sone as*, as soon as IVg/2.

aneuer, nanauer *n.* 'enewer': name for a hawk that flies at ducks, causing them to dive into the water I/228; II/111. [<ME *eneuen* 'to drive waterfowl into the water'.] See also ANEWYTH.
anewyth *pr. 3sg.* enews: (of a waterfowl) plunges into (or remains in) a body of water (for fear of a hawk) II/139. [Cf. ME *eneuen* 'to drive waterfowl into the water' <OF *enewer* (*en* + *eau*) 'to moisten'.]
angeles *n. pl.* parasitic intestinal worms IVh/68n (MS Ry). [<OF *aiguille* 'needle', infl. by *anguille* 'eel'.] See also AGELES.
anodyr *adj.* another I/223.
anodyre *pron.* another (one) I/236.
appetently *adv.* eagerly, with appetite I/112.

assayle *v.* of a dog: to cover, mate (with) III/95, 100.
assauted *pa.p.* assaulted; of a badger: dug out of its set IVa/10.
autelys, awteles *n. pl.* atteals: small ducks of some sort (possibly widgeon) II/234; III/43. [ME *autele*.]
awyse *n.* See GOOD AWYSE.

B

baak *n.* back III/61.
bad(e) *n.* wildcat, spec. a mountain cat (prob. the European wildcat *Felis silvestris*) I/179; III/56. [ME *badde*.]
baeyis *n. pl.* boys I/95.
bayris *n. pl.* See BEYRE.
y-bakkid *ppl.adj.* 'backed', i.e. possessing a back III/92.
barrene *n.col.* of mules: a 'barrenness, infertility' I/50.
bastarde, basterd *n.* 'bastard' = hybrid; (of an animal or bird) a cross-breed I/213; II/150; IVh/14; **basterdys** *pl.* I/182.
bastart *n.* a sweet wine from the Iberian peninsula IVi/39.
be *prep.* by, beside II/133.
bechyng(e) *n. & ger.* a 'beaching' = a beakful, a morsel I/270; II/23.
beddyte, beyddyte *pr. 3sg.* beds, withdraws to bed I/122, 123.
beyre *n.* bear IVa/8; **bayris** *pl.* I/45.
beyted *pa.p.* baited = set upon with dogs IVa/8.
beyttyþ *pr. 3sg.* See BETYS.
ben(e), byn, by(yn)ne, bith, bythe *pr. ind. pl.* are I/171, 172, 173, 182, 205; III/66; IVh/3, 26, passim.
beseged *pa.p.* beseiged IVa/10.
betys, beteth, beyttyþ *pr. 3sg.* of a hart: swims, makes its way upstream, against the current I/196; II/178; III/74; IVg/6. [ME *beten* <OF *batre* 'beat'.]

betterys *n. pl.* See BYTTERE.
bevy, beve(e), beuy *n.col.* of ladies, quails, roes: a 'bevy' = a group, herd, flock I/8, 9, 10; II/202, 203, 204; III/6, 7, 8. [ME *bevey* <AN *bevée* – original sense obscure.]
byege *adj.* big, large I/169.
byfe *n.* beef I/242.
byldynge *n.col.* of rooks: a 'building' = a 'nesting, building of nests' I/27.
byn, by(y)ne *v.* See BEN(E).
byne *n. pl.* bees I/24.
byrre *n.col.* of conies (rabbits): a 'berry' = a burrow, warren I/38. [prob. <OE *beorg* 'hill'; possibly <OE *burg, burh* 'fortified dwelling'.]
byttere *n.* bittern I/135; **betterys, bytorus, botowrys** *pl.* I/11; II/230; III/39.
byttonnere *n.* 'bitterner': name for a hawk that flies at bitterns I/228.
bytwix *prep.* between III/106.
blanket(t) *n.* a type of woollen cloth, often undyed II/72; threads of the same, given to a hawk to regurgitate as 'casting' II/76.
ble(e) *n.* colour, hue; *of voone* ~, *of on* ~, of a single colour I/268; II/55.
bocher houndys, bochere hovndis, bocheres hundis *n. pl.* butcher hounds: large dogs (usually mastiffs) kept by butchers to help them to keep control of animals being led to slaughter I/184; III/68–9; IVe/11.
bock, boke *n.* See BUCKE.
bomynabul *adj.* abominable I/66.
borges *n. pl.* burgesses: citizens with full municipal privileges; perh. here in the sense of town officials, members of the town assembly I/79. [ME *burgeis*.]
borys *n. pl.* boars I/51.
botowrys *n. pl.* See BYTTERE.
bowere *n.* bower (bougher) = a young, fledged hawk that clambers out of its

nest to perch on an adjoining bough I/225; II/107. [ME *bower* <*bough.*]
brace, braas *n.col.* 'brace': (of dogs) a pair or couple (on a shared leash) I/57; III/70.
branchere, brawncher *n.* brancher: a young hawk, older than a BOWERE (*q.v.*), that is capable of short flights near its nest I/225; II/107. [ME *braunchier* <OF.]
brasse *n.* brass or bronze used in pots and other (kitchen) utensils II/29. [ME *bras.*]
brawlyng, braulyng *pr.p.* making a noise, clamouring II/190; III/86.
brayle, braile, brayell *n.* **1.** abdomen, bowels (of a hawk) I/231; III/119; IVh/29. **2.** collectively, a hawk's undertail feathers II/122. [ME *brail* <OF *braiel* 'belt, girdle'.]
breke *v.*[1] of an illness (spec. REE, *q.v.*): 'break', begin to dissipate IVh/42; **brekith** *pr. 3sg.* IVh/39.
brekyth *v.*[2] *pr. 3sg.* rends, tears apart II/87.
brekyþe, brekþ, breykythe *v.*[3] *pr. 3sg.* of a hart: swims or makes its way upstream, against the current I/196; II/178; III/74; IVg/6.
brennyth *pr. 3sg.* burns II/39; **brent** *pa.p.* burned II/11.
brewseworte *n.* bruisewort, a name given to several different plants (including the common daisy) for their supposed healing properties IVh/48.
brydys *n. pl.* birds I/141.
brovkyne *pa.p.* broken; i.e. dismembered, carved I/128.
bruschyd *pa.p.* ?'bruised, hurt' [<ME *brisen*], or ?'purged' [<ME *brushen*, 'to brush clean'] II/77.
bucke, buk(e), bock, boke *n.* buck, the male fallow deer (*Cervus dama*) I/174;

II/168; III/54, 81, passim; **bukkys** *pl.* II/198; III/3.
bustterd, bustard(e) *n.* bustard, spec. the great bustard (*Otis tarda*) I/204; III/104; IVh/3.
but *conj.* unless, except IVh/42.

C

canell *n.* cinnamon IVh/52.
canvas *adj.* the colour of canvas (?light brown) II/161.
cappone *n.* capon, a castrated cockerel I/130.
caprike *n.* a type of sweet wine IVi/36. [ME *cap(r)ik* <L *Capria.*]
carlys *n. pl.* carls, churls II/240, 242.
carte sadill *n.* cart-saddle: the small saddle to which are attached the shafts of a horse-drawn cart III/99.
carttars *n. pl.* carters I/97.
cast *n.col.*[1] of bread: a measure or quantity, a ration I/71.
cast *n.col.*[2] of hawks: a pair I/72. [<ME *casten* 'to launch a hawk (to make it fly) from the fist'.]
cast *v.*[1] of a hawk: to regurgitate indigestible matter; also, to vomit generally II/64, 66; **castyþe** *pr. 3sg.* II/83. See also CASTYNG.
cast *v.*[2] *v. imp.* hold, restrain (a hawk) I/239.
castyng *n.* casting: a pellet of indigestible matter regurgitated by a hawk II/62; also, any indigestible matter added to a hawk's food to allow it to regurgitate ('cast') such a pellet II/67, 70.
catte *n.* ~ *of the mountayne*, prob. the European wildcat (*Felis silvestris*) IVd/16. See also BAD(E).
cavs *n.* cause I/205.
cege(e) *n.col.* See SEGE.
celedony, solondon *n.* celandine, a name formerly used of two plants that

were thought to be the same species: greater and lesser celandine – here, most likely the former (*Chelidonium majus*) II/64; IVh/82. [ME *celidoine*, L *celidonia*.]
centtans *n.col.* of judges: a 'sentence, sentencing' I/76.
cete *n.col.* of badgers: ?a 'city' I/36. [?<OF *cité*.]
chate *n.* a horn signal of any kind; also, a specific horn signal (of unknown character) III/64. [<AN *chater* 'to sound the horn'.]
cheyuen *n.* chevin: the chub, a river fish of the carp family I/153.
chennans *n. pl.* canons, members of a religious community I/63.
chermyng *n.col.* See CHYRME.
chese *v.* choose II/101.
chyne *n.* chine = spine, backbone; hence, the back generally I/170.
i-chynyd *pa.p.* of a samon: filleted (the flesh being cut away from the chine, or backbone) I/149.
chyrme *n.col.* a 'chattering, warbling, twittering' (of birds) I/25. [ME *chirm* <OE *cirm* 'noise, uproar'.] See also CHYRMYNG.
chyrmyng *pr.p.* chattering, warbling, singing (of birds) II/21; **chyrmyng, chermyng** *n.col.* II/210; III/15. [ME *chirmen*.]
chiteryng *n.col.* of starlings: a 'chittering' = chattering (imitative) III/16. [<ME *chiteren*.]
chyuerys *n.* See CLYUERSE.
chov3this *n. pl.* jackdaws (possibly also choughs: see Appendix I, 33n) I/29.
chourllys *n. pl.* churls I/88.
clarrey *n.* clary, a spiced wine sweetened with honey IVi/40.
clatteryng *n.col.* of 'choughs' (i.e. jackdaws): a 'clattering, chattering' I/29. [Cf. ME *clateren*.]

clepyd *pa.p.* called, named II/122.
clyuerse, chyuerys *n.* cleavers (or clivers), also called goosegrass, a climbing plant (*Galium aparine*) I/259; II/45. [ME *cliver*.]
clowdir, clowdre, clovdyre *n.col.* of carls, cats: a 'clodder, cludder'; i.e. a clotted mass, a dense group; hence, a crowd I/54; II/240, 241; III/49, 50. [ME *cloddre*.]
clostyr, clvsture *n.col.* of churls, grapes, knaves, nuts: a cluster I/86, 87, 88.
clowte *n.* clout, a piece of cloth II/8.
cnavys *n. pl.* knaves: prob. 'boys', but possibly 'churls' (see Appendix I, 113n) I/94.
comfortynge, confortyng *pr.p.* encouraging I/191; III/71.
commente *n.* commonalty, the commons I/161. [Var. of ME *communite*.]
cony, conny(e) *n.* the European rabbit *Oryctolagus cuniculus* (spec. a fully grown specimen) I/125, 138, II/191; **connys** *pl.* I/38.
coorze *n.* a type of wine IVi/14. [? <Italian *corso*, a wine of Corsica.]
cordyt *pa.p.* 'corded'; i.e. of a lamprey: has its 'cord' removed I/146 (see Appendix II, 48n).
corllowe *n.* curlew I/134; **corlewis, kurloews** *pl.* II/200; III/4.
cormmeravnttys *n. pl.* cormorants I/74.
cottys *n. pl.* coots, i.e. the bald coot (*Fulica astra*) I/20.
couerkele *n.* cover; (*attrib.*) ~*federis*, the two central feathers of a hawk's tail, its 'deck feathers' II/118. [<ME *covercle*, 'lid, protective covering' <OF.]
coursed *pa.p.* coursed, i.e. hunted with gazehounds IVa/5.
covee *n.* cow I/267.

covey, couy *n.col.* of partridges: a 'covey' = a hatching, a brood I/7; II/206; III/10. [ME *covei* <OF *covée* 'brood'.]
covpul *n.col.* of spaniels: a couple, pair (on a shared leash) I/59.
covrtears *n. pl.* courtiers I/89.
cowert *n.col.* of coots: a 'covert', i.e. a 'nest', a 'brood' I/20. See Appendix I, no. 42n. [<OF *couvert*.]
cownteryuer *n.* 'counter-river', a beater located on the far bank of a river or pond, and tasked with driving waterfowl towards the austringer II/134. [Cf. L *contrariveator, contraripator*.]
cray(e) *n.* cray, a form of constipation in which the hawk's mutes (droppings) appear thick and chalky I/232, 253; II/30, 54; III/119; IVh/30, 75. [<OF *craie* 'chalk'.]
crannys *n. pl.* cranes (the European crane, *Grus cinerea*) I/5.
crowys *n.pl* crows I/28.
crowyth *pr. 3sg.* 'crows', makes a noise; of a hawk's belly: 'grumbles' II/80.
curattys *n. pl.* curates I/65.
cuttelle *n.* any of the ten primary (outer) feathers on a hawk's wing, named for their resemblance to a knife-blade II/114. [Cf. ME *coutel* 'knife, blade' <OF.]

D

d *n.* penny IVh 48, passim; *d-worþe*, a pennyworth IVh/51–2. [<L *denarius*.]
damnynge *n.col.* of jurors: a 'damning, condemning' I/78.
davberis *n. pl.* daubers, craftsmen who apply plaster, lime or daub during the building of a structure I/98.
deth *n.* 'death' = a horn call signalling the success of a hunt (spec. here for hare, otter or wolf) III/62, 63.
dyngnete *n.col.* a 'dignity' I/63.

dysmemmyrde *pa.p.* dismembered I/132.
dyswygurte *pa.p.* disfigured (with reference to the carving of a peacock) I/133.
dyssayt *n.col.* See DYSSEYTE.
dysseyfe *subj. sg.* deceive, mislead II/129.
dysseyte, dyssayt *n.col.* of lapwings: a 'deceit' I/15; II/235. See Appendix I, no. 116n.
dyvyng, dyuyng *n.col.* of atteals: a 'diving' II/234; III/43.
do *v. imp.* apply II/12.
dog(ge) for the bowe *n.* a type of bloodhound III/61; IVe/16.
dokys *n. pl.* ducks II/111.
doo, dwo *n.* doe, the female fallow deer I/175; II/168; III/54; IVa/4, passim;
dooys, dooeys, doys *poss.* I/203; III/103; IVh/2.
doppyng *n.col.* of 'herles', sheldrakes: a 'ducking, diving' II/233; III/42. [<ME *doppen* 'to dive, plunge' (underwater).]
doubbe, dubbe *v.* ~ *in*, flavour with I/247; *v. imp.* disguise II/64. [ME *dubben*.]
doues, dowys *n. pl.* doves I/75; III/31.
dovt *n.col.* of wild cats: a 'horror', a 'peril' I/55. [ME *doute* <OF *dote, doute*.]
down(e) *n.col.* of hares: a multiplicity (exact sense and origins obsc.) II/218; III/24. See Appendix I, no. 89n. [?<ME *doune* 'down, open country'; ?<ME *don* 'dun coloured'.]
drawythe *pr. 3sg.* of a hunting dog: searches for game by scent IVe/16;
drawyn *pr. 3pl.* IVe/15.
dryfte *n.col.* of tame swine: a 'drift', a drove = a herd of animals that are driven I/53. [<OE *drifan* 'to drive'.]
drovfe *n.col.* of 'neat' (cattle): a drove, a herd I/81. [ME *drove* <OE *draf*.]
dubbe *v. imp.* See DOUBBE.

dukys *n. pl.* ducks II/223.
dull *adj.* listless, cheerless II/70.
dunghylle currys, dovnghyll currys *n. pl.* dunghill curs: nondescript dogs, or more spec. dogs living on a dunghill, a refuse heap I/184–5; IVe/12.
dwo *n.* See DOO.

E

egkyl, neygule *n.* eagle I/201; II/143.
egles *n. pl.* See AGELES.
elk(e) *n.* 'elk', a name used of a certain type of deer (identity unknown; perh. a young stag) II/169; III/55, 103; IVh/3; also defined as a two-year-old red deer stag I/176, and a 200-year-old hart IVd/12. [Cf. ME *elk*.]
ellerun *n.* common, or European, elder (*Sambucus nigra*), a shrub with white flowers and black berries IVh/62. [ME *ellern*.]
ellys *adv.* else I/147; II/28.
ellys *n. pl.* eels I/148.
emparovre *n.* emperor I/201.
endue *v.* endue, endew = of a hawk: to pass food from crop to stomach and there to digest it II/84. [ME *endeuen*.]
enlurryd, enlurid *pa.p.* of a hawk: recalled to (or by means of) a lure I/205, IVh/4. See also LURYD.
enseymyd *ppl.adj.* 'enseamed' = of a hawk: purged of excess body fat II/75. [ME *enseimen*.]
entyrmuer, ventteremuere *n.* intermewer = a half-mewed hawk, one that is taking on its first adult plumage I/226; II 109. [<OF *entremué*; cf. ME *meuere*.]
erbis *n. pl.* herbs IVh/50.
ere *n.* year III/96.
erthe *n.col.* of foxes: an 'earth' = the lair of a burrowing animal I/37.
essye *adj.* easy I/166.
euyrey *adj.* every I/213.

F

facon(e) *n.* See FAUCON.
faysanddare, fesoner *n.* 'pheasanter': the name given to a hawk that is flown at (or perh. adept at catching) pheasants I/227; II/110.
fayssant, faysand *n.* pheasant I/136; III/90; **faysandis, feysandys, fesawntys** *pl.* I/6; II/205; III/9.
faucon, fawcone, facon(e), favkone, fawkyn *n.* falcon: any of the long-winged hawks, such as a lanner, peregrine and the like II/105, 182; ~ **gentell, ~ gentill, ~ ientyl(l)**, 'falcon-gentle', a byname for the peregrine falcon (*Falco peregrinus*) I/210; II/147; III/108; IVh/10; ~ *of the rock*, ~ *of þe roche*, ~ *of þe rokke*, 'falcon of the rock', another byname for the peregrine falcon I/211; II/148; III/108; IVh/12; ~ *peregryne*, ~ *perygryne*, peregrine falcon I/212; II/149; III/108–9; IVh/13.
faukenere *n.* falconer III 122.
faulle *n.col.* of woodcocks: a 'fall' = an 'alighting' I/17. [<ME *fallen* 'to alight'.]
favne *n.* fawn, the young of a deer I/203; **fowne** III/103; IVh/2.
fawcone *n.* See FAUCON.
fawyr *n.* favour, goodwill I/160.
fayre *adj.* ~ *watyr*, fresh (clean) water II/5.
fechowe, fechewe, fuche *n.* the fitchew, or polecat I/179; II/171; III/56; IVd/15.
fechyng *pr.p.* fetching, retrieving I/188.
federys, fedyrs *n. pl.* feathers II/71, 94, 114, 118, passim.
feyllyschype *n.col.* of yeomen: a fellowship; perh. as in a company of infantry I/23.
felaundres *n. pl.* See FILAWNDYRS.
ferde *n. for* ~, in fear II/139.

GLOSSARY

fereth *pr. 3sg.* fears IVb/3.
fesoner *n.* See FAYSANDDARE.
festyn *pr. 3pl.* Read *fettyn*: fetch, retrieve IVe/19. [ME *fetten*.]
fewte *n.* See FUT(E).
fyane *adj.* See WYNE FYANE.
fyȝttynge *n.col.* of beggars: a 'fighting' I/106.
filawndyrs, fyllavndyrs, felaundres, felaundirs, felawndirs *n. pl.* filanders, thread-like intestinal worms I/231, 245; II/15, 53; III/118; IVh/29, 58. [ME *filanders*.]
fynnyde *pa.p.* finned; of a fish: to be 'carved' by having its fins cut off I/153.
flaggys *n. pl.* flags, the secondary flight feathers (cubital feathers) on a hawk's wing II/116.
flat *adj.* of a horse's leg: not overly rounded, not bulging I/170.
flawyre *n.* odour, fragrance I/265. [ME *flavour*.]
fle *pr. 3pl.* See FLYITH.
fleeth, fleth, flyth, fleyth *pr. 3sg.* flees I/199; II/181; III/77; IVg/7. [ME *flen*.]
flettythe, flittyth, fletys, fletis *pr. 3sg.* swims; spec. of a hart: swims, makes its way, downstream I/194; II/177; III/73; IVg/5; **fletyng** *pr.p.* swimming about (or ?away) II/129. [ME *fleten*.]
flyȝth *n.col.* of doves, larks: a 'flight' II/224, 225.
fly(y)th, flyith, fleyth, fleth *v.*[1] *pr. 3sg.* flies I/200; II/125, 182; III/77, 78, passim; **fleythe, fle** *pr. 3pl.* I/218; III/111, 113; IVh/19, 24. [ME *flien*.]
flyth, fleyth, fleth *v.*[2] *pr. 3sg.* See FLEETH.
flyntys *n. pl.* flint stones, or other hard stones, such as quartz, basalt and the like II/50.
fol(e)mard *n.* See FULMARD.

foote, fut(e), fewte *n.* footprint, track, spoor I/173, 174; II/170, 171, passim; III/53, 54. [ME *fot* <OE; perh. also ME *fute* <OF *fuite* 'flight'.]
forget *n.* See FERRE IOTEE.
forme *n.* form = the lair, resting-place of a hare I/124.
formyd *pa.p.* 'formed'; of a hare: to be in its form (its lair) II/189; III/85.
fowle *adj.* foul, befouled II/122.
fowne *n.* See FAVNE.
frech *adj.* fresh II/55.
freris, freres, freyrs *n. pl.* friars I/91; II/227; III/33.
fro, frove *prep.* from I/218; III/111.
i-frosschyde *pa.p.* 'frushed', broken apart; i.e. carved, cut up I/145. [ME *frushen* <OF *froissier*.]
frounce, frownce, frounse, frovns, fronse *n.* frounce: a canker or sore in the mouth and throat of a hawk I/229, 239; II/6, 53; III/116; IVh/27, 44, 54. [ME *frounce*.]
frove *prep.* See FRO.
fuche *n.* See FECHOWE.
fulmard, fol(e)mard, fulmer *n.* foumart, the European polecat I/178; II/171; III/56; IVd/14. [ME *ful-mard*.]
fut(e), fewte *n.* See FOOTE.

G

gagelyng, gagyllyng *n.col.* of geese, women: a 'gaggling', a gaggle II/214; III/20. See also GAGULLE.
gagulle *n.col.* of geese, women: a 'gaggle' (imitative) I/84, 85.
gayte *n. pl.* See GETE.
gale *n.* gall, gallbladder I/248.
gallantye *n.* galantine, a sauce made from the cooking juices of fish or meat, spiced and thickened with breadcrumbs I/146.
gefe *v. imp.* give IVh/59. See also ȝEVE.

gellonder, ielonere *n.* ?a hawk that flies at hens I/228; II/111. [?<ME *geline*, a hen <OF.]

gerfaucon, gerefacone, garfavkone, ierfawkyn *n.* gerfalcon (also, gyrfalcon, or gyr – *Falco rusticolus*), the largest of the falcons I/209; II/146; III/107; IVh/8.

gete, geette, gayte *n. pl.* goats I/82; II/217; III/22.

gyees, gyse *n. pl.* geese I/84; III/20.

gytte *n.* See IOTEE.

glayre, gleyre *n.* glair, the white of an egg I/253; II/31; IVh/75.

glede *n.* the red kite (*Milvus milvus*) II/110. [<OE *glida* 'kite'.] See also MILLONE.

gleymyd *pa.p.* congested with 'gleam', the oily mucus of a hawk's stomach II/78. [<ME *gleim* 'slime, rheum, phlegm'.]

i-gobenyd *pa.p.* cut into pieces, or chunks I/152. [ME *gobonen*.]

Go bette! *imp.* Make haste! III/97.

good-awyse *n.col.* of burgesses: a 'good advice' I/79.

gorchyd *pa.p.* gorged; i.e., of a hawk: fully fed, having a full gorge or crop II/80.

gorgys *n. pl.* meals, spec. those of a hawk II/88.

gose *n.* goose I/129.

gosehawke, gossehauke, goshavke *n.* the goshawk (*Accipiter gentilis*), a large, short-winged hawk I/219; II/156; III/112; IVc/1.

gouernyd *pa.p.* trained I/207.

grappus *n. pl.* grapes I/86.

gray(e), grey *n.* badger I/180, 188; II/172; III/56; IVd/17; **grayis** *pl.* I/36.

grehounde, greund(e) *n.* greyhound III/91, 95; IVe/1, 2, passim; **greundes** *pl.* III/48.

greke *n.* a sweet wine from Greece, or one made elsewhere in the style of such a wine IVi/13.

grekeseke *n.* ?dry wine from Greece IVi/28. [*Greke* + *secce* <OF *sec* 'dry'.]

greybichies *n. pl.* 'grey-bitches'; i.e. female greyhounds III/100.

ȝ

ȝeye *n.* eye; ~ *lyddys*, eye lids I/230; **ȝeyin** *pl.* eyes I/167. See also YE(E).

ȝeyte, ȝyt *adv.* yet = also, further I/247; II/135.

ȝeve, ȝeyfe *v. imp.* give I/249, 269; IVh/38, 53, 69. See also GEFE.

ȝelow *adj.* yellow II/76.

ȝeman *n.* yeoman II/157, 188; IVh/20. See also YOVMEYNE.

ȝif *conj.* if IVh/39.

ȝyt *adv.* See ȝEYTE.

H

hagarde, hagberte *n.* haggard = a hawk that has been caught after taking on its adult plumage; hence, a hawk that has moulted in the wild I/226; II/109. [<OF *hagard* adj.]

hagberte *n.* See HAGARDE.

hay-de-mew *n.* See MURE-DE-HAY.

hayed *pa.p.* netted, caught in a net, or hay IVa/11. [<AN *haie* 'net'.]

Hay! *interj.* an exclamation of encouragement, esp. for one or more hunting hounds.

hayryfe *n.* hairif = cleavers, or goose-grass, a climbing plant II/45. See also CLYUERYS. [ME *hei-rive*.]

halowed *pa.p.* hallooed, pursued with shouts IVa/9. [ME *halouen*.]

hallywatter clarke, holy watir clerke *n.* holy-water clerk: a clerk in minor orders who carried the vessel

containing holy water at religious ceremonies I/222; II/159; IVh/23.
hanffulle *n.* handful I/259.
y-hangid *ppl.adj.* hanged; having certain feature(s) that hang down (precise sense unclear) III/93. .
haras, harres *n.col.* of horses: a 'stud' I/46; II/219; III/25; of harlots: (*fig.*) a 'brothel' II/220. [ME *haras* 'breeding pen', 'stud animal' <OF *haraz, haras.*]
harborowth, herborovthe *pr. 3sg.* (*refl.*) 'harbours'; i.e., of a hart: withdraws to its lair I/118; of a knight: withdraws to his chamber, goes to bed I/119; **is herborowyde, (is) herborowid** *pa.p.* (as *adj.*) II/183, 184; III/79, 80.
harde *adj.* hardy, strong, resilient II/162.
harlottys *n. pl.* lechers, rogues; or, perh., prostitutes, whores II/220.
harres *n.col.* See HARAS.
harrys *n. pl.* hares I/126, 127.
harte, hert(e) *n.* hart, the male red deer (*Cervus elaphus*), esp. one over five years old I/171; II/165; III/51; IVa/1, passim; **hertes, harttus, hart(t)ys** *pl.* I/1, 190; II/175, 197; III/1, 70, passim
hawke, havke *n.* hawk: generically, any of the birds of prey used for the sport of hawking, or falconry, including short-winged (true) hawks, falcons and eagles I/225, 226, 227; II/1, 7; IVh/26, passim; **hawkys, haukis, havkys** *pl.* I/201, 208; II/142, 145; III/101, 107; IVh/t, 33, passim; **havkys, hawkis** *poss.* I/235; II/3, 16, 19, passim.
hawkys of towre, haukis of the toure, havkys of þe toure *n. pl.* byname for falcons (long-winged hawks), so-called because they soar to a great height and circle there waiting for their prey I/72; II/145; III/107, 110; IVh/19. [<OF *tourn, tour* 'a turn, a circle', confl. with OE *tūr* 'tower'.]

heddyte *pa.p.* 'headed' = beheaded, decapitated I/142.
heyhond *n.* Read *heyhoue* = hayhove, the herb ground ivy (*Nepeta hederacea*) II/49. [ME *hei-hove, heyhowun.*]
heyle *n.* eel I/147.
heyris *n. pl.* ears I/168.
heyroner, herrovnneer *n.* 'heroner': name for a hawk that flies at, or is used for hunting, herons I/228; II/111. [<ME *heiroun.*]
heyte *v. imp.* heat I/255.
hende *n.* end II/120.
herborowyde *pa.p.* See HARBOROWTH.
herkenythe *pr. 3sg.* listens IVb/2.
herne *n.* heron I/132.
herreles *n. pl.* shelducks (formerly called sheldrakes): a species of duck (*Tadorna tadorna*) with multicoloured plumage III/42. [<AN *herle, herele.*]
herrovnneer *n.* See HEYRONER.
hert(e) *n.* See HARTE.
hesyll *n.* hazel; (*attrib.*) ~ *styke*, hazel stick II/71.
hete *v.* eat II/22.
hewe *n.* ?Error for VEWE (*q.v.*), 'view'. Or, ?call, shout [ME *heue*]; *fle to þe ~*, of a hawk: ?fly at a quarry raised by shouts, ?fly (at a quarry) when summoned to do so by the hawker IVh/24.
hyen *n. pl.* eyes II/103.
hynd *n.* hind, the female of the red deer I/203; **hyndis, hynde** *poss.* III/103; IVh/2.
hite *pron.* it I/255.
hob(b)y, hobye *n.* hobby (*Falco subbuteo*), one of the smallest species of falcon I/217; II/154; III/110, IVh/18.
hole *adj.* whole II/52.
holpyn *pa.p.* helped II/123.
honye, honne *n.* honey I/234; IVh/34; *tere of ~*, honey-tear = virgin honey, nectar IVh/41.
hont *n.* See HUNT(E).

horhonde *n.* horehound (or hoarhound), the herb *Marrubium vulgare*, commonly used for medicinal purposes II/49.

hoste, ost, nost *n.col.* of men, sparrows: a multitude, ?a force I/21, 22; II/212, 213. See Appendix I, nos 130, 190n.

hostelers *n. pl.* hostelers: taverners, innkeepers I/103.

y-howghid *ppl.adj.* 'hocked', possessing hocks III/94. [<ME *hough* 'hock'.]

hundees, hundis *n. pl.* hounds III/47, 71.

hunt(e), hont *n.* hunter I/189; II/174, III/59, 66, 70.

husk(e) *n.col.* of hares: a group (original sense obscure) II/218; III/23.

I / Y

i-, y- As prefix to a participle, see either the base form of the verb or the participle as headword ignoring the prefix.

ye(e) *n.* eye; ~ *lidis*, ~ *ledis*, eye lids III/117; IVh/27.

i-illyde *pa.p.* winged; of a bird: to have its wings cut off I/136. [<OF *aile, ele* 'a wing'.]

ynow *adv. gode* ~, good enough III/98.

ypocras *n.* hippocras, a sweet, spiced wine IVi/42.

isope *n.* hyssop, a bushy aromatic herb (*Hyssopus officinalis*) I/262.

iwys *adv.* indeed II/242.

I = J

ielonere *n.* See GELLONDER.
ierfawkyn *n.* See GERFAUCON.
iocondlye *adv.* jocundly, joyfully I/116.
ioiste *n.* See IUS(S)E.
iolly *n.* jelly I/155.
iotee, iuttye, gytte *n.* a water-bank, river-bank, embankment (a sense not well exemplified in the J.B. texts).
  a. of hawks / a hawk: *flye ... to þe fare* ~, *flyyth to ferre* ~, *fle to þe forget* (error), to fly spontaneously at game that rises unexpectedly nearby I/224; II/131 (see II/131–3n); IVh/25.
  b. of hawks / a hawk: *fle to the* ~ *ferre*, ~ *ferre*, fly at waterfowl that has been driven towards the hawk(er), prob. from the far side of a river (or pool) II/134; III/114. [ME *gete* 'a jetty, embankment'; see also *OED*, s.vv. *jutty* n. 1, *jetty* n. 2.]

iouke, ioke *v.* jouk, roost I/258; IVh/81.
iovghelars *n. pl.* jugglers I/99.
iugys *n. pl.* judges I/76.
iurrears *n. pl.* jurors I/78.
ius(s)e, (error) **ioiste** *n.* juice I/245, 260; II/2, 17, 45; IVh/50, 59.

K

kemmyssteris *n. pl.* kempsters, (female) wool-combers I/105.

ken *v.* know, perceive II/16.

ken(n)ettys, kenettis *n. pl.* kennets = small hunting hounds (running dogs) that pursue a quarry by its scent I/184, 186; III/68; IVe/9, 17. [ME *kenet* <AN *kenit*, dim. of OF *chien*.]

kesterell *n.* kestrel, a small species of hawk (*Falco tinnunculus*), also known as the windhover II/160.

key *n.* key; ~ *of þe foote*, the 'key' for opening the foot (referring to the long, middle toe of a hawk's foot) II/113.

kynd *adj.* natural II/71.

knave, knafe *n.* boy II/160; ~ *childe*, young boy, a boy child IVh/61.

knyth *n.* knight II/184; **knyȝttys** *pl.* I/41.

knyȝttys See KNYTH.

L

lache *n.col.* of carters: a 'lash' (as of a whip) I/97.

layth *pr. 3sg.* ~ *ouyr*, drives (waterfowl) towards (the hawker) II/134.

GLOSSARY

lame *n.* lamb I/143.
laner, lannyr, layner *n.* lanner = the lanner falcon (*Falco biarmicus*), spec. the female of the species I/215; II/152; III/109; IVh/16; **lan(n)eret, lanrett, laynerett** *dim.* lanneret, the male lanner falcon I/215; II/152; III/109; IVh/16. [ME *laner, laneret* <OF.]
lappwynngys, lapwynkys *n. pl.* lapwings I/15; II/235.
lat *imp. aux.* ~ *not*, let not II/135.
lauandyr cotyn *n.* lavender cotton: a name formerly used for several plants, especially ground cypress and southernwood, both used medicinally II/49.
lavȝttyre *n.col.* of hostelers: a 'laughter' I/103.
lawandere *n.* lavender I/262.
laweris *n. pl.* lawyers I/77.
leberttys *n. pl.* leopards I/44.
leyne *adj.* lean, thin, emaciated I/167; (of beef) not fatty I/241.
leys *n.col.* See LESSE.
lemors *n.* See LYMOURE.
lenyng, leneyng, leynnyng *pr.p.* of a hare: crouching (in its form, or lair) I/124; II/189; III/85.
lepe *n.col.* of leopards: a 'leap, leaping' = a 'pouncing' I/44.
leppe *v.* leap I/166.
lere *v. imp.* learn II/141.
lesse, lese, leys *n.* leash, a thong or strap for holding one or more hunting dogs IVe/3; *n.col.* a 'leash' = a group of three or more dogs (spec. greyhounds) I/56; a group of (three) hawks II/153. [ME *les(se.*]
leuyr(e) *n.* liver I/249; II/21.
lewde *adj.* ignorant, unskilled or unlettered II/141.
lewre *n.* See LURE.
lyeme *n.* lyam = a leash for hounds, spec. for a limer or lyam-hound (a dog used for tracking) III/61. [ME *liam, lime* 'leash'.]
i-lyfte *pa.p.* 'lifted' = dismembered, carved I/131. [ME *liften.*]
lyght See LITHE.
lymoure *n.* limer, or lyam-hound: a type of bloodhound used for tracking and locating game, esp. before the start of a hunt IVe/6; **lymures, lymors, lymmorous, lemors** *pl.* I/183, 186; III/67; IVe/15. [ME *limer.*]
lithe, lyght *pr. 3sg.* lies II/193; III/86, 89.
lyse *n. pl.* lice III/117.
logythe, lodgeth *pr. 3sg. (refl.)* 'lodges'; of a buck: retires to its lair I/120; of a squire: retires to his chamber, goes to bed I/121; **is logged, is loggid** *pa.p. (as adj.)* II/185, 186; III/81, 82. [ME *loggen.*]
loynes *n. pl.* loyns, lunes = short leather leashes, or straps, formerly fastened to the jesses to secure a hawk (to a perch etc.) IVh/84. [ME *loine* <OF *longe, loigne.*]
londwyne *n.* land-wine = any locally made wine IVi/1.
longithe *impers.* there ~ *to*, there belongs to I/162, 201; **longeth, longyn** *pr. 3pl.* ~ *for*, ~ *to*, are suitable, fitting for II/142; III/101; IVh/6.
lowryng *adj.* louring: threatening, angry II/103.
lure, lewre *n.* lure = a feathered bait for training and recalling a hawk (spec. a falcon) I/218; III/111; IVh/19.
luryd, lurid *pa.p.* lured; of a hawk (spec. a falcon): recalled to the lure II/143; III/105. [ME *luren.*] See also ENLURRYD.

M

mad *pa.p.* ~ *in*, made into I/242.

maydynewort *n.* a name used of maythe, or stinking camomile (*Anthemis cotula*), and certain other plants resembling it I/262. [ME *maithe*.]

mayle *n.* mail = the breast feathers of an adult hawk II/161.

May-buttire *n.* unsalted butter set aside in the month of May for medicinal purposes IVh/49.

mallapertnys *n.col.* of peddlers: a 'malapertness' = impudence, shamelessness I/101. [<ME *malapert* adj. <OF.]

mallarttus *n. pl.* mallards (the familiar green-headed dabbling duck) I/14.

malmesey *n.* malmesy, a variety of strong, sweet wine IVi/21. [ME *malvesie* <OF.]

mane *n.* man I/163, 164.

mantelettes, mantellettys, manteletis *n. pl.* mantles: the dorsal feathers of a hawk, its 'mantle' II/116; III/117; IVh/28. [<OF *mantel, manteau*.]

marchandys *n. pl.* merchants I/80.

mard-haye *n.* See MURE-DE-HAY.

marlyone *n.* See MERLYNE.

martryn, marteron, mertrone, martorn *n.* the marten, a weasel-like animal much sought after for its valuable pelt I/180; II/172; III/57; IVd/20.

martemasse, marttylmas, martymes *n.* Martinmas, the feast of St Martin (11 November); ~ *befe*, ~ *byfe*, Martinmas beef: the flesh of an ox slaughtered and salted at Martinmas for winter provision I/241; II/11; IVh/46.

marys, maris *n. poss.* mare's I/246; II/17; IVh/58.

mastowe *n.* mastiff: a large, fierce breed of dog used for hunting dangerous game IVe/4; **mastyffys, mastiues** *pl.* I/183; III/67.

mategors *n.* A variety of wine (of unknown origin and character) IVi/33.

medell, medylle *v. imp.* mix I/268; IVh/34.

megnelonde *n.* 'mainland' = dry land III/77.

melonne *n.* See MILLONE.

merlyne, merlyon, marlyone *n.* the merlin (*Falco columbarius*), a species of small falcon I/216; III/110; IVh/17; **marlyons** *pl.* II/153. [ME *merlioun*.]

mete *n.* food I/112, passim; II/18, passim; IVh/74, passim.

mewte *n.col.* a 'mute' = a pack (of hounds) III/47. [ME *mute* <AN.]

myddynges kurris *n. pl.* dunghill curs III/69. [ME *midding* 'dunghill' + *curre*.]

my3th *aux. subj.* might II/129.

millone, melonne, melowne, mellannd *n.* milan: prob. the red kite (*Milvus milvus*) I/202; II/143; III/102; IVh/1. [<OF *milan* 'kite'.] See also GLEDE.

mylonere *n.* ?a person who flies milans (kites) [<OF *milan* 'kite']; or, read ?*myrlonere*, ?*merlyonere*, one who keeps and flies merlins [<ME *merlioun*] III/122.

mytis, mytes, myt(t)ys *n. pl.* mites, parasites on a hawk I/230, 243; III/116; IVh/28, 56.

moo *adj.* more I/172; II/166; III/52.

moryng *pr.p.* ?lingering, staying in one place II/128. [?<OF *morer*, 'to linger'.]

mormeracyone *n.col.* of starlings: a 'murmuration, murmuring' I/30.

morthere *n.col.* of crows: a 'murder, murdering' I/28.

moser *n.* ?mouser, a hunter of mice [<ME *mous*]; or, ?a hunter of titmice or similar small birds [<ME *mose* 'titmouse'] II/110.

mosture *n.col.* of peacocks: a 'muster' = a 'show, exhibition, display' I/16. [ME *moustre* <OF.]
motis *n. pl.* motes = notes sounded on a (hunting) horn III/64. [ME *mot* <OF.]
movnkys *n. pl.* monks I/66.
mownterose *n.* A variety of wine (of unknown origin and character) IVi/11.
muer *n.* mewer = a hawk that has mewed or moulted II/109. [ME *meuere* <*meuen* 'to mew, moult'.] See also MURE-DE-HAY.
mullys *n. pl.* mules I/50.
mure-de-hay, mard-haye, hay-de-mew *n.* 'hedge-mewer' = a hawk that has moulted in the wild (lit. 'in a hedge') I/226; II/108; IVc/5. [<ME *meuere*; OF *mué de haie*.]
muscaden *n.* muscadel, muscatel: a rich, sweet wine made from muscat grapes IVi/10. [ME *muscadelle*.]
musket(t) *n.* musket: the male sparrowhawk I/222; II/159; III/113; IVc/4; IVh/23.
mutacyone *n.* transformation, esp. in the form of rebellion or civil strife I/161; ~ *n.col.* of throstles: a 'mutation', transformation I/34.
mute *n.* faeces of a hawk or falcon; spec. faeces that falls down and is not ejected ('sliced') to a distance II/81, 122. [ME *mute*.]
mute *v.* defaecate (said of birds, esp. hawks) II/25. [ME *muten*.]

N

nanauer *n.* See ANEUER.
nas *n.* ass I/164, 169.
neyder, neydir *adv.* neither, II/133; III/105.
neygule *n.* See EGKYL.
neyte *n. pl.* neat = cattle I/81.
nerle, norle *n.* earl I/212; II/149.

nerrer *adv.* nearer, more closely; or, ?more thoroughly II/73.
nerthyn *adj.* earthern II/28.
nessthe *adj.* nesh = soft, tender IVh/38.
neuertreyuyng *n.col.* of jugglers: a 'never-thriving' I/99.
ny(e) *n.col.* of pheasants: a 'nest' = a brood or hatch I/6; II/205; III/9. [ME *nie* <OF *ni* <L *nidus* 'nest'.]
nyes *n.* eyas = a young, unfledged hawk I/225; II/107. [ME *nyesse* <OF *niais* 'nestling'.]
ny3ttynngalys *n. pl.* nightingales I/33.
nodyre *conj.* nor I/205.
noynon *n.* onion IVf/4
nonnys *n. pl.* nuns I/67.
nost *n.* See HOSTE.
note *n.* nut II/38; **nottys** *pl.* I/87.

O

odyre *adj.* other I/243.
odyre *conj.* other = or I/160.
oyle *n.* oil; ~ *dolive*, olive oil IVh/79.
oke *n.* oak I/250.
okefern *n.* oak-fern: a name for the common polypody (*Polypodium vulgare*) and several other similar ferns found growing on oak trees IVh/72.
on *adj.* one II/104.
one *prep.* upon I/166, 265.
onkyndenes *n.col.* See VNKYNDENES.
opyn *adj.* of a hawk's foot: bare, lacking feathers II/102.
ordeyne, ordenne *v. imp.* ordain: prepare, arrange I/262; IVh/80.
orpyment, orpamente, orpemente *n.* orpiment: the trisulphide of arsenic, also called yellow arsenic, used as a treatment for mites and lice I/244; II/14; IVh/57.
osey *n.* any of a number of varieties of sweet Portuguese wines, spec. from around Lisbon IVi/41. [ME *oseie*.]
ost *n.* See HOSTE.

ostreger(e), ostrigere *n.* ostreger = austringer: someone who keeps and flies goshawks II/127, 132; III/122. [<OF *ostruchier*, <*ostour* 'goshawk'.]

otyr, ottyre *n.* otter II/173; IVd/22.

oþer *adj.* other = another IVh/24.

ovte *adv.* out I/239.

ow3te *v. aux.* ought I/157.

P

palys, palleys *n.* 'palace' = the palate or roof of the mouth I/235; IVh/35. [<OF *palais*.]

parcare *n.* parker, an official in charge of a park II/192.

pardnars *n. pl.* pardoners I/102.

partrikkys *n. pl.* partridges II/206.

pase *n.col.* of asses: a (slow, steady) pace I/49. [ME *pase*.]

passyth *impers.* exceed; *þer ~ not* there are no more than II/119.

pe(e)re *n.* a form of constipation producing hard faeces suffered by hawks (later called 'the stone') I/231, 250; II/24, 54, 81, 123; III/119; IVh/30, 71. [<AN *pere* 'stone'.]

peycokys *n. pl.* peacocks I/16.

peyne *n.* pain (error for PYN(E), *q.v.*) IVh/31, 80.

peys *n.* See PIES.

peletyr of Spayne *n.* pellitory of Spain (*Anacyclus pyrethrum*), a herb used for various medicinal purposes II/98.

pelyownde *n.* See POLIONE.

penywi3t *n.* a penny-weight = 24 grains (1/20 troy ounce) IVh/47, 48.

penyworte *n.* pennywort, a name formerly used of several plants with rounded leaves employed for medicinal purposes IVh/47.

percely *n.* parsley IVh/72.

perke *n.* perch, the stand or support on which a hawk perches II/48.

perspere *n.* samphire (*Crithmum maritimum*), a plant with fleshy leaves that grows on rocks beside the sea II/26; IVh/71. [ME *pers-pere*.]

pese *n. sg.* pea II/37. [ME *pese*.]

pyament *n.* piment, a wine that has been spiced and sweetened IVi/43. [ME *piment*.]

pygyne *n.* pigeon I/139.

pies, pyes, pyis, peys *n.* a disease which causes a hawk to become dizzy or to swoon and so fall off its perch, or from the hawker's hand I/233, 261; II/47, 59; III/121; IVh/31, 82. [Origins obscure; see I/229–33n.]

pyis *n. pl.* pies = magpies I/35.

pyn(e), (error) peyne *n.* pin = a hard, painful nodule or growth on the underside of a hawk's foot I/232, 257; II/37; III/120; IVh/31, 80. [Origins obscure; see I/229–33n.]

pith *n.* inner tissue, contents (of a sore, spec. the FROUNCE, q.v.) IVh/44.

pyttyvsnys *n.col.* of turtledoves: a 'piteousness' I/32.

playn(e) *adj.* *a ~ grovnd, a ~ grond, ~ grounde*, an open (often flat) stretch of countryside I/204; III/104; IVh/4.

plays *n.* plaice, a species of flat-fish I/156.

plowe *n.* plough III/98; *~ beme*, plough-beam: the central wooden support of a plough III/92; *~ padill*, plough-paddle: a spade for removing earth from a plough III/99.

pokkes, pokys, pokkis, poxe *n.* pocks: a condition characterised by sores, esp. those caused by external parasites such as mites I/229, 243; III/116; IVh/27, 56. [<ME *pok* 'sore, skin eruption'.]

polione, polyon, pellyone, pelyownde, polyownde *n.* a swelling of a hawk's lower leg (or knee), above the jess I/233, 255; II/33; III/120; IVh/31, 77.

[Obscure; perh. related to ME *poleine* 'knee armour'.]
polypody, pollypodyi, polepody *n.* polypody, a fern of the genus *Polypodium* IVh/71; *oke* ~, ~ *of an oke*, oak polypody: a name given to the common polypody and similar ferns found growing on oak trees I/250; II/26–7. See also OKEFERN.
pondrews, pondors *adj.* heavy I/206; III/106. [ME *ponderous*.]
pontyfycalle *n.col.* of prelates: a 'priestliness, popishness' I/61.
poot *n.* See POT(T)E.
poppe *n.* Pope I/158.
pop(p)ys *n. pl.* 'puppies' = small pet dogs, lapdogs I/185; IVe/13.
portatyfe, portatiff *adj.* portative, portable; *perch(e)* ~, a large, portable perch used in the field, esp. for transporting heavier raptors I/206; III/106; IVh/5.
pot(t)e, poot *n.* pot I/255; II/28, 34; IVh/77.
povdyr(e) *n.* powder I/237, 242, 244.
povdore *v. imp.* (put) powder (on) I/241.
povre *adj.* poor I/219.
powertte *n.col.* of harpers: a 'poverty' I/100.
pownce *n.* pounce = toe, claw (of a hawk), spec. any of the front three claws on each foot II/112.
poxe *n.* See POKKES.
prefe *v.* prove, establish II/74.
preys *n.col.* of priests: prob. a 'press' = a crowd, throng I/68. (See no. 161 and note in Appendix I.)
preysttys *n. pl.* See PRYST.
prelettus *n. pl.* prelates I/61.
pryce *n.* 'prise': a horn call signalling the success of a hunt, esp. a hart hunt III/62. [ME *pris, price* <AN <OF *prise* 'the capture', 'the kill'.]

pryste, prest *n.* priest I/221; II/158; **preysttys, prystes** *pl.* I/68; III/36.
proferyth *pr. 3sg.* attempts II/25.
provd *adj.* proud I/164.
put *v. imp.* add IVh/51.

Q

quarraye, quarre, qwarre, qwerre *n.* quarry, prey (of a hawk) I/223; II/127; III/113; IVh/25; *fleyth to þe* ~, of a hawk: flies at game (waterfowl) found for it by the hawker II/127. [But see also II/126–30n.]
quele *n.* quill, the shaft of a feather IVh/44.

R

rac(c)hys, rechis *n. pl.* raches = running hounds that pursue a quarry by following its scent I/58, 184; III/68; IVe/8. [ME *racche*.]
rafulle *n.col.* of boys, 'knaves': a 'raffle' = a rabble I/94, 95. [ME *rafle* <*raf* 'a group of people'.]
rage *n.col.* of colts: a 'boistrousness, playfulness' I/48.
rayndeere, reynedere *n.* reindeer I/175; II/169; III/55.
ram(m)age *adj.* wild, untamed; ~ *havke*, ~ *hawke*, a young hawk that has left the nest and the tree in which it fledged I/226; II/108. [ME *ramage* <OF.]
ravynnys, rawynnys *n. pl.* ravens I/26; II/236.
receuyd *pa.t.* eaten, ingested II/63. [ME *receiven* 'ingest'.]
rechate *n.* rechate, recheat: a horn signal for summoning hunters and hounds during a hunt, or at its close III/64. [ME *rechate* <AN *rechater*.]
rechis *n. pl.* See RAC(C)HYS.
reclaymyd, reclaymid, reycleymyd *pa.p.* of a hawk: recalled by means of a lure I/205; II/144; III/105; IVh/4.

ree, rye *n.* rye = a disease of hawks manifesting as congestion of the nares and swelling of the head (prob. a type of head-cold) I/229, 234; II/1, 53, 97; III/116; IVh/27, 34. [ME *re* <AN.]
reycleymyd *pa.p.* See RECLAYMYD.
Reynesshe *adj.* Rhenish; ~ *wyne*, wine from the Rhine region and Alsace IVi/2.
reyryde *pa.p.* 'reared'; of a goose: carved by having its limbs lifted and severed I/129. [<ME *reren* 'to lift, raise'.]
reyservynge *pr.p.* retaining, setting aside I/248.
reytornnyth(e) *pr. 3sg.* returns I/198; *pr. 3pl.* I/187.
remowntyng *ppl.adj.* restoring, reviving II/32, 95; **a remowntyng** *ger.* a tonic II/96. [<ME *remounten* 'restore, revive' <AF.]
rennyn, rennythe *pr. 3pl.* run I/187; IVe/17; **ronnon** *pa.p. is* ~, is run (at), i.e. hunted with hounds IVa/3.
reppe *n.* ?Error for *roppe*, intestine IVh/66. [ME *rop, roppe.*]
respoyse *n.* raspis, a type of sweet red, or rose-coloured, wine IVi/34. [ME *raspice.*]
retryuyn *pr. 3pl.* retrieve IVe/18.
rewe *n.* rue, a name used of any evergreen shrub belonging to the genus *Ruta*, but esp. *Ruta graveolens* whose bitter leaves were used medicinally IVh/34.
ribbe *n.* ribcage III/92.
rye *n.* See REE.
rynde *n. seconde* ~, pith (of a plant stem) IVh/62.
Rochel *n.* wine exported from the port-city of La Rochelle, western France IVi/54; (*attrib.*) *Rocell wyne* II/5.
roche *n.* roach, a small freshwater fish of the carp family I/154.

romanyske *n.* prob. romanesco: a variety of wine produced in the vicinity of Rome IVi/15. [? <Italian *romanesco*, remodelled with English -*isk* suffix.]
romeney *n.* rumney (also romney), a sweet wine, originally from Greece; ~ *of Modon*, from Modon (Methóni) in the Peloponnese IVi/20. [ME *romenei(e.*]
ronnon *pa.p.* See RENNYN.
roo, rowe *n.* the roe deer (*Capreolus capraea*); also, occasionally, the female of the species (when set against 'roebuck') I/122; III/54, 103; IVb/3; **rooes, roys, rossys** *pl.* I/8; II/202; III/7; **roo-boke, roo-buk(e)** *n.* roebuck, the male of the roe deer I/175; II/187; III/55, 83; IVd/ 8; **roo-doo** *n.* roe-doe, the female of the roe deer I/175; IVd/9; IVh/2.
roode *n.* rod II/92.
rookys *n. pl.* rooks I/27.
rossys *n. pl.* See ROO.
rostere *n.* 'roaster': name given to a large eel, prob. indicating the way it was cooked (by roasting) I/147. [<ME *rosten.*]
rottys, rotis *n. pl.* roots I/251; IVh/72.
rowe *n.* See ROO.
route, rovte, rowt(e) *n.col.* of knights, wolves: a 'rout' = a host, a throng (prob. threatening) I/41, 42; II/207, 208; III/11, 12.
ruptarge *n.* an Iberian wine IVi/35. [ME *riptage.*]

S

saker, sakyr, sakore, sacre *n.* the saker falcon (*Falco cherrug, Falco sacer*), spec. the female of the species I/214; II/151; III/109; IVh/15; **sakeret, sakyrret, sakorret, sacrett** *dim.* sakret (sakeret), the male saker falcon

GLOSSARY 243

I/214; II/151; III/109; IVh/15. [ME *sacre, sacret* <OF.]
sadly *adv.* steadfastly, purposefully, earnestly I/110.
saferon, safyrne, safrovne, saforne *n.* saffron I/247; II/18, 56; IVh/59.
sandragon(e), sancdragon *n.* sandragon, or 'dragon's blood': name given to the red juice or resin of the dragon-tree (*Dracæna draco*) I/242; II/10; IVh/46. [ME *san-dragoun* <OF.]
i-savssyd *pa.p.* prepared or served in a sauce; also, spiced, seasoned I/156. [ME *saucen.*]
sawte *n.col.* of a lion or lions: an 'assault, attack', combined with the notion of a 'leap, bound' I/60. [ME *saut*, aphetic of *assaut* + OF *salt, saut* 'a leap'.]
saxifrage, sax(e)frage *n.* saxifrage, a name used of any plant belonging to the genus *Saxifraga*, esp. those used medicinally I/250; II/26; IVh/72.
scall *n.* scab II/7. [ME *scale.*]
i-schallyd *pa.p.* scaled; of a fish: to have its scales removed I/154.
i-schapte *pa.p.* shaped, formed; *welle* ~, well formed IVf/7.
scheldrakys *n. pl.* sheldrakes (now called shelducks) : a species of duck (*Tadorna tadorna*) with multicoloured plumage II/233. [ME *sheldrake.*] See also HERRELES.
schene *n.* shin, the lower leg (below the knee) II/102, 106.
schyp *n. pl.* sheep III/21.
scholderynge, schulderyng *pr.p.* crouching I/124; II/189; III/85. [ME *shuldren.*]
scholdyrt *pa.p.* 'shouldered'; of a lamb: to have its shoulder cut off I/143. [<ME *shulder.*]
schlandure *n.* slander, defamation I/161. [ME *sclaundre.*]

schoe *pron.* she I/258.
scle *v.* slay, kill III/102.
scrate *v.* scratch II/242.
seymy *adj.* of a hawk: to be (or, to have become) fat II/76. [Cf. ME *seime* 'grease, lard' <OF *saime*; also, cf. ME *enseimen* 'to cause a hawk to lose excess fat'.]
sege, cege(e) *n.col.* of bitterns, herons: a 'siege' I/11, 12; II/229, 230; III/38, 39 (see Appendix I, no. 99n).
sekyth *pr. 3sg.* seeks, probes II/72. [ME *sechen.*]
semen lumbricorum *n.* wormseed: a name given to several plants considered effective as a purge for worms IVh/65. [L *semen* 'seed' + *lumricus* 'intestinal worm'.]
sere *n.* cere: the yellow, wax-like membrane above a hawk's beak; also, the skin around its eyes, and the bare skin of its lower legs and feet II/103. [<L *cera* 'wax'.]
sese *subj.* seize II/136.
sesse *v.* cease II/135. [ME *cesen.*]
sethe, seþen *v. imp.* seethe, boil I/251; IVh/62.
sewgir *n.* See SUGIRE.
sydyte, sydyd *pa.p.* 'sided'; of a pig: carved by having its sides (ribs) cut away from the spine I/142; *ppl.adj.* possessing sides, flanks IVf/4.
sygnett *n.* signet, seal; (*fig.*) one of the 'tokens' (features) of a hawk's foot II/113. [ME *signet* <OF.]
syʒte *n.col.* a 'spectacle', 'display' = a multitude; *A bomynabul* ~, an abominable horde I/66 (see Appendix I, no. 136n).
sikill *n.* sickle III/94.
singler, syngelare *n.col.* of boars: a 'singler' = confl. of *sanglier* (an adult, male wild boar) + 'loner', 'one that has

left the herd' I/51; III/14. [OF *sengler* 'boar' + L *singularis* 'solitary'.]
sittid *pr. 3sg.* sits III/87.
skolke *n.col.* of foxes, friars, thieves: a skulk, skulking I/91, 92, 93.
skoue *n.col.* of fish: a shoal, 'school' I/69. [var. of ME *scole*.]
slothe *n.col.* of bears: a 'slowness' I/45. [ME *slouthe* <*slou* adj.)
smegrene *n.* sengreen, the houseleek (*Sempervivum tectorum*), which was used medicinally IVh/49. [var. of ME *singrene*.]
snyttys *n. pl.* snipes, a name formerly used of several similar species of wading bird, esp. the common snipe (*Gallinago gallinago*) I/18. [ME *snite* <OE.]
soyleth, soylyth, soyelys, sowles, swllyth *pr. 3sg.* 'soils'; of a hart, a waterfowl: plunges into a river or pool to escape from its pursuers (e.g. hunters, a hawk) I/193; II/140, 176; III/72; IVg/2. [ME *soilen* <*soile* 'a wallow', 'a water-refuge' <OF *soil, souil* 'an animal's wallow'.]
solondon *n.* See CELEDONY.
sondyre, sundir, sovneder *n.col.* of (wild) swine: a 'sounder' I/52; II/209; III/13. [ME *soundre* <AN *sundre*; cf. OE *sunor*.]
sore *n. grete* -, error for ?*gete fere* (see IOTEE, IUTTYE, GYTTE) IVh/25.
sore hauke *n.* sore-hawk: a juvenile in its first (red-coloured) plumage; hence, a hawk in its first year II/108–9. [ME *sore* 'sorrel, reddish-brown' <OF *sor*.]
sorraye *n.* sorré: a spicy sauce for eels and other fish; or, a dish of this name, sometimes coloured red I/148. [ME *sore*.]
sorde, (error) **swerde** *n.col.* of mallards: a 'rising-up' (in flight), a 'soaring' II/232; III/41. [ME *sourde* <*sourden*

'to rise up' <OF *so(u)rde*.] See also SORDYTH, SORT.
sordyth *pr. 3sg.* rises, soars up (in flight) II/133. [ME *sourden*.] See also SORDE.
soryth *pr. 3sg.* soars, rises II/137. [ME *soren*.]
sorselle *n.* sarcel: a hawk's pinion feather, the first of the ten primary (phalangeal, or digital) flight feathers II/115. [<OF *cercel*.]
sort *n.col.* of mallards: a 'flock' I/14. [ME *sorte* 'a group, troop' <OF.] Cf. SORDE.
sothyrnewode, suthernwode, sovthornwood *n.* southernwood (*Artemisia abrotanum*), a fragrant shrub once commonly used for medicinal purposes I/245; II/17; IVh/59.
sovdears *n. pl.* soldiers I/90.
sovneder *n.col.* See SONDYRE.
sovrly *adv.* surely, securely; of sleep: soundly I/117. [ME *seurli*.]
sowles *pr. 3sg.* See SOYLETH.
sparrovs *n. pl.* sparrows I/22.
spend *v. imp.* use, employ II/29.
sparowehawke, sperrehauke, sparhauk, sperawke *n.* the sparrowhawk (*Accipiter nisus*), a species of small hawk; also, spec., the female of the species II/158; III/112; IVc/3; IVh/22. Cf. MUSKETT.
speruere *n.* sperviter: one who keeps and flies sparrowhawks III/122. [ME *sperver* <OF *espervier*.]
spyarde *n.* spayard: a three-year-old male red deer, but defined (erroneously) by MS Eg as a 300-year-old hart IVd/13. [ME *spaiard* <AF *espeyard* 'three-year-old male red deer'.] See also SPYCARDE, SPYTARD.
spycarde *n.* a three-year-old male red deer; one that has unbranched antlers I/177. [confl. of ME *spike* + *spaiard*

GLOSSARY

<AN *espeyard.*] See also SPYARDE, SPYTARD.
spychecoke *n.* a large eel; one that is cooked by being skewered on a roasting spike I/147.
spytard *n.* spittard: a young, male red deer with unbranched antlers III/56; also, defined (erroneously) by MS H as a 100-year-old hart II/169. [confl. of ME *spite* 'spit' + *spaiard* <AN *espeyard.*] See also SPYARDE, SPYCARDE.
i-spyllyde *pa.p.* 'spoiled'; of a hen: dismembered, carved I/144. [ME *spoilen* <OF *espoillier* 'to strip, skin, undress'.]
i-splate *pa.p.* 'splatted', split; of a fish, cut lengthwise and laid open I/150. [ME *splatten.*]
spryng *n.col.* of teals: an 'upsurge', a 'leaping, flying' (into the air) I/13. [<ME *springen.*]
squat *n.col.* of dawbers: a slapping-down, or -on, (of daub, plaster); or, perh., ?a smoothing-down (of the same) I/98. [<ME *squatten* 'squash, smash', 'let fall'.]
squier *n.* ~ *of þe fyrst hede*, a young squire II/154–5.
staffisakyr, staffwysavkyre *n.* stavesacre (*Delphinium staphisagria*), a plant (esp. the seeds) used for medicinal purposes I/236; II/4. [ME *staphis-agre.*]
stallethe *pr. 3sg.* stalls, i.e. stands motionless IVb/1. [ME *stallen.*]
staris, stares *n. pl.* starlings I/30; III/16.
stode *n.col.* of mares: a 'stud' I/47. [ME *stode* 'place where animals are kept (esp. for breeding)'; also, 'animals kept for breeding'.]
stokedowfe *n.* stock-dove, the wild pigeon *Columba aenas* II/91.
sto(t)te *n.* the stoat, ermine I/181; II/173; III/58. See also WHITRATH.

stottys *n. pl.* disreputable women: sluts, bawds I/107. [ME *stot.*]
styngand(e) *adj.* stinking II/168, 171.
strakes *n. pl.* complex sets of notes on a hunting horn, constituting one or more specific horn calls III/64. [ME *strake* <*straken* 'to sound a horn'.]
streke *v.* stretch (forth, out) II/42.
sugire, sewgir *n.* sugar; ~ *-candey*, sugar-candy, ~ *roce*, rock sugar (names for crystallised sugar) II/56; IVh/65.
supereflovite *n.col.* of nuns: a 'superfluity, overabundance'; also, perh., ?an 'immoderation' (of behaviour) I/67.
swerde *n.col.* See SORDE.
swet *adj.* ~ *mylke*, fresh milk (not sour or curdled) I/237–8.
swete *subj.* sweat(s) IVh/78.
swyuenyng *ger.* a swooning, giddiness II/59. [ME *sweven/swevenen* 'dream'.]
swllyth *pr. 3sg.* See SOYLETH.

T

takythe *pr. 3sg.* attains, reaches I/199; **take** *subj.* attain, reach IVg 7; ~ *agayne*, go against (the stream) IVg/6; ~ *ouer*, go across, cross (a river) IVg/3; ~ *with*, move downstream (with the current) IVg/5.
talon *n.* the single, posterior claw of a hawk's foot II/113.
tapyr *n.* tabor, a small drum used when fowling or falconing to flush game, or to drive it in a certain direction II/135. [ME *tabour.*]
tapyse *v.* tapis: to take cover, lie low so as not to be seen II/155. [ME *tapisen.*]
tappestrs *n. pl.* tapsters: beer- or wine-drawers (often spec. feminine: barmaids, alewives) I/104.
tars(s)ell *n.* See TERSELL.
tassell *n.* See TERSELL.
teyllys *n. pl.* See TELYS.

teynt *n.* tent, a dark-red Spanish wine IVi/37. [ME *teint.*]
telys, teyllys *n. pl.* teals: small freshwater ducks of the genus *Anas*, esp. the European teal (*Anas crecca*) I/13; II/231.
temparatly *adv.* temperately, in moderation I/114.
temppure *v. imp.* temper, blend I/237.
tere of honey *n.* See HONYE.
terer *n.* terrier IVe/19; **terryars, teeryovrs, terowres, teerors** *pl.* I/184, 187; III/68; IVe/10.
terowres *n. pl.* See TERER.
tersell, tar(s)sell, tassell *n.* tercel, tiercel: the male of any type of hawk or falcon I/220; III/107, 112; IVc/2; IVh/8, 10, 21; also, **terselet, tars(s)elet, taselett** *dim.* (from the fact that the males are about a third smaller than the females) I/209; II/146, 154, passim.; *tarsell gentill, tarselet ientylle,* 'tercel gentle': byname for the male peregrine falcon I/210; IVh/10. [ME *tercel, tercelet.*]
tewell *n.* anus, vent (cloaca); also, by implication, the lower bowels (of a hawk) III/119. [ME *teuel.*]
tharfe *n.col.* of threshers: read *thrafe* = a 'thrave', 'threave'; i.e. a measure of wheat, straw, corn etc.; hence, a multitude I 96. [ME *threve.*]
theis *pron.* these IVh/24.
theuys, thewys *n. pl.* thieves I/92; II/228.
i-thyide *pa.p.* thighed; of a pigeon, a quail: carved for the table by having its thighs cut off I/139, 140.
thrum *n.col.* of greyhounds: a group, troop III/48. [ME *thrum* 'host, band, troop'.]
thus *pron.* these III/102.

tyle-ston *n.* a masonry tile used for preparing food or medicine, esp. when heated II/11.
tyre *n.* a sweet wine of the Levant, prob. from Syria, named after (?exported from) the city of Tyre IVi/38.
tirynge *n.* tiring: a piece of tough meat given to a hawk to tear at for exercise IVh/38. [<ME *tiren* 'struggle (with)', 'tear at'.]
tysyke *n.* phthisic: a wasting lung disease II/79. [ME *tisike.*]
typingys *n.col.* of magpies: a 'tidings', a 'bringing of news' I/35.
todyr *adj.* other II/180.
togedirs, togaydure *adv.* together I/235; IVh/35, 49, passim.
tokynnys *n. pl.* tokens, characteristic features II/112.
toþer *pron.* other(s) II/118.
toure, towre *n.* See HAUKIS OF THE TOURE.
tras *n.* tress: a lock or length of hair [ME *trace*]; or, perh. (*fig.*) a head of hair [<ME *tresse*] I/166.
trase *n.col.* of hares: a 'trace' = a 'track', (set of) footprint(s) I/127. [ME *trace* 'footprint'.]
trene *adj.* treen, wooden II/34. [ME *treen.*]
trewloufe, trewloue *n.col.* of turtledoves: a 'true-love' II/237; III/46.
tribiane *n.* Prob. trebbiano, a white Italian wine from Tuscany and Marche IVi/12.
triete *n.col.* of courtiers: either, ?a threat, threatening [<ME *thret*]; or, ?a negotiation, negotiating, council, accord [<ME *trete*] I/89.
trype *n.col.* of goats, hares: a 'trip' = a 'herd, flock' I/82, 126; II/217. [ME *trippe* <AF.]
tryse *adv.* thrice I/260.

i-tronchnide *pa.p.* 'truncheoned'; of a carp: cut into truncheons, pieces I/151. [<ME *tronchoun* <OF *tronçon* 'piece, fragment'.]
y-trussid *ppl.adj.* neat, compactly formed III/92. [<ME *trussen*.]
turtyllys, turteles *n. pl.* turtledoves I/32; II/237; III/46.

þ

þis, þeis *pron.* these I/204; IVh/4, 8, passim.
þred *n.* third I/159.
þreysschars *n. pl.* threshers I/96.
þrestyllys *n. pl.* throstles; = the song thrush, but also the blackbird I/34. [ME *throstel*.]

V = U

vnbrassyde *pa.p.* 'unbraced', i.e. undone; hence, of a mallard: carved by being dismembered I/137. [ME *unbracen* 'undo, loosen, detatch'.]
vngynttyte *pa.p.* unjointed; of a curlew: carved by being dismembered I/134. [ME *unjointen*.]
vnguyte *n.* Error. See III/113–4n.
vnkyndenes, onkyndenes, wnkyndnys *n.col.* of ravens: an unkindness, unnaturalness I/26; II/236; III/45.
vnlassyde *pa.p.* unlaced, undone; of a cony: carved by being dismembered I/138. [<ME *unlasen*.]
vntachyd *pa.p.* 'detached'; of a bittern: carved by being dismembered I/135. [<ME *untachen* 'to unfasten'.]
vssyde *adj.* used I/255.
vus *v. imp.* use = accustom, familiarise, train I/247.

V = V

vantage *n.* an advantageous position; *at a ~*, (of a hawk) positioned to its advantage II/138. [ME *vauntage*.]
vaweture, vowtour, wautoure, watter *n.* vulture I/202; II/143; III/101; IVh/1. [ME *vulture*.]
ventteremuere *n.* See ENTYRMUER.
vermulond *n.* a type of wine (of uncertain origin and character); perh. a red Italian variety IVi/25. [<?ME *vermiloun, vermulon* 'vermilion', 'bright red'.]
vernache *n.* vernage, a strong, sweet white wine from Italy IVi/26. [ME *vernage* < Italian *vernaccia*.]
vewe, vve, wyue *n.* view; *fleyth to þe ~, fle to the ~, flye to ~*, of a hawk (or hawks): to fly at game that the hawk has located by itself I/223; II/126; III/113. [ME *veue*.]
vinne cottinn *n.* ?wine from the Cotentin peninsula of north-west Normandy IVi/45.
vonne *pron.* one; i.e. the first (of an enumerated set) I/158.
voone *adj.* one; *of ~ blee*, of one (a single) colour I/267.
vowtour *n.* See VAWETURE.
vve *n.* See VEWE.

W

wache *n.col.* of nightingales: a 'watch, watching' = wakefulness I/33.
wappure *n.* vapour, fumes I/266. [ME *vapour*.]
ware *adj. be ~*, be aware, vigilant, wary II/128.
watter, wautoure *n.* See VAWETURE.
weche, wessche *v. imp.* wash I/240, 246, passim.
wederyng *ger.* weathering: exposure (of a hawk) to open air and light II/68.

wedir-seke *adj.* weather-sick; of a hawk: ill from a lack of weathering (exposure to open air and light) II/68.
wermyn *n.* 'vermin', such as lice, mites and the like, that can cause a hawk to become ill I/243.
wesyll(e), wessole *n.* weasel I/180; II/172; IVd/19.
whitrath, (error) **whyterache** *n.* 'white-rat', a name for the stoat or (in its white winter coat) ermine II/173; III/57. [ME *whit-rat*.]
whyth *adj.* white II/5, 72.
wyne cute *n.* 'cuit': a sweet, syrupy liquid made by boiling wine (or must) down to a half or a third of its original volume IVi/52. [ME *cute* <OF *cuire* 'to cook, boil', *cuit* 'boiled'.]
wyne de Grecia *n.* a sweet wine made in the Greek manner (known as GREKE, q.v.); or, spec., a Portuguese wine (known as *vinho de Grecia*) made from over-ripe grapes IVi/16.
wyne de Lepe *n.* a strong white wine from the town of Lepe in south-west Spain IVi/44.
wyne fyane *n.* Enigmatic; the element *fyane* is perh. a mistake for *fyne* in either of two senses: 'fine wine', 'wine of quality' [ME *fin* adj.]; or 'clarified, fined wine' [<ME *finen* v.] IVi/27.
wynegure *n.* vinegar I/241.
wynkys *n.pl.* wings II/106.
wyue *n.* See VEWE.
wnkyndnys *n.col.* See VNKYNDENES.

Y

yovmeyne *n. pl.* yeomen: farmers of small freeholdings I/23. See also ȜEMAN.

Place-Names

Algarbe the Algarve, southern Portugal IVi/46.
Arphax Unidentified IVi/31.
Bare ?Bari, port-city in south-east Italy IVi/23.
Bayone Bayonne, port-city in south-west France IVi/53.
Bilbowe Bilbao, port-city in northern Spain IVi/49.
Bunne Bonn, city on the river Rhine, Germany IVi/4.
Burgoyne Burgundy, France; as *adj.* Burgundian IVi/55.
Cayser Unidentified IVi/50.
Calabria Calabria, region of south-west Italy IVi/24.
Candyne Crete IVi/21. [<L *Candia*.]
Cavelence Unidentified IVi/3.
Cherow Unidentified IVi/5.
Cosderam Unidentified IVi/32.
Elceter ?Alsace [<L *Elisatia, Alisatia*] IVi/7.
Gemerant Unidentified IVi/30.
Gascone Gascony, France; as *adj.* Gascon IVi/56.
Grecia Greece IVi/16.
Lepe Lepe, town in Andalucia, south-west Spain IVi/44.
Mamorant Unidentified IVi/29.
Neker *þe* ~, the Neckar valley, Germany IVi/9.
Paytors Poitou, historical region of west-central France IVi/51.
Rennca ?Rhens in the Rhine valley, Germany IVi/6.
Robedore Ribadeo, north-west Spain IVi/48.
Rocell, Rochel La Rochelle, port-city in western France II/5; IVi/54.
Roodes the island of Rhodes IVi/22.
Sclauonia Slavonia, historic region of northern Croatia IVi/19.

Tartarea Tartary; here, prob. a vague designation for eastern Europe IVi/18.
Tromyn Unidentified IVi/8.
Tullouse Toulouse, city in southern France IVi/47.

APPENDIX I

COLLECTIVE NOUNS

This Appendix sets out a complete collation of phrases containing collective nouns (or 'terms of association') found in all J.B. witnesses – a total of nineteen. Each phrase typically consists of two main elements, a collective noun (sometimes a noun phrase) and a plural end-noun (X), that are set out in the formula 'a [collective noun] of [Xs]'. The J.B. lists of these collocations fall into two main categories: long lists, ranging from 105 phrases (Pl) to 164 (*StA*), and short lists, ranging from twenty phrases (Dg*) to seventy-three (C).

The collation is arranged alphabetically into 226 headwords representing the end-nouns of these phrases. This means that alternative versions of the same phrase can fall under different headwords, as in 'a drove of beasts' and 'a drove of neat' (nos 9, 139) – a division that often reflects the divergent traditions of the long and short lists. Roman type is used for headwords that have lemmata in the *OED*, even if obscure or obsolete (e.g. Gete, Wypes), and italic type for headwords that are either not recorded by the *OED*, are of indeterminate meaning, or are significantly different in sense from their modern counterparts (e.g. *Herles*, *Triaclers*). In such cases, wherever possible, the lemmata used by the *MED* are used.

Under each headword, phrases are arranged into groups according to the collective noun used (e.g. 'a swarm of bees' and 'a charm of bees', both under 'Bees', no. 10), as well as variant forms of the end-noun itself (e.g. *roes*, *rossys*, *robukes*, all under 'Roes / Roebucks', no. 171). Introductory headings and closing remarks are also included as nos 1 and 228 respectively. The collation closes with an index of the collective nouns themselves, and is followed by its own set of explanatory notes.

Witnesses are listed by their sigla in alphabetical order, a sequence broken only by pairs that are closely related, viz. Dg–Rg, H–L, *HSG–LJ*, Pl–Prk. For further details about the relationships between different versions of the J.B. lists of collective nouns, see the main Introduction. To view typical lists of these terms in their proper context, see Prk (I/1–107), H (II/197–241) and Ha (III/1–50).

1. Headings

Distretac*i*o rerum	Addl
Termys of venery &c.	Eg
A litel boke of doct*r*ine for ionge gentil me*n*	Rd
The compaynys of beestys and fowlys.	St*A*
De venatorib*us* in Angl*i*cis	T

2. Apes

A schrewdnesse of apus	Adv
A schrewdenys of apys	Eg
A schreudenes of apys	Pp
A shrewdnes of apes	Rd
A shrewdenes of apis	St*A*
A srewd[n]ess*e* of apes	T
A shrewdenesse of apes	W

3. Asses

i.	A paas of assus	Adv
	A passe of assys	Eg
	A pase off assys	Pl
	A pase of assys	Prk
	A passe of assys	Pp
	A pase of asses	Rd
	A pase of assis	St*A*
	A pase of asses	W
ii.	A posse of asses	T

4. Atteals

i.	A dyvyng of autelys	H
	A dyvinge of autelis	L
	A dyuyng of awteles	Ha
	A dyuyng*e* of altelis	Harl
ii.	A dryvyng off awtelez	C

5. Bakers

A tabernacle of bakers	Pp
A tabernacle of bakers	Rd
A tabernacle of bakers	St*A*
A tabarnacle of bakers	T
A tabernacle of bakers	W

6. Barbers

A scrape of barbures	W

7. Barons

i.	A trought of barronnysse	Eg
	A trouthe of barons	*HSG*
	A trowthe off baronys	Pl
	A trothe of barrovns	Prk
	A trowthe of barons	W
ii.	A bryghtte of baronez	C
	A bry3ght of barons	Dg*
	A bri[3]t of barons	T
iii.	A route of barons	Pp
iv.	A corte of barons	Rd
v.	A thongh of barons	St*A*

8. Bears

i.	A slouth of beres	Adv
	A slouthe of beerys	Eg
	A slouth of beres	*HSG*
	A slowthe off berys	Pl
	A slothe of bayris	Prk
ii.	A slewthe of berys	Rd
	A sleuth of beeris	St*A*
	A slevth of beres	T
	A sl[ew]the of berys	W
iii.	A slawnys of berys	Pp

9. Beasts

A drove off beestiz	C
A drove of beestes	Dg
A droue of bestys	Rg

(*See also* Neat)

---

2 T srewdness*e*] srewdvesse   7 T bri3t] brizt *(Roman 3-stroke z sans tail)*   8 W slewthe] slwethe

APPENDIX I 253

10. Bees

i.	A swarme of bees	Adv
	A swarme of beys	Eg
	A swarme of bees	HSG
	A swerme off been	Pl
	A swarme of byne	Prk
	A swarme of beyn	Pp
	A swarme of beene	Rd
	A swarme of bees	StA
	A swa[rm]e of bene	T
	A swarme of been	W
ii.	A charme of bees	L

11. Beggars

i.	A fyȝghtynke of beggars	Adv
	A fighting of beggers	HSG
	A fighting of beggers	LJ
	A fyȝteyng off begarys	Pl
	A fyȝttynge of beggars	Prk
	A fightynge of beggers	Rd
	A fightyng of beggers	StA
	A feythtynge of [b]eggars	T
	A feytyng of beggers	W
ii.	A faytre of beggers	Pp

12. Birds (All, Small)

i.	A dissimulacione of birdys	Rd
	A dissimulacion of breddis	StA
ii.	A dyssymulacion of all bryddes	Adv
	A dissymulacoun of all byrdys	Pp
	A dissemulacione of all byrdes	T
iii.	A dyssymylacyon of alle smalle bryddys	Eg
iv.	A pype of bryddes	Dg*
v.	A pympe of birdez	C

13. Bitterns

A sege of byttores	Adv
A sege off betores	C
A sege of bytours	Dg
A sege of betorys	Rg
A sege of betowrys	Eg
A sege of botowrys	H
A sege of bettoris	L
A sege of bytorus	Ha
A sege of betoris	Harl
A siege of bittours	HSG
A cege off byttorys	Pl
A cegee of betterys	Prk
A sege of byttors	Pp
A sege of bitturos	Rd
A sege of betouris	StA
A seage of buttors	T
A sege of butors	W

14. Boars (Wild)

i.	[A] syngler of bores	Adv
	A syngler of boores	Dg
	A synguler off bores	Rg
	A synguler of boorys	Eg
	A singler of bores	Ha
	A synggular off boreys	Pl
	A syngelare of borys	Prk
	A syngler of borys	Pp
	A singlar of bores	Rd
	A synguler of boris	StA
	A synglare of bores	T
	A singuler of bo[r]es	W
ii.	A syngulerez of wyld bores	C

15. Bottles

A couple or a payer of botillis	StA

10 Prk of] *add* go *canc*   T swarme] swamre   L] *added by second scribe*   11 T beggars] ?leggars   14 Adv A] *om*   W bores] boyes *(scribal error)*

16. Boys

i.	A raskall of boyes	HSG
	A raskall of boyes	LJ
	A rascayle of boyes	Pp
	A rascalle of boyes	Rd
	A rascall of boyes	StA
	A rascall of boyes	T
	A rascall of boyes	W
ii.	A rafull of boyes	Adv
	A raffull off boyys	Pl
	A rafulle of baeyis	Prk
iii.	A blush of boyes	StA
iv.	A singuler of boyes	W

17. Bread

A cast of brede	L
A caste of breed	HSG
A caste off bred	Pl
A cast of bred	Prk
A cast of brede	Pp
A caste of bred	Rd
A cast of brede	StA
A cast of brede	T
A caste of brede	W

18. Brewers

i.	A festre of bruers	Rd
	A festre of brweris	StA
ii.	A rable of brewers	W

19. Bucks

A herde off bukkez	C
A heerde of bukkes	Dg
A herde of buckes	Rg
A herde of bukkys	H
A herd of buckis	L
A herde of bukkys	Ha
A heerde of bukkys	Harl

20. Burgesses

i.	A good-awyse of borges	Prk
	[*olim?*]	Pl
ii.	A route of burgesez	C

21. Butchers

A goryng of bochouris	StA

22. Butlers

A draght of buttelers	Adv
A draught of buttelerys	Eg
A drawght of buttelers	Pp
A draufthe of boteleris	Rd
A draught of boteleris	StA
A drawght of butelers	T

23. Calves

A cloder of calvys	Pp

24. Canons

A dygnite of chanons	Adv
A dignite off chanonez	C
A dignyte of chano*n*ns	Dg
A dignyte of chanons	Rg
A dygnyte of chanonnysse	Eg
A dignite of chanones	Ha
A dignite of shanons	Harl
A dignyte of chanons	HSG
A dyngyyte off chano*n*ys	Pl
A dyngnete of chennans	Prk
A dignite of channons	Pp
A dignite of chanons	Rd
A dignyte of chanonys	StA
A dignite of chanons	T
A dignite of chanons	W

---

16 Prk baeyis] e *super*   W boyes] *error for* bores *(boars, q.v.)*   17 L] *added by second scribe*   20 Prk good-awyse] goodawyse   Pl] *MS damaged*

APPENDIX I 255

25. Carls
i. A clust*ur* of karl*es*   Adv
    [A] cluster of carles   HSG
    A clust*er* of carles   L
ii. A clowder of karles   Dg
    A clowder of karlys   Rg
    A clowdyr of carlys   H
    A clowd*re* of karles   Ha
(*See also* Churls)

26. Carters
A lassche of carters   Adv
A lasshe of carters   HSG
A lasshe of carters   LJ
A lache off cartarys   Pl
A lache of carttars   Prk
A lasche of carters   Pp
A layshe of carters   Rd
A lash of carteris   StA
A lasche of carters   T
A lasshe of carters   W

27. Carvers
i.   An vmbrekyng of carvers   Adv
ii. A nombryng*e* of keruers   Rd
iii. An vnbrewyng of kerueris   StA

28. Castle
A sege vnto a castelle   Eg

29. Cats (Tame)
i. A cludder of catt*es*   Adv
    A cluther off kattez   C
    A clowder of cattes   Dg
    A clowder of cattys   Rg
    A clowdyr of cattys   H
    A clouder of catt*es*   L
    A clowdir of catt*es*   Ha
    A clodr*e* of cattes   Rd

A cloudr*e* of cattes   T
A clo⟨u⟩dre of cattes   W
ii. A cloudyr of cattys,
    Non dicitur *a clouster*   Eg
iii. A gloryng*e* of cattis   Harl
iv. A clowder off tame cattys   Pl
    A clovdyr*e* of tame cattys   Prk
v. [A] cluster of tame cattes   HSG
vi. A covert of catt*es*   Pp

30. Cats, Wild
i. A dowte off wylde cattys   Pl
    A dovt of wyld cattys   Prk
ii. [A] destruct*io*n of wilde
    cattes   HSG

31. Cats, Young
A kyndyll of yong cattis   StA

32. Chickens
i. A pype of chekynnysse   Eg
    A pepe of chykennys   StA
    A pype of chykyns   T
    A pyppe of chekyns   W
ii. A pympe of chekens   Rd
iii. A tryppe of chekyns   Pp

33. *Choughs*
i. A clatering of chowhis   HSG
    A clatteryng off chow3eys   Pl
    A clatteryng of chov3this   Prk
    A clateryng of chagheys   Pp
    A claterynge of chokwes   Rd
    A clateryng of choughes   StA
    A clat*e*rynge of chowes   T
    A clattryng of chowes   W
ii. A chaterynge of choughys   Eg
(*See also* Daws)

25 HSG A] *om* 29.i. W cloudre] ?clondre ii. Eg A] *add* coud *canc* v. HSG A] *om*
vi. Pp cattes] *error for* cottes *(coots, q.v.)* 30 HSG A] *om*

256   APPENDIX I

34. Churls

i. A cluster of cherlez — Dg*
    A clowster off chorleys — Pl
    A clostyr of chourllys — Prk
    A cluster of churlys — Pp
    A cloustere of chorles — Rd
    A clustre of cho⟨r⟩lis — StA
    A cluster of chorles — T
    A cloystre of churles — W

ii. A cluther of churlez — C

(*See also* Carls)

35. Clerks

i. A scole off clarkys — Pl
    A skole of clarkys — Prk
    A scole of clerkys — Rd
    A scole of clerkes — StA
    A scole of clerkes — W

ii. A prese of clerkis — T

iii. A frape of clerkez — C
     A frape of clerkes — Dg*

36. Cobblers

i. A dronkesyp of coblers — Rd
    A dronkship of coblers — StA
    A drunkynshyp of cobelers — W

ii. A plukke of cobelers — Rd

(*See also* Shoeturners)

37. Collegians

A n⟨o⟩bs*er*uaunce of coligeners — T

38. Colts

i. A rage of coltys — Eg
    A rage off coltys — Pl
    A rage of colttys — Prk
    A rage of coltys — Pp
    A rag*e* of coltes — Rd
    A rage [of] coltes — T

ii. A ragg of coltes — HSG
iii. A ragg of coltis or a rake — StA
iv. A ragge of coltes or of folus — Adv
v. A harresse off horsez, mares or coltez — C

39. Conies

i. A bery of connys — Eg
    A bery of conyes — HSG
    A bere off conys — Pl
    A byr*r*e of connys — Prk
    A bery of conneys — Pp
    A beri of conynges — Rd
    A bery of conyes — StA
    A bery of conyng*e*es — T
    A bery of conyng*es* — W

ii. A barow of conys — Adv

iii. A syght off conyes — C
     A sy3ght of conyes — Dg*

40. Controllers [i.e. comptrollers]

A seet of covntrollers — Adv

41. Cooks

i. A temp*er*avnce of cokus — Adv
    A temporans of cokys — Eg
    A temp*er*ans of cokys — Pp
    A temp*er*ans of kokes — Rd
    A temp*er*ans of cokys — StA
    A te*mper*ance of cokes — T

ii. A hastynes of cookes — HSG
    A hastynes of cookes — LJ

iii. A bawdyng of cokes — W

---

34 Rd chorles] chor les   StA chorlis] *broken type*   37 T nobseruaunce] ?nebseruaunce
37 T of] *om*

APPENDIX I

42. Coots

A couerete of cootys	Eg
A couerte of cootes	HSG
A coue*r*te off cotys	Pl
A cowert of cottys	Prk
A covert of c[o]tt*es*	Pp
A couertt of coteys	Rd
A couert of cootis	StA
A coue*r*te of cotes	T
A covet of cotis	W

43. Cordwainers

A trynkette of cordwaners	HSG
A try⟨nkette⟩ of co⟨rd⟩waners	LJ
A trynget of cordyners	Rd

(*See also* Corvisers)

44. Cormorants

A flight of cormerants	HSG
A fly3te off cavmerawntys	Pl
A fly3t of cor*m*meravnttys	Prk
A flyth of carmeront*es*	Rd
A flight of corm*er*auns	T
A flyght of carmeraunt*es*	W

45. Corn

i. A g*r*ete fouiyson of corne   C
ii. A foyson of corne   Dg*

46. Corvisers

A trynket of corueseris	StA
A trynket of korvesers	W

(*See also* Cordwaners)

47. Courtiers

i.
[A] threte of cortyars	HSG
A thret off cortearys	Pl
A threte of courtres	Rd
A threte of couurtyers	T
A thrette of curtyers	W

ii.
A thretynge of curtyers	Eg
A thretenyng of courteyeris	StA

iii.
A trete of courtyours	Pp
A triete of covrtears	Prk

iv. A charge of cortyurs   Pp

48. Cranes

An herd of cranes	Addl
An herd [of] cranys	Adv
A herd of cranes	C
A heerde of cranes	Dg
A herde of cranys	Rg
A herde of cranys	Eg
A herde of cranys	H
A herde of cranes	L
A herde of cranes	Ha
A heerde of cranes	Harl
An herde of cranys	HSG
A herde off cranys	Pl
A herd of cra*n*nys	Prk
A herde of cranys	Pp
A herd of cranes	Rd
An herde of cranys	StA
A herde of kranes	T
An herde of cranes	W

42 Pp cottes] cattes *(scribal error)*   43 *LJ* trynkette of cordwaners] *leaf damaged*   46 W korvesers] *olim* korverers, r² *changed to* s   47.i. HSG A] *om*   W curtyers] *olim* curtayers, *with* y *overwriting* a   iii. Prk triete] i *super*   48 Adv of] *om*

258   APPENDIX I

	49. Crows		A herde of curlewys	Eg
i.	A mursher of crowys	Eg	A herde of corlewis	H
	A murther of crowes	HSG	A herde of curlewes	L
	A morther off crowys	Pl	A herde of kurloews	Ha
	A morthere of crowys	Prk	A herde of curlewys	Harl
	A murther of crowes	W	A herd of corlewse	Pp
ii.	[A] byggyng of rockes		A herd of curluys	Rd
	or crowes	Adv	An herde of corlewys	StA
			A herde of curlvus	T

50. Cuckolds

			54. Curriers	
i.	An vncredybeletee of		A smere of coryers	HSG
	cokwoldes	Adv	A smere of coryers	LJ
	An vncredibelite of		A sm[e]re of coryers	Rd
	cukkoldys	Pp	A smere of coryouris	StA
	An vncredibilite of cocoldis	StA	A smere of coriers	W
ii.	A noncredibilite of cokkoldes	T		

51. Curates

		55. Curs	
		A cowardnesse of curres	Adv
A charge of curates	Adv	A cowardenys of currys	Eg
A c[h]arge of curettysse	Eg	A cowardys of currys	Pp
[A] charge of curates	HSG	A cowardnes of curris	StA
A charge off kurettys	Pl	A cowardens of curres	T
A charge of curattys	Prk		
A charge of curates	Rd	**56. Cygnets**	
A charge of curatis	StA	A teeme off signettes	C
A charge of curates	W		

52. Curgers

		57. Daubers	
A threte of curgers	Adv	i. A squat off dawberys	Pl
		A squat of davberis	Prk
53. Curlews		A sqwatte of dawbers	Pp
An heerd of curlues	Addl	A squat of dauberys	Rd
A herde of curlews	Adv	A squatte of dawberis	StA
A heerd off curlewz	C	A squatte of dowbars	T
A heerde of curlewes	Dg	A sqwatte of dawbers	W
A herde of curlewes	Rg	ii. A sawtte of dawbars	Adv

---

49 Adv A] *om*   51 Eg charge] carge   HSG A] *om*   53 T curlvus] v *super*
54 Rd smere] smre, *or* ?suire

APPENDIX I

58. Daws
A clateryng of dawes	Adv

(*See also* 'Choughs')

59. Deer (All)
i.	An herd of all dere	Adv
	An herde of alle dere	HSG
	A herde off alle dere	Pl
	A herd of all dere	Pp
	A herde of al deres	T
	An herde of all dere	W
ii.	A herd of all mannere dere	Prk
	A herd of alle maner of dere	Rd
	An herde of all maner dere	StA
iii.	An heerd of dere	Addl
	A herde of dere	Eg
	An herde of dere	HSG
iv.	A tryppe off deere	Adv

60. Doctors
A doctryne of doctersse	Eg
A doctrine of doctours	Rd
A doctryne of doctoris	StA
A doctryne of doctors	T

61. Doves
A flyght of dowes	Adv
A flyght of doovys	C
A fly3ghte of doves	Dg
A flyth of dowys	Rg
A flyght of douys	Eg
A fly3th of dowfys	H
A flight of dovis	L
A flyght of doues	Ha
A flyght of dowfis	Harl
A flight of douues	HSG
A fly3te off dovys	Pl
A fly3t of dowys	Prk
A [f]lyght of dovys	Pp
A [f]lyth of doues	Rd
A flight of doues	StA
A flight of dowues	T
A flyght of doves	W

62. Ducks
i.	A padelynge of dookysse	Eg
	A padlyng of dokys	Pp
	A padlynge of dukkes	T
ii.	A badelyng of dokis	StA
iii.	A bablyng of dokes	W
iv.	A teme of dukys	H
	A teme of dokis	L
	A teme of duckys	Harl

63. Ducks / *Digges*, Wild
i.	A teeme of wylde dokes	Dg
	A teme of wylde dokes	Rg
	A teme of wyld dokes	Ha
ii.	A teeme off wyldigges	C

64. Faitours
[i.e. impostors]
A w⟨a⟩nderyng of feyters	W

65. Falcons
A lure of fawkons	Adv
A lure of fawconez	C
A lure of favcons	Dg*

66. Fawns
A neste of fawnes	C

67. Ferrets
A byssenesse of fyrrettes	Adv
A besynys of ferettys	Eg
A besynes of fyrettes	Pp

59.iv. Adv] *heading to the carving terms* 61 Rg of] *add* do (*partial dittography*)
Pp flyght] lyght   Rd flyth] slyth   64 W wanderyng] *first two letters poorly formed*

A besynes of feryttes	Rd	A stalke of fostres	Rd
A besynes of ferettis	StA	A stalke of fosteris	StA
A besynese of ferettes	T	A sta[l]ke of forsters	T
A besynes of forettes	W	A stalk of forsters	W

68. Fieldfares

74. Foals

i. A flok of feldyfares	Adv	A ragge of coltes or of folus	Adv
A floke of feldefares	T		

75. Foxes

ii. A herd of felfares	C	i. An erthe of foxes	Adv
A herd of feldfares	Dg*	A nerthe of foxys	Eg
(See also Weldefares)		An erthe of foxes	HSG
		[olim?]	Pl

69. Finches

A chyrme of fynches	HSG	An erthe of foxis	Prk
(See also Goldfinches)		An erth of foxys	Pp
		A nerthe of foxis	Rd

70. Fish

		A nerth of foxes	T
		A herthe of foxes	W
i. [A] scole of fysshe	HSG	ii. A sculke of foxues	Adv
A scole of fysch	Rd	A s[k]ulk off foxez	C
A scoll of fysh	StA	A skulke of foxes	Dg
A scole of fyche	T	A sculke of foxys	Rg
ii. A scoue off fyche	Pl	A sculke of foxys	H
A skoue of fyche	Prk	A skulke of foxis	L
A scoue of fysshe	W	A skulke of foxis	Harl
		[A] skulke of foxes	HSG

71. Fishers

		A scolke off foxys	Pl
A dryfth of fischers	Rd	A skolke of foxys	Prk
A drifte of fishers	StA	A skolke of foxys	Pp
		A sculke of foxys	Rd

72. Flies

		A skulke of foxis	StA
A besynes of flyes	HSG	A sculke of foxis	StA

73. Foresters

		A sculke of foxes	T
A stalke of fosters	Adv	A skulke of foxes	W
A stalke of fostersse	Eg	iii. A skulf of foxes	Ha
A stalke of fosters	L		
A stalke of fosters	Pp		

70.i. *HSG* A] *om*   73 L] *added by second scribe*   T stalke] stake   75.i. Adv foxes] fyoxes   Pl] *MS damaged*   ii. C skulk] sulk   *HSG* A] *om*   StA²] *phrase repeated on a later leaf*

APPENDIX I

76. Friars

i.	A sculke of freurs	Adv
	A skulke off frerez	C
	A skulke of frerees	Dg
	A sculke of fryers	Rg
	A sculke of freyrs	H
	A skulke of freris	L
	A skulk of freres	Ha
	A skulke of freres	HSG
	A scolke off frerys	Pl
	A skolke of freris	Prk
	A skoulke of frerys	Pp
	A sculke of fryers	Rd
	A sculke of freris	StA
	A sculke of freres	T
	A skulk of freyris	W
ii.	A bewperis of freris	Harl

77. Geese

i.	A gagyll of ghees	HSG
	A gagull off gesse	Pl
	A gagulle of gyse	Prk
	A gagalle of gese	Rd
	A gagle of gees	StA
	A gagle of geyse	T
	A gagle of gese	W
ii.	A gagelyng of geese	Dg
	A gagelynge of gese	Rg
	A gagelynge of gesse	Eg
	A gagyllyng of gese	H
	A gagelinge of geese	L
	A gagelyng of gyees	Ha
	A gagelynge of gese	Harl
	A gaglyng of gese	Pp

iii.	A gayling of gees	Adv
iv.	A company or a gaglyng of gese	C

78. Gentlemen

A rowte of gentyllemen	Eg

79. Gentlewomen

i.	A company of gentylweme⟨n⟩	Adv
ii.	A rowte of gentilwomen	Pp

80. Gete
[i.e. goats]

A tryppe of gete	Adv
A tryppe off geyte	C
A tryppe of geete	Dg
A trepy of gete	Rg
A tryppe of gete	Eg
A trype of gete	H
A tryppe of gete	L
A trip of geette	Ha
A trippe of gete	Harl
A trippe of gete	HSG
A trype off gete	Pl
A trype of gayte	Prk
A tryppe of geyte	Pp
A trypp of gete	Rd
A trippe of gete	StA
A trype of gete	T

81. Gold

A somme of gold	C
A somme of goold	Dg*

---

76 T of] *add* fre *canc*   77 T geyse] *add* of *canc*   W of] *add* G *canc*   78 Eg gentyllemen] gentylle men   79 Adv gentylwemen] *word cut off by tight MS binding but traces of a final* n *are apparent, as is a possible macron over the final* e   80 Adv tryppe] *letter (indistinct) canc after* y   H of] *add* l *canc*

82. Goldfinches

i.
A chyrme of goldefynchys	Eg
A cherme off goldeffynchys	Pl
A chyrme of goldfynchys	Prk
A chyrme of goldefynchys	Pp
A chirme of goldfinches	Rd
A cherme of goldefynches	StA
A chirme of goldfe[n]ch	T
A chyrme of goldefynchys	W

ii.
A chyrmyng of goldfynch	C
A chirmyng of goldfynches	Dg
A chyrmynge of goldefynches	Rg
A chermyng of goldfy*n*chys	H
A chirmynge of goldfynchis	L
A chyrmyng of goldfynches	Ha

iii. A tremynge of goldefynchis   Harl

(*See also* Finches)

83. Good fellowship

A solaz of gode felychyp   C

84. Goshawks

i.
A flyght of goshawk*es*	Adv
A flyght of gossehawkys	Eg
A flight of goshaukes	HSG
A fly3te off gosshawky[s]	Pl
A fly3t of goshavkys	Prk
A [f]lyth of gosehaukys	Rd
A flight of goshaukes	StA
A flight of gosehaukes	T
A flyght of gosehawk*es*	W

ii. A flyght of a gossauke   Pp

85. Gossips

A gagelyng of gossippes   Harl

86. Grapes

A clust*ur* of grap*es*	Adv
A cluster off grapez	C
A cluster of g*r*apes	Dg
A clowster of grapys	Rg
A clustyr of grapys	H
A clust*er* of grapis	L
[A] cluster of grapes	HSG
A clowster off grapys	Pl
A clvstur*e* of grappus	Prk
A clustyr of grapys	Pp
A clouster*e* of g*r*apys	Rd
A clustre of grapys	StA
A cloustre of grapes	T
A cloystre of grapys	W

87. Greyhounds

i.
A leassch of grehond*es*	Adv
A lesse of grehoundys	Eg
A lees of grehoundes	HSG
A lesse off greyhowndys	Pl
A leys of grayhoundys	Prk
A lesche of grewhond*es*	Pp
A lese of grehondys	Rd
A lese of greyhundes	T
A lese of greyhound*es*	W

ii. A lece of grehoundis of .iij   StA

iii. A brase of grewhond*es*   Pp

iv. A brace of grehoundis of .ij   StA
A bracc of ij grcyhu*n*dis   T

v. A lech, a brase, an hardlyng of grehoundez   C

vi. A thru*m* of greundes   Ha

---

82 Pp goldefynchys] golde fynchys   Rd chirme] i *super*,   goldfinches] gold finches T goldfench] goldfech   84 Eg gossehawkys] gosse hawkys   Pl gosshawkys] gosshawky Rd flyth] slyth,   gosehaukys] gose haukys   85 Harl] *interpolated by a different hand* 86 HSG A] *om*   87 W of] *add* Gy *canc*   C lech] *add* ff *canc*

APPENDIX I

88. Greys

i.	A cety of greyes	HSG
	A cete off greyys	Pl
	A cete of grayis	Prk
	A cyte of greys	Pp
	A cete of greys	Rd
	A cete of graies	StA
	A cytee of greyes	T
	A cyte of greyes	W
ii.	A sawte of greyes & a farewyng	C
iii.	A sawte of grayes	Dg*
iv.	A dysseit of greys	Adv
v.	A syght of grayys	Eg

89. Hares

i.	A trippe of hares	HSG
	A trype off hareys	Pl
	A trype of harrys	Prk
	A trypp of hares	Rd
	A trippe of haaris	StA
	A trype of hares	T
ii.	A huske of hares	Dg
	A husk of hares	Ha
	A huske of haris	Harl
	A huske of harys	Pp
iii.	A don of hares	Dg
	A down of hares	Ha
iv.	A huske or a downe of hars	Adv
	A huske of harys or a dunne of hares	Rg
	A huske or a downe of harys	H
	A huske or a dov[n]e of haris	L

v.	A huske or a denne of harez	C
vi.	A droue or a huske of harrys	Eg
vii.	A herde of harys	L
viii.	A trase of an hare	HSG
	A trasse off a hare	Pl
	A trase of harrys	Prk

90. Harlots

i.	A haras of harlottes	H
	A haras of harlotys	L
ii.	An herde of harlottys	StA

91. Harpers (& Luters)

i.	A meledy of harpers	Adv
	A melody of harpers	Pp
	A melodi of harpers	Rd
	A melody of harpers	StA
	A melody of harperes	T
	A melody of herpers	W
ii.	A melody of harpers ⟨&⟩ luters	L
iii.	A pouerte off harperys	Pl
	A powertte of harppers	Prk

92. Harts

	An heerd of hertis	Addl
	An herd of hertes	Adv
	A herde off hertes	C
	A heerde of hertes	Dg
	A herde of hertys	Rg
	A herde of hertys	Eg
	A herde of hartys	H
	A herd of hertis	L
	A herd of hertes	Ha

---

88 T cytee] *a letter (?i) canc after* t   89.i. Pl, Prk] *phrase appended to the resting terms*
ii. Dg A] *add* huscke *canc*   iii. Dg] *phrase added with caret interlinearly after* A huske of hares   89.iv. L dovne] dove   vii. L] *phrase added in margin after A* herd of hertis *by a later (third) hand*   viii. Pl, Prk] *phrase appended to the resting terms*   91.ii. L] *phrase added by second scribe,* &] *traces of a grapheme, prob. brevigraph for* et, *partially lost through trimming*

APPENDIX I

A heerde of hertis	Harl
An herde of hertes	HSG
[*olim?*]	Pl
A herd of harttus	Prk
A herde of hert*es*	Pp
An herde of hertis	St*A*
A herde of hertes	T
An herde of hertys	W

93. Hawks (of the Tower)

i.	A cast of hawk⟨s⟩ of tour*e*	Adv
	A caste of hawkys of the towre	Eg
	A caste of haukys of the toure	Harl
	A caste of hawkes of the tour	HSG
	A ⟨c⟩aste off hawkys off þe towre	Pl
	A cast of havkys of þe tour*e*	Prk
	A cast of hawkys of the towre	Pp
	A caste of haukys of the toure	Rd
	A cast of haukis of þe tour .ij	St*A*
	A cast of hauk*es* of to*ur*	T
	A caste of hawkes of the toure	W
ii.	A cast of havkes	L
iii.	A lece of thessame haukis .iij	St*A*

94. Haywards

A waywardenes of haywardes	Rd
A waywardnes of haywardis	St*A*
A waywardnes of heyward*es*	T

95. Hens

i.	A broode of hennysse	Eg
	A brude of hennys	Pp
	A brode of hennys	St*A*
	A broode of hennes	T
	A brode of hennes	W
ii.	A grale off hennez	C
iii.	A garule of he*n*nes	Dg*
iv.	A padelyng*e* of hennes	Rd
v.	A tryppe of hennes	W

96. Heralds

A knowlege of heraldes	W

97. *Herles*

A doppyng of herreles	Ha
A doppynge of herles	Harl
(*See also* Sheldrakes)	

98. Hermits

A n⟨ob⟩ser*u*ans of hermyt*es*	Rd
An obs*er*uans of herimytis	St*A*
A nobs*er*uaunc*e* of heremyt*es*	T

---

92 Pl] *MS damaged*   93.i. Adv hawks] s *obscured by MS binding*   Pl caste] *hole in MS,* þe towre] þetowre   St*A* þe] y^e   93.ii. L] *added by second scribe*   98 Rd nobseruans] *first three letters poorly formed*

APPENDIX I 265

99. Herons

i.
A sege of herons	Adv
A sege of herovnnes	Dg
A sege of hayrons	Rg
A sege of hayrynnys	Eg
A sege of heyro*n*nys	H
A sege of heyrones	L
A sege of herones	Ha
A sege of herons	Harl
A siege of heyrons	HSG
A cege off heronys	Pl
A cege of herronns	Prk
A seche of herons	Pp
A sege of hayrons	Rd
A sege of heronnys	StA
A seage of hero[n]s	T
A sege of herons	W

ii. A beuy or a sege of heronez C

iii. A bevy of herons Dg*

100. Horses

i.
An haras of horsys	Adv
A harresse of horses	Dg
A hares of hors	Rg
A harrys of hors	Eg
A haras of horse	H
A haras of hors	L
A haras of horses	Ha
A haras of horsis	Harl
A hareys of hors	HSG
A hares off hors	Pl
A harres of horssys	Prk
A harres of horses	Pp
A hares of hors	Rd
An harrasse of horse	StA
A hares of horse	T
A hares of hors	W

ii. A harresse off horsez, mares or coltez C

101. Horses, Old

A stalyn of olde hors Eg

102. Hostelers

An lau3ghter of hostyllars	Adv
A lawghtur of ostylersse	Eg
[A] lau[f]ters of hostelers	HSG
A law3eterys off ostelerys	Pl
A lav3ttyr*e* of hostelers	Prk
A laughter of ostylers	Pp
A laughtr*e* of host*e*rers	Rd
A laughtre of osteloris	StA
A laughter of ostelers	T
A laught*er* of hostelers	W

103. Hounds

i.
A brace of hownd*es*	Adv
A brasse of houndys	Eg
A brase of houndes	HSG
A brasse off howndys	Pl
A brace of hovndys	Prk
A brace of houndis	Rd
A brace of houndes	W

ii.
A mute of hovndes	Dg*
A mewte of hundees	Ha
A mute of houndes	StA

iii. A packe of houndis Rd

iv. A mewte, a pakke & a kenell of houndes C

104. Hounds, Running

A couple of rennyng houndis StA

---

99 T herons] herovs 102 HSG A] *om*, laufters] lausters

105. Hunters

A blaste of hvnters	Adv
A blaste of huntersse	Eg
A blast of hvnters	L
A blast of hounters	Pp
A blaste of huntres	Rd
A blast of hunteris	StA
A blast of hunters	T

106. Husbands

i.	A multeplying of husbondus	Adv
	A multiplieng of husbondis	StA
	A multiplynge of husbondes	T
ii.	A multeplynge of hosbandri	Rd
iii.	A nowmbyr of housbandes	Pp

107. Jays

A gayling of iaes	Adv

108. Jewellers

A ryches of iuelers	Pp

109. Judges

i.	A sentence of iuges	Adv
	A centens off iugys	Pl
	A centtans of iugys	Prk
	A sentence of iugys	Pp
	A sentens of iuges	Rd
	A sentence of iuges	StA
	A sentence of ivgges	T
ii.	A sedent of iuggysse	Eg
iii.	A sadnes of iugis	W

110. Jugglers

i.	A neuerthryvyng of iuglars	Adv
	A neuerthryvyng off ioglerys	Pl
	A neuertreyuyng of iovghelars	Prk
	A neuerthryuyng of iogulers	Rd
	A neuerthriuyng of iogoleris	StA
	A neuerthryuynge of iogulers	T
	A neverthryvyng of iogulers	W
ii.	An ouerthryngyng of iuglers	Pp

111. Jurors

A dampnyng of iorus	Adv
A dampnynge of iuryersse	Eg
[olim?]	Pl
A damnynge of iurrears	Prk
A dampnyng of iurrors	Pp
A dampnynge of iurers	Rd
A dampnyng of iurrouris	StA
A dampnynge of iurrers	T
A dampnyng of iurers	W

112. Kempsters / Kembers

i.	A scaldyng of kempsters	Adv
	A scolding of kempsters	HSG
	A scolding of kempsters	LJ
	A scoldeyng off kemstarys	Pl
	A skoldynge of kemmyssteris	Prk
	A skoldenge of kempsters	Rd
	A scoldyng of kemsteris	StA
	A [s]coldynge of kempstars	T
	A scoldyng of kempsters	W
ii.	A skoldyng of kymbers	Pp

---

105 L] *added by second scribe*   106 T husbondes] u *has long looped tail normally used to indicate an omitted* n   111 Pl] *MS damaged*   112 T scoldynge] coldynge

APPENDIX I 267

113. Knaves

i.	A rafull of knaue*s*	Adv
	A rafull of knaues	HSG
	A rafull of knaues	LJ
	A raffull off knavys	Pl
	A rafulle of cnavys	Prk
	A rawfell of knaves	Pp
	A rafle of knaues	Rd
	A rafull of knauys	StA
	A rawfull of knaues	T
	A rafle of knavys	W
ii.	A cluster of knaves	Harl

114. Knights

i.	A rowte of knyght	Adv
	A rowte of kny3ttes	Dg
	A rowte [of] k[n]ytys	Rg
	A rowte of knyghtys	Eg
	A rowte of knytys	H
	A rowte of knyghtis	L
	A rowt of knyght*es*	Ha
	A rought of kynghtis	Harl
	A rowte of knyghtes	HSG
	A rowte off knghtty⟨s⟩	Pl
	A route of kny3ttys	Prk
	A rowte of knyghtys	Pp
	A rowte of knygtes	Rd
	A route of knyghtis	StA
	A route of knyghtes	T
	A rowt of knyghtis	W
ii.	A my3ghtenes of knys*tes*	Adv
iii.	A ray of knyghtez	C
	A ray of kny3ghtes	Dg*

115. Ladies

i.	A bevy of ladyes	Addl
	A beyve of ladyes	Adv

A bevy of ladyes	Dg
A bewy of ladyes	Rg
A beuy of ladyes	Eg
A beve of ladys	H
A beve of ladies	L
A beuy of ladyes	Ha
A bevy of ladies	Harl
A beuye of ladyes	HSG
A bevy off ladyys	Pl
A bevy of ladys	Prk
A bevy of ladys	Pp
A beuy of ladyes	Rd
A beuy of ladies	StA
A beve of ladys	T
A beve of ladyes	W

ii.	A bevy of ladyes or a company	C
iii.	A eloquence of ladys	Pp

116. Lapwings

i.	A dyssayte off lappy*n*g	C
	A deseyte of lapewynkes	Dg
	A desyte off lepewy*n*kes	Rg
	A dyssayte of lepwynkys	Eg
	A dysseyte of lapwynk*ys*	H
	A disseyte of lepwynckes	L
	A deceyte of lapewyng*es*	Ha
	A disseit of lapwynkis	Harl
	A disceite of lapwinks	HSG
	A dysseyte off lapwyng	Pl
	A dyssayt of lappwyn*n*g*ys*	Prk
	A dyssate of lypewyng*es*	Pp
	A disseyte of lypwynkys	Rd
	A disseyt of lapwynk*es*	W
ii.	A desserte of lapwyng*is*	StA

(*See also* Wypes)

113.ii. Harl] *phrase added by a different hand* 114.i. Rg of knytys] of *om*, kytys Pl knghttys] *hole in MS* Rd] *phrase added interlinearly* 116 Dg lapewynkes] lape wynkes

117. Larks

i.
A exsaltyng off larkys	Pl
A exsalttynge of larkys	Prk
A exaltyng of larkys	Pp
A exaltynge of lerkys	Rd
An exaltyng of larkis	StA
A nexaltynge of larkes	T
An exaltyng of larkes	W

ii.
An exaltacion of larkes	Adv
A exaltacyon of larkys	Eg
A exaltacion of larkes	HSG

iii. A beuye of larkes — HSG

iv.
A fly3hte of larkes	Dg
A flyth of larkys	Rg
A fly3th of larkys	H
A flight of larkis	L
A flyght of larkes	Ha
A flyght of larkis	Harl

v. A flok off larkez — C

118. Lawyers

An eloquence of lawers	Adv
A eloquens of lawyers	Eg
A eloquens off lawyereys	Pl
A ellequens of laweris	Prk
A elaquens of lawyers	Rd
An eloquens of laweyeris	StA
A neloquens of lawyers	T
An eliquens of lawyers	W

119. Leopards

A leype of lybardes	Adv
A lepe of lybardys	Eg
A lepe of lebardes	HSG
A lepe off lybbartes	Pl
A lepe of leberttys	Prk
A lepe of libartes	Pp
A lepe of lybardes	Rd
A lepe of lebardis	StA
A lepe of leopardes	T
A lepe of lebardys	W

120. Liars

| A glorifyeng of lyers | HSG |
| A glorifyeng of lyers | LJ |

121. Lice

A flock of lyse — HSG

122. Lion(s)

i.
A pryde of lyons	Adv
A pryde of lyons	Eg
A pryde of lyons	HSG
A pryde off lyonys	Pl
A pryd of lyonnys	Prk
A pride of lyons	Pp
A pride of lyons	Rd
A pride of lionys	StA
A pryde of lyons	T
A pride of lyons	W

ii. A lepe of lyons — Pp

iii. A sowte off a lyonen — Pl

A sawt of a lyone — Prk

iv. A sowse of a lyonas — Eg

123. Lyam / Limer

i.
A sewyt of a lyam	Pp
A sute of a lyame	Rd
A sute of a lyam	StA
A sute of a lyame	T
A sute of a lyam	W

ii. A sute of a lyhmer — HSG

---

123 T of] *add* l *canc*

APPENDIX I

124. Maidens

i. A rage of madyns — Pp
    A rage of maydnes — Rd
    A rage of maydenys — *StA*
    A rage of maydyns — T
ii. A lure of maydons — Adv
    A lure of maydenez — C
    A lure of maydenes — Dg*

125. Mallards

i. A sourde off mallard — C
    A sovrde of malardes — Dg
    A sowrde off malardys — Rg
    A sorde of malardys — H
    A soorde of malardes — Harl
    A sourd of malardes — *HSG*
ii. A swerde of malardis — Ha
iii. A sor*te* of malar*des* — Adv
    A sorte of malardis — L
    A sorte off mawlardeys — Pl
    A sort of mallarttus — Prk
    A sorte of mawler*tes* — Pp
    A sorth of malerdes — Rd
iv. A surt of malar*des* — T
    A surte of malardis — W
v. A sorde or a sute of malardis — *StA*
vi. A flusche of mallardys — Eg

126. Mares

i. A stode of mars — Adv
    A stoode of marys — Eg
    A stode of mares — *HSG*
    A stode off marys — Pl
    A stode of marys — Prk
    A stode of marys — Pp
    A stede of mares — Rd
    A stode of maris — *StA*
    A stode of mares — T
    A stode of mares — W
ii. A harresse off horsez, mares
    or coltez — C

127. Mariners

A grete-science of maryners — Pp

128. Martens

i. A rychesse of martrons — Adv
    A riches of martronys — *StA*
    A riches of martres — T
    A riches of martrons — W
ii. A ryches of martyrs — Pp
    A reches of marterys — Rd

129. Masters

A nexmapell*e* of maysters — Rd
A example of maisteris — *StA*

130. Men

i. An host of men — Adv
    A hoost of men — Dg
    A hoste of men — Rg
    A oste of men — Eg
    A ost of men — H
    A oste of men — L
    A hoste of men — Ha
    A ost of men — Harl
    An hoost of men — *HSG*
    A oste off men — Pl
    A nost of mene — Prk
    An ost of men — Pp
    A noste of menne — Rd
    An hoost of men — *StA*
    A nost of me*n* — T
    An oste of men — W
ii. An hoste of men or a
    companye — C

APPENDIX I

131. Merchants

i. A faythe of marchauntysse	Eg	
[*olim?*]	Pl	
A fayth of marchandys	Prk	
A fayth of marchant*es*	Pp	
A feyth of marchant*es*	Rd	
A faith of marchandis	*StA*	
A feyth of marchaunt*es*	W	
ii. A feyth al*ius* deseyt of marchauntes	T	

132. Merlins

A lesshe of marlions	Harl

133. Messengers

A dylygence of messangers	Adv
A dylygens of massyngers	Eg
A deligence of messyngers	Pp
A dilygen[c]e of messyngers	Rd
A diligens of messangeris	*StA*
A diligens of messengers	T
A diligence of messangers	W

134. Millers

i. A franchesse of mylnars	Adv	
A franchize of millers	T	
ii. A franchype of millers	Rd	
iii. A fraunch of mylneris	*StA*	
iv. A fra‹u›dysnes of mylners	Pp	

135. Moles

A labyr of mollys	Eg
A laber of molles	Rd
A labor of mollis	*StA*
A lobour of molles	T
A labur of moll*es*	W

(*See also* Mouldwarps, Wants)

136. Monks

i. An abhominabul sy3ght of mvnkus	Adv
An habomynable syght off monkys	C
A abho*mi*nable sy3th*e* of monkes	Dg
An abhomynabylle sy3te of monk*es*	Rg
A abhominable syght of monkes	Ha
A bomynabull sy3te of mo*nn*kys	Pl
A bomynabul sy3te of movnkys	Prk
A bomynabyll syght of monkes	Pp
A bhomynable sight of mo*n*kis	*StA*
A nobhomnable sight of monkes	T
A abhominable sight of munk*es*	W
ii. A obho*mi*nabell*e* of monkes	Rd
iii. A deuowtenesse of mo*n*kys	Harl
iv. A lordship of monkes	HSG

137. Mouldwarps [i.e. moles]

A labur of muldwarpus	Adv

(*See also* Moles, Wants)

---

131 Pl] *MS damaged*   T alius deseyt] *added super*   133 Rd dilygence] dilygente   134 Pp fraudysnes] ?frandysnes   136 Pl monnkys] kys *super*

APPENDIX I   271

138. Mules
i. A baren off mewlys   Pl
    A barren*e* of mullys   Prk
    A boryane of mulys   Pp
    A bareyne of mules   Rd
    A baren of mulis   *StA*
    A bareyn*e* of mules   T
    A baren of mules   W
ii. A burdynne of mulysse   Eg

139. Neat [i.e. cattle]
i. A droffe of nete   Eg
    A droue of nete   *HSG*
    A drove off nete   Pl
    A drovfe of neyte   Prk
    A drave of nete   Pp
    A droue of nete   Rd
    A droue of nete   *StA*
    A drowe of nete   T
    A drowe of nete   W
ii. A dryfte of nette   Adv

(*See also* Beasts)

140. Nightingales
i. A wacch of nyghtgales   Adv
    A waycche of nyghtynggalys   Eg
    A wache off nyghteynggalys   Pl
    A wache of ny3ttyn*n*galys   Prk
    A wach*e* of nightyngalys   Rd
    A wache of nyghtingalis   *StA*
    A wache of nyghty*n*gales   T
ii. A wecche of nayngales   W
iii. A wage of nyghtyngals   Pp

141. Nuns
i. A super*f*luyte of n‹v›nes   Adv
    A super*f*luite off nonnez   C
    A super*f*luite of no*n*nes   Dg
    A super*ff*lewyte of nunnys   Rg
    A super*f*luite of nu*n*nes   Ha
    [A] super*f*luyte of nonnes   *HSG*
    A super*f*luete off nonys   Pl
    A super*e*flovite of non*n*ys Prk
    A super*f*luite of nonnys   Pp
    A super*f*luite of nonnes   Rd
    A super*f*luyte of nunnys   *StA*
    A super*f*luyte of nonnes   T
    A super*f*luite of nonnes   W
ii. A holynesse of nu*n*nys   Harl

142. Nuts
A clust*ur* of nott*es*   Adv
A cluster off nottez   C
A cluster of notes   Dg
A clowster of notys   Rg
A clustyr of nottys   H
A cluster of nottis   L
[A] cluster of nottes   *HSG*
A clowster off nottys   Pl
A clostyr of nottys   Prk
A clustyr of notty*s*   Prk
A cluster of nott*es*   Pp
A cloustere of nott*es*   Rd
A clustre of nottis   *StA*
A clouster of nottes   T
A cloystre of nuttes   W

---

139 T A] *add* g *canc*   141 Adv nvnes] *olim* nones, o *changed to* v   Rg superfflewyte] super fflewyte   *HSG* A] *om*   142 *HSG* A] *om*   Prk²] *written as catchwords on previous leaf*

143. Officers

i.
An execucion of offycers	Adv
A execucyon of offycers	Eg
A nexecuc*io*ne of offycers	Rd
An execucion of officerys	StA
A nexecuc*io*ne of officers	T
An exe‹c›ucon of officers	W

ii.
An excusion of officers	Pp

144. Oxen

A teme of oxon	Adv
A teeme off oxon	C
A tyme of oxen	Dg
A teme of oxen	Rg
A teme of oxyn	H
A teme of oxen	L
A teme of oxn	Ha
A teme of oxen	Harl

145. Painters

A mysbelefe of peynters	Adv
A mysbeleve of payntours	Pp
A misbeleue of paynters	Rd
A misbeleue of paynteris	StA
A mysbeleue of peynto*ur*s	T
A misbyleve of peynters	W

146. Panters
[i.e. pantrymen]

A kerffe of pantersse	Eg
A carfe of pantlars	L
A kerf of pawnters	Pp
A kerfe of panters	Rd
A kerff of panteris	StA
A kerfe of panters	T

147. Pardoners

i.
A lying of p*ar*doners	Adv
A lyynge of pardynersse	Eg
A lyeng of pardoners	HSG
A lyeng of p*ar*doners	LJ
A lying of pardnars	Prk
A lyeng of pardon*er*s	Rd
A lyeng of pardeneris	StA
A lyyng*e* of p*ar*doners	T
A lying of p*ar*doners	W

ii.
A lesyng of pardoners	Pp

148. Partridges

A covy of partrik*es*	Addl
A couy of p*ar*trych	Adv
A couy of p*er*trychez	C
A covey of p*ar*tryches	Dg
A couy of p*ar*tryches	Rg
A couaye of parterygys	Eg
A couy of p*er*tr*i*kkys	H
A covey of p*er*triches	L
A couy of partryches	Ha
A cove of partrichys	Harl
A coueye of partrichs	HSG
A covy off p*ar*tregys	Pl
A covey of parttrygys	Prk
A covy of pertrychys	Pp
A couy of p*ar*tirigges	Rd
A couy of partrichis	StA
A covy of p*ar*trich	T
A coue of pertriches	W

---

143 W execucon] c *indistinct*   145 Adv peynters] *omitted by scribe, but added by a different hand infra*   Rd paynters] y *super*   146 L] *added by second scribe*

APPENDIX I

149. Peacocks

A must*ur* of pecokke*s*	Adv
A mo⟨u⟩styr of pecockys	Eg
A muster of pecoks	HSG
A mowster off pecokekys	Pl
A mostur*e* of peycokys	Prk
A musture of pekockys	Pp
A moustere of pok⟨e⟩kys	Rd
A mustre of pecockys	StA
A mustyr of pecokes	T
A muster of pacokkes	W

150. Pedlars

[A] malapertnes of pedlars	Adv
A mallapertnys of pedlers	Prk
A malep*er*tynesse of pedlers	Pp
A malap*er*tenes of pedlers	Rd
A malepertnes of pedleres	StA
A malap*er*tenesse of pedlers	T
A malapertnes of pedelers	W

151. People

A congregacon of pepull	Adv
A co*n*gregacou*n* of pepyll	Pp
A congregacion*e* of pepyll*e*	Rd
A congregacion of peple	StA
A co*n*gregacon*e* of peple	T

152. Pheasants

i.	An iye of fesauntz	Addl
	An iee of fesauntez	C
	A ie of fesavntes	Dg
	A ye of fes*r*auntes	Harl
	An yʒe of fezaunt*es*	Pp
	A ye of fesauntes	W
ii.	An nye of fesant*es*	Adv
	A ny of fesauntys	Eg

A nye of fesawnt*ys*	H
A nye of feysantes	L
A nye of faysandis	Ha
A neye of fesantes	HSG
A ny off fessantys	Pl
A ny of feysandys	Prk
A nye of fesantes	Rd
A ny of fesant*es*	Rg
A nye of fesaunttys	StA
A nye of fesa*n*ces	T

153. Pies
[i.e. magpies]

i.	A tydynge of pyys	Eg
	A tydyngys off pyys	Pl
	A tyþingys of pyis	Prk
	A tythyng*es* of pyys	Pp
	A tydyng*e* of pypys	Rd
	A titengis of pies	StA
	A tydyng*e* of pyes	T
	A tydyng of pyes	W
ii.	A chat*ur*yng of pyes	Adv

154. Pinders

i.	A frowardnes of pyndars	Adv
ii.	A waywerdnes of pynders	Pp

155. Pipers

A pouerte of pyp*er*s	Adv
A pouerte of pypers	Pp
A pou*er*te of pyp*er*s	Rd
A pauuerty of pypers	StA
A pou*er*te of pypers	T
A poverte of pypers	W

149 Eg moustyr] ?monstyr   Rd pokekys] ?pokokys   150 Adv A] *om*, malapertnes] *olim* homelenesse *canc*, A malap *added and canc*, malapertnes *added by a different hand below*   Pp malepertynesse] male pertynesse   152 Harl A] *add* o *canc*

156. Plovers

i. A congregacyon of plouers — Eg
    A co*n*gregac*i*on of plou*e*rs — HSG
    A co*n*gregasyo*n* off plou*e*rys — Pl
    A co*rn*ngregacon*e* of plouerys — Prk
    A conggregacou*n* of plovers — Pp
    A congregacion*e* of plou*e*rys — Rd
    A congregacion of pleu*e*rs — StA
    A co*n*gregacon*e* of plou*e*rs — T
    A congregacon of plowers — W

ii. A broode of plovers — Adv

iii. A haunte off plou*e*rz — C

157. Pope, The

The pope in his holy see — Adv

158. Porters

i. A sauegarde of porterysse — Eg
    A savegard of porters — Pp
    A sauegard of porters — Rd
    A safegarde of porteris — StA
    A sauegarde of porters — T

ii. A suffrage of porters — Adv

159. Preachers

A conuertynge of precherrysse — Eg
A co*n*u*e*rtyng*e* of p*r*echours — Rd
A conu*e*rtyng of prechouris — StA
A co*n*u*e*rtynge of p*r*echours — T

160. Prelates

i. A pontifical of prelates — HSG
    A po*n*tyfycalle off p*r*elattys — Pl
    A pontyfycalle of p*r*elettus — Prk
    A pontificall of prelat*e*s — Pp
    A pontificall*e* of p*r*elatys — Rd
    A po*n*tifical of p*r*elates — T
    A pontifical of p*r*elatt*es* — W

ii. A pontificalite of prelatis — StA

iii. A pontificatenes of p*r*elates — Adv

161. Priests

i. A discretnes of prustes — Pp
    A dis[c]retenes of pryst*es* — Rd
    A discretenes*s*e of p*r*estes — T

ii. A dyscrecyon of prestys — Eg
    A discrecion of prestis — StA

iii. [A] prees of prestes — HSG
     A pres off pres‹b›ys — Pl
     A preys of preysttys — Prk
     A prese of preystes — W

iv. A state of p*r*estes — Dg
    A state of prestys — Rg
    A state off preestez — C
    A state of prystes — Ha
    A state of p*r*istis — Harl

v. A dyspetenesse of prystes — Adv

vi. A pontyfycalle of prestysse — Eg

162. Princes

i. A state of p*r*inces — Adv
    A state of pryncysse — Eg
    A state of princes — HSG
    A state off prynsys — Pl
    A stat of prynsys — Prk
    A state of princes — Pp
    A state of p*r*inc*es* — Rd
    A state of pry*n*ces — StA
    A state of p*r*inces — T
    A state of pry*n*ces — W

ii. A pontificall*e* of pry*n*ces — Rd

163. Prisoners

A pyte of prysoners — HSG
A pyte of prysoners — LJ

161.i. Rd discretenes] distretenes   iii. HSG A] om   W prese] *olim* peese, e¹ *changed to* r
Pl prestys] t *indistinct*

164. Quails

A beve of quayles	Addl
A beuy of quayles	Adv
A beuy of quaylez	C
A bevey of quayles	Dg
A bewy of quayles	Rg
A beuy of quaylys	Eg
A bevee of qu*a*ylys	H
A beve of quailles	L
A beuy of quayles	Ha
A bevy of quayles	Harl
A beuye of quayles	HSG
A bevy off quaylys	Pl
A bevy of quayllys	Prk
A bevy of qu*a*yles	Pp
A bevy of queyles	Pp
A beuy of quayles	Rd
A beuy of quaylis	StA
A beue of quales	T

165. Rabbits

i.	A neste of rabettys	Eg
	A neste of rabettis	HSG
	A neste off rabattys	Pl
	A nest of rabettys	Prk
	A nest of rabbyts	Pp
	A neste of rabett*es*	Rd
	A nest of rabettis	StA
	A nest [of] rabettes	T
	A neste of rabett*es*	W
ii.	An nest or a dow of rabett*es*	Adv

166. Raches

i.	A kenell of ratches	Adv
	A kenelle of raycchys	Eg
	A kenel of recches	HSG
	A kenell off racheys	Pl
	A kennel of racchys	Prk
	A kennell of rachys	Pp
	A keny*lle* of raches	Rd
	A kenell of rachis	StA
	A kenel[l]e of raches	T
ii.	A kenette of reches	W

167. Rails

A raskall of railes	Pp

168. Ravens

An vnkyndenesse of ravens	Adv
A vnkyndnez of ravenz	C
A vnkyndenes of ravenes	Dg
A vnkyndenys off rawynnys	Rg
A vnkyndenys of rauynnys	Eg
A onkyndenes of ravynnys	H
A vnkyndenes of ravenes	L
A vnkyndenes of rauenes	Ha
A vnkyndenesse of rauons	Harl
An vnkindnes of rauons	HSG
A vnkyndenys off ravenys	Pl
A wnkyndnys of rawynnys	Prk
A vnkyndenes of ravenys	Pp
A nonkendenes of rauons	Rd
An vnkyndenes of rauenes	StA
A nonkyn*e*dness*e* of reveness*e*	T
An onkyndenes of ravens	W

169. Rebels

A rysyng of rebellez or of shrewez	C

---

164 L quailles] Quailles, *with* Q *retraced by a later (third) hand*   Pp¹] *phrase added by a different hand*   165 T of rabettes] *of om, olim* rebettes, e *changed to* a   Adv dow] *gap follows, word possibly incomplete*   166 Adv of] *add* of (*dittography*)   T kenelle] kenelte   167 Pp] *phrase added by a different hand*   168 Dg of] *add* lapewynkes of *canc*

170. Ribalds
i. A foly or a lewdnez
   off rebawdez   C
ii. A foly of rebawdes   Dg*

171. Roes / Roebucks
i. A bevy of roes   Addl
   A beuy of roos   Adv
   A beuy off rooz   C
   A bevy of rooys   Dg
   A bewy of roys   Rg
   A beuy of roys   Eg
   A bevee of roys   H
   A beve or rooys   L
   A beuy of rooes   Ha
   A bevy of roes   Harl
   A beuye of roos   HSG
   A bevy of roys   Pp
   A beuy of roes   Rd
   A beuy of roos   StA
ii. A bevy off rossys   Pl
   A bevy of rossys   Prk
iii. A beve of robukes   T

172. Rooks
i. A byldynge of rookys   Eg
   A byldyng of rooks   HSG
   A byldyng off rokeys   Pl
   A byldynge of rookys   Prk
   A byldyng of rokys   Pp
   A byldynge of rokes   Rd
   A beldyng of rookes   StA
   A bildynge of rukes   T
ii. A beloyng of rokes   W
iii. [A] byggyng of rockes
    or crowes   Adv

173. Scholars
[A] scole of scolers   HSG

174. Scots
A dysworschyp of Scottes   Adv
A disworship of Scottis   StA,
A dysworshyppe of Scottes   W

175. Sergeants
A sotelty of sergeauntis   StA

176. Servants
i. An obecyence of ser*u*andys   Pp
   A nobbecians of ser*u*antes   Rd
   An obeisians of ser*u*auntis   StA
   A nobbeysaunce of ser*u*ante   T
   An ob‹b›esyaunce of seruauntes   W
ii. An obedience of ser*u*antes   Adv
   A obedyens of seruandys   Eg

177. Sewers
i. A credens of sewers   Rd
   A credens of seweris   StA
ii. A devydyng of sewers   Adv

178. Sheep
i. A flocke of schepe   Adv
   A flokke off shepe   C
   A flocke of schepe   Eg
   A floke of schepe   H
   A flock of shepe   L
   A flok of schyp   Ha
   A floke of shepe   Harl
   A flock of shepe   HSG
   A floke off schepe   Pl
   A floke of schepe   Prk
   A flocke of schepe   Pp

(*continued overleaf*)

172.iii. Adv A] *om*   173 HSG A] *om*   176 W obbesyaunce] ?oblesyaunce

A flok of shepe	Rd
A flocke of shepe	*St*A
A floke of shepe	T
A flok of shepe	W
ii. A flok of chepe	Dg
A [f]locke of chepe	Rg

179. Sheldrakes

i. A doppyng of scheldrakys	H
ii. A drowping of sheldrakis	L

(*See also* Herles)

180. Shipmen

A venture of schippemen	Pp

181. Shoe-turners

A plocke of shoturneris	*St*A
A plu[k]e of schoturne	W

(*See also* Cobblers)

182. Shrews
[i.e. rogues]

A rysyng of rebellez or of shrewez	C

183. Silver

i. A mace or a verge of sylu*er*	C
ii. A mace of silu*er*	Dg*

184. Singers

i. A musyn of syngars	Adv
A musyon*e* of syngers	T
ii. A mvsycion of synger‹s›	L
A musycion of syngers	Pp

185. Snipes

i. A walke of snytys	Eg
A walke of snytes	*HSG*
A walke off snytys	Pl
A walke of snyttys	Prk
A walke of snytes	Pp
A walke of snytes	Rd
A walke of snytis	*St*A
A walke of snytes	T
A walke of snytes	W
ii. A fall of snypys	Adv

186. Soldiers

i. A bost of sowgeers	Adv
[A] boste of souldyours	*HSG*
A boste off sawdyarys	Pl
A bost of sovdears	Prk
A boste of sawdiers	Rd
A boost of saudiouris	*St*A
A boste of sawdyers	T
A boste of sawdyers	W
ii. A blast of sowdyurs	Pp

187. Sots
[i.e. fools]

A disworschyp of sot*es*	Rd

188. Souters
[i.e. cobblers]

A blecche of sowters	*HSG*
A blecche of sowters	LJ
A bleche of soutres	Rd
A bleche of sowteris	*St*A
A blea[c]he of sowters	W

---

178 Rg flocke] slocke *(crossbar omitted)* 181 W pluke] plube 184 L] *added by second scribe*, syngers] *letter lost through trimming of leaf* 186 *HSG* A] *om* 188 W bleache] bleahe

189. Spaniels

A cowpull of spayneel*es*	Adv
A copylle of spaynellys	Eg
A copill of spaynels	HSG
A copulle off spaynelys	Pl
A covpul of spannelis	Prk
A copyll of spanyels	Pp
A copyll*e* of spaynell*es*	Rd
A coupull of spaynellis	StA
A cowpyl of spanels	T
A cople of spanell*es*	W

190. Sparrows

An host of sparow*es*	Adv
An hoste of sparowz	C
A hoost of sparovns	Dg
A hoste of sparowys	Rg
A oste of sparowys	Eg
A ost of sparowys	H
A oste of sparowis	L
A hoste of sparowes	Ha
A ost of sparowys	Harl
An hoost of sparowes	HSG
A oste off sparowys	Pl
A hoste of sparrovs	Prk
An ost of sparouse	Pp
A noste of sp*a*rous	Rd
An ost of sparowis	StA
A nost of sparows	T
An [oste] of sparows	W

191. Squires

A route of squyers	C

192. Stars / Starlings

i.
A murmuracyon of starys	Eg
A murmerac*i*on of stares	HSG
A mormerasyo*n* off starys	Pl
A mormeracyon*e* of staris	Prk
A murmuracou*n* of starys	Pp
A m*ur*muracio*n*e of stares	Rd
A murmuracion of stares	StA
A m*ur*m*u*racio*n*e of stares	T
A murmuracon of stares	W

ii.
A murmuracion of sterlyng*es*	Adv

iii.
A chateryng of stares	C
A chateryng of stares	Dg
A chateryng*e* of starys	Rg
A chaterynge of staris	L

iv.
A chateryng of sterlyngys	H

v.
A chiteryng of stares	Ha

vi.
A claterynge of staris	Harl

193. Stewards (of House)

i.
A prouision of stywardes	Adv
A preuysyon of stywardysse	Eg
A provision of steward*es*	Pp
A p*ro*[v]icio*ne* of steward*es*	T

ii.
A p[ro]uisio*ne* of stuardes of howse	Rd
A p*ro*uision of steward*i*s of hous	StA

194. Stots
[i.e. disreputable women]

A disworship of stottes	HSG
A disworship of stottes	LJ
A dysoworchyp of stottys	Pl
A dysworschype of stottys	Prk
A dysworschip of stott*es*	Pp
A diswyrschepe of stottes	T

---

189 Rd spaynelles] a *super* preceding phrase in the MS, An oste of men scribe omits stroke through descender *of* p   190 W oste] *omitted by scribe, here supplied from the*   193 T provicione] probicione Rd prouisione]

195. Subtleties

A non*cr*edibilite of soteltes   Rd

196. Summoners

i. A nontrouthe of su*m*ners   Rd
    A nonetrewyth of su*m*ners   T

ii. A vntrowth of su*m*ners   Adv
    A vntrowth of sumners   Pp
    An vntrouth of sompneris   StA

197. Swallows

i. A flyght of swalow*es*   Adv
    A flyght of swaloez   C
    A fly3ght*e* of swalowes   Dg
    A flyth [of] swaleus   Rg
    A flyght of swalys   Eg
    A flyght of swalows   Ha
    A flyght of swalowys   Harl
    A flyth of swalous   Rd
    A flight of swalowes   StA
    A flight of sualous   T
    A flyght of swalowes   W

ii. A slyght of swallous   Pp

198. Swans

i. A herde of swa*n*nez   C
    A herde of swa*n*nes   Dg*
    A herde of swannys   Eg
    An herde of swannys   HSG
    A herde off swanys   Pl
    A herd of swannys   Prk
    A herde of swannys   Pp
    A herd of s[w]annes   Rd
    An herde of swannys   StA
    A herde of swa*n*nes   T
    An herde of swannys   W

ii. A teme of swans   Adv
    A teeme of swa*n*nes   Dg
    A teme of swannys   Rg
    A teme of swa*n*nys   H
    A teme of swannes   L
    A teme of swa*n*nes   Ha
    A teme of swannes   Harl

199. Swine

A sowndyr of swyne   Rg

(*See also* Swine, Wild)

200. Swine, Tame

A dryfte of tame swyne   Eg
A drifte of tame swyn   HSG
A dryfte off tame swyne   Pl
A dryfte of tame swyne   Prk
A dryfte of tame swyne   Pp
A dryft of tame swyne   StA
A dryfte of tame swyne   T
A dryft of tame swyne   W

201. Swine, Wild

i. A sownder of wylde swyne   Adv
    A sound*er* off wyld swyne   C
    A sovnder of wylde swyne   Dg
    A sovneder of wyld swyn   H
    A sundyr of wylde swyne   Eg
    A sundir of wyld swyn   Ha
    A sowndir*e* of wylde swyne   Harl
    A sondre of wilde swyn   HSG
    A sonder off wylde swyne   Pl
    A sondyr*e* of wyld swyne   Prk
    A sowndyr of wylde swyne   Pp
    A sondr*e* of wyld swyne   Rd
    A soundre of wilde swyne   StA
    A sondre of wilde swyne   T
    A sondre of wilde ‹s›vyne   W

---

196 Pp vntrowth] vn trowth   197.i. Rg of] *om*   ii. Pp slyght] *error for* flyght, *but written with round* s   198 Rd herd of swannes] herd *written super*, sannes   201.i. Adv wylde swyne] wyldeswyne   T wilde swyne] wildeswyne   W wilde svyne] wilde‹ss›vyne

APPENDIX I

ii. A gendir of wild swyne   L
iii. A dryfte of wylde swyne   Adv

202. Tailors
i. A dysgesyng*e* of taylers   Rd
    A disgysyng of taylours   St*A*
ii. A proude-shewyng of taloris   St*A*

203. Tapsters
A promys of tapsters   Adv
A promys of tapsterysse   Eg
A promesse of tapsters   *H*SG
A promesse of tapst*er*s   L*J*
A promes off tapstarys   Pl
A pro*mm*es of tappestrs   Prk
A promys of tap[s]ters   Pp
A p*ro*mise of tapsters   Rd
A promyse of tapsteris   St*A*
A promes of tapsters   T
A p*ro*myse of tapsters   W

204. Taverners
An glosyng of tau*er*ners   Adv
A glosyng of tauernerysse   Eg
[A] glosyng of tauerners   *H*SG
A glosyng of taverners   Pp
A glosyng*e* of tau*er*ners   Rd
A glosyng of tauerneris   St*A*
A glosyng*e* of tau*er*ners   T
A glosyng of taverners   W

205. Teals
i. A spryng of teales   Adv
    A sprynge of teles   Dg
    A sprynge of telys   Rg
    A sprynge of telys   Eg
    A spryng of telys   H

A sprynge of telis   L
A spryng of teles   Ha
A sprynge of telis   Harl
A spryng of teeles   *H*SG
A spryng off tellys   Pl
A spryng of teyllys   Prk
A spryng of telys   Pp
A sprynge of teles   Rd
A sprynge of telis   St*A*
A sprynge of teles   T
A spryng of telys   W
ii. A turbe or a spryng of teles   C
iii. A turbe of teles   Dg*

206. Teeth (The)
i. A rage of teth   Pp
    A rage of tethe   Rd
    A rage of teth   T
ii. A rage of the teethe   St*A*

207. Thieves
i. A sculke of theu*e*s   Adv
    A sckulke of thefes   Dg
    A sculke of thewes   Rg
    A sculke of theuys   H
    A skulke of thevis   L
    A skulke of theues   *H*SG
    A scolke off thevys   Pl
    A skolke of thewys   Prk
    A sculke of theues   Rd
    A skulke of theuys   St*A*
    A sculke of theues   T
    A skulke of thevys   W
ii. A denne off theves   C
    A denne of thefes   Dg*

201.iii. Adv wylde swyne] wyldeswyne   203 Pp tapsters] tapfters   204 Adv An] *add* eloq *canc*   *H*SG A] *om*   T glosynge] *olim* glasynge, a *canc and* o *added super; in margin,* le lo   206 T of] *add* th *canc*

208. Threshers

i.	A thrave of thressars	Adv
	A thraue of thresshers	HSG
	A thraue of thresshers	LJ
	A thrave off thrachearys	Pl
	A thraue of throsheris	StA
	A [t]hrawe of thressers	T
	A th[r]awe of tresshers	W
ii.	A tharfe of þreysschars	Prk
iii.	A tawght of threschers	Pp
iv.	A barne of tharshsers	Rd

209. Throstles

A mutacion [...]	HSG
A mewtasyon off threstylys	Pl
A mutacyone of þrestyllys	Prk
A mutacoun of thristelys	W

210. Tinkers

A wondryng of tynkars	Adv
A wondryng of tynkkers	Pp
A wondrynge of tynkers	Rd
A wonderyng of tynkeris	StA
A wonderyng of tynkers	W

211. Triaclers

i.	A poysone of triaclers	Rd
	A poysyne of treaclers	T
	A poyson of treaclrers	W
ii.	A poysonyng of tryaclars	Adv
iii.	A provision of tryakullers	Pp

212. Turtle(dove)s

i.	A duell of turtyls	Pp
	A duell of turtillis	StA
	A dule of turtyls	T
	A duell of turtelys	W
ii.	A dole of turtyles dowes	Adv
iii.	A petuysnys off tyrtylys	Pl
	A pyttyvsnys of turtyllys	Prk
iv.	A truluff of tertyll	C
	A trewlove of turteles	Dg
	A trewloufe of turtyllys	H
	A trewloue of turtelis	L
	A trewloue of turteles	Ha
	A treweloue of turtelis	Harl
	A trewloue of turtellys	Rd
v.	A trewloue of turtuldowys	Rg

213. Ushers

i.	A sete of huscherysse	Eg
	A sete of ischers	Pp
	A sete of vssheris	StA
	A seete of vsshers	T
ii.	A fete of vshers	Rd

214. Vicars

A prudence of vycarres	Adv
A prudens of vycarysse	Eg
A prudence of vicarys	Pp
A prudens of vygares	Rd
A prudens of vikeris	StA
A prudens of vicars	T

215. Wants
[i.e. moles]

A labour of wantys	Pp

(See also Moles, Mouldwarps)

216. Weldefares

An haunt of weldefares	W

---

208 T thrawe] chrawe   W thrawe] thawe   209 HSG] phrase left incomplete by compositor
212 Harl treweloue] trewe loue   Rd trewloue] trew loue

217. Whelps

A lytt*er* of whelp*es*	Adv
A lyttur of whelpys	Eg
A lytter of whelpes	*HSG*
A letur off whelpys	Pl
A lytter*e* of whelpus	Prk
A littyr of whelpys	Pp
A litter of welpis	*StA*
A lyter of whelpes	T
A littre of wh⟨e⟩lpys	W

218. Wives

i. [*olim?*] — Pp
   A nonpaciens of wyues — Rd
   A noonpaciens of wyues — *StA*
   A nonpaciens of wyue — T
ii. An impacience of wyves — Adv

219. Wolves (Wild)

i.
A rowte of wolues	Adv
A route of wolues	C
A rovte of wolffes	Dg
A rowte of wolfys	H
A rowte of wolues	L
A rowt of wolfes	Ha
A route of wolfis	Harl
A rowte of wolues	*HSG*
A rowte off wolleuys	Pl
A rovte of woluys	Prk
A rowte of woluys	Pp
A rowte of wolfes	Rd
A route of woluess	*StA*
A route of wolves	T
A rowte of wolves	W

ii. A rawte of woluys — Rg
iii. A rowte of wylde wolfys — Eg

220. Women

i.
A gagyll of women	*HSG*
A gagull off wmen	Pl
A gagulle of wemene	Prk
A gagall*e* of wymmen*e*	Rd
A gagle of women	*StA*
A gagle of wyme*n*	T
A gagle of women	W

ii.
A gagelynge of woemen	Dg
A gagelyng*e* of wommen	Rg
A gagyllyng of wome*n*	H
A gagelinge of women	L
A gagelyng of wemen	Ha
A gaglyng of wemen	Pp

iii. A gayling of wemen — Adv

iv. A co*m*pany or a bablyng off women — C

v. A feleschyp of wemen — Adv
   A felyschyp of wemen — Pp

221. Woodcocks

i.
A fall of wodecokk*es*	Adv
A falle of woodecockys	Eg
A falle of wodecoks	*HSG*
A falle off wodcokekys	Pl
A faulle of wodcokys	Prk
A falle of wodecokkys	Pp
A falle of wodekokys	Rd
A fall of woodecockis	*StA*
A fall of wodcokes	T
A fall of wodecokkes	W

ii. A daryng of wodcokk*es* — C

222. Woodwalls

A discencion of wodewalis — *HSG*

---

217 W whelpys] e *indistinct* 218 Pp] *a line expunged in the MS where this phrase would usually be found* 221 Eg woodecockys] woode cockys Pp wodecokkys] wode cokkys

223. Wooers
A wanhope of w⟨o⟩uers	W

224. Wrens
An herd of wrennes	Addl
An herd of wrennes	Adv
A herd of wre*nn*ez	C
A heerde of wrannes	Dg
A herde of wrannys	Rg
A herde of wrennys	H
A herde of wrennes	L
A herde of wrennes	Ha
A heerde of wrennys	Harl
An herde of wrennys	HSG
A herde off wranys	Pl
A herd of wrennys	Prk
A herde of wrannys	Pp
A herd of wrannes	Rd
An herde of wrennys	StA
A herde of w*r*ennes	T
An herde of wranes	W

225. Writers
A worship of writeris	StA

226. Wypes [i.e. lapwings]
A dysseyt of wypes	Adv
A disseyet of wypes	T

(*See also* Lapwings)

227. Yeomen
i.	A felyschyppe of yemen	Eg
	A felouship of yomen	HSG
	A fellychype off yemen	Pl
	A feyllyschype of yovmeyne	Prk
	A felychipe of yome*n*	T
	A felesshipp of yomen	W
ii.	A felishippyng of yomen	StA
iii.	A felysypp*e* of yema[n]ri	Rd

228. Closing remarks
Explicit &c	C
ex p*ar*te p*r*eced[e]*n*ti	Dg
Lat catt*es* scrate carlys with sorow iwys. Lerne or be lewde – I tell þe thys.	
Explicit I. B.	H
Explicit	L
Explicit	HSG
¶ Here endeth a lytyll treatyse called the booke of curtesye or lytyll John. Enprynted atte westmoster.	LJ
Explicit Iulyan Barne	Pp
¶ Explicit	StA

---

223 W wouers] *o* indistinct   228 Dg precedenti] precedonti   H iwys] I wys

Index of Collective Nouns

In this Index, italic type is used for Middle English words that have not been modernised. This may indicate, variously, that no suitable modern term exists, that the modern reflex would be misleading, or that the meaning of a specific lexical item is uncertain or unusual. Where *v=u* and *y = i*, they are alphabetised accordingly.

abominable *sight* 136
bablyng 62, 220
badelyng 62
barn 208
barren 138
barrow 39
bawdyng 41
beloyng 172
bery 39
besynes 67, 72
bevy 99, 115, 117, 164, 171
bewperis 76
byggyng 49, 172
blast 105, 186
bleche 188
blush 16
boast 186
brace 87, 103
briʒt 7
brood 95, 156
building 172
burden 138
cast 17, 93
cete 88
charge 47, 51
charm 10
chattering 33, 153, 192
chirm 69, 82
chirming 82
chittering 192
clattering 33, 58, 192
cloder, clowder, cludder 23, 25, 29

cluster 25, 29, 34, 86, 113, 142
cluther 34
company 77, 79, 115, 130
company or a babbling 220
congregation 151, 156
converting 159
couple 104, 189
couple or pair 15
court 7
covert 29, 42
covey 148
cowardness 55
credence 177
damning 111
daryng 221
deceit 88, 116, 131, 226
den 89, 207
desserte 116
destruction 30
devoutness 136
dignity 24
diligence 133
discencion 222
discreetness 161
discretion 161
disguising 202
dyspetenesse 161
dissimulation 12
disworship 174, 187, 194
dividing 177
diving 4
doctrine 60

dole 212
don, down, dunne 89
dow 165
dowte, dovt 30
doppyng 97, 179
draught 22
drift 71, 139, 200, 201
dryvyng 4
dronkship 36
drowping 179
drove 9, 89, 139
drunkenness, see *dronkship*
duell 212
earth 75
eloquence 115, 118
enbrewyng, see *unbrewyng*
exalting 117
exaltation 117
example 129
excusion 143
execution 143
faith 131
fall 185, 221
farrowing 88
faytre 11
felishippyng 227
fellowship 220, 227
fester 18
fete 213
fighting 11
flight 44, 61, 84, 117, 197
flock 68, 117, 121, 178
flush 125
folly (or lewdness) 170
(great) *foyson* 45
franchype 134
franchise 134
frape 35
fraudysnes 134

fraunch 134
frowardnes 154
gaggle 77, 220
gaggling 77, 85, 220
gayling 77, 107, 220
garule 95
gendir 201
glorifying 120
glorynge 29
glosyng 204
good-advice 20
goring 21
grale 95
great-science 127
hardlyng 87
harras 38, 90, 100, 126
hastiness 41
haunt 156, 216
herd 19, 48, 53, 59, 68, 89, 90, 92,
   198, 224
holiness 141
host 130, 190
huske 89
iee, iye, ye 152
impatience 218
in his see 157
kennel 103, 166
kennette 166
kerff 146
kindle 31
knowledge 96
labour 135, 137, 215
lash 26
laughter 102
leap 119, 122
leash 87, 93, 132
lesyng 147
lewdness 170
litter 217

APPENDIX I

lordship 136
lure 65, 124
lying 147
mace (or verge) 183
malapertness 150
melody 91
mightiness 114
misbeleue 145
morthere 49
multiplying 106
murder, see *morthere*
murmuration 192
musycion 184
musyn 184
muster 149
mutation 209
mute 103
nest 66, 165
never-thriving 110
nye 152
noncredibilite 50, 195
nonpaciens 218
nontrouthe 196
number 106
numbering 27
obedience 176
obeisians 176
observance 37, 98
ouerthryngyng 110
paas, *pase* 3
pack 103
paddling 62, 95
peep, *pype* 12, 32
pympe 12, 32
piteousness 212
pity 163
pluck 36, 181
poison(ing) 211
pontifical 160, 161, 162

pontificality 160
pontificateness 160
posse 3
poverty 91, 155
press 35, 161
pride 122
promise 203
proud-showing 202
provision 193, 211
prudence 214
rabble 18
rafull 16, 113
rage 38, 124, 206
ragg 38, 74
rascal 16, 167
rawte 219
ray 114
riches, *ryches* 108, 128
rising 169, 182
rout 7, 20, 78, 79, 114, 191, 219
sadnes 109
safeguard 158
sawte, *sawtte* (57), 88, 122
school 35, 70, 173
scolding 112
scoue 70
scrape 6
sedent 109
seet 40, 213
sentence 109
shrewdness 2
siege 13, 28, 99
sight 39, 88, (136)
singular 14, 16
skulk 75, 76, 207
slawnys 8
sleuth 8
sloth 8
smear 54

solace (*solaz*) 83
somme 81
sorde, sourde 125
sort, sorth 125
sotelty 175
sounder 199, 201
sowse 122
sowte, sawt 122
spring 205
squat 57
stalk 73
stalyn 101
state 161, 162
stud 126
suffrage 158
superfluity 141
surt 125
sute 123, 125
swarm 10
swerde 125
tabernacle 5
tawght 208
team 56, 62, 63, 144, 198
temperance 41
tharfe 208
thongh 7
thrave 208
threat 47, 52
threatening 47
thrum 87
tiding, *tydyngys* 153
trace 89
tremynge 82
trenket 43, 46
trete, triete 47
trip 32, 80, 89, 95
troth 7
true-love 212
turbe (or spring) 205

unbreaking 27
vnbrewyng 27
vncredibilite 50
unkindness 168
untruth 196
venture 180
verge 183
walk 185
wandering 64, 210
wanhope 223
watch 140
waywardness 94, 154
wonderyng, see *wandering*
worship 225

COLLECTIVE NOUNS — NOTES

As I argue in the main Introduction ('Development of the *J.B. Treatise*'), the lists of phrases containing collective nouns constitute one of the central components of the *J.B. Treatise* in its many different forms. While these lists have no clearly traceable ancestry, we may observe that broadly similar lists were compiled from as early as the 13th century for Anglo-Norman primers, notably Walter de Bibbesworth's *Tretiz* (late 13th century),[1] *Nominale sive verbale* (*c*. 1340),[2] and the trilingual didactic poem *Femina* (1420),[3] all of which are referred to in the explanatory notes below. There are also brief lists of collectives in some sporting manuals, such as William Twiti's *The Art of Hunting* (*L'Art de venerie*), *Prince Edward's Book of Hawking*, and its corrupt derivative *The Tretyse off Hawkyng*. Some phrases, it will be found, are identical in all these disparate sources, but there are also certain notable discrepancies between the J.B. lists and the others, which suggest that the J.B. lists developed as a separate, parallel tradition, which itself bifurcated into the long and short J.B. versions of these phrases. In the case of C and Dg* only, there is evidence of cross-fertilisation from the Anglo-Norman lists by way of texts that have yet to be discovered.

Like the brief lists of collectives in the sporting manuals cited above, the contents and structure of the J.B. lists suggest strongly that they probably arose from the desire to assemble the terms used by hunters, fowlers and falconers for their quarries seen as a plurality, or in abundance. This may be deduced from the fact that deer and game birds feature prominently among the lists' opening items. These are interspersed with phrases referring to other birds and animals, as well as humans when the same collectives are used of them. Thus, in H, we find the

---

[1] 'The Treatise of Walter de Biblesworth' [*sic*], in *A Volume of Vocabularies*, ed. Thomas Wright (London, 1857), pp. 142–74 (BL, MS Arundel 220); Annie Owen, *Le traité de Walter de Bibbesworth sur la langue française* (Paris, 1929) (CUL, MS Gg.1.1). Except where otherwise indicated, all my references are to the most recent edition of the Cambridge manuscript: Walter de Bibbesworth, *Le tretiz*, ed. William Rothwell, A-NTS, Plain Texts Series 6 (London, 1990).

[2] *Nominale sive verbale* (CUL MS Ee.4.20), ed. W.W. Skeat, *TPS*, 25:3 (1906), pp. 1*–50*.

[3] *Femina: Now First Printed from a Unique MS. in the Library of Trinity College, Cambridge*, ed. William Aldis Wright, The Roxburghe Club (Cambridge, 1909). This work has been newly edited by William Rothwell for the Anglo-Norman On-Line Hub (2005): <www.anglo-norman.net/texts/femina.pdf>.

sequence: 'A herd of harts ... a herd of curlews ... A bevy of roes ... a bevy of ladies'. It would seem that the medieval predilection for cataloguing and ordering then led to a rapid expansion of these lists beyond their initial purpose.

The next stage in the development of these lists (especially the long versions) is that compiling them seems to have become something of a joke, with ever more imaginative collectives being invented for both animals and humans, especially where opportunities for unflattering comparisons presented themselves, as in 'a gaggle of geese / a gaggle of women'. The lists grew as they might in a 19th-century parlour game, with results ranging from the sardonic and even insulting ('a superfluity of nuns') to the ingenious ('a damning of jurors'). The game has remained popular into modern times, with writers, artists, and logophiles of all persuasions assembling new versions, or even inventing contemporary additions of their own.[1] And yet, underlying even some of the more amusing phrases, a serious purpose can be discerned: the attempt to categorise each group in terms of its essential characteristics. The phrase 'a pride of lions' is now so familiar that we are easily inured to its metaphoric implications. But when it is followed by 'a leap of leopards, a sloth of bears, a shrewdness of apes', the thrust of the original allusion appears fresh again.

In the notes that follow I refer frequently to the groundbreaking work of John Hodgkin, who undertook the first serious study of collective nouns in several J.B. witnesses and derivative printed books down to the 19th century ('Terms I', 1909). Hodgkin's project was vast in scope and has never been comprehensively updated, let alone equalled. Yet it is not without its problems, perhaps chief among them being Hodgin's verdict that 'the majority of [the collectives] are not company terms, and ... there are no solid grounds for supposing them to be such' ('Terms I', p. 5). Such a view could not fail to colour the author's approach to his subject.

Hodgkin was also overly eager to find sarcasm in these terms wherever possible, and to reject as fundamentally flawed those phrases that apply collectives to non-gregarious people and animals (such as hermits and badgers), since logic dictates that they exist in isolation and are not found in large numbers. But Hodgkin exhibits greater inflexibility than many of the phrases he analyses. An adult badger may indeed be a solitary animal by nature, but the *J.B. Treatise* can be seen as offering a company term for those occasions where several badgers are found together, as perhaps a mother and young in their set. At other times, it has to be admitted that a J.B. collective is simply perverse, as in 'a singular of boars', even allowing for the obvious wordplay on *sanglier*. In spite of such occasional paradoxes, I believe

---

[1] See, for example, James Lipton, *An Exaltation of Larks or, The Venereal Game*, 2nd edn (Harmondsworth, 1977); Steve Palin, *A Dissimulation of Birds* (London, 1998), and *A Menagerie of Animals* (Liverpool, 2000); Mark Faulkner et al., *A Compendium of Collective Nouns: From An Armory of Aardvarks to A Zeal of Zebras* (San Francisco, 2013); Samuel Fanous, Thomas Bewick and Bill Oddie, *A Conspiracy of Ravens: A Compendium of Collective Nouns for Birds* (Oxford, 2014).

it would be wrong to cast doubt on the larger issue of whether these lists contain company terms at all, or to impugn their integrity as a whole.

Hodgkin ('Terms I') printed and commented on the collective nouns in the following J.B. witnesses: Addl, Dg, Eg, H, Harl, *HSG, LJ*, Prk, Rg, *StA*. (He also reprinted ('Terms I', pp. 58–9) the list of 50 collectives that Francis Junius recorded in his posthumously published *Etymologicum Anglicanum* (Oxford, 1743), from an unidentified manuscript. Since there is nothing unusual in Junius's list, and the identity of the manuscript is unknown, I have not included it in the present study.)

Subsequently, Hope E. Allen ('Fifteenth-century associations') published the collectives in Rd, and Rachel Corner ('More terms') those in C, Dg* and L. Rachel Hands (née Corner) later provided a thorough commentary on the collectives in *StA* in her facsimile edition of that incunable (*EHH*), and Tom Burton published the collectives of Pp with commentary: 'Late fifteenth-century "terms of association" in MS. Pepys 1047', *N&Q*, 25 (1978), 7–12 (hereafter, 'Terms'). Appearing for the first time in this collation are Adv, Ha, Pl, T and W.

1 The headings in Eg and T are noteworthy for explicitly associating these terms with the sport of hunting.

2 *schrewdnesse* 'wickedness, depravity, maliciousness', perhaps passing into the weaker sense of 'mischievousness', 'naughtiness'; see *MED*, *shreuednesse* n. Early senses of this word, derived from the adjective *shreued*, are invariably pejorative, the association with astuteness or sagacity emerging only during the later 16th century, as can be seen in *OED*, s.v. *shrewdness* n.

3 *pase, passe* Interpreted by Hodgkin ('Terms I', pp. 21–2) as referring to the 'walk', 'track' or customary path followed by an ass to its feeding grounds or elsewhere. His main evidence comes from Cotgrave's *Dictionarie* of 1611, in which the noun *passée* is given the general gloss 'A passage, course, passing along', and, when used in the phrase *Les passées d'un Cerf*, the particularised sense of 'His racke, or passages; the places which he has gone through or by'. Hodgkin also cites a 15th-century *Nominale*, which has: 'Hic Passus, a rayke' (ME *raike* = 'a course, passage' <ON); see Thomas Wright, *Anglo-Saxon and Old English Vocabularies*, 2nd edn, rev. Richard Paul Wülcker, 2 vols (London, 1884), I, 679. Hands offers the more plausible suggestion that *pase* 'refers simply to the characteristic speed of the animal', i.e. its plodding gait, and so means 'a (slow) pace' (*EHH*, p. 161/1984n) – which accords with *MED*, s.v. *pase* n.(1) 2a.

(ii) *posse* Most likely, scribal misreading of *passe*, but since *posse* is also recorded as a variant of *post*, it is not impossible that the phrase is intended to evoke an image of several asses tied to a post or stave; see *MED*, s.v. *post* n.(1).

4 Although sometimes identified with the widgeon, the exact identity of the atteal is obscure. It appears to be a small duck of some kind, wintering in the Shetland and Orkney Islands: see *OED, atteal* n.; *MED, autele* n.; also, W.B. Lockwood, *The Oxford Book of British Bird Names* (Oxford, 1984), s.v. *Atteal*. The collective indicates the bird's characteristic action: that of diving below the surface, a motion also associated with the sheldrake (no. 179).

(ii) *dryvyng* Probably scribal error for *dyvyng*, perhaps inspired by the notion of hunting for waterfowl by 'driving' them into nets, or into the air for a falconer.

5 *tabernacle* The principal senses of this word, as recorded by the *MED* (s.v. *tabernacle* n. 1.) are 'a movable dwelling', 'tent', 'hut' and the like; leading to a speculative gloss for the J.B. phrase of 'booth, stall', with reference to such a stand or enclosure set up by a vendor in a market. As Hodkin points out ('Terms I', no. 200), bakers were required to sell their bread at the marketplace – presumably in a stall – and forbidden to sell it at the bakehouse.

6 *scrape* The term summons up a range of unpleasant ideas associated with shaving. It could indicate the 'scraping away' (of skin) that results in razor burn, especially when caused by a blunt razor; alternatively, it can suggest a 'scratch, scatching', or a 'cut', or even a 'laceration', from being shaved by a clumsy barber. See *MED, scrapen* v. 1. (a), 2. (e).

7 (i) *trothe* Possibly, 'fidelity', 'allegiance', with reference to the pledge of fealty taken by lords temporal at the coronation of a monarch; see Hodgkin, 'Terms I', p. 38, and no. 147 below. T.L. Burton suggests that such an allusion to loyalty could have been intended sarcastically, with the idea of rebellious – rather than loyal – barons in mind: 'Terms'; p. 10/92n. On the other hand, the word could also evoke a general sense of moral virtue, as symbolised by Gawain's pentangle 'In bytoknyng of trawþe' (*SGGK*, 625 and 619–665). According to *MED*, the form *trought* in Eg is an acceptable variant of ME *treuth*.

(ii) *briȝt* ?'brightness' = 'brilliance, resplendence'. The intended meaning is uncertain, but there may be a parallel with the phrase 'a ray of knights' (no. 114. iii), if *ray* is interpreted as 'a ray of light'. Among the AN lists, both *Nominale* (p. 14) and *Femina* (p. 4) give the collective for barons as *brut* – glossed by *MED* (s.v. *bruit* n.) as 'fame, renown', but also 'commotion, tumult'. (The two senses are closely connected, since the type of renown referred to here was often won through the commotion of battle.) It is possible that the J.B. terms could have developed through modification of AN *brut, brust* (*q.v.* in *A-ND*).

In MS T this word appears as *brizt*, with a tail-less Roman *z* that cannot be confused with the grapheme yogh. At some point in the transmission of this word, yogh must have been read as a tailed *z*, and then modified to Roman *z*.

(iii) *route* 'host, company', 'throng'; the word often has connotations of an unlawful assembly, which may or may not be intended here; see *MED, route* n.(1). Burton ('Terms', p. 10/92n) suggests that the word in Pp could represent a corruption of the AN collective *brut, bruit*, referred to in (ii) above, through loss of initial *b*.

(iv) *corte* 'court' – a self-explanatory allusion.

(v) *thongh* Possibly, as Hands suggests (*EHH*, p. 156/1949n), a compositor's scrambling of *troth*, which is how it is treated by *MED*, s.v. *treuth*, n. 15a. But the word could equally be an error for *throng*, a word with strong military connotations (see *MED, throng* n.), or it could refer to the legendary 'thong' of oxhide used for demarcating an area of land (*MED, thong* n. 2c); hence, a 'demesne'.

8 Although it is tempting to interpret *slouth* and *sleuth* as 'sloth', with reference to the bear's long winter hibernation, the intended sense here is more likely to be the more neutral 'slowness, sluggishness' – rendered *slawnys* in Pp. Although identical in meaning, *slouth* and *sleuth* have different origins. *Sleuth* derives from OE *slæwþ*, while *slouth* is a later construction formed on the ME adjective *slou* (<OE *slaw*), under influence of *sleuth*. See *MED*, s.vv. *sleuthe* n.; *slouthe* n.

9 *drove* 'herd' (<OE *draf*), referring to animals that are driven, with the end-noun *beestes* 'beasts' indicating domesticated farm animals: here, probably cattle. Cf. 'a drove / drift of neat' (no. 139).

10 (ii) *charme* 'buzzing, humming'; a variant of *chirm*, the collective used of finches and goldfinches (nos 69, 82).

11 (i) *fyʒttynge* Although Hodgkin ('Terms I', no. 219) pleads for the sense 'lying', from ME *fiton* (var. *fyttyn, fytten*) 'an untruth, a falsehood', the medial -*ʒ*- or -*gh*- in most instances suggests that 'fighting' is the intended meaning here (though see Pp's *faytre* below). Presumably, beggars were viewed as antagonistic rivals for whatever scraps they could find.

(ii) *faytre* a 'deception, fraud'; see *MED, faiterie* n. Hodgkin seems to have had an uncanny instinct about this phrase (see (i) above), since he did not know of the existence of Pp.

12 (i–iii) The collective here must refer to the habit of many birds, especially ground-dwelling species, of feigning injury or drawing attention to themselves in some other way in order to distract predators from their eggs or young. The same collective is applied to lapwings/wypes: nos 116, 226.

(iv) *pype* 'peep, chirp, squeak' (onomatopoeic) <AN *pipe, pipée*; see *MED, pipe* n.(3), and cf. the OF verb *piper*, glossed by Godefroy as 'pousser un petit cri'. In the AN lists, there is the phrase, 'pipee des oyseuz' (Bibbesworth, p. 8); 'pipe de oseaux ... a pipe of bryddys' (*Femina*, pp. 2–3).

(v) *pympe* Variant of *pype*; see *MED, pimpe* n. Chickens (no. 32) are also classed as a *py(m)pe*.

13 *sege* 'siege', with reference to the bittern's habit of standing motionless as it waits for a fish to swim within striking distance. The same collective is used of the heron (no. 99), which also hunts in this way. In Eg the phrases for bittern and heron are followed by *A sege vnto a castelle* (no. 28), which emphasises the notion of a long, patient wait.

14 (i) *syngler* Combines the senses of 'singler' ('loner') + *sanglier*, a full-grown wild boar, aged four years or more: one that has left the herd or 'sounder' to live on its own. See *BH*, 1314–16, and *CV*, 21–23: 'A when he [the boar] is of age of iiij ȝere, he schall departyn out of companye by kynde of age & schal gone alone; & when he is alone, he schall þen be called synguler for þe causes fore-seid'. ME *singler* derives from OF *sengler*, with influence from L *singularis*, adj. 'single, solitary'. See *OED*, *sanglier* n.; *MED*, *singler* n. The term is clearly incongruous as a collective noun, since the animal it refers to is by definition solitary.

(ii) *syngulerez* Apparently an attempt to create a plural form for a word that expresses singularity; see *MED*, *singuleres* n.

15 Hodgkin ('Terms I', no. 124) proposes plausibly that bottles may have been 'coupled', or tied together in pairs, for easy transportation slung over a horse's back: hence, 'a couple or pair'.

16 (i) *rascall* 'rabble, mob'; see *MED*, *rascaile* n. 2b.

(ii) *rafull* 'raffle' = 'rabble', 'riff-raff': *OED*, *raffle*, n.^{2}. For *MED*, the term is not so explicitly pejorative, and indicates merely 'A group of young men or boys': s.v. *rafle* n.(2). However, this dictionary also recognises the strong negative associations commonly evoked by the etymon *raf* n.(1). This phrase is undoubtedly a variant of the more usual formula 'a raffle of knaves' (no. 113), which occurs also in the same three J.B. sources.

(iii) *blush* The word is associated by both Hands (*EHH*, p. 159/1984n) and Hodgkin ('Terms I', no. 141) with involuntary blushing. However, the word also meant 'a look, glimpse', and may therefore be no more than a variant of the collective 'sight', used of conies, greys (badgers) and monks (nos 39, 88, 136). See *MED*, *blish* n.; *blishen* v. 3.

(iv) *boyes* Error for *bores* (see no. 14). I have included this phrase under the headword 'Boys' in case other texts are discovered repeating this error.

17 *cast* Indicates a particular quantity of bread: a ration, either for a meal or a day. See *MED*, *cast* n. 2d; Hodgkin, 'Terms I', no. 121; also, the account of hunters' rations in *The Boke of Curtasye*, lines 631–2: 'Þo vewter, two cast of brede he tase, / Two lesshe of grehoundes yf þat he hase' (*Babees Book*, p. 320).

18 (i) *festre* ?Error for *sestre*, a measure of beer or wine; see *MED*, *sester* n. (b), and Hodgkin, 'Terms I', no. 194, for examples. However, *festre* may have been intended, and in *StA* the word is printed with a capital *F* (and written with a minuscule *f* in Rd). Hands suggests that *festre* could be 'an allusion to the process of fermentation used by brewers' (*EHH*, p. 163/1989n); whereas *MED* associates it with a fistula or ulcerous sore: s.v. *festre* n.(2).

(ii) *rable* It is not immediately obvious why brewers should be assigned such a pejorative collective. Perhaps brewers, like their more bibulous customers, were inclined to overindulge and become unruly.

19 It is strange that this phrase appears only in the short lists of collectives, since it appears in embryonic form in the earliest lists of collective nouns for hunters, such as the question and answer of Twiti's *Art of Hunting*: 'How many herdes be there of bestes of venery?' / 'Sire, of hertis, of bisses ['hinds'], of bukkes & of doos. A soundre of wylde swyn; a beuy of roos.' (Twiti-C, 170–2; cf. Twiti-F, 184–6; *BH*, 1257–63).

20 (i) The original meaning of this phrase is obscure. Possibly it was devised as a deliberate and more respectful alternative to *route* (see (ii) following), with the suggestion that it was sage to follow the advice of the more illustrious burgesses – especially those who sat on the town council (see *MED*, *burgeis* n.). Or perhaps important burgesses had a reputation for wisdom, such as Chaucer's four guildsmen: 'Wel semed ech of hem a fair burgeys / To sitten in a yeldehalle on a deys. / Everich, for the wisdom that he kan, / Was shaply for to been an alderman' (*CT*, I.369–72). For a succinct account of the status and privileges of burgesses, see D.M. Palliser, 'Urban Society', in *Fifteenth-Century Attitudes: Perceptions of Society in Late Medieval England*, ed. Rosemary Horrox (Cambridge, 1994), pp. 132–49 (p. 139).

Pl is damaged at the point where this phrase occurs in Prk.

(ii) Cf. *Nominale*, which reads *Route de Burges* (p. 14), a phrase probably intended to convey the sense of an 'assembly, gathering', a 'company'. By the late 15th century, *route* had acquired the additional sense of 'a disorderly crowd', which may have rendered it too ambiguous for this context, thereby inspiring the alternative *good-awyse* in Prk. That some scribes were sensitive to such matters can be seen in the treatment of monks and nuns (nos 136, 141) in MS Harl. See also *MED*, *route* n.(1), senses 1, 3.

21 *goryng* Hands reads this as 'piercing, stabbing' (*EHH*, p. 163/1990n), and rejects Hodgkin's interpretation that it refers to butchers as being blood-splattered ('Terms I', no. 196) on the grounds that this sense did not emerge until the mid-16th century. But there is a cluster of words deriving from OE *gor*, 'dung, filth', that could be even more apt. The ME noun *gore* retained the primary meaning of its OE etymon, and was also used as a dismissive term for a worthless person. The related verb *goren* referred to the process of festering in wounds, as did the gerund *goring*; and the adjectival participle *gor-wounded* indicated the possession of a filthy or festering wound: see *MED*, *gore* n.(3); *goren* v.(2); *goring* ger. It therefore seems very likely that *StA*'s *goryng* could mean either 'filthiness', or 'putrefaction', with sarcastic reference to the insanitary conditions in which butchers worked, or the quality of their wares.

22 *draught* Probably, a 'drawing' (of liquor), though the sense a 'drinking, swallowing' is also possible; see *MED, draught*, n. 1c, 7a. The butler was the domestic official responsible for the cellar (the buttery, where butts of ale or wine were stored), and for serving liquor at table.

23 *cloder* 'clodder, cludder' = 'a clotted mass', 'a dense group'. See *MED*, s.v. *cloddre* n.; *cloddred* ppl.; *OED*, s.vv. *clodder*, n.; *cludder* n. This collective is usually reserved for carls and cats (nos 25, 29). It seems likely that *calvys* is an error for *cattys*.

24 *chanons* 'canons': clergymen belonging to a religious order, especially those living in a clergyhouse or cathedral.

25 (ii) *clowder* 'a dense group'; see note 23 above. *MED*, s.v. *carl* n., defines this phrase rather prosaically as 'a group of male persons'. The unflattering connotations of the collective suggest that one or more of the other senses of *carls* was intended: 'knaves, rascals, serfs, peasants', as with churls (no. 34.ii).

26 *lasche* 'lashing', with reference to the unrestrained use of a whip.

27 (i) *vmbrekyng* 'unbreaking' = 'breaking', 'dismembering'; hence, 'carving'. The prefix *um-* (*un-*) is redundant.

(ii) *nombrynge* 'numbering', probably in the sense of 'reckoning' or 'allocating'; a carver had to ensure that his division of each dish provided enough for everyone, according to his or her merit, at each table.

(iii) *vnbrewyng* Probably an error for *enbrewyng, embrewyng* = 'soiling', as in the injunction to young persons at table: 'But from embrowyng the clothe yee kepe clene' (*The Babees Book*, p. 6, line 147). A carver's work could presumably become quite messy. In John Russell's *Boke of Nurture*, the carver is explicitly enjoined to avoid soiling the table: 'enbrewe not youre table for þan ye do not ryght' (line 331). See also *MED, embreuen* v.

28 *sege* See note 13 above.

29 (i, ii, iv) *cludder, clowder*, etc. 'clodder, cludder', 'a dense group'; see note 23 above. As a collective noun for cats, the word suggests a family or group of cats lying together in a heap. It is curious that Eg explicitly proscribes the use of *cluster*, since this is precisely the term used in *HSG* (v).

Note that the collective in both T and W could easily be read as *clondre*, perhaps a felicitous neologism derived from *clondren*, 'to drone, hum', producing the sense 'a purring of cats'. See *MED, clondren* n. [*sic*]; also, *OED, clondre*, v. I am grateful to Mrs Hands for this intriguing suggestion.

(iii) *glorynge* 'glaring, staring'; also, 'glinting, gleaming' (presumably of cats' eyes); see *MED, gloren* v.; *OED, glore*, v.

(v) *cluster* NB the prohibition in Eg (ii) against this collective.
(vi) *cattes* Error for *cottes*, 'coots'; see no. 42. I have included this phrase under the headword 'Cats' in case other texts are discovered repeating this error.

30 (i) *dovt* 'horror, peril' (<OF *dote, doute*), indicating something to be feared; see *MED, doute* n. The destructiveness of wild cats, especially for poultry farmers, is well known, even today. This is to disagree with Hodgkin ('Terms I', no. 20), who reads the word as deriving from the verbal phrase *do out*, meaning 'to expel, extirpate, extinguish'; see *MED*, s.v. *don* v.(1) 6. (g); *OED*, s.v. *do* v., PV2 (phrasal verbs with adverbs). Typical citations in both dictionaries suggest that Hodgkin's argument is somewhat strained in this instance.

31 *kyndyll* 'kindle' = 'brood, litter'; the noun was used of the young or offspring of any animal, not necessarily only those that were born in litters; see *MED, kindel* n., and *kindelen* v.(2), 'to give birth'.

32 (i, ii) *pype, pympe* 'peep, chirp, squeak' (onomatopoeic); see note 12 (iv, v) above. The birds referred to here are not chickens in the modern sense, but their young, i.e. 'chicks'.

(iii) *tryppe* 'herd, flock' (<AF): see *MED, trippe* n.(2). In the J.B. lists of collectives, this term is usually reserved for goats (no. 80) and hares (no. 89), though in W we find it used of hens (no. 95), and here of chicks. The word is also found in the AN lists as the collective noun for sheep, as in *Nominale*: 'Vn tripe de berbis ... A trip of schepe' (p. 23). Hands gives some interesting examples of its wider usage: *EHH*, p. 156/1943n.

33 (i–ii) ME and EMnE *chough(e)* was used rather loosely for several smaller members of the crow family distinguished by their chattering calls, notably the jackdaw and the Cornish chough, both cliff-dwelling species. The alternative forms of the word – *choȝe, chouȝhe, chowȝe, chowe* – all point to its imitative origins. Either bird (jackdaw or chough) may be intended here, but perhaps the jackdaw is the more likely, given its tendency to nest in high buildings in close proximity to humans. This hypothesis is strengthened by Adv, which employs the same collective with the end-noun *dawes* (no. 58 below). Lockwood, *British Bird Names*, discusses the history of the word *Chough* (see s.v.); and see also Shakespeare's allusion to 'russet-pated choughs' (i.e. jackdaws) in *A Midsummer Night's Dream*, III.ii.21; Randle Holme, *The Academy of Armory* (Chester, 1688; repr. Menston, 1972), p. 248, col. 1: 'The *Jack-Daw*, or *Daw* ... In some places it is called a Caddesse or Choff'. Cf. *ibid.*, p. 247, col. 2, where Holme describes the '*Cornish Chough* proper'.

The collective *clattering* (cognate with OE *clatrung*, 'noise') indicates 'noisy chattering'; see *MED, clatering* ger. (c), and *clateren* v. 2. (a): 'To talk noisily, chatter, babble'. Cf. *Promptorium* (ed. Way), III, 76: 'C(h)yrpynge, or claterynge of byrdys ... Garritus'.

(ii) *chaterynge* Essentially synonymous with 'clattering' above, but apparently onomatopoeic in origin. See *MED*, *chatteren* v.

34 (i) This formulation is essentially synonymous with 'a cluster of carls' (no. 25); the end-noun probably refers to 'villeins', 'peasants', rather than just 'men'.

(ii) *cluther* 'clodder, cludder' = 'a dense group' (with negative associations); see note 23 above.

35 (i) *scole* 'school' (<OE *scol*, 'place of learning'). In the J.B. lists, the phrase 'a school of clerks' is usually paired with 'a *scole* of fish' (no. 70) for the purpose of paronomasia, the ME reflex deriving in the latter instance from an entirely different root (<OE *scolu*, 'shoal, multitude'). Such humorous juxtaposition occurs elsewhere in these lists; see e.g. falcons and maidens (nos 65, 124).

(ii) *prese* 'crowd, throng', 'multitude'. This collective is more often applied to priests (no. 161), probably for the sake of alliteration.

(iii) *frape* 'host, multitude', or 'mob, rabble'; see *MED, frape* n. (<OF *frap*). This is the term used by the AN lists; e.g. *Nominale: Frape de Clers* (p. 14).

36 (i) It is not clear why cobblers should have been singled out as representatives of drunkenness, though Hodgkin observes primly that alcoholic overindulgence is 'a habit that to this day is too prevalent amongst this class of workmen' ('Terms I', no. 210).

(ii) *plukke* 'pulling, tugging', probably referring to the cobbler's action of pulling tight the threads while sewing a shoe. See *MED*, s.vv. *plukken* v; *plukke* n.

37 The collective 'observance' is normally applied to hermits (see no. 98). Collegians, or members of a college, were presumably expected to observe their duties with the rigour associated with hermits. The noun *coligener* is not recorded by *MED*, and the earliest citation in *OED* is 1546 (s.v. *collegianer* n.).

38 (i) *rage* 'boistrousness, playfulness', with reference to the skittishness of young horses; see *MED, rage* n. 7. Girls ('maidens', no. 124) are also described collectively as 'a rage', presumably for displaying the same characteristics. In the group of texts cited here, the phrase that follows immediately after refers to the slow and steady pace of asses (no. 3), apparently so as to effect a humorous contrast.

My reading of this term disagrees with Hodgkin ('Terms I', pp. 20–2, and no. 36), who conflates *rage* with *ragge* (iii below), and equates both with *rake* [ME *raike*], 'a track or walk'. The friskiness of colts may be a more typical characteristic.

(ii–iv) *ragg(e)* Probably, a 'raggedness', with reference to a colt's shaggy coat; cf. the proverb, 'Of a ragged Colt comes a good horse' (Whiting, C376). As Hands observes, this collective 'may have originated in a miscopying of *rage* (i above), resulting in an independent term': *EHH*, p. 155/1940n. See *OED*, s.vv. *rag*, n.² 10, *ragged* adj.¹; *raggy* adj.¹.

(iii) The term *rake*, which is given as an alternative by *StA*, here probably indicates swift motion – a 'rushing' – along the lines of *rage* in (i), rather than a 'course' or 'path', as proposed by Hodgkin ('Terms I', pp. 20–2). The most likely source of this word is the verb *raken* (<OE *racian*), glossed by *MED* as 'to hasten, move quickly, rush': s.v. *raiken* v. (b); see also *OED*, *rake*, v.[1] 2. There may also be some influence from the unrelated noun *rak* (var. *rake*), which referred principally to a storm or storm cloud, but could also indicate 'a rapid movement, a rush': *MED*, *rak* n.(1) b.

(v) *harresse* 'stud'; see note 100 below.

39 (i) *bery* 'den, burrow', 'warren'. As *MED* shows (s.v. *beri* n.), the origins of this word are uncertain, but its most likely root is OE *beorg*, whence ME *bergh, berȝ* ('a hill, mound, or barrow'; cf. the *balȝ berȝ* of the Green Knight in *SGGK*, 2172).

Conversely, Erik Björkman proposes a derivation from OE *byrig*, dative singular of *burg, burh*, 'a fortified dwelling', and compares this with 'a *cete* [= city] of greys' (no. 88): 'Wortgeschichtliche kleinigkeiten', *Beiblatt zur Anglia*, 28 (1917), 251–4 (pp. 251–53).

Note that the animals referred to here as 'conies' are what are now called 'rabbits', specifically the common European rabbit, *Oryctolagus cuniculus*. In the 15th century, however, the term *rabbit* was reserved for the young of the species (see no. 165), with *cony/coning* indicating a mature animal over a year old. See *MED*, s.vv. *coning* n. and *rabet* n.(1).

(ii) *barow* Either, a 'den', 'burrow' <OE *byrig*, dat. sing. of *burg, burh* (see *MED*, *burgh* n.(2), var. *burh, borewe, borwȝ*); or, a 'barrow', 'mound' (= a 'warren') <OE *beorg, beorh*, 'hill' – inspired by the notion that a rabbit warren often forms a slight mound of excavated earth; see *MED*, *bergh* n.

(iii) *syght* 'large number, multitude', 'a group': see *MED*, *sighte* n. 3a. This sense of the word seems to derive from the notion that a multiplicity of people, animals etc. provides a spectacle or display. In the J.B. lists, the term is used chiefly of badgers (greys: no. 88) and monks (no. 136), but see *OED*, s.v. *sight*, n.[1] 2, for examples of its wider currency.

40 *seet* Probably, 'a sitting', 'a seatedness', referring to the way the controller – a steward with responsibilty for his lord's accounts – was perennially seated at his desk checking records; see *MED*, s.vv. *sete* n.(2) 1(a); *setten*, v. 34 (a). This collective was also used of ushers (no. 213).

41 (i) *temperans* Most likely, a 'mixing, blending', with sarcastic equivoque on the additional sense of 'temperateness, moderation'; see *MED*, *temperaunce* n. 1, 3, 5; *tempringe* ger.

(iii) *bawdyng* Either 'filthiness', with sarcastic comment on the hygiene of cooks; or 'cutting, trimming', with reference to the preparation of food. This noun is not recorded in either sense by *MED*, but could have arisen from *bauden* v.(1), 'to make filthy', or *baudi* adj., 'soiled, filthy, dirty'.

For my suggested alternative, 'cutting', see the somewhat obscure verb that appears in two recipe collections: 'þan take þin Purpays ... & ... bawde it & leche it in fayre pecys': *Two Fifteenth-Century Cookery Books*, ed. Thomas Austin, EETS os 91 (London, 1888; repr. 1964) (hereafter *Harley Cook Books*), p. 18; see also p. 76, under 'Herbe-blade'). *MED*, s.v. *bauden* v.(2), glosses this verb tentatively as meaning '? to trim'.

42 *couert* 'refuge', 'nest' – probably a figurative allusion to a brood or hatch of young birds, on the model of 'a covey of partridges' and 'a nye of pheasants' (nos 148, 152). The end-noun *coot* (ME *cote*) is probably imitative of a short, high-pitched call. In the 14th century, this word appears to have been used loosely of various diving waterfowl, especially the guillemot, but by the 15th century it was increasingly restricted to the bald coot (*Fulica astra*), the bird most likely to have been intended here. On the origins of the word, see Lockwood, *British Bird Names*, s.v. *Coot*. The end-noun in Pp is *cattys* (see no. 29), undoubtedly scribal error for *cottys* (coots), which I have emended accordingly.

43 *trynkette* 'trenket' = the knife used by a shoemaker or leatherworker. The end-noun, 'cordwainers' refers to shoemakers, especially those who worked with cordwain (*corduan*: Spanish leather, named for the city of Cordova). The collective is applied also to 'corvisers' (no. 46), another name for shoemakers.

44 *flight* Hodgkin ('Terms I', no. 61) is on insecure ground in arguing that cormorants were 'flown' at fish in the same way that goshawks were 'lett fli' at their own quarry; in other words, that cormorants were used for hunting fish by being 'flown' at them. Cormorants were certainly used for catching fish (an ancient practice still pursued in rural China), but they have to dive for their prey. What is more, the quotation on which Hodgkin bases this argument states clearly that the expression *lett fli* is *not* to be used of a goshawk; see further note 84 below. Since cormorants are solitary birds, the 'collective noun' probably refers to their characteristic skimming flight over water.

45 *fouiyson, foyson* 'abundance', 'a large amount' especially of food and drink; see *MED, foisoun* n. (<OF *foison*). The addition of the modifier *grete* in C can be taken to indicate a very large quantity, 'a profusion'. This collective appears nowhere else in the J.B. lists, but is given in *Femina* as the term for a group of beasts: 'ffusoun ... of quyk bestayle' (p. 3).

46 For *trynket*, refer to note 43 above. Corvisers were leatherworkers, especially shoemakers; see *MED, corveiser* n.

47 (i) *threte* Probably, a 'threat', a 'menace', with caustic reference to the dangers of life at court. Hands (*EHH*, p. 162/2008n) suggests that there could be equivoque on the word's earlier meaning of 'crowd, multitude', but *MED*, s.v. *thret* n. (a), has no citations showing that this sense survived into the 15th century.

(ii) *thretenyng* 'threatening' – not recorded by *MED*.

(iii) *triete, trete* Possibly, variant forms of *threte* – see *MED*, s.vv. *trete*; *threten* v.(1); or, perhaps, forms of *trete*, 'negotiation, bargaining', a 'treaty, accord', a 'conference, council': see *MED*, *trete*, n.(2). Conducting negotiations and arranging agreements were important duties of experienced, ambassadorial courtiers. Chaucer himself was charged with many such commissions, as is briefly discussed in the account of Chaucer's life in *The Riverside Chaucer*, pp. xv–xvii.

(iv) *charge* Normally reserved for curates (no. 51); see the note below.

48 One of the oldest phrases, found also in the AN lists – e.g. Bibbesworth, p. 8: 'E des gruwes ausi une herde'; *Femina*, p. 2: 'Des grues ensy vn herde ... Of cranes also an herde.'

49 (i) Hodgkin ('Terms I', nos 112–13) is surely mistaken in arguing that *murhser* (Eg) and *morther* were intended 'to represent the noise of crows'. It is far more likely that Eg's *murhser* is simply scribal error for *murther* or *morther*, both forms of the same word, meaning 'murder'; see *MED*, s.vv. *morther* n.(1); *murthen* v. Hence, 'a murder, murdering', with reference to the crow's predilection for killing and eating the young of other birds.

(ii) *byggyng* 'edifice, dwelling' = a rookery; see *MED*, *bigginge* ger. 1b, 3a.

50 (i) *vncredibelite* There is probably equivoque in this collective, combining the senses of 'incredulity', 'disbelief' with 'incredible number'. For the former sense, see *MED*, *uncredible* adj.

(ii) *noncredibilite* The notion that men are naturally incredulous about having been cuckolded is emphasised by this form of the collective.

51 *charge* 'protecting, safeguarding'; a 'dutifulness'; a 'caring', a 'solicitude'; see *MED*, *charge* n., senses 3a, 4, 5. The earliest attestation of the sense 'people or district committed to the care of a minister of religion' is 1530, according to *OED*, s.v. *charge* n.[1] 14. a.

52 *curgers* The collective 'threat' is normally reserved for courtiers (no. 47), for which *curgers* may be a mistake. Otherwise, the enigmatic end-noun could be an early form of *ciergers*, meaning 'cierge-bearers', a cierge (ME *cerge*) being a large wax candle used in religious ceremonies. Perhaps the phrase refers to the rivalry among possible candidates for the honour of being assigned this duty. Further evidence is needed in this matter as the word *cierger* is not recorded by *MED*, and the earliest (in fact, the only) attestation in *OED* is 1624.

53 Among birds, the collective 'herd' is assigned also to cranes, fieldfares, swans and wrens (nos 48, 68, 198, 225). There does not appear to be a specific pattern of association to account for this.

54 *smere* 'smear, smearing', with reference to the compounds used by a currier – a tradesman who darkens leather after it has been tanned. Hodgkin supplies a useful quotation describing a currier's work: 'Terms I', pp. 27–8.

APPENDIX I — NOTES 301

56 An adaptation of the more common phrase 'a team of swans' (no. 198.ii), with 'team' indicating 'a brood'. For more on this word, see note 62.iv below.

57 *squat* Possibly, a 'dropping', 'slapping down', or 'slapping on' (of daub or plaster); or a 'smoothing down' of the same; see the different senses given by *MED* (s.v. *squatten* v.). Hodgin cites a 17th-century use of the verb meaning 'to ... make flat by letting fall' ('Terms I', no. 199).

(ii) *sawtte* Most likely a scribal error for *sqwatte*, perhaps phonetically confused with *sorte*, 'a group, company, band', as used of mallards (no. 125).

58 *clateryng* 'noisy chattering'. This phrase is essentially a variant of 'a clattering /chattering of choughs' (no. 33), ME *choughe* being another name for the jackdaw.

59 (iv) This phrase is not part of the main list of collectives in Adv, but appears inexplicably as a heading to the carving terms and the J.B. material as a whole: see Appendix II, no. 1, and my description of Adv in the Introduction. The phrase is also enigmatic for going against the widespread consensus, even among the AN lists, that the collective noun for deer is 'herd'. The term *trip*, a 'troop, host', is most commonly applied to goats and hares (nos 80, 89), as well as certain fowls (nos 32, 95).

60 *doctryne* Refers to the teachings and precepts of a doctor of divintity.

61 *flyght* ?'flying (through the air)'; or, ?'taking flight'. Hodgkin supports the latter reading by pointing to the way that a flock of doves, or even a pair, take flight in unison: 'Terms I', no. 62. In the case of other birds, the collective probably refers to some characteristic aspect of their flight: cf. nos 44, 84, 117, 197.

62 (i) *padelynge* The origins of this word are obscure, and its use as a collective noun for ducks is not recognised by *MED* (s.v. *padelinge* n.), which acknowledges the term only in relation to hens (see no. 95 below). The collective appears to refer to the habit that ducks have of walking around in shallow or muddy water, as in the example provided by John Palsgrave in his *Lesclarcissement de la langue francoyse* (London, 1530), ed. F. Genin (Paris, 1852), p. 651: 'I paddyll in the myre, as duckes do or yonge chyldren.'

(ii) *badelyng* It is not now clear whether this represents a compositor's error for *padelyng*, or an otherwise unrecorded variant of that term (but see *bablyng* in W: iii). Either way, the fact that this word appeared in print led to its repetition and formal acceptance; see the *StA*-derived texts cited by Hodgkin, 'Terms I', no. 98, and *OED*, s.v. *badling* n.².

(iii) *bablyng* Most likely, 'babbling' = 'chattering, quacking' (<OF *babiller*); see *MED*, *babelen* v.(1) and *babelinge* ger. (1); cf. 'A ... bablyng off women' (no. 220.iv); 'a clattering of choughs' (no. 33). Another, more remote, possibility is that the word means a 'bobbing', 'oscillating', referring to the way that ducks

up-end themselves, or even disappear underwater completely, to feed, and then bob back to the surface; see *MED, babelen* v.(2); cf. 'a diving of atteals' (no. 4).

(iv) *teme* 'brood'; the collective here refers to the progeny or hatchlings of a duck – see *MED, teme* n.(1), 1b, 1h. Analagous terms are 'brood', 'covert', 'covey' and 'nye'. Cf. also 'a team of cygnets/swans' (nos 56, 198.ii).

63 For the collective *team*, see note 62.iv above. The term *wyldigges* represents a combination of ME *wild* + *digge*, 'a duck' (dialectical, origins obscure): *MED, digge* n.; *OED, dig* n.². The word is used in the *Parlement of the Thre Ages*, 244–5: 'Spanyells full spedily þay spryngen abowte, / Be-dagged for dowkynge when digges bene enewede'.

64 *feyters* 'faitours' = impostors, esp. beggars, vagabonds, who feign illness to beg for alms; see *MED, faitour* n.; *faiterie* n. The collective refers to the peripatetic disposition of such scroungers.

65 *lure* 'luring', referring to the lure – a stuffed leather bag decked with feathers, which a falconer swings in the air so as to recall his birds, especially when training or exercising them. This phrase is rare in the J.B. texts, but occurs also in the AN lists; e.g. 'A lure of ffaukones & damezelez' (*Femina*, p. 3). In all three J.B. texts in which it appears, 'a lure of falcons' is paired with 'a lure of maidens' (no. 124) – though in Dg* the juxtaposition is interrupted by 'a turb of teals'. See note 124.ii below on the humour of the implied comparison.

66 The collective *nest* is normally reserved for rabbits (no. 165). Fawns are the young of fallow deer, as *BH* explains: 'And ye speke of the Bucke the fyrst yere he is / A fawne sowkyng on his dam ...' (1370–1). In the wild, does and fawns congregate separately from the bucks, except during the rut. Perhaps the intended image is of several fawns forming a recumbent group to chew the cud, and so appearing as if clustered in a nest. Alternatively, *nest* may refer simply to the flattened patch of grass in which a young fawn has been lying, the equivalent of a hare's form.

67 *besynes* a 'busyness', an 'industriousness', probably referring to the vigour and energy that can be observed in a caged ferret, or one introduced into a rabbit warren; see *MED, bisinesse* n.; *OED, business* n. 1 (this sense now differentiated in MnE as *busyness* (q.v.), first attested 1809).

68 Of the AN lists, *Nominale* employs both collectives used in the J.B. group of texts: 'Vn herde de gryues ... A floc of feldefares' (p. 25). By contrast, *Femina* has the strange formula, 'Et des griuez sanz .h. erde ... And of feldfares wi*th*oute .h. erde' (p. 2), repeated by Bibbesworth: 'E des grives sauns .h. eerde' (p. 8).

69 *chyrme* 'chattering, warbling, twittering' (<OE *cirm*, 'noise'): *MED, chirm* n. The usual form of the end-noun is 'goldfinches' (no. 82).

70 (i) *scole* 'school, shoal' (<MDu *schole* = OE *scolu*, 'shoal, troop, multitude'). This phrase usually occurs alongside 'a *scole/skole* of clerks' (no. 35; <OE *scol*, 'place of learning').

(ii) *scoue* Variant form of *scole*, 'shoal'; see *MED*, *scole* n.(3). Hodgkin ('Terms I', no. 120) declares that *scoue* 'is evidently a North Country writing for "scole" ', but offers no evidence for this assertion.

71 *drifte* 'drifting', 'floating', with equivoque on the homonym *drift* = 'a drove, herd'; see *MED*, *drift* n., and nos 139, 200, 201. Hodgkin ('Terms I', no. 213) offers a quotation from the *Lex Londinensis* of 1680 to show that *drift* referred to a 'recognized fishing-ground', but this sense appears to be a later development.

72 *besynes* 'busyness', an 'industriousness'; see note 67 above.

73 *stalke* 'stalk, stalking'. A forester would need to move cautiously and stealthily in all aspects of his work, whether quietly observing and counting his master's deer, tracking an individual hart before the start of a hunt, or patrolling his territory on the lookout for poachers. I have elected to treat *stake* in T as scribal error for *stalke*, though it could be seen as an independent term, perhaps alluding to a forester's duties in staking out a boundary (of a park or chase).

74 *ragge* 'raggedness'; see note 38.ii–iv above.

75 (i) *erthe, nerthe* 'earth' – the correct term for a fox's burrow or lair, and widely used of other burrowing animals as well; see *MED*, *erthe* n. 6d. This phrase occurs only in the long versions of the lists of collectives; the fact that it is not in *StA*, while the alternative 'a skulk of foxes' occurs twice, probably indicates a printer's error. Pl is damaged where this phrase occurs in Prk.

(ii) *sculke* 'skulking' – an allusion to the stealthy manner in which a fox will prowl around, looking for any opportunity to pounce on a hen or other booty. Since foxes do not hunt in packs, this is clearly a term invented for the nonce. In the long lists, this phrase often occurs in addition to 'an earth of foxes', though at some remove. It also often appears alongside 'a skulk of friars' and 'a skulk of thieves' (nos 76, 207).

(iii) *skulf* Most likely scribal error for *skulk*, with the *f* transferred from the end of the following word, *of*.

76 (i) *skulke* a 'skulking, prowling', as of a mendicant friar in pursuit of alms. The anti-clerical bias that is evident in the majority of these lists is curious, given that many J.B. scribes would have had some ecclesiastical training. Cf. the treatment of clerks, monks, nuns and priests (nos 35, 136, 141, 161).

(ii) *bewperis* 'good fatherliness' <OF *beau pere*. In ME, *bew-pere* was used both as a noun and a respectful form of address for a priest, confessor or ecclesiastical superior; see *MED*, *beau* adj. 2e. MS Harl is notable for eschewing

the anti-clericism that is apparent in the other J.B. witnesses; see also its treatment of monks and nuns (nos 136, 141).

77 The collectives 'gaggle' and 'gaggling' are clearly onomatopoeic in origin, as are 'peep' and 'chattering' (nos 32, 33, 153, 192). They are applied also to gossips and women (nos 85, 220) as sardonic comment on the sound and content of their chatter.

(iii) *gayling* Probably, a 'noise', an 'outcry' <ME *gale*, 'song', 'noise'. In its various senses, this noun refers to the sounds made by a voice, usually human, sometimes animal. The related verb *galen* (<OE *galan*) refers even more often to the voices of birds or animals, as in the *Promptorium* (ed. Mayhew): 'Galyn, as crowys or Rokys: Crocito ... crosco' (col. 204). More generally, it means 'to shout', 'to make a loud or harsh sound' (with one's voice). See, for example, the words of Chaucer's Host in *The Friar's Tale*: 'Now telleth forth, thogh that the Somonour gale' (*CT*, III.1336).

(iv) The term 'company' appears also in *Nominale*, 'Vn cumpanye de owes, A cumpanye of gees' (p. 25); Bibbesworth, 'Des dames dist hom compaignie / E des ouwes ne chaungez mie' (p. 8).

78 In Eg, this phrase is grouped with 'a rout of knights' and 'a rout of wild wolves' (nos 114, 219). In essence, ME *route* (<OF *rote, route*) designates a large group, a throng (of people, soldiers, men-at-arms, birds or animals), but it was also used specifically of any assembly of disreputables, such as scoundrels, outlaws, rioters and devils. It is likely that wolves incurred this more pejorative sense, but whether the opprobrium was meant to extend by sarcastic implication to knights and gentlemen as well is difficult to judge. See *MED*, *route* n.(1), and note 79.ii.

79 (ii) In Pp, this phrase forms an unusual trio with 'a rout of knights' and 'a rout of wild wolves'. The end-noun of this phrase may originally have been 'gentlemen', as in Eg (see note 78 above); if so, it is difficult to account for the alteration to 'gentlewomen', which makes less sense in the overall context.

80 *tryppe* 'herd, troop', 'flock'; see note 32.iii above.

81 The AN *Femina* has a very similar phrase, but with a different end-noun. The entire line reads, *Summe du blé, summe du bienez*, which is glossed as *Summe of corn, summe of goud* (p. 3). This could be read as 'a quantity' of corn and goods, possessions (*goud*), or as 'a load' (as for a horse or wagon) of the same. The J.B. phrase may represent a mutation of *goud* to *gold*, with a corresponding shift of meaning: 'a quantity, sum, amount of gold'. The expression is found in Chaucer's *Shipman's Tale*, which tells how, 'This marchant ... hath ... payd eek in Parys / To certayn Lumbardes ... The somme of gold' (*CT*, VII.365–8).

82 (i–ii) *chyrme, chyrmyng* 'chattering, warbling, twittering'; see note 69 above. This word is used in a J.B. hawking remedy that describes how a hawk afflicted with

worms will shriek, unprompted by the twittering of another bird: 'sche scremyth sodenly heryng no chyrmyng of no byrde' (MS H: II/20–1).

(iii) *tremynge* Read *?tremlynge* = 'trembling, quivering', 'twitching', possibly 'flittering' – with reference to the way a flock of goldfinches can be seen flitting rapidly among seedheads, and pecking up the seeds with rapid, darting movements. See *MED*, s.v. *tremblen* v. (var. *tremle, tremlin*).

83 *solaz* 'solace', 'joy, cheer' (ME *solas* <OF *solaz*).

84 (i) This phrase probably refers to the twisting, turning flight of a goshawk in pursuit of its quarry. The bird belongs to the category of short-winged hawks, which are flown from the fist and accelerate rapidly towards their prey over short distances (see Prk, I/219–24, and the associated notes).

Hodgkin ('Terms I', nos 57, 60) claims that a goshawk was *lett fli*, while a falcon was *cast*, but the passage that he quotes from the *StA* hawking treatise is concerned explicitly with a goshawk when offering the following caution: 'And if yowr hawke reward to any fowle by countenance for to flee ther to ye shall say "cast the hawke ther to", and not "lett fli ther to"' (*PH*, 252–4; punctuation mine). In other words, this passage states exactly the opposite of what Hodgkin claims for it.

(ii) The explicitly singular end-noun in Pp is typical of the inconsistencies and incongruities sprinkled throughout these lists.

85 *gossippes* Probably, 'friends, chums', 'companions', perhaps in the specific sense of 'female friends'; see *MED, god-sibbe* n. 2a. This item has been interpolated in the manuscript by a revising hand to accompany the phrase 'a gaggling of geese', which is elsewhere normally paired with 'a gaggle/gaggling of women' (no. 220).

86 This phrase normally accompanies 'a cluster of nuts' (no. 142), and sometimes also 'a cluster of churls' (no. 34), as in Prk (I/86–8).

87 (i–iv) The distinction between a 'brace' and a 'leash' of greyhounds is explained by the phrases in *StA*, and also by *Femina*: 'A lese of grehoundes ys y named / When .iij. en lese beþ to gedere ... And a bras of grehoundes ys / When ij en lese beþ to gedere' (*Femina*, p. 4). *StA* makes a similar distinction in relation to hawks of the tower (see no. 93); and *THawk 2* indicates that a leash of dogs might consist of more than three: '... of Grey houndes .ij. is a brace, and as many as thou might lede in a lese after the, is but a lesh' (p. 144).

The origins of this particularised sense of *brace* (<AN *brace* 'a leather strap') are not altogether certain. *OED* (s.v. *brace* n.[2] 15. a.) speculates that, 'Perhaps the band or cord with which dogs were coupled in coursing was called a *brace*'; but why it should apply to only two dogs is unclear. We do know, however, that the term was applied also to other types of hound; see note 103.i below.

(v) *hardlyng* 'tying together (of several brace of dogs)', <OF *hardel*, 'cord, rope'; the word is discussed in more detail by Corner, 'More terms', p. 241/57n. See also *MED, hardel* n.; *hardlen* v.; and *MG*, p. 108: 'þan shuld þe sergeaunt of þe

mute of þe hert houndes ... make alle hem of the office ... hardle her houndes, and in euery hardel suffisen ii or iii couple of houndes atte þe moost'.

(vi) *thrum* 'group, bunch'; a 'crowd, troop' <OE *þrymm*; see *MED*, *thrum*, n.(1).

88 (i) *cete, cety, cyte* Probably, 'city, town' (<OF cité), as argued by Erik Björkman (see note 39.i above) and endorsed by *MED*, s.v. *cite* n. By contrast, *OED*, s.v. *cete* n.², offers a tentative derivation from L *coetus/cetus*, 'meeting, assembly, company', a notion rightly dismissed by Hodgkin, 'Terms I', pp. 13–15. Owing to its publication in *StA*, and subsequent repetition in numerous derivative texts, the form *cete* prevailed over all others, and may be the origin of MnE *set*, meaning a badger's lair or earth, a term first attested, according to the *OED* (s.v. *set*, n.¹ 32), in 1898: 'A badger's earth or warren is properly and generally called a "set" or "cete" '.

(ii) *farewyng* 'farrowing'; cf. other phrases based on the notion of giving birth: 'a kindle of young cats', 'a litter of whelps' (nos 31, 219).

(ii–iii) *sawte* Sense obscure. Corner ('More terms', pp. 240–1/55n) suggests interpreting this word as *salt* (ME *saut*) in the sense 'sexual desire, arousal (of a female)', which would provide a connection with 'farrowing', but she admits that this is unsatisfactory. My own view is that *sawte* may refer to the way a badger is besieged or 'assaulted' when dug out of its den; the word would thus evoke the notion of a military assault, as on a city (or *cete*; cf. (i) above). See *MED*, *saut* n.(1), the aphetic of *assaut*; and *sauten* v.(1); and see also the phrase 'a grey is beseged or assauted' in the J.B. 'hunting terms' of Adv (IVa/10).

(iv) The notion that badgers are deceitful is obscure. Hands suggests (*EHH*, p. 154/1927n) that it 'may well be an attempt to rationalize an already obscure word', i.e. *cety* (i above). Alternatively, perhaps the end-noun *greys* is a remnant of scribal misunderstanding of OF *gryves*, 'fieldfares'. Although fieldfares (no. 68) are not normally classified as a 'deceit', other birds are: cf. 'a dissumulation of all (small) birds' and 'a deceit of lapwings' (nos 12, 116, 226).

(v) *syght* 'spectacle' = 'large number, multitude'; see note 39.iii above.

89 (i) *trippe* 'herd, flock'; see note 32.iii above.

(ii–vi) *huske* Sense obscure. Neither *MED* nor *OED*, s.v. *huske* n., offers any useful information about the origins of this word, especially as it is used here. It is unclear why *MED* lists 'a group or company of hares' with other senses referring to outer coverings of various sorts, principally the husk of a nut (s.v. *huske* n. 1–3). And the *OED* entry, which relies on Joseph Strutt's *Sports and Pastimes of the People of England* (London, 1801) for its only citation of this term, is clearly in need of updating.

(iii–v) *don, down, dunne* Perhaps, 'a down', referring to grassy uplands or open countryside (ME *doune* <OE *dun*), the sort of countryside in which hares are commonly found. The form *denne* in MS C shows scribal manipulation of this term,

and is best understood in the sense of 'hiding place', rather than 'underground lair', since hares do not dig burrows as rabbits do.

Hodgkin ('Terms I', no. 7) suggests a possible connection with Scots *donie*, 'a hare', and the related adjective *dunny*, 'dun-coloured', but the evidence is slim: see John Jamieson, *Dictionary of the Scottish Tongue* (Edinburgh, 1867), and *The Scottish National Dictionary* by William Grant and David Murison (Edinburgh, 1932–76), s.v. *donie*. If these collectives do refer to the colour of the hare, the necessary sense would be provided by the ME adjective *don* – var. *donne, dun(ne* – without recourse to Scots words.

(vi) *droue* 'drove, driving', perhaps referring to the act of chasing hares into nets, a practice illustrated in Gaston Phebus's *Livre de chasse*, p. 286 (cap. 82). See also note 9 above concerning cattle ('beasts') that are also driven; and note the hare's complaint in the the poem *The Hunted Hare*: 'ffrov dale to doune I am I-drevfe' (*Secular Lyrics*, no. 119, line 7).

(vii) This item is interpolated in the manuscript by a contemporaneous revising hand, and is positioned immediately after the opening phrase 'a herd of harts'. The collective seems to have been chosen for reasons of alliteration.

(viii) *trase* 'trace, footprint'; also, 'a trail' consisting of a series of footprints. See *MED*, *trace* n.(1) senses 2–3, and the following: 'Also ȝe may knowe a greete hert bi þe steppis þat in Engelond is callid trace ...' (*MG*, p. 77); '... if there be many huntesmen, they shall soyle ['mar, destroy'] the traces and footing of the Hare' (*Noble Arte*, p. 166). In later usage, the term 'trace(s)' could refer specifically to a hare's footprints in snow: e.g. 'also in time of Snowe we say the *Trace* of an Hare' (*Noble Arte*, p. 239); cf. Nicholas Cox, *The Gentleman's Recreation*, I.12. These two senses – of 'footprints' and 'trail' are closely connected and are impossible to distinguish in the J.B. phrases.

In all three J.B. texts, this phrase is paired with 'a trip of hares' of group i; and in Pl and Prk both phrases are located at a remove from the main list of collective nouns (see Prk, I/126–7). The singular end-noun 'a(n) hare' in Pl and *HSG* – so incongruous in the context – is probably an attempt to rationalise the fact that a trace (either a footprint or a series of footprints) must belong to an individual animal. Prk eliminates this discrepancy by altering the end-noun to plural 'hares', which may also have been intended equivocally, producing the additional sense, 'a tress [i.e. 'lock'] of hairs' (see *MED*, *trace* n.(2); *tresse* n.; and cf. 'a fayre tras' in I/165–6).

90 (i) Probably, 'a stud (?brothel) of rogues, lechers', with the collective *haras* ('a horse stud', 'a breeding pen') being used in a transferred sense for comical effect. Cf. *Of Arthour and of Merlin*, where *haras* indicates a mob of lechers: 'Sche seyd sche was a liȝt woman / And comoun hore to alle man. / Of þat chaunce mani nam kepe ... For ribaudye gret haras / Tofolwe[d] hir bodi – allas'; ed. O.D. Macrae-Gibson, EETS os 268–9 (1973, 1979), lines 787–82.

Alternatively, *harlots* could refer to 'female prostitutes, whores' – a sense that had developed by the late 15th century – creating another possible meaning for this phrase: 'a stud (= brothel) of whores'. It may be significant that the preceding phrase in both H and L is 'a haras of hors(e)', with a possible equivoque on 'whores'. See *MED*, s.v. *harlot* n. 3a, 3b, and no. 100 below.

(ii) Perhaps to be read as 'a multitude of rogues, knaves', or '~ of vagabonds', against the more colourful version in H and L.

91 It will be seen that harpers feature only in the longest lists of collectives – with the exception of L, where 'a melody of harpers ⟨&⟩ luters' has been interpolated below the original list (with the Tironian nota for *et* partially lost through trimming of the leaf). In all the manuscripts cited in group i, 'a melody of harpers' is contiguous with 'a poverty of pipers' (no. 155). In Prk and Pl, however, these two phrases have been conflated, resulting in the loss of 'a poverty of pipers' in both.

92 Ignoring the fragmentary lists of collectives in *LJ*, and the supplementary list in Dg*, this phrase ('A herd of harts') opens all the lists of collectives, with the notable exception of Rd, from which it is inexplicably absent. It is also technically missing from Pl owing to physical damage to the manuscript, but its erstwhile presence can be inferred from Prk.

On the question of what constitutes a herd, see *THawk 1*: 'II is a copil euermore and III is a herd of dere and no fewer. For if þu se II dere and no mo, þu may say "þer pasturs II dere, II hertis, II bukkis, II roesse"' (lines 244–6).

93 (i) The expression 'hawks of the tower' refers to long-winged hawks, or falcons, some of which are listed in the J.B. Hierarchy of hawks; see Prk I/208–18, and the associated notes. The collective *cast* derives from the correct technical term for releasing a hawk from the fist, as set out in *StA*'s hawking treatise: '... ye shall say cast yowre hawke to the perch, and not set youre hawke vppon the perch'; likewise, '... ye shall say cast the hawke ther to, and not lett fli ther to' (*PH*, lines 214–5; 253–54).

(ii) *thessame haukis* – i.e. hawks of the tower, referred to in the preceding phrase in the *StA* sequence (cited in group i). The collective *lece*, 'leash', refers to the leather thong – or pair of such thongs, also sometimes called *lunes* or *lewnes* (ME *loines*) – by which a hawk was secured to her perch or the falconer's hand. The phrase was probably inspired by the equivalent notion of a leash (= a threesome) of tethered greyhounds (see no. 87), though hawks themselves were never tied to one another. The expression appears to have had general currency, as can be seen in *PPF*: 'Yf ther be III [falcons] in numbur sette, / Lees is here name; it is but skylle, / Whethir hit be laner, faucon, or sacrete, / Or eny þat is namyd in this bille / Of haukys of toure ...' (lines 621–5). See also *MED*, *lesse* n.(1) 1a (b).

94 The hayward referred to in this phrase is presumably the manorial hayward, who safeguarded his master's fields, hedges and fences – rather than the village hayward,

APPENDIX I — NOTES

who minded the community's animals grazing on the common, making sure they did not stray out of bounds. The manorial official also had responsibility for supervising the harvest, protecting it from theft, and paying the labourers. Although there is an obviously neat rhyme in the pairing of 'wayward' and 'hayward', the collective 'waywardness' – meaning 'depravity', 'perversity, recalcitrance' – probably points to a history of tension between haywards and villagers, and also hints at corruption amongst holders of this office. For a full account of the duties and misdemeanours of haywards, see H.S. Bennett, *Life on the English Manor: A Study of Peasant Conditions 1150–1400* (Cambridge, 1960), pp. 55, 178–80.

95 (i) *broode* 'brood' = 'hatch, hatching' (<OE *brod*). Cf. 'covey' (no. 148) and 'team' (nos 56, 62, 63, 198), which also refer to groups of hatchlings.

(ii–iii) *grale*; *garule* 'chattering, clucking'. Both words have the same meaning, though their origins are different: *grale* <OF *grailler* 'to squawk, croak, call'; *garule* <OF *garuler* (of birds) 'to chatter, twitter'. In the AN lists, *Nominale* has 'Vn grele de gelyns ... A floc of hennes' (p. 25); cf. *Femina*, 'Greyle dez geleynez ... A greyle of hennes' (p. 3); Bibbesworth, 'Greile de gelins' (p. 8). Corner discusses both words at length in 'More terms', pp. 235–7/22n. See also *MED*, s.vv. *greile* n.; *grallen* v.; *A-ND*, s.vv. *greile*, *grele* s.

(iv) This phrase most likely represents a conflation of 'a brood of hens' and 'a paddling of ducks' through scribal miscopying. In the long lists, hens, chickens (no. 32), and ducks (no. 62) normally occur in that order. Rd combines the end-noun *hens* with the collective for ducks. followed by the phrase for chickens, but makes no reference to ducks.

(v) *tryppe* Cf. 'a trip of chickens' in Pp, and note 32 above.

96 As the officer supervising a tournament, a herald needed to have a good memory and a thorough knowledge of all the coats of arms that might appear on the field. His expertise would also enable him to identify individual commanders, both friend and foe, on a field of battle, to monitor their actions, and report accordingly to his master. The establishing of the College of Arms in London in 1484 created a repository for the recorded knowledge of the royal heralds.

97 *doppyng* 'diving' <ME *doppen*, 'to dive'; cf. also the nouns *dopping* and *domping* in *MED*, which are both glossed as names for unidentified diving birds. Hodgkin ('Terms I', nos 93–4) identifies the end-noun *herles* with the red-breasted merganser (*Mergus serrator*) and the goosander (*Mergus merganser*), both called *harle* in Modern French. However, the AN lists agree that a *herle* is a sheldrake (now known as a shelduck): the brightly multicoloured species *Tadorna tadorna*. For example, *Femina* (p. 55): 'In mareis demurmt la herele ... In mereis duellyþ þe sheld drake'. See also 'Sheldrakes', no 179.

98 As Hodgkin points out, 'A hermit is essentially a *solitary* dweller, and to speak of a *company* of them is a contradiction in terms' ('Terms I', no. 159). Cf. 'a singular of boars' (no. 14), which is similarly contradictory. The collective 'observance' refers to the devotion, or sense of duty, which a hermit owes to the rules of his (or her) religious order.

99 (i–ii) *sege, cege* 'siege', referring to the patience with which a heron stalks or waits for its prey; see also nos 13, 28, and cf. the phrase *a heyron stalkyth* in the J.B. Resting terms, Appendix III, no. 15. The expression is elucidated by Nicholas Cox, *Gentleman's Recreation*, II.7: '*Hern at seidge*, is when you find a *Hern* standing by the water-side watching for Prey, or the like.' A related but slightly different image occurs in the *Parlement of the Thre Ages*, in the description of falcons attacking a heron: '... to the heron þay hitten hym full ofte, / ... and brynges hym to sege' [i.e. to a defensive position beside the water] (lines 223–4).

(ii–iii) *beuy* 'bevy' = 'group', 'flock' (<AN *bevée*). This is the preferred collective for herons in the AN lists, appearing as *beuee* (*Nominale*, p. 25), *Bovee / Bevée* (Bibbesworth, p. 8), *deueye* (*Femina*, p. 3). In the J.B. lists, 'bevy' is more commonly used of ladies, quails and roes (nos 115, 164, 171).

100 *haras* 'stud' (<OF *haraz*). The term referred originally to the enclosure or building where horses (stallions and mares) were kept for breeding, but was extended to denote the breeding animals themselves; see *OED*, s.v. *haras* n. In H and L, this phrase is followed by 'a haras of harlots' (no. 90), suggesting deliberate word-play on *horse / whores* (ME *hores*); see H, 219–20 in Part II above. See also note 90 in this appendix; and *MED, hore* n.(2).

101 *stalyn* 'stallion', with *olde hors* indicating an adult male horse – one that is sexually mature and capable of breeding. See *MED, staloun* n.; and *hors* n. 1b, where this phrase is cited.

102 In the J.B. lists, this phrase is invariably followed by 'a promise of tapsters' or 'a *glosyng* of taverners' (nos 203, 204), and often both. It therefore seems most likely that the end-noun refers to hostelers or innkeepers, rather than to ostlers, or grooms (ME *hostiler* (var. *ostiler*) was used in both senses; see *MED, hostiler* n. 2a, 2c). Joviality, such as we see in Chaucer's Harry Ballly (*CT*, I.4358), has probably always been an important asset for a successful innkeeper.

103 (i) *brace, brase* 'couple', 'pair' (<AN *brace* <OF), referring to the fact that hunting hounds were led to the field tethered in pairs (see also notes 87, 104). It is interesting to note that a century or so after the J.B. texts were written, the term *brace* was no longer considered appropriate for hounds. According to Gascoigne, 'We finde some difference of termes betwene houndes, and Greyhoundes. As of Greyhoundes two make a *Brase*, and of houndes a *Couple*' (*Noble Arte*, p. 242). Cf. the hunting treatise in Nicholas Cox's *Gentleman's Recreation*: 'Of Grey-hounds, two make a *Brace*; of Hounds, a *Couple*. Of Grey-hounds, three make a *leace*; and of Hounds, a *Couple and a half*' (I.16).

(ii) *mute* 'pack' (<AN *mut, mute*); cf. *SGGK*, 1451, 1720. This is the preferred

term in all three AN lists, and is explicated thus in *Femina*: 'A mut of houndes ʒe shul say / xxiiij Racchez y coupled to gedere'. See also *Modus et Ratio* for the claim that a 'mute' consists of no fewer than twelve running hounds and a limer ('douze chiens courans et un limier': 3.77–82).

(iii–iv) As a collective noun, or a term for an assembly of people, things or animals, *pack* often carried tones of disparagement or opprobrium; cf. Chaucer's *Legend of Good Women*, G 299: 'And yit they were hethene, al the pak'.

(iv) *kenell* See 'a kennel of raches' (no. 166) and note 166 below.

104 *couple* Synonymous with *brace*; see 'Hounds' (no. 103.i), and the poem *The Hunted Hare*, lines 13–15: 'hontteris ... cowpullyʒt þer howndes more & lase'. In the J.B. lists, *couple* is normally reserved for the spaniel (*q.v.* no. 189), but see the quote from Gascoigne in note 103.i above. The 'running hounds' referred to here were the mainstay of the hunt 'with strength'. They were generally smallish dogs such as kennets, raches and harriers, which pursued their quarry principally by scent. This distinguished them from bigger dogs – such as alaunts, greyhounds, hart-hounds and mastiffs, which hunted only by sight – and from limers, used solely for tracking. Following Gaston de Foix, Edward of York devotes an entire chapter to running hounds: *MG*, pp. 58–61 (cap. 14).

105 *blast* Indicates the enthusiastic blowing of a hunting horn. Horn calls consisted of an elaborate system of signals, as described by Baillie-Grohman, *MG*, Appendix, s.v. 'Hunting Music'; see also Hands, *EHH*, p. 146/1843n.

106 (i–ii) *multiplieng* An ambiguous term, interpreted by Hodgkin ('Terms I', no. 139) as referring to 'the loose morals of married women', but intimating to Hands (*EHH*, p. 161/1989n) 'the procreative enthusiasm of the male'. Another possibility, suggested by the collective *nowmbyr* in Pp, is that the phrase refers to the willingness of widows to remarry, as seen in Chaucer's Wife of Bath, who, '... was a worthy womman al hir lyve: / Housbondes at chirche dore she hadde fyve' (*CT*, I.459–60; and cf. the account of what women most desire in the *Wife of Bath's Tale*: *CT*, III.927–8). In the J.B. lists, this phrase is normally paired with 'a non-patience of wives' (no. 220), indicating that 'married men' rather than 'husbandmen, farmers' are intended in this context.

(ii) *hosbandri* Glossed by *MED* as 'husbands collectively', rather than a plural form of *hous-bonde* (s.v. *hus-bondrie* n. 4). It is not clear, however, why the scribe should have chosen to make such a distinction, especially as he uses another word modelled on this very form elsewhere in his list of collectives: *yema[n]ri* (no. 227).

107 *gayling* 'noise', 'outcry' (<ME *gale*; see note 77.iii above), with possible word-play on ME *gaie*, 'a jay' (<OF *gaye*).

108 *ryches* 'richness', 'wealthiness'. In Pp, this phrase follows 'a richness [i.e. 'opulence'] of martens' (no. 128), a more common item in the long lists.

109 (i) *sentence* 'sentencing'.
(ii) *sedent* 'sitting' (L *sedent*, 'they are sitting').
(iii) *sadnes* 'seriousness, gravity'; also, a 'prudence': *MED, sadnesse* n. 2b.

110 (i) A 'never-thriving'. This description of jugglers usually accompanies the phrase 'a poverty of harpers/pipers' (nos 91, 155) – impecunious performers all.

(ii) *ouerthryngyng* 'overthronging', 'overcrowding' (<ME *thring*, 'a crowd, throng'; or <*thringen*, 'to gather in a crowd, to throng together'). This collective suggests that Pp's compiler may have had in mind an additional sense of *iuglers*: 'parasites, rogues', as well as 'entertainers, performers'; see *MED, jogelour* n. 3; William Langland, *Piers Plowman*, ed. W.W. Skeat (Oxford, 1886; repr. 1961), B VI.71–2: 'I shal fynden hem fode that feithfulliche libbeth. / Saue Iakke the iogeloure and Ionet of the stues'.

111 *dampnyng* 'damning', 'condemning'. Unlike today, jury trials were apparently not thought to favour the accused. Jurors also had a reputation for being corrupt, slanderous and covetous, as in the moralising of 'The Fable of the Cat and the Fox' in the *Gesta Romanorum*, ed. Sidney J.H. Herrtage, EETS ES 33 (London, 1879) 'But bi the foxe are vndirstondyn vokettes ['advocates'] ... courteers, Iurrours, and wily men, that han xviij[en] sleightes' (II.52, p. 372). Cf. *Promptorium*, col. 241: 'Iorowre: *susurro*'; and *MED, jurour* n. (c): 'a tale-bearer, slanderer; whisperer'.

112 'A scolding, chiding of wool-combers'. The favoured form, *kempsters*, implies female wool-combers; Pp's *kymbers* is more gender-neutral; see *MED, kembestere*, n; *kembere* n. It is not immediately clear why kembers and kempsters were considered an ill-tempered group.

113 (i) *rafull, rawfull, rafle* 'raffle' = 'rabble', 'riff-raff'; see note 16.ii above. In this context, *knaves* probably indicates 'boys', as in the variant phrase 'a raffle of boys' (no. 16.ii).

(ii) This phrase was added to Harl's list of collectives by a second interpolating hand (Hand no. 3). The end-noun, which Hodgkin ('Terms I', no. 123) reads as *knottes*, is cramped, but the central letters -*av*- are not in doubt. Elsewhere, grapes, nuts and churls (or carls) occur in sequence together, all sharing the same collective, 'cluster' (see e.g. Prk, I/86–8), so perhaps *knaves* should here be understood as 'peasants, villeins', 'churls'.

114 (i) *rowte, route* 'host, company', 'throng'; cf. 'a rout of barons' (no. 7.iii). In the J.B. lists, this phrase is commonly paired with 'a rout of wolves' (no. 219); see e.g. Prk, I/41–2. This sequence may have been prompted by the innocent realisation that knights and wolves share the same collective noun in everyday locutions; or by a mischievous desire to draw a comparison, perhaps inspired by the pejorative associations of the word *rout*. A throng of armed knights would doubtless be a fearsome spectacle, as implied by the collective 'mightiness' in Adv (ii). See also notes 78, 79 and 219 for further discussion of *rout*.

(ii) *knystes* Scribal error for *knytes*, or *kny3tes*.

(iii) *ray* Most likely, an 'array', a 'battle order', being the aphetic of ME *arrai*, *araye* (<AN *arraie*, *arai*); see *MED*, *raie* n.(1). This is the collective used in two of the AN lists: *Nominale*, 'Aray de Chiualers' (p. 14), and *Femina*, 'Aray dit homme dez chiualers ... Aray seyþ man of kny3ttys' (p. 4).

Although less likely, it seems possible that the sense 'ray of light' – hence, a 'gleaming', a 'resplendence' – could have been understood, forming a parallel with 'a bright of barons' (no. 7.ii); see *MED*, *rai* n.(1).

115 (i) *bevy* 'group', 'flock' (<AN *bevée*).

(iii) Elsewhere, eloquence is normally ascribed to lawyers (no. 118), for which *ladys* is very likely a mistake, positioned as this phrase is in Pp between judges and jurors.

116 (i) *dyssayte*, *deseyte* 'deceit', referring to the female lapwing's habit of feigning injury to draw predators away from her nest and chicks. Cf. Chaucer, *The Parliament of Fowls*, 347: 'The false lapwynge, ful of trecherye'; also the J.B. phrase 'a dissimulation of birds' (no. 12).

Hodgkin suggests ('Terms I', no. 80) that *dyssayt* could be a corruption of *dix-huit*, a colloquial, imitative French name for the lapwing; but this seems implausible when the Old French form of the word is considered: *dis et oit* (Godefroy, s.v.).

See also no. 226 for texts that refer to lapwings by their onomatopoeic name, *wypes*.

(ii) *desserte* Unquestionably a compositor's error for *desseite*; but in a vivid demonstration of the power of the printed word, this term was dutifully reprinted in all subsequent and derivative editions of *StA*, and so became the accepted collective noun for lapwings; see *OED*, *desert* n.^{2} 4 (an entry that had still to be updated in November 2019).

117 (i–ii) Both 'exalting' and 'exaltation' allude to the skylark's habit of soaring into the air and hovering while pouring forth its song; <ME *exalten*, 'to elevate, raise up'; *exaltacioun*, 'zenith', 'exalted position'. The title of James Lipton's popular book *An Exaltation of Larks* (Harmondsworth, 1977) has made this phrase one of the best known to modern audiences, yet it is interesting to see that Lipton's preferred formulation occurs in only three J.B. sources.

(iii) *beuye* 'bevy' = 'group', 'flock' (<AN *bevée*). It will be seen that *HSG* has two phrases for larks, with this one added at the beginning of the usual sequence 'a bevy of ladies / quails / roes' (see e.g. Prk, I/8–10).

(iv) Like *exalting / exaltation*, the collective *flight* probably refers also to the skylark's habit of rising high into the air to sing. There is a clear division here between the long lists, which use *exalting / exaltation*, and the short lists, which prefer *flight*.

(v) The term 'flock' occurs also in *THawk 2*: 'A Flok of larkes, and eke of Shepe' (p. 144); also *THawk 1*: 'a flok of larkis and of schepe' (line 240).

119 *leype, lepe* 'leap, leaping', as onto the animal's prey. Cf. Trevisa, *Properties of Things*, II, 1219: 'Þe leopardus is a ful resynge beste and heedstronge and þursteþ blood ... And seweþ [pursues] his pray startelyng and lepyng and nought rennyng.'

120 The liars referred to here must be vainglorious persons, boasting fatuously about themselves in a self-aggrandising manner.

122 (i) Pride is an appropriate attribute of the king (or prince) of beasts. See the 12th-century bestiary translated by T.H. White, *The Book of Beasts* (London, 1954), p. 7: 'A lion, proud in the strength of his own nature, knows not how to mingle his ferocity with all and sundry, but, like the king he is, disdains to have a lot of different wives.' For Trevisa, '*Leo* in grew hatte *rex* in latyn, kyng in englisshe, and hatte leo "kyng" for he is kyng and prince of alle bestes ...' (*Properties of Things*, II, 1214). Cf. Lydgate's, *Reson and Sensualyte*, where it is said that Venus cautioned Adonis, 'Teschewe bestys that be proude: / As boors, lippardys, and lyouns': ed. Ernst Sieper, EETS ES 84, 89 (London, 1901, 1903), lines 3714–5.

(ii) Cf. 'a leap of leopards', and note 119 above.

(iii) *sowte, sawt* Probably, an 'attack', 'assault' (ME *saut* <*assaut*), conflated in meaning with the homonym signifying 'a leap, bound' (<OF *salt, saut*); see *MED*, *saut* n.(1) (b), and *saut* n.(2) (a); also Godefroy (s.v. *saultee*, s.f.); Palsgrave, *Lesclarcissement*, p. 699: 'I scoupe ['bound'], as a lyon or a tygre dothe, whan he doth folowe his pray. *Je vas par saultés*. I have sene a leoparde scoupe after a bucke ... : *jay veu ung leopart aller par saultées apres ung dayn* ...'. The notion of an attack accords well with Eg's collective, *sowse* ('a heavy blow', see iv below), and the idea of leaping, bounding is manifest in Pp's choice of *lepe* (ii).

(iv) *sowse* 'striking' (as of a blow); a 'heavy blow'; see *OED*, *souse* n.², *MED*, *soushen* v., and the description of the beaters in the *Parlement of the Thre Ages*, 216–8: 'to floodes þay hyen ... to rere vp the fewles: / Sowssches thaym full serely, to seruen thaire hawkes'.

123 (i) *MED*, s.v. *sute* n. 2c, glosses this phrase mistakenly as 'a set of leash-hounds', despite the obvious fact that all sources refer to a single hound: *u lyum* = a lyam-hound, or limer (see *MED*, *liam* n. (b) and *limer* n.). Such singularity makes perfect sense, since the limer – a type of bloodhound – was always used on its own when tracking game, especially before the start of a hunt: see *MG*, pp. 83–91. The phrase most likely means 'a pursuit / searching of a limer' (*MED*, *sute* n. 3a), though there may also be an added sense of 'a retinue, following', referring to the main body of running hounds that follow the limer's lead (see *MED*, *sute* n. 2a). As elsewhere, this is a strange phrase to have in a list generally concerned with expressing the notion of plurality.

(ii) In both editions of *HSG*, the end-noun appears as *lyhm*, with two dots above the *m* – a character overlooked by William Blades in his inventory of Caxton's typecase: *The Biography and Typography of William Caxton* (London, 1877; repr. Totowa, NJ, 1971), Plate XIII. Dr Lotte Hellinga has suggested to me that the character could represent a mis-casting of *m* with a single long bar above it, usually read as *mm* or *mme*. Alternatively, the two dots could be taken as a variation of the apostrophe that indicates *er*, perhaps with a doubling of the *m* also intended, to produce *lyhm(m)er*. Although the term *limer* appears in no other J.B. source, I have opted to represent the end-noun as *lyhmer* rather than *lyhm(m)e*; the deliberate use of the dotted *m* in both editions of *HSG* suggests that the compositors regarded it as a distinct character, and not simply an alternative for the single-barred *m*. For further discussion of the issues raised briefly in this note, see my article 'Caxton's Printings of The Hors, the Shepe and the Ghoos: Some Further Considerations', *Transactions of the Cambridge Bibliographical Society*, 13 (2004), 1–13.

124 (i) *rage* 'playfulness', probably with the added sense of 'flirtatiousness', and possibly 'love-sickness'; see *MED*, *rage* n. 6, 7; *ragen* v. 4. Hands reads *rage* as 'wanton behaviour' (*EHH*, p. 159/1982n); cf. Chaucer's description of Nicholas and Alisoun, who 'rage and pleye' while Alisoun's husband is away on business (*CT*, I.3273). With the exception of *StA*, in which the proper sequence has been disarranged, this phrase is contiguous with 'a rage of teeth' (no. 206).

(ii) *lure* 'luring', 'alluring' – a metaphor derived from falconry; see the accompanying phrase 'a lure of falcons' (no. 65), and *Femina*: 'A lure of ffaukones & damezelez' (p. 4). Bibbesworth offers a curious comment: 'luyre de puceles. / Mes pucele ceo set saunz juper / Les gentils faucouns aluirer' (p. 8). There is, however, a vital distinction in the way that *lure* relates to falcons and maidens: falcons are recalled by means of a lure, whereas maidens, because of their alluring qualities, may be identified with the lure itself.

125 (i, v) *sorde, sourde* 'sord' = 'rising-up' (in flight), an 'up-soaring' (<OF *sourde*, 'to rise up, spring up'). There is evidence that this collective is not simply an invention of the J.B. lists, since it appears also in *StA*'s main hawking treatise: 'when ther be in a stobull tyme sordes of mallardes in the felde' (*PH*, 1111–2). See also the related verb in the J.B. 'flying terms' in MS H: '... whan þe hawke hath not fowndyn hyr game ... but it spryngyth or sordyth vp sodenly be hym' (II/131–3).

(ii) *swerde* Error for *sorde, sourde* through association with ME *sorde/ swerd*, 'a sword'. See *MED*, *sword* n. (with variants *sorde, swerde, surd*).

(iii) *sorte, sorth* 'flock' (<OF). This word serves in many contexts as a general term for a group, troop, company, multitude; see *MED*, *sorte* n. With the exception of Eg, *HSG* and *StA*, this is the preferred term of the long lists, with the short lists opting for 'sord' (i above); it is a noteworthy feature of L that the scribe has here departed from the model offered by H, which he usually follows closely. Hodgkin is mistaken in treating *sorte* and *sorde* as the same word ('Terms I', p. 28 and no. 96): each has its own independent tradition.

(iv) *surt(e)* Most likely a variant of *so(u)rde* or of *sorte* (i, iii above).

(v) *A sorde or a sute* The second term, *sute*, is most likely a simple compositor's error for *surte* (iv above). My conjecture is that the manuscript source of *StA* contained only *surte* and that the printer added *sorde* because of his knowledge of the term from *StA*'s hawking treatise (see the quote in (i) above), thereby creating this unique pairing of collectives. However, *sute* can also be regarded as an independent term: *MED* treats it as an example of 'a band, retinue, company' (s.v. *sute* n. 2), while Hands (*EHH*, p. 153/1938n) suggests 'the sense of "pursuit" (with the image of the disturbed birds flying off "after each other")'.

For *sorde* ('rising-up'), see (i) above, *pace MED*, which glosses it as a form of *sorte*, 'flock' (s.v. *sorte* n. 1a); see (iii) above.

(vi) *flusche* 'rushing, whirring' – perhaps onomatopoeic. This noun is not in *MED*, but see *flusshen* v. and *flusshing* ger.

126 Both *stode* and *harresse* (<AN *haras*) refer to the same things: the place or enclosure where animals were kept for breeding, as well as the breeding animals themselves: see *MED*, *stode* n.(1) and note 100 above. See also *Nominale*, p. 23*, 'Vn harasse de poleyns, A stode of coltes'; and cf. *Sir Perceval of Galles*, 326–7: 'He sawe a full faire stode / Offe coltes and of meres gude'; in *Middle English Metrical Romances*, II, 531–603.

127 Followed by 'a venture of shipmen' (no. 180), which is also unique to Pp. See Chaucer's description of the Shipman for some indications of the knowledge (ME *science* <L *scientia*) required for maritime navigation: *CT*, I.401–4.

128 (i) *ryches* 'wealth, opulence', with reference to the high value placed on a marten's pelt. Hodgkin provides some interesting illustrative quotes on this topic: 'Terms I', no. 56.

(ii) There is very likely no difference in meaning between this pair of phrases and those of group i, since Rd's *marterys* and Pp's *martyrs* are both possible variant forms of ME *martrin* (<OF *martre*), 'a marten'. However, there is the interesting possibility that *MED*, s.v. *richesse* n. 5(c), could be correct in interpreting Rd's *marterys* as 'martyrs'; the collective should then be understood as referring to their spiritual wealth.

129 Hodgkin ('Terms I', no. 191) sees this as referring to the failure of masters (probably in the sense of 'master tradesmen' or 'master craftsmen') to follow the example they set for others; however, the phrase need not be sarcastic in intent. See *MED*, s.v. *maister* n. 5. (a).

130 (i, ii) *host* Probably an 'army', an 'armed throng', rather than just a 'multitude'. This phrase is usually paired with 'a host of sparrows' (no. 190) – perhaps referring to the destructive power of a large flock of these birds – and in eight of the long lists there follows 'a fellowship of yeomen / yeomanry', another phrase with strong military associations.

(ii) As a collective noun for men, 'company' appears also in *THawk 2*: 'a company of men and of women' (p. 144).

131 (i) Pl is damaged at the point where this phrase occurs in Prk's sequence. It seems likely that the phrase is sarcastic in intent, and Hodgkin ('Terms I', no. 192) suggests that 'faith' may refer to the treachery involved in the 'false packing' of goods. But it could equally stand for the whole gamut of mercantile sharp practices.

(ii) The words *alius deseyt* ('or deceit') are written above *feyth*, apparently as an afterthought or personal interjection. Perhaps the copyist, John Benet, had recently been hoodwinked by an untrustworthy merchant.

132 Cf. 'Hawks (of the Tower)', no. 93.iii. The merlin is a type of falcon, or 'hawk of the tower', so the collective is appropriate.

133 Presumably this refers to the diligence with which a messenger carries out his duties – or is supposed to.

134 (i–iii) *franchesse, franchize, fraunch* 'privilege', referring either to the toll, or multure, forfeited to a miller by his clients, or the right to exact such a toll; similarly, the collective could point to the monopoly that a miller enjoyed over a particular area. See MED, *fraunchise* n.; *fraunche* n.; also, Bennett, *Life on the English Manor*, pp. 129–35, for an account of the mill as a manorial monopoly, and the penalties for taking one's corn to a rival mill. Rd's *franchype* is probably no more than scribal error for *franchyse*.

(iv) *fraudysnes* ?'fraudulence', such as one sees in the behaviour of the miller in Chaucer's *Reeve's Tale* (*CT*, I.4092–9). Bennett, *Life on the English Manor*, p. 135, observes that the good character and honesty of millers was often questioned. The two elements of this collective noun, *fraudys* + *-nes*, suggest a formation based on the OF adjective *fraudeux, fraudieux*, with the addition of the English suffix *-ness*, to produce a unicum synonymous with the usual noun, *fraudulence* (see MED, s.v.).

136 (i) 'A horrible spectacle of monks': an expression of anticlerical sentiment sustained by the next phrase in several J.B. lists: 'a superfluity of nuns' (no. 141). The collective 'sight', meaning 'large number' occurs elsewhere in association with conies and greys (nos 39, 88), but nowhere else is it qualified as it is here.

(ii) It seems likely that the word *sight* has been omitted by the scribe, rather than that *abominable* is here used as an otherwise unattested collective noun, as is asserted by both MED, s.v. *abhominable* adj. 3. and OED, s.v. *abominable*, adj., n., and adv. (n. 1).

(iii–iv) It is interesting to see both Harl and HSG opting for more respectful collectives for monks, although Harl alone does the same for nuns (see no. 141). There may, however, be some implied criticism in HSG's 'lordship', suggesting, as it does, a figure such as Chaucer's Monk, 'daun Piers', with his many wordly pretensions: *CT*, I.165–207.

137 The term 'labour' is the usual collective for moles (see no. 135), with reference to their constant digging through the ground. The end-noun *muldwarpus*

– literally, 'earth-throwers' – survives in MnE (chiefly in northern England) in various permutations, such as *moudiewart, mouldywarp*; see *OED, mouldwarp* | *moldwarp* n.; *MED, molde-werpe* n.; Clive Upton *et al., Survey of English Dialects: The Dictionary and Grammar* (London and New York, 1994), s.v. *mouldy-warp* n. Cf. modern German *Maulwurf* 'mole' <MHG *moltwerf*, rendered as 'Erdaufwerfer', lit. 'earth up-thrower' by Gerhard Wahrig, *Deutsches Wörterbuch* (Gütersloh, 1968).

138 (i) *baren, bareyne* 'barrenness', alluding to the mule's sterility. *MED* recognises the adjective *baraine*, but not this noun. There may be a pun here on ME *beren*, 'to carry', with reference to the mule as a beast of burden. Pp's *boryane* looks like scribal error for *barayne*.

(ii) The allusion to the mule's status as a beast of burden is obvious, but the collective may also contain a pun on Latin *burdo*, 'a hinny' – the progeny of a horse and a she-ass (the term *mulus* being reserved for the mule proper; i.e. the offspring of a jackass and a mare). In Middle English the term *mule* was used for both types of animal – see *MED, mule* n.(1) – but *burd* ('a hinny') was also known, though less commonly used. *MED* does not record the noun *burd*, but it is used by Trevisa, *Properties of Things*, II, 1219, lines 9–11.

139 (i) 'A drove of neat' = 'a herd of cattle', referring to the fact that these animals are 'driven' before a herdsman. This phrase occurs only in the long lists, but three short lists contain the synonymous formulation 'a drove of beasts' (no. 9).

(ii) *dryfte* 'drift' = 'drove, herd'; see *MED, drift* n. 1. This collective is most commonly applied to tame swine (no. 200).

140 (i, iii) *wache, wecche* 'wakefulness', with reference to the nightingale's nocturnal singing. The expression could also be suggestive of nightingales as 'standing watch', like sentinels; see *MED, wacche*, n. 1. (a), 6. (b).

(ii) *nayngales* It is difficult to account for this word except as scribal error, since it resembles nothing recorded by *MED*, s.vv. *nighte-gale* n. or *nightin-gale* n.

(iii) *wage* Most likely an error for *wacche*, perhaps influenced by ME *waggen*, 'to make rapid movements', 'to flutter'.

141 There is a strong streak of anticlericalism apparent in many of the J.B. lists, especially the long ones, which can be seen also in the treatment of clerks, friars, monks and priests (nos 35, 76, 136, 161).

(i) The principal sense of *superfluity* must be 'excessive number', 'overabundance', but there may also be an additional sarcastic sense of 'extravagance' or 'immoderation', implying behaviour contrary to that expected of a nun; see *MED*, s.v. *superfluite* n. 1a, 1c, 1d. When Trevisa describes 'bestes þat vseþ superfluite and continuance of seruice of Venus', the term indicates libidinous excesses: *Properties of Things*, II, 1103.

142 This phrase is often grouped with 'a cluster of grapes' and 'a cluster of churls/carls' (not necessarily in that order); see e.g. Prk, I/86–8 and H, II/238–9.

143 (i) The officers referred to here would have been court officials, charged with executing, or enforcing, a legal judgement, carrying out a sentence, and the like. In all witnesses bar *StA*, the sequence is: judges, lawyers, jurors, officers.

(ii) *excusion* Probably scribal error for *execusion*, since *excusion* makes no sense as an independent term.

144 'A team', such as that which pulls a plough or a cart. In the case of ducks and swans (nos 56, 62, 63, 198), however, the word indicates a 'brood', 'hatching'.

145 'A misbelief of painters' – an enigmatic statement. Hands glosses *StA*'s *misbeleue* as 'disbelief, incredulity' (*EHH*, p. 163/2011n); Hodgkin proposes an allusion to portraitists who 'misbelieve' the real appearance of their subjects and paint them in a flattering way ('Terms I', no. 197); and *MED* glosses the noun *misbileve* as 'heathen belief', 'heresy' and 'religious disbelief'. Perhaps the collective indicates 'someone not to be believed' – a refererence to the fact that painters create simulacra of reality: paintings that can only ever be parodies of God's creation, and that need, accordingly, to be treated with strong scepticism. Perhaps the phrase represents Lollard antipathy towards religious images and those who create them.

146 The panter (ME *panetere*) was the household official who supervised the pantry or bread-closet (<AN *paneterie*), and had responsibility for the cutting and serving of bread, particularly in the form of trenchers; his duties are described in detail in *BK*, p. 266. Hence, *kerf, carfe*: a 'carving, slicing' (of bread). This phrase normally occurs only in the long lists of collectives; in L it is one of eight phrases interpolated by a second scribe.

147 One need look no further than the forged Papal bulls and other tricks of the trade employed by Chaucer's Pardoner for justification of this phrase: *CT*, I.686–706; VI.335 ff.

(ii) *lesyng* 'lying' (<OE *leasung*); see *MED, lesinge* ger.; *lesen* v.(2).

148 The collective 'covey' (ME *covei(e)* <AN *covee, cove, coveie* <OF 'a hatching') must have referred originally to a brood of partridge chicks, but came to be used of the adult birds as well, as can be seen in *StA*'s hawking treatise: 'and let yowre spanyellis fynde a couy of partrichys' (*PH*, 426–7); *THawk 2*: 'And þou shalt sey, thou hast j founde a Covey of Partriches' (pp. 143–4). *THawk 1* offers the following definitions: 'How many is a covi of partrykkes? Als many as hawntis in a place and kepis hem togedir passyng II ... How few may be a covy? Þu may say III resonabely and no fewer' (lines 241–4). Cf. 'a team of cygnets / swans', 'a brood of hens' (nos 56, 98, 198) for other phrases modelled on the same idea.

149 *mustur, mosture* 'muster' = 'exhibition', 'display', such as the peacock makes with his tail; see *MED, moustre* n. Hodgkin ('Terms I', no. 88) reads Eg's collective as *monstyr*, which *MED* allows as an acceptable variant of the term (<OF *moustre*,

monstre, 'spectacle'); my own examination of the manuscript inclines me to prefer *moustyr* over *monstyr*.

150 Pedlars were presumably thought to be malapert – i.e. presumptuous, impudent, shameless – in the way that they pressed an uninterested public to buy their wares; see *MED*, *malapert* adj.; *malapertnesse* n. In the J.B. lists, pedlars usually fall into a sequence that includes pardoners and tinkers, sometimes also jugglers and harpers – all peripatetic vagabonds: see e.g. Prk, I/99–102. If Langland's depiction of pedlars is anything to go by, they were not an especially wholesome group; in the words of Coueytise: 'I haue as moche pite of pore men as pedlere hath of cattes, / That wolde kille hem, yf he cacche hem my3te for coueitise of here skynnes' (Langland, *Piers Plowman*, B V.258–9).

151 *congregacon* 'gathering, assembly'; the term does not necessarily indicate a group assembled in church. This phrase is often paired with 'a congregation of plovers' (no. 156).

152 I have separated *iye* from *nye*, although they are but two forms of the same word: ME *nie*, 'a nest' (<AN *ni*, *ney*, *nid* <OF <L *nidus*), with *an iye* representing a misdivision of *a nye*. (See *AND*, s.v. *ni*¹ s.) The collective thus indicates a 'nest' or 'brood' of pheasants, equivalent to 'a covey of partridges' and 'a covert of coots' (nos 42, 148). Cf. *Femina*, 'Nye dez fesauntez ... A nye of fesauntes' (p. 2); *Nominale*, 'Vn Ny de fesauntz, A hep of fesaundes' (p. 25). The collective must have referred originally to a brood of pheasant chicks, but came to be used of the adult birds also, as in the hawking treatise *THawk 2*: 'And þou shalt sey, thou hast j founde ... an ye a [*sic*] of Fesauntes' (pp. 143–4).

153 (i) *tydynge*, *tydyngys* 'tiding(s)', 'bringing of news (or gossip)' – a role traditionally attributed to the magpie; cf. Chaucer, *Troilus and Criseyde*, III.526–27: 'Dredeles, it cler was in the wynd / Of every pie and every lette-game'. Hodgkin ('Terms I', p. 33) offers a different interpretation by referring to the superstition that when a person encounters magpies, the exact number seen can be an augur of the future.

(ii) *chaturyng* 'chattering' (onomatopoeic).

154 The pinder was a manorial official with responsibility for impounding stray animals – particularly those belonging to villagers or tenant farmers – that had strayed out of bounds. It is not difficult to imagine how unpopular pinders would have been, or how they might be conceived as a *frowardnes*, a 'contrariness, maliciousness', or a *waywerdnes*, a 'waywardness, perversity, injustice'.

155 Although it is not difficult to imagine that musicians such as pipers might have been well known for their indigence, the collective that has been ascribed to them may also have been chosen for reasons of humorous alliteration. Cf. no. 91.iii (harpers) and the related note above.

156 (i) 'A gathering, assembly ~'. This phrase is often paired with 'a congregation of people' (no. 151), probably for humorous effect.

(ii) 'A brood ...' (<OE *brod*) = a 'hatch, hatching'.

(iii) *haunte* 'gathering', 'flock' (<AN *hant* 'a place frequented by birds and animals', especially for feeding). Although both noun and verb (*haunten*) could be used of humans in a wide range of contexts, they were also the correct technical terms to be used of birds and animals in relation to their regular retreats for feeding or resting, as in *MG*, 19: 'And ʒif he [the hart] may not abide he takeþ þan his leeue of his haunte'; T.S., *A Jewell for Gentrie* (London, 1614; facs. edn, Amsterdam and Norwood, NJ, 1977): 'It is the nature of the Plouer ... to flye together in shoales or companies, and for the most part they wil after feeding, haunt one place' (sig. K1v). The noun also came to refer to 'a large number of birds', perhaps because many are in the habit of congregating in the same place; see e.g. *Sir Orfeo*, 285–6: 'Of game they founde well gode haunt – / Maulardes, hayroun, and cormeraunt'; in *Middle English Verse Romances*, ed. Donald B. Sands (Exeter, 1986; repr. 1996).

158 (i) Hodgkin's suggestion that the collective *safeguard* may refer to a long protective apron of that name is not convincing; no such sense is recorded by *MED* (s.v. *sauf-garde* n.), and the earliest attestation of anything remotely similar (a woman's outer skirt or petticoat) is first attested by the *OED only* in 1585 (s.v. *safeguard* n. 7).

Hands (*EHH*, p. 162/2006n) points out that the end-noun *porters* could refer to 'doorkeepers' (<OF *portier*) as well as 'carriers' (<OF *porteour*). Since this phrase occurs in a sequence of statements about household officials (in Rd: servants, stewards, ushers, pantrymen, butlers, sewers, carvers, porters), its most likely sense would appear to be 'a protection, safe-keeping of doorkeepers'. See the description of the porter's office in *The Boke of Curtasye*: 'The porter falle to kepe þo ʒate, / Þe stokkes with hym erly and late; / ʒif any man hase in court mys-gayne, / To porter warde he schalle be tane... Of strangers also þat comen to court, / Þo porter schalle warne ser at a worde' (lines 361–70; cf. also 351–5; in *Babees Book*, pp. 309–10).

(ii) *suffrage* 'assistance', 'aiding'; see *MED*, *suffrage* n.

159 Presumably, 'a converting' (to Christianity), as well as 'a turning aside' (from unrighteousness).

160 (i) *pontifical* = pontificals (or pontificalia), the name given to the robes or vestments of high ecclestiastics, such as bishops, cardinals and abbots.

(ii) *pontificalite* 'the tenure of a pope', hence, a 'popishness'; see *MED*, *pontificalite* n. and *pontifical* adj. The collective probably represents a caustic broadside at posturing prelates for behaving as if they were the pope himself.

(iii) *pontificatenes* Probably identical in meaning to *pontificalite*; see *MED*, *pontificate* n.

161 (i–ii) 'A discreetness ~' = 'prudence, discretion'; but cf. Hodgkin ('Terms I', no. 154), who sees this as a sarcastic dismissal of priests who are unable to safeguard the secrets entrusted to them in confessionals.

(ii) As above, though this form of the collective may also refer to the honorific title 'Your Discretion', used when asking an official to exercise his powers of judgment; see *MED, discrecioun* n. 4.

(iii) *pres(e), prees, preys* 'press', 'crowd, throng': an unflattering term, with the humorous benefit of alliteration, suggesting a plethora, if not a surfeit, of priests; see Hodgkin ('Terms I', no. 162), and cf. 'a superfluity of nuns' (no. 141).

The form of the word in Prk (*preys*) has been interpreted by *MED*, s.v. *preis(e* n. (b), as meaning 'praise' (= ?praising, ?praiseworthiness), but this is to disregard a number of factors. In the first place, this phrase occurs in Prk as the last item in a sequence of unflattering references to clerics: 'an abominable sight of monks', 'a superfluity of nuns', 'a *preys* of priests'. Then there is the logic underlying these terms and the ways in which they are usually constructed. With an abstract noun such as *praise*, we might expect the word to be refashioned as the gerund *praising* if it is intended to suggest the typical activity of the group (cf. 'converting', no. 159). Alternatively, where the collective describes a state, rather than an action, the suffix *-ness* is often added, as with 'discreetness' (no. 161.i), 'richness' (no. 128). According to *MED*, s.v. *presse* n., variants of that word include *preise, prisse, prise, price*; and since Prk's *preys* derives from Pl's *pres*, I have elected to treat it as a permutation of the latter word, rather than as a separate term with entirely different associations altogether.

(iv) Hodgkin ('Terms I', no. 166) suggests that this phrases originated as scribal error for 'a state of princes' (see no. 162). However, the two phrases belong to different traditions: 'a state of priests' occurs only in the short lists, and 'a state of princes' only in the long lists. The collective can be understood as indicating the 'high estate' to which priests belong.

(v) *dyspetenesse* 'haughtiness, disdainfulness' (<ME *despit*, n.; *despitous*, adj.): another unflattering term.

(vi) An error for 'a pontifical of prelates' (see no. 160). The scribe appears to have conflated two phrases with the loss of one.

162 (i) *state* 'sovereignty', 'authority', 'dominion'; see *MED, stat* n. 11 (a), and *estat* n. 12.

(ii) *A pontificalle of prynces* In Rd, this phrase is followed by 'a pontifical of prelates' and 'a state of princes'. Rather than being an independent item, it probably represents an erroneous conflation of the two quoted phrases, but was not deleted when they had themselves been correctly copied into the manuscript.

163 A curiously compassionate sentiment for an age that treated malefactors with severity. Perhaps the originator of this phrase had in mind some current political prisoner, someone who had incurred his sovereign's displeasure or suspicion – a common enough event in the turbulent years of Yorkist and Lancastrian rivalry for the English crown.

164 This phrase is usually grouped with 'a bevy of ladies' and 'a bevy of roes' (nos 115, 171); see e.g. Prk, I/8–10; H, II/202–4; and Ha, III/6–8.

165 'Rabbits' here refers specifically to young rabbits, born in the nest prepared for them by their mother in the depths of their burrow or warren; the adult animals were referred to as 'conies' (see no. 39). See *Noble Arte*, p. 178: 'The Conie beareth hyr Rabettes .xxx. dayes, and then kindeleth'.

(ii) *dow* Read ?*dower*, a 'burrow', variant of ME *douver* (<OF *douvre*, 'a ditch, cave'), referring to the underground warren in which these animals live. It is unclear whether *dow* is itself a variant of *douver/dower*, or whether the word is incomplete in the manuscript: there is a large gap between the words *dow* and *of*, perhaps indicating the scribe's uncertainty about the final letters of *dow⟨...⟩* in his exemplar. Alternatively, perhaps the scribe simply realised that the next word, *rabettes*, would not fit on the line, and decided to spread out those words that could be accommodated.

166 (i) 'A pack of hunting hounds', with the collective *kennel* referring to the place where the dogs are lodged. Cf. 'a haras of horses' and 'a stud of mares' (nos 100, 126) for other phrases modelled on the same idea. Raches, which pursued the quarry by scent, were one of the main groups of 'running hounds' used in a hunt; see note 104 above.

(ii) *kenette* Very likely, scribal error for *kenelle*, under the influence of ME *kenet* (*kenette*), 'a small hunting hound'.

167 The name 'rail' (ME *rale*) has long been used for both the landrail (or corn-crake) and the water rail. The two species are so alike that the landrail, a summer visitor to the British Isles, was previously believed to metamorphose into the water rail during winter: see Lockwood, *British Bird Names*, p. 125. The collective *raskall*, a 'rabble, mob', is normally reserved for boys (no. 16). Perhaps the harsh, grating voice of the landrail inspired the choice of this term. It seems unlikely that the hunting sense 'animals not hunted as game' was intended, *pace* Burton ('Terms', p. 9/12n), though the related sense of 'worthlessness' (suggesting disagreeable qualities) may be implied. For these different senses, see *MED*, *rascaile* n. 2a, 3b.

168 *vnkyndenes* Most likely, 'unnaturalness', 'lacking in natural affection', with reference to the belief that the raven forces its young to fend for themselves until it recognises them as its own by the appearance of glossy black feathers; see White, *Book of Beasts*, pp. 141–2 and Trevisa, *Properties of Things*, I, 621: 'Þe rauen biholdeþ þe mowþe of hire briddes whanne þay ȝaneth, but he[o] ȝeueþ hem no mete or heo knowe and see þe liknesse of here owne blaknesse and of here owne colour and feþeres.' In setting out this item, I have not distinguished 'an unkindness' from 'a non-kindness' because of the ease with which the one form can mutate into the other; cf. H, T and W.

169 *rysyng* an 'uprising', a 'rebellion'; see also note 182.

170 *rebawdez* 'ribalds' = 'rascals, dissolutes, good-for-nothings'; see *MED*, s.v. *ribaude* n. The AN lists prefer the collective 'rout' for this group – e.g. 'Dez rebaudez ... vn route' (*Femina*, p. 4); 'Route de Ribaudes' (*Nominale*, p. 14) – with 'folly' reserved for villeins: 'ffolye ... dez vileynez' (*Femina*, p. 3); 'Grant fouleie dist hom des vileins' (Bibbesworth, p. 8).

171 'Roes' (male and female roe deer) commonly occur in sequence with ladies and quails (nos 115, 164), with all three classified as a 'bevy'; see note 164 above. Only T restricts the collective to the male of the species. The term 'bevy' appears to have been in common use, appearing as it does in hunting treatises, e.g. Twiti-C, 172; *BH*, 1275–80.

172 (i) 'A building of rooks', 'a rookery ~', referring to the huge communities of nests constructed by these birds.

(ii) *beloyng* Perhaps scribal error for *beldyng*, influenced by *belowyng*, as an allusion to the general din generated by a rookery: hence, 'a cawing of rooks'. This would broaden the range of senses admitted by *MED*, which associates bellowing with a sound more akin to roaring (s.v. *belwing* ger.; *belwen* v.).

(iii) *byggyng* 'building', 'edifice' – synonymous with (i) above. See also note 49.ii.

174 'A disworship' = 'a disgrace, dishonour'. In other J.B. lists, the end-noun appears variously as 'sots' and 'stots', perhaps according to the scribe's personal prejudice; see nos 187, 194 and the related notes below.

175 Hands (*EHH*, p. 158/1974n) reads this as referring to an elaborate dish (a 'subtlety' – see no. 195) carried in by a serving man, known as a 'sergeant'. However, the sequence in *StA*, which places this phrase between pipers and bakers, and so prompts Hands to this interpretation, is idiosyncratic, since it has been disarranged by the compositor. My preference is for a more conventional exposition: 'a sagacity, shrewdness of sergeants-at-law (i.e. barristers, lawyers)', with perhaps the added sense of 'skill, cunning (at argument)'; see *MED*, *sotilte* n., senses 1, 3, 4; *sergeaunt* n. 4; and Chaucer's description of the 'Sergeant of the Lawe' in *CT*, I.309–330.

176 (i) The obeisance alluded to here could be one (or more) of three things: obedience itself (as in group ii); a gesture or bow acknowledging someone's authority; or a general disposition of deference; see *MED*, *obeisaunce* n. Whether the phrase was intended sarcastically, as claimed by Hodgkin ('Terms I', no. 183a) is open to debate.

177 The sewer was an attendant who served, carved and tasted his master's food; the noun *credence* referred to the act of tasting, or taking an assay, to prove that a dish had not been poisoned. See *MED*, s.vv. *credence* n. 4; *seuere* n.(3); *OED*, s.v. *credence* n. 5, 6. and Russell's *Boke of Nurture*, 1199: 'Credence is vsed, & tastynge, for drede of poysenynge'. It seems likely that the notion of a credence as 'A side table or sideboard for vessels and dishes ready for being served at table', first attested 1576 (*OED*, *credence* n., sense 7), developed as a transferred sense through references to the serving table where the sewer did his tasting. Cf. the later, parallel borrowing *credenza* < Italian (first attested in English in 1834).

(ii) *devydyng* Probably, a 'carving' (of food), though the word could refer instead to the action of 'separating' (the guests), i.e. seating them at table – one of the main duties of the *asseour*, a domestic official whose duties and name sometimes overlapped with those of the sewer. The title *sewer* itself is thought to be the aphetic form of ME *asseour* <AF *assaiour*, OF *asseeor*.

178 This phrase is a strong marker of disparate traditions among extant lists of collectives. In the AN lists, sheep are invariably a 'trip' (*trip, tripe, trippe*), whereas the J.B. lists consistently prefer 'flock' for sheep, reserving 'trip' for goats and hares (nos 80, 89); see e.g. Bibbesworth p. 8, 'trippe de berbiz'. The form *chepe* in Dg and Rg is a recognised variant of ME *shep*.

179 (i) *doppyng* 'diving' <ME *doppen*, 'to dive'. Sheldrakes (now known as 'shelducks' or 'sheld ducks') are also referred to as 'herles'; see no. 97 and the associated note above.

(ii) *drowping* Perhaps an error for *doppyng*, influenced by ME *drouping*, 'cowering, hiding, lurking', as in the *Promptorium* (ed. Mayhew): 'Daryn, or drowpyn, or privyly to be hyd: *Latito* ...' (col. 135).

180 Most likely, 'A risk (i.e. a perilous undertaking) of seamen', with reference to the dangers of life at sea, and complementing the preceding phrase in Pp, 'a great science of mariners' (no. 127); see *MED*, *venture* n. 2. Alternatively, Tom Burton proposes ('Terms', pp. 10–11/106n) that *schippemen* could refer to ships' masters, rather than the ordinary sailors, and that *venture* conveys the notion of a hazardous business enterprise (a sense first attested by the *OED*, s.v. *venture* n. 4.a, in 1584). Cf. the question asked of Antonio's apparent losses in Shakespeare's *The Merchant of Venice*: 'Hath all his ventures failed? What, not one hit?' (III.ii.265).

181 There is little evidence to determine precisely what 'shoe-turners' were, and how they differed from cobblers, who are also classed as a *plukke* in one J.B. list (see no. 36.ii). The word is not glossed by *MED*, and *OED*, citing only *StA*, suggests a 'workman who "turns" or cuts to shape the soles of shoes': s.v. *shoe* n., Compounds C3; see also s.v. *turner* n.[1] 1.a. Hodgkin ('Terms I', no. 207), on the other hand, suggests a maker of 'turned shoes': i.e. shoes that are made inside-out and then 'turned' into the right shape. But he offers no evidence to support this assertion, and the first attestation of such a sense is 1882: see *OED* s.v. *turned* adj. 6.c.

Hodgkin is probably also mistaken to associate the collective *pluck* with 'a wooden peg', a 'pegging awl' (related to modern German *Pflock*). The term probably describes the characteristic action of a shoe-maker as he 'plucks', or pulls tight, the thread as he sews on the sole of a shoe.

182 *shrewez* 'rascals, rogues'; see *MED, shreue* n. 1(a). The collective *rysyng* depicts them as being in uprising, rebellion.

183 Both *mace* and *verge* indicate the same object: a rod, or staff, of office. Cf. the AN versions: 'Mace dargent ... Mas of seluer' (*Femina*, p. 3); 'Masse de argent' (Bibbesworth, p. 8); and see *A-ND*, s.v. *mace*¹ s. In both C and Dg* this phrase is preceded by 'a sum of gold' (no. 81).

184 (i) *musyn, musyone* Variants of ME *musicien*, 'musician', 'a performer or composer of music'; hence, presumably, a 'musicianship'.

(ii) Explained in note 184.i above.

185 (i) *walke* Presumably, an allusion to the way in which this wading bird strides through the shallows in search of prey. The form *snite* derives from OE; *snipe*, used by Adv alone, probably comes from ON; see *MED*, s.vv. *snipe* n., *snite* n.

(ii) *fall* The collective normally applied to woodcocks; it probably means an 'alighting' – see the discussion in note 221.

186 Cf. Shakespeare's portrait of the soldier, 'Seeking the bubble reputation / Even in the cannon's mouth': *As You Like It*, II.vii.152–3.

(ii) *blast* Most likely referring to a blast on a horn, or military trumpet. The collocation evokes the general clamour associated with a band of soldiers.

187 'A disgrace of fools, dolts'; perhaps also 'rascals, villains'; see *MED, sot* n.(1). It is unclear whether *sotes* here represents scribal error or an intentional emendation of 'Scots' or 'stots' (nos 174, 194), the two groups normally associated with the collective 'disworship'.

188 *blecche* 'blackening', referring to the black dye (ME *blacche*) used by cobblers to darken leather – especially the cut edges of a piece of leather – in shoe-making.

189 Hunting hounds were commonly led to the field in pairs, or couples; cf. 'a brace of hounds' (no. 103). It is not known when spaniels were introduced to England, but they were clearly familiar to Edward of York in the early 15th century; see e.g. *MG*, cap. 17, which refers to spaniels as 'hounds for the hawk' (*chienz d'oisel* in his source: *LC*, cap. 20).

190 This phrase is usually paired with 'a host of men' (no. 130), which has unmistakable military connotations. Hodgkin ('Terms I', no. 72) could well be correct in claiming that the collective noun refers to the 'destructive habits' of a flock of sparrows, and therefore evokes the notion of an army or hostile force, equivalent to that of 'a host of men'.

191 In the J.B. lists, the collective 'rout' is usually applied to knights (no. 114), not squires. Matters are different in the AN lists, however, with which C here agrees; see specifically *Nominale* ('Route de Esquiers': p. 14) and *Femina* ('A Route seyþ man of squiers': p. 4).

192 Note the clear division between the long lists, which have 'a murmuration', and the short lists, which prefer some form of 'chattering'. Both words describe the low, continuous chirruping, twittering and warbling of a flock of starlings.

(v) *chiteryng* 'twittering'. This is the word used in several manuscripts of Chaucer's *Miller's Tale,* when Alisoun's singing is compared with that of a swallow: 'But of hir song it was as loude and yerne / As any swalwe sittyng [*var.* chitering] on a berne' (*CT*, I.3257–8); for the reading *chitering*, see *The Text of the Canterbury Tales*, ed. John M. Manly and Edith Rickert, 8 vols (Chicago, 1940).

(vi) *claterynge* 'chattering' <ME *clateren*, 'to chatter, babble, gossip'. This collective is normally applied to 'choughs' and 'daws' (nos 33, 58).

193 The steward was the official in charge of a household: the major-domo. His responsibilities would have included exercising foresight, making advance arrangements for all the staff under his control, and ensuring that the household was adequately stocked with all necessities. These several duties are all encompassed by the different senses of ME *provisioun*.

194 *stottes* disreputable women: 'prostitutes' or 'bawds'; see *MED*, *stot* n. 2.(a), (b). Hence, 'an unworthiness of sluts'.

Hodgkin ('Terms I', no. 229) offers an alternative interpretation, drawing on the primary sense of *stot* as a 'steer, bullock or horse' (see *MED*, *stot* n. 1). In Hodgkin's view, this phrase alludes to the custom of Plough Monday (the first Monday after 6 January), when a number of men, drawing a plough in the manner of 'steers', would ask for money or refreshment. If refused, they would plough up the ground in front of the niggard's house, regardless of his station. Hence, Hodgkin's reading: 'a disrespectfulness of "steers"'.

Owing to the haphazard capitalisation of nouns and the similarity of *c* and *t* in many scribal hands, it is not always easy to determine whether the end-noun of this phrase should be read as 'stots' (as here) or as 'Scots' (no. 174), who are also classed as a 'disworship'. Some witnesses are clearer than others in this regard.

195 *MED* interprets the end-noun *soteltes* as referring to 'contrived or specious deductions', as well as 'dissembling' or 'blandishments', both eminently plausible suggestions: see s.vv. *non-credibilite* n.; *sotilte* n. 4(b). However, the word may also be understood as alluding to something entirely different: viz. culinary 'subtleties' (see *MED*, *sotilte* n. 5). These comprised a diverse range of dishes that were created for special effect, especially at grand banquets. Some were elaborate sculptures made from sugar; others were intended to create surprise or amusement – such as the 'four-and-twenty blackbirds baked in a pie' of the

nursery rhyme; and some were no more than dishes in which the ingredients were disguised to appear as something else: e.g. fish or almond paste disguised to look like eggs during Lent. The menus of great feasts show that subtleties were often included with each course. See *Curye on Inglysch*, p. 39, no. 1; p. 153, no. 15; *An Ordinance of Pottage*, pp. 67, 110; Mrs Alexander (Robina) Napier, *A Noble Boke off Cookry* (London, 1882), p. 37; Russell, *Boke of Nurture*, pp. 164–70; and the denunciation of such extravagances by Chaucer's Parson (*CT*, X.443–4). Some subtleties appear to have been dramatic tableaux, such as those brought forth during the coronation banquet of Henry VI: *Secular Lyrics*, pp. 98–9. The essence of a culinary subtlety was that it should provoke amazement and incredulity: hence, a *noncredibilite*. It is surely no coincidence that painters – a group responsible for another form of artifice – are also presented as challenging credulity or belief: see no. 145.

196 Needs no explanation in the light of Chaucer's depiction of this profession: *CT*, I.623 ff. and III.1321 ff.

197 (i) *flyght* Presumably, a reference to the fast, skimming flight of the swallow. Cf. nos 44, 61, 84, 117 for other phrases that employ this collective.

(ii) *slyght* Most likely, an error for *flyght*, though the scribe has used a round *s*, and has not simply forgotten to add a crossbar to a long *s* / *f*.

198 With the exception of Adv, C and Dg*, there is a clear distinction between the long lists, which prefer 'herd' as the collective for swans, and the short lists, which opt for 'team'.

(ii) *teme* Presumably, a 'brood' or 'hatching' of young swans; see *MED*, *teme* n.(1) 1b, and *temen* v.(1) 1(a) 'to produce offspring'. Cf. the variant 'a team of cygnets' (no. 56), and see also notes 62, 63. Birds, especially waterfowl, are often categorised in terms of their broods of chicks.

199 This phrase belongs properly with 'a sounder of wild swine' (no. 201), the scribe having omitted the modifier 'wild'. I have placed it under a separate headword in case other texts are discovered in which this formulation is repeated.

200 *dryfte* 'drove, herd', referring to animals that are driven. In *MG*, the collective *trip* is used to distinguish tame from wild swine: 'þat men calle a trip of a tame swyne is called of wilde swyne a soundre' (p. 30).

201 (i) Cf. *Femina*, 'Soundre dez porks ... A sondre of hogges' (pp. 2–3). As the correct term for a herd of wild pigs, 'sounder' was clearly in common usage. See the quotation from *MG* in note 200 above, and *SGGK*, 1439–40: 'On þe sellokest swyn swenged out þere / Long sythen fro þe sounder þat siʒed for olde'. See also *BH*, 1281–6, for the different names used of a sounder according to its size.

(ii) *gendir* 'litter' (of young) <ME *gendren* 'to give birth'. *MED* s.v. *gendre* n. glosses the word more prosaically as 'herd, group' (<OF).

(iii) Scribal error must lie behind this formulation, since the collective *drift* fails to make sense here: tame swine (no. 200) may be driven, but not wild swine.

202 (i) *disgysyng* 'dressing in showy attire', 'dressing in a newfangled fashion' (<OF *desguiser*). The phrase may be critisising tailors for their own extravagant attire, as much as for dressing their clients in lavish clothes. The absurdities of high fashion were often lamented, as in *The Simonie*, a satirical poem on the evil times of Edward II: 'Knihtes sholde weren weden in here manere ... Nu ben theih so degysed [*sic*] and diverseliche i-diht, / Unnethe may men knowe a gleman from a kniht, / wel neih' (lines 253–7): *The Political Songs of England*, ed. Thomas Wright, Camden Society (London, 1839), pp. 323–45.

(ii) Expresses essentially the same idea as 'disguising'. Hodgkin ('Terms I', no. 189) suggests an allusion to the custom whereby yeoman tailors adopted a new livery or suit every year. Cf. the term *proud tailor* as a name (now historical and obsolete) for the gaudily feathered goldfinch: *OED*, s.v. *proud* adj., n., and adv., Compounds C3 (attested 1770).

203 *tapsters* As *MED* demonstrates, the noun *tappestere* was used indiscriminately in Middle English of both men and women who drew and served ale, or who otherwise kept a tavern or alehouse. Their promises might then be understood in terms of the quantities of alcohol they have to offer, together with the carousing that goes with it. But it is also apparent that *tappestere* came to be used as a derogatory term for women, suggesting that some female tapsters, or alewives, were known for offering their clients more than just liquid refreshment. In his essay on 'Rural Society', Mark Bailey has an intriguing reference to a certain Joanna Skeppere who, in 1471, was said to have 'maintained a "tapster" in her [ale]house which attracted "lecherous and suspicious men"'; in *Fifteenth Century Attitudes* (ed. Horrox), pp. 150–68 (p. 165).

204 *glosyng* 'flattering', 'smooth-talking' – suggesting a taverner's deferential or obsequious professional demeanour, adopted to keep his customers happy.

205 *spryng* 'upsurge', a 'flying' (into the air); see *MED*, s.vv. *spring* n. 4, 5, and *springen* v. 5(a), and cf. 'a sord (= a rising-up) of mallards' (no. 125), which is normally the next item in the J.B. lists.

(ii-iii) *turbe* 'flock', 'troop' (<AN *turbe* 'crowd', 'flock' <OF). Cf. *Nominale*: 'Vn tourbe de cercels, A hep of telus' (p. 25).

206 *rage* 'aching', 'pain' (see *MED*, *rage* n. 5(b)), a distressing reminder of the poor dental health from which many people suffered at this time. The phrase might then be understood as meaning something like, 'an attack of toothache'. In T, the end-noun *teth* is preceded by the cancelled letters *th*, suggesting that the lost exemplar from which T was copied also contained 'the teeth', as found in *StA*.

207 'A skulk of thieves': usually occurs in sequence with 'a skulk of foxes / friars' (nos 75, 76; see the relevant notes above).

208 (i) *thrave, thrawe* Refers to a measure of wheat, corn etc.: usually twelve or twenty-four sheaves (depending on locality); hence, figuratively, a 'multitude, crowd', 'many', as in Langland, *Piers Plowman*, B XVI.55: 'Ac I have thou3tes a threve'. See further *MED*, *threve* n. This word is singularly and felicitously apt in combination with the end-noun *threshers*.

(ii) *tharfe* Although I have separated this formula from others in group i, the collective *tharfe* is probably best read as scribal error for *thrafe* = *thrave* (ME *threve*), examined above. On the other hand, it is remotely possible that ME *tharf* (<OE *þearf*), 'a need', 'a poverty', was intended, though it would appear from quotations in the *MED* that this word had largely faded from use by the mid-13th century.

(iii) *tawght* Obscure. If not a mistake, perhaps it can be read as a variant of *tough*, which *MED* (s.v. *tough* adj.) also records in the forms *tou3t(e, togh(e, to3t*. Toughness or strength would have been desirable attributes for the exhausting task of threshing.

(iv) *barne* Refers to the storage building in which threshing would have taken place in winter or bad weather.

209 This phrase is incomplete in both editions of *HSG*, but since the collective *mutation* occurs in conjunction with no other end-noun, it seems likely to belong with others in this group.

The exact nature of the throstle's mutation is obscure. In ME, the name *throstel* could indicate both the blackbird (*Turdus merula*) and the song thrush (*Turdus philomelos*), both known for their complex, musical singing. Perhaps this phrase refers to the mutation that takes place when a blackbird moults from its speckled brown juvenile plumage into its adult black; or to the way in which the song of a thrush becomes ever more complex as it grows up; or perhaps to the thrush's ability to mimic other birds and sounds. Hodgkin ('Terms I', no. 89) suggests a possible connection with the folk belief that a thrush grows new legs, and casts its old ones, when about ten years old. However, his citations for this belief all belong to the 19th century.

210 *wondryng* 'wandering', 'roving', with reference to the peripatetic life of a tinker. The spelling with an *o* is an acceptable variant of ME *wandringe*.

211 *triaclers* Apothecaries who made and sold *triacle* ('treacle') – any of a variety of remedies for a range of ills, but especially an antidote for venom or poison; see *MED*, *triacler* n.; *triacle* n. This phrase seems to contain a strong hint – emphasised by the form *poysonyng* in Adv – that the treaclers' concoctions may have been worse than the poisons they were meant to neutralise.

(iii) *provision* The collective in Pp is difficult to explain, except as the result of scribal misreading and conflation with the phrase 'a provision of stewards'.

212 (i–ii) *duell, dole* 'dole, dolefulness', a 'mourning' (<AN *duel, duil, doel*), with reference to the turtledove's cooing, which sounds like soft weeping, traditionally interpreted as grief for the bird's lost mate; see e.g. Chaucer, *CT*, I.3705–6 and IV.2077–80, and cf. the following passage from the bestiary in MS Bodley 764: 'The dove sighs rather than sings; and so do preachers, not caring for love songs, sigh for their own sins and those of others': *Bestiary: Being an English Version of the Bodleian Library, Oxford, M.S. Bodley 764*, trans. Richard Barber (Woodbridge, 1993), p. 162.

(iii) 'A piteousness' expresses the same idea as above.

(iv–v) 'A truelove' alludes to the traditional fidelity of the turtledove, as described in MS Bodley 764: 'It is said that the turtle-dove, as soon as it loses its partner and is widowed, hates the idea of marriage and the marriage bed ... . So she refuses any new match, and will not dissolve the oaths and bonds that tie her to her dead mate. She continues to love him alone, and to keep the name of wife for him only'; *Bestiary ... Bodley 764*, p. 163. See also Chaucer, *The Parliament of Fowls*, 355: 'The wedded turtil, with hire herte trewe'.

213 (i) The usher was the domestic official responsible for admitting people to a room and then directing them to their seats at a feast; he often occupied a seat at the door to a hall or chamber, as described in *The Boke of Curtasye*, 'Þo vssher alle-way shalle sitt at dore / At mete, and walke schalle on þe flore, / To se þat alle be seruet on ryȝt' (lines 473–5). These duties make possible two readings for the J.B. collective: (1) 'a seatedness', and (2) 'a seating', 'a showing to seats' (the two senses co-exist comfortably together). ME *setten* could be used transitively to mean 'to place on a seat', 'to cause to sit down' (e.g. *CT*, I.748: 'And to the soper sette he us anon'), *pace OED*, which cites Shakespeare and Fletcher (*Henry VIII*, 1623) as the first attestation of this sense of the word (s.v. *seat* v. 1.a). See also no. 40, where the same collective is applied to controllers.

(ii) *fete* Most likely, scribal error for *sete*. However, the word was transcribed without comment as *fete* by Hope Allen ('Fifteenth-century associations', p. 604, col. 1), and accepted as such by *MED*, which includes it with the gloss 'a celebration', s.v. *fete* n.

214 This phrase provides a fine example of how difficult it can be to judge the intended tone of some items. For Hands, the phrase refers to 'the prudence, wisdom and discretion' which should be a vicar's 'chief characteristic' (*EHH*, pp. 156–7/ 1950n); whereas for Hodgkin it's exactly the opposite: 'a sarcastic allusion to the imprudence or improvidence of vicars, e.g. large families and infinitesimal incomes' ('Terms I', no. 163).

215 *wantys* 'wants' = 'moles' <OE *wand*, perhaps a shortened form of OE *wande-weorpe*. This term for a mole is still in dialectical use; see Upton, *Survey of English Dialects*, s.v. *want* n.; *OED*, s.v. *want* n.[1]. The usual form of this phrase is 'a labour

of moles' (no. 135), and there is also another version in Adv, which employs the synonymous end-noun *muldwarpus* (no. 137).

216 The meaning of the end-noun *weldefares*, which is not recorded by *MED*, is not immediately apparent, but it could represent a variation of ME *felde-fare*, *veldevare*, the fieldfare (literally, 'field-goer') of no. 68, with the first element *(felde-)* replaced by ME *wold* in the sense of 'field', 'open country' (see *MED*, *wold* n.(1), 1(a)). Alternatively, *welde-* could indicate 'a wood, forest', yielding the sense of 'forest-goer' (see *MED*, *wold* n.(1), 1(b)). The word might then refer to a bird, an animal or even a human – perhaps a brigand – along the lines of OE *weald-genga*, 'bandit, thief'. The collective *haunte* ('a place frequented', 'a feeding-ground') could apply equally well to an animal, a bird (cf. no. 156), or something more sinister.

217 'A litter of puppies', so named after the place where they are born: a litter, or bed, of straw; see *MED*, s.v. *litere* n. 1–3; *A-ND*, s.v. *litere* s. Cf. 'a kindle of young cats' and 'a brood of hens', amongst others, where the collective noun also refers to the multiple progeny of a creature.

218 *wyues* In Adv, Rd and T, this phrase is preceded by 'a multiplying / number of husbands' (no. 106), suggesting that the particular sense 'married women' is intended here, rather than just 'women'. In Pp, fol. 4r, the entry following 'a number of husbands' has been thoroughly expunged. Given the pattern established elsewhere, it seems very likely that some form of this phrase once stood there, and that it incurred the wrath of an early (possibly, a female) reader who deleted it. The alteration to the manuscript can be clearly seen in the facsimile edition *Stere Htt Well*, p. (7).

219 This phrase commonly occurs in combination with 'a rout of knights', and in Eg it is paired with 'a rout of gentlemen' (see notes 78 and 114.i above). It appears to have been in common use: *BH*, 1262, gives 'Rowte of wolues' as the correct expression to be used of these animals.

(ii) *rawte* Variant (?or erroneous) form of *rowte*.

220 In general, the long lists prefer 'gaggle', and the short lists 'gaggling', as the collective for both women and geese (no. 77), with the two phrases often being paired with one another. See also no. 85, 'a gaggling of gossips', for a different alliterating end-noun.

(iii) *gayling* Probably, 'noise', 'outcry'; see note 77.iii.

(iv) The term 'company' appears also in the AN lists; e.g. 'Compaignie de damys' (*Nominale*, p. 14); 'Des dames dist hom compaignie' (Bibbesworth, p. 8). See also *THawk 2*: 'a company of men and of women' (p. 144); but cf. 'A company of gese and of ladyes' in *THawk 1*, lines 239–40.

(v) In both Adv and Pp, this phrase falls precisely where 'a fellowship of yeomen' (no. 227) normally occurs, as can be seen in Prk, I/23. If the phrase had occurred in only Adv or Pp, the end-noun *wemen* could have been regarded as a scribal error; however, its occurrence in two independent witnesses affords it a certain legitimacy. In this instance, the collective indicates 'comradeship, friendship', 'a comradely band'.

221   (i) *fall* This collective, which is also used of snipes (no. 185), probably refers to the 'settling' or 'alighting' (from flight) of a large number of birds, a sense attested by *MED*, s.v. *fallen* v. 29(d). There is also the possibility of a further dimension, as suggested by Steve Palin, a dedicated bird-watcher and illustrator, who remarks on a notable characteristic of the woodcock's flight – namely, the way that this bird 'collapses', or drops quickly to the ground when landing: *A Dissimulation of Birds* (London, 1998), under *F*. There might then be an affinity with the collective *discencion*, used of woodwalls (see note 222 below).

I am not convinced by Hodgkin's suggestion ('Terms I', no. 87) that the phrase is analagous to the expression 'a fall of snow'. He quotes from the nonconformist Charles Morton (1627–98), who describes how woodcock are often found in large numbers in the morning, where there had been none the previous evening. For Morton, this phenomenon provides an image for understanding the Book of Jeremiah, as he explains by means of the following simile: 'Consider their coming, which is so sudden ... that it is as if they dropped down upon us from above': 'Enquiry into the Physical and Literal Sense of Jeremiah viii:7', in *The Harleian Miscellany*, 12 vols (London, 1744–46, repr. 1808–13), II, 578–88 (p. 583). Hodgkin's proposal would have more force had he been able to provide evidence of a widespread perception of woodcock as birds that drop collectively from the sky, but this does not seem to have been the case.

(ii) *daryng* 'hiding, concealment'; see *MED*, *daren* v.; *daring* ger.

222 A problematic phrase for several reasons. In the first place, the name *woodwall* was used in the Middle Ages for several different types of bird. In Bibbesworth's *Tretiz*, it indicates the golden oriole (*Oriolus oriolus*), known for its flute-like call: 'Plus est delit en la oriol (*de la chambre*) / Escoter la note de l'oriol (*a wodewale*)' (ed. Wright, p. 166), an identification that matches cognate names for that bird in other languages: *wiedewaal* (MDu), *witewal* (MHG); cf. *witwol*, *witwall* in EMnE (see *OED*, s.vv. *witwall* n., *woodwall* n.). On the other hand, several Anglo-Latin glossaries identify the woodwall with the kingfisher (*Alcedo atthis*); e.g. 'Hec alcedo, a wodewale' (Wright, *Anglo-Saxon Vocabularies*, col. 702; also col. 562/38 for another text). And, to complicate matters further, the *Promptorium* relates *Wode-wale* to *Reyne fowle*, the 'rain-fowl' or woodpecker (cols 369, 533). Indeed, by the mid-16th century, *woodwall* had become the preferred name for the green woodpecker (*Gecinus viridis*), and this association eventually supplanted its earlier meanings: see Lockwood, *British Bird Names*, pp. 170–1.

(As an aside: the *wodewales* that Chaucer mentions in a list of songbirds in his *Romaunt of the Rose* (657–60, 912–15) are probably intended to be orioles – though many editors follow Skeat in glossing the word, somewhat incongruously in this context, as '(green) woodpeckers'.)

In relation to the J.B. phrase, however, the collective *discencion*, 'descent, descending', 'swooping (down)' makes least sense in relation to orioles, but could apply equally well to green woodpeckers (referring to the characteristic downward swooping flight of these birds) and kingfishers, indicating the way they dive into water after their prey. Such a reading of the noun is not currently recognised by *MED* s.v. *descensioun* n.; but see *descense* n., esp. sense 1(a):'downward movement; a downward rush or swoop'.

223 'A hopelessness of wooers': a resonant phrase, recalling the wretched Absolon of Chaucer's *Miller's Tale* and any number of other suffering literary lovers. As *MED* shows, s.vv. *wanhope* n. 2. and *wouer* n., both words have a range of meanings that add to the rich suggestiveness of this collocation. *Wanhope* could indicate 'hopelessness, despair', as well as 'unjustified, false confidence'; and a *wouer* might be someone who courts a woman with honourable intent, a go-between, or even a duplicitous seducer. The alliteration is a felicitous bonus.

224 Hodgkin ('Terms I', no. 71) proposes that the wren is here allocated the collective 'herd' because it is 'king of birds' – an allusion to Aesop's fable in which the wren flies higher than all other birds by riding on the eagle's back. But other birds are also classified as a herd, viz. cranes, curlews, fieldfares and swans.

225 Hodgkin, who is always on the lookout for sarcasm in these phrases, suggests an allusion to the custom of prefacing a new work with one or more panegyrics dedicated to the writer's patron, or hoped-for future patron: 'Terms I', no. 201. But it seems to me more plausible that the straightforward sense of 'honour', 'worthiness' is intended, perhaps with nothing more than a tongue-in-cheek reference to his own profession by the scribe who devised this phrase.

226 *wypes* 'lapwings' – an onomatopeoic name, still in dialectical use, and so comparable to a number of MnE bird names, such as *pewit, peewit, peewee*; see *MED*, *wipe* n.; *OED*, *wype* n., *peewit* n. Although the majority of witnesses prefer the end-noun 'lapwings' (no. 116), they all agree on the collective 'deceit', analysed in note 116 above.

227 (i) This phrase occurs in the following sequence: 'a host of men', 'a host of sparrows', 'a fellowship of yeomen'. Its most likely sense is, therefore, 'a companionship of freeholders', or perhaps 'a military company of freeholders', complementing the martial sense of 'a host of men' (no. 130). For the sense 'armed band', see *MED*, *felaushipe* n. 5(c).

Hodgkin ('Terms I', no. 193) interprets the phrase as alluding to 'a guild of attendants' – for which, see *MED*, *felaushipe* n. 6(b) – but this is to ignore the generally rustic tone of the sequence in which it occurs.

APPENDIX I — NOTES 335

(iii) *yemanri* Probably indicates small freeholders generally, or an army's infantry composed of such freeholders, rather than the general body of freemen of a livery company: cf. *OED, yeomanry* n., senses 1.a and 1.b.

Rd's end-noun is noteworthy for having a similar form to another word occurring elsewhere in the same list: *hosbandri* (no. 106).

228 Dg: Added later by the scribe below the main list of collectives on fol. 160r to direct the reader back to the shorter, supplementary list of collectives on fol. 157v (Dg*). My asterisk represents a *signe-de-renvoi*, which is repeated in the margin and again at the end of Dg*.

APPENDIX II

CARVING TERMS

This Appendix presents a complete collation of statements (phrases) containing Carving terms found in all J.B. witnesses – a total of thirteen. Typically, each phrase consists of two major elements, a noun and a verb, the latter either a past participle employed adjectivally (as in 'a deer broken', no. 9), or an active, imperative verb, as in 'break that deer'. As will be seen, several verbs have nothing to do with cutting or carving, although all are broadly relevant to the preparation or serving of food – for example, nos 4 ('a capon sauced'), and 12 ('a fire *timbered*'). They are included in this collation because they form an integral part of the lists in which they occur.

The J.B. lists of Carving terms fall into two main categories: long lists, which include 'fish', and short lists, which do not.[1] The short lists range from thirteen items (Am) to twenty-two (W); and the long lists from twenty-nine items (Pl, Prk) to forty-one (Eg). BS is unique in that it intersperses its thirty-nine carving terms with the names of nineteen different sauces; these sauces are not included in the collation itself, but are recorded in the apparatus.

The collation is arranged into two main divisions, consisting, first, of animals, birds and miscellaneous items (nos 2–34), and, secondly, of 'fish' (nos 36–59). This reflects the arrangement of the lists in the witnesses themselves, of which only two introduce their terms for fish by means of a separate heading (no. 35). Within these two divisions, entries are arranged alphabetically by headwords identifying each creature or dish that is the subject of the 'carving' verb. Introductory headings and closing remarks are also included as nos 1 and 60 respectively. The collation is followed by an index of the carving terms (the verbs) themselves, along with its own set of explanatory notes.

As in Appendix I, witnesses are listed by their sigla in alphabetical order, a sequence broken only by pairs that are closely related to one another, viz. Am–*HSG*, Pl–Prk. For further details about the different versions of the J.B. lists of Carving terms, and the relationships that can be plotted between them, see the main Introduction. To view a typical list of these terms in its proper context, see Prk (I/128–56).

---

[1] I have placed inverted commas around the word *fish* because it needs to be understood rather loosely. In the J.B. lists, the category 'fish' includes porpoises and various shellfish.

1. Headings

A tryppe off deere		Adv
¶ Termes of a keruer.		BK
Here begynnythe the termys of keruynge of foulys ande of fyschysse &c.		Eg
Longing for keruers		Rd
Here folow the dew termys to speke of breekyng or dressyng of dyuerse beestis and fowlis &c. And thessame is shewed of certayn fysshes.		StA
This longeth to a keruer		T

2. Bittern

i.	A bittore vntached	Am
	A byttore vntached	HSG
	A byttoure ys vntachyde	Eg
	A byttor vntacheyd	Pl
	A byttere vntachyd	Prk
	A burtor vntachyde	Rd
	A beture vntachid	StA
	A bittor vntached	T
	A bittor vntached	W
ii.	Vnioint þe betore	Adv
	Vnioynt that bytture	BK
	Vniointe þat bittour	BS

3. Brawn

i.	Brawyn ys leyschyde	Eg
	Brawne is lechyde	L
	Brawne lechyd	Rd
	Brawne leechyd	StA
	Brawne y-lechyd	T
	Brawne lesshed	W

ii.	Leche þe brane	Adv
	Lesche þat brawne	BK
	Lech þat [b]rane	BS

4. Capon

i.	A capon sawsyd	Am
	A capon sawsyd	HSG
	A caponne ys sawsyde	Eg
	A capon sawced	L
	A capon savced	L
	A capon sawsyde	Pl
	A cappone sawsyd	Prk
	A capone y-sawsed	Rd
	A capoon sawsede	StA
	A capone y-sawssyd	T
	A capon sawsed	W
ii.	Sawce þe capon	Adv
	Sauce that capon	BK
	Sause þat capon	BS

5. Chicken

i.	A shekyn frusshed	Am
	A chekyn frusshed	HSG
	A chekyn frusshed	L
	A cheken y-frocheyd	Pl
	A chekyne i-frosschyde	Prk
	A cheken y-frushed	Rd
	A checoon ⟨fr⟩usshyd	StA
	A chekyne fruschide	T
ii.	A chekyn fynshid	W
iii.	A chekynne ys fassyde	Eg
iv.	Frussh þe chekyn	Adv
	Frusshe that chekyn	BK
	Frusch þat chekyn	BS

---

1 Adv A] *red lombard initial*   2 Pl vntacheyd] vn tacheyd   Prk vntachyd] vn tachyd   BS bittour] *add* Sause ganell   3 BK þat] y^t BS brane] krane (*scribal error*); *add* Sause mustard   4 L^1] *interpolated by a revising hand*   BS capon] *Add* Sause wyne or ale and fyne powder   5 L frusshed] *olim* thrusted *canc*; frusshed *added by a different hand* StA frusshyd] *broken type*   BS chekyn] *add* Sause sorell

6. Cony

i.	A cony vnlaced	Am
	A cony vnlaced	HSG
	A conyng ys vnlasyde	Eg
	A cony vnlased	L
	A cone vnlasyde	Pl
	A conny vnlassyde	Prk
	A conynge vnlaced	Rd
	A cony vnlaciedde	StA
	A conynge vnlasyde	T
	A connyng onlaced	W
ii.	Vnlace þe cony	Adv
	Vnlace that cony	BK
	Vnlace þat cone	BS

7. Crane

i.	A crane dysplayd	Am
	A crane displayd	HSG
	A crane ys dysplayde	Eg
	A crane dysplat	L
	A crane dysplayde	Rd
	A crane d‹i›splayde	StA
	A crane displeyed	T
	A crane displayed	W
ii.	Dysplaye that crane	BK
	Dysplay þat crayne	BS
iii.	Asplay þe crane	Adv
iv.	Lech þat krane	BS

8. Curlew

i.	A curlew vnyoynted	Am
	A curlew vnioynted	HSG
	A cvrlew vnyoyned	L
	A corlu vnioyneteyd	Pl
	A corllowe vngynttyte	Prk
	A curlew vnyoyndide	Rd
	A curlew vnioyntede	StA
	A corlow vnyontyd	T
	A curlu onioyntyd	W
ii.	A corlowe ys vnrowtyde	Eg
iii.	Vntache þe curlew	Adv
	Vntache that curlewe	BK
	Vntach þat curlew	BS

9. Deer

i.	A dere broken	Am
	A dere broken	HSG
	Fryste a dere ys brokynne	Eg
	A dere brokyn	L
	A dere y-broken	Pl
	A dere brovkyne	Prk
	A dere brokynge	Rd
	A dere brokenne	StA
	A dere brokyne	T
	A dere broken	W
ii.	Breke tho dere	Adv
	Breke that dere	BK
	Brake that dere	BS
iii.	Vndo the dere	Adv

10. Egg

i.	A negge tyrede	L
	A neg y-teryde	Rd
	An egge tyred	StA
	And eg tyryd	T
ii.	Tyre þe egge	Adv
	Tyere that egge	BK
	Thyre þat egge	BS

6 Eg vnlasyde] vn lasyde   Pl vnlasyde] vn lasyde   Prk vnlassyde] vn lassyde   BS cone] *add* Sause vinegur & fyn powder   7 StA displayde] *broken type*   BS[1] crayne] *add* Sause pykett   BS[2] krane] *recte* brane, *i.e. 'brawn'*   8 Pl vnioyneteyd] vn ioyneteyd   Prk vngynttyte] vn gynttyte   T vnyontyd] *olim* vnyonted, e *changed to* y   BS curlew] *add* Sause galymafray   10 BS Thyre] *transcribed by Griffiths as* Shyre

11. Egret

A egrete ys i-kneyde	Eg
A negrete y-kneed	T

12. Fire

i.	A fyre tymberde	L
	A fyre tymbered	StA
	A fuyr tymbred	T
ii.	Tymbre that fyre	BK
	Tymber þat fire	BS

13. Goose

i.	A goos reryd	Am
	A ghoos rerid	HSG
	A gosse ys rerryde	Eg
	A gosse y-reryde	Pl
	A gose reyryde	Prk
	A gose reryd	Rd
	A goose rerede	StA
	A gose y-rered	T
	A gose reryd	W
ii.	A gooce arered	L
iii.	Reare þe goos	Adv
	Rere that goose	BK
	Rere þat gouse	BS

14. Gull

A gulle ys i-brawynde	Eg

15. Hen

i.	A hen spoyled	Am
	A hen spoyled	HSG
	A henne ys i-spoylyde	Eg
	A hen spoylyde	Pl
	A hene i-spyllyde	Prk
	An hen spoylede	StA
	A hene spoylyd	T
	An hen spoylyd	W
ii.	A hene y-swylyd	Rd
iii.	Spwlle þe henne	Adv
	Spoyle that henne	BK
	Spoule þat hene	BS

16. Heron

i.	A heron dysmembryd	Am
	A heron dismembrid	HSG
	A hayryn ys dysmemberyde	Eg
	A heron dysmembred	L
	A heron dysmembryde	Pl
	A herne dysmemmyrde	Prk
	A herone dysmembryde	Rd
	An heron dysmembrid	StA
	A herone dismenbride	T
	An heron dismembryd	W
ii.	Dysmenbre þe heron	Adv
	Dysmembre that heron	BK
	Dysmembyr þat herne	BS

17. Kid

A kede y-shuldrede	Rd
A kidde shulderide	StA

(*See also* Lamb and Kid)

18. Lamb

i.	A lame schollderyd	Pl
	A lame scholdyrt	Prk
	A lambe shulderide	StA
ii.	A lame sydyde	Rd

(*See also* Lamb and Kid)

19. Lamb and Kid

i.	A lambe & kyde shuldred	HSG
	A lame and a kyde shuldred	T
	A lam & a kede shuldred	W
ii.	A lambe, A kydde: shuldrede	L

---

13 Rd BS gouse] *add* Sause gansall   15 BS hene] *add* Sause powncy   16 BS herne] *add* Sause rosett   19 W & a] *add* kyd *canc*   L] *two nouns bracketed*

20. Mallard

i.
A malard vnbrased	Am
A malard vnbrased	HSG
A mallerde ys vnbrassydde	Eg
A malarde vnbrased	L
A mawlarde vnbrasyde	Pl
A mallard vnbrassyde	Prk
A malard vnbrasyde	Rd
A malarde vnbrasid	StA
A malarde vnbrasyd	T
A malard vnbraced	W

ii.
Vnbrace the malard	Adv
Vnbrace that malarde	BK
Vnbrace þat mallard	BS

21. Partridge

i.
A partriche eyled	HSG
A partrich alet	StA
A parterriche elyd	W

ii. A partriche y-eked   T

iii. A pertrych wynged   L

iv. A parteryche, A quayle: alle thes benne wyngyde   Eg

v.
Wynge þe partrich	Adv
Wynge that partryche	BK
Wyng þat pertrych	BS

22. Pasty

i.
A pastey ys brouderydde	Eg
A paste borderd	L

ii.
Border that pasty	BK
Brodur þat pasteth	BS

23. Peacock

i.
A pecok dysfuguryd	Am
A pecok disfigured	HSG
A pecocke ys dysfyguryde	Eg
A pecok dysfygured	L
A pecoke dysvygoryd	Pl
A peycoke dyswygurte	Prk
A pocok dy[s]fugryde	Rd
A pecoke disfigured	StA
A pecoke disfugred	T
A pocok disfigured	W

ii.
Dysfygure þe pecok	Adv
Dysfygure that pecocke	BK
Dysfygur þat pekoke	BS

24. Pheasant

i.
A fesant eyled	HSG
A fesonde ys i-haylyde	Eg
A fesavnt ellyd	L
A fessante y-ellyde	Pl
A fayssant i-illyde	Prk
A fesant y-layde	Rd
A fesawnt alet	StA
A fesaunt y-aled	T
A fesaunt [e]leyd	W

ii.
Alay þe fesond	Adv
Alaye that fesande	BK
Hale þat fasaynt	BS

---

20 Eg] Mons dei *written in the red lombard initial opposite*   Pl vnbrasyde] vn brasyde   Prk vnbrassyde] vn brassyde   BS mallard] *add* Sause dudnett   21 Eg] *two nouns bracketed*   Adv] *preceded by* vn the canc   BS pertrych] *add* Sause watere   23 L dysfygured] olim de canc; dysfygured *added by a different hand*   Rd dysfugryde] dyffugryde   BS pekoke] *add* Sause dewcett   24 W eleyd] cleyd   BS fasaynt] *add* Sause Robertyn

25. Pig

i. A pigge heded & syded — HSG
   A pygge hedyd & syded — L
   A pege heded & sydeyd — Pl
   A pyge heddyte and sydyte — Prk
   A pigge ⟨hede⟩de and sydede — StA
   A pyge heded and sydyd — T
ii. A pyge heddyde — Rd
iii. A pygge heded and thyed — W

26. Pigeon

i. A pegyn y-thyyde — Pl
   A pygyne i-thyide — Prk
   A pegeone y-thyed — Rd
   A pegeon thyghed — StA
ii. Thygh þe pygeon — Adv
   Thye that pegyon — BK
   Thy þat pygyon — BS
iii. A woodecocke, A pegonne:
   Alle thes benne i-schrydde — Eg

(*See also* Pigeon and Small Birds)

27. Pigeon and Small Birds

i. A pegone and all small
   byrdes y-thyed — T
ii. A woodecok, A pegyn &
   All smalle byrdes: thyed — L

(*See also* Small Birds, Woodcock)

28. Plover

i. A plouer ys mynschyde — Eg
   A plover mynst — L
   A plouer y-mensyde — Rd
   A plouer mynsed — StA
   A plouer y-mynssyd — T

ii. A plover mynied — W
iii. Mynce þe plover — Adv
   Mynce that plouer — BK
   Mince þat plouer — BS

29. Poper

A popyr ys lowryde — Eg

30. Quail

i. A quayle y-whyngged — T
   A quayle y-whynged — Rd
   A quayle wyngged — StA
   A quale wynged — W
ii. Wyng þe quayll — Adv
   Wynge that quayle — BK
   Wyng þat qwhayle — BS
iii. A parteryche, A quayle:
   Alle thes benne wyngyde — Eg
iv. A quayle y-thyyde — Pl
   A quaylle i-thyide — Prk

31. Rail

A rayle ys brestyde — Eg
A rayle brest — L
A rale y brested — Rd
A raale brestyde — StA
A rayle y-brested — T
A rayle brested — W

---

25 StA hedede] *broken type*   26 Adv Thygh] *olim* Thegh, e *changed to* y   BS pygyon] *add* Sause phasur   Eg] *two noun phrases bracketed*   27 L] *three noun phrases bracketed*
28 BS plouer] *add* Sause mustard   30 Eg] *two noun phrases bracketed*

32. Small birds

i. Alle smale birdes thyed — *HSG*
ii. Al smalle berdys [y-thyed] — *Rd*
iii. Thygh all man*er* smale
    brydd*es* — *Adv*
    Thye all maner of small
    byrdes — *BK*
    Thy þ*at* smal byrde — *BS*
iv. A quayle y-thyyde, And
    alle smale byrdeys — *Pl*
    A quaylle i-thyide, And
    alle smalle brydys — *Prk*
v. A woodecok, A pegyn &
    All smalle byrdes: thyed — *L*
vi. And alle smalle bryddys
    ben i-schrydde — *Eg*
(*See also* Pigeon and Small Birds)

33. Swan

i. A swan lyfte — *Am*
   A swan lyfte — *HSG*
   A swau*n*ne ys lyfte — *Eg*
   A swanne lyfte — *L*
   A swan y-lefte — *Pl*
   A swane i-lyfte — *Prk*
   A swanne y-lyfte — *Rd*
   A swanne lyfte — *StA*
   A swan*e* y-lyft — *T*
   A swa*n*ne lyft — *W*
ii. Lyft þe swane — *Adv*
   Lyft that swanne — *BK*
   Lyft þ*at* swane — *BS*

34. Woodcock

i. A wodecok thyed — *HSG*
   A wodecok y-thyed — *Rd*
   A wodecoke thyghed — *StA*
   A wodcoke y-thyed — *T*
   A wodecok thied — *W*
ii. Thygh þe wodecok — *Adv*
   Thye that wodcocke — *BK*
   Thy þ*at* wodcok — *BS*
iii. A woodecok, A pegyn &
    All smalle byrdes: thyed — *L*
iv. A woodecocke, A pegonne:
    Alle thes benne i-schrydde — *Eg*

35. Headings for Fish

Alle the termys that longgythe
    vnto fysche. — *Eg*
Now of fysshes — *StA*

36. Barbel

i. A barbule ys i-tuskydde — *Eg*
   A barbel tusked — *L*
   A barbell*e* tusked — *Rd*
   A barbill tuskyd — *StA*
   A barbell tusked — *T*
ii. Tuske þe barbell — *Adv*
   Tuske that barbell — *BK*
   Tuske þ*at* barbyll — *BS*

---

32 Rd] *preceded by* A pegeone y-thyed, *so the two entries together could have been meant as* A pegeone y-thyed [&] Al smalle berdys   BS smal byrde] smalbyrde   L] *three noun phrases bracketed*   Eg] *conjunction links this to the previous entry,* A woodecocke, A pegonne: Alle thes benne i-schrydde *(noun phrases bracketed)*   33 BS swane] *add* Sause chawden   34 BS wodcok] *add* Sause powder & salt   L] *three noun phrases bracketed* Eg] *two noun phrases bracketed*

37. Bream

i.	A breme ys splayde	Eg
	A breme splayed	*StA*
	A breme splayed	T
ii.	A breyme y-sprayd	Rd
iii.	A breem splat	L
iv.	Splay þe breme	Adv
	Splaye that breme	*BK*
	Splay þ*at* breame	BS

38. Carp

i.	A carpe trownsonnyd	Pl
ii.	A carpe i-tronchnide	Prk
iii.	A carpe langed	T

39. Cheven

i.	A cheuynne ys vynnydde	Eg
	A cheven [f]ynde	L
	A cheffen y-vynyde	Pl
	A cheyuen fynnyde	Prk
	A cheuien*e* vynnyd*e*	Rd
	A cheuen fynned	*StA*
	A cheuan*e* fynned	T
ii.	Fyn þe cheven	Adv
	Fynne that cheuen	*BK*
	Fyn þ*at* cheueyn	BS

40. Conger

A conggyr g‹n›owod	T

41. Crab

i.	A crabbe ys mynyde	Eg
ii.	Carve þe crabbe	Adv
iii.	Tayme that crabbe	*BK*
iv.	Trayeme þ*at* crabe	BS

42. Crayfish

A crauys ys vnmaylyde	Eg

43. Eel

i.	An ele tronsoned	*StA*
	A nele tronsenett	T
ii.	Transsene that ele	*BK*
	Trunson þ*at* ele	BS
iii.	A ele ys crowsyde or	
	ellys i-colpynnd*e*	Eg

44. Eel, Great

A [...] callyd a rostar other	
elles a spychecoke	Pl
A gret heyle callyd a rostere	
or ellys a spychecoke	Prk

45. Eels, Small

A[nd] alle oþ*er* ellys y-calyde	
e‹llys› yn sorrey	Pl
And all ellys small in sorraye	Prk

46. Gurnard

A gornarde chynyde	Eg
A gornard chyned	L
A gornard y-chyned	Rd
A gurnarde chyned	*StA*
A gornard chonyd	T

---

39 L fynde] synde *(crossbar omitted)*   40 T gnowod] *the second letter has been altered and is smudged, but has the shape of an* n   43 *StA* tronsoned] trousoned *(turned* n*)*
44 Pl *ellipsis*] *MS damaged*;   spychecoke] spyche coke   Prk spychecoke] spyche coke
45 Pl And ...ellys[2]] *MS damaged*

47. Haddock

i. A haddocke ys sydyde — Eg
A hadok syded — L
A haddok y-syded — Rd
An haddoke sided — *StA*
A haddoke sydyd — T

ii. Syde that haddocke — *BK*
Syde þ*at* haddok — BS

iii. Syth þe haddok — Adv

48. Lamprey

i. A lampray ys cordyde — Eg
A lavmprey corded — L
A lamproye cordyd — T

ii. A lamppray cordyt i*n* gallantye — Prk
[*olim?*] — Pl

iii. Strynge that lampraye — *BK*
Stryng þ*at* lamp*ray* — BS

iv. A lampray y-coudyd — Rd

v. Chyne þe lawmprey — Adv

49. Lobster

i. A lomster barbed — L

ii. Barbe the lopster — Adv
Barbe that lopster — *BK*
Barbe þ*at* lopst*er* — BS

50. Perch and Roach

A perche & a roche scalyd — Pl
A perche and a roche i-schallyd — Prk

(*See also* Roach)

51. Pike

i. A pyke splatted — L
A pyke i-splate — Prk
A pyke splatted — *StA*

ii. A pyke y-splyte — Pl
A peke y-splett — Rd
A pyke splett — T

iii. Splat þe pyke — Adv
Splatte that pyke — *BK*

iv. A pyke splayde — Eg

v. Spla þ*at* pyk — BS

52. Plaice

i. A playsse ys sawsyde — Eg
A playse y-sawsyd — Pl
A plays i-savssyd — Prk
A playse y-sauset — Rd
A playse saussyd — T

ii. Sauce that playce — *BK*
Sause þ*at* playce — BS

iii. A playce, A tenche: savced — L

53. Porpoise

i. Vndertraunche þe purpoos — Adv
Vndertraunche þ*at* purpos — *BK*

ii. Vntrench þ*at* porpas — BS

54. Roach

A roche i-bonyde or rybbyd*e* — Eg

(*See also* Perch and Roach)

---

48 Pl *olim?*] *MS damaged*   BS lampray] *add* Sause galyntyn   52 L] *two noun phrases bracketed*   53 *BK* þat] y^t

55. Salmon

i.	A samon ys chynyde	Eg
	A samond chynede	L
	A samon chynyde	Pl
	A samon i-chynyd	Prk
	A samone y-chyned	Rd
	A sawmon chyned	StA
ii.	Chyne that samon	BK
	[C]hyne þat salmon	BS

56. Sole

A soyle y-loynyde	Rd
A sole loyned	StA
A soile laynyd	T

57. Sturgeon

i.	Traunche þe sturgeon	Adv
	Traunche that sturgyon	BK
ii.	Trench þat sturgen	BS

58. Tench

i.	A tenche y-sauset	Rd
	A tenche sawced	StA
ii.	A playce, A tenche: savced	L
iii.	Sauce þe tench	Adv
	Sauce that tenche	BK
	Sause þat tench	BS
iv.	A tenche sousyd	T
v.	A tenche sowsyde, or ellys he may be take yn a iollye	Eg
vi.	A tenche yn iele	Pl
	A tenche in iolly	Prk

59. Trout

i.	A trowte gobbonde	Pl
	A trout i-gobenyd	Prk
	A troyte gobonyd	Rd
ii.	A trought gobettid	StA
iii.	Culpen þe troute	Adv
	Culpon that troute	BK
	Colpon þat trowte	BS
iv.	A trouȝt cowponyd	T
v.	A trought i-colpynnyde, or ellys he ys cheuernyde or ellys ynvndate	Eg

60. Closing Remarks

¶ Here hendeth the goodly termes.	BK
Explicit &c.	Eg

---

55 Eg] *Omnes colles* ‹...› *written in the red lombard initial opposite; cf. 20n supra* BS Chyne] ?Thyne   57 Adv þe] *add* ele   58 L] *two noun phrases bracketed*

Index of Carving Terms

In this index, where $y = i$ and $v = u$, they are alphabetised accordingly

aled, alet, see eyled
arered 13
asplay 7
barbe, barbed 49
i-bonyde 54
border, bordered 22
i-brawynde 14
break, broken 9
breasted 31
carve 41
cheuernyde 59
chine, chined 46, 48, 55
i-colpynnde 43, 59
corded 48
y-coudyd 48
cowponyd 59
crowsyde 43
disfigure, disfigured 23
dismember, dismembered 16
dysplay, displayed 7
y-eked 21
eyled, ellyd, aled, alet,
   i-illde, etc. 21, 24
fassyde 5
fin, finned 39
fynshid 5
frussh, frusshed 5
gnowod 40
gobettid 59
gobonyd, i-gobenyd 59
heded etc. 25
i-illyde, see eyled
yn a iolly 58
ynvndate 59
y-kneed 11
langed 38
leche, lechyd 3, 7
lyft, y-lyft 33
loined 56
lowryde 29

mince, minced 28
mynyde 41
rere, reryd 13
rybbyde 54
sauce, sawced 4, 52, 58
scaled 50
i-schrydde 26, 32
shouldered 17, 18, 19
side, sided 18, 25, 47
syth 47
sowsyde 58
splay, splayed 37, 51
splat, splatted, i-splate 37, 51
splett, y-splyte 51
spoyle, spoylyd 15
stryng 48
y-swylyd 15
tayme 41
thigh, thighed 25, 26, 27, 30,
   32, 34
tymber, tymbered 12
tyre, tyred 10
trayeme 41
traunche 57
trench 57
i-tronchnide 38
trunson, tronsoned, trowsonnyd
   38, 43
tusk, tusked 36
vnbrace, vnbrased 20
vndertraunche 53
undo 9
unjoint, unjointed 2, 8
unlace, unlaced 6
vnmaylyde 42
vnrowtyde 8
vntache, vntached 2, 8
vntrench 53
wing, winged 21, 30

CARVING TERMS — NOTES

Ostensibly, the J.B. lists of Carving terms present the correct terminology for describing the action of carving every type of flesh or fish that might appear at table; those phrases that use the verb imperative may be taken as offering the exact command to be addressed to one's attendant carver. In consequence, some modern writers on medieval foods have taken these terms seriously, treating them as if they were part of the established etiquette of table manners in the 15th century.[1] However, this is to overlook the principle that patently underlies so much of the J.B. material: the attempt to assemble a comprehensive set of terms to cover every possible contingency — in this case, a specific verb for describing the cutting up of every type of fish, flesh or fowl.[2]

Examining the lists more closely, we soon perceive that by no means all the verbs catalogued pertain to acts of cutting; some relate to the preparation of an ingredient for cooking, to different ways of cooking, and even to the presentation of a dish at table. Moreover, even those verbs that do refer specifically to cutting are not always clearly the actions of a carver, rather than a cook or a butcher. In other words, it would be more accurate to describe these lists as having an imagined relevance for the kitchen as much as for the table; and it is important to recognise that their contents are, at times, patently artificial. Their aim is to be comprehensive, and they achieve this by collecting and, where necessary, inventing an elaborate vocabulary that Hodgkin colourfully describes as 'a kind of heraldry applied to the kitchen'.[3]

As with the Collective nouns, the Carving terms commence with a phrase that employs a technical, but straightforward, hunting term concerning deer: *A dere broken* (W, no. 9). And this may well be how the lists originated, as 'a vestige of the elaborate rituals connected with the slaughter of hunted deer'.[4] Before long, however, the language appears to have become more contrived, and it is evident that the available verbs for describing the act of cutting things up ran out long before the

---

[1] For example, P.W. Hammond, *Food and Feast in Medieval England* (Stroud, 1993), p. 112.

[2] The J.B. Carving terms are not recognised as an independent category in Keiser's *Manual X*, but are included as a sub-category (II, III) of 'Proper Terms', 3702 [470]. See also 3682 [406] for Wynkyn's *Boke of Kervyng*.

[3] 'Terms II', p. 53.

[4] Kate Mertes, 'Aristocracy', in *Fifteenth-Century Attitudes*, ed. Horrox, pp. 42–60 (p. 54).

different viands themselves. In consequence, the lists grew to include imaginative synonyms (e.g. *aled/wynged, rere/lyft*), then any term to describe the act of cutting or dressing (e.g. *fin, side*). At some point, they expanded to include cooking terms, as in *a plaice sauced* (no. 52), and even alternative names for an ingredient, indicating how it is cooked – *A gret heyle callyd a rostere or ellys a spychecoke* (Prk, no. 44). In this way, the lists of carving terms became increasingly anomalous, though they managed to maintain a broad connection with cooking and serving food. We are even told the correct term for starting a fire (presumably in the kitchen, or perhaps in the dining hall): it is *timbered* (no. 12).

From a linguistic point of view, the J.B. carving terms are intriguing for demonstrating the sheer inventiveness of their compilers, who often created new meanings for many words, as well as new grammatical forms unrecorded anywhere else at this time. It is also noteworthy that many terms can be grouped together through their use of essentially the same imagery – e.g. *disfigure* and *spoyle*; *unbrace, unlace* and *undo*. No less interesting are the origins and connotations of many terms, though these aspects are often ignored in the cursory glosses offered by both the *OED* and the *MED*. For example, all the *OED* has to say about the verb *lift* (sense 9) is that this is 'The technical word for: To carve (a swan)'. And the *MED* tells us only that *loinen* v.(1) means 'To carve (a sole)'. There is so much more to say, and the explanatory notes that follow attempt to go some way towards remedying that neglect.

John Hodgkin printed and commented on the carving terms in the following J.B. texts: Am, *BK*, Eg, *HSG*, Prk and *StA*. Subsequently, Hope E. Allen published the terms in Rd ('More terms', 1936), Auvo Kurvinen reprinted those in Prk ('MS Porkington 10', 1953), Rachel Hands commented extensively on the version in *StA* (*EHH*, 1975) and Jeremy Griffiths published the terms in the Tollemache *Book of Secrets* (BS, 2001). Appearing for the first time in this collation are Adv, L, Pl, T and W.

Two important recent studies, by Ville Marttila and Magdalena Bator, examine many of the terms found here as they are used in medieval recipe collections.[1] It is regrettable that neither takes account of the J.B. lists, which would have added significantly to the corpora from which they derive their statistical information. Of particular interest is chapter 3 in Bator's study, entitled 'Verbs of Cutting', which divides such verbs into four categories: verbs of dividing, reducing, removing and penetrating.[2] Also relevant to many of the J.B. terms is Bator's analysis in Chapter

---

[1] Ville Marttila, 'Mincing words: A diachronic view on English cutting verbs', in *Selected Proceedings of the 2008 Symposium on New Approaches in English Historical Lexis (HEL-LEX 2)*, ed. R.W. McConchie, Alpo Honkapohja and Jukka Tyrkkö (Somerville, MA, 2009), pp. 104–22 (also available online at: <http://www.lingref.com/cpp/hel-lex/2008/paper2171.pdf>). Magdalena Bator, *Culinary Verbs in Middle English*, Studies in English Medieval Language and Literature, 46 (Frankfurt-am-Main, 2014).

[2] Bator, *Culinary Verbs*, pp. 67–123 (p. 69).

4, of 'Cooking verbs'.[1] The fact that many of the J.B. carving and cooking verbs are found also in recipes of the period is an important reminder that, whatever flights of fancy they may contain, these lists maintained some contact with spoken and practical usage.

1   Adv: It is difficult to account for this heading, which has the appearance of a phrase from the list of collective nouns, but would be unique even there, since the collective *trip* is applied to deer nowhere else. In all respects, it is singularly inappropriate as a heading for the carving terms.

   StA: By referring to *dressyng* 'preparing', as well as *breekyng* 'carving', the heading in *StA* points out usefully that the carving terms extend beyond expressions that might be used of, or by, a carver.

2   (i) *vntached* 'unfastened, detached', hence 'dismembered'; see *MED*, *untachen*, v. (<*tachen*, 'to fasten, attach; secure'). As with *vnbrased* (no. 20) and *vnlaced* (no. 6), *vntached* expresses the idea of cutting up an animal in terms of 'loosening' or 'unfastening' it.
   (ii) *vnioint* 'unjoint', 'dismember'.

3   (i) *brawne is lechyde* 'meat (flesh) is sliced'; see *MED*, *braun* n. and *lechen* v.(1). *Brawn* does not here refer to jellied meat loaf, which, paradoxically, was called *leche* in the Middle Ages, indicating that it was served in slices: *MED*, *leche* n.(2). See the instructions in *BK*: 'Take your knyfe in youre hande, and cut brawne in þe dysshe as it lyeth, & laye it on your soueraynes trenchour' (p. 272); also, the cookery book in MS Harley 279: 'an þenne take clene Freysshe Brawn ... an þan leche it in pecys': *Harley Cook Books* (ed. Thomas Austin), p. 12, no. 32.

4   *sawsyd* Contains the double sense of 'cooked or served in a sauce', and 'spiced, seasoned', notions that both derive from the noun *sauce*; see *MED*, s.vv. *saucen* v. (a), *sauce* n. (a). A similar ambiguity can be seen in an instruction in *BK* that, 'the chekyn shall be sauced with grene sauce or vergyus' [verjuice = the juice of acidic fruits] (p. 275). In another recipe book preserved in a manuscript at Holkham Hall, Norfolk, it is clear that sauce ('seasoning') might be nothing more than a sprinkling of salt: 'Quayle rost ... and no sauce but salt and serue it': Mrs Alexander Napier, *A Noble Boke off Cookry* (London, 1882) (hereafter, *Noble Cookry*), p. 61. *MED* makes an unnecessary and unsatisfactory distinction in treating the J.B. texts' use of the verb as a special case, which it glosses as 'to prepare (sth.) for the table': s.v. *saucen* v. (b).

5   (i) *frusshed* 'cut up', 'broken up'. The primary sense of *frushen* (<OF *froissier*, glossed by Godefroy as 'briser, rompre') is 'to strike, crush, smash, shatter, splinter,

---
[1] *Ibid.*, pp. 125–56.

slash', hence 'to cut up'; see *MED, frushen*, v. 1. It is unhelpful of *MED* to state that *frushed* in the J.B. texts simply means 'carved', since the word carries such strong connotations. The word's literal sense is probably 'cut up small', as Hands suggests (*EHH*, p. 164/2022n), but it conveys an image of something that is 'shattered' – as in the fate suffered by Sir Jakes de Neys, who is 'al toffrusschyd' by a band of Saracens in the romance *Richard Coeur de Lyon*; see *Der Mittelenglische Versroman über Richard Löwenherz*, ed. Karl Brunner (Vienna/Leipzig, 1913), ll. 5069–71.

The noun *chekyn* refers to a chick – the young of a domestic fowl.

(ii) *fynshid* ?'finished off', 'decorated, garnished'; see *MED, finshed*, pa.ppl. of *finishen* v.

(iii) *fassyde* ?Read *farsyde* 'stuffed' (with seasoned stuffing), or 'spiced', 'garnished with spices'; see *MED, farsen* v. 1.

6   *vnlaced* 'unlaced, loosened, unfastened', hence 'dismembered'. This is one of several verbs that depict dismembering an animal as a form of loosening or unfastening. Others are *vnbrased* (no. 20), *vndo* (no. 9), *vntached* (nos 2, 8). All could usefully be classified as 'dividing verbs' according to Bator's system, though they are not included in her inventory (*Culinary Verbs*, pp. 70–91). *MED*, s.v. *unlasen* v. 3, distinguishes between cutting up a game animal (as in *SGGK*, 1605–6), and dressing or dismembering an animal for cooking or serving – a distinction that can be difficult to sustain.

7   (i) *dysplayd* 'displayed, spread out'. Hodgkin ('Terms II', p. 71) suggests that a crane was said to be 'displayed' because of the elaborate way in which it was presented at table, with its bill thrust through the hole left by the removal of its windpipe (this is described in *Noble Cookry*, p. 62). Yet the principal sense of *displaien* is 'to spread (something) out' – such as a banner, cloth, wings, limbs (see *MED, displaien* v.). It therefore seems more likely that a 'displayed' crane is simply one that has been dismembered and spread out, rather as *BK* describes: 'Take a crane, and vnfolde his legges, and cut of his wynges by the Ioyntes: than take vp hys wynges and his legges, and sauce hym ...' (p. 276). As this text makes clear elsewhere, fowls that had their legs and wings removed were presented in a dish with the severed limbs artistically arranged – presumably, 'displayed' – around the carcass (*BK*, p. 272).

(iii) *asplay* Either an error for *display*, or a variant of *splay*, itself the aphetic form of *display*, with a redundant *a*- prefix. See *MED, splaien* v., and note 37 below.

(iv) *krane* Scribal error for *brane* 'brawn' – see no. 3.

8   (i) *vnyoynted* 'unjointed', 'dismembered'.

(ii) *vnrowtyde* 'broken up', 'dismembered'. The verb expresses the idea of breaking something up, especially a group or assembly (of people, animals); see *MED, route* n.(1), *routen* v.(7), *unrouten* v.; also Godefroy, *desrouter*, verbe.

(iii) *vntache* 'unfasten, detach', hence 'dismember'; see note 2 above.

9 (i–ii) *breke, broken* 'cut up', 'dismember(ed)'; the image of breaking a carcass into its constituent parts is a graphic one. In the context of preparing food for the table, the verb *breken* is more usually applied to fowls, as in the cookery book *The Forme of Cury* (first compiled c. 1390): 'and serue the chykens hole oþer ybroke': in *Curye on Inglysch*, ed. Constance B. Hieatt and Sharon Butler EETS ss 8 (Oxford, 1985), IV.35. So too in John Russell's *Boke of Nurture*: 'Good syr, y yow pray þe connynge of kervynge ye wille me teche ... and alle wey where y shalle alle maner fowles breke, vnlace, or seche ...' (lines 313–5): in *The Babees Book*, ed. F.J. Furnivall, EETS os 32 (London, 1868; repr. 1997).

In a different context, *breken* was also the correct technical term for butchering a hunted deer (see *BH*, 1748), and it is from here that the word seems to have been appropriated for the J.B. lists of carving terms. At table, however, *breken* is clearly suitable for a fowl in a way that it cannot be for a deer, simply because of the animal's size. Perhaps it should be treated as a term of dressing or preparation, though it may equally have been used in a transferred sense to mean simply 'cut, carve' – i.e. as 'a general carving term', as Hands suggests (*EHH*, p. 164/2018n). See also *MED, breken* v. 1c; and Appendix I, where one of the collective nouns for carvers is an *vmbrekyng* (no. 27). In terms of its figurative import, the word can be grouped with *frush* (no. 5), and rather more loosely with *dismember* (no. 16) and *unjoint* (nos 2, 8).

(iii) *vndo* 'undo', hence 'dismember'. The word belongs with a group of synonyms that present dismembering in terms of loosening or unfastening; see note 6 above, and *MED, undon* v. 9a. As with *breken*, the word often describes the dismembering of deer slain in the hunt (see *BH*, 1750, 1771), as well as boar (*BH*, 1730–2). It occurs occasionally in cookery books to describe the action of cutting up, or cutting open, a variety of creatures, especially fish and fowl: e.g. *Curye on Inglisch*, IV.110; III.11. As with *breken*, *undo* was not principally a verb describing carving or slicing, but rather the action of cutting something apart. It, too, has been appropriated from the hunting field to provide a 'carving' term for deer.

10 The usual glosses of the verb *tyre, tyred* in this context are decidedly vague: Hands, *EHH*, p. 165/2042n, has 'prepared as food'; *MED*, s.v. *tiren* v.(3) 2b, offers simply 'of an egg: prepared'; and Hodgkin ('Terms II', no. 16) suggests the action of heating or swinging an egg, though his evidence (Jehan Palsgrave's *Lesclarcissement de la langue françoyse*, 1530) hardly supports his conclusions. As *MED* reveals, the main senses of *tiren* (the aphetic form of *atiren*) are 'to dress, equip, make ready, adorn, ornament'. Perhaps the J.B. compilers had in mind some elaborate process of preparing an egg, as in the recipe for making counterfeit 'rost eggs in lent'. The eggs were blown and then carefully filled by stages with 'mylk of almonds', some of it coloured yellow to represent the yolk; see *Noble Cookry*, p. 37. Alternatively, in the context of so many other terms describing carving and dismembering, perhaps *tiren* here implies the process of breaking and separating an egg – the figurative equivalent of dismembering it. Once again, inspiration could

have come from the hunting field, as when King Mark's hunter says to Sir Tristrem, '3ond liþ a best vnflain; / Atire it, as þou wold ...': *Sir Tristrem*, ed. E. Kölbing (Heilbronn, 1882), lines 468–9.

In the little treatise *For to Serve a Lord*, the verb *tyre* is used explicitly as a synonym for 'dismember': 'To tyre or ellis to dismember an heronsew ...' [*heronsew* = *heronshaw*, ME *heironseu* 'a (small) heron']. See *Babees Book*, pp. 366–77 (p. 374).

(ii) The verb in BS is undoubtedly *Thyre*, not the unintelligible *Shyre* in the printed edition: *The Tollemache 'Book of Secrets'*, ed. Jeremy Griffiths (London, 2001) (hereafter *Book of Secrets*), p. 96.

11 *y-kneed* 'kneed', 'has its legs broken off at the knee'; this participle is not recognised by *MED*, but clearly derives from the noun *knee*. Presumably, the egret's long legs had to be snapped off prior to cooking or serving, as in the following recipe in MS Harley 4016: 'Take a Heron ... roste him and ... breke awey the bone fro the kne to þe fote, And lete the skyn be on' (*Harley Cook Books*, p. 78). In the Beinecke recipe collection (MS W), the heron's legs are broken prior to cooking: 'Do hym on a spitte ... & breke awey the bone fro the kne to the foute ...': *An Ordinance of Pottage*, ed. Constance B. Hieatt (London, 1988) (hereafter *Pottage*), no. 145.

12 *tymbered* 'laid, built, made'. The verb *timbren* (<OE *timbran, timbrian*) was used to mean 'to build, construct, make', both literally and figuratively in a wide variety of situations. The sense 'to build a fire' is not, however, recorded by *MED*, s.vv. *timbren* v.(1); *itinbred* p.ppl.

13 *reryd, arered* 'raised, lifted', but here used in the particularised sense of 'cut up, carved'. Under *reren* v.(1) sense 8, *MED*, cites Rd as evidence of the sense 'To carve (a goose)'. It is not clear how the verb *reren* (<OE *ræran*, 'to lift, raise') acquired the meaning 'to cut, slice, carve', which occurs only occasionally outside the J.B. lists of carving terms. The word appears in Russell's *Boke of Nurture*, where it is applied to a variety of birds: '... partriche, stokdove & chekyns, in seruynge, with your lifft hand take þem by þe pynon of þe whynge, & þat same with þe fore parte of þe knyfe be ye vp rerynge' (lines 397–9). So too in *For to Serve a Lord*: 'To unlose, tire or display a crane: ... rere legge and whyngge as of a capon' (*Babees Book*, pp. 374–5). Perhaps the association between lifting and cutting arose through the notion of lifting something (a slice of meat, a joint) away with the stroke of a knife.

It is noteworthy that only L among the J.B. texts uses *arered*, of which *rered* is the aphetic form. The use of *areren* to mean 'cut (away)' is not recognised by *MED* (s.v. *areren* v.), though the word occurs in this sense in the *StA* printing of *BH*: 'And so forth ['onward to'] the fillittis that ye vp arere' (line 1796; manuscript variants: 'ye rere'; 'ye vp rere' – see Hands, *EHH*, p. 178, line 315 and 315n).

In many texts, a far more commonly used word is the synonym *reisen* (<ON *reisa*, 'to lift, raise') and its related forms *araisen, areisen*: 'Every goos ... & also

swanne, reyse vp þo leggis of alle þese furst, ... afftur þat, þe whynges ...' (*Boke of Nurture*, 402–4); 'Feysaunt, partriche ... y yow say, areyse þe whynges furst' (*ibid.*, 417–8). In *BK*, by contrast, the form *reyse* is standard (see pp. 275–6), as it is in *Pottage* (nos 37, 40, 96 *et seq.*). See *MED*, s.vv. *araisen* v. 12, *reisen* v.(1) 7, though it should be noted that the *MED* makes no connection between these two terms, and that its treatment of the relevant sense of *reisen* needs to be amplified beyond the hunting field. It seems likely that *reisen* acquired the sense 'to cut (off)' through influence from OF *raser* (whence also ME *rasen*, 'to cleave, slice, cut'; see *MED*, s.v. *rasen* v.(1) 3), but this does not adequately explain why *reren* should have acquired this meaning as well, except perhaps by association and analogy. At any rate, the association between lifting and cutting seems to have become sufficiently well established to inspire the parallel use of *liften* itself as a carving term, as in no. 33.

Finally, it should be observed that *reisen* was also used in some recipes to indicate the act of setting up, or arranging, the severed wings and legs of a fowl around the cooked carcass (e.g. *Noble Cookry*, pp. 62–3), a sense recognised by *MED*, s.v. *reisen* v.(1) 2.

14 *i-brawynde* 'filleted', 'breasted', 'has its breast meat removed'. A recipe in the collection known as *Diuersa Servicia* makes it clear that *brawn*, when used of birds, refers specifically to the breast meat: 'tak braun of caponys oþer of hennys and þe þyes ...': *Curye on Inglisch*, II.29. See also *MED*, *braun* n. 2a, and cf. no. 31.

15 *spoyled* 'stripped' (of parts); hence, 'dismembered'. The verb *spoilen* derives from OF *espoillier*, 'to strip, skin, undress', 'remove' (arms etc.), and overlaps considerably with ME *despoilen* (<OF *despoillier*), which includes the senses 'to undress; strip; ravage; devastate'. The *Promptorium* (ed. Mayhew) glosses the word as follows: 'Spoylyn [*var.* Spylyn], ore Dysmembryn, as men Done caponys or oder ffoulys: Arcuo [*var.* Artuo]' (col. 463). The underlying notion is similar to that expressed by *disfigure* (no. 23).

(ii) *y-swylyd* Even allowing for scribal misunderstanding, it seems unlikely that the intended sense here is that a hen should be 'washed' (*MED*, *swilen* v.); more likely, the word represents an error for *y-spwyled* (i.e. *y-spoyled*) along the lines of *spwlle* in Adv.

16 The notion of dismembering a carcass – removing its 'members', or limbs – is essentially the same as that expressed by the terms *break* (no. 9) and *unjoint* (nos 2, 8). Unfortunately, when Auvo Kurvinen published the carving terms from Prk ('MS Porkington 10', p. 60), she misread *herne* as *heene*, and her mistake has been taken up and repeated several times in *MED*, s.vv. *dismembren* v. 1b; *unjointen* v. b.

17 *shulderide* 'shouldered', 'has its shoulder removed'. Presumably this represented a symbolic initial stage in carving a kid (and a lamb), as hinted at in *BK*: 'Fawne, kyde, and lambe, laye the kydney to your souerayne, than lyf[t]e vp

the sholder & gyue your souerayne a rybbe' (p. 273; cf. the equivalent passage in Russel's *Boke of Nurture*, 441–3).

18 (i) *shulderide* See note 17 above.

(ii) *sydyde* 'sided', 'has its sides [i.e. ribs] removed'. It is unclear whether this phrase describes a stage in the carving process, or in the dismembering of a carcass prior to cooking. Several cookery books contain recipes for the 'syde of a dere': e.g. *Pottage*, no. 159; *Noble Cookry*, p. 66; MS C, fol. 44v (unpublished).

19 *shuldred* See note 17 above.

20 *vnbrased* 'released, undone, loosened, detached'; hence, 'dismembered'. See *MED*, s.vv. *bracen* v.(1), and *unbracen* v. The same image is evoked by the verbs *unlaced* (no. 6), *vntached* ('unfastened', nos 2, 8) and *undo* (no. 9).

21 (i) *eyled, alet* 'winged', 'has its wings cut off' <OF *aile* (var. *elle*), 'a wing'. See *MED*, *ieled* ppl. As a description of carving a bird, this is obviously incomplete, and is probably best considered a synecdoche, indicating only one action but implying many more. As *BK* reveals (pp. 272–8), it was standard procedure to cut off the wings and legs of a bird when serving it. See also Russell, *Boke of Nurture*, lines 397 ff. (esp. 469–76), for several ways of mincing, boning and presenting a bird's wings to one's 'souerayne'.

(ii) *y-eked* Most likely, scribal error for *y-eled* 'winged'.

22 *bordered* Referred to here is the operation of providing a pasty (a pie wholly enclosed in pastry) with an ornamental border around the edge of its lid.

23 *disfigured* The choice of this verb was probably influenced by the elaborate preparations for cooking and serving a peacock. The bird was first carefully skinned, roasted and then meticulously re-cloaked in its skin – with feathers intact and comb gilded – prior to being served, a process described in MS Sloane 7, fol. 105r (see *Pottage*, p. 109, A.8), and more fully in MS Arundel 334, in a text that has been printed under the title 'Ancient Cookery from Arundel MS 344' [*sic*] by Richard Warner, *Antiquitates Culinariæ, or Curious Tracts relating to the Culinary Affairs of the Old English* (London, 1791; repr. 1981), pp. 51–90. Presumably, the peacock was 'disfigured', or marred, when a carver began to slice through this immaculate presentation. The image is very similar to that evoked by *spoiled* (see note 15). The Arundel text is quoted by Hodgkin, together with a similar Latin recipe from MS Sloane 1986: 'Terms II', p. 77.

Note that *MED* follows Allen ('Fifteenth-century associations', p. 604) in representing the carving term in Rd as *dyffugryde* – a simple scribal error in the manuscript, which I have corrected in my transcription.

24 *eyled, alet, i-illyde*, etc. 'winged'; see note 21 above.

25 (i–iii) *heded* 'beheaded'. The word is more straightforward in meaning than the gloss offered by *MED*, s.v. *heden* v.(1) 1b: 'of a pig: ?cut up after slaughtering, prepared for serving'.

(i) *syded* 'butchered by having its sides cut off'; cf. note 18.ii above, and *SGGK*, 1354: 'And syþen sunder þay þe sydez swyft fro þe chyne'. See also the recipe in MS Harley 279: '& loke þat þow haue fayre sydys of Pyggys, & fayre smal Chykenys' – *Harley Cook Books*, p. 25 (no. 109). It seems very likely that the terms 'headed' and 'sided' – even more so than the verbs used of a deer (no. 9) – describe butchering procedure, or the dressing of a carcass, rather than carving at table.

(iii) *thyed* Most likely introduced by scribal error from the preceding entry in the manuscript: 'a woodcock thighed'.

26 *y-thyyde* 'thighed', 'has its thighs cut off' – the complementary action to being winged: see note 21 above. The verb is not recorded by *MED*.

(iii) *i-schrydde*: 'shredded', 'chopped up small' – equivalent in meaning to *minced* (no. 28) and perhaps *frushed* (no. 5). *MED* has plenty of examples of herbs and vegetables being shredded for cooking, but not meat: s.v. *shreden* v. (a).

27 *thyed* See note 26 above.

28 (i) *mynsed* 'minced', 'chopped up small' – equivalent to *shredded* (nos 26, 32) and perhaps *frushed* (no. 5). A curious item in the will of Hugh Willoughby of Wollaton (proved 15 December 1448) shows that smaller birds were indeed served in this way; the will refers to 'a chaffar [chafer] of silver, for partrich mynced': *Testamenta Eboracensia: A Selection of Wills from the Registry at York* (Part II), ed. James Raine Jun., Surtees Society, 30 (Durham, 1855), p. 133.

(ii) *mynied* ?'mined'. Very likely no more than scribal error for *mynced*, but perhaps understood by the scribe to mean 'broken into', hence 'broken apart': see *MED, minen* v. 1a (d), 2b (a); and cf. no. 41.i.

29 *popyr* Most likely, the popeler or European spoonbill, also known as the shovelard; see *OED*, s.vv. *poper*, n.[1]; *popard*, n.; *popeler*, n.; *shovelard*, n; *MED*, s.vv. *poper* n.; *popelere* n.; and Lockwood, *British Bird Names*, p. 120. There is no need to pursue Hodgkin's suggestion ('Terms II', pp. 75–6) that the word denotes some sort of wild goose.

The participle *lowryde*, 'lowered', probably represents a deliberate inversion of *lyfte, y-lyft* (no. 33), *reare, reryd* (no. 13), and *raise* (discussed in note 13), adopted so as to create a unique carving term for this bird.

30 See notes 21 and 26 above for discussions of birds that are, respectively, 'winged' and 'thighed'.

31 It is not clear why a rail (probably the landrail or corn-crake, *Crex crex*) should be 'breasted' – that is, have its breast meat removed – rather than being winged or thighed. *MED* (s.v. *ibrested* ppl.) is somewhat vague here, defining the verb simply as 'Of a rail; cut up, carved'. As Hands observes (*EHH*, p. 165/2040n), the term most likely derives from the noun *brest*, rather than from the verb *bresten*, 'to break, burst, shatter', though the possiblity of intentional wordplay cannot be discounted. The operation described by this verb is identical to that expressed by *i-brawynde* (no. 14).

32 For 'thighed' and 'shredded', see note 26 above.

33 (i) *lyfte, y-lyft* 'lifted' = 'cut up', 'carved'; (ii) *lyfte* as imperative, 'cut up'. It is not immediately obvious how the verb *liften* acquired the meaning 'to cut (up)', except perhaps by analogy with the synonyms *reren* and *reisen* (see note 13 above). In the J.B. carving lists, the term is restricted to the swan, but in *BK* it is applied to other birds and small animals as well: 'Capon or henne of grece, lyfte the legges, than the wynges ...'; 'Fawne, kyde, and lambe ... lyf[t]e vp the sholder & gyue your souerayne a rybbe' (pp. 272–3; cf. Russell, *Boke of Nurture*, lines 409–10, 441–3). Since *BK* adapts large parts of the *Boke of Nurture* for its own use, it is interesting to observe how some of the original terms are altered; for instance, '& þat same [the wings] with þe fore parte of þe knyfe be ye vp rerynge' (*Boke of Nurture*, 399), becomes 'with the foreparte of your knyfe lyfte vp your wynges' (*BK*, p. 272). Whoever adapted the *Boke of Nurture* for *BK*, clearly saw *lift* and *rear* as synonyms. Under *liften* v. 8, *MED* defines the word as meaning 'to carve (a swan)', but fails to connect this with 'cut off a head' (sense 3), and overlooks the examples in *BK* that would have supported a more inclusive definition of the cutting, severing, carving senses of this word.

34 For 'thighed' and 'shredded', see note 26 above.

36 *tusked* 'has its "tusks" removed'. The barbel gets its name from the two pairs of sensory filaments known as 'barbels' or 'barbules' (<OF <L *barba*, 'a beard') on either side of its mouth. Presumably, these were considered to have the appearance of projecting teeth or tusks, like those of a boar, and were trimmed off before the fish was cooked or served – hence 'tusked'. It is difficult to assess how important a procedure such as this actually was, since the instruction is not repeated by medieval cookery books. Moreover, the barbel is not the only fish in these lists to possess barbules; the carp, tench and sturgeon also have these filaments, though theirs are all different in appearance.

37 (i, iv) *splay, splayde* 'split and lay (laid) open' – see *MED*, *splaien*, v. 2d. This is a shortened form of the verb *displaien*, which is used of the crane (no. 7) to mean 'spread out'. It appears to be synonymous with *splatten* in both the J.B. carving terms and medieval recipe books (see L (iii) and no. 51).
   (ii) *y-sprayed* Read *y-splayed*.
   (iii) *splat* 'split and laid open'; see note 51 below.

38 It is odd that the carp, which was such a common fish in manorial and monastic ponds, should be so rare in these lists.

(i) *trownsonnyd* 'cut into pieces, fragments' <OF *tronçonner* 'to cut up' (into *tronçons* 'pieces, bits'; cf. *A-ND*, s.v. *trunçuner*, *trounsoner* 'to shatter, smash to pieces'). Godefroy gives one of the senses of *tronçon*, s. m., as 'partie coupeé d'un poisson'. The medial *n* in this form of the word is important; Hands omits it by representing the term as *trowsonnyd*: *EHH*, p. 166/2027n. Other spellings are *tronsoned, tronsonett, trunson, transsene*: see no. 43 (eel). This verb is identical in meaning to *i-tronchnide* (ii below), but the form suggests a derivation directly from OF *tronçonner*, rather than, as is the case with *i-tronchnide*, from ME *tronchoun*. The same idea is expressed by *i-colpynnde* (nos 43, 59), and *gobbonde, gobettid* (no. 59).

(ii) *i-tronchnide* 'truncheoned', 'cut into truncheons' – i.e. 'fragments, pieces'; see *MED, itronchned* ppl.; *tronchoun* n. (<OF *tronçon*); *OED*, s.v. *truncheon* n.

(iii) *langed* Obscure. This may represent a corruption of *lanced* (<OF *lancier, lanchier*), 'cut, slashed, pierced'; see *MED, launchen* v. Alternatively, it may be a corrupt derivation from the noun *longe* 'lung', which often occurs in the collocation *livere and longe(s)*, meaning the inner organs generally; see *MED, longe* n. Perhaps a *langed [longed]* carp is one that is eviscerated, with the removal of its lungs referring by synechdoche to all the organs.

39 *fynned* 'finned', 'has its fins cut off'. There is no obvious reason why the chevin, or chub, should be 'finned', as there is nothing remarkable about its fins – unlike the perch, which has a large dorsal fin armed with very sharp spikes, but which is said to be 'scaled' (no. 50). In recipe books, the fish that most commonly has its fins cut off is the sturgeon, as in MS Harley 4016: 'Take a Sturgeon, and cut of the vyn fro the tayle to þe hede, on the bakke' (*Harley Cook Books*, p. 104). See also *Noble Cookry*, p. 71 (sturgeon); *Pottage*, nos 63 (turbot), 175 (sturgeon). In the J.B. lists, paradoxically, the sturgeon (no. 57) is not finned, but is *traunched*.

40 *gnowod* Read ?*gnowed* = 'gnawed', in the sense 'cut into', 'scored' (with a knife); see *MED, gnauen* [var. *gnoue, gnouen*] v. 2, which is defined as follows: 'Of sharp instruments, knots: to bite into (flesh)'. This would mean that the conger is 'scored, hatched', a notion expressed also by the verb *crowsyde* 'crossed' (no. 43.iii). Although the conger is common enough in cookery books as an ingredient (e.g. *Pottage*, nos 90, 100, 180; *Harley Cook Books*, p. 14; *Antiquitates Culinariæ*, p. 87), nowhere else is it said to be 'gnawed'.

41 (i) *mynyde* 'mined', 'excavated' (= 'scooped out'), 'shelled'. This sense of the verb *minen* is not recorded by *MED*.

(ii) Cf. Russell, *Boke of Nurture*, 590: 'Crabbe is a slutt ['awkward creature'] to kerve and a wrawd ['perverse'] wight'.

(iii) *tayme* 'cut into', 'pierce, broach' – see *MED, tamen* v.(2).

(iv) *trayeme* Most likely, a corruption of *tayeme* (<*tamen*), but it could also be an otherwise unrecorded verb derived from *tram(me)*, 'a siege engine'; hence, 'besiege' – an appropriate image for the struggle to get at the flesh of a crab.

42 *is vnmaylyde* Hodgkin ('Terms II', no. 42) remarks, '*Unmaylyde* is the correct expression for taking a crayfish out of his shell ... the *mail* is, of course, his shell or *armour*.' The newly updated *OED* entry concurs, glossing the solitary J.B. instance of this usage as 'To remove the shell (of a crustacean)': s.v. *unmail* v. 2. But this does not quite match how the word appears to have been used in the Middle Ages. In Caxton's *Foure Sonnes of Aymon* (*c.* 1489), for example, the verb applies to hauberks of mail, not their wearers: 'And thenne began the batell ... ye sholde haue seen many speres broken, and sheldes bresten ... and many a goode haubergen vnmayled.' *The Right Plesaunt and Goodly Historie of the Foure Sonnes of Aymon*, ed. Octavia Richardson, EETS, ES 44–5 (London, 1885), p. 79. Similarly in Lydgate's *Tale of Two Merchants* (*Fabula duorum mercatorum*), the assaults of Fortune are described as destroying a man's defences, represented as metaphorical hauberks: 'How many a man hath Fortune assayled ... Her habiriownys of steel also vnmayled!' *The Minor Poems of John Lydgate*, Part II, ed. Henry Noble MacCracken, EETS OS 192 (1934), p. 508 (l. 668). In both cases, the verb describes the breaking open of a chain-mail tunic, rather than its removal, which suggests that a better way to read the phrase *A crauys ys vnmaylyde* might be 'A crayfish has its mail-coat (*sc.* its shell) split open'. The sense 'to remove a coat of mail' appears to be a somewhat later development, first attested by the *OED* in 1578: see s.v. *unmailing* n.

43 (i–ii) *trunson, tronsoned* 'cut into fragments, pieces' <OF *tronçonner* 'to cut up' (into *tronçons* 'pieces, bits'). See note 38.i above. Note that *StA* prints *trousoned*, which I have treated as containing a turned *n* and corrected accordingly. The same idea is expressed by *i-colpynnde* (below and no. 59), and *gobbonde*, *gobettid* (no. 59).

(iii) *crowsyde* Possibly 'crossed', 'scored, hatched (with a knife)', as in *BK*, p. 281: 'A playce, put out the water than crosse hym with your knyfe'. However, as both Hodgkin ('Terms II', no. 43) and Hands (*EHH*, p. 166/2027n) suggest, it is possible that this word represents a miscopying of *trowsynde* or *trownsynde*.

i-colpynnde 'cut into pieces, chunks' – see *MED*, *culpoun* n. ('a piece, chunk, segment'), whence, *culpounen* v. In medieval cookery books, one is often instructed to 'culpon' one or more eels; see *Pottage*, no. 15; *Noble Cookry*, p. 86. The action appears to have become strongly associated with eels, judging by the following account of Hector's dispatching of an enemy in the *Laud Troy Book*, ed. J. Ernst Wülfing, EETS OS 121 (London, 1902), lines 6254–5: 'He carf a-two bothe flesche and bon, / He culpunte him as he were an ele'.

44 *a rostere* 'a roaster', something that is roasted; *spychecoke*: something skewered on a roasting spike. These terms both seem to refer to essentially the same method of cooking a large eel – i.e. by roasting it (on a skewer). See *MED, rostere* n.; *spiche-coke* n. The lacuna in Pl is the result of damage to the manuscript.

45 *sorrey, sorraye* According to *MED*, s.v. *sore* n.(2), this term refers to 'a dish of chopped eels or other fish, sometimes coloured red', and the phrase *eles in sore* indicates the same dish made specifically with eels. This essentially repeats the gloss in *OED*, s.v. *sorré* n. As Hieatt and Butler point out, the word *sore* (also *soree*) is probably not derived from OF *sor* 'red', though an association with that colour seems to have arisen fairly early: *Curye on Inglisch*, p. 215, s.v. *soree*.

While *MED*'s principal definition is beyond dispute, its gloss of *eles in sore* is not wholly satisfactory. In medieval recipe books, the phrase is often used in a way that suggests that there was something called *sore* (*sorré*) that existed independently of the eels and other fish that were commonly associated with it – namely, a particular spicy sauce or stock, from which the dish gets its name; see, for example, *Pottage*, no. 14; *Antiquitates Culinariæ*, p. 85. In much the same way, the heading *Felets yn galentyne* (*Pottage*, no. 24) indicates a dish in which fillets are combined with galantine, another spicy sauce.

46 (gurnard) *chyned* 'chined', *sc.* 'filleted', 'has (its) flesh cut away from the chine, or backbone', which is essentially how the *MED* glosses the word, s.v. *chinen* v.(2). This is the same action denoted by *sided*, the term used for lamb, pig and haddock (nos 18, 25, 47).

In the J.B. lists, only fish are 'chined', specifically gurnard, lamprey and salmon, and we find that the word is also used in recipes for fish, such as the following: 'Take a fressh Salmon ... and chyne him as a swyne, and leche ['slice'] him flatte with a knyfe' (*Harley Cook Books*, p. 102). But this instruction should make us pause and consider how exactly a pig would be 'chined' and how the same action might be applied to a salmon. The question is important because the verb has also been interpreted as meaning 'split open, divided along the backbone'. Hodgkin reads it thus ('Terms II', no. 38), and M.Y. Offord makes a comparable claim for the moment in the *Parlement of the Thre Ages* when the poacher is said to have 'chynede hym [the hart] chefely' (line 89): p. 75, s.v. *chynede*. It has to be admitted that Hodgkin's hypothesis concerning fish is plausible, not least because there are other verbs – *splayed* and *splatted* – that clearly refer to the action of cutting a fish along its spine and splitting it open (see notes 37 and 51). But while a fish can easily be split in two with a cleaver, the same cannot be said of a larger animal, such as a deer (or a pig). It would seem that a quadruped was said to be chined by having its usable parts – particularly its 'sides' or ribs – cut away from both sides of the spine: the process referred to in *SGGK* during the butchering of the deer: 'And syþen sunder þay þe sydez swyft fro þe chyne' (line 1354).

To summarise, a fish could not have been 'chined' in precisely the same way as a deer, but in an analagous way, by having its flesh cut away from the backbone; hence, in modern parlance, it was 'boned', 'filleted'.

47 (haddock) (i–ii) *sided* 'has its sides [*sc.* fillets] removed'; hence, 'boned, filleted' – a synonym for *chined* (no. 46). *MED* does not record the active form of the verb, found in *BK* and BS, and its gloss for the participle as 'carved into sides' leaves a lot to be desired: s.v. *sided* adj. (b). See also nos 18 and 25 (lamb and pig), where the term is applied to animals, rather than fish.

(iii) *syth* 'seethe' – meaning either 'boil, cook in liquid', or 'bake, roast'. See *MED*, *sethen* v.(1), senses 1 and 2. The use of this term in Adv can very likely be attributed to scribal misreading of *syde*.

48 The lamprey, an eel-like fish, of which there are several species, was highly prized as food in the Middle Ages, not least because it was considered to be more like flesh than fish in flavour.

(i–iii) *corded, strynge* These phrases must mean that a lamprey has its 'cord' or 'string' removed, though it is not clear what this organ might be. *MED* (s.vv. *corde* n. 3; *streng* n. 3a) suggests a muscle, tendon, ligament, nerve and the like, and the *OED* (s.v. *string*, n. 2. b.) admits to uncertainty over what this might be, 'In certain fishes. ? *Obs.*' Two possibilities suggest themselves, however: the animal's entrails, and its primitive backbone.

Regarding the former, several medieval recipe books refer to the lamprey's entrails as its 'string(s)'. A good example occurs among the recipes in MS Beinecke 163:

> Then wesch hym [a lamprey] ... & cut hym a lytyll overtwarte a straw brede byfore the navyll so that the stryng be lose. Then slete hym a lytyll at the throte & take out the stryng ... Yf he be a femaule, thrist hym in thy honde from the navill upward so that the spauner ['roe'] come out theras thu takest out the stryngys. (*Pottage*, no. 118)

These instructions, employing the same terminology, are repeated in the Holkham recipes (*Noble Cookry*, pp. 49–50), and abbreviated accounts of the operation occur also in MS Harley 5401 and the *Forme of Curye*, where the word *gut* (pl. *guttes*) is used in place of *string*; see Constance B. Hieatt, 'The Middle English culinary recipes in MS Harley 5401: An edition and commentary', *Medium Ævum*, 65 (1996), 54–71 (recipe no. 29); *Curye on Inglisch*, IV.130. Elsewhere in the Beinecke recipes, precisely the same instructions are given for eviscerating the conger, and again the word used is *gutte* (*Pottage*, no. 180).

It seems likely, then, that the noun *string* was used to refer to the simple digestive tract of the lamprey. Living, as they do, either as filter-feeders or as parasitic blood-suckers, lampreys do not have a highly evolved intestinal structure, but something more akin to a simple tube. The term *string* is therefore wholly appropriate, as would be *cord*, though I have yet to find an incontrovertible example of the latter used in this sense.

Turning to my alternative suggestion, it is clear that the word *string* referred also to the lamprey's primitive backbone – in the 17th century at least. Randle Cotgrave glosses the French word *cordé* as follows: 'Corded; twisted as a cord; ... also, out of season; (a Metaphor from Lampreyes, which being out of season, haue a hard string in their backes).' *A Dictionarie of the French and English Tongves* (London, 1611), s.v. *Cordé*. Cotgrave is here referring to the lamprey's peculiar anatomical feature, known to biologists as a notochord. This is a proto-backbone, which exists in the embryos of all vertebrates, but survives in the lamprey into adulthood as a flexible, cartilaginous rod located between the spinal cord and the gut. This organ can be removed intact, since it is not composed of individual vertebrae, and is not attached to a ribcage, as a true backbone would be. The recipe quoted above from the Beinecke collection goes on to describe precisely this operation:

> Yf thu wilte bone hym [a lamprey], slyt hym a lytyll in the same place withyn so that thu may come to the bone, & louse ['loosen'] the bone with a pyke fro thy fysch &, as esily as thu may, draw awey the bon fro thy tayle that hit come out hole ... (*Pottage*, no. 118)

Although I have yet to find a medieval text that refers explicitly to the notochord as a 'string' or 'cord', it seems possible that the cryptic J.B. verbs 'string' and 'corded' could very well allude to the removal of this organ. The instruction in Adv, to *Chyne þe lawmprey* (v), also focuses on that aspect of the creature's anatomy.

For more on the anatomy of these fish, see *The Biology of Lampreys*, ed. M.W. Hardisty and I.C. Potter, 4 vols (London, 1971–82), especially III, 95–190, 333–76.

(ii) *gallantye* 'galantine', a thickened sauce; see Glossary. Pl is badly damaged at this point, but almost certainly once contained some form of this statement, judging by the cognate text of Prk. Auvo Kurvinen, 'MS Porkington 10', p. 65, glosses *cordyt* as 'curded', which could be understood in the sense of 'jellied' (see *MED*, *crudden* v.). This interpretation receives some support from a recipe that describes cooking a lamprey and then serving it cold in its own jelly, accompanied by a sauce of hot galantine: *Curye on Inglisch*, III.24. On the other hand, there seems to be little point in reading *cordyt* as having a different sense in this one instance.

(iv) *y-coudyd* 'cut up into cuds' (*sc*. lumps, pieces, gobbets): see *MED*, s.vv. *icouded* ppl.; *cude* n. This participle, which is printed as *y condyd* by Allen ('Fifteenth-century associations', p. 604), probably represents a scribal misreading and modification of *y-cordyd*, the action recommended by the majority of other J.B. texts.

(v) *chyne* With other fish, this imperative verb can be interpreted to mean 'bone', 'fillet' (see note 46 above), but because of the lamprey's unusual anatomy it is probably more usefully understood as an instruction to 'remove the backbone', *sc*. the lamprey's notochord, described in (i–iii) above.

49 *lomster* The form *lomster* in MS L appears to be an unicum, unattested by *OED* (s.v. *lobster* n.[1]) or *MED* (s.v. *lopster*). As one might expect of the ME reflex of OE *loppestre*, the first syllable of the word normally ends with *p* or *b*, suggesting that this is a phonetic spelling.

Precisely what is meant, or implied, by *barbe(d)* is mysterious if one wishes to analyse the verb beyond the rather mundane gloss supplied by the *OED* (s.v. *barbe* v. 2. d.): 'The specific term for carving a lobster'. Given the way these phrases often focus on some notable feature of the creature that is to be dissected, an allusion to the lobster's protective shell, or its prominent claws, might be expected.

Hodgkin ('Terms II', no. 48) suggests that *BK*'s imperative *barbe* derives from the noun *barb* (<*bard*), denoting the armour of a war horse, and that the expression thus indicates that a lobster has its 'armour' removed, by analogy with the crayfish, which is 'unmailed'; see *OED*, *bard*, n.[2]; *barb*, n.[2]. To this ingenious interpretation we must object that there is no record of the verb *barb* being used in this sense; the relevant verb is *to bard* (first attested 1521), and it always indicates the action of arming, not disarming (see *OED*, s.v. *bard*, v.[1]).

None of these terms is recorded by the *MED*, but the verb *barben* (<AN *barber* <OF *barbiier* 'to shave', 'to trim') is, so perhaps a 'barbed' lobster is one that is 'trimmed' of its claws. Alternatively, the verb could derive from an (unattested) notion that the lobster's claws are sharp, or dangerous, weapons, like the barbs of an arrow, or the edge of an axe (see *MED*, s.v. *barbe* n. 3). The animal might therefore be '(un)barbed' in the sense that it is 'disarmed'.

50 *scalyd, i-schallyd* 'scaled', 'has its scales removed' – see *MED*, *scalen* v.(1). The scales of both perch and roach are large, and those of the perch are also noticeably rough, so scaling these fish before cooking makes sense, as in a recipe in MS Arundel 334: 'Take roches, or elles loches, and scale hom, and wasshe hom, and frie hom in oyle ...' (*Antiquitates Culinariæ*, p. 87). Recipe books do not always specify that these fish must be scaled; conversely, the instruction is often applied to other fish, such as bream, bass and mullet: see e.g. *Pottage*, nos 171, 179.

51 (i, iii) *pyke ... splatted* In essence, the verb *splatten* means 'to split open' or, when applied to a fish, 'to split (and spread) open' – see *MED*, *splatten* v. (of uncertain origin, but related to MDu and MLG *splitten*, *spletten*). It would seem that a *splatted* fish was cut lengthwise down the back, with its belly left intact, in exactly the same manner as kippers are prepared to this day. See, for example, *Noble Cookry*, p. 71: 'To dight a tenche ... splat hym by the bak through the hed let the belly be hole'; and MS Harley 4016: 'Take a gurnard rawe, and slytte him endelonge the bak, þorgh þe hede and tayle, and splatte him ...'; 'And take the pike, and roste him splat on a gredire ... And ley the pike in A charger, the wombe side vpward; and then caste the sauce there-on al hote ...' (*Harley Cook Books*, pp. 104, 101).

This is one of the few J.B. phrases to find an echo in literature. In the *Laud Troy Book*, the death of Antenor is described thus: 'The noble vaylaunt Menescene / Smot Antenor – & that was sene ... He layde him as brod & flat / As is a pike when he is splat' (lines 14003–8). See also Whiting, P194.

(ii) *splett, y-splett, y-splyte* Identical in meaning to *splatted* (past participle of *splatten*), defined in (i) above. The closely related forms of these past participles reveal their direct descent from MDu or MLG *splitten, spletten* – unlike ME *splatten*, which betrays some intermediary influence, such as Anglo-Latin *splattare*; see R.E. Latham, *Revised Medieval Latin Word-List from British and Irish Sources* (London, 1980), s.v. *splatto*.

(iv–v) *spla, splayde* 'split and lay (laid) open'; see *MED, splaien*, v. 2. (d), and note 37 above. The sense is identical to that of *splatten, splatted*, defined in (i) above.

52 *playse ... sawsyde* 'sauced', which could mean either 'served in a sauce', or 'seasoned, spiced'; see note 4 above. Fish were often served in a sauce, as in the following recipe for a gurnard from MS Harley 4016: '... and ley hym in a dissh. And þen cast þe sauce on hym in þe dissh, and serue him forthe hote' (*Harley Cook Books*, p. 104). See also the recipe for 'Pyke in sauce' in *Pottage*, no. 62.

53 The numerous medieval recipes for cooking porpoise, and records of its being served at important feasts, indicate that it was a prized foodstuff. For a brief account of porpoises as food in the Middle Ages, see Ove Fosså, 'A whale of a dish: Whalemeat as food', in *Disappearing Foods: Studies in Foods and Dishes at Risk*, ed. Harlan Walker (Totnes, 1995), 78–102 (esp. pp. 81–2).

(i) It is by no means clear what is intended by *vndertraunche*, which is not recorded by *MED*, and which *OED* (s.v. *undertranch* v.) glosses unhelpfully as 'To carve (a porpoise)'. It is also difficult to tell whether the word describes the butchering of a porpoise, its preparation in the kitchen, or its final carving at table. Hodgkin ('Terms II', no. 52) treats *vndertraunche* as little more than a synonym for *traunche* (see note 57 below), indicating the action of cutting or slicing. But the prefix *under-* also suggests that the word could mean more: possibly, 'cut from below', or 'cut (deeply) into'. It is equally possible that the prefix is redundant, or had lost its original meaning – as described by *MED*, s.v. *under-* pref.

Other sources offer little insight. *BK* declares that large pieces of salted porpoise should be carved like venison: 'ye must loke yf there be a salte purpos, or sele turrentyne [salted], & do after þe fourme of venyson' (p. 280). However, the porpoise was also cooked in stews and broths, in which presumably it had already been cut up fairly small; see *Curye on Inglisch*, IV.13, 70, 111.

(ii) *untrench* See note 57 for analysis of the verb *trenchen*. The prefix *un-* could be considered as having an intensifying effect on the simplex form of the verb, as in *unlesen*, 'unloosen', but most likely represents scribal error for *under-*, discussed in (i) above.

54 'A roach boned or ribbed', *sc.* filleted, with the flesh being cut from the fish's bones, or ribs. The action is the same as that described by the verbs *chined* (no. 46), *loined* (no. 56) and *sided* (no. 47). The past participle *rybbyde* is not attested by the *MED*, but is most likely a formation from the noun *ribbe* – as in the rib(s) of a human or animal – rather than from the homonym that referred to a scraper (usually for cleaning flax): see *MED*, s.vv. *ribbe* n.(1) and n.(3).

55 *chyned* 'boned, filleted'; see note 46 above. The instruction is repeated in a recipe in MS Harley 4016: 'Take a fressh Salmon ... and chyne him as a swyne, and leche him flatte with a knyfe' (*Harley Cook Books*, p. 102).

Note that Griffiths (*Book of Secrets*, p. 96) prints the verb in BS as 'Thyne', which makes little sense in the context. If this is indeed what was intended by the scribe, it should be treated as a misreading of *T* for *C*, and be corrected, as in my transcription.

56 *loyned* 'boned, filleted'. This verb clearly derives from the noun *loine*, which, strictly speaking, can only be used of a person or a quadruped, to designate the lower back area, between the last rib and the pelvis. As the citations in the *MED* show, s.v. *loine* n.(1), the word was never used of fish. Yet here is a verb that implies that a sole can be thought of, if only in a transferred sense, as having 'loins' – this presumably being the flesh on either side of the backbone: flesh that is cut away from the bone when the sole is 'loined'. The action so described would make this term synonymous with *i-bonyde* and *rybbyde* (no. 54), *sided* (no. 47) and *chyned* (no. 46). Cf. *MED*, s.v. *loinen* v. (1), which offers little insight with its gloss, 'To carve (a sole)'.

57 The presence of the sturgeon in these three witnesses is an interesting feature, given that it was (indeed, still is) a so-called 'royal (or regal) fish', meaning that it is legally regarded, along with the whale (and, later, the porpoise), as a prerogative of the Crown – a notion enacted by the statute *Prerogativa Regis* of about 1322, cap. 13; see <www.legislation.gov.uk./1322>. (In the printed *Statutes of the Realm*, 10 vols (London, 1810–22), vol. I, this statute is assigned to 17 Edward II (AD 1324), but it is now accepted as being of *temp. incert.*, and more likely to have been enacted in 15 Edw. II). By all accounts, sturgeon was a rare luxury on medieval tables. A fully grown fish can be over 20 feet (6 m) long, yielding some 60 stone (380 kg) of rich, fatty flesh, that would have been especially prized on fast days. Recipes for mock sturgeon – as in *Curye on Inglisch*, pp. 155–6 – suggest that the fish was not as readily available as consumers would have liked.

(i–ii) *traunche, trench* Although neither of these verbs is attested by *MED*, they must both derive from OF *tranchier*, 'to cut, hew, sever, slice'. See *OED*, *tranch* v.; *trench* v.; and Caxton's *Lyf of Charles the Grete*, ed. S.J. Herrtage, EETS ES 36–37 (1880–81), p. 63, lines 29–33: 'Fyerabras ... came wyth a course vpon Olyuer, & gaf hym a stroke vpon his helme so sharply that he trenched moo than vc maylles ...' (capitals mine).

We are presumably being told that the sturgeon needs to be sliced or chopped into pieces. This would concur with the instructions of recipe books, which usually specify that this fish needs to be chopped up, or else filleted, and then boiled; see *Curye on Inglisch*, II.71; *Noble Cookry*, p. 71; *Harley Cook Books*, p. 104.

In Adv, the entire entry reads *Traunche þe ele sturgeon* – no doubt an uncorrected scribal error in which two adjacent entries have been conflated, with the loss of one, probably similar to *BK*'s instruction to *Transsene that ele* (see no. 43.ii).

58 (i–iii) *sauce, sawced* As with the capon (no. 4) and the plaice (no. 52), this verb could indicate either that tench should be served in a sauce, or simply spiced, seasoned. Perhaps the former sense is more likely here, especially in the light of the many recipes that describe preparing or serving tench in sauces such as *cyuee* 'civy', an onion sauce (see *Curye on Inglisch*, III.9, IV.123), or *brase*, a braising sauce (see *Pottage*, no. 173; *Noble Cookry*, p. 71). See also Russell's description of 'Tenche in Iely or in Sawce' (*Boke of Nurture*, 586).

(iv–v) *sousyd, sowsyde* 'soused', i.e. 'preserved, pickled'; see *MED, sousen* v. It seems likely that the use of this term arose from a misreading of 'sauced', but that it became an accepted independent variation.

(v–vi) For the suggestion that tench should be served in jelly, see Russell, *Boke of Nurture*, 586 (quoted above), and *BK*, which includes in its second course for dinner between Michaelmas and Christmas, 'tenche in gelly' (p. 280). The expression *may be take* in Eg signifies 'may be eaten'; see *MED*, s.v. *taken* v. 12a.

59 (i) *gobbonde* 'cut into gobbons', i.e. pieces, chunks; see *MED*, s.vv. *gobonen* v.; *goboun* n. References to gobbons (of fish) are fairly common in medieval recipe books (e.g. *Pottage*, nos 14, 100; *Curye on Inglisch*, I.19, 43, 50; *Harley Cook Books*, p. 10, no. 25), but the related verb is not found as easily. However, see *Curye on Inglisch*, I.9 for 'appleen igoboned' (chopped apples), and Russell's instructions for salted lamprey: 'goben hit a slout ['aslant'] .vij. pecis y assigne' (*Boke of Nurture*, 566).

(ii) *gobettid* 'cut into gobbets', i.e. pieces, chunks – see *MED*, s.vv. *gobeten* v.; *gobet* n. The sense is identical to that of *gobbonde* above. Some recipes specify the type of gobbet required, as in *Curye on Inglisch*, III.1: 'Take eles & fle hem & cut hem on thynne gobetes'.

(iii–v) *culpon* 'cut into pieces, chunks, slices' – see *MED*, s.vv. *culpounen* v.; *culpoun* n. Hence the participial forms *i-colpynnyde, cowponyd*. See also note 43.iii above.

(v) *cheuernyde, ynvndate* Both terms are obscure and unrecorded by the *MED*. Hodgkin ('Terms II', no. 58) is probably correct in suggesting that they indicate scoring the fish with a knife to form either a chevron or a wavy pattern: *cheuernyde* <*cheveroun*, 'a heraldic charge in the shape of a chevron'; *ynvndate* <*unde, ounde* 'wavy' (a heraldic term) <OF *undee, ondee*, 'a wave'; see *MED*, s.vv. *ounde* adj.; *ounded* adj.; *OED, undee, undé(e*, adj.

If Hodgkin's hypothesis about *ynvndate* is correct, the word may be regarded as another form of *undated* (= *undee*, 'having the form of waves'), with the addition of the prefix *yn-*. *Undated* is the term used in the description of paled ('striped') arms in *StA*'s treatise on the blazoning of arms: 'Palyt armys oftyme ar founde *vndatyt*, that is to say watteri ...' (italics mine): Dame Juliana Berners, *The Boke of Saint Albans, 1486* (facsimile edn), The English Experience, No. 151 (Amsterdam & New York, 1969), sig. d²6v. See also *OED*, s.v. *undated* adj.[1]. But the addition of *yn-* is not easily accounted for. Perhaps it was inspired by the notion that the required wavy, or 'watery', pattern should be incised *into* the fish.

Alternatively, *ynvndate* could be read as 'inundated', i.e. covered in sauce. The verb is not attested by *MED*, and the first citation of a verbal usage in *OED* comes from 1623. *MED* does, however, record the noun *inundacioun*, meaning 'an overflowing of water, a flood' (<L *inundatio* 'a flood, deluge'). Perhaps, in this context, 'an abundance of liquid' (*sc*. sauce) could be intended? As with so many other hapax legomena in the J.B. lists, additional attestations of how the word was used would make interpretation so much easier.

APPENDIX III

RESTING TERMS

This Appendix sets out a complete collation of Resting terms found in all J.B. witnesses – a total of fourteen. Typically, the Resting terms are found in statements that consist of a noun phrase and a verb (or a verb phrase). The verb may be active and intransitive in form (*A hart harborowth*, Prk); or it may consist of a past participle employed either with or without the auxiliary *is* in a quasi-passive construction (*An harte is herborowyde*, H; *An hert harburght,* Adv). The J.B. lists vary somewhat in length, with the great majority containing between eight and fourteen statements, but there can be as few as six statements (W), and as many as eighteen (Adv).

In order to give some sense of the diversity to be found in the lists of Resting terms, four complete lists are set out in full – those of Adv, Am, T and W – all of them distinctive in some way. W, in particular, deserves attention because the six statements that it preserves can be regarded as the nucleus of this item in all its forms. These six statements – three pairs really – occur in all fourteen witnesses, albeit with an occasional omission, as with Eg and Rg, which both lack the formula 'a squire is lodged'. It will be seen that these three pairs of statements describe, respectively, how hart and knight, buck and squire, roebuck and yeoman go to rest, in each case, by means of matching verbs: e.g. *An harte is herborowyde / A knyth is herborowyde* (H). The conjugates of each pair are usually written sequentially, and their relationship is occasionally emphasised by means of linking braces. W departs from this pattern only insofar as its statements relating to animals and humans are grouped separately, so that the pairings are not as obvious.

The collation that follows is arranged alphabetically by headwords identifying the animal, bird or human that is the subject of each statement (nos 2–29). Introductory headings and closing remarks are included as nos 1 and 30 respectively. The collation closes with an index of the resting terms themselves, and is followed by its own set of explanatory notes.

As in Appendices I and II, witnesses are listed by their sigla in alphabetical order, a sequence broken only by pairs that are closely related to one another, viz. Am–*HSG*, Dg–Rg, H–L, Pl–Prk. For further details about the different versions of the J.B. lists of Resting terms, and relationships that can be plotted between them, see the main Introduction. To view complete lists of these terms in their proper context, see Prk (I/118–27), H (II/183–96), and Ha (III/79–90).

Adv

An hert harburght	f. 63r
A knyght harburght	
A hynde chamburd	
A lade chambred	
A buck lodgeth	5
A squier lodgeth	
A bere coureth	
A woman cowreth	
A gray scratteth	
A schrewed quene scrattet[h]	10
A roo beddeth	
A yomon beddeth	
A fox lyggeth	
A boy lygge[t]h	
A cur cowcheth	15
A knave coucheth	
An hors lyttereth	
A carle lytterde	
&c	

T

A herte harboreth	f. 35v
A knyght harboryth	
A buke lugeth	
A squyer lugeth	
A roo beddeth	5
A yomone beddyth	
A hare in a forme schuldyrynge	
or ellis lenynge	
A conynge s[yt]tynge	
A wodcoke syttynge	
A wodcoke bekynge	10
A gosehauke tyreth, fedyth,	
gorgeth, bekyth, rusyth,	
endeuth, mutyth, perchyth,	
pruneth and plumeth	
Explicit qui vult	15

Am

An hare in hys forme is	f. 211r
sholdryng or lenyng	
A dowue sittethe	
An herte is herbored	
A knyght is herbored	
A bucke is logged	5
A squier is logged	
A roo is bedded	
A yoman is bedded	

W

An herte herboryth	f. 186r
A bucke loggith	
A roo beddyth	
A knyght herboryth	
A sqvyer lodgith	5
A yoman beddyth	

Adv 3 hynde] ? hyende, e¹ *smudged*   Adv 4 A] *add* ?Prof *canc*; *add* lad‹.› *in fainter ink supra*; lade *added by a revising hand*
Am 3 is] *add* her *canc*
T 8 syttynge] stytynge   13] perchyth] *add* ayer prue

APPENDIX III

1. Headings

¶ ye shall say thus.   *StA*

2. Bear

A bere coureth   Adv

3. Boy

i.   A boye is beddyd brawlyng   H
     A boye is beddid brawlynge   L
ii. A boy lygge[t]h   Adv
iii. A boy walkethe   Dg
     A boy walkyd   Rg
     A boy walkyth   Ha

(*See also* **Knave**)

4. Buck

i.   A buck lodgeth   Adv
     A boke logeyth   Pl
     A boke logythe   Prk
     A bucke lodgith   *StA*
     A bucke loggith   W
ii. A buke lugeth   T
iii. A bucke is logged   Am
     A bucke is logged   HSG
     A buk ys logged   Dg
     A bugke ys loggyd   Rg
     A bucke ys loggyde   Eg
     A bukke is logged   H
     A buck is logid   L
     A buk is logged   Ha

5. Carl

A carle lytterde   Adv

6. Cony

i.   A cony syttyng   Pl
     A connye syttynge   Prk
     A cony sittyng   *StA*
     A conynge s[yt]tynge   T
ii. A cony syttethe   Dg
     A conynge syttyth   Rg
     A conyng syttythe   Eg
     A cony syttyth   H
     A cony sitteth   L
     A cony sittid   Ha

7. Crane

A crane stalkyth   H
A crane stalketh   L

8. Cur

A cur cowcheth   Adv

9. Dove

A dowue sittethe   Am
A douue sitteth   HSG

10. Fox

A fox lyggeth   Adv

11. Goshawk

A gosehauke tyreth, fedyth,
gorgeth, bekyth, rusyth,
endeuth, mutyth, perchyth,
pruneth and plumeth   T

12. Grey [badger]

A grey scratteth   Adv

---

6 T syttynge] stytynge   11 T perchyth] *add* ayer prue

13. Hare

i. An hare in hys forme is
    sholdryng or lenyng   Am
    An hare in his forme is
    sholdring or lening   *HSG*
    A hare yn hys forme
    scholderyng lenyng   Pl
    A hare in here forme
    scholderynge ore
    leynnyng   Prk
    An haare in her forme
    shulderyng or leenyng   *StA*
    A hare in a forme schulderynge
    or ellis lenynge   T
ii. A hare ys formed schulderyng
    or lenyng   Dg
    A hare ys furmyd schuldrynge
    or lenynge   Rg
    A hare is formyd schulderyng
    or lendyng   H
    An hare is fourmed shuldryng
    or lenynge   L
    A hare is formyd schulderyng
    or lenyng   Ha
iii. A hare ys formyde   Eg
iv. A trype off hareys   Pl
    A trype of harrys   Prk
v. A trasse off a hare   Pl
   A trase of harrys   Prk

14. Hart

i. A harte harbrowythe   Pl
   A hart harborowth   Prk
   An hert herbourghith   *StA*
   A herte harboreth   T
   An herte herboryth   W

ii. An hert harburght   Adv
    An herte is herbored   Am
    An herte is herbored   *HSG*
    A hert ys herborowred   Dg
    A hert ys herbrowyd   Rg
    An harte is herborowyde   H
    An hartt is herbrowed   L
    A hert is herborowid   Ha
iii. A herte, A knyghte: ben
     herborowde   Eg

15. Heron

A heyron stalkyth   H
A heyron stalkethe   L

16. Hind

A hynde chamburd   Adv

17. Horse

An hors lyttereth   Adv

18. Knave

i. A knave ly3the in hys bed
   brawlyng   Dg
   A knaue lyth on ys bedde
   brawlynge   Rg
   A knaue lyght in his bedde
   braulyng   Ha
ii. A knave coucheth   Adv
(*See also* Boy)

19. Knight

i. A knyght harborwythe   Pl
   A kny3t herborovthe   Prk
   A knyght harboryth   T
   A knyght herboryth   W

---

13 Pl[1] scholderyng] *add* deryng *supra*   Rg furmyd] *add* A   14 Am is] *add* her *canc*

ii. A knyght harburght   Adv
     A knyght is herbored   Am
     A knyght is herbored   HSG
     A kny3t ys herbowred   Dg
     A knyte ys herbrowyd   Rg
     A knyth is herborowyde   H
     A knyght is herbrowed   L
     A knyght [is] herborowid   Ha
iii. A herte, A knyghte: ben
     herborowde   Eg

20. Lady
A lade chambred   Adv

21. Parker
A parcare walkyth   H
A parker walketh   L

22. Partridge
A partryche lyethe   Dg
A partryche lyth   Rg
A parterygge lythe   Eg
A perterych lythe   H
A pertriche lieth   L
A parterich lithe   Ha

23. Pheasant
A fesavnte stalkethe   Dg
A fesante stalkyth   Rg
A fesaunt stalkythe   Eg
A fesawnte stalkyth   H
A feysand stalketh   L
A faysand stalkyth   Ha

24. *Quene*
A schrewed quene scrattet[h]   Adv

25. Roe(buck)
i.   A roo beddeth   Adv
     A roo bedythe   Pl
     A roo beddyte   Prk
     A roo beddith   StA
     A roo beddeth   T
     A roo beddyth   W
ii. A roo is bedded   Am
     A roo is bedded   HSG
     A roobuk ys bedded   Dg
     A robugke ys beddyd   Rg
     A roobucke ys beddyde   Eg
     A roo-buke is beddyd   H
     A robuck is beddid   L
     A roobuk is beddid   Ha

26. Squire / Esquire
i.   A squier lodgeth   Adv
     A squyar logeyth   Pl
     A squyere logythe   Prk
     A sqvyer lodgith   W
ii. An esquyer lodgith   StA
iii. A squyer lugeth   T
iv. A squier is logged   Am
     A squyer is logged   HSG
     A squyer ys logged   Dg
     A squier is logged   H
     A squier is logid   L
     A squier is loggid   Ha

27. Woman
A woman cowreth   Adv

---

19 Ha is] *supplied editorially to match the phrasing of other statements in the MS* Eg] *two noun phrases bracketed*   20 Adv A] *add* ?Prof *canc*; *add* lad‹.› *in fainter ink supra*; lade *added by a revising hand*   25 H roo-buke] roo buke

28. Woodcock

i. A wodcoke syttynge — T
ii. A wodecoke beekyng — StA
   A wodcoke bekynge — T

29. Yeoman

i. A yomon beddeth — Adv
   A yeman bedythe — Pl
   A yoman beyddyte — Prk
   A yoman beddith — StA
   A yomone beddyth — T
   A yoman beddyth — W

ii. A yoman is bedded — Am
   A yoman is bedded — HSG
   A ʒoman ys bedded — Dg
   A yeman ys beddyde — Eg
   A ʒeman is beddyd — H
   A yoman is bedded — L
   A yeman is beddid — Ha

30. Closing Remarks

&c — Adv
Explicit — Eg
Explicit qui vult — T

Index of Resting Terms

In this index, the symbol + indicates statements that are commonly paired with one another (e.g. nos 25 + 29); a comma is used between numerals where there is no special connection between the relevant statements. Where $y = i$, it is alphabetised accordingly.

beddeth, is bedded 25 + 29
is beddyd brawlyng 3
beekyng 28
bekyth 11
chambered 16 + 20
coucheth, cowcheth 8 + 18
coureth, cowreth 2 + 27
endeuth 11
fedyth 11
is formyd schulderyng or lenyng 13
gorgeth 11
harboreth, (is) harboured 14 + 19
lyggeth 3 + 10
lythe 22
lyth ... brawlynge 18
lyttereth, lytterde 5 + 17
lodgeth, is logged 4 + 26
mutyth 11
perchyth 11
plumeth 11
pruneth 11
rusyth 11
scratteth 12 + 24
(is) shouldering or leaning 13
sitteth, sitting 6, 9, 28
stalkyth 7, 15, 23
tyreth 11
walkyth 3, 21

30 Eg] *underlined in red*

RESTING TERMS — NOTES

The overall impression created by the J.B. lists of Resting terms suggests strongly that they had their genesis in an attempt to assemble the correct terminology for referring to the actions by which different animals of the chase withdraw to their lairs to rest or sleep. The first phrases assembled for this purpose were probably those referring to hart, buck and roe, as well as knight, squire and yeoman – with the animals and humans perhaps grouped separately, as in W, before being combined so as to present statements with matching verbs as juxtaposed pairs. The hierarchical arrangement of these statements, and their implied assumption of an ordered relationship between the animal and human worlds, is reminiscent of the conceit underlying the J.B. Hierarchy of hawks.

Beyond this central sextet of phrases, many versions also contain the formulas 'a hare is formed shouldering or leaning', and 'a cony sitting'. And most of the longer lists conclude with several disconnected statements, some of which pertain more to locomotion than resting, such as *A boy walkethe*, *A fesavnte stalkethe* (Dg). By contrast, Adv contains only matching pairs of statements, and has more of them than any other list. The notes that follow specify which phrases are paired with one another in the lists, a relationship also signalled by means of the symbol + in the Index of Resting Terms.

External evidence suggests that the formulations pertaining to humans are, for the most part, rather contrived: I have, for example, yet to find corroboration in literature or any other non-J.B. source that a knight going to, or located in, his chamber was said to 'harbour' or 'be harboured' there. Indeed, hunting treatises of the 16th century often contain many of the J.B. resting terms for animals, but none of the corresponding statements about humans. See, for example, the collection of ten resting terms for beasts of venery and the chase in Nicholas Cox's, *The Gentleman's Recreation* (London, 1677), I.10, under the heading 'Terms for their Lodging'.

Regarding the grammatical composition of these statements, I have already referred to those employing past participles as having a quasi-passive construction. At first sight, the declaration *An harte is herborowyde* may look like a straightforward assertion in the passive voice, but it is important to recognise that the hart is not being acted upon, except by itself. The expression '(is) harboured' – the auxiliary *is* being sometimes omitted – may therefore be most usefully understood as having the force of an adjectival participle, indicating a state rather than an action. The entire statement can therefore be understood as meaning, 'a [resting] hart is [one that has] harboured [itself]' – a sense essentially identical to that conveyed by versions that use an active verb, such as *A hart harborowth* (Prk).

Of the fourteen J.B. witnesses containing these terms, only five have previously appeared in print, viz: H, *HSG*, L, Prk, and *StA*.[1] Appearing here for the first time are Adv, Am, Dg, Rg, Eg, Ha, Pl, T and W.[2]

2 *coureth* 'cringes, cowers'; perhaps also, 'remains secluded'; see *MED*, s.v. *couren* v. A matching statement in Adv assigns the same verb to a woman (no. 27).

3 (i) *is beddyd brawlyng* 'goes to bed noisily', or '~ in a quarrelsome manner'; see *MED*, *braulen* v.(1); *brauling* ger. Cf. the variant, 'a knave [i.e. boy] lies in his bed brawling' (no. 18.i).

(ii) *lyggeth* 'lies (down)'; see *MED*, *lien* v.(1). A matching statement in Adv assigns the same verb to a fox (no. 10).

4 The buck referred to here is the male fallow deer, an animal that lacked the high status of the hart, but was nevertheless an important quarry of the hunt. This raises the question as to whether the verb that is here applied to it, *to lodge* (ME *loggen*), could also be used in a technical hunting sense – hitherto unattested, but possibly modelled on *harbour* as used of a hart – as I explain below.

In the present context, the meaning of the verb in its different forms is accurately glossed by the *MED*, s.v. *loggen* v. 5: 'To conceal (sb., onself), shelter; of a buck: go to his lair; *ppl.* **logged**, concealed; of a buck: safe in his lair.' But we may also plausibly ask if *lodge* (both noun and verb) was used of the buck in ways equivalent to *harbour*, the technical name for a hart's lair; for example, a hart 'harbours' when it goes to its lair; and a hunter 'harbours' the hart when he tracks it to its lair (see further note 14.iii below). It would be fascinating to find evidence that a buck's lair was known as its 'lodge', and equally gratifying to discover proof that the tracking of a buck to its lair was known by this word prior to the first attestation (1575) in the *OED*. This comes from George Gascoigne, who declares 'we lodge and rowse a Bucke, and he lieth also in his layre' (*Noble Arte*, p. 241; see also p. 141). Hunting manuals of the 15th century are not helpful on this point: *BH* states that the hart, buck and boar are *reride* or *vpreryde* ('tracked and started') with a limer (lines 1361–5), while the earlier *Master of Game* (following Gaston Phébus's *Livre de chasse*) specifically excludes the buck from this practice (p. 22).

---

[1] For the resting terms in H, see Joseph Haslewood's Introduction to the facsimile edition, *The Book containing the Treatises of Hawking ... Wynkyn de Worde* (1810), p. 26. For those in *HSG*, see Sykes's facsimile edition of Lydgate's *The Hors, the Shepe & the Ghoos* (1822) [s.n.]; in L, see Corner, 'More fifteenth-century terms', p. 233; in Prk, see Kurvinen, 'MS Porkington 10', p. 60; in *StA*, see Hands, *EHH*, p. 86.

[2] The J.B. resting terms are not recognised as an independent category in Keiser's *Manual X*, but are included as a sub-category (IV) of 'Proper Terms', 3702 [470].

With the exception of Eg and Rg, the witnesses cited here all contain a matching statement that assigns the same verb, in its various forms, to a squire or an *esquyer* (no. 26).

(i–ii) *lodgeth, lugeth* 'withdraws to its lair'; see *MED, loggen* v. 5. The form of the verb used by T occurs also in the *Parlement of the Thre Ages*, when the poacher declares, 'Als I ... lugede [var. *logid*, 'sheltered'] me in the leues þat lighte were & grene' (661–3).

(iii) *is logged* 'is secluded, concealed, withdrawn' (in its lair). Cf. note 14.ii–iii on the grammatical structure of the analagous expression 'is harboured' as used of the hart.

5 *carle* 'a carl, churl, villein'; *lytterde*: 'bedded down in litter', *sc.* straw, rushes or similar material. This signification is not recorded by *MED*, s.v. *literen* v., where the only sense assigned to this verb is 'to provide (an animal) with litter'. A matching statement in Adv assigns the same verb to a horse (no. 17).

6 (i) *syttyng* 'sitting, crouching, squatting'.

(ii) *sittid* (Ha) 'sits' (*pr. 3 sg.*). This form of the verb appears also in the poem *The Hunted Hare*, lines 23–5: 'The furst mane þat me doþ fynde ... "lo," he sayth, "where syttyt an haare" '. See *Secular Lyrics*, pp. 107–10.

As can be seen in the complete text of T provided at the start of this Appendix, the cony often introduces a change of focus from pure resting terms to a range of other descriptive verbs. The forms *sitting, sits* imply that the animal is above ground, rather than in its burrow, the place it would naturally go to hide or rest. In sources other than the J.B. texts, it is clear that the verb *sit* was also used of the hare (an animal that does not live in a burrow); see, for example, *The Hunted Hare*, lines 22, 37, 42, 62; and *Noble Arte*, p. 24: 'both the Hare and Conie do sit and squat'.

7 *stalkyth* Provides an image of the slow, careful movements with which a crane hunts its prey. In H and L, this statement forms a trio with matching formulae about the heron (no. 15) and the pheasant (no. 23). See the complete text of H in Part II, esp. lines 194–6.

8 *cowcheth* Combines the two senses of 'goes to bed' and 'cowers, crouches, lies submissively'; see *MED, couchen* v. 1. (a), (b), <AN *coucher* <OF *couchier*. A matching statement in Adv assigns the same verb to a knave (no. 18.ii).

10 *lyggeth* 'lies (down)' – a rather vague term for an animal that makes its den underground. A matching statement in Adv assigns the same verb to a boy (no. 3.ii).

11 Nothing like this appears anywhere else in the J.B. material, and it is unclear what it is doing in a list of resting terms. Its contents are all technical terms for a hawk's behaviour, namely: *tyreth* 'tires' = 'tears or plucks at tough meat'; *fedyth* 'eats (specifically flesh)'; *gorgeth* 'fills its gorge, or crop' (in feeding); *bekyth* 'wipes its beak' (after feeding); *rusyth* 'rouses' = 'shakes its feathers and body';

endeuth 'endues' = 'digests' (its food); *mutyth* 'mutes' = 'defaecates'; *perchyth* 'perches' = 'sits on a bough or perch'; *pruneth* 'prunes' = 'preens (itself)'; *plumeth* 'plumes' = 'plucks out feathers' (its own or those of its prey). T's little set of hawking expressions bears a striking resemblance to a heading in *PH*, beginning 'An hawke tyrith, fedith, goorgith ... ' (lines 1000–3). *PH* has two further terms omitted by T: *joykith* 'jouks' = 'sleeps'; and *puttithouer* 'puts over' = 'passes food from the crop to the stomach'.

In T, *perchyth* is followed by the words *ayer prue*, which I have treated as a scribal error; *prue* looks suspiciously like partial dittography of the next word, *pruneth*, and *ayer* makes no sense in the context – though it is tempting to think that the scribe may have had in mind the hawking term *aire*, meaning 'to nest', 'to breed'; see *MED* s.v. *airen* v.(2), and *PH*: 'And we shall say that hawkis doon eyer, and not brede, in the woodes' (21–2).

12 *scratteth* 'scratches', perhaps in the sense 'digs in the earth'; see *MED*, s.v. *scratten* v. A matching statement in Adv assigns the same verb to a shrewish woman (*quene*, no. 24).

13 (i) *forme* 'form' – the correct technical term for a hare's nest or resting place, which is often no more than a shallow depression in the ground, or under a hedge. *MED* (s.v. *forme* n., *formen* v.) slips up lamentably when it refers to a hare's form as its 'burrow'. One of the key distinguishing features of all species of European hares is that they do not dig burrows or live underground, which is precisely what makes them such excellent quarries for the sporting hunter.

(i–ii) *sholdryng ... lenyng* Both terms convey the sense of 'crouching, lying low' (with shoulders close to the ground).

(ii–iii) *ys formed* 'is seated in its form'. Cf. the active and intransitive use of the verb in *MG*, p. 13: '... for whan an hare abideþ and formeth in a playn contre ...'.

(iv–v) These phrases, containing collective nouns, have been mysteriously appended to the resting terms in Pl and Prk; see s.v. 'Hares' (no. 89) and the associated notes in Appendix I.

14 With the exception of *StA*, the witnesses listed here all contain a matching statement assigning the same verb, in its various forms, to a knight (no. 19).

(i) *harboreth* 'withdraws to its lair'; see *MED, herberwen* v. 6b. The verb suggests that a hart's lair may have been known as its 'harbour', though this sense of the noun is not attested before 1575: 'And note you well, that some Harts be so craftie, that they haue two layres wherein they harboure: and when they haue bene three dayes on that one syde of the forrest, they will take an other harborough ...' (*Noble Arte*, p. 73). This slightly antedates the earliest citation in the *OED*, s.v. *harbour* n.[1] 2c, which comes from Abraham Fleming, *Of Englishe Dogges* (1576).

In the *Master of Game* (1410), Edward of York always refers to the hart's lair as its *leire, liggyng* ('lying': *MED*, s.v. *liing(e* ger. (1) 2.) and its *strength* – the last being a direct translation of OF *fort* ('a place of strength', hence 'a thicket'): pp. 76, 83,

86, 90–1. Gascoigne also generally prefers *lair*, but occasionally employs *harbour* as a synonym (see quotation above). It is tempting to speculate that *harbour* may have been used in this way in the 15th century too.

(ii–iii) *harburght, is herbored*: 'in its lair', 'is withdrawn in its lair'; see *MED*, *herberwen* v. 6b. It is essential to distinguish this intransitive, quasi-passive use of '(is) harboured' from the identical, true passive, which has an entirely different, though related, meaning, referring to the preliminary stage of a hart hunt, when the hart was tracked to its lair by an expert huntsman, known as a 'harbourer'. In the technical language of the hunt, the harbourer set out to 'harbour' the hart; or, as Edward of York puts it, 'whan an hunter goþ to fynde of an hert and to herborowe hym' (*MG*, p. 73; see also pp. 7, 18, 22, 83–4). Likewise, in the passive voice: 'Whan þe hert is harboured, as bifore is said' (*MG*, p. 94); see *MED*, s.v. *herberwen* v. 6a. Thereafter, the hart had to be 'moved' or 'unharboured' – i.e. driven from its lair – so that the chase could begin.

The available evidence does not reveal how the intransitive sense of the J.B. verb 'harbour(ed)' emerged: whether from the widely used transitive sense, 'to track to its den', or from a noun, unattested at this date, referring to the hart's den as its 'harbour' (see note 14.i above).

15 See my remarks on the matching statement concerning the crane in note 7 above.

16 *hynde* 'hind', the female of the red deer; *chamburd*: 'in its lair', 'is withdrawn in its lair'. This statement, which is paired in Adv with a matching counterpart referring to a lady (no. 20), is surely an artificial construction, inspired by the desire to equate lady and hind by analogy with knight and hart. The same association will later provide the central metaphor for one of Thomas Wyatt's best known sonnets: 'Whoso list to hunt, I know where is an hind': *The Complete Poems*, ed. Ronald A. Rebholz (Harmondsworth, 1978), p. 77.

17 *lyttereth* 'beds down in litter', i.e. straw, rushes, or the like. A matching statement in Adv assigns this verb also to a carl (no. 5; see the relevant note above).

18 (i) *lyȝthe in hys bed brawlyng* 'lies in his bed making a noise', or 'lies in his bed quarrelling, squabbling'; cf. the variant, 'a boy is bedded brawling' (no. 3.i). In this context, *knave* probably indicates a young boy, though 'page' or 'servant boy' would also make sense.

(ii) *coucheth* 'goes to bed'; perhaps also 'cowers': see note 8 above. A matching statement in Adv assigns this verb also to a cur (no. 8), which suggests that *knave* here probably denotes a servant boy.

19 The witnesses listed here all contain a matching statement assigning the same verb, in its various forms, to a hart (no. 14).

(i) *harboryth* 'withdraws, retires' – to bed, to his closet, or somewhere private, equivalent to a hart's lair; see note 14 above. This particularised sense of the verb is not recognised by *MED*, although it records the animal equivalent: 'of a hart: to go to his lair' – s.v. *herberwen* v. 6b. Of humans, *MED* records only a variety of senses of lodging, sheltering, entertaining, taking refuge, and the like (senses 1–5). Yet the J.B. usage suggests that a knight harbours (himself) somewhere *within* a building – in a room or private apartment: the equivalent of a lady's chamber (no. 20) – in a more specific sense than *MED* allows. Of course, this sense may not have had much, or any, currency outside the J.B. texts, and may simply have been coined here as a conceit for establishing a symmetry between the animal and human worlds.

(ii) *harburght, is herbored* '(is) withdrawn, retired' (somewhere private).

20 *chambred* 'is withdrawn, has retired' (to her chamber). The participle must derive from the noun *chaumbre*, 'a private chamber, bedroom', 'a woman's apartment', but is unrecorded in this sense by *MED* (s.vv. *chaumbren* v.; *chaumbred* ppl.). In Adv, this statement is preceded by its matching counterpart, 'a hind chambered' (no. 16), though the inspiration for the pairing must have come from the notion of a woman retiring to her apartment; hence the term *chambred*, which is then applied by analogy to the hind.

The reverse process is likely to have taken place in relation to knight and hart, which share the verb *harbours* (nos 14, 19). In that case, the expression derives from the language of the hunt in relation to the hart, and is applied by analogy to the knight.

21 *walkyth* 'walks'; presumably, referring to the main activity of a parker doing his rounds and carrying out his duties as guardian of an enclosed hunting reserve.

22 *lyethe* 'lies', 'squats' (close to the ground) – typical behaviour of a ground-nesting bird. Cf. *THawk 1*, which insists that, 'Thow sal say hole-fotyd fawlis ['fowls'] lyeng and noȝt sittyng ... For all hole-foted fewles lyggys in [this] kynd of speche. So dos partrik, fesaund and whayle ['quail']' (lines 234–8). ('Whole-footed fowls' are waterfowl with webbed feet.)

23 *stalkethe* 'stalks', 'walks carefully or stealthily' – an apt description of the motion of a pheasant through underbrush. See note 15 above on the little group of matching phrases in H and L.

24 'A shrewish hussy (or harlot) scratches'. The noun *quene* here probably carries its full potential of negative connotations as a term of abuse for a woman; see *MED*, *quene* n.; *OED*, *quean*. A matching statement in Adv assigns this verb also to a badger (a grey: no. 12). I have amended the verb from *scrattet* to *scratteth*, as the latter spelling of *3 sg.* verbs is standard in Adv.

25 With the exception of Rg, these witnesses all have a matching statement that assigns the same verb, in its various forms, to a yeoman (no. 29).

(i) *beddeth* 'withdraws to its lair'. As a technical term, this word is not attested in medieval hunting manuals, but is specified by Gascoigne in 1575 as one of the correct terms to be used of the roe deer: '... we seeke and finde the rowe and he beddeth' (*Noble Arte*, p. 241).

(ii) *is bedded* 'is in its lair'.

26 These witnesses all contain a matching statement that assigns the same verb, in its various forms, to a buck (no. 4; see the relevant note above).

(i–iii) *lodgeth, lugeth* 'withdraws, retires' – to bed, or somewhere private, equivalent to a buck's lair.

(iv) *is logged* 'is withdrawn' (somewhere private).

27 A matching statement in Adv assigns the same verb to a bear (no. 2; see the relevant note above).

28 (i) *A wodecoke syttynge* This statement, an unicum, is probably the result of scribal error. As can be seen from the complete text of T at the start of this Appendix, it is preceded by 'a cony sitting' and followed by 'a woodcock *bekynge*' (see 28.ii) – which suggest that the scribe may have miscopied 'sitting' from the preceding statement, before noticing his error and then writing down the correct expression for the woodcock, but without deleting the faulty one.

(ii) *beekyng*: 'basking, warming'; see *MED*, *beken* v.(1). As Hands observes (*EHH*, p. 167/2043n), this verb was probably chosen for equivoque on the ME name for a woodcock or snipe, *beke* (<AN *bekas, bibikaz*).

29 The witnesses cited here all contain a matching statement that assigns the same verb, in its various forms, to a roe (no. 25).

(i) *beddeth* 'takes to, withdraws to, his bed'.

(ii) *is bedded* 'is abed', 'is in his bed'.

30 T: This *explicit* occurs at the foot of fol. 35v, where it appears to separate all the items that precede it (the collectives, soiling terms and resting terms) from the carving terms, which begin at the top of fol. 36r with their own heading (see Appendix II, no. 1). The phrasing is noteworthy, however, for allowing the reader to choose whether or not to stop at this point.

www.ingramcontent.com/pod-product-compliance
Lightning Source LLC
Chambersburg PA
CBHW030517230426
43665CB00010B/646